Politics In China: An Introduction

Politics In China: An Introduction

EDITED BY
William A. Joseph

UNIVERSITY PRESS

2010

OXFORD
UNIVERSITY PRESS

Oxford University Press, Inc., publishes works that further
Oxford University's objective of excellence
in research, scholarship, and education.

Oxford   New York
Auckland   Cape Town   Dar es Salaam   Hong Kong   Karachi
Kuala Lumpur   Madrid   Melbourne   Mexico City   Nairobi
New Delhi   Shanghai   Taipei   Toronto

With offices in
Argentina   Austria   Brazil   Chile   Czech Republic   France   Greece
Guatemala   Hungary   Italy   Japan   Poland   Portugal   Singapore
South Korea   Switzerland   Thailand   Turkey   Ukraine   Vietnam

Published by Oxford University Press, Inc.
198 Madison Avenue, New York, New York 10016

www.oup.com

Oxford is a registered trademark of Oxford University Press.

Library of Congress Cataloging-in-Publication Data
Politics in China: an introduction / edited by William A. Joseph.
p.   cm.
Includes index.
ISBN 978-0-19-533530-9; 978-0-19-533531-6 (pbk.)
1. China—Politics and government.   I. Joseph, William A.
JQ1510.P655 2010
320.951—dc22   2009027998

9 8 7 6 5 4 3 2 1
Printed in the United States of America
on acid-free paper

To my Sino-mentors,

John Wilson Lewis and Harry Harding

子曰、 學而時習之、不亦說乎

The Master said, "To learn something, and then to put it into practice at the
right time: is this not a joy?"

Confucius, *The Annalects, Chapter 1, Verse 1*
Translated by Simon Leys, Norton, 1997

Acknowledgments

In the most immediate sense, this project began when Oxford University Press invited me to submit a proposal for an introductory textbook on Chinese politics more than three years ago. But its true origins go back over four decades to the summer of 1966, when I took my first college course on China. My interest had been piqued by events unfolding in Beijing (we called it "Peking" then) as the Red Guards—university students like myself—were challenging professors about their political views and methods of education during the very early stages of China's Great Proletarian Cultural Revolution. It was a tumultuous time on American and European college campuses, too, and the youthful rebellion against authority in China seemed to many to be part of a global generational movement.

The news from the People's Republic of China (we called it "Communist China" or "Red China" then) reaching Western audiences in the mid-1960s was, at best, piecemeal and sketchy because of Cold War hostilities and the PRC's increasing self-imposed isolation from much of the world. It would be quite a few years before the terrible destructiveness of the Cultural Revolution and the atrocities committed by the Red Guards would become widely known and well-documented.

By then, I was immersed in Chinese Studies. I had been intellectually captivated by that summer school course, taken at Berkeley, with the incomparable Benjamin I. Schwartz of Harvard. When I returned to Cornell for my sophomore year in the fall of 1966, I took the plunge into learning Chinese. I also began my study of Chinese politics with Professor John Wilson Lewis. What an extraordinary time that was to be learning—and teaching—about Chinese politics! I still vividly recall Professor Lewis' lecture on why the philosophical debate that had raged a few years before in China over whether "one divides into two" or "two unites into one" was crucial to understanding Chairman Mao Zedong's ideological motives for launching the Cultural Revolution. John became my undergraduate advisor, and I was very fortunate to be able to continue my study of Chinese politics with him at Stanford, where I completed an M.A. in East Asian Studies and a Ph.D. in political science. I also benefited enormously in my training at Stanford as a China Watcher, political scientist, and teacher from the guidance and inspiration provided by Harry Harding. I dedicate this book with deepest gratitude to my academic mentors, John Wilson Lewis and Harry Harding.

I am especially indebted to the following people at Oxford University Press for their superb work during the many stages of this project from conception to publication: David McBride, Senior Editor for Politics and Law; Alexandra Dauler, Assistant Editor for Politics and Law; and Brian Desmond, Senior Production Editor.

The contributors are what make this book unique. Each is a broadly-trained China scholar and practitioner of her or his discipline (mostly political science); but each is also a specialist in the study of the particular subject of the chapter of which he or she is the author. It has been a pleasure and an honor to work closely with them, and I want to thank them for being part of this project. I learned a great deal from them, as I have from so many other colleagues in the China field.

The contributors and I are very grateful to the following China scholars for their valuable comments on the chapters in this volume: Marc Belcher, Edward Friedman, Thomas B. Gold, Merle Goldman, J. Megan Greene, David M. Lampton, Kenneth Lieberthal, Barrett McCormick, Kevin J. O'Brien, Margaret Pearson, Michael Sheng, Wenfang Tang, Fengshi Wu, and several anonymous reviewers.

As editor, I assume full responsibility for any and all errors. I invite readers to send comments and corrections directly to me at wjoseph@wellesley.edu.

William A. Joseph
Wellesley College
March 2010

Contents

Illustrations

TABLES

Abbreviations

ACWF	All-China Women's Federation
AR	autonomous region
CC	Central Committee
CCP	Chinese Communist Party
CCRG	Central Cultural Revolution Group
CCTV	China Central Television
CCYL	Chinese Communist Youth League
CMC	Central Military Commission
CMS	Cooperative Medical Scheme
CPSU	Communist Party of the Soviet Union
DPP	Democratic Progressive Party
ELG	Export-Led Growth
ExCo	Executive Council
HIV/AIDS	Human Immunodeficiency Virus/Acquired Immune Deficiency Syndrome
HKSAR	Hong Kong Special Administrative Region
HLLAPCs	Higher-Level Agricultural Producer Cooperatives (Collectives)
IMF	International Monetary Fund
KMT	Kuomintang
LegCo	Legislative Council
LLPAPCs	Lower-Level Agricultural Producer Cooperatives (Cooperatives)
NCNA	New China News Agency (Xinhua)
NPC	National People's Congress
PAP	People's Armed Police
PBSC	Politburo Standing Committee
PLA	People's Liberation Army
PRC	People's Republic of China
ROC	Republic of China
SAR	special administrative region
SARS	Severe Acute Respiratory Syndrome
SASAC	State Asset Supervision and Administration Commission
SEZ	Special Economic Zone
SMEs	small- and medium enterprises
SOE	state-owned enterprise
TAR	Tibet Autonomous Region

TVE	township and village enterprise
USSR	Union of Soviet Socialist Republics
VRA	Villager Representative Assembly
WTO	World Trade Organization
XUAR	Xinjiang Ugyhur Autonomous Region

Contributors

ROBERT BARNETT is Director of the Modern Tibetan Studies Program at Columbia University in New York and an Associate Research Scholar there. From 2000–2005 he was director of the joint Columbia/University of Virginia summer program at Tibet University in Lhasa, where he also taught in 2001. He has written on Tibetan cinema and television within Tibet, women and politics in the TAR, post-1950 leaders in Tibet, contemporary exorcism rituals and other subjects. His books include *Tibetan Modernities: Notes from the Field* (with Ronald Schwartz, 2008), *Lhasa: Streets with Memories* (2006) and *The Poisoned Arrow: the Secret Petition of the 10th Panchen Lama* (1997).

GARDNER BOVINGDON is Assistant Professor of Central Eurasian Studies and East Asian Languages and Cultures and Adjunct Assistant Professor of Political Science at Indiana University. A specialist on nationalism and identity politics with a geographical focus on Xinjiang, he has published a number of journal articles and book chapters on these topics. His book, *The Uyghurs: Strangers in Their Own Land*, is forthcoming from Columbia University Press.

BRUCE GILLEY is Assistant Professor of Political Science in the Mark O. Hatfield School of Government at Portland State University. His research centers on the comparative politics of China and Asia as well as the comparative politics of democracy and political legitimacy. He is the author of *China's Democratic Future* (2004) and *The Right to Rule: How States Win and Lose Legitimacy* (2009). He is a member of the board of directors of the *Journal of Democracy* and a frequent commentator and speaker on issues relating to China's democratization.

WILLIAM HURST is Assistant Professor of Government at the University of Texas at Austin. Previously, he served for two years as a postdoctoral fellow in Modern Chinese Studies at Oxford University. He is the author of *The Chinese Worker after Socialism* (2009) and co-editor of *Laid-off Workers in a Workers' State: Unemployment with Chinese Characteristics* (2009). His ongoing research focuses on Chinese legal system reform.

WILLIAM A. JOSEPH is Professor of Political Science at Wellesley College and an Associate in Research of the John King Fairbank Center for Chinese Studies at Harvard University. He is the author of *The Critique of Ultra-Leftism in China* (1984) and editor or co-editor of *New Perspectives on the Cultural Revolution* (1991), *China Briefing* (1991, 1992, 1994, 1997), *The Oxford Companion to Politics of the World* (2nd ed., 2001), *Introduction to Comparative Politics: Political Challenges and Changing Agendas* (5th ed., 2009), and *Introduction to Politics in the Developing World* (5th ed., 2009).

JOAN KAUFMAN is Lecturer on Global Health and Social Medicine Harvard Medical School, Distinguished Scientist at the Heller School for Social Policy and Management, Brandeis University, senior fellow and founder of the AIDS Public Policy Project at Harvard's Kennedy School of Government, and China team leader for the International AIDS Vaccine Initiative. She worked for Ford Foundation and the UN in China, was a Radcliffe fellow at Harvard and a Soros Reproductive Health and Rights Fellow. Dr. Kaufman works and writes on AIDS, gender, international health, infectious diseases, reproductive health, health sector reform, and health governance issues, with a focus on China.

JOHN JAMES KENNEDY is Associate Professor of Political Science at the University of Kansas. His research focuses on rural social and political development including village elections, tax reform and rural education. He frequently returns to China to conduct fieldwork and collaborate with Chinese colleagues at Northwest University, Xian, Shaanxi province. Prof. Kennedy has published several book chapters as well as articles in journals such as *Asian Survey, The China Quarterly*, the *Journal of Chinese Political Science, Journal of Contemporary China*, and *Political Studies*.

RICHARD CURT KRAUS is Professor Emeritus of Political Science, University of Oregon. He is the author of *Class Conflict in Chinese Socialism* (1981), *Pianos and Politics in China* (1989), *Brushes with Power: Modern Politics and the Chinese Art of Calligraphy* (1991); *The Party and the Arty* (2004); and coeditor of *Urban Spaces: Autonomy and Community in Contemporary China* (1995). He is now writing about the politics of China's cultural influence abroad.

CHENG LI is Research Director and Senior Fellow of the John L. Thornton China Center at the Brookings Institution. He is the author or the editor of *Rediscovering China: Dynamics and Dilemmas of Reform* (1997), *China's Leaders: The New Generation* (2001), and *China's Changing Political Landscape: Prospects for Democracy* (2008). His academic writings have appeared in *World Politics, China Quarterly, China Journal, Journal of Asian and African Studies*, and other scholarly journals. He is the

principal editor of the Thornton Center Chinese Thinkers Series published by the Brookings Institution Press. Dr. Li is a columnist for the Hoover Institution's online journal, *China Leadership Monitor*.

SONNY SHIU-HING LO is Professor of Political Science at the University of Waterloo, Ontario, Canada. His recent works include *The Politics of Cross-Border Crime in Greater China: Case Studies of Mainland China, Hong Kong and Macao* (2009); *The Dynamics of Beijing-Hong Kong Relations: A Model for Taiwan?* (2008); and *Political Change in Macao* (2008).

KATHERINE MORTON is a Fellow in the Department of International Relations, Australian National University. She is a specialist on China and Global Politics with over a decade of experience working on environmental problems at the local, national, and international levels. Her book on *International Aid and China's Environment: Taming the Yellow Dragon* (2005) investigates the effectiveness of international ideas and practices in building capacity to address environmental problems in China. For the past six years she has been conducting research on the Tibetan Plateau looking at the emergence of environmentalism and more recently the local and regional impacts of climate change.

SHELLEY RIGGER is Brown Professor of East Asian Politics at Davidson College. She has been a visiting researcher at National Chengchi University in Taiwan and a visiting professor at Fudan University in Shanghai. She is the author of two books on Taiwan's domestic politics, *Politics in Taiwan: Voting for Democracy* (1999) and *From Opposition to Power: Taiwan's Democratic Progressive Party* (2001); a monograph, "Taiwan's Rising Rationalism: Generations, Politics and 'Taiwan Nationalism'" (2006); and articles on Taiwan's domestic politics, the national identity issue in Taiwan-China relations and related topics.

R. KEITH SCHOPPA is Doehler Chair in Asian History at Loyola University, Maryland. He has authored many books and articles, including

Blood Road: The Mystery of Shen Dingyi in Revolutionary China (1996), which won the 1997 Association for Asian Studies' Levenson Prize for the best book on twentieth century China, and textbooks on modern China and East Asia. He has received fellowships from the National Endowment for the Humanities, the American Council of Learned Societies, and the John Simon Guggenheim Memorial Foundation.

FREDERICK C. TEIWES is Emeritus Professor of Chinese Politics at the University of Sydney. He is the author of numerous works on Chinese Communist elite politics during the Maoist era, including *Politics and Purges in China* (1979), *Politics at Mao's Court* (1990), *The Tragedy of Lin Biao* (1996), *China's Road to Disaster* (1999), and *The End of the Maoist Era* (2007) (the latter three studies co-authored with Warren Sun). He thanks the Australian Research Council for generous research support over many years.

TYRENE WHITE is Professor of Political Science at Swarthmore College. She is the author of *China's Longest Campaign: Birth Planning in the People's Republic, 1949–2005* (Cornell, 2006), and many articles on rural politics and population policy in China. She is the editor of *China Briefing: The Continuing Transformation* (2000) and co-editor of *Engendering China: Women, Culture, and the State* (1994). Her current research is on the local political influence of Chinese NGO's and on the use of litigation to improve the status of Chinese women. She teaches courses on contemporary China, East Asia, and population politics.

DAVID ZWEIG is Chair Professor, Division of Social Science, and Director of the Center on China's Transnational Relations at The Hong Kong University of Science and Technology. He has been a Post-doctoral Fellow at Harvard University. He is the author of four books, including *Agrarian Radicalism in China, 1968–1981* (1989), *Freeing China's Farmers* (1997), and *Internationalizing China: Domestic Interests and Global Linkages* (2002). He is co-editor of two special issues on migration in the *Journal of International Migration and Integration* and *Pacific Affairs*.

Politics In China: An Introduction

1

Studying Chinese Politics

William A. Joseph

On October 1, 2009, the **People's Republic of China (PRC)** celebrated the sixtieth anniversary of its founding. And what an eventful and tumultuous six decades it had been!

During that time, China was transformed from one of the world's poorest countries into the world's fastest growing major economy through a process that is widely called a "miracle,"[1] producing what has been "one of the biggest improvements in human welfare anywhere at any time."[2] Thirty years ago, China was isolated from much of the rest of the world and engaged in little international economic activity. Now it is the world's third-largest trading country (after the United States and Germany) and its export and import policies have an enormous impact in literally every corner of the globe. China has also gone from being a weak state, barely able to govern or protect its own territory, to a rising power that is challenging the United States for global influence. It now sits with the great powers in international organizations, such as the United Nations where it is one of the five permanent veto-bearing members of the Security Council. The PRC has the world's largest armed forces, a formidable arsenal of nuclear weapons, and a rapidly modernizing oceangoing navy.

Over those same sixty years, the PRC also experienced the most deadly famine in human history, caused largely by the actions and inactions of its political leaders. Not long after that catastrophe, there was a collapse of government authority that pushed the country to the brink of (and in some places actually into) civil war and anarchy, a reign of terror that tore at the very fabric of Chinese society, and a destabilizing power struggle among the top leadership.

Today, China is, for the most part, peaceful, prospering, and proud. This is the China that was on display for the international community during the 2008 **Beijing** Olympics and the 2010 World Expo in Shanghai.

The story of this incredible political journey and politics in contemporary China are the subjects of this book. The two go together: it simply is not possible to understand politics in China today without an understanding of the Chinese past, and not just the last few decades, but the last century and a half, or even better, at least passing familiarity with the last millennia or two.

The famine and political chaos mentioned above occurred during the period (1949–1976) when **Mao Zedong** was chairman of the **Chinese Communist Party (CCP)** and the undisputed and largely indisputable leader of the People's Republic. The Maoist era was not without its accomplishments (which are discussed in this book), but overwhelming scholarly opinion is that it was, as a whole, a disaster for China, economically, politically, culturally, environmentally, and in other ways. Those who followed Mao in power in China have taken the country in a very un-Maoist direction, and with spectacular economic results.

But one thing about China has not changed throughout the history of the People's Republic from the beginning of the Maoist era to the present: the Chinese Communist Party has

A VERY BRIEF CHINESE LESSON

Chinese is spoken by more people than any other language in the world. Yet "Chinese" really comprises many dialects, some of which are so different from one another that they are mutually incomprehensible and are considered by linguists to be separate languages. About seventy percent of China's population speaks the Mandarin dialect, which is the dialect of Chinese spoken mainly in the northern, central, and southwestern parts of the country, as their native tongue. Other major dialects include Wu (a subdialect of which is spoken in the area that includes China's largest city, Shanghai) and Cantonese, which is the dialect native to the southern coastal region adjacent to Hong Kong.

But people who speak different Chinese dialects share the *same* written language. For example, Mandarin and Cantonese speakers cannot understand each other in face-to-face conversations or over the telephone, but they can communicate by letter and read the same newspapers or books because written Chinese is made up of *characters* rather than phonetic letters. These characters, which have evolved over time from symbolic pictures, depict meaning more than sound, so that speakers of various Chinese dialects often pronounce the same written character very differently. There are about 50,000 different Chinese characters, although basic literacy requires knowledge of about 4,000 because the vast majority of characters are ancient and have fallen out of common usage.

Chinese does not have an alphabet; both the meaning and the pronunciation of Chinese characters can only be learned by memorization. Like many of the world's other languages—including Arabic, Greek, Hebrew, Japanese, and Russian—that do not use the Roman alphabet on which English is based, Chinese characters must be "Romanized" (or "transliterated") if English speakers are to have any idea how to pronounce them. The most common way of Romanizing Chinese is the *pinyin* (literally, "spell sounds") system used in the People's Republic of China and by the United Nations. But because linguists have differed about how best to approximate distinctive Chinese sounds using Roman letters, there are still several alternative methods of Romanizing Chinese.

This book and most other English-language publications use the *pinyin* Romanization for Chinese names, places, and phrases, with a few exceptions for important historical names where an alternative Romanization is commonly given. In most cases, a word in *pinyin* is pronounced as it looks. However, there are a few *pinyin* letters that appear in Chinese terms in this book for which a pronunciation guide may be helpful:

"c" is pronounced "ts" (e.g., Empress Dowager *C*ixi)
"x" is pronounced "sh" (e.g., Empress Dowager Ci*x*i; Deng *X*iaoping)
"z" is pronounced "dz" (e.g., Mao *Z*edong)
"q" is pronounced "ch" (e.g., Emperor *Q*in; *Q*ing dynasty)
"zh" is pronounced "j" (e.g., *Zh*ongguo, the Chinese word for "China")

A couple of important points about Chinese names: in China (as in Japan and Korea), the family name, or surname (for instance, Mao), comes *before* the personal, or given, name (for instance, Zedong). Some people interpret this as a reflection of the priority given to the family or the group over the individual in East Asian culture. Chinese who have immigrated to the United States or other countries often adapt their names to the "Western" order of personal names before family names. For example, "Li" is the family name of one of the contributors to this volume, Dr. Cheng Li of the Brookings Institution; in China, he is known as Li Cheng.

Chinese has relatively few family names: in fact, one term for the common folk is the "old hundred names" (*laobaixing*), which cover about 85 percent of the people in China. The most common family name in China is Wang; there are more than 93 million Wangs in China, followed by 92 million Li's, and 88 million Zhangs. On the other hand, there is an almost infinite variety of given names in Chinese, which often have descriptive meanings such as "beautiful bell" (*meiling*) or "bright and cultivated" (*bingwen*).

never been seriously challenged as China's ruling party. There have been sporadic protests by students and **peasants**, labor unrest, ethnic uprisings, and deep pockets of dissent and discontent, but all have been quelled before they could become threatening to the CCP's hold on power. The party itself has been through violent internal purges and almost inexplicable ideological and policy turnabouts, the most recent of which cause some to question just how "communist" the Chinese Communist Party really is.

Communist rule has not only survived in China, but the CCP has thrived in power while most other such regimes have long perished from this earth. The *hows* and *whys* of this fundamental political continuity—and the prospects for continued CCP rule—is a central theme in this volume, and it is one of the most important questions that political scientists ask about contemporary China. One part of the answer to this question is that it is the Chinese Communist Party that has presided over China's recent economic success, which has won the party a great deal of popular support, reflecting a strong desire among many sectors of the population for political stability and continuity.

But there has also been significant political change within the CCP, and it is much less dictatorial in its exercise of authority than it was during the Mao years. This has also contributed to the party's staying power. Nevertheless, the PRC is still regarded by many outside observers as having one of the world's most repressive political regimes. For example, *The Economist*, a highly respected British weekly magazine, ranked China 136th out of 167 countries on its 2008 "Index of Democracy," which is based on measures of "electoral processes and pluralism," "functioning of government" (which includes corruption), "political participation," "political culture," and "civil liberties."[3]

The contradiction between China's increasingly open, globalized economy and its still "closed," authoritarian political system raises several more fascinating questions for students of Chinese politics, and comparative politics in general: What does the Chinese experience say about the kind of government best able to promote rapid economic development? Is a strong, authoritarian regime required for such a task? How has the Chinese Communist Party been able to resist the pressures for democratization that usually accompany the social, economic, and cultural changes that modernization brings? Will it be able to continue to do so in the future? These questions, too, are addressed, directly and indirectly, in many of the chapters in this book.

The next part of this introduction provides a brief overview of the land and people of China in order to set the geographic and demographic contexts of Chinese politics. Then comes a discussion of what I call the "four faces" of contemporary China—China as China; China as a **communist party-state**; China as a developing country; and China as a rising power—that are offered as ways in which to frame the analysis of contemporary Chinese politics. This is followed by a review of the major approaches used by political scientists to study politics in China. Finally, the chapter concludes with a summary of the organization of the book and the content of its chapters.

China: A Geographic and Demographic Overview

Geography is the multi-faceted study of physical space on the surface of the earth, and demography is the study of the size, composition, distribution and other aspects of human population. In all countries, there is a close relationship between geography and demography, and both have important implications for politics and policy-making. In China, as one of the world's largest countries in terms of physical space and the largest in terms of population, this is especially the case.

The People's Republic of China is located in the far eastern part of the Asian continent that is usually referred to as East Asia, which also includes Japan and the two Koreas, the communist Democratic People's Republic of Korea (North Korea) and the capitalist democracy, the Republic of Korea (South Korea). China shares land borders with fourteen countries, the longest being with Russia and Mongolia in the north, India in the west, and Burma (Myanmar) and Vietnam in the south. China's eastern border is made up almost entirely of an 11,200-mile-long (18,000 kilometers) coastline along the western edge of the

WHERE DID "CHINA" COME FROM?

The name "China" is of totally non-Chinese origin. In fact, its origins are uncertain. Its first use in English has been traced to 1555 CE and the term is believed to have come via Persian and Sanskrit in reference to the ancient Qin (pronounced "chin") kingdom in what is now northwest China and whose capital lay at the eastern end of the Silk Road that connected East Asia, Central Asia, the Middle East, and ultimately Europe. The king of Qin became the founder of China's first imperial dynasty in 221 BCE by bringing neighboring kingdoms under his control and is therefore known as China's first emperor.

The Chinese term for China is *Zhongguo*, which literally means "Middle Kingdom." This name dates from the sixth century BCE, several centuries prior to the unification of the Chinese empire, and even then was meant to convey the idea of being the center of civilization, culture, and political authority. The Qin emperor was the first political leader to be able to claim the title of ruler of the entire Middle Kingdom.

The term "Sino" is also often used to refer to China, as in "Sino-American relations." Scholars who specialize in the study of China are called "sinologists." Sino comes from the Latin for China (*Sinae*).

Pacific Ocean. The country stretches for about 3,200 miles (5,200 kilometers) from east to west, and 3,400 miles (5,500 kilometers) from north to south.

In terms of total area, China (5.6 million square miles/9.6 million square kilometers) is a bit smaller than the United States, making it the fourth largest country in the world, with Russia first and Canada second. China's population of a little over 1.3 billion is the largest in the world, but India, with 1.16 billion people, is expected to surpass China in population in 2030–2040. Although China and the United States are quite similar in geographic size, China's population is about four times that of the United States. Therefore, China, with 359 people per square mile, is much more densely populated than the United States, which has 81 people per square mile. Both countries have large areas that are sparsely populated or uninhabitable. By comparison, India, which is only about a third the geographic size of China, has 890 people per square mile and very few areas with low population density. China has about 20 percent of the world's population, but only 7 percent of its arable land—that is, land used for planting edible crops. Feeding its people is—and long has been—a central challenge for the Chinese government.

Like the United States, China is a land of great geographic and climatic contrasts, but China tends to have greater extremes. One the world's largest deserts (the Gobi) and the highest mountains (the Himalayas, which include Mount Everest—or as it is called in Tibetan, *Jomolangma*) are located in the far western part of the country. Climate varies from semitropical in the southeast to subarctic in the northeast, which borders on Russian Siberia. Most of the country is much more temperate. Beijing (China's capital city) is located at about the same latitude in the Northern Hemisphere as New York.

One way to think about China's geography is to imagine a 2,000-mile line cutting diagonally across the country from just north of Beijing to the PRC's border with Burma in the far southwest (see Map 1). To the east of this line lies "**China Proper**" (or Inner China), which consists of **provinces** that early on became part of the Chinese empire. This area, which is about one-third of China's total, is largely populated by the ethnic group to which the vast majority of Chinese people belong, the **Han**, a term taken from the name of imperial China's second dynasty, which lasted for more that four centuries (206 BCE–220 CE) and is considered the early golden age of Chinese civilization.

China Proper can itself be divided into several geographic regions. The three provinces of the **Northeast**, sometimes referred to as Manchuria, have vast tracts of forestland, but it was also once China's industrial heartland; now it is considered a rust belt because of the closing of aged, inefficient factories and high unemployment. The area that stretches from Beijing to the **Yangtze River**, which flows into the East China Sea near Shanghai, is referred to as **North China**. Agriculturally, this is a one-crop a year growing area with some similarities to the American Plains states. **South China** is the region that lies below the Yangtze and is warmer and wetter than the north, which allows for rice farming and in some areas year-round cultivation. Almost the entire coastal area of China Proper, from north to south, has become industrialized during the country's recent economic development spurt. China's population is also heavily concentrated along the eastern coastline and the adjacent provinces of China Proper. About 90 percent of the Chinese people live in this area, which is only about 30 percent of the country's total land area.

To the west of the imaginary diagonal line lies "**Outer China**." Outer China comprises about two-thirds of the country, but it is very sparsely populated. Most of the region was incorporated into the Chinese empire during its later periods, particularly in the seventeenth and eighteenth centuries, and is home to most of China's non-Han **ethnic minorities**, including **Tibetans**, **Uyghurs**, and Mongols. The **Great Wall** of China was begun by China's first emperor more than two thousand years ago and expanded through many

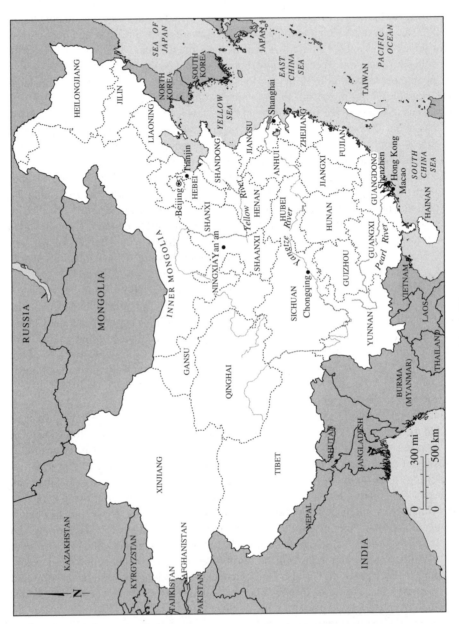

Map 1 China

other **dynasties** largely as a fortification to keep non-Han peoples out of China—a strategy that failed twice in Chinese history when the country was conquered by the Mongols in 1279 CE and by the **Manchus** in 1644 CE. Today, Han make up 91.5 percent of the PRC's population, with the other 8.5 percent divided among fifty-five ethnic minority groups that range in size from about sixteen million to under three thousand.

The other major geographic and demographic divide in China is that between the urban and rural areas. China developed large and, for the times, very "advanced" cities early in its imperial history. When Marco Polo visited the country in the fourteenth century, he marveled at the splendor of its cities and the system of canals that linked them for commercial and other purposes. From his experience, there was nothing comparable in Europe.[4] But China has always been, and still remains, a largely rural society. At the time of the founding of the PRC in 1949, only about 10 percent of the total population lived in urban areas. In recent decades, China has experienced extensive modernization and urbanization, and today 45 percent of the people (585 million) are urban.

China has over 120 cities with a population of more than one million (the U.S. has nine). The largest are Shanghai (18.8 million), China's financial center, and Beijing (16.9 million), the political capital. In both of these mega-cities, as in most all urban areas in China since the 1980s, there has been a massive influx of people—perhaps 150 million—from the countryside in search of jobs and a better life. In Beijing such migrants—referred to as the "**floating population**"—make up one-quarter of the population; in Shanghai, it is a third. This is just one way in which urban-rural boundaries are shifting in the People's Republic, which, in turn, reflects geographic and demographic transitions with enormous political implications.

Administratively, the People's Republic of China is a **unitary state**, which means that the national government has ultimate authority over all lower levels of government. The United Kingdom and France also have this form of government, in contrast to federal systems, such as the United States and Canada, in which there is significant sharing of power between the national and subnational levels of government (see Figure 1.1).

The PRC has twenty-two provinces (similar to states in the U.S.), four cities that are considered the equivalent of provinces and are directly administered by the central government (Beijing, Shanghai, Tianjin, and **Chongqing**), and five **autonomous regions** (Guangxi, Inner Mongolia, Ningxia, **Tibet**, and **Xinjiang**—all located in "Outer China") with large concentrations of ethnic minority groups. Autonomous regions do have limited autonomy when it comes to some cultural matters, but are completely under the political and military control of the government in Beijing.

There are also two **special administrative regions** (SAR) of the PRC: the former British colony of **Hong Kong**, which reverted to Chinese sovereignty in 1997, and **Macao**, a former Portuguese possession that became an SAR of the PRC in 1999. The SARs do have considerable political and economic autonomy, although ultimate sovereignty over their affairs lies in Beijing.

The island of **Taiwan**, located about seventy-five miles off the coast of southeastern China, is a politically contested area. It has been part of China since the mid-seventeenth century, but fell under Japanese control from 1895 until 1945. When the Chinese Communist Party won the civil war in 1949, its rivals, the **Nationalist Party (Kuomintang** or Guomindang) fled to Taiwan, where, with U.S. support, they were able to establish a stronghold. Despite many political changes on both the mainland and the island in the intervening years, Taiwan still remains a separate political entity, although Beijing claims that it is rightfully a province of the PRC.

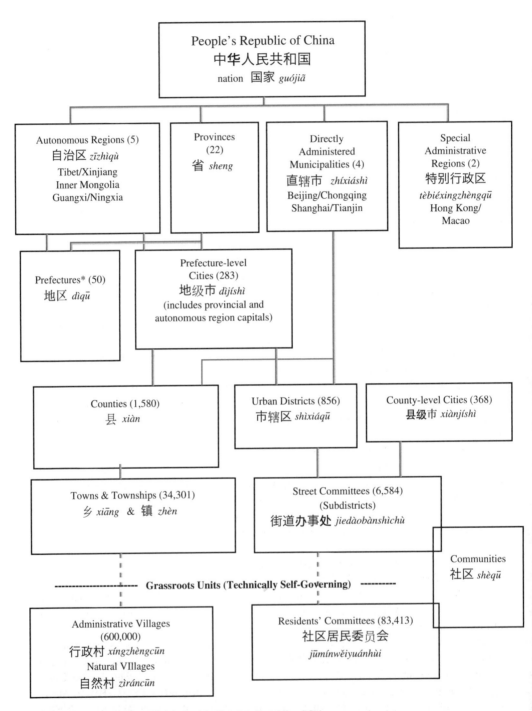

Figure 1.1 Administrative Divisions of the People's Republic of China
* Prefectures are being phased out as a unit of administration in the PRC as they are incorporated into surrounding urban areas.
Source: China Statistical Yearbook 2009.

Four Faces of Contemporary China

Hopefully, readers have already gotten the sense that Chinese politics is extremely important in today's world, and perhaps they will also find it immensely fascinating. But Chinese politics is quite complex and can be more than a bit confusing to someone new to the subject. Not only are the stages of political change that China has gone through in modern times full of twists and turns—a very involved and convoluted (and somewhat unbelievable) plot line, one might say, if we were talking about a novel; and for those unfamiliar with the Chinese language, the cast of characters that have played or now play influential roles in Chinese politics can also be somewhat bewildering. Furthermore, the People's Republic of China has a type of political system—a communist party-state—about which most readers will know very little, in terms of its structure of power and policy-making process. As readers progress through the chapters in this book, it might be helpful, in order to understand China's unique political development and current politics, to keep in mind what can be called the "four faces" of contemporary China.

China as China

By "China as China," I mean taking note of the influence of the Chinese past and culture on politics in the PRC. In the broadest and boldest strokes, Chinese political history can be broken down into three periods: the **imperial period** of dynastic monarchy (221 BCE—1912 CE); the **republican period** (1912–1949) characterized by weak central government, powerful regional **warlords**, several stages of civil war, and the invasion and occupation by Japan that started World War II in the Pacific; and the **communist period** (1949–to the present) that began with the victory of the Chinese Communist Party in the civil war and continues through the present day.

But Chinese *cultural* history dates back to well before the beginning of the imperial period in 221 BCE. Human beings have lived in the area that is now called China for more than a million years. The first dynasties—systems of hereditary rule over a specific geographic area—appeared as small, independent kingdoms more than four thousand years ago. The earliest artifacts of Chinese material culture, such as exquisite bronze and jade vessels, are from this period. Chinese as a written language took shape in the Shang dynasty (1600–1046 BCE) as inscriptions etched on "oracle bones" made from turtle shells and animal scapula for the purpose of divination and record-keeping.

The foundation of the Chinese empire—or China as a unified political entity—and the start of the imperial period in Chinese history is dated from 221 BCE, when a number of kingdoms where brought under the authority of the king of Qin, who is known as the first emperor of a unified China. The **Qin dynasty** lasted less than twenty years, giving way to the Han, as noted above. But the imperial system founded by Qin lasted for over two thousands years, through the rise and fall of more than a dozen different dynasties, until it was overthrown by a revolution and replaced by the Republic of China in 1912.

The philosopher-scholar Confucius, whose ethical, social, and political teachings are the foundation of Chinese culture, lived in 557–479 BCE, centuries before the founding of the Qin dynasty. In fact, the emperor Qin was profoundly suspicious of scholars and ordered many of them executed and their books burned. He favored a school of philosophy called **Legalism**, which advocated harsh laws rather than Confucian education and morality as the basis for maintaining the ruler's authority and commanding the obedience of his subjects. Later dynasties restored the prominence of **Confucianism** and imbedded it in the very structure of imperial Chinese society and government. Over the millennia, Legalism and other schools of thought combined with and influenced the evolution of Confucianism. Today, not only are the areas encompassed by "**Greater China**" (the PRC, Taiwan Hong Kong, and Macao) considered to be part of the Confucian cultural region, but so, too, are Japan, Korea, Vietnam, and Singapore, all of which were deeply influenced by the spread of many aspects of Chinese civilization.

This book focuses on Chinese politics during the communist period (with one chapter on the earlier periods) and mostly on very recent decades. From that perspective, we are concentrating our attention on but a tiny slice (see Figure 1.2) of the grand span of China's political history. It should come as no surprise that such a long and rich history should be considered when trying to understand almost any aspect of China today, including its politics.

But it is not just the imperial past or Confucian culture that should be taken into account when studying contemporary China. The process that brought the Chinese Communist Party to power and the radicalism of the Maoist era may seem far removed from the rapidly modernizing rising power that China is today. But as one leading scholar of Chinese politics, Elizabeth J. Perry, has recently observed, "China's stunning economic strides in the reform era can only be understood against the backdrop of a revolutionary history that remains highly salient in many respects."[5] In fact, she goes further and argues that legacies of the CCP's revolutionary past—notably its practice of the politics of divide-and-rule when dealing with opposing forces—are an important part of the answer to the question set out earlier about the durability of communist power in China.

The government of the PRC places great emphasis on nationalism in its messages aimed to audiences both at home and abroad. It expresses pride in the antiquity, greatness, and uniqueness of Chinese culture and civilization, as well as in as its growing stature in world affairs. Nationalism, along with the country's economic success, is now a core element on which the Chinese Communist Party bases its claim to the Chinese people that it has the right, or political legitimacy, to continue governing China. Chinese nationalism, with its roots in both the past and present, is an important matter not only in the PRC's foreign policy, but also in Chinese domestic politics.[6]

Scholars may disagree on the extent to and ways in which China today is shaped by its imperial history, traditional culture, and revolutionary heritage. But none would deny that

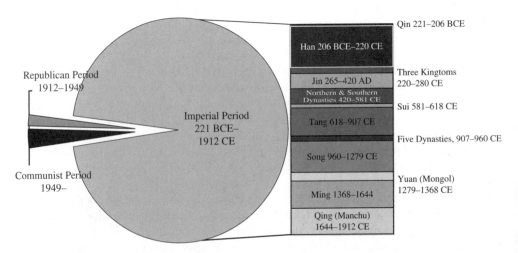

Figure 1.2 Chinese History from Imperial Times to the Present

the past and the knowledge, memory, and imagination of China's long history play a prominent role in contemporary Chinese politics.[7]

China as a Communist Party-State

In the early 1980s, about two dozen countries in Africa, Asia, Europe, and Latin America, with more than one-third of the world's population, were ruled by communist parties. Today, there are only five countries with an *unelected* ruling communist party: China, Cuba, Laos, North Korea, and Vietnam.[8] Despite many important differences, past and present communist party-states have several things in common as a unique type of political system.

First, as the term "party-state" implies, the communist party controls the state, that is, the formal institutions of government at the national level and below. The party and state are organizationally separate—for example, there may be a prime minister who heads the government and a general secretary who heads the communist party. But it is the party that is ultimately in charge of the state, and the leader of the communist party is the most powerful individual in the country. In a sense, it is the party that makes policy and the state that implements the party's policies, and there is a web of ways in which the communist party makes sure that it controls the state. For example, top state leaders, such as the prime minister and the president are also always top communist party officials

Second, the party-state proclaims, at least formally, an adherence to some variant of **ideology** based on **Marxism-Leninism** and is committed to guiding the country in building **socialism** and ultimately creating a truly egalitarian communist society. This is taken to be the party-state's official and exclusive ideology in guiding policy and framing political life. Competing ideologies are considered illegitimate and even subversive, and are, therefore usually vigorously suppressed.

Third, the communist party sees itself as a "**vanguard party**" and claims the right to exercise the "leading role" over society, the economy, culture, and most other aspects of life because only the party, which is made up of a relatively small "ideologically advanced" minority of the population, is said to be able to lead the country towards socialism and **communism**. In China, less than 6 percent of the population belongs to the CCP, or about 8 percent of the age-eligible (over 18) population.

Fourth, as an extension of its exclusive ideology and leading role in society, the communist party claims to govern in the interests of all the "people," and therefore holds a monopoly on political power that precludes any meaningful opposition or contestation from other political parties or organizations. The definition of which groups fit into the category of the "people" may shift over time—as it often has during the history of the CCP and the PRC. This is important because the "people" are those who support socialism and the party, while those who oppose them are labeled as "enemies of the people." One of the roles of the ruling communist party is to exercise control over these enemies through what has been called the "**dictatorship of the proletariat**" or, as in China today, the "**people's democratic dictatorship**."

Fifth, communist party-states are particularly concerned with their authority over the economy because economic growth is so critical to advancing the cause of socialism and building a strong nation. There are times when communist party politics and ideology may have a negative influence on economic growth (as during much of the Maoist era in China). And some communist party-states may greatly reduce the role of the party-state in the economy, and even introduce extensive elements of free-market **capitalism** (as in China today). But the party's claim to a leading role in determining the country's economic destiny remains a defining feature of a communist party-state.

Communist party-states have diminished greatly in number since the height of the Cold War, and those few that remain, other than North Korea and to a lesser extent Cuba, are markedly different from the kind that Stalin and Mao (themselves very different) built.

And China's political system is certainly in a time of transition (another theme of this volume), with great scholarly debate (including among scholars in China) about where it may be headed. But Chinese politics must still be described and analyzed within the communist party-state framework since remains the essential nature of the PRC's political system.

China as a Developing Country

Despite its astounding economic growth over the last few decades, China is a developing country. It may have the second- or third-largest economy in the world (depending on the method of calculation), but, by many measures, it is relatively poor and less modern than developed countries, such as the United States, Japan, and Western Europe. The World Bank classifies China as a lower middle income country, along with, for example, Angola, Bolivia, Egypt, Guatemala, and Indonesia. The group above this category (upper middle income) includes countries such as Argentina, Mexico, Poland, and South Africa, while the category below (low income) has Ghana, Haiti, Pakistan, and Uzbekistan among its members. Table 1.1 provides an idea of China's level of development in comparison to some of the world's other very large economies.

China faces many of the same challenges that other developing countries do: raising the living standards and bringing health care, education, and other social services to its citizens, tens of millions of whom live in absolute or relative poverty; overcoming the huge inequalities between the more prosperous and the poorer regions of the country, particularly between the urban and rural areas and the coastal and inland regions; balancing economic growth and environmental concerns—to name just a few of the dilemmas of development. The PRC very much sees itself as part of the developing world and as speaking and acting on behalf of the shared interests of the less developed countries in various international forums such as the United Nations.

But China also has some important advantages when it comes to economic development. It has had for more than thirty years a variation of what political scientists refer to as a **developmental state**, that is, a government that sets its highest priority on and effectively uses its power to promote economic growth.[9] This contrasts sharply with many developing countries classified as **predatory states,** where political power is used to further private, rather than national interests.

China certainly has a big problem with corruption (as several chapters note). Still, the government of the PRC and the Chinese Communist Party have, overall, a remarkable record in promoting or at least presiding over economic growth and modernization since the early 1980s. China's other development advantages include a generally well-educated and healthy labor force and abundant natural resources, although its rapidly growing economy has generated a demand that exceeds domestic supplies of oil, coal, lumber, and other commodities, all of which are now imported in huge quantities.

There is considerable irony in the fact that the PRC has been considered as a model for "Third World" development at two very different times and in two very different ways since 1949. The Maoist model was much praised from the mid-1960s through the early 1970s. At that time, China was seen as a trailblazer in areas like providing preventive health care and at least basic education to almost all its people, paying attention to rural development and limiting the "urban bias" endemic to most other developing countries, promoting gender equality, creating structures for worker participation in management, basing

Table 1.1 China's Economic Development in Comparative Perspective

	China	United States	Russia	Brazil	India	Nigeria
World Bank Classification	Lower Middle Income	Upper Income	Upper Middle Income	Upper Middle Income	Lower Middle Income	Lower Middle Income
Gross Domestic Product per capita (2008)	$6,000	$47,500	$16,100	$10,200	$2,900	$2,300
Labor force by occupation (1999-2007)	agriculture: 43% industry: 25% services: 32%	agriculture: 0.6% industry: 22.6% services: 76.8%	agriculture: 10.2% industry: 27.4% services: 62.4%	agriculture: 20% industry: 14% services: 66%	agriculture: 60% industry: 12% services: 28%	agriculture: 70% industry: 10% services: 20%
Life expectancy at birth in years (2009)	male: 71.61 female: 75.52	male: 75.65 female: 80.69	male: 59.33 female: 73.14	male: 68.43 female: 75.73	male: 67.46 female: 72.61	male: 46.16 female: 47.76
Infant mortality: number of deaths per 1,000 live births (2009)	male: 18.87 female: 21.77	male: 6.94 female: 5.55	male: 12.08 female: 8.94	male: 26.16 female: 18.83	male: 34.61 female: 25.17	male: 100.38 female: 87.97
Personal computers per 100 people (2007)	5.7	80.5	13.3	16.1	3.3	0.8

Sources: CIA World Factbook; World Bank World Development Indicators.

15

policy choices on a national commitment to the common good, and breaking dependency on the international economy through promoting self-reliance. This model was embraced by many—including China scholars in the United States and elsewhere[10]—before the huge and tragic human cost and the less than stellar economic performance of the Maoist experiment became widely known.

And now, in the early twenty-first century, China is once again being touted as a model for the developing world for its sustained high rate of **export-led growth**, the rapid rise in the standards of living of most of its population, and successful poverty reduction. These achievements have been realized by stimulating ferocious economic competition between firms and individuals, which has resulted in a huge rise in unemployment, the appearance of large income and general welfare inequalities, and a consumer culture that many see as being crassly materialistic. In both means and consequences, the current widely watched and admired Chinese model of development is the complete opposite of the Maoist model.

China as a Rising Power

There is general scholarly, political, and public opinion consensus that the rise of China to great power status is one of the most important developments in global politics over the last decade or so. China's rise is certainly well under way, as measured by its global economic clout, military might, and diplomatic influence.

China's growing power and influence is changing the terrain of international relations in both theory and practice. A new acronym, **BRIC**, which stands for Brazil, Russia, India, and China, has made its way into the vocabulary of international relations to reflect the growing influence of the world's largest "emerging economies," and among the BRIC countries, China is widely regarded as the showcase. There is also little doubt that the PRC is now the dominant power in East Asia, having surpassed America's ally, Japan, in influence, even if Japan is a far richer country than China.

But the impact of China's rise goes far beyond the emerging economies and a shifting **regional power hierarchy** in East Asia. We are talking here of the very rare historical event of the ascendancy of a new superpower. The rise of the PRC is often compared to that of Britain in the nineteenth century and the United States in the twentieth, and it is not uncommon to hear or read that the twenty-first century will be the Chinese century.[11]

Many scholars and diplomats have noted the shift from a post–Cold War unipolar world, in which American power was unrivaled, to an emerging bipolar world in which the United States is learning to share center stage with China. Sino-American relations are considered by many knowledgeable observers to be the most important bilateral relationship in world politics today. Indeed, when leaders from the world's twenty largest economies—the G-20—met in London in early 2009 to discuss the global recession, there was particular attention paid to the words and actions of the "G-2"—the United States and China—as the countries most crucial to dealing with the crisis.

The quest for national wealth and power has been a preoccupation of Chinese governments since late imperial times. In the mid-1800s, China suffered devastating military defeats and other humiliations by Western powers intent on expanding "free trade" to East Asia. Prior to this momentous encounter with Europe and America, China considered itself to be the cultural (and by extension, the political) center of its known world, able to repel or absorb any challenge to the superiority of its civilization.

The shattering of this worldview was one of the most important ingredients in the decline and collapse of China's two-thousand-year-old imperial system in the early twentieth century and the country's turn toward the revolutionary process that led to the rise of the Chinese Communist Party and the establishment of the People's Republic in 1949. The tasks of **state-building** and the restoration of national pride fell to that new regime, and in both areas there were both triumphs and setbacks during the Maoist era. But the emergence of China as a global power that we are witnessing today did not begin until the early 1980s with the onset of the post-Mao economic reforms under the leadership of **Deng Xiaoping**, who along with Mao Zedong ranks as the most influential Chinese political leader of modern times.

If there is little debate about the fact of China's rise as a world power, there is lots of controversy among scholars, politicians, journalists, and others about what this means to the United States, East Asia, and the world. One side in this debate argues that the rise of China is threatening to American interests and a destabilizing factor in regional and international affairs. Those who are part of the "China Threat" school urge the United States and other countries to be wary of China's intentions and prepare for the worst, even war.[12] They express alarm, for example, at the PRC's vigorous development of a "blue water" navy with battleships and aircraft carriers that can sail for long periods of time far from the country's coastal waters.

The other side in this debate sees China's global ascendency as another chapter in the rise (and fall) of great powers that has occurred throughout much of history. They understand that China's rise will create challenges for other countries, particularly the United States, but they see these as an incentive for healthy competition, rather than a source of potentially disastrous conflict. They see many areas of mutual interest between the United States and the PRC and many opportunities for cooperation that could be of potential benefit to whole world, and they emphasize China's use of **soft power**, or noncoercive influence through means such as diplomacy and foreign aid, more than its reliance on or development of the mostly military instruments of hard power.[13]

Approaches to the Study of Chinese Politics

Like China itself, the study of Chinese politics has gone through dramatic changes since the founding of the People's Republic in 1949.[14] Indeed, as one might expect, political changes in China have often led to changing approaches to studying Chinese politics.

The first generation of American scholars to focus on politics in the PRC were not permitted to travel to China and had little access to materials of academic interest due to Cold War hostilities. Many of them spent time in Hong Kong, which was then still a British colony, conducting interviews with refugees from the China mainland and scouring valuable, yet relatively meager collections of local Chinese newspapers and a hodgepodge of official documents held by research centers devoted to the study of contemporary China. Although most of this pioneer generation had fairly strong Chinese language skills (often honed in Taiwan), they still had to rely heavily on translations of PRC radio broadcasts provided by organizations like the Central Intelligence Agency and the British Broadcasting Corporation for news about what was happening in China since very few Western reporters were permitted on the mainland.

Given the limits on research, these first-generation scholars tended to study large issues in Chinese politics. They produced numerous works that remain classics in the field, such as *Leadership in Communist* China (John Wilson Lewis, 1963), *Cadres, Bureaucracy, and Political Power in Communist China* (A. Doak Barnett, 1967), and *The Spirit of Chinese Politics* (Lucian W. Pye, 1968).

Once détente and normalization in Sino-American relations set in during the 1970s, scholarly access to China gradually opened up. Subsequent generations of specialists in Chinese politics have been able to carry out field research, work in archives, conduct surveys, interview people in all walks of life, including government and communist party officials, and engage in collaborative projects with colleagues in the PRC. There is now a literal flood of research material available from the PRC, such as books by Chinese academics, memoirs by important political figures, uncountable newspapers and journals, as well as massive amounts of data and statistics. There are still restrictions on scholarly activity (for both Chinese, as well as foreign researchers), and some subjects remain taboo because of their political sensitivity. Occasionally a foreign scholar is accused of crossing the line between academic work and "spying" and may be detained for a while before being expelled from the country. The PRC has also banned American scholars whose work has been judged to be objectionable from traveling to China. Nevertheless, the study of Chinese politics is a rich and dynamic field of scholarship that continues to attract superb graduate students, which bodes well for the future of this very important subject.

Not only have the methods and materials for studying politics in China changed greatly over the last six decades, but so, too, have the approaches, models, and topics that scholars employ and emphasize in their analysis. These can be broadly grouped into the following categories:

- elite politics
- factional politics
- informal politics
- bureaucratic politics
- center-local relations
- political institutions and processes
- political development
- political economy
- political culture
- ideology
- state-society relations
- policy- and event-centered studies

While each of these approaches has been especially popular among scholars at certain times, all of them are still "in the mix" when it comes to studying Chinese politics, and most are reflected in the chapters in this book.

Elite Politics

Because so much of China's history in the twentieth century was dominated by towering political figures, it is not surprising that scholars have often focused on the country's top leaders in studying Chinese politics. Through much of the 1950s and 1960s, a "Mao-in-Command" model of analysis reflected the extraordinary power of the Chairman of the Chinese Communist Party in determining the country's domestic and foreign policies. In the 1980s and 1990s, it was Deng Xiaoping who was clearly the PRC's "paramount leader," even though he never held the highest formal offices in the party or the government. China's more recent leaders have had neither the personal clout nor the historical stature of Mao and Deng. They have governed more collectively, and there are many more sources of influence at work in China's political system than in the earlier periods. Nevertheless, power remains highly concentrated in the upper echelons of the CCP, particularly in the two dozen or so members of the party's top organizations. Therefore, many China specialists still take an elite-centered approach—sometimes called **"Beijingology"**—to analyzing Chinese politics, closely studying who's who in the leadership, the formal documents issued by the central authorities, and the debates in journals containing articles by intellectuals and policy specialists who serve as advisers to party-state leaders.[15]

Factional Politics

This is really a subcategory of the elite approach to studying Chinese politics, but the emphasis is on divisions, or factions, within the ruling communist party leadership. **Factions** are groups of individuals who are united by some common bond and whose purpose is to maximize their power, especially that of their own leader. Factions may be motivated by shared ideology, policy preferences, personal loyalties, or simply the desire for power. All political parties have factionalism to one degree or another. In the case of the CCP, high-stakes factional politics has deep roots, and during the Maoist era led to bloody internal purges and vicious vendettas that spilled over into national cataclysms such as the Cultural Revolution in the latter half of the 1960s. Factionalism remains an important feature of leadership politics and policy-making in the PRC, but it plays out in a much more routine and institutionalized manner that may cost leaders their jobs, but no longer their lives, nor does it engulf their entire families.[16]

Informal Politics

Factional politics is a type of informal politics that involves power relationships outside of the constitutional institutions and processes of the state. It is not governed or regulated by formal rules or laws and is often seen as reflecting traditional, rather than modern aspects of politics. In fact, informal politics is frequently said to be a means of resistance to or a way of overcoming the inefficiencies of the modern state. Political scientists have long noted the importance of various kinds of informal politics in China, especially in the form of *guanxi,* or "connections" among individuals based on common bonds such as native place, school ties, military unit, or a network of shared friends, which has deep roots in Confucian culture.[17] A related type of informal politics studied by China scholars is **patron-client relations**, which involve exchanges between a more powerful patron and a less powerful client. The patron may offer resources (such as land or a job) or protection to the client, while the client provides various services, including labor, personal loyalty, and political support to the patron. Patron-client relations are particularly potent in rural China where the forces of tradition remain strong.[18] Kinship groups and folk religion temple associations are another source of informal politics that has been identified as very influential in Chinese **villages**.[19]

Bureaucratic Politics

The bureaucratic politics model of Chinese politics seeks to explain policy outcomes by looking at the interaction of officials in different, and often competing, government agencies who are mostly motivated by their organization's interests.[20] In this sense, it might be considered a variant of the factional model, with the common bond among members being their positions in a specific part of the bureaucracy. The bureaucrats' goals may include enhancing their organization's authority, increasing its budget, or protecting its turf. What's important is that individual political behavior is determined by the individual's place in the bureaucracy.

One of the first goals of the CCP when it came to power in 1949 was to rebuild the Chinese state, which had been weakened and torn apart by more than a century of rebellion, revolution, world war, and civil war. They did so with quite astounding speed and effectiveness. They also created a state that had greater control over the country's vast territory and reached deeper into the most basic levels of society, particularly the rural villages, than any government in Chinese history. As discussed above, the kind of political system they constructed—a communist party-state on the Soviet model—is, by definition, a highly bureaucratized and centralized one that seeks to exercise authority, not just over the economy, but also over many or even most other areas of society. This, in turn, requires a huge and powerful bureaucracy. In such an institutional environment, bureaucratic politics can become entrenched and intense. Scholars who take this approach to studying Chinese politics also often point to the deep and lingering influence of the legacy of bureaucratic government that was one of the distinguishing features of China's imperial system.[21]

Center-Local Relations

An important variant of the bureaucratic politics model of Chinese politics focuses on the relations between national and local levels of the party-state. In China, "local" refers to any of several levels of administration below the center (based in the capital, Beijing), including provinces, cities, rural **towns**, and villages. China has a long tradition of a strong central government, reaching far back into imperial times, but it also has a tradition of powerful centrifugal forces due to its historical patterns of development and regional variations. At times in its not so distant past, the country has disintegrated in fact, if not name, most recently in the early twentieth century during the so-called **Warlord Era** when real power was in the hand of more than a dozen "local" strongmen rather than the central government of the Republic of China.

As noted above, the PRC is a unitary state in which the national government has ultimate authority over lower levels. Even so, ever since the founding of the country, leaders in Beijing have had to contend with recalcitrance, obstruction, opposition, and even outright resistance from subordinate authorities when it comes to the implementation of party-state policies. The **market reform** of the economy has led to a decentralization of both authority and resources, and center-local relations is a timely and important topic in the study of Chinese politics.[22]

Political Institutions and Processes

Many studies of China by political scientists focus on specific institutions of the party-state. For example, there are studies of the Chinese Communist Party, of the **National People's Congress** (the PRC's legislature), and the **People's Liberation Army** (which encompasses all branches of China's military).[23] Other studies describe and analyze specific political processes, such as the **mass mobilization campaigns** that were a hallmark of the Maoist era (and have not altogether disappeared), elections for village leaders in rural China, or the rise of the Internet (especially blogs) as a form of political participation by "netizens" in the PRC.[24] A variation on these approaches to Chinese politics can be found in studies that ask questions about state-building, that is the construction of institutions and processes, at the national and local levels, designed to carry out various government functions, such as taxation or the delivery of social services.[25] This may be most crucial in the formative years of a new nation (the early 1950s for the PRC), but it is also a challenging task for a country going through a period of major transformation, as is now the case with China—which leads to the next approach to the study of Chinese politics.

Political Development

In this context, political development refers to the process of change within a political system or the transformation from one type of system to another within a country. China has experienced particularly, and perhaps uniquely, dramatic political change over the last century. Changes that occurred before the CCP came to power are largely, but not entirely, within the purview of historians rather than political scientists.[26] Some political development studies of the PRC analyze the evolution of the Chinese communist party-state from one form of non-democratic regime to another. At the height of Mao's rule, China's political system approximated the totalitarian model first used to describe Nazi Germany under Hitler and the Soviet Union under Stalin. **Totalitarianism**, as the name implies, is a form of government that presumes the right of total control over almost every aspect of society and life, including thought and reproduction, and seeks to dissolve as completely as possible the autonomy of the individual.

There is a lot of scholarly debate about the totalitarian model and its applicability to Maoist China. But there is consensus that since the 1980s the PRC has developed a much less intrusive party-state that has been variously referred to by political scientists as "revolutionary authoritarianism," "consultative authoritarianism," "soft authoritarianism," and "Market-Leninism,"[27] all of which are meant to convey that the CCP, while maintaining a very firm grip on political power has, at the same time, greatly reduced the scope of its authority, particularly in economic matters. A recent trend in the study of Chinese political development concerns the progress toward and prospects for democratization in China. This is another area in which there is vigorous academic (and political) debate that reflects divergent views about whether China is "ready" for democracy or even whether democracy is "right" for China.[28]

Political Economy

Political economy as a subfield of political science is concerned with the interaction between politics and the economy (how one influences the other), and especially with the role of the state versus the market in "governing the economy."[29] These have both been matters of great importance and contention in contemporary Chinese politics. Mao Zedong used his near absolute power to steer the PRC forcefully in the direction of his radical vision of socialism and communism and away from the both the bureaucratic Soviet model and the "capitalist road" down which he had concluded some of his closest comrades were leading the country. The results of this Maoist political economy were, in the first case, the disastrous **Great Leap Forward** (1958–1960) and the murderous **Great Proletarian Cultural Revolution** and its aftermath (1966–1976).

Since the late 1970s, Chinese leaders have remade the PRC economy into one that is almost the mirror opposite of that pursued by Mao, although still subject to the ultimate political authority of the Chinese Communist Party leadership and with a large state-controlled sector. China's spectacular economic success is a testament to the wisdom of their policy choices (or at least their willingness to "let go" of the economy), but one of the major challenges they face in the early twenty-first century—particularly in light of the global recession—is to keep the economy growing not only for the sake of the livelihoods of the Chinese people, but also because the party's political legitimacy now hinges heavily on its record of economic success.[30]

Political Culture

Political culture refers to the attitudes, values, and beliefs that people have about politics, which, in turn, shape their political behavior and how they perceive their relationship to political authority. In the case of China, scholars who have taken a political culture approach emphasize the enduring influence of Confucianism and other traditions in contemporary Chinese politics. More specifically, they stress attitudes such as deference to authority, the tendency toward an imperial style of rule on the part of government officials, a preference for an ordered hierarchy of power and a fear of disorder or chaos, the priority attached to the group rather than the individual, and an emphasis on duties over rights.

Although influential in the 1950s and 1960s as a way to understand Chinese politics, the political culture model was criticized by many scholars because of its alleged ethnocentric biases and over simplification. It fell out of favor for much of two decades, but has regained adherents who apply a much more sophisticated and nuanced understanding of Chinese culture and history to explaining what is unique about politics in China.[31] Some China specialists draw attention to aspects of the Confucian tradition, such as reverence for education, advancement by merit, and the strength of community ties, as partial explanations for the PRC's economic achievements, as well as those of Taiwan, Hong Kong, South Korea, and Singapore,[32] which is rather ironic since in earlier times other aspects of Confucianism were given as reasons why China fell behind the West in terms of industrialization.

Ideology

Ideology can succinctly be defined as a comprehensive set of ideas about how society should be ordered to achieve certain desired goals. It addresses fundamental political questions such as: Who should have political power? How should that power be used? How should resources be allocated among competing needs and demands?

One of the defining characteristics of a communist party-state is a formal commitment to some variant of Marxism-Leninism as the party's and the state's guiding ideology. The PRC is no exception; in fact, the case could be made that ideology has been an especially important and virulent variable in Chinese politics. Maoist **campaigns** such as the Great Leap Forward and the Cultural Revolution were largely driven by ideology. Post-Mao China is rightly seen as much less ideological in its politics and policy-making, and the party has drastically revised what "communism" means in China today. But ideology still matters as the foundation of the political culture of China's leadership and their approach to governing. It also marks the formal boundaries of what is politically permissible in the PRC. Some political scientists continue to study Mao's ideology (formally called "Mao Zedong Thought") both because of its uniqueness as a variant of communism and its impact on China. Others examine communist ideology in China as it has evolved since Mao and its role in legitimizing the profound policy changes the country has experienced and the continuing rule of a communist party.[33] In fact, there are those who argue that the CCP's ideological adaptability is one of the reasons it has been able to hold on to power.[34]

State-Society Relations

Political science has traditionally focused mainly on the formal institutions and agents of government—the state and state actors—as the most important units of analysis. This is still an influential approach to the study of politics in general, sometimes referred to as "bringing the state back in" or the "new institutionalism,"[35] and, as noted above, in the study of Chinese politics, as well. Somewhat recently, many scholars have argued that a state-centered approach is insufficient as a method of political analysis. They have instead concentrated on relations between the state and various components of the society over which its exercises power. These may be classes (such as industrial workers and peasants), non-economic groups (such as intellectuals, artists, and youth), and groups defined by other forms of **collective identity** (including religion, ethnicity, and gender).

The key questions in the state-society approach are: What impact does state policy have on the group in question? How does the state gain compliance for those policies? How does society respond to state demands or press its own demands on the state? Under what conditions is the state regarded as legitimate by various groups under its authority, and under what conditions is that legitimacy challenged or rejected? What forms of resistance to state power do social groups take? These have been, and remain, big questions in the study of Chinese politics. In fact, they are becoming increasingly crucial as Chinese society becomes more complex through the processes of modernization and globalization, which have given rise to new social groups such as private entrepreneurs and a middle class.[36]

The concept of **civil society** is very relevant here. The term is generally taken to mean the formation and operation of private organizations and associations composed of civilians who join together to pursue a common purpose *other than the direct pursuit of political power* and which operate independently of government authority. Most simply, it consists of those associations that exist and operate in the social space between the family and the state. Civil society can be composed of an almost infinite variety of types of associations, ranging from trade unions to religious groups, sororities and fraternities to professional organizations (e.g., for medical doctors or political scientists), charities and nongovernmental organizations—and even, as in one famous study, bowling leagues.[37] Many political scientists see the vigor of civil society as an important indicator of the health of a democracy. On the other hand, nondemocratic regimes tend to be wary of too much autonomy for private associations lest they develop political aspirations. The Maoist party-state managed to largely obliterate civil society in China. Civil society has reemerged to a limited degree in the much more open social space of contemporary China, which has led scholars to gauge (and debate) both the scope of its autonomy and its potential for planting the seeds of democratization.[38]

Policy- and Event-Centered Studies

There are numerous important works on Chinese politics that focus either on a particular policy issue or a specific event in the history of the People's Republic. These works most often draw on one or more of the approaches or models discussed above for their analytical framework. For example, one study of health policy in the PRC applies the bureaucratic politics model,[39] while one on population policy combines the political economy and state-society relations approaches.[40] Similarly, there are works on the Great Leap Forward that also stress bureaucratic politics or state-society relations,[41] as well as those that give priority to elite politics and the role of Mao Zedong.[42] Even when there are contending approaches to analyzing a specific issue or event, the result is most often vigorous academic debate that enhances our overall understanding of that aspect of Chinese politics.

The Contribution of Other Disciplines

Finally, a word should be said about the important contributions of disciplines other than political science to the study and analysis of Chinese politics. Most China scholars have had at least some interdisciplinary training and consider themselves to be an area- or country-specialist as well as a specialist in their specific discipline. China is literally too big, its history too long, its culture too deep, and its society (including its politics) too complex to be analyzed with a set of tools from just a single academic discipline. Most of the contributors to this volume are political scientists, but they would readily acknowledge (and many do so in their reference notes and suggested readings) how much they have learned about China from colleagues in a wide variety of fields such as history, sociology, anthropology, economics, art history, and language and literature. The other contributors would likewise recognize not only the insights they have gained from political science, but from many other disciplines as well.

The Organization of the Book

This is a rather unusual introductory textbook about Chinese politics. There are several superb single-authored texts on this subject written by some of the leading scholars in the field.[43] In this book, each chapter was written by a China scholar who is a specialist in the subject matter of that chapter.

The chapter topics are those most often taught in introductory courses on politics in China. You will note that there is not a chapter on China's foreign policy. This is, of course, a topic of great importance, particularly in light of the emphasis we have put on the rise of China as a world power. But it is usually the case that Chinese foreign policy is taught as a separate course or as part of a course on the international relations of East Asia. It is pretty ambitious for an instructor to try to cover both Chinese domestic politics and foreign policy in a single course. (Imagine trying to do that for the United States!) Several of the chapters in this book do, however, touch on aspects of China's international relations as they bear on the topic at hand.

Each chapter contains boxes that are set off from the main body of the text. These are meant to highlight and go into a little more detail about particularly important individuals, events, policies, or other topics that will enhance the reader's understanding of the main subject of the chapter. Following the main chapters of the book, there is a timeline of modern Chinese political history and a glossary of key terms. The key terms are printed in bold in their first appearance in the text.

Part I: The Political History of Modern China

The first three chapters following this introduction are analytical chronologies of Chinese history from imperial times to the present. "From Empire to Peoples' Republic" (by R. Keith Schoppa) briefly discusses pre-modern Chinese history, but focuses mostly on the period from the late eighteenth through the mid-twentieth centuries. It traces the surprisingly rapid and radical decline of, as well as the ultimately futile efforts to save, the last Chinese imperial dynasty (the **Qing**). The author then turns his attention to the overthrow of the Qing dynasty in the Revolution of 1911, the founding of the Republic of China in 1912, the disintegration of the Republic in the 1920s, and the brief period of relative stability and progress under the leadership of Chiang Kai-shek and the Nationalist Party. This is followed by a discussion of the origins of the Chinese Communist Party and the rise to power within the party of Mao Zedong, the onset of civil war between the Nationalists and the Communists, which ended in 1949 with the victory of the CCP, the establishment of the People's Republic, and the flight of the Nationalists to Taiwan. In the final section of the chapter, the author offers an analysis of why the CCP won the civil war, and why the

Nationalists lost—obviously very crucial questions, given the impact of the outcome of the conflict, not just on Chinese history, but world history as well.

"Mao Zedong in Power (1949–1976)" (by Frederick C. Teiwes) mostly covers the period during which Chairman Mao wielded nearly absolute authority in Chinese politics from the founding of the People's Republic until his death. But it also discusses in some detail the process by which Mao Zedong consolidated power in the CCP in the 1940s since that had such a strong influence on the way he exercised power after the founding of the PRC in 1949. The early years of communist rule in China were marked by considerable successes, particularly in the areas of initial industrialization and raising health and education standards, but they also saw a tightening of the party's grip over society and the first post–1949 political fissures within the party's top leadership. In the latter part of the 1950s, Mao took a sharp "leftward" turn ideologically that had a profound effect on politics and policy in the PRC, most notably in the Great Leap Forward (1958–1960), a utopian push for accelerated economic development that plunged the country into famine and depression, and the Great Proletarian Cultural Revolution that began in 1966 and led to a terribly destructive period that combined elements of a witch hunt, a crusade, an inquisition, armed conflict, and cut-throat palace politics. The author not only describes *what* happened during this dramatic and fateful era, but also *why* it happened, as well as offering a perspective on how we should evaluate the overall influence and legacy of Mao Zedong, who was surely one of the most important and complex political figures in modern times.

The next chapter, "Deng Xiaoping and His Successors (1976 to the Present)" (by Bruce Gilley) takes up the chronology of Chinese politics from the aftermath of Mao's death through the first decade of the twenty-first century. The central theme here is political context of the phenomenal economic transformation of China during the last three decades. This transformation was only possible because of the improbable political resurrection and consolidation of power by Deng Xiaoping, who became China's top leader about a year after Mao's death, despite the fact that he had been purged during the Cultural Revolution for allegedly opposing the Chairman. Deng presided over the implementation of reforms that moved China toward a globalized **market economy**, although with strong state controls. Deng's greatest crisis came in the spring of 1989 when hundreds of thousands (some estimated that the crowd peaked at over a million) of people gathered in and near **Tiananmen Square** in the center of Beijing to protest about a variety of issues, including government corruption and soaring inflation, as well as asking for greater political freedom. Deng and most of China's other key leaders decided to use massive force to end the demonstration, resulting in the so-called **Beijing Massacre** of June 4, 1989, in which a still unknown large number of civilians were killed by the Chinese army. Deng's successors (Deng died in 1997), **Jiang Zemin** (formally in power from 1989–2002) and **Hu Jintao** (in power since 2002) have continued the combination of economic reform and unchallengeable communist party rule that has been the basic pattern of Chinese politics in the post-Mao era.

Part II: Ideology, Governance, and Political Economy

The second part of the book consists of three chapters that focus on broad aspects of Chinese politics that are important for understanding how the PRC has been and is governed. Chapter 5, "Ideology and Chinese Politics" (of which I am the author) discusses how communism (Marxism-Leninism) first came to China in the early twentieth century and its growing influence in shaping the course of the Chinese revolution. It explores how, in the 1940s, Mao Zedong's adaptation of Marxism-Leninism became the ideological orthodoxy of the Chinese Communist Party and the essential components of "**Mao Zedong Thought**" (as it is formally called) and their impact on Chinese politics and policy during the Maoist era. There is a brief review of how Mao Zedong Thought is now officially evaluated and embraced in a "communist" China that has, in so many ways, become the obverse of what the Chairman believed should be the ideological direction of the PRC. The chapter then turns to the topic of "**Deng Xiaoping Theory**," which is said by the CCP to be its guiding ideology in the era of reform and opening to the world, and is notable for the ideological justification it provides for introducing large elements of capitalism into a country still governed by a communist party. Both Jiang Zemin and Hu Jintao have gone to considerable lengths to put their personal stamps on party ideology by continuing to adapt Mao Zedong Thought and Deng Xiaoping Theory to changing historical circumstances. The chapter concludes with an exploration of contending ideologies in China today and the role of Chinese communist ideology in contemporary Chinese politics.

The next chapter, "China's Communist Party-State: The Structure and Dynamics of Power" (by Cheng Li) first provides a description of how the political system of the PRC is organized and functions in governing the People's Republic. As the chapter title indicates and as discussed earlier, China's political system is what political scientists classify as a communist party-state. This chapter looks at the key institutions and offices of both the Chinese Communist Party (the party) and the People's Republic of China (the state) and the multiple and multifaceted connections between them that ensure that the state remains under the authority of the party. It then takes up the important question of the changing composition of the membership and particularly the top leadership of the CCP as it has evolved from a revolutionary organization designed to seize power and pursue radical objectives to a ruling party managing a complex modern state committed above all to economic development. In the last part of the chapter, the author offers his analysis of several important trends that now shape elite politics and policy-making in the PRC and that might provide some guidance for understanding how the party-state evolves in the near future.

Economic policy-making is one of the most crucial tasks of any government, and economic performance is a major standard by which a people judge their government. It also influences nearly every other aspect of politics; thus the topic is included in this part of the book, along with the chapters on ideology and the party-state. The chapter on "China's Political Economy" (by David Zweig) examines the CCP's overall development strategies and the specific economic policies made by the party leadership and implemented by the state machinery. Since this is one of the ways in which China has changed most dramatically in recent decades, the author provides a brief overview of the "Maoist political economy" that prevailed before the beginning of the **reform era** in the late 1970s. He then lays out the stages and strategy of economic reform begun by Deng Xiaoping, followed by a discussion of a series of issues that lie at the heart of the political economy of contemporary China, including the **decollectivization** of agriculture, the decline of the public sector and the growth of privatization, corruption, property rights, and the tension between market forces and the still heavy hand of the party-state in the economy. The chapter concludes with a section on the internationalization of China's economy and the PRC's rapidly expanding role in the global economy.

Part III: Politics and Policy in Action

The first two chapters in Part III of the book look at Chinese politics in the spatial dimensions of rural and urban China, while the following chapters present four case studies of policies that are particularly important in the political life of the PRC. Chapter 8, "Rural China: Reform and Resistance" (by John James Kennedy) focuses on politics in the countryside, where 55 percent of the Chinese people (over 700 million) *technically* live—technically, that is, because as many as 150 million of those rural residents have migrated to the cities in search of work, an important subject that is treated in the following chapter on urban China. The chapter on rural China explains the administrative organization of the Chinese countryside and how that fits into the overall party-state structure of the PRC. The author pays particular attention to politics in China's villages, of which there are more than 600,000. In recent years, village governance in China has changed dramatically with the introduction of elections for leaders and the formation of village representative assemblies. The chapter describes and evaluates just how democratic these trends are and the relationship between elected village officials and the village communist party leader, who is still the most powerful person on the local level. Finally, the author takes up the issue of unrest in the Chinese countryside, which has been growing significantly as rural people take action to protest against corrupt officials, unscrupulous land grabs, polluting factories, and other matters they find harmful to their interests.

There are intentionally many parallels and connections between the chapter on rural China and the chapter, "Urban China: Change and Contention" (by William Hurst). As noted above, this chapter looks in some depth at the situation of rural migrants—called the "floating population"—who now make up a sizable portion of the inhabitants of many Chinese cities. It also describes the administrative structure of China's urban areas and its ties to adjacent rural regions. The author discusses the rise in urban unemployment as state-owned enterprises are shut down, streamlined, or privatized and, in contrast, the rise of a new urban middle class of professionals and entrepreneurs, as well as the political views and career expectations of the urban youth. He then explores the challenges that environmental concerns, growing socioeconomic inequality, and the need for urban planning pose to city and national leaders in China.

The final four chapters in this part of the book deal with key areas of public policy in the PRC. The first concerns policies toward the arts and culture (by Richard Curt Kraus). Although the nature and extent of censorship has changed greatly since Mao was in power and the arts are, in many ways, flourishing in China, culture is one of the areas of life in which the Chinese communist party-state still claims the right to exercise a "leading role," enforcing limits on freedom of expression if its watchdogs feel a certain and undefined ideological or political line has been crossed.

The environmental desecration that has been a severe downside of China's economic miracle is the subject of the next chapter (by Katherine Morton). Maltreatment of the environment is, ironically, one the things that the Maoist and reform eras in China have in common. The section discusses the causes and most egregious consequences of China's environmental crisis, its international implications, the government's response, and the growth of grassroots environmental activism in the PRC. The author also assesses the limitations on reform of China's environmental policy and the possibilities that the country will shift toward a model of **sustainable development**.

The chapter on public health (by Joan Kaufman) takes note of the extension of basic health care to the vast majority of the Chinese people that counts as one of the major achievements of the Maoist era. But the focus of this chapter is on the decline in primary and preventive care, especially in the rural areas, that has taken place due to the impact of marketization and privatization of social services in general. The author stresses the impact of the **Severe Acute Respiratory Syndrome (SARS)** crisis in 2003 in opening the eyes of the PRC leadership to the appalling condition of the country's health care system. The chapter also looks at the evolution of China's policy toward HIV/AIDS, which is spreading fast in the PRC and has recently been given a high priority by the government officials, as has overall health care reform.

The issue addressed in the next chapter is population control, in particular China's **one-child policy**. This is probably among the most widely known and controversial policies—both at home and abroad—of the Chinese government. Among the questions that this chapter (by Tyrene White) addresses are: When and why did China's leaders become so concerned about the rate of population increase in the country that they decided to implement the most restrictive and intrusive family planning policy in history? What were the components of the one-child policy, and how has it evolved over time? Why was it so effective in urban areas, but not in rural areas, where it met with significant resistance? And where it was effective, did it have the positive effect on development that is claimed by Chinese leaders? What have been some of the other results or consequences of that policy? For example, how did the one-child policy contribute to a situation in which China has an unnatural gender imbalance of more males than females in certain age groups, and what are the social and political implications of that imbalance? The rapid "graying" of China's population and the public policy challenges this presents to the government are also discussed.

Part IV: Politics on China's Periphery

The last part of this book is called "Politics on China's Periphery." This is not meant, in any sense, to convey that the areas or topics covered are only of peripheral, or minor, importance in understanding Chinese politics. They are, in fact, of central importance and are only peripheral in the geographic sense that they concern places that are on the periphery, or edges, of the People's Republic. Three of these areas—Tibet, Xinjiang, and Hong Kong—are formally administrative parts of the People's Republic of China, although Tibet's and Xinjiang's status as autonomous regions is quite different from that of Hong Kong as a special administrative region of the PRC. The fourth area—Taiwan—is not under the control of the PRC and acts, in many ways, as an independent country, although Beijing insists that it is rightfully part of China.

The first two chapters in this section are on Tibet (by Robert Barnett) and Xinjiang (by Gardner Bovingdon). Both Tibet and Xinjiang are autonomous regions of the PRC located in the far western part of the country. As noted in the earlier discussion of geography, autonomous regions are areas, equivalent in administrative status to provinces directly under the central government, that have a high concentration of ethnic minority population and are allowed some leeway to adopt certain national policies to their culture and customs while remaining firmly under the political and military authority of Beijing. Tibet and Xinjiang are the two largest, if sparsely populated, territorial units in the PRC and both lie along strategically important borders; both regions have also been the site of substantial ethnic conflict and challenges to the central government. The situation in Tibet has been particularly volatile and gained widespread international attention because of the visibility and prominence of the **Dalai Lama**, the spiritual leader of Tibetan Buddhism who has been in exile from Tibet since 1959. The majority of the population in Xinjiang is Muslim, and the largest ethnic group among them is the Uyghurs, who have very strong religious and cultural ties to the Islamic nation-states and peoples of Central Asia. These ties have given rise to separatist movements in Xinjiang and serious incidents of violence that, while not as large scale as the protests in Tibet, are a matter of urgent importance in contemporary Chinese politics.

The next chapter is about Hong Kong (by Sonny Shiu-Hing Lo), which was a British colony from the mid-nineteenth century until 1997, when it was returned through negotiations to Chinese sovereignty. In contrast to Tibet and Xinjiang, Hong Kong is a densely populated, territorially tiny part of the People's Republic of China. It is also one of the world's great financial centers and by far the richest part of the PRC—with a very free market capitalist economy. Hong Kong is officially a Special Administrative Region (SAR) of the PRC that does have significant degrees of self-government and democracy. How these are exercised in practice and the tensions this creates with Beijing—which has the final say in matters related to the SAR—is a major theme of this chapter.

The subject of the next chapter (by Shelley Rigger) is Taiwan. The PRC claims sovereignty over this island, which is just a bit farther from the Chinese mainland than Cuba is from the United States. But, in fact, Taiwan has not been under the PRC's control since the end of the **Chinese civil war** in 1949. At that time, the losing side in the conflict—the Nationalists under Chiang Kai-shek—was able to retreat to Taiwan and, with U.S. support, establish a viable political system and economy separate from the mainland. The author describes the transition that Taiwan has made since then from an authoritarian regime to a multiparty democracy with one of the highest standards of living in East Asia. After decades of hostile estrangement, Taiwan and the PRC have recently developed commercial and other ties. The future of Taiwan-China relations is a hot political topic on both the island and the mainland—and of strategic importance to the region and the United States. And, as the author emphasizes, politics in Taiwan (with a population not much smaller than Iraq and larger than Australia) is interesting and important on its own terms.

Conclusion

In 1949, a book titled *China Shakes the World* was published.[44] It was written by Jack Belden, one of the very few Western journalists who was able to cover the Chinese Communist Party during the war against Japan and the civil war against the Nationalists. Belden's message was that what was happening then and there in China—the anticipated victory of the CCP—was destined to be of global significance. But the book appeared at a time when most Americans had little interest in China, which they had given up for lost to chaos and communism. With the onset of the "Red Scare" in the United States, Belden's book gained hardly any attention and soon went out of print.

In 2006, another book with the same title, *China Shakes the World*, was published. But it was published at a time of enormous international and American interest in the PRC. The author, James Kynge, was also a journalist in China and his bottom-line message was not that different from Belden's, which both sought to capture in the title of their books. Both Belden and Kynge were right—China was shaking the world—though Kynge's book, with the subtitle *A Titan's Rise and Troubled Future—and the Challenge for America*, was a much greater commercial success than Belden's; it won the *Financial Times* 2006 Business Book of the Year award.

But the message conveyed by the shared titles of Belden's and Kynge's books, and even the words they used, has deeper roots. It was Napoleon Bonaparte, emperor of France in the early nineteenth century, who is said to have remarked, when looking at a map of Europe and Asia, "Let China sleep. For when she wakes, she will shake the world."[45] In the long run, Napoleon was right, too, although when he died in 1821, imperial China was in decline and was about to be badly shaken by a new world order dominated by the rising powers of Western Europe.

Imperial China's decline led to more than a hundred years of tumultuous and often hugely violent change, culminating in the reawakening of China that was reflected in Chairman Mao Zedong's proclamation, just before the founding the PRC on October 1, 1949, that "the Chinese people have stood up!"[46] China shook the world during the Maoist era, but because of the Cold War and Mao's own disastrous policies, its global influence was limited and great pain was inflicted on the country.

Now a changed and changing China is again shaking the world, this time with a very different impact on global affairs and the Chinese people. The editor and authors of this book hope that their contributions help readers better understand China's modern political history and contemporary politics and why these are matters that should command the attention of anyone who wants to be an informed citizen of the twenty-first century.

Notes

1. See, for example, "China's Economic Miracle," in Susan Shirk, *China: Fragile Superpower; How China's Internal Politics Could Derail Its Peaceful Rise* (New York: Oxford University Press, 2007), 13–33.

2. "When China Wakes," *The Economist*, November 28, 1992, 15.

3. *The Economist*, The Economist Intelligence Unit's Index of Democracy 2008, available at http://www.eiu.com/.

4. See Jonathan Spence, *The Chan's Great Continent: China in Western Minds* (New York, W. W. Norton, 1998), 1–18. For an argument that Marco Polo never made it as far as China, see Frances Woods, *Did Marco Polo Go To China?* (Boulder, CO: Westview Press, 1998).

5. Elizabeth J. Perry, "Studying Chinese Politics: Farewell to Revolution?," *The China Journal* 57 (January 2007): 5.

6. See, for example, Peter Hays Gries, *China's New Nationalism: Pride, Politics, and Diplomacy* (Berkeley: University of California Press, 2005); and Suisheng Zhao, *A Nation-State by Construction: Dynamics of Modern Chinese Nationalism* (Stanford, CA: Stanford University Press, 2004).

7. See Paul A. Cohen, "Remembering and Forgetting National Humiliation in Twentieth-Century China," in Paul A. Cohen, *China Unbound: Evolving Perspectives on the Chinese Past* (New York: Routledge, 2003).

8. In recent years, Cyprus, Nepal, and Moldova have had ruling communist parties that were *elected into* power in multiparty states. Communist party-states such as China do not permit free, multi-party elections. On Nepal's communist party, see the Box "Maoism Outside of China" in chapter 5.

9. See, for example, Phil Deans, "The People's Republic of China: The Post-Socialist Developmental State," in Linda Low, ed., *New Thinking on the Developmental State* (Hauppauge NY: Nova Science Publishers, 2004).

10. See, for example, The Committee of Concerned Asian Scholars, *China! Inside the People's Republic* (New York: Bantam Books, 1972); Michel Oksenberg, ed., *China's Developmental Experience* (New York: The Academy of Political Science, Columbia University, 1973); Victor Nee and James Peck, eds., *China's Uninterrupted Revolution: From 1840 to the Present* (New York: Pantheon Books, 1975); and Ross Terrill, ed., *The China Difference* (New York: Harper Collins, 1979).

11. See, for example, Martin Jacques, *When China Rules the World: The End of the Western World and the Birth of a New Global Order* (New York: Penguin Press, 2009); Ted Fishman, "The Chinese Century," *The New York Times*, July 4, 2004; and Oded Shenkar, *The Chinese Century: The Rising Chinese Economy and Its Impact on the Global Economy, the Balance of Power, and Your Job* (Philadelphia, PA: Wharton School Publishing, 2004).

12. See, for example, Peter Navarro, *The Coming China Wars: Where They Will Be Fought and How They Can Be Won* (Upper Saddle River, NJ: FT Press, 2008); and Steven W. Mosher, *Hegemon: China's Plan to Dominate Asia and the World* (New York: Encounter Books, 2000).

13. See, for example, Joshua Kurlantzick, *Charm Offensive: How China's Soft Power Is Transforming the World* (New Haven, CT: Yale University Press, 2007); C. Fred Bergsten et. al., *China's Rise: Challenges and Opportunities* (Washington, DC: Peterson Institute for International Economics, 2008); and William H. Overholt, *The Rise of China: How Economic Reform Is Creating a New Superpower* (New York, W. W. Norton, 2008).

14. For reviews of the evolution of the study of Chinese politics, see: Richard Baum, "Studies of Chinese Politics in the United States," in *China Watching: Perspectives from Europe, Japan and the United States,* eds. Robert Ash, David Shambaugh, and Seiichiro Takagi (New York: Taylor & Francis, 2006), 147–68; Lowell Dittmer and William Hurst, "Analysis in Limbo: Contemporary Chinese Politics amid the Maturation of Reform," in *China's Deep Reform: Domestic Politics in Transition,* eds. Lowell Dittmer and Guoli Liu (Lanham, MD: Rowman & Littlefield, 2006), 25–46; Sujian Guo and Jean-Marc F. Blanchard, eds., Special Issue on "The State of the Field: Political Science and Chinese Political Studies," *Journal of Chinese Political Science*, 14, no. 3 (September, 2009).

15. See, for example, Joseph Fewsmith, *China since Tiananmen: From Deng Xiaoping to Hu Jintao*, 2nd ed. (New York: Cambridge University Press, 2008). Also see many of the suggested readings in chapter 3 by Frederick C. Teiwes in this volume.

16. See, for example, Victor C. Shih, *Factions and Finance in China: Elite Conflict and Inflation* (New York: Cambridge University Press, 2003). The influence of leadership factions (or coalitions) on Chinese politics is a central theme of chapter 6 by Cheng Li in this volume.

17. See, for example, Lucian W. Pye, *The Dynamics of Chinese Politics* (Cambridge, MA: Oelgeschlager, Gunn & Hain, 1981).

18. See, for example, Jean Oi, "Communism and Clientelism: Rural Politics in China," *World Politics* 32, no. 2 (January 1985): 238–266, and her book, *State and Peasant in Contemporary Chin: The Political Economy of Village Government* (Berkeley: University of California Press, 1989).

19. See Lily L. Tsai, *Accountability Without Democracy: Solidary Groups and Public Goods Provision in Rural China* (New York: Cambridge Studies on Comparative Politics, Cambridge University Press, 2007).

20. See, for example, Kenneth G. Lieberthal and David M. Lampton, eds. *Bureaucracy, Politics, and Decision Making in Post-Mao China* (Berkeley: University of California Press, 1992).

21. See, for example, Harry Harding, *Organizing China: The Problem of Bureaucracy, 1949–1976* (Stanford, CA: Stanford University Press, 1981).

22. See, for example, Thomas P. Bernstein and Xiaobo Lü, "Taxation without Representation: Peasants, the Central and the Local States in Reform China," *The China Quarterly* 163 (Sept. 2000): 742–763; and their book, *Taxation without Representation in Contemporary Rural China* (New York: Cambridge University Press, 2003).

23. See, for example, David L. Shambaugh, *China's Communist Party: Atrophy and Adaptation* (Berkeley: University of California Press, 2008); Kevin J. O'Brien, *Reform Without Liberalization: China's National People's Congress and the Politics of Institutional Change* (New York: Cambridge University Press, 1990); and David L. Shambaugh, *Modernizing China's Military: Progress, Problems, and Prospects* (Berkeley: University of California Press, 2002).

24. See, for example, Gordon Bennett, *Yundong: Mass Campaigns in Chinese Communist Leadership* (Berkeley: Center for Chinese Studies, University of California, 1976) and Tyrene White, *China's Longest Campaign: Birth Planning in the People's Republic, 1949–2005* (Ithaca, NY: Cornell University Press, 2006); Baogang He, *Rural Democracy in China The Role of Village Elections* (New York: Palgrave Macmillan, 2007); Guobin Yang, *The Power of the Internet in China: Citizen Activism Online* (New York: Columbia University Press, 2009).

25. See, for example, Elizabeth Remick, *Building Local States: China during the Republican and Post-Mao Eras* (Cambridge, MA: Harvard University Asia Center, 2004).

26. For an example of a study by a political scientist of political development in China in the 1920s and 1930s, see Suisheng Zhao, *Power by Design: Constitution-Making in Nationalist China* (Honolulu: University of Hawaii Press, 1996).

27. Perry, "Studying Chinese Politics: Farewell to Revolution?," 5; Harry Harding, *China's Second Revolution: Reform after Mao* (Washington, DC: Brookings Institution Press, 1987), 200; Minxin Pei, "China's Evolution Toward Soft Authoritarianism," in Edward Friedman and Barrett L. McCormick, eds., *What if China Doesn't Democratize? Implications for War and Peace* (Armonk, NY: M. E. Sharpe, 2000) . 74–95; Marc Blecher, *China against the Tides: Restructuring through Revolution, Radicalism and Reform*, 3rd ed. (New York: Continuum Books, 2009), 72.

28. See, for example, Bruce Gilley, *China's Democratic Future: How It Will Happen and Where It Will Lead* (New York: Columbia University Press, 2004).

29. The term comes from Peter A. Hall, *Governing the Economy: The Politics of State Intervention in Britain and France* (New York: Oxford University Press, 1986). It is also one of the four themes applied to the study of comparative politics in Mark Kesselman, Joel Krieger, William A. Joseph, eds., *Introduction to Comparative Politics*, 5th ed. (Boston: Wadsworth/Cengage, 2009).

30. There are numerous studies by political scientists that focus on political economy issues. For a listing of some of these, see the suggested readings at the end of chapter 7 by David Zweig in this volume.

31. See, for example, Jeffrey N. Wasserstrom and Elizabeth Perry, eds., *Popular Protest and Political Culture in Modern China*, 2nd ed. (Boulder, CO: Westview Press, 1994). Among the most early important works that take the political culture approach to Chinese politics are those of Lucian Pye, for example, *Asian Power and Politics: The Cultural Dimensions of Authority* (Cambridge, MA: Harvard University Press, 1988). See also, Peter R. Moody, "Trends in the Study of Chinese Political Culture," *China Quarterly*, 139 (September, 1994), 731–740

32. See, for example, Ezra F. Vogel, *The Four Little Dragons: The Spread of Industrialization in East Asia* (Cambridge, MA: Harvard University Press, 1991); and Daniel A. Bell, *China's New Confucianism: Politics and Everyday Life in a Changing Society* (Princeton, NJ: Princeton University Press, 2008).

33. For a list of suggested readings on the subject of the ideology of the CCP, including Mao Zedong Thought, see chapter 5 by William A. Joseph in this volume.

34. See, for example, John W. Lewis and Xue Litai, "Social Change and Political Reform in China: Meeting the Challenge of Success," *The China Quarterly* 176 (December 2003): 926–42; and Bruce J. Dickson, *Wealth into Power: The Communist Party's Embrace of China's Private Sector* (New York: Cambridge University Press, 2008).

35. Peter B. Evans, Dietrich Rueschemeyer, and Theda Skocpol, *Bringing the State Back In* (New York: Cambridge University Press, 1985); and B. Guy Peters, *Institutional Theory in Political Science: The New Institutionalism*, 2nd ed, (New York: Continuum, 2005).

36. This is another subfield in the study of Chinese politics with a very rich and varied scholarly literature. For some examples, see the suggested readings at the end of the chapters by Kennedy, Hurst, and Kraus in this volume. Among the excellent edited volumes on the topic is Peter Gries and Stanley Rosen, eds., *State and Society in 21st Century China* (New York: Routledge Curzon, 2004).

37. Robert D. Putnam, *Bowling Alone: The Collapse and Revival of American Community* (New York: Simon & Schuster, 2000).

38. See, for example, Timothy Brook and B. Michael Frolic, *Civil Society in China* (Armonk, NY: M. E. Sharpe, 1997); Jonathan Unger, ed., *Associations and the Chinese State: Contested Spaces*. Armonk, NY: M. E. Sharpe, 2008.

39. David M Lampton, *Health, Conflict, and the Chinese Political System* (Ann Arbor: Michigan Papers in Chinese Studies, 1974).

40. White, *China's Longest Campaign*.

41. David Bachman, *Bureaucracy, Economy, and Leadership in China: The Institutional Origins of the Great Leap Forward* (New York: Cambridge University Press, 1991); and Ralph A. Thaxton Jr., *Catastrophe and Contention in Rural China: Mao's Great Leap Forward Famine and the Origins of Righteous Resistance in Da Fo Village* (New York: Cambridge University Press, 2008).

42. Frederick C. Teiwes and Warren Sun, *China's Road to Disaster: Mao, Central Politicians, and Provincial Leaders in the Unfolding of the Great Leap Forward 1955–1959* (Armonk, NY: East Gate Book, 1998). Elite-centered studies of the Cultural Revolution include the pathbreaking work by Roderick McFarquhar: *The Origins of the Cultural Revolution*, Vols. 1–3 (New York: Columbia University Press, 1974; 1983; 1999); and with Michael Schoenhals, *Mao's Last Revolution* (Cambridge, MA: Harvard University Press, 2008).

43. See, notably, Blecher, *China against the Tides;* June Teufel Dreyer, *China's Political System*, 7th ed. (New York: Longman, 2009); Kenneth J. Lieberthal, *Governing China: From Revolution to Reform*, 2nd ed. (New York: W. W. Norton, 2003); and Tony Saich, *Governance and Politics of China*, 2nd ed. (New York: Palgrave Macmillan, 2004).

44. Jack Belden, *China Shakes the World* (New York: Harper, 1949). The book was republished in 1970 by Monthly Review Press and in 1989 by New World Press. The other classic book from a similar time and on a similar topic is Edgar Snow, *Red Star Over China* (New York: Random House, 1938; reprinted by Grove Press, 1994).

45. James Kynge, *China Shakes the World: A Titan's Rise and Troubled Future—and the Challenge for America* (Boston, MA: Houghton Mifflin Harcourt, 2006). Parts of the quote attributed to Napoleon have been used in numerous titles of books and articles about China since the 1980s; see, for example, Nicholas D. Kristof and Sheryl Wudunn, *China Wakes: The Struggle for the Soul of a Rising Power* (New York: Times Books/Random House, 1994); Yu Guangyuan, *Deng Xiaoping Shakes the World: An Eyewitness Account of China's Party Work Conference and the Third Plenum*, edited by Steven I. Levine and Ezra F. Vogel (Norwalk, CT: EastBridge, 2004); and "When China Wakes," *The Economist*, November 28, 1992.

46. *Selected Works of Mao Tsetung*, Vol. V (Peking: Foreign Languages Press, 1977), 15–19.

Suggested Readings

China Brief, The Jamestown Foundation, http://www.jamestown.org/programs/chinabrief/

China Leadership Monitor, The Hoover Institution, http://www.hoover.org/publications/clm/

Cohen, Paul A. *Discovering History in China: American Historical Writing on the Recent Chinese Past*. New York: Columbia University Press, 1986.

Dillon, Michael. *Contemporary China: An Introduction*. New York: Routledge, 2008.

Fairbank, John King, and Merle Goldman. *China: A New History*. 2nd ed. Cambridge, MA: Harvard University Press, 2006.

Fenby, Jonathan. *Modern China: The Fall and Rise of a Great Power, 1850 to the Present*. New York: Harper Collins, 2008.

Grasso, June, Jay Cornin, and Michael Kort. *Modernization and Revolution in China: From the Opium Wars to the Olympics*. 4th ed. Armonk, NY: M. E. Sharpe, 2009.

Guo, Sujian and Baogang Guo, *Challenges Facing Chinese Political Development*. Lanham, MD: Lexington Books, 2007.

Hutchings, Graham. *Modern China: A Guide to a Century of Change*. Cambridge, MA: Harvard University Press, 2001.

Kang, David C. *China Rising: Peace, Power, and Order in East Asia*. New York: Columbia University Press, 2007.

Lampton, David M. *The Three Faces of Chinese Power: Might, Money, and Minds*. Berkeley: University of California Press, 2008.

Lawrance, Alan. *China since 1919: Revolution and Reform; A Sourcebook*. New York: Routledge, 2004.

Mitter, Rana. *Modern China: A Very Short Introduction*. New York: Oxford University Press, 2008.

Ross, Robert, ed., *China's Ascent: Power, Security, and the Future of International Politics*. Ithaca, NY: Cornell University Press, 2008.

Schoppa, R. Keith. *Revolution and Its Past: Identities and Change in Modern Chinese History*. Upper Saddle River, NJ: Prentice Hall, 2001.

Schoppa, R. Keith. *The Columbia Guide to Modern Chinese History*. New York: Columbia University Press, 2000.

Schoppa, R. Keith. *Twentieth Century China: A History in Documents*. New York: Oxford University Press, 2004.

Spence, Jonathan. *The Search for Modern China*. 2nd ed. New York: W. W. Norton, 1999.

Wasserstrom, Jeffrey M. *China in the 21st Century: What Everyone Needs to Know*. New York: Oxford University Press, 2010.

Wilkinson, Endymion. *Chinese History: A Manual*. Revised and Enlarged ed. Cambridge, MA: Harvard University Press, 2000.

THE POLITICAL HISTORY OF
MODERN CHINA

2

From Empire to People's Republic

R. Keith Schoppa

The Chinese empire was born amid the turmoil and wars of the second century BCE. In the first two dynastic regimes, the Qin (221–206 BCE) and the Han (202 BCE–220 CE) several patterns emerged that would persist throughout the empire until 1912. First, when the brutal leader of the Qin state, known historically as Qin Shi Huangdi (literally, "first emperor of Qin"), established a centralized empire, he momentarily put to rest the political centrifugal forces endemic in Chinese feudalism; but relations between center and region and/or locality remained an ongoing issue throughout the empire and the Republic (1912–1949). Tensions between center and locality continue to be problematic in early twenty-first century China in the wake of the economic reforms begun in the 1980s.

Second, while Qin Shi Huangdi tried to burn all books dealing with history, literature, or philosophy, the Han dynasty began to rally around the ideas and approach of Confucius (Kong Fuzi), who had lived in the late fifth century BCE (see Box, **Confucius on Government and Politics**). The Han instituted a rudimentary **civil service examination system** with a strong emphasis on testing mastery of Confucianism. By the Song dynasty (960–1279), the examination had become the jewel in the crown of the imperial Chinese government. It provided political, social, ideological, and cultural unity for China's complex diversity of regional and local cultures. Those who passed the examinations became government officials and the social elite. While the Confucian-based exam was abolished in 1905, the early twenty-first century saw the Chinese government establishing Confucius Institutes around the world to promote the learning of Chinese language and culture.

A third pattern that appeared in the late Han dynasty was the continual interaction between Han Chinese within the Great Wall (which began to be constructed in the Qin dynasty) and non-Han peoples of the steppe beyond the Wall—Mongols, Manchus, and Turks. Over the centuries, these peoples, defined by their mobility in herding flocks, raided and even invaded China within the Wall, a more sedentary society of farmers. At times of greater Chinese strength, the Han Chinese pushed further into steppe lands. From the late thirteenth century on, the interaction between the Han and non-Han peoples became more an ongoing "dialogue" of power, with these outsiders ruling parts of North China from the late eleventh century on, and with the Mongol Yuan dynasty (1279–1368) and Manchu Qing dynasty (1644–1912) ruling all of China. The heritage of these relationships is the early twenty-first century Chinese government's ambivalence in its policies toward ethnic minorities.

Late imperial China reached its zenith of wealth and power during the reign of the Manchu emperor, Qianlong (1736–1795), in a period is known as "**High Qing**."

CONFUCIUS ON GOVERNMENT AND POLITICS

Confucius (551–479 BCE) was an ancient Chinese philosopher whose ideas have had an enduring impact on Chinese culture and history. Much of his philosophy is concerned with politics and government, and like other great political thinkers, such as Plato, Confucius focuses on the "good" state that he believes will be the best way for society to be organized and governed. His teachings, including the following observations on political matters, are found in *The Analects of Confucius*, which were compiled by the philosopher's disciples in the generations after his death.

2.3   The Master said: "Lead them by political maneuvers, restrain them with punishments: the people will become cunning and shameless. Lead them by virtue, restrain them with ritual: they will develop a sense of shame and a sense of participation."

12.19   Lord Ji Kang asked Confucius about government, saying, "Suppose I were to kill the bad to help the good: how about that?" Confucius replied: "You are here to govern; what need is there to kill? If you desire what is good, the people will be good. The moral power of the gentleman is the wind; the moral power of the common man is grass. Under the wind, the grass must bend."

12.11   Duke Jing of Qi asked Confucius about government. Confucius replied: "Let the lord be a lord; the subject a subject; the father a father; the son a son." The Duke said: "Excellent! If indeed the lord is not a lord, the subject not a subject, the father not a father, the son not a son, I could be sure of nothing anymore—not even of my daily food."

12.7   Zigong asked about government. The Master said: "Sufficient food, sufficient weapons, and the trust of the people." Zigong said: If you had to do without one of these three, which would you give up?"—"Weapons."—"If you had to do without one of the remaining, which would you give up?"—"Food; after all, everyone has to die eventually. But without the trust of the people, no government can stand."

2.21   Someone said to Confucius: "Master, why don't you join the government?" The Master said: "In the *Documents* it is said: 'Only cultivate filial piety and be kind to your brothers, and you will be contributing to the body politic.' This is also a form of political action; one need not necessarily join the government."

13.13   The Master said: "If a man can steer his own life straight, the tasks of government should be no problem for him. If he cannot steer his own life straight, how could he steer other people straight?"

From *The Analects of Confucius*, translated by Simon Leys (New York: W. W. Norton, 1997), 6, 8, 56, 57, 58, and 62.

Mid-eighteenth-century military campaigns in central Asia brought the empire 6 million square miles of new territory, and China made Tibet its protectorate. In the foreign policy dubbed the **"tributary system"** by Western scholars, South, Southeast, and East Asian states sent gifts and performed the **kowtow** (*ketou*—literally, "knock head") before the Chinese emperor as symbolic ritual in Chinese eyes of their superiority vis-à-vis the tributary states' subordinate status. Exceptional government leadership created an age of economic prosperity marked by agricultural commercialization and diversification and the importation of crops from the New World. An indication of this remarkable time was the Qianlong emperor's cancellation of annual taxes four times in his reign because the government was so fiscally wealthy. Prosperity brought greater elite wealth, new occupational opportunities, new markets and commercial relationships, and from 1749 to 1790, a 70 percent increase in population up to 301 million. It is not surprising that in the late eighteenth century, the number of people fascinated with China ("Sinophiles") in Europe and the recently established United States grew, impressed with China's "enlightened despotism," meritocracy (a ruling elite based upon the examination), and material culture. Historians have recently focused on the Qing regime, not only for its rule in China, but as the leader of a multi-ethnic empire—establishing effective rule over Turks, Tibetans, and Mongols as well.

The Decline of the Imperial State

Amid the glories of the late eighteenth century were unfortunately many signs of decline and danger. Military campaigns and suppressing rebellions, especially the religious-based White Lotus Rebellion (1796–1804), eroded state wealth. A weakening economy and military did not bode well for continuing successes. The emperor's patronage of He Shen, his corrupt personal favorite at the court in the 1780s and 1790s, opened the floodgates to widespread corruption as the courtier parleyed his position into bureaucratic influence and great wealth. His corruption proliferated far beyond his clique to every administrative level. Like a cancer on the body politic, it metastasized into widespread corruption that robbed economic resources and undermined popular respect for the dynasty. The population surge, a sign of growing wealth, ironically posed the greatest long-term danger: the Chinese system of partible inheritance (where inheritance was divided among a family's sons) meant that land per capita shrank markedly. Poverty and bankruptcies rose. The increasingly fiscally strained government had difficulty providing charitable relief and public works for the people, two keys for insuring respect and support for the regime.

China also faced a growing threat from Western empire-building nations, propelled by the alliterative triad of merchants, missionaries, and the military. Chinese culture frowned on commerce with outsiders, seeing itself as being the "Middle Kingdom," and "everything under Heaven," and therefore self-sufficient in all important things. But pressure from the West prompted China to allow trade at the southern city of Guangzhou under a modified tributary arrangement, where the Chinese government orchestrated the music to which Westerners danced. Westerners bought teas and silk; but because they offered nothing the Chinese wanted (woolen textiles for a tropical climate!), Great Britain, in particular, suffered from an unfavorable trade balance with China—until they began to smuggle in opium. Why this drug became such an addiction among the Chinese is still unclear, but the number of chests of opium smuggled into China increased exponentially in the first decades of the nineteenth century—at least as measured by the extent of drug addiction and related currency outflow and soaring inflation. When the Chinese emperor sent an imperial commissioner who used strict measures to quash the smuggling, Great Britain saw it as a cause for war.

In the **Opium War** (1839–1842) Great Britain exacted China's humiliating defeat and forced on it the **Treaty of Nanjing**, the first of many such agreements, called the "**unequal treaties**" because China gave all yet received nothing. This war opened a century of aggression by Western nations against China, transforming the Middle Kingdom into a semi-colony, subject to the demands of many foreign nations. The treaties opened trading ports along the coast and along the Yangtze River, where foreign settlements were carved into existing Chinese cities; some Chinese came then to be ruled by foreigners. These settlements installed **extraterritoriality** with consular jurisdiction under which an accused foreigner would be tried for a crime in a Western, not a Chinese, court. Though Chinese who worked with or were converted by Westerners were not covered by extraterritoriality, Westerners, because of their special legal status, often tried to use their power to protect their Chinese business agents (compradors) or their religious converts. In addition, China lost its right to control and collect its own tariffs. It could not regulate foreign ships' entries into inland waterways, the loss of an important right for any sovereign nation. China's tributary system was nullified: ambassadors of foreign states could now reside permanently in Beijing.

The open propagation of Christianity was guaranteed by the unequal treaties. This meant that missionaries could go anywhere, could purchase property for church and school, and could proselytize at will. Though the impact of late Qing missionaries was complex, on the whole, it was an unhappy one. The political landscape was studded with episodes of violence sparked by the actions of culturally arrogant missionaries who believed they alone had the "Truth"; at core, these episodes were spawned by the cultural imperialism of the missionaries and the tenacious cultural chauvinism of the Chinese.

The nineteenth century was also ravaged by domestic rebellion. The **Taiping Rebellion** (1851–1864), the largest uprising in world history, devastated much of east central and south China, reached militarily into most provinces, and killed an estimated 20 million people. Incubated in an area marked by ethnic rivalry, unemployment, and poverty, and forged into a utopian crusade based on a bastardized Christianity, the rebellion (turned would-be dynasty) was a major threat to traditional Chinese culture. It promised to dethrone Confucianism and the family as cultural hallmarks, raise the status of women, institute primitive economic communism, and replace social hierarchy with equality (see Box, **The Taiping Plan for Reorganizing Chinese Society**). Though many elements caused its demise, including its poor administration, its inability to fulfill its promises to the people, and a leadership that politically cannibalized itself, its coup de grace came from Beijing-authorized provincial armies that were formed and led by Han Chinese officials who were concerned about the rebellion's cultural threat. The rebellion's destruction is almost unfathomable; in the populous and prosperous Jiangnan (the Lower Yangtze) region, the population, which stood at 67 million in 1843, plummeted to 45 million half a century later.

The decades of the 1850s into the 1870s saw other areas raked by rebellions as well. The first phase of the Robin Hood–like Nian rebellion in north China (1853–1868) was primarily extended **guerrilla warfare**. Chinese scholar-officials again dealt successfully with the rebels' challenges, copying the rebels' own strategy of employing scorched earth tactics while building fortified settlements to keep rebels away from the masses. The rebellion's second phase was mostly a struggle between cavalries that ranged across the North China plain; Han officials suppressed it as well.

Two Muslim rebellions in southwest (1855–1873) and northwest China (1862–1873) had different dynamics. In the southwest's Yunnan, the key struggle (the Panthay rebellion) emerged from the treatment of Chinese Muslims (called Hui), who had for many years controlled mining in the province, by interloping ethnic Han Chinese who moved in to seize the mines. Massacre followed by countermassacre marked the bloody affair; siege warfare

THE TAIPING PLAN FOR REORGANIZING CHINESE SOCIETY FROM *LAND SYSTEM OF THE HEAVENLY DYNASTY* (1853)

The division of land must be according to the number of individuals, whether male or female; calculating upon the number of individuals in a household, if they be numerous, then the amount of land will be larger, and, if few, smaller....All the fields in the empire are to be cultivated by all the people alike. If the land is deficient in one place, then the people must be removed to another....Thus, all the people in the empire may together enjoy the abundant happiness of the Heavenly Father, Supreme Lord, and Great God. There being fields, let all cultivate them; there being food, let all eat; there being money, let us all use it so that nowhere does inequality exist, and no man in not well fed and clothed.

All men and women, every individual of sixteen years and upwards, shall receive land, twice as much as those of fifteen years of age and under....Throughout the empire the mulberry tree is to be planted close to every wall, so that all women may engage in rearing silkworms, spinning the silk, and making garments. Throughout the empire every family should keep five hens and two sows....At the time of harvest every sergeant shall direct the corporals to see to it that of the twenty-five families under his charge each individual has a sufficient supply of food, and, aside from the new grain each may receive, the remainder must be deposited in the public granary...for the whole empire is the universal family of our Heavenly Father....

....[T]he sergeant must keep an account of money and grain figures in a record book....For every twenty-five families there must be established one public granary and one church where the sergeant must reside. Whenever there are marriages, of births, or funerals, all may go to the public granary; but a limit must be observed, and not a cash be used beyond what is necessary. Thus, every family which celebrates a marriage or a birth will be given one thousand cash and a hundred catties of grain. This one rule is applicable throughout the empire. In the use of all things, let there be economy, to provide against war and famine....In every circle of twenty-five families, all young boys must go to church every day, where the sergeant is to teach them to read the Old Testament and the New Testament, as well as the book of proclamations of the true ordained Sovereign. Every Sabbath the corporals must lead the men and women to the church, where the males and females are to sit in separate rows. There they will listen to sermons, sing praises, and offer sacrifices to our Heavenly Father, the Supreme Lord and Great God.

From J. Mason Gentzler, *Changing China: Readings in the History of China from the Opium War to the Present* (New York: Praeger, 1977), 54–58.

ended in the murders of all caught inside city walls. Unlike the Taiping and the Nian, the Qing regime used their own military forces, not those under the leadership of Han civilian officials. The dynamic of the rebellion in the northwest, in contrast, was more religious/ideological, with the leaders of a New Sect charting the way. Like the Panthay, this rebellion featured vicious and brutal siege warfare. Another Han scholar-official led in quelling the movement in a bloody five-year campaign.

Efforts to Save the Qing Dynasty and the Imperial System

One impact of these devastating foreign and domestic crises facing the Qing dynasty in the mid-nineteenth century was the financial exhaustion of the government. Already by 1850—after the Opium War but before any of the rebellions—the Qing government was taking in only about 10 percent of what it was spending. It followed that the reconstruction work after the rebellions—such as rebuilding bridges, fixing irrigation works, and reclaiming devastated farmland—could not be undertaken by the central government, but that local elites had to take over any reconstruction if it was going to occur in their areas. In other words, the crises that were wracking the Chinese state, in the end, had to be solved by Han leaders of Chinese society rather than the Manchu-led central state. Or, seen another way, the center was losing power to the provinces and localities; it was the old center-locality tension that events brought once again to the fore.

Leaders of the so-called **Self-Strengthening Movement** argued that Western technology (particularly armaments and ships) should be used to protect Chinese traditions. They argued that Western technology would serve as the techniques ("means") by which Chinese traditions, or essence ("ends"), could be protected and preserved. They did not seem to understand that ultimately the "means" necessarily affect the "ends." While self-strengthening involved a multi-pronged effort in the spheres of diplomacy, education, and technology, advances in military technology were usually taken as a measure of successful self-strengthening for they were most clearly related to defense. In this regard, the main fruits of the self-strengtheners' labor were an arsenal built near Shanghai and a shipyard at Fuzhou, one of the first five treaty ports; these institutions were established by the same Han scholar-officials who had quelled most of the rebellions. Though self-strengtheners did not call for major institutional change in the imperial government, they did establish the Zongli Yamen (Office for General Management), a kind of foreign ministry, to oversee many diplomatic, educational, and technological efforts.

The self-strengtheners continually had to fight conservatives in the imperial court who argued that contact with the West was contaminating, that Chinese traditions must be revivified; these were, for the most part, men who were overwhelmed by fears of change and what that change would portend for the traditional Chinese world and their own lives.

Even as Chinese debated their proper actions, foreign threats and crises did not abate. In the twenty-one years from 1874 to 1895, China lost control of the Ryukyu Islands (Liuqiu in Chinese), Vietnam, and Korea, its three most important tributary states, that is, states that most frequently dispatched missions to the Middle Kingdom. Aggressive actions by Japan in the first and third instances and by France in the second pointed to a new wave of imperialism in the closing quarter of the nineteenth century. The losses of Vietnam to France (1883–1885) and of Korea to Japan (1894–1895) had significant national security implications.

It was the **Sino-Japanese War** that was most shocking to the Chinese: the huge land empire of China had been militarily humiliated by the Japanese, a people whom the Chinese had denigrated as "dwarf bandits." In the war with Japan, China lost the island of Taiwan, and, if three European countries had not stepped in, the Liaodong Peninsula in southern Manchuria would have been lost as well. In 1897 and 1898, in an even more ominous development, Western nations demanded the right to "lease" areas of China for from twenty-five to ninety-nine years. Russia, Great Britain, and France queued up to "carve up the Chinese melon"—where they could extract mineral resources and build and operate rail lines.

During this crucial period, the most powerful leader in China was the Empress Dowager Cixi, who had ruled as regent for child emperors from 1861 to 1891, and after that as a meddler in the rule of her nephew, the Guangxu emperor. Cixi was, for the most part, a strong backer of conservative political forces in the imperial government.

In the contexts of the defeat by Japan and the leasehold mania, a movement to reform state institutions emerged full-blown in the summer of 1898 after brewing for three years in the provinces. The rationale for this change was set down by scholar-official, Kang Youwei, who reinterpreted classical Confucian texts in a quite revolutionary way—all with a view of supporting radical institutional change. Gaining support from the Guangxu emperor, Kang provided the policy agenda; in the summer of 1898, in what is known as the **Hundred Days Reform**, the emperor issued over a hundred decrees calling for institutional innovations in many arenas. These included revamping the examination system and establishing a national school system; restructuring the government and abolishing sinecure posts; modernizing the police, military, and postal systems; and setting up new institutions to promote agriculture, commerce, and industry (see Box, Memorial from Kang Youwei to the Guangxu Emperor). However, the reforms thoroughly threatened the political establishment and the power of the empress dowager. Cixi therefore opposed them and staged a coup d'état, putting the emperor under house arrest and executing those reformers who did not flee Beijing in time.

Despite this failure, the reforms and their ideological base were important in China's political development. Kang's call for institutions undergirded by and infused with Western ideas began to stimulate, as nothing had before, an interest in Western things beyond guns and ships. It might be said that Kang's work began to prime the pump of greater change. Perhaps more significant, Kang's reinterpretation of Confucianism was crucial in bringing China into the modern world, in effect, undercutting Confucianism itself. Before, Confucianism had been *the* Way, an unquestioned article of faith; but Kang had turned it into an ideology among other ideologies. When Confucianism became simply an ideology, it could, for example, be seen as a tool legitimizing the elevation of certain groups (fathers, husbands, parents, elder brothers, males in general) and demeaning others (sons, wives, women in general, all children, younger brothers). Thus, though it was an unintended consequence, Kang's work was the first step in dethroning Confucianism as the unchallenged basis of Chinese culture. It was also an important precursor to the "New Policies" adopted by the Qing regime in the first decade of the twentieth century in a last ditch effort to save the dynasty.

But sadly the Qing did not move toward reform until they were pounded by one more wretched and seemingly quite insane episode. The decline of the traditional state was punctuated at century's end by the tragic **Boxer Uprising** in North China. These rebels were called Boxers because of their martial arts rituals, which allegedly brought them invulnerability. The Boxers, mostly peasant young men and women, particularly targeted Chinese Christian converts and foreign missionaries. They attacked the converts because of the special privileges that they often enjoyed and the missionaries because they refused to allow converts to participate in traditional Chinese festivals and offended Chinese customs and beliefs in other ways. Alarmed Western nations pressed Cixi to suppress the Boxers and made plans to intervene. Instead, at this time of political, cultural, and international crisis, the Empress Dowager became an active ally of the Boxers: "China is weak," she allegedly said, "the only thing we can depend upon is the hearts of the people."[1]

In the end, Western and Japanese forces marched on Beijing to suppress the Boxers; and the Chinese government, in what seems an episode from the theater of the absurd, declared war on all eight nations (Germany, Russia, France, Japan, the United States, the United Kingdom, Italy, and Austria-Hungary). In the face of the Western offensive, most Boxers simply disappeared into the northern Chinese countryside, while Cixi fled to the western city of Xi'an. The foreign powers forced the Qing court to sign a peace treaty called the **Boxer Protocol** in September 1901. Of all the Protocol's humiliating provisions, the most disastrous

MEMORIAL FROM KANG YOUWEI TO THE GUANGXU EMPEROR ON REFORM (1898)

A survey of all states in the world will show that those states which undertook reforms become strong while those states which cling to the past perished. The consequences of clinging to the past and the effects of opening up new ways are thus obvious. If Your Majesty, with your discerning brilliance, observes the trends in other countries, you will see that if we can change, we can preserve ourselves; but if we cannot change, we shall perish. Indeed, if we can make a complete change, we shall become strong, but if we make only limited changes, we shall still perish. If Your Majesty and his ministers investigate the source of the disease, you will know that this is the right prescription.

Our present trouble lies in our clinging to old institutions without knowing how to change. In an age of competition between states, to put into effect methods appropriate to an era of universal unification and laissez-faire is like wearing heavy furs in summer or riding a high carriage across a river. This can only result in having a fever or getting oneself drowned.

It is a principle of things that the new is strong but the old weak; that new things are fresh but old things rotten; that new things are active but old things static. If the institutions are old, defects will develop. Therefore there are no institutions that should remain unchanged for a hundred years. Moreover, our present institutions are but unworthy vestiges of the Han, Tang, Yuan, and Ming dynasties; they are not even the institutions of the [Manchu] ancestors. In fact, they are the products of the fancy writing and corrupt dealing of the petty officials rather than the original ideas of the ancestors...Furthermore, institutions are for the purpose of preserving one's territories. Now that the ancestral territory cannot be preserved, what good is it to maintain the ancestral institutions?....

Nowadays the court has been undertaking some reforms, but the action of the emperor is obstructed by the ministers, and the recommendations of the able scholars are attacked by old-fashioned bureaucrats....Rumors and scandals are rampant, and people fight each other like fire and water. A reform in this way is as ineffective as attempting a forward march by walking backward....Your Majesty knows that under the present circumstances reforms are imperative and old institutions must be abolished,

....As to the republican governments of the United States and France and the constitutional governments of Britain and Germany, these countries are far away and their customs are different from ours....Consequently I beg Your Majesty to adopt the purpose of Peter the Great of Russia as our purpose and to take the Meiji Reform of Japan as the model of our reform. The time and place of Japan's reform are not remote and her religion and customs are somewhat similar to ours. Her success is manifest; her example can easily be followed.

From J. Mason Gentzler, *Changing China: Readings in the History of China from the Opium War to the Present* (New York: Praeger, 1977), 86–87.

for China was a staggering indemnity to pay the cost of the war for the foreign powers that proved a crushing burden to the imperial government's already crippled economy.

The 1911 Revolution

The last decade of Manchu rule in China ended with a tidal wave of reformist and revolutionary activity, the degree and rate of which varied from place to place throughout much of the country. The decade was marked by a surge of urban nationalism, driven by fears of national dismemberment by the British in Tibet, the Russians in Mongolia, and the French in parts of Southwest China. Chinese in various provinces rose together to try to recover "rights" taken by the imperialists through the unequal treaties and other means, especially their ownership and control of railroads. Newspapers and magazines that focused on current developments proliferated. Cities were being paved, lighted, and better policed. In them came the spiraling of wide-ranging reformist efforts to deal with social ills—opium smoking, gambling, and foot-binding. Once subordinated social groups, especially women and the youth, began to emerge as social and political players. Chinese living overseas, still motivated by native place loyalties, played an increasingly active role in China's developments, sending money for specific reformist and revolutionary goals and investing in China's cities.

In this context, the Empress Dowager moved to make major reforms. In August 1905, after an unsuccessful attempt to structure a dual modern school-traditional examination system, she ordered the outright abolition of the civil service examination—arguably the single most revolutionary act of twentieth-century China. The exam system had been the chief conveyor of traditional Confucian orthodoxy and the recruiting source for political and social elites for millennia. With the examination system gone, there was no way to promulgate an official ideology. Indeed, there was now no ideology of state in China. Furthermore, the source for the recruitment of officials and political and social elites in general was a giant question mark. There was now simply no way to stop the tides of change. Military reforms led to the founding of a modern army, the New Army, organized by longtime official Yuan Shikai, with academies producing well-trained cadets inculcated with patriotic ideas. The government departments, called Boards, in place since the Tang dynasty, were transformed into modern ministries.

Perhaps the most surprising change was Cixi's championing of constitutional government in 1908. Chinese leaders had interpreted the victory of Japan over Czarist Russia in the Russo-Japanese War (1904–1905) not only as the first victory of an Asian nation over a European nation, but also as the victory of a constitutional power over an authoritarian monarchy. In 1906, the Qing court sent missions abroad to study constitutional systems in Japan, Europe, and the United States. For the court, Japan's constitutional monarchy seemed a relevant and advantageous system for China to emulate. For one thing, it would shore up the Qing regime as it structured a more "modern" political system. While the system would set up representative bodies in the provinces and localities, where elites would presumably flex their political muscles, such a system also potentially provided a vehicle for the Qing court to regain some of the political power that had devolved to provinces and localities in the late-nineteenth-century post-rebellion reconstruction.

In August 1908, Cixi announced a projected constitutional calendar, which would be fully realized by 1917. Representative bodies at township, county, and provincial levels began to be formed from 1909 to 1913. These bodies provided forums in which to debate, demand, and legislate. Had Cixi lived, she might have been able to lead China into that new system, but she died in November 1908, a day after the death of the thirty-seven-year-old Guangxu emperor, who died without an heir. She had arranged for a three-year-old member of the royal family to succeed Guangxu. The regents of the child emperor seemed incapable of dealing with what became obstreperous provincial and national assembly elites and whose own foot-dragging on the pace of reform antagonized many Han Chinese.

Japan was not only the model for China's developing constitutionalism, but the rapidly modernizing nation was also a school for young Chinese intellectuals. China began sending students to Japan in the late 1890s, with numbers soaring from two hundred in 1899 to thirteen thousand in 1906. Students formed politically oriented associations, many of them based on provincial native place. Seeing Japan's developing modernity and its role as a growing world power in the context of China's weakness, these students asked what was wrong with China. The answer more and more frequently was "the Manchus," the ethnic group that had controlled China for over two and half centuries. Among these students, strong anti-Manchu feelings developed. In 1905, Sun Yat-sen (Sun Zhongshan in *pinyin*), a medical doctor turned full-time revolutionary who had spent part of his youth in Hawai'i, established the Revolutionary Alliance in Tokyo. It called for overthrowing the Manchus and establishing a republic. Other revolutionary organizations sprang up as well.

Motivated by anti-Manchu nationalism and a deep sense of things gone terribly wrong for the country, revolutionaries rose up in October 1911 in a series of largely unplanned and uncoordinated actions that culminated in the **1911 Revolution.** These revolutionaries were not closely associated with Sun—indeed, he was fund-raising in Denver, Colorado, at the time. Fighting soon raged between the Qing and revolutionary forces. Yuan Shikai, the founder of the New Army, emerged as power broker in the struggle. A powerful dynastic official and a Han Chinese who had faithfully served the Manchu Qing dynasty, Yuan had had no experience with and had not even announced support for republicanism in China, but a political deal committed the presidency of the new Republic to him if he engineered the Qing abdication. Part of the reasoning for acquiescing to Yuan was the widespread fear that continued fighting might tempt some imperialist powers to make hay out of the unrest for their own advantage.

The reality was that the signs of ever more threatening imperialism were everywhere. Two examples suggest the range of imperialist tentacles at that point in the early twentieth century. In the month the revolution erupted, the Chinese government defaulted on its Boxer indemnity payments. The British Foreign Office, meeting with representatives from the Hong Kong and Shanghai Banking Corporation, agreed that in order to secure their loans, they would have to take control of crucial institutions in the Chinese government. The other example shows Western treaty "rights" in China as supreme: because an earlier agreement had declared that China could not interfere in the soybean trade, one provincial governor could not stop the export of soybeans from his province, even at a time when people were dying from famine.

The Qing dynasty abdicated on February 12, 1912, and was replaced by the Republic of China. White flags were flown as a sign that Han Chinese rule had been restored in the overthrow of the ethnic outsiders. But it was more than a "restoration." Despite the lack of major social and economic change in its aftermath, this *was* a revolution—for when the revolutionaries overthrew the Manchus, they also destroyed the imperial system that had existed since 221 BCE. The Republic of China got off to a rousing democratic start in the winter of 1912–1913 with elections to the National Assembly. Sun Yat-sen turned his Revolutionary Alliance into a political party, the Kuomintang (KMT),* or Nationalist Party, to vie with a number of other hopeful parties. Although there were gender, age, educational, and economic qualifications for voting and serving in office, the elections went remarkably smoothly, given no history of electoral government in China's past. They were ironically the high point of electoral democracy in the twentieth and twenty-first centuries on the Chinese mainland and in Taiwan until the 1980s. The Nationalists won about 43

* *Kuomintang,* which literally means "National People's Party," is an older form of romanization. In *pinyin*, it is *Guomindang* (GMD). Both romanizations are commonly used in scholarly writing. It was the editor's decision to use Kuomintang (KMT) to refer to the Nationalist Party founded by Sun Yat-sen in this book.

percent of the vote, a plurality among the multiple parties: they took 269 of the 596 House of Representative seats and 123 of the 274 Senate seats; they would control 45 percent of the seats in each house. Nationalist Party leader Song Jiaoren, believed to be headed to the prime ministership under President Yuan Shikai, left for Beijing from Shanghai in March 1913; but he was shot dead at the Shanghai train station.

Conferring the presidency of the republic on Yuan Shikai turned out to have been a huge mistake. Yuan was indeed concerned with modernizing the Chinese state, but he thought that a republican government was too unwieldy to produce focused modernization. Yuan targeted the republic as a system and its components for destruction. Song was simply the first hit—Yuan was implicated in his assassination.

After republican revolutionaries rebelled against Yuan in the summer of 1913 because of his other highhanded actions, the president did not slow down in his efforts to dismantle the republic. In November 1913, he outlawed the Nationalist Party. In February 1914, he abolished the representative assemblies established in the last decade of Qing rule—at all levels, from county to province to nation. Then he announced his plan to become "Grand Constitutional Emperor" and thus reinstate the monarchy and take the throne. In late 1915 a rebellion blazed up out of southwest China to move against the would-be emperor. Yuan died suddenly in June 1916 of natural causes before he could found a new dynasty, but his death plunged the young Republic into political chaos.

The Agony of Warlordism

As long as Yuan Shikai was alive, he was able to control the generals who had been trained under his command in the New Army. With his death, the destructive genie of military struggle was unloosed; the struggle among these provincially based generals, now referred to as "warlords," produced one of the most disastrous and chaotic periods in modern Chinese history.

The goal of each warlord was to take control of Beijing and its government institutions in order to be recognized as president of the Republic. Governmental institutions in the 1920s became pawns in the warlords' struggles. The concerns of civilian politicians and bureaucrats focused increasingly on keeping their positions and maintaining their own political power, frequently cultivating connections with warlords. In this context, corruption tended to become a crucial dynamic and often decided policies and elections. The most famous case was that of Cao Kun, who won the presidency in 1923 by bribing national assemblymen with $5,000 each to vote for him. In the decade from 1916 to 1926, referred to as the "Warlord Era," the Republic of China had six different presidents and twenty-five cabinets. The high hopes of 1912 and early 1913 lay in shambles: the hopes of establishing a republican ethos—carrying the voice of the people into the institutions of government—were aborted.

Instead, it was the ethos of the military and militarization that was carrying the day; it began to emerge as a major dynamic in twentieth-century China. There was a wide spectrum of warlord types. Some probably had the abilities, character, and potential to lead the Chinese nation. Wu Peifu, for example, had a traditional civil service degree, was a graduate of the Baoding Military Academy, and was a student of the Buddhist canon and the Confucian classics. Both Feng Yuxiang and Yan Xishan were able reformers in the areas they held, the latter often called the "Model Governor" in Shanxi province. But other warlords were simply outrageous thugs, wreaking terror and havoc in the areas they controlled. Easiest to mock was Zhang Zongchang, the "Dog-Meat General," whose Shandong troops were notorious for their practice of "opening melons"—that is, splitting skulls—and for stringing human heads on telegraph poles, all in order to elicit "respect" for their brutal power.

Those warlords who were serious about trying to gain national power were involved in shifting coalitions, often armed by Western nations, who hoped "their" warlord would come out on top and then offer them advantages. These coalitions fought major wars in north China in 1920, 1922, 1924, and 1925, while many smaller conflicts erupted throughout the country. These were bloody wars, not merely minor skirmishes and political posturing. For many Chinese, the main scourge of the times was what the warlords did to pay for the weapons and supplies their armies needed. One means was outright and outrageous taxation: every conceivable item, service, or situation bore extraordinarily high taxes, from consumer goods to licenses to everyday situations (getting married, owning a pig, going to a brothel). Land taxes were collected far in advance, in some areas up to a decade ahead. The other warlord strategy for getting needed money was to force farmers to plant opium, since that crop brought in huge profits. The tragic irony of this was that in the late Qing, the cultivation of opium had been eliminated in most areas. The acreage of cultivated land devoted to opium production was at 3 percent from 1914 to 1919; but it skyrocketed to 20 percent from 1929 to 1933. The Western powers that had first brought opium to China had long gotten out of the trade. In sum, the warlords, who arose in the context of growing nationalism in the early twentieth century, came to be the antithesis of nationalism. They rendered the Republic of China an empty shell.

The May Fourth Movement

In the midst of this military and political chaos emerged an intellectual and cultural revolution that would change China's political destiny. Though Confucianism in the political and educational realm had been dethroned, it retained its stranglehold on Chinese society. Confucian social bonds elevated the status and power of age over youth, of males over females. In one of his strongest metaphors, famous writer Lu Xun argued that something had to be done to awaken the Chinese to the destructiveness of traditional culture.

> Imagine an iron house without windows, absolutely indestructible, with many people fast asleep inside who will soon die of suffocation. But you know since they will die in their sleep, they will not feel the pain of death. Now if you cry aloud to wake a few of the lighter sleepers making those unfortunate few suffer the agony of irrevocable death, do you think you are doing them a good turn? But if a few awake, you can't say there is no hope of destroying the iron house.[2]

Now, the old verities, which formed the iron house, slowly began to collapse. Slogans like "Down with Confucius and sons" filled the press and echoed in street demonstrations. The journal, *New Youth*, which began to be published in 1915, offered a forum for students to discuss issues and called on youths to take charge of their lives and world. A language revolution was part of this **New Culture Movement**. Written literary Chinese (*wenyan*), a difficult grammatical form that was an obstacle to increasing the rate of literacy among the people, was discarded in favor of the vernacular (*baihua*), where the written language was the same as the spoken language, a style that facilitated the spreading of public literacy. Beijing University's new chancellor, Cai Yuanpei, set out beginning in 1916 to make the university the laboratory to shape the new culture. He brought professors to campus with wide-ranging ideas—from radical and liberal to conservative and reactionary—and then gave them complete academic freedom to debate all issues and possibilities for the most appropriate cultural route ahead.

The emphasis on individualism was greater in this period than in any of modern China's history; its goal was to cast off ideological shackles of patriarchy and family authority. Two imaginary characters, "Mr. Democracy" and "Mr. Science," became watchwords of the cry for progress during this time.

The New Culture Movement took place in the larger context of the **May Fourth Movement** (ca. 1915–1924), which has been called both China's Renaissance and its Enlightenment.[3] The movement added a powerful political dynamic to the pivotal events of the era. Its name came from a student demonstration in Beijing on May 4, 1919, to protest the decision at the Versailles peace conference to let Japan keep the former German leasehold in Shandong province that it had taken in World War I's opening days. Japan's claim to this territory had been agreed to via secret treaties with the Allied powers during the war. China's position on the matter was weakened by the fact that the government in Beijing had itself in 1915, admittedly under duress, agreed to Japan's **Twenty-One Demands,** which gave the Japanese empire many "rights" in China, much like the leaseholds the Qing had given other nations in the late 1890s.

The Beijing demonstration of May 4, 1919, was the first salvo in a nationwide protest, which successfully pressured China's delegates at Versailles to refuse to sign the peace treaty. This political "victory" gave rise to two alternative strategies for the remaking of Chinese culture and the nation. In the struggle between the proponents of these alternatives, the May Fourth Movement would come to be shattered. One approach held that the new China could best be constructed through direct, even violent political action; its proponents pointed to the impact of the Beijing demonstration and others, especially in Shanghai, that had direct and desired political results. These proponents of political action argued that other changes, for example cultural advances, would follow once the political system was changed. They contended that unless the foundation of the current political system—warlords bolstered by imperialists—was destroyed, nothing would ever change in China because such conservative forces would always hold the balance of power and impede further progress.

Those who proposed the alternative approach contended that any meaningful political change could only be built upon cultural change, through a process that was more evolutionary than revolutionary. They argued that if the culture was not changed, then even if the current cast of political power-holders was ousted, similar groups with deep roots in traditional culture would simply take their place. This group attacked various political "isms," like socialism, Marxism, and **anarchism**, that claimed to offer overarching systemic blueprints of a holistic way out of China's predicament. Instead, led by pragmatists, they favored solutions to specific problems; in the words of Hu Shi, "liberation means liberation from this or that institution, from this or that belief, for this or that individual; it is liberation bit by bit, drop by drop."[4] The results of this approach would be a long time coming, which seemed to many a dangerous prospect, given China's internal weakness and especially the external threats posed by imperialist nations. For many Chinese, the persistently urgent question after 1919 became how to build national power as quickly as possible so as to forestall deepening national humiliation and perhaps even dismemberment.

The Birth of the Chinese Communist Party

As the realization of China's plight became more widespread, the "ism" of Marxism–Leninism received increasing attention for its potential to deal with China's multiple problems, particularly after the successful communist revolution in Russia and the founding of the Soviet Union in 1917. Intellectuals and journalists formed Marxist study groups in Shanghai and Beijing. Agents from the Moscow-based **Comintern (Communist International)** made contact with these groups and formally organized the Chinese Communist Party (CCP) in July 1921. Because of the tiny number of CCP members (only fifty to sixty in 1921), Comintern agents pushed the CCP to join with the largest and best-known "bourgeois" party, Sun Yat-sen's Nationalists, which had remained in opposition to the warlord-dominated Republic from its political base in the southern province of Guangdong. Comintern agents also met and wooed Sun, who at this point was willing to accept help from whatever source. He eventually agreed to link up the KMT with the CCP in a **united front** through a "bloc within" system, where the two parties would not combine organizationally but individual CCP members could also join the Nationalist Party. Throughout the years of the united front, the CCP was directed by the Comintern and ultimately by Soviet leader V. I. Lenin, until his death in 1924, and then by Joseph Stalin.

Comintern agent Mikhail Borodin, who emerged as a major force in these political developments, pushed to restructure the loosely organized parliamentary-like KMT on the Leninist model of "**democratic centralism.**" In this model, along which the CCP was already organized, a façade of democratic-style discussion in party ranks is trumped by the decision-making of a centralized leadership. Borodin was also instrumental in the establishment of a KMT army, the results of a realistic recognition that attaining the party's political goals in the militarized culture of the time required armed forces of its own. The party thus established a military academy at Whampoa (Huangpu in *pinyin*) near Guangzhou. Its commandant was a relatively young officer, Chiang Kai-shek (Jiang Jieshi, in *pinyin*), who at the time was not a member of Sun's inner circle.

While the new Nationalist Party constitution and army had Borodin's fingerprints all over them, the party's central ideology was Sun's own Three Principles of the People: nationalism, democracy, and socialism (see Box, **The Three Principles of the People, Sun Yat-sen**). The achievement of nationalism meant uniting the country by eliminating warlords and imperialists. The attainment of democracy would come only after a period of party tutelage of the Chinese masses in the ways of democracy. The specific policy aims in Sun's concept of "socialism," or as it is often called, "people's livelihood," were somewhat ambiguous. Sun did not buy into the CCP position that China's central socioeconomic problem was the uneven distribution of wealth; rather, he argued that the central problem was the "grinding poverty" of the Chinese people. His solution: equalization of land ownership (without specifics), the development of government-owned enterprises (fitting the traditional model of socialism), and a tax on the increase in the value of landed property (the "unearned increment"—since whoever owned the land did nothing to earn the amount of the increased land value over time).

By the mid-1920s, the KMT had become increasingly polarized. Rightists in the party argued that the Soviets had too much power in Chinese affairs and that the CCP bloc within should be discontinued. Leftists, on the other hand, supported some CCP social and economic aims. Sun was temporarily able to keep the lid on these differences, but his death from liver cancer in March 1925 opened the floodgates of factional bitterness. Intra-party rivalry only worsened in the aftermath of the killings of Chinese protestors by British troops in Shanghai and Guangzhou in May and June 1925, acts that galvanized the deepening sense of national peril. The country erupted in demonstrations, street marches, and some violence in their anger against imperialists. In August a leader of the KMT left wing was gunned down, with some in the party's right wing implicated. From November 1925 to January 1926, a right-wing faction met in Beijing to disparage both the CCP and the left wing; in March 1926, they held their own party congress while the CCP and KMT left wing had met separately in January. The united front had disintegrated.

THE THREE PRINCIPLES OF THE PEOPLE, SUN YAT-SEN (1924)

Nationalism. In view of the ruthless exploitation of China by foreign powers, China is in fact a subcolony, a status that is much worse than that of a colony....China has concluded unequal treaties with many countries all of whom, because of the existence of these treaties, are China's masters....Today our urgent task is to restore our lost nationalism and to use the combined force of our 400 million people to avenge the wrongs of the world....Only when imperialism is eliminated can there be peace for all mankind. To achieve this goal, we should first rejuvenate Chinese nationalism and restore China's position as a sovereign state.

Democracy. There is a difference between the European and Chinese concept of freedom. While the Europeans struggle for personal freedom, we struggle for national freedom. As far as we are concerned, personal freedom should never be too excessive. In fact, in order to win national freedom, we should not hesitate to sacrifice our personal freedom. The revolutionaries in Europe and America are fond of saying that men are born equal....But is it really true that men are born equal? No stretch of land is completely level; nor are two flowers exactly identical. Since there is no such thing as equality in the sphere of nature, how can there be equality among men? True equality...has nothing to do with equality of achievement; it merely means that all people in a democratic society should enjoy the same political rights.

Among the popular rights in a democracy the foremost is the right to vote...; besides the right to vote for officials, the people should also have the right to recall them.

Insofar as the enactment of legislation is concerned, the people should have the right of initiative, as well as the right of referendum. Only when people have these four rights...can they be said to have direct control over their government or to enjoy full democracy.

People's Livelihood. The purpose of social progress cannot be more than the realization of the utmost good for the largest number of people in the society, and such realization lies in the harmonization, rather than conflict, between different economic interests....

What is the basic fact about China? It is the grinding poverty of the Chinese people....The so-called disparity in wealth is really a disparity between the poor and the extremely poor, since all Chinese are undeniably poor.

Different countries have different ways of solving their land problem....The true solution of our land problem is to make sure that farmers own the land which they till; land ownership by tillers is in fact the final goal of the principle of people's livelihood. Though China does not have "great landlords" in the Western sense, more than 90 percent of the farmers till land they do not own. This is a serious problem. Unless this problem is solved, it is senseless to talk about the principle of people's livelihood.

From Dun Jen Li, *The Road to Communism: China since 1912* (New York: Van Nostrand Reinhold, 1969), 115–125.

Commandant Chiang, suspicious of Communist aims, struck out at Communists at Whampoa in March 1926, but he only sacked a relatively small number. Throughout the factional struggle, Stalin continued to call for the CCP to work with the Nationalists. Four months later Chiang began the **Northern Expedition**, a long-planned two-pronged military campaign (one headed to Wuhan in central China, the other to Shanghai on the coast) to unite the country by getting rid of warlords and imperialists. When armies associated with the left (the CCP and left-wing KMT) began to mobilize farmers and workers as they reached their initial destination of Wuhan, Chiang's hostility to the Communists intensified. He took Shanghai in late March 1927, with much help from CCP-led labor unions and leftist organizations. But, in early April, Chiang had his forces attack union headquarters and leftist groups. In the ensuing bloodbath, sometimes referred to as the "**White Terror**," hundreds were killed and thousands fled in panic. Even after the Terror had begun, Stalin from Moscow claimed that although the purge showed Chiang's true political color, the CCP should continue to work with the Kuomintang left; CCP General Secretary Chen Duxiu commented that these orders from Stalin were "like taking a bath in a toilet."[5]

The KMT left wing broke with the CCP in early summer 1927, with Borodin and the other Comintern agents fleeing for their lives. The White Terror spread over the country well into 1928; it broke the back of the CCP. In the fall of 1927, there were several desperate attempts by Communists to rise up, but they were all bloodily suppressed. In August 1928, Chiang Kai-shek reached Beijing and, at least on the map, had unified China for the first time since the death of Yuan Shikai in 1916.

The Nanjing Decade

On the verge of national victory in 1927, Chiang had declared that the capital of the Republic of China would be in the central Chinese city of Nanjing (which means "southern capital") in order to be closer to his base of political power. The period from 1927 to 1937, when the Japanese invasion forced Chiang and his government to flee and abandon the capital, is known as the **Nanjing Decade**. Beijing, which means "northern capital," was renamed Beiping, or "northern peace."

Even under the best conditions, Chiang would have had to struggle mightily to overcome or even begin to solve China's many problems during the Nanjing Decade. But he had to confront extraordinary difficulties. His power lay in three positions: head of state, chairman of the Nationalist Party, and commander in chief of the army, but there were challenges to his control of all three. "Residual warlordism" remained a problem; during the Northern Expedition, Chiang had co-opted, rather than defeated, warlords. They challenged him in four wars from March 1929 to September 1930. Further, the KMT itself was not unified; it was split among factions vying for power; disgruntled party **cadres** aligned themselves with residual warlords and continued to make trouble. Chiang, who was usually called "Generalissimo" because of his command of the national army, did not firmly consolidate his power in the party until after 1935. He himself received his main backing from the Whampoa Clique, men who owed him personal loyalty from the days when he was their military commandant. The active core of the clique was an organization called the **Blue Shirts**, many of whom saw **fascism**, the ideology chosen by Germany and Italy at the time, as the way to restore China.

Another military challenge was a revived Communist movement in southeast China. From 1931 to 1937, Japan also became an aggressive military threat in the northeast— before its outright invasion of China proper in 1937. From October 1928, when he assumed power as head of state, until October 1934, Chiang's forces were involved in or on the brink of actual warfare forty-five of the seventy-two months—about 62.5 percent of the time. In 1934, six years after he had taken power, he firmly controlled just seven of the eighteen provinces; when the Japanese invaded in summer 1937, fully one-third of the provinces were still beyond Chiang's control. He thus faced huge obstacles in being able to reconstruct China in effective fashion.

Chiang Kai-shek emerged as heir to the long line of self-strengtheners, focusing on crucial infrastructure for defense and further modernization of the Republic of China. But lack of funds blocked almost all accomplishment or even significant progress; the economic difficulties confronting the government were debilitating. The worldwide depression made it especially hard to make headway in modernizing projects. Furthermore, the Republic had an insufficient and poorly structured tax base. The government gave up national claims to the land tax, since levying it effectively after so many years of war required a national census for which there was neither time nor money. So, by default, national revenues came from tariff duties (nonsensical, at a time of having to import many items to build industries) and from regressive excise taxes on commodities for which the poor had to pay a larger percentage of their income than the wealthy By 1937, China, with a population of 500 million, had less industrial production than Belgium, which had 8 million people. "China had the same mileage of modern highways as Spain, one-third of the telegraph lines in France, and less railroad mileage that the state of Illinois."[6]

Like Yuan Shikai, Chiang saw state-building as a top-down process. He was determined to have the Kuomintang state penetrate more deeply into society than had the imperial state, utilizing a system of townships, wards, villages, and urban neighborhoods, alongside the traditional *baojia* **system** of group mutual surveillance. But lack of effective administration and control prevented its successful realization. In culture, Chiang attempted a return to the past, resurrecting Confucianism as part of his **New Life Movement** to revive traditional virtues and cultivate civic virtue. The Blue Shirts became his standard-bearers in the campaign of the New Life Movement, which essentially became a war against the legacy of the May Fourth Movement. The Generalissimo made it clear: "In the last several decades we have in vain become drunk with democracy and the advocacy of free thought. And what has been the result? We have fallen into a chaotic and irretrievable situation."[7] He said it most clearly in 1932: "The Chinese revolution has failed."[8]

The Rise of Mao Zedong

Born in 1893 into a peasant family in the central province of Hunan, Mao Zedong had been a founding member of the CCP who, as a "bloc within" member of the KMT, had been active during the Nationalist Revolution in organizing peasant associations. Driven underground in the cities and to southeast mountainous areas by the White Terror of 1927–1928, the CCP rebuilt in the countryside. It was there that Mao Zedong began his rise to power within the party. He worked closely with military figure Zhu De, who built the **Red Army**. Even while most of the party was in the rural mountains, CCP headquarters remained underground in Shanghai and was run by former students educated in the Soviet Union. As traditional Marxists, they believed that the revolution would be engineered by the urban industrial **proletariat**; it made sense to them to keep the party center in the city. Mao and Zhu developed a **base area** on the border of Jiangxi and Fujian provinces. In late 1931, it became known as the Chinese Soviet Republic, or the **Jiangxi Soviet**,* in late 1931.

During this period, the CCP experimented for the first time with **land reform** and implementing **class struggle.** Given that 80 to 85 percent of China's population were peasants and that there were relatively few urban workers, Mao began to see the peasants,

---

* The term *soviet* is a Russian word literally meaning *council* and is used to refer to a type of political organization in which power is in the hands of the workers.

rather than the proletariat, as key to revolutionary success. For land reform, Mao divided peasants into rich, middle, and poor categories. Although the largest group by far was the poor peasants, what constituted each group varied according to locale and to the particular people who made the categories; these groupings were not hard and fast—and they were always subject to reevaluation. Once people had been labeled, land would be confiscated from landlords and sometimes from rich peasants and then distributed to poor and middle peasants and hired laborers. Obviously, the rankings turned people's worlds upside down: landlords lost all their land, while poor peasants overnight received the land resource they had never had.

But the capriciousness of class rankings and re-rankings alienated many people in the base area. The category of rich peasant was a political hot potato; it was defined in different ways, and policies toward rich peasants varied by location. In some areas, rich peasants were grouped with other peasants and seen as allies of the revolution. In other areas, they were put in the category of exploiters along with landlords. In one wave of radicalism from June to October 1933, many formerly designated middle peasants were reclassified as landlords and had their land confiscated. In another reclassification from October to December 1933, many landlords were relabeled middle peasants. In one county, out of 3,125 households, 1,512 (48 percent) were reclassified from landlord and rich peasants to middle and even poor peasants. Then early in 1934, rich peasants again fell under bitter attack. With such rapid changes, a peasant might be a middle peasant in May, a landlord in October, and a poor peasant in December—all without any change in economic status whatsoever. The confiscation of land and the reclassifications sparked frequent violence and unrest.

In the end, Mao called a temporary halt to land reform partly because it was antagonizing too many people at a time when the CCP needed all the support that it could attract, but also because of the lack of unity among the party elite. Although the CCP center had moved from Shanghai to the Jiangxi Soviet in the 1930s, the leadership remained in the hands of the USSR-trained party **cadres** and the Comintern representative assigned to China. There were other smaller communist base areas in central China that had their own programs and policies; the CCP at the time was thus not a monolithic movement, but was diverse and polycentric.

The reborn CCP frightened Chiang Kai-shek. Between 1930 and 1934, he launched five **extermination campaigns** against the Jiangxi Soviet. Three of the first four failed because of faulty and weak military strategy; the other failed when the Generalissimo had to pull out his troops in the wake of Japan's invasion of Manchuria. Only the fifth succeeded, when his forces adopted better strategy: constructing a network of roads to maintain supply lines and building blockhouses to tighten the noose around the soviet. To save themselves, about 86,000 Communists fled, on a 370-day forced march of about 6,000 miles: the fabled **Long March**. Pursued by Jiang's troops and bombers, they marched over snow-covered mountain ranges and through quicksand-like bogs. About 8,000 survived to reach **Yan'an** in Shaanxi province in China's remote northwest. En route, Mao began his climb to the top as party leader.

Once the marchers reached Yan'an, Mao admitted that the Long March and what led to it were a worse defeat than the White Terror in the late 1920s. But in orthodox party history the Long March is treated as a great victory, a verdict that came in part because of those heroes who survived the brutal natural and human forces, even though those survivors numbered less than 10 percent of those who began. For the survivors it was a story of triumph over superhuman odds, and it produced among the survivors, especially Mao himself, a sense of mission and destiny. Indeed, until the late 1990s, veterans of the Long March monopolized the political leadership of the People's Republic.

The War with Japan, 1931–1945

In contrast to the difficulties that dogged China in its efforts to build a modernizing nation state, Japan, beginning with the "restoration" of the Meiji emperor in 1868, had seemed to be almost immediately successful, industrializing rapidly and adopting a constitution in little over two decades. Already in the early 1870s some Japanese leaders had begun casting lustful eyes on the Asian mainland, in the beginning at Korea in particular. Japan proceeded to "open" Korea with an unequal treaty in 1876; and for the next eighteen years the Japanese pitted themselves against China for realizing the predominant role on the Korean peninsula. Korea had been China's closest tributary state, and China did not want to give up its long-standing interests there. Japan won control over Korea as a result of its defeat of China in the Sino-Japanese War (1894–1895). Between 1905 and 1910, Japan swallowed Korea piece by piece; Korea became, along with Taiwan, another spoil of war, a formal part of the Japanese empire. Japan increased its interests on the mainland, specifically in Chinese Manchuria, with its war against Russia (1904–1905).

Japan showed its determination to move more aggressively into China proper with the Twenty-One Demands in 1915. One group of those demands cut particularly deeply into Chinese sovereignty: it required that the Chinese attach Japanese advisers to the key governmental executive, military, financial, and police bodies—in effect, making China a protectorate of Japan. Although Yuan Shikai was compelled to sign the Demands, the Japanese in the end dropped these flagrantly arrogant conditions. But Japan insisted that it be allowed to hold on to parts of Shandong province after the war, a decision, as noted above, that led to the May Fourth incident in 1919. The Japanese also pushed Koreans to move into Manchuria to increase the numbers of its people in the Chinese territory, which Japan saw increasingly as its own. Japan's objectives in the area were furthered in the 1910s and 1920s through collaboration with the Manchurian warlord Zhang Zuolin. But the Japanese were not sure they could trust Zhang, so the Japanese military blew up his train and killed him in June 1928.

From 1928 until 1931, Chiang Kai-shek tried to expand Chinese interests in Manchuria, building railroads to compete with those of the Japanese. A series of seemingly minor incidents over water rights and boundary disputes ratcheted up tensions between Korean and Chinese farmers in Manchuria. Japanese newspapers exaggerated the importance of the incidents, declaring them examples of China's "disrespect" for Japan—which helped fuel anti-Chinese riots in both Japan and Korea. The Japanese military command in Manchuria also magnified the situation into a towering threat to the Japanese position in the area. In this frame of mind, Japanese field officers, without the agreement or even knowledge of the military authorities or the government in Tokyo, blew up a length of track on Japan's South Manchuria Railroad in September 1931, blamed it on the Chinese, and, in "retaliation," launched a full-scale military assault on the Chinese forces and quickly took full control of Manchuria.

The Chinese did not resist; appeasement of Japan was a pattern that Chiang Kai-shek would follow for six more years. The irony was heavy: Chiang had come to power riding the wave of nationalism. And he had begun to recover some unequal treaty system "rights": tariff autonomy, reduction of numbers of foreign concessions, and negotiations over extraterritoriality (finally achieved in 1943). But he was unwilling to resist the Japanese as, over the next several years, Japan established a puppet state in Manchuria (Manchukuo); attacked Shanghai for six weeks in early 1932; advanced into several provinces of Inner Mongolia; and made demands, seized territory, and took China's sovereign rights in northern China.

Generalissimo Chiang did little except to explode verbally against his own Nineteenth Route Army when it dared to resist Japan in the Shanghai attack. Chiang argued that he did not resist the Japanese because his army was not yet strong enough, and, to his mind, the CCP was a greater threat to China. According to Chiang, "The Japanese are a disease of the skin; the Communists are a disease of the heart."[9] Obviously, a heart problem is more serious and needs to be treated first, unless, of course, the skin disease was a malignant melanoma, an apt analogy given Japan's malevolent actions in China.

Chiang's appeasement stirred a loud and vigorous chorus of dissent from all across the country—from party leaders, journalists, students, and average citizens. Jiang responded in his White Terror mode: making arrests, engineering assassinations, raiding university dormitories, and closing campuses. A government decision in December 1935, which basically handed eastern Hebei province with the cities of Beiping and Tianjin over to the Japanese, gave rise to a student movement whose protest demonstrations and rallies spread beyond cities to rural areas as well. National Salvation Associations, which were established across the nation, called for the removal of Japanese troops and puppet governments in Manchukuo and East Hebei.

In this politically volatile context a bizarre episode, the **Xi'an Incident**, occurred in December 1936. Chiang's top general, former Manchurian leader Zhang Xueliang, whose main military assignment was to keep the Communists bottled up in the Yan'an area, kidnapped the Generalissimo while he was in the northwestern city of Xi'an, which is not far from Yan'an. Zhang held Chiang until he agreed to another united front with the CCP to fend off Japan. Although after he was freed Chiang claimed that he made no such commitment, when Japan next directly challenged China in July 1937, he ended his policy of appeasement and at last resisted the outright Japanese invasion and formed, at least in name, an anti-Japanese united front with the CCP.

In the war, Jiang's government traded space for time, retreating from Nanjing, first to the nearby city of Wuhan, then to Chongqing in the far southwestern province of Sichuan, where it remained until war's end. Sichuan and neighboring Yunnan province came to be called "**Free China**," that is the part of China controlled by neither the Japanese nor the Communists and under Nationalist Party authority. Retreating along with the government were tens of millions of civilians; schools and factories were floated into the interior on barges. Though the main refugee corridor was westward along the Yangtze River, millions of others fled to the south and southwest. By October 1938, much of eastern China, containing the major industrial cities and much of the best cropland, had fallen to the Japanese army.

The Japanese invasion was marked by rampant and gratuitous atrocities to terrorize the population. The most infamous of these was the "**Rape of Nanjing**" in late 1937, during which the Chinese have estimated that 200,000 to 300,000 were killed and tens of thousands raped. In several provinces of China, the Japanese military also used chemical warfare (poison gas) and biological warfare (spreading diseases like bubonic and pneumonic plague and cholera) against the civilian population. Despite the atrocities, Chinese collaboration with Japanese military occupiers was common; although later Chinese condemned these people as traitors, those who continued to live in occupied areas had to continue with their lives in some fashion even under the Japanese sword. Not all Chinese could flee to Free China; the ill, elderly, pregnant, and poor were groups that could not easily become refugees. A national collaborationist regime was established at Nanjing in March 1940 under longtime Kuomintang leader Wang Jingwei, who had been a close associate of Sun Yat-sen. Wang came to be regarded as a national traitor by both the KMT and the CCP.

With the attack on Pearl Harbor in December 1941, the United States became China's ally in the war against Japan. Their joint goal was to strengthen Chiang Kai-shek's position sufficiently to win back eastern China, which could then be used as a base from which to bomb Japan. But logistical problems were severe: Chiang's regime in remote Chongqing was cut off from its supply lifelines and had to make do with supplies and armaments that were airlifted in. Further, bad relationships between the Generalissimo and General Joseph Stilwell, the top U.S. military commander assigned to work with Chiang, helped to thwart that strategy, and Nationalist Chinese forces remained in Chongqing until the war ended in 1945 and the government of the Republic of China returned to Nanjing.

The war's legacy for China was tragic. About 20 million Chinese were killed, almost 16 million of those being civilian casualties. Scorched earth policies—blowing up dikes and bridges and destroying railroads and roads—used by the Chinese resistance to slow Japanese aggression destroyed much of the infrastructural gains that Chiang had accomplished during the Nanjing Decade.

One of the most destructive legacies of the war was a malignant inflation. Whereas prices increased about 40 percent during the war's first year, from the attack on Pearl Harbor in 1941, they shot up more than 100 percent each year. Thus, something that cost about 1 *yuan* in 1937 would have cost 2,647 *yuan* in 1945. Nothing erodes the political support of a people for its government faster than inflation, especially the marauding type of inflation China faced during and after the war. The inflation led to the hoarding of commodities, creating scarcities and even higher prices, corruption that reached new heights, and ravaged standards of living. But the Chinese Communists benefited enormously from the war. At war's end there were nineteen Communist base areas in North China; and the CCP governed an area that spread across roughly 250,000 square miles. Mao claimed that there were 1.2 million CCP members by the end of the war. Communist military forces had increased almost tenfold from 92,000 in the beginning to 910,00 in 1945. The war of resistance against Japan gave the Communist movement breathing room from Chiang Kai-shek's obsessive efforts to exterminate it. It also gave the CCP the time to expand its popular support in several ways: through its own nationalistic appeal to the Chinese people by fighting the Japanese; its policies of mass mobilization for economic, literacy, and other programs; and its insistence that the 8th Route Army (its main army) respect and even help the masses.

Civil War

Even before Japan surrendered, attention in China began to shift from the war to the postwar reality of an intensely polarized Chinese political world. The united front did not work effectively, especially after an incident in January 1941, when Kuomintang troops in the New Fourth Army opened fire on Communist troops, killing three thousand and wounding many more. During the first years of the war against Japan, thousands migrated to Yan'an, the CCP's base, where Mao consolidated his political and ideological domination of the party. He was formally elected Chairman of the Chinese Communist Party in 1945.

While in Yan'an, Mao also worked to adapt Marxism-Leninism to China's situation, emphasizing peasants as key to the revolution. At Yan'an, the party devised policies that would guide it for decades to come. These included the "**mass line**," a leadership style of relying on and actively using input from the masses in decision-making. The CCP under Mao also devised a strategy for the "re-education" of those party cadres was who were recalcitrant to follow or who opposed the official "line." The goal was to change their minds. This involved a process called a **rectification campaign,** which included small-group sessions studying documents the party selected; writing detailed self-criticisms;

being criticized in mass meetings; and confessing their errors. If there were no confessions, the party might isolate the targeted cadres; apply various psychological pressures; and/or send the cadre to do hard labor among the peasantry. Finally, as part of the repertoire of party's strategic policies, the revolutionary roles of art and literature were defined at a 1942 forum:

> In the world today all culture, all art and literature belong to definite classes and follow definite political lines. There is no such thing as art for art's sake, art which stands above classes or art which runs parallel to or remains independent of politics. Proletarian art and literature are part of the whole cause of the proletarian revolution.... Therefore, the Party's artistic and literary activity occupies a definite and assigned position in the Party's total revolutionary work and is subordinated to the prescribed revolutionary task of the Party in any revolutionary period.[10]

The United States attempted to mediate in the CCP-KMT dispute but to no avail; it was never an impartial broker, for it continued to aid the Nationalists with arms and supplies. When General George Marshall ended his failed mission to broker peace in China in January 1947, it was only a matter of time before the parties' intransigence turned into civil war. In one of the largest wars of modern times, Chiang Kai-shek's Nationalists held huge initial advantages in quantity of men and materiel: its forces numbered about three million soldiers with roughly six thousand artillery pieces; the CCP, on the other hand, had armies of about one million and just six hundred artillery pieces. The Nationalists did win the early battles in 1946; but the Communists regrouped in Manchuria, launching a campaign to isolate the major cities. Chiang then blundered badly, sending half a million of his best troops to Manchuria before consolidating his control south of the Great Wall. The Communists quickly transformed the Manchuria theater into islands of isolated KMT-controlled cities in a Communist sea. Instead of pulling out, Chiang began costly airlifts. He used, for example, his entire military budget for the last half of 1948 to supply one city for two months and four days.

By mid-1948, the numbers of Communist troops were roughly equal to those of the KMT and they had more artillery pieces, many of the new troops coming through defection or surrender and the weapons captured from the fleeing enemy. The Communist victory in Manchuria was disastrous for the KMT: Chiang lost 470,000 of his best troops, who were killed, defected to the Communists, or became prisoners of war. Essentially the KMT had lost the civil war even before the main battles shifted to China proper.

The decisive battle for central China came at the battle of Huai-Hai in Shandong and Jiangsu provinces from October 1948 to January 1949. Communist party leaders showed themselves to be superior strategists. For leadership positions and strategic advice, Chiang was partial to Whampoa graduates and downplayed the roles and views of others. In this case, he did not follow the advice of former militarily knowledgeable warlords to make a stand at a more favorable place along the Huai River. He chose instead to stand at the railroad center of Xuzhou, where his forces were exposed on three sides. Furthermore, Chiang personally insisted on directing the battle, even though he was two hundred miles away from the fighting. Communist forces annihilated Chiang's forces: he lost half a million men and almost all of his mechanized troops. By early 1949, China north of the Yangtze River was mostly in Communist hands, and in April, they took the Nationalist capital in Nanjing. Although sporadic fighting continued in the south and west until the end of the year, on October 1, 1949, Chairman Mao Zedong declared the founding of the People's Republic of China with its capital in renamed Beijing. In December, Generalissimo Chiang Kai-shek and the government of the Republic of China fled to Taiwan.

Postmortem on the Civil War

Although the military struggle was decisive in determining the outcome of the Chinese civil war, underlying political and economic factors were crucial. Chiang never attempted to reach out to non-KMT groups or to liberalize politics in areas under his authority. When the opportunity came to expand his base by joining with the Democratic League, a party formed by an unusual coalition of old line militarists and Western-style political liberals in 1944, Chiang did not even seriously consider it. Instead, he arrested or had assassinated many of its key figures before totally outlawing the Democratic League in October 1947. Chiang's government became known for its incompetence and its corruption. He may not have been corrupt personally, but many members of his family and close associates were deeply involved in graft and other shady dealings to enrich themselves.

The most crucial reason for the failure of the KMT was the ravaging inflation that undermined both the economy of the Republic and public support for Chiang's regime. By 1945, the government's revenue was covering only one-third of its expenses. Chiang's answer was simply to print more money, a "solution" that added more fuel to fires of inflation. The exchange rate for Chinese *yuan* to U.S. dollars stood at 7,000 to 1 in January 1947 and 45,000 to 1 just seven months later. Prices in July 1948 were three million times higher than in July 1937. Inflation itself was demoralizing to the Chinese people, but even more so was having "a government with neither the will nor the ability to do anything but watch over the deterioration of the nation's urban economy."[11] In the end, the economic collapse was total, engulfing the rural economy as well.

> By late 1947 and 1948, the very fabric of rural society seemed to be unraveling. Banditry, the traditional sign of feeble political control and deteriorating economic conditions, was pervasive....Landlords fled the countryside for the relative security of walled towns....Ordinary peasants, too, abandoned the farms, becoming recruits to the growing ranks of the hungry and destitute, many of whom died in the streets and alleyways of cities.... 10 million people were threatened with starvation in 1948; 48 million—about one of every ten Chinese—were refugees....The most desperate reportedly sold their wives and daughters—in 1946, the price of fifteen- and sixteen-year-old girls in [Zhejiang] was said to be 4,000 yuan...."[12]

The outcome of the Chinese civil war was not only determined by KMT failures and losses; the CCP did not win the struggle simply by default. The communists were obviously successful in terms of military strategy. But that was only part of the equation that equaled victory. The main elements of its success were the party's ability to mobilize the masses to join their cause and its generally pragmatic approach in dealing with local situations.

The most important element of the CCP's mass mobilization strategy was class struggle, used in both base areas and guerrilla zones under their control. During the war against Japan, class struggle was the vehicle to reduce rents, taxes, and interest, and carry out land reform. The party sent work teams to villages to mobilize peasant associations to challenge village elites. It is clear that the "rise of peasant associations fundamentally changed rural power relations,"[13] and won the CCP massive popular support. A second wave of mass organizing in the base areas concentrated on setting up women's and workers' associations as part of mobilizing the population for war.

Mobilizing the masses was slow and difficult work. The first hurdle for a work team sent to a village was to gain the trust of the people in a culture based on personal connections. If the mobilizers were from the village or had close ties to residents of the village, the effort would be easier. In situations in which the work team members had no connections to the village, cadres had tough, sometimes intractable problems. Mobilizers had to have networking skills and, as a matter of course, had to spend a great deal of time winning the confidence of the community by cultivating new social ties and building grassroots networks. Only after they had succeeded in this work could they move on to mobilizing the population in various organizations for action, such as land reform.

The timing of the CCP's mobilizational efforts varied by locale. In some bases in North China, the efforts were underway by 1939 and 1940; in others, they were not begun until 1943 or 1944. In central China bases, they started in 1941. Class struggle became most tangible in the "**struggle meeting**," which was "the most intense, condensed form of peasant mobilization."[14] These often-violent meetings were launched in North China against local despots by 1942, but did not begin in central China until late 1943. Party cadres targeted the village bosses and landlords and encouraged the expression (often explosion) of latent peasant anger against them, which was not easy to do. The traditional relationship between peasants and local elites, where peasants "knew their place" and were careful not to antagonize those in power, had to be overcome. Allaying peasant fears about throwing off these old relationships was a formidable task. The staged struggle meetings were pivotal in "shattering mass apathy and passivity and disrupting what former solidarity had existed among targets and community."[15]

In the period from 1946 to 1948, class struggle became the means to carry out radical land reform, the same policies it had attempted and abandoned in the Jiangxi Soviet. Party leaders argued that the inauguration of land reform during the civil war was important because it was the best way to mobilize the masses against attacks by Nationalist forces. When the party began the land reform campaign, a main dynamic of struggle meetings was vengeance against elites and even middle and poor peasants who had collaborated with the Japanese.

A party directive in March 1946 instructed party cadres to stay out of the land reform process and leave it to peasant associations, which could themselves expropriate and redistribute land and property; it was a policy that actually encouraged extremism among the masses, which often led to the killing of landlords and other violent acts. By 1948, the party pulled back on the "leftist excesses" that had both symbolized and encouraged the extremism that had become the hallmark of the land reform process. Party leaders wanted to move away from the frequent killings of landlords and rich peasants, from taking land from middle peasants, and from attacking commercial and industrial enterprises.

In the mobilization that occurred alongside land reform, men formed militia units; peasant associations spearheaded army recruiting; women's associations managed surveillance posts; local self-defense units transported supplies and ammunition; and cultural teams did propaganda work. The continual CCP emphasis was on the connection between land reform and mobilization of the masses in support of party policy. The process of mass mobilization brought people to the party and gave them a shared purpose with the party and its undertakings, a crucial element in the party's overall success.

Finally, an important factor in communist revolutionary success was its pragmatic strategy that varied according to place and time. One size did not fit all when it came to revolutionary strategies and approaches. Not every attempt at mobilization succeeded; sometimes the party failed. Sometimes contingencies gave the CCP their success. But, generally, when they achieved success, it came because party cadres understood the specific locale: its natural environment; its social, economic, and political structures, networks, and relationships; and its particular needs and grievances. Then, it carefully built coalitions with local leaders to mobilize the local populace on issues of significant concern and import to that particular area.

In the end, successful military and political strategies, marked by pragmatism about local situations, brought communist success. The trajectory from empire to a Republic to the People's Republic was unpredictable and violent. Unfortunately, most of the first thirty years of communist rule in China saw a continuation of those trends.

Notes

1. Quoted in John K. Fairbank, Edwin O Reischauer, and Albert M. Craig, *East Asia, The Modern Transformation* (Boston: Houghton Mifflin, 1965), 397, 400.

2. Lu Hsun [Xun], "Preface to the First Collection of Short Stories, 'Call to Arms'" in Lu Hsun, *Selected Stories of Lu Hsun* (Beijing: Foreign Languages Press, 1972), 5.

3. See, for example, Jerome B. Grieder, *Hu Shih and the Chinese Renaissance: Liberalism in the Chinese Revolution, 1917–1937* (Cambridge, MA: Harvard University Press, 1970). Vera Schwarz, *The Chinese Enlightenment: Intellectuals and the Legacy of the May Fourth Movement of 1919* (Berkeley, CA: University of California Press, 1986).

4. Quoted in R. Keith Schoppa, *Revolution and Its Past* (Upper Saddle River, NJ: Pearson Prentice Hall, 2006), 176.

5. Quoted in C. Martin Wilbur, *The Nationalist Revolution in China, 1923–1928* (Cambridge, MA: Harvard University Press, 1983), 131.

6. Schoppa, 213.

7. Lloyd Eastman, *The Abortive Revolution* (Cambridge, MA: Harvard University Press, 1974), 42.

8. Eastman, 1.

9. Theodore H. White and Annalee Jacoby, *Thunder Out of China* (Cambridge, MA: Da Capo Press, 1980; first edition, 1946), 129.

10. Quoted in Schoppa, 281.

11. Suzanne Pepper, "The KMT [GMD]-CCP Conflict, 1945–1949" in *Cambridge History of China*, Vol. 13, *Republican China, 1912–1949*, Part 2, John K. Fairbank and Albert Feuerwerker, eds. (Cambridge: Cambridge University Press, 1986), 742.

12. Lloyd Eastman, *Seeds of Destruction* (Stanford, CA: Stanford University Press, 1984), 81–82.

13. Ch'en Yungfa. *Making Revolution: The Communist Movement in Eastern and Central China* (Berkeley: University of California Press, 1986), 221.

14. Ch'en Yungfa, 220.

15. Schoppa, 279.

Suggested Readings

Averill, Stephen. *Revolution in the Highlands: China's Jinggangshan Base Area*. Lanham, MD: Rowman & Littlefield, 2005.

Coble, Parks. *Facing Japan: Chinese Politics and Japanese Imperialism*. New York: Cambridge University Press, 1991.

Cohen, Paul A. *China Unbound: Evolving Perspectives on the Chinese Past*. New York: Routledge Curzon, 2007.

———. *History in Three Keys: The Boxers as Event, Experience, and Myth*. New York: Columbia University Press, 1997.

Ding Ling. *Miss Sophie's Diary and Other Stories*. Beijing: Panda Books, 1985.

Eastman, Lloyd. *The Abortive Revolution: China under Nationalist Rule, 1927–1937*. Cambridge, MA: Harvard University Press, 1974.

Fogel, Joshua, ed. *The Nanjing Massacre in History and Historiography*. Berkeley: University of California Press, 2000.

Lu Xun. *Selected Stories of Lu Xun*. Beijing: Foreign Languages Press, 2000.

Preston, Diana. *The Boxer Rebellion: The Dramatic Story of China's War on Foreigners that Shook the World in the Summer of 1900*. New York: Walker and Company, 2000.

Rhoads, Edward J. M. *Manchus and Han: Ethnic Relations and Political Power in Late Qing and Early Republican China*. Seattle: University of Washington Press, 2000.

Schoppa, R. Keith. *Blood Road: The Mystery of Shen Dingyi in Revolutionary China*. Berkeley: University of California Press, 1995.

Spence, Jonathan. *God's Chinese Son: The Taiping Heavenly Kingdom of Hong Xiuquan*. New York: W. W. Norton, 1996.

Wakeman, Frederic E., Jr. *Spymaster: Dai Li and the Chinese Secret Service*. Berkeley: University of California Press, 2003.

Westad, Odd Arne. *Decisive Encounter: The Chinese Civil War, 1946–1950*. Stanford, CA: Stanford University Press, 2003.

White, Theodore H., and Annalee Jacoby. *Thunder out of China*. New York: William Sloane, 1946.

Zou Rong. *The Revolutionary Army: A Chinese Nationalist Tract of 1903*. Trans., John Lust. The Hague: Mouton and Co., 1968.

3

Mao Zedong in Power (1949–1976)

Frederick C. Teiwes

Chairman Mao Zedong was the absolute ruler of China from the founding of the People's Republic on October 1, 1949, to his death on September 9, 1976. Under his leadership the communist regime achieved initial successes followed by two decades of wrenching failures, most notably the Great Leap Forward (1958–1960) and the Cultural Revolution (1966–1968), and periods of partial, tortured recovery. During these final two decades Mao's prestige was adversely affected among the public and even sections of the Chinese Communist Party (CCP), but his authority never wavered. Despite claims during the Cultural Revolution that he had been opposed by various party leaders, claims unfortunately echoed in much academic writing, every clear order from the Chairman was obeyed, however destructive to national, party or individual leader's interests.

What is more remarkable than the oft-noted formulas of "no Mao, no Great Leap" and "no Mao, no Cultural Revolution," is that even after the disastrous effects of these movements became clear to the great majority of the CCP elite, they were curbed only when Mao decided that the costs were too great. Equally if not more telling, continuing (if watered down) aspects of Cultural Revolution radicalism persisted during the last period of Mao's life from 1972 when his health was extremely fragile, including his final two months when he was in a virtual coma. Only with the Chairman's death did his surviving colleagues turn decisively against his policies, but not against his sacrosanct position as the founding father of the country.

Mao's power derived precisely from his accepted position as the father of the nation, a status culturally enhanced as the "severe and brilliant" founding emperor of a new dynasty.[1] For the broad sections of the population, both as a result of a genuine perception of the new order and incessant official propaganda, Mao had overturned an exploitative social system, brought peace and order, launched economic construction, and, above all, expelled the foreign powers and restored China's national dignity. For top CCP leaders and lower-level officials and cadres, Mao was the strategic genius whose leadership converted the party's seemingly hopeless, or at best an extremely marginalized situation, into the unimaginable victory of 1949. For such communists, opposing Mao was simply out of the question. Much more significant than any calculation of the futility of any challenge was the Chairman's moral authority: whatever his errors, Mao's achievements could not be ignored, as his brilliance, in the elite's view, had created the revolutionary success that gave meaning to their life endeavors. To deny Mao would have amounted to denying themselves.

While Mao's authority was beyond challenge, the Chairman himself was jealous of his power and wary of possible threats, sometimes readjusting the distribution of authority among institutions and individuals to reinforce his own dominance. At worst, notably during the Cultural Revolution, he showed signs of paranoia, but overall he evinced supreme confidence. Unlike Stalin, who generally stayed close to the levers of power in the Kremlin, Mao toured the provinces regularly, often at critical turning points returning to Beijing (or convening leadership councils elsewhere) to enforce his views on his colleagues. In the chronological discussion that follows, the changing distribution of power at Mao's hand and his fluctuating views of his colleagues are examined. This is related to a larger issue concerning Mao's method of rule—he was both the great unifier of the CCP and, in his later years, the figure who ripped the party apart.

In addition to shifting approaches to power, Mao's policies varied greatly. Two broad tendencies can be identified: the "revolutionary romantic" and the pragmatic.

"Maoism" is often equated with "revolutionary romantic" endeavors, the Great Leap above all others, when, in fact, the flesh-and-blood Mao had a highly pragmatic side. From his earliest days as a radical intellectual in the late 1910s he promoted both sweeping visions of a powerful China and the practicality required to achieve it, with pragmatism dominating for the majority of his career. Even in his most radical periods, Mao adopted pragmatic, rational approaches to specific issues.

Another aspect of Mao's rule is that, like any leader, he had particular interest in specific policy areas, with significant consequences for the sectors concerned. Most broadly, Mao took responsibility for the overall course of the revolution, for the ideology and goals of the regime. He also believed he had a special understanding of rural China, and played a direct role in overseeing the transformation of agriculture. This was in sharp contrast to economic policy, an area where Mao confessed a lack of understanding and, apart from his disastrous Great Leap program, largely stayed aloof. Finally, the Chairman kept an iron grip on foreign and military policy. In this latter regard, a crucial concern of his leadership was relations with the Soviet Union. For Mao was not simply a Chinese nationalist or committed Marxist; he and the CCP were part of the international communist movement headed by Moscow. The development of this complex and often tense relationship had an enormous impact on People's Republic of China (PRC) domestic as well as foreign policy.

This chapter first briefly examines the background to the establishment of the PRC— Mao's position within the CCP, the structure of leadership power, the party's policy orientation, and the resources the regime-in-waiting possessed on the eve of taking power. It then analyzes five distinct periods involving different political dynamics, policy programs, and impacts on Chinese society, before concluding with an overall assessment of Mao and his rule. As the discussion unfolds, readers should keep in mind the question of how and why Mao changed over these years, and whether, as is sometimes claimed, there was an underlying causality connecting the earlier Mao with the destructiveness of his later years.

Mao's Rise to Power, 1935–1949

Contrary to official CCP histories, Mao did not assume leadership of the party in 1935 during the Long March. Instead, this was a gradual process that was only completed a decade later. The fundamental reason for Mao's rise to power during this period was the successful political, military, and diplomatic policies he designed for the dual struggles against the Nationalists (Kuomintang) and the Japanese. These policies contributed to CCP survival from the seemingly hopeless position of the early Long March, were crucial to developing substantial communist power in base areas behind Japanese lines while outmaneuvering the Nationalists within the ostensible anti-Japanese united front, and then led to the stunning, much quicker than expected victory in the civil war of 1946–1949.

But the solidification of Mao's power also reflected other developments. Ironically, given tensions soon apparent in Mao's independent tendencies and his unwillingness to sacrifice CCP forces for Soviet priorities, one of the most crucial was Stalin's endorsement of his leadership in late 1938. Stalin's decision was apparently based on the calculation that, as a strong capable leader, Mao was preferred over the historically pro-Moscow, but less politically successful "Returned Student" faction of CCP leaders. Another major factor was the development of, and through the rectification campaign of 1942–1944, the party's indoctrination in a new ideological canon, Mao Zedong Thought, an ideology that both supported his policy approach and sanctified his person as a significant Marxist theorist. Finally, a series of organizational steps completed the process—notably a 1943 decision giving Mao the authority to personally decide critical matters, and the formation of a new Maoist leadership at the Seventh **Party Congress** in 1945 in Yan'an, the town in Shaanxi province that served as party headquarters in 1937–1947.

The key to Mao's political ascent, though, was the pragmatic ideology and policy that produced revolutionary success. In ideological terms, despite some theoretical pretension, Mao Zedong Thought was intensely practical and oriented toward contemporary problems. The focus was on concrete Chinese conditions, as exemplified in Mao's famous dictum that Marxism-Leninism was the arrow, but its significance was in hitting the target of the Chinese revolution. Another seminal concept was "truth from facts"—that theory must never blind leaders from the reality of the situation. In concrete terms this led to cautious military policies, as befit the weaker forces of the CCP, and flexible rural policies that pushed mild or more far-reaching social reforms according to prevailing conditions and the party's needs.

Overall, as reflected in the rectification campaign's heavy criticism of the "left lines" of the late 1920s and early 1930s, Mao's cautious policies could be considered "rightist" in that, by and large, he avoided unnecessary struggles, sought to maximize the united front of potential allies, and bided his time until the balance of forces shifted to the CCP's favor. Also significant was that, notwithstanding the undercurrent of tensions with Stalin, Mao's theoretical claims were modest, the Soviet Union's role as the leader of the communist world was never questioned, and Stalin's writings were part of the curriculum studied during the CCP rectification campaign. Furthermore, in particular areas where the CCP had little experience, such as urban policy, when communist forces moved into cities in the Northeast from 1946, careful attention was given to Soviet precedent. Mao's pragmatism extended to both accepting the international communist order led by Moscow and utilizing what appeared to be valuable foreign experience.

One of Mao's greatest achievements in the 1935–1945 decade was to fashion a unified party. In contrast to the bitter and often violent inner-party factionalism of the early 1930s, Mao created a unified leadership around his person and policies, a process that was not based on advancing over the broken bodies of opponents, as often claimed, but instead on a shrewd process of garnering broad support. Apart from the crucial matter of propagating a successful revolutionary strategy, Mao accomplished this by moderate treatment of former political opponents, eschewing a **Politburo**[*] made up of or even including his

---

[*] The Politburo (or Political Bureau) was at that time (c. 1945), the highest leadership body of the CCP. It consisted of thirteen members and was headed by Mao. In 1956, the size of the Politburo was expanded to about twenty and a new top organization, the Standing Committee, with five members, was established, again headed by Mao. Although the memberships fluctuated somewhat in size over time, the Politiburo and its Standing Committee remain the most powerful leadership bodies of the CCP.

own closest supporters, but instead, drawing widely on talent and from representatives of different party constituencies or "mountaintops" to staff key positions. He also presided over a flexible and consultative policy process that devolved responsibility as required by a decentralized war situation, and where policies could be argued by his colleagues in a diluted form of "collective leadership," what has been called the "Yan'an roundtable," even as Mao retained the final say.

Of particular importance was his sensitivity to the various constituencies in the party, something seen in the promotions to the number two and three positions in the CCP. Liu Shaoqi, the leader most associated with the party's urban underground or "white area" forces, who although closest to Mao in criticism of past "leftist" excesses had limited personal connection to him, became the widely acknowledged successor. Zhou Enlai, a leader of higher status in the party's early days with extensive military and political connections who had been a political opponent of Mao's in the early 1930s, but one careful to maintain as positive relations as possible, assumed the critical political and diplomatic roles he would retain until his serious illness in the 1970s. (See Table 3.1)

More extensive than specific Politburo appointments was the broad distribution of power among the "mountaintops" of the decentralized party structure—the top generals of various armies, the leaders of base areas where the CCP had established viable governing structures and garnered popular support, and leading figures of the underground struggle. Thus, in addition to belief in the revolutionary cause, the wide sharing of the spoils of power among the party elite deepened the commitment of the disciplined forces that soon defeated the larger, better equipped but factionalized armies of the Kuomintang. Of course, this could not eliminate all perceptions of unfairness concerning the distribution of power, particularly the belief of some army and base area leaders that they were the crucial actors in the CCP's success and that the underground or "white area" leaders were less deserving of rewards. This, however, was a latent tension that did not become significant until the first major post-1949 power struggle, the Gao Gang affair in 1953–1954 (see below); for now, different groups had a vested as well as an ideological interest in success, and for that unity was essential.

A final factor to be noted in Mao's unification of the party was that while it involved intense psychological pressure in indoctrinating leaders and ordinary cadres alike in Mao's political line, Mao's program contained an explicit "organizational line" that promised a break with the violent party practices of the past (in which he too had played a prominent role): patient education would replace the "ruthless struggles and merciless blows" of the early 1930s.[2]

Despite some excesses, notably the so-called rescue campaign in 1943 that, under the direct leadership of Politburo security chief Kang Sheng, involved the torture and imprisonment of thousands of party members accused of disloyalty or subversion and for which Mao apologized, by and large this approach was honored, earning Mao further loyalty and resulting in deeper commitment to the CCP's cause. While future rectification movements after 1949 would cause trepidation, leaders and ordinary cadres generally accepted that ideological self-examination was an appropriate method of enforcing the party's policies, and if excesses did occur they would be corrected, yet again demonstrating the greatness of the party and Mao. This conviction began to fray from the late 1950s, but it remained surprisingly robust to the end of Mao's life.

Two aspects of the situation in the years immediately preceding the establishment of the PRC should be mentioned: the expectation of a seamless shift from a rural-based revolution to an urban-oriented state-building approach, and the vast diversity of conditions facing the communists as they seized national power. While hopeful Westerners regarded the communists as mere agrarian reformers, a view also darkly hinted at by Stalin, who

Table 3.1 Top Leaders of China 1949–76

Name and Birth/Death	Key Titles and Dates	Comments
Mao Zedong (1893–1976)	CCP Chairman (1945–76) PRC President (1949–59) Military Commission Chairman (1949–76)	One of the founders of the Chinese Communist Party in 1921. Assumed a position among the top leadership of the CCP in 1934–35 during the Long March, although not elected Chairman of the Politburo until 1943 and of the Central Committee until 1945. The absolute ruler of China from the founding of the PRC in 1949 until his death in 1976. Still revered in China despite acknowledgement of his serious mistakes.
Zhou Enlai (1898–1976)	PRC Premier (1949–76) PRC Foreign Minister (1949–58) CCP Vice-Chairman (1956–69, 1973–76)	Long March veteran. Headed the machinery of government after the founding of the PRC. Key role in détente with United States in early 1970s. Valued by Mao as a skilled administrator and diplomat, but not particularly respected by the Chairman. Some regard Zhou as a moderating influence during the Cultural Revolution; others see him as an obsequious underling to Mao, who nevertheless became increasingly unhappy with Zhou in 1973–74.
Liu Shaoqi (1898–1969)	PRC Vice-President (1949–59) PRC President (1959–66) CCP Vice-Chairman (1956–66)	Most significant leader of CCP "white area" forces operating in urban areas and behind enemy lines during the civil and anti-Japanese wars. Regarded as Mao's successor from the 7th CCP Congress in 1945 until he was purged as a "capitalist roader" during the Cultural Revolution. Died in detention. Posthumously rehabilitated in 1980.
Deng Xiaoping (1904–1997)	CCP General Secretary (1956–66) CCP Vice-Chairman (1975–76, 1977–82) Vice-Premier (1952–66, 1973–76, 1977–80) Military Commission Chairman (1981–89)	Long March veteran. One of Mao's favorites in the post-1949 CCP leadership until the Cultural Revolution, when he was ousted as a "capitalist roader" but protected from physical harm by Mao. Returned to leadership positions in 1973 after making self-criticism, but removed a second time in 1976 for political mistakes. Again returned to the leadership in mid-1977, about nine months after the arrest of the Gang of Four. Consolidated power as China's paramount leader from late 1978. See also Fig. 4.1.
Chen Yun (1905–1995)	CCP Vice-Chairman (1956–66, 1978–82) PRC Vice-Premier (1949–66, 1979–80)	Veteran revolutionary who became one of China's leading economic planners after 1949. Architect of successful economic recovery and development policies in 1949–57. Criticized by Mao as too cautious during Great Leap Forward in 1958, but called back by him in 1959 and 1962 to deal with severe economic difficulties. Again criticized by Mao in 1962 as "always a rightist," and remained on the sidelines until late 1978 when he played a key role in altering the CCP's leadership equation. Subsequently had a major influence on economic policy, initially supporting reform but increasingly cautious and conservative from the mid-1980s. See also Fig. 4.1.

(continued)

Table 3.1 *Continued*

Name and Birth/Death	Key Titles and Dates	Comments
Lin Biao (1907–1971)	CCP Vice-Chairman (1958–71) PRC Vice-Premier (1954–66) PRC Defense Minister (1959–71)	Long March veteran, and one of the CCP's greatest military leaders during the civil and anti-Japanese wars. A Mao favorite, he became defense minister in 1959 following the dismissal of Peng Dehuai for criticism of the Great Leap Forward. Mao chose Lin as his successor at the start of the Cultural Revolution, an appointment written into the 1969 CCP constitution. Mao grew increasingly unhappy with Lin over a number of bizarre matters starting in 1970. Lin and other members of his family were killed in a plane crash while trying to flee China after an alleged (but unlikely) failed coup attempt against Mao.
Jiang Qing (1914–1991)	Deputy Director, Central Cultural Revolution Group (1966–69) Member, CCP Politburo (1969–76)	Former movie actress who married Mao in Yan'an in 1939. Kept on the political sidelines until the early 1960s when Mao called on her to counter bourgeois influences in the arts. She took on increasingly powerful roles during the Cultural Revolution and its aftermath. She and three of her radical colleagues were arrested after Mao's death in 1976, denounced as the Gang of Four, and accused of plotting to seize power. Sentenced to life in prison, where she committed suicide in 1991.
Hua Guofeng (1921 - 2008)	CCP Chairman (1976–81) PRC Premier (1976–80) Military Commission Chairman (1976–81)	Chosen by Mao to succeed Zhou Enlai as premier in January 1976 in a move that caught everyone by surprise. Had worked in support of Deng's program in 1975, but was seen as a beneficiary of the Cultural Revolution. Played the decisive role in the purge of the Gang of Four, becoming CCP Chairman by unanimous Politburo decision. Worked largely cooperatively with Deng in 1977–78 in eliminating the influence of the Cultural Revolution, but from the end of 1978 was undermined by his lack of Party seniority. Removed from key posts in 1980–81. See also Fig. 4.1.

doubted the Chinese party leader's communist credentials, Mao and his colleagues were good Marxists. For all their indebtedness to the rural revolution that "surrounded the cities," they ultimately saw the rural phase as a necessary prelude to a modernizing program to create a "rich and powerful" China, a program that had to embrace an industrializing society. As Mao put it in mid-1949, "The serious task of economic construction lies before us. We shall soon put aside some of the things we know well and be compelled to do things we don't know well."[3]

This transition, however, would have to occur in a regionally fragmented China, where not only did conditions differ significantly from area to area in social, economic, and even ethnic terms, but the CCP's strength and local history varied enormously. The fundamental difference was between, on the one hand, the base area regions of North China where "the countryside surrounded the cities," that is, the rural revolution that initiated the reform of village society, built up the political and military forces that defeated the Nationalists on the battlefield, and took over the cities of that region and the Northeast, and, on the other hand, the vast areas south of the Yangtze River where communist forces were weak to nonexistent, a straightforward military seizure of the cities took place, and CCP cadres fanned out from the cities to bring the first stages of land reform to the villages.

Under these conditions, daunting problems faced Mao's new regime. Chinese society and polity were fragmented, public order and morale had decayed, a war-torn economy suffered from severe inflation and unemployment, and the country's fundamental economic and military weakness created monumental obstacles to the goal of national wealth and power. Yet the CCP's revolutionary experience bequeathed the new regime some potent resources. A unified leadership around an unchallenged leader, a leader whose authority was being elevated to the even more imposing level as a dynastic founder, promised strong nonfactionalized direction from the top. The pragmatic nature of Mao's policies in navigating the difficult currents of political and military struggle indicated an ongoing approach of dealing in realities. A disciplined party organization, although small for a huge country and short in critical skills, provided the core of an effective administration. Added to this, the population's positive anticipation of the prospects of peace, order, and economic development gave the new regime support during what would come to be regarded, albeit with some exaggeration, as the PRC's golden years.

Mao as All-Powerful Chairman of the Board, 1949–1956

The New Democracy Period

This initial period of the PRC was, in the party's own terms, a great success. The economy was restored more or less on schedule by 1953, before beginning rapid growth along the lines of Soviet-style central planning. All of the country except for Taiwan, Hong Kong, and Macau had been brought under Beijing's control by 1951. Through skillful diplomacy and especially by fighting the world's foremost power to a stalemate in the **Korean War**, China's national pride and international prestige had grown significantly. After a period of careful reassurance to the general populace and key groups, the CCP began to penetrate society and establish totalitarian control through organizational measures reaching into urban neighborhoods and villages. The party also used political campaigns that embodied Marxist notions of class struggle and targeted specific groups, whether to attack those considered hostile to the regime, sometimes using chilling violence, or to indoctrinate those who could be won over to the party's cause. Economic gains translated into general popular support, while those who benefited from land reform, such as poor peasants, and activists, who secured positions in the expanding industrial structure, were even more supportive of the regime.

Land reform, a priority socioeconomic program of the new regime, was basically implemented from 1950 to 1952. This program, which had been carried out in the base areas of North China during the revolutionary struggle, was now extended to virtually the entire country, notably the "newly liberated areas" south of the Yangtze. Since the PRC was, economically and socially, in the pre-socialist stage of "**New Democracy**," the movement confiscated and redistributed landlord land to peasants on the basis of individual ownership. The initial approach laid down by the agrarian reform law of June 1950 was mild; its main objective was to advance the economy by "freeing rural productive forces" rather than aiding the village poor. But the approach was radicalized by late 1950 as resistance developed in the villages. Now class struggle and mass mobilization were emphasized, with poor peasants assuming village leadership and landlords humiliated, with perhaps 1 to 2 million executed. A substantial redistribution of land to poor and middle (more productive but not rich) peasants occurred, but the most significant outcome of land reform was the destruction of the old rural power structure.

From 1953 the party moved steadily toward the Marxist objective of the **socialist transformation** of the economy and society. This process had its twists and turns, producing considerable yet quite containable popular discontent during its "high tide" in 1955–1956, but the result not only achieved the ideological objective, it also extended the party's political and economic control, and with it the leadership's sense of a fundamental breakthrough. According to Mao at the Eighth CCP Congress in fall 1956: "we...have gained a decisive victory in the socialist revolution [and] our Party is now more united, more consolidated than at any time in the past."[4]

As the new emperor, Mao's authority was absolute, but his manner of rule was less intrusive or disruptive than in any subsequent period of the PRC. Although imposing his views in a small albeit crucial number of cases, generally Mao served as the chairman of the board, allowing his more specialist colleagues, notably Premier Zhou Enlai and economic czar Chen Yun, to shape programs in the areas of their special competence, and largely acting as a synthesizer and arbiter of policy decisions. Mao continued the consultative style of the 1940s, acknowledged his own lack of expertise, and reflected his relatively centrist position on the issues of the day. In contrast to the full-blooded Maoism of the Great Leap or Cultural Revolution, Mao's ideological position up to 1956 was largely the orthodox Marxism that saw socialist victory in terms of seizing ownership of the forces of production, and his political task was the relatively incremental one of adjusting the pace of socialist transformation. Even in the relatively few cases in which he imposed his views, his approach was systematic and rational, the process involved considerable discussion and efforts to persuade his colleagues, and although his initiatives were bold and impatient, they were still in many respects moderate.

To a large extent, Mao's less intrusive role was due to the focus on economic development and the broad elite consensus that China should follow the Soviet model, a position Mao fully shared. As Mao subsequently declared, "Since we had no experience...we could only copy the Soviet Union and our own creativity was small."[5] This overstated the case for various areas, notably rural policy, where Mao oversaw considerable adjustments from Soviet precedent, but on key matters including economic strategy and methods, military modernization and government institutions, extensive borrowing and even blind copying of Soviet practices occurred with the aid of Soviet experts.

Such excessive copying undoubtedly frustrated Mao, and at the same time he endured tense relations with Stalin during negotiations in Moscow for the 1950 Sino-Soviet alliance and subsequently over the Korean War. Chinese entry into the Korean conflict was the first case in which Mao enforced his personal view, overcoming fears of an apparent majority of the Politburo that getting involved would jeopardize China's security and economic recovery. In any case, in his relations with the Soviet Union, Mao accepted Stalin's and subsequently Moscow's leadership of international communism. He swallowed some bitter pills in the 1950 treaty, such as the imposition of joint Sino-Soviet stock companies allowing Soviet exploitation of Chinese resources, and despite some theoretical innovations he largely stayed within the Stalinist version of Marxism-Leninism, as graphically suggested by his nocturnal visits to the Beijing residence of the Soviet ambassador for ideological tutorials. Clearly, any dealings with Stalin involved considerations of international politics where Mao took personal control, but the acknowledgment of broad Soviet ideological authority only added to the weight of Russian pronouncements on building socialism. And on core economic planning issues, Mao's role was relatively limited.

Meanwhile, power was being redistributed within the CCP. This involved less the rise or fall of individuals as the main power holders remained members of the **Central Committee**[*] elected in 1945, with all the various mountaintops still represented, than their reshuffling and the establishment of new institutions. The key aspect was the centralization and civilianization of power over the 1950–1954 period. Given the diverse conditions facing the CCP in 1949, an initial period of regional administration based on the various armies that took control of different areas was logical. Large regional Military-Administrative Committees and subordinate military control committees were established, but this was a transitional arrangement from the first. Army commanders initially playing key roles in regional governments were gradually transferred to strictly military positions. Indeed, from the start the key leaders in five of the six large regions were civilians, including Deng Xiaoping in the Southwest. The principle Mao demanded during the revolutionary period that "the party commands the gun, and the gun must never be allowed to command the party"[6] was again enforced. Another aspect of centralization concerned Mao personally. While his authority was never in question, he enhanced his administrative control in 1953 by requiring that he sign off on all Central Committee documents.

With the new 1954 state constitution and other organizational changes, a permanent institutional structure was in place: the party was in overall control and primarily concerned with political movements, particularly in the rural areas; the **State Council** headed the expanding state bureaucracy and took charge of economic policy; and the reorganized **Central Military Commission** (CMC) oversaw the **People's Liberation Army (PLA)**. Mao as party, state, and CMC chairman was at the top of all three pillars of power, although significantly Zhou Enlai as premier was crucial in state administration and, along with Chen Yun, economic policy. Finally, the new structure reaffirmed Mao's control of the military and his now personalized principle that "the party commands the gun." Both Liu Shaoqi (Mao's presumptive successor) and Zhou Enlai were excluded from the CMC. The Chairman and his then favored junior colleague, Deng Xiaoping (who also assumed a key role as CCP secretary-general, charged with overseeing the party's day-to-day business),

---

[*] The Central Committee of the CCP is larger, but less powerful than the Politburo. In 1945, there were forty-four full members and thirty-three alternates. Mao was elected Chairman of the Politburo in 1943, and of the Central Committee in 1945, hence the title, "Chairman Mao." The Central Committee was expanded greatly in size over the years that the CCP has been in power. It now has over 370 full and alternate members.

were the only civilians on the reorganized CMC. At the same time, virtually all the leading generals promoted to the highest rank of marshal in 1955 took on strictly military responsibilities.[7] Although six of the ten marshals were elected to the Politburo in 1956, it is clear that in the entire period from then until the Cultural Revolution began in the mid-1960s, the military played a limited, generally minimal role in civilian affairs.

At the leadership level the most important redistribution of power concerned the transfer of leading regional figures to key positions in Beijing in 1952–1953—a development picturesquely referred to at the time as "five horses enter the capital." Deng Xiaoping was one of those horses, but the "leading horse" was Northeast leader Gao Gang, another favorite of Mao's. This resulted in turf battles as Gao's new assignment as head of the State Planning Commission apparently produced tension with both Zhou Enlai and Chen Yun over economic policy.

But the main disruptive impact was a much more fundamental challenge to leadership unity. In late 1952 to early 1953, Gao had at least several private conversations with Mao in which the Chairman expressed dissatisfaction with Liu Shaoqi and Zhou Enlai as too cautious concerning the pace of socialist transformation. Even more ominous, according to Gao's secretary, in summer 1953 Mao raised the issue of Liu's possibly traitorous activities in the Northeast in the late 1920s, and tasked Gao with investigating the matter.

Gao then began to lobby other key leaders, including Deng Xiaoping and Chen Yun, with an aim to securing their support for a challenge to Liu and/or Zhou. He particularly argued that as a CCP leader in the so-called white areas under Kuomintang control, Liu did not deserve his high position, while he, Gao, represented the red "base areas." Mao's attitudes and motives were opaque, and other leaders did not know how to respond. After some hesitation, Chen and Deng approached Mao and reported on Gao's lobbying. Mao's reaction was to lure Gao into taking further steps in his plotting against Liu and Zhou, turn on him for disrupting party unity, and reaffirm Liu Shaoqi's position as the Chairman's successor. Gao, apparently believing he had been betrayed by Mao, committed suicide. The end result was that the first significant challenge to party unity since the consolidation of Mao's leadership had been repulsed, while the Chairman's all powerful ability to determine the fate of his subordinates had been reemphasized, and his ultimate aims and attitudes remained uncertain. In the end, Mao opted for leadership unity and stability—on this occasion.

The Transition to Socialism

In policy terms, the key turning points in the early 1950s concerned the pace of the transition to socialism: the **general line** for the transition in 1953, and the "high tide" of agricultural **cooperativization** in 1955. In both cases the initiatives to move faster came from Mao, while Liu Shaoqi and other leaders advocated a slower pace. Given the outcomes achieved, Mao's interventions were viewed within the CCP as successful, and (together with his decision on the Korean War) as further proof of his unmatched strategic insight. In neither case, however, was Mao's position wildly radical. Prior to the fall of 1952, the consensus CCP position was that the "New Democracy" period of communist rule in China, which allowed multiple forms of economic ownership, including private property, would last for 10 to 20 years, and *only then* would the transition to socialism begin.

Now, however, Mao pressed for a more ambitious schedule whereby the transition would start almost immediately, but the process itself would be gradual. When the general line was laid down by Mao unilaterally in June 1953, it stipulated that socialist transformation would be completed "within a period of ten to fifteen years or a bit longer," and warned against "errors either of 'left' deviation or of right deviation."[8] In the buildup to the general line, analogous to his handling of the Gao Gang affair, elements of both Mao's awesome power and reasonableness were present. Mao caused individual panic in early 1953 by criticizing Finance Minister Bo Yibo's tax policies as "beneficial to capitalism," yet Bo suffered only a mild career setback. In the summer of 1953, moreover, despite his impatience over the speed of transformation, Mao backed the softer, more pragmatic approach to commercial capitalists advocated by Chen Yun over the harsher preferences of Gao, who urged faster movement toward the nationalization of commerce.

Similar phenomena can be seen concerning the implementation of the transition to socialism in the countryside. Following the conclusion of land reform, the party took the first major step in that direction in 1953–1955 by gradually establishing **lower-level agricultural producer cooperatives** made up of twenty-five to fifty families. Land, although still technically owned by the farmers, as well as tools and draft animals, were pooled; agricultural production was under the direction of cooperative officials. Members were paid partly on the basis of how much work they did and partly according to how much property they had contributed to the **cooperative**.

After two years of fluctuating development in the cooperativization movement during which Mao again warned his comrades about going too fast (left deviation) or too slowly (right deviation), a consensus emerged at the start of 1955, with Liu Shaoqi and CCP Rural Work Department Director Deng Zihui most prominent, that a limited contraction of the number of existing cooperatives was necessary after overexpansion in 1954. Mao accepted this, but by the spring of 1955, based on his own investigations, he became concerned that this policy, by loosening state control of agriculture, was undermining the state procurement of grain needed to feed the cities and was contributing to class polarization in the countryside, as some families were getting quite a bit richer than others. This led Mao to argue for a relatively modest increase in the number of cooperatives. While this was formally accepted by the party leadership in May, Mao pressed for further increases in June and July, which all of the highest leaders apparently accepted. Deng Zihui, however, argued against Mao's latest proposal, leaving his colleagues in the Rural Work Department astonished that he dared to "offend Chairman Mao merely over hundreds of thousands of cooperatives."[9]

Mao rejected Deng's advice and subjected him to criticism as a "right deviationist," yet Deng retained his position, although his career was more adversely affected than that of Bo Yibo. What was significant was that in turning on Deng Zihui, the Chairman had raised an economic question to a political one, and although his latest proposal on the cooperatives was still far from radical, his rhetoric mobilized the party apparatus into an intense campaign mode. This resulted in the "high tide" that by the end of 1956 had basically formed the whole countryside into **higher-level agricultural producers cooperatives,** or **collectives**. Not only were these much larger—250 families—than the earlier cooperatives, but the collective also now owned the land and peasants were paid only according to their labor. Only a small portion of the collectively owned land was set aside for private cultivation. This was a far more radical outcome than Mao's mid-1955 plan, which had only called for establishment of lower-stage (less socialist) cooperatives in *half* of China's villages by spring 1958. But since the achievement of agricultural **collectivization** was a key socialist goal, Mao's intervention to speed things up was seen by his comrades as further evidence of his superior insight and inspirational leadership.

The "high tide" in agriculture was soon followed by the similarly rapid socialist transformation of industry and commerce. By early 1957, the nationalization of these sectors was basically complete and private ownership largely eliminated from the urban economy. At about the same time, an effort had been undertaken to significantly increase the pace of economic development, an effort later regarded as the "little leap forward." But all of these programs produced dislocations in the economy, and measures were taken to relax the pace of change starting in the spring of 1956.

At a late April meeting of the Politburo, however, Mao said that he wanted to increase the already high rate of investment, despite mounting evidence that the economy could not effectively absorb it. Although there was an almost unanimous Politburo preference for a more restrained policy, the meeting dutifully approved Mao's wishes. Zhou Enlai, however, went to see Mao a few days later to argue against the decision and, after a temper tantrum, Mao agreed. The incident not only demonstrated that the Chairman responded to rational argument, but that despite the earlier attacks on Bo Yibo and Deng Zihui, even a cautious leader like Zhou Enlai was willing to approach him, believing that Mao's consultative leadership style still applied. Similarly pragmatic adjustments were made in other areas in 1956–1957, notably increasing the scope of private peasant production within the collective framework and reestablishing a limited rural free market.

Mao and the leadership as a whole did not regard such scaling back as defeats, but rather as sensible adjustments in the context of the overwhelming—and much more quickly achieved than anticipated—victory of socialist transformation. This, as previously noted, was orthodox Marxism. With the economic structure transformed and private property in both city and countryside largely abolished, there was now not only the basis for socialist modernization, but the class enemy also no longer had the wherewithal to challenge the regime. To be sure, there were still opposing political and ideological tendencies, or contradictions, in socialist society, but these were nothing to worry about. As Mao put it in early 1957, "large scale, turbulent class struggles . . . have in the main come to an end."[10]

In this context, party priorities were to shift to economic construction and handling "**non-antagonistic contradictions** among the people." In other words, most problems in China could be resolved through discussion, debate, persuasion, and other noncoercive means. The populace was believed to fundamentally support the CCP and possess creative skills that the regime should enlist, but at the same time, society had legitimate grievances that the party should alleviate. In this context, Mao sought to encourage the expression of different opinions, including complaints about regime shortcomings. This was famously expressed in Mao's spring 1956 slogan addressed to intellectuals in particular: "let a hundred flowers bloom, let a hundred schools of thought contend." In 1956 this by and large only produced tepid academic discussion, but the following year a more determined effort by Mao set in motion a series of policy failures with ultimately catastrophic consequences for the PRC.

Experiments and Disasters, 1957–1960

The Hundred Flowers Movement and the Anti-Rightist Campaign

Three major developments followed the declaration of fundamental victory at the fall 1956 Eighth Party Congress—the **Hundred Flowers movement** in the first half of 1957, the **Anti-Rightist campaign** in the summer and fall, and the **Great Leap Forward** that emerged in late 1957 and extended into 1960. These movements were interconnected; Mao played an initiating role in each, and the Hundred Flowers and Great Leap were virtually unique experiments in the history of international communism, drawing Soviet puzzlement and criticism as a result. The Anti-Rightist campaign and Great Leap in particular had dire consequences that left deep scars on society. These campaigns grew out of the 1956 consensus on giving priority to economic development, but the originally envisioned concessions to society of the Hundred Flowers soon gave way to increasing emphasis on class struggle against perceived enemies of the revolution. Finally, notwithstanding Mao's decisive role in each campaign, the Hundred Flowers and Anti-Rightist campaign both had broad support in the top leadership, albeit with more reservations in the former case. But even with widespread initial enthusiasm in the elite and populace, the third movement was fundamentally a case of "no Mao, no Great Leap."

Leadership consensus existed on the assumption underpinning the Hundred Flowers that the party should solicit feedback from the public. But encouraging open criticism of the government, which was only mildly encouraged in 1956, was always fraught with difficulty and met resistance from lower-ranking officials who were vulnerable to direct criticism in their work units. Facing this resistance, Mao began to push for a more vigorous Hundred Flowers in February 1957. The response from intellectuals who had been subject to various ideological remolding campaigns since 1949 was cautious, but under repeated official urging, by May an outbreak of extensive criticism of the regime unfolded. In fact, much of this criticism remained guarded and was along the themes Mao himself had set, but bitter attacks on lower-level cadres plus comparatively rare extreme statements attacking the party and even Mao himself caused deep concern within the CCP. By mid-May, without admitting it, Mao realized he had miscalculated, and began to plan for a counterattack on the critics. For several weeks he waited to "lure the snakes out" (something erroneously thought by many to have been his plan from the beginning), and then in early June launched a systematic attack in the form of the Anti-Rightist campaign against those who had spoken out.

What was significant about the Anti-Rightist campaign was its intensity and scope. It was conducted in all official organizations, it deeply touched intellectuals and other segments of the urban population in particular, and it resulted in the extensive use of the "rightist" label that would curse people so designated for the rest of the Maoist era, as well as the widespread sending of "rightists" to the countryside for reform through labor. Even more fundamentally, the campaign sent a chill of fear through society, something hitherto not felt on such a broad basis. In the early years of the PRC, although there had been many threatening movements directed at particular groups, for those not directly affected, there was the sense that these efforts were justified, or in any case not personally relevant. Now fear was much more widespread, with an intimidating effect for the future.

For all that, the Anti-Rightist campaign initially seemed designed to restore the *status quo ante*, the situation of unchallenged party dominance without major policy readjustments. The broad thrust of the moderate economic policies that had prevailed since the "little leap" continued into the early fall of 1957, and there were no signs of a redistribution of power either among leading institutions or individuals.

However, various developments created pressure on existing economic policy. At one level, the perceived unreliability of intellectuals as a result of the Hundred Flowers called into doubt the assumption that specialists could be relied on as a key "positive factor" for economic development. Also, the assumption of society's support of the regime that underpinned the relaxation of 1956–1957 was undermined by waves of industrial strikes and substantial peasant withdrawals from poorly performing collectives—something that led to socialist education efforts among workers and peasants in the summer of 1957 to bring them back in line with party policy. Finally, the pace of economic growth, particularly in agriculture, lagged behind expectations. Thus there was a basis for an altered approach to development. These considerations fed into Mao's fundamental desire to transform China into a powerful industrializing state at the quickest possible pace.

Other factors also came into play in pushing policy in a more radical direction. One was the ever-significant relationship with the Soviet Union. At the policy level, without any intention of straying from the broad parameters of the Soviet model, by 1956 CCP leaders focused on the differences between Soviet and Chinese conditions and the need for appropriate policy adjustments, something equally persuasive to an economic specialist like Chen Yun and to Mao, who offered the most systematic statement of the need for readjustment in April 1956.[11]

Furthermore, by the time Mao attended the fortieth anniversary of the Bolshevik revolution in Moscow in November 1957, he had shed any latent sense of inferiority to Stalin, who had died in 1953. Indeed, Mao felt superior as an international communist leader to Stalin's successor, Nikita Khrushchev. He also believed that China had attained a new status by mediating between the Soviets and Eastern Europe first during the Polish October that brought Poland a degree of autonomy from Moscow and then following the crushing of the Hungarian revolution in 1956 by the Soviet army. Mao thought that the Russians had handled both matters badly.

There was also a sense of growing optimism and competitiveness in the communist world, generated by rapid Soviet economic advances and Moscow's technological breakthroughs with the *Sputnik* satellite and intercontinental ballistic missile in 1957. Mao's reaction was to declare that internationally "the east wind is prevailing over the west wind," and to match Soviet boasts that they would overtake the United States economically in fifteen years with the claim that China would overtake Britain in the same period. In terms of international communist politics, Mao strongly affirmed Soviet leadership while in Moscow, which undoubtedly facilitated a Soviet promise to provide the PRC with nuclear weapons technology. Subsequently, despite an overlay of competing national pride and some suspicion, in March 1958, Mao declared "complete support" for every recent Soviet foreign policy initiative.

Meanwhile, following the Moscow meeting, the CCP called for significant increases in production, and the idea of a Great Leap Forward was first propagated. Yet these developments were to pale in comparison to what actually emerged in the first half of 1958.

The Great Leap Forward

A psychological factor was also arguably at play in the new turning point. After a period of virtually unbroken success since assuming unchallenged leadership of the CCP in the 1940s, Mao suffered his first notable failure with the Hundred Flowers. Seemingly unable to accept personal responsibility and seeking a new success, Mao undertook an unusually personal initiative in pushing the Great Leap, much to the surprise and consternation of his colleagues. Beginning in January 1958 he convened a series of ad hoc meetings that led to drastically increased production targets, including a frenzy in June that doubled the national steel target over 1957's actual production.

In this process, several drastic changes took place in Mao's leadership style and the distribution of power within the CCP. Mao now took personal control of the economy, the area in which he subsequently acknowledged he had no particular understanding. He complained that in the past the Politburo had become a mere "voting machine" that simply endorsed the policies of Zhou Enlai, Chen Yun, and others, and he went on to subject these leaders to severe criticism.

In attacking their 1956–1957 policies, Mao not only overlooked his own consistent approval of those policies, he also made the specious assertion that those policies were responsible for the "rightist" onslaught during the Hundred Flowers. In sharp contrast to the situation in the spring of 1956, when Zhou approached Mao on the question of overinvestment, the Premier was now denied the right to speak on economic matters and considered resigning. The overall result was a fundamental change from the first eight years of the regime, when a diluted form of collective leadership existed. Now any leader, no matter how prestigious, could be shunted aside at Mao's whim; it had truly become a case in which no one dared challenge the Chairman's word.

A consequence of both Mao's turn against the leaders of the State Council's economic ministries and the Great Leap approach of relying on mass mobilization rather than technical expertise was that the party apparatus now assumed the key organizing role in economic development. With this came the further elevation of one of Mao's favorite colleagues, Deng Xiaoping, who as CCP general secretary exerted intense pressure on lower level officials to meet fanciful targets. Mao's continuing favoritism was reflected in his spring 1959 remark at the very time of Liu Shaoqi's long fore-shadowed elevation to state chairman—the position equivalent to president of the PRC that Mao had held since 1949—that while he himself was the "main marshal," Deng was the "vice marshal."[12] Deng thus played key roles in the various stages of the Great Leap: the initial escalation of targets in the first half of 1958, the extreme radicalism of the summer and fall, and the "cooling off" phase from late 1958 until the summer of 1959.

In each phase Mao was the key player. After forcing the dramatic escalation of steel targets in June 1958, Mao was again at the center of events at the leadership's annual summer meeting in the coastal resort city of **Beidaihe** that saw not only the further escalation of targets, but also the nationwide launching of the **people's commune** movement that virtually eliminated private property in the countryside and created larger (5,000–25,000 families) and more radical forms of collective living, as well as promising a quick transition to full **communism** within a very few years. This extremism was arguably fed by Mao's newly contentious relations with the Soviet Union, caused mainly by his resentment of proposals from Moscow for joint military facilities on Chinese soil that he took as disrespecting PRC sovereignty. Meanwhile, Moscow openly criticized claims that would have China reach communism not only in a ridiculously short time, but also before the senior communist state.

Finally, it was the Chairman who was the first of the top leaders to speak out against the radical excesses of the summer and fall, resulting in late 1958 in a significant lowering of industrial targets, moderated policy concerning the people's communes, and the relegation of the transition to communism to a more distant future. While this indicated that Mao still retained pragmatic sensibilities, more significantly it demonstrated that none of his colleagues was willing to risk the Chairman's ire, even as excesses ran riot and the first signs of famine emerged until he had spoken.

While the situation in the first half of 1959 trended toward "cooling off," it was inhibited by two factors. The first overarching factor was Mao's ambivalence about slowing down the Leap. Although he temporarily enlisted Chen Yun in mid-1959 to provide some control over the economy, Mao was unwilling to entertain any fundamental reconsideration of *his* Great Leap. Related to this was the fact that, with the undercutting of the role of the centralized economic ministries, policy implementation rested with provincial party authorities, and these leaders varied considerably, from extreme radicalism to a more measured if still highly ambitious approach. In this Mao generally sided with the more cautious local leaders, but he was periodically excited by the claims of the radicals, some of whom even considered Mao's efforts to deflate their wild claims about their achievements in leaping forward as "rightist," and he never insisted on bringing them back to reality. Nevertheless, when the party leadership convened in July 1959 for a meeting at Lushan—another scenic spot, but this one located in the high cool mountains of central China—Mao's signals indicated an intention for a further retrenchment of the Leap, and he called for an open discussion of the problems facing the regime.

The **Lushan Conference** was truly seminal in the history of the CCP, although it can also be seen as an extension of the harsh pressures that Mao brought on his colleagues at the early 1958 meetings. The hopes of many leaders for a further readjustment of Leap policies were shattered when Minister of Defense Peng Dehuai wrote a "letter of opinion" to Mao that was highly critical of Great Leap shortcomings. Although Peng—a Long March veteran, a marshal of the PLA, and the commander of Chinese forces in the Korean War—attributed errors in the Leap to the failure of others to implement the Chairman's directives correctly, Mao was deeply offended. Peng's effort was a clumsy misreading of Mao's psychology: whereas Peng's aim was to prod Mao into taking further steps in the direction of slowing the Leap that he had already signaled, the Chairman interpreted it as a personal challenge.

Other leaders, including those with difficult political relations with Peng, attempted to calm the situation to no avail as Mao insisted on Peng's dismissal and began an intense campaign against "right opportunism"—this time aimed at targets in the party—that frightened officials from addressing problems and intensified radical policies. This took matters further than in early 1958 in terms of how differences within the leadership were handled; now leaders earning Mao's displeasure were not merely criticized and sidelined, they were subjected to even harsher denunciation and dismissed from office. More tragic was that Mao's new lurch to the left at this time was a key factor in deepening the famine that would eventually account for anywhere from 15 to 46 million peasant lives. Significantly, throughout this drama and despite the military's concern for the famine's impact on the morale of peasant troops, there was no PLA position on the Leap nor concerted support for Peng after Mao acted.

Although there was grumbling within the top leadership over Mao's arbitrariness at Lushan, the Chairman remained unchallenged. Much as they had been in the last half of 1958, other leaders were tentative in the extreme, even as evidence of much more severe disasters accumulated in late 1959 and the first half of 1960. Mao, as before, was ambivalent about how to respond, calling for remedial measures but still endorsing high targets in mid-1960. Significantly, it was only in the fall of 1960 when Mao personally ordered a concerted effort to combat the Leap's excesses that a systematic retreat from the Great Leap began. It was also the period when Mao began his own retreat to the so-called second front of leadership, an arrangement whereby he concerned himself with matters of ideology and overall political direction, while other leaders on the "first front" assumed responsibility for the daily administration of the party and state. This involved no lessening of Mao's authority, although in the circumstances it meant leaving the task of cleaning up the mess he had created to Liu Shaoqi, Zhou Enlai, Deng Xiaoping and others.

The Limits of Recovery, 1961–1965

The crisis created by Mao's failed Great Leap Forward was the deepest in PRC history. As the famine deepened, widespread demoralization affected cadres and population alike, social order declined, black markets and superstitious practices multiplied. Throughout 1961, a series of measures were implemented to cope with the situation: drastic cuts in excessive investment; shifting resources to agriculture and consumer industries; ending radical decentralization to enhance economic coordination; adjusting commune organization to increasingly vest authority in production teams, the smallest rural unit; allowing peasants private plots and free markets; emphasizing material incentives in both urban and rural areas; restoring the authority of factory managers and technical personnel; and appealing to intellectuals by indicating that providing expertise alone (rather than being "**red and expert**") was enough to demonstrate political loyalty.

In key functional areas, party documents laying down systematic policies were drafted, each under the direction of a party leader with relevant expertise. Mao approved each document, but overall leadership on the "first front" was provided by Liu Shaoqi. Mao's attention was focused on the further deteriorating relations with the Soviet Union and on the broader problem of reorienting the regime from the excessive high pressure approach of the Great Leap to one emphasizing **inner-party democracy** and cautious policy-making, the "truth from facts" approach of the revolutionary period whereby careful investigation and research were required before decisions were made.

The depth of the crisis, as well as the damage to Mao's personal prestige, was evident at the **7,000 cadres conference** in January–February 1962. An undercurrent of discontent with the Chairman was present at this massive gathering of officials from different institutions and administrative levels, to the extent that Mao felt it necessary to offer a self-criticism. In many respects this was very restrained, and he reasserted the correctness of the Great Leap policy line. But Mao acknowledged responsibility for the current dire situation, declared that he was subject to the will of the majority (in the restricted sense that if everyone disagreed with him he would concede the point), and admitted that the party had been unable to "regularize a whole set of guiding principles" during the Leap in contrast to the "fully persuasive" policies of the Soviet model period.[13]

What was particularly striking was the fact that the leadership rallied around the Chairman. Although Beijing Mayor Peng Zhen suggested that even Mao had made mistakes (the boldest statement of any leader in the 1949–1976 period, but one that largely echoed Mao's self-criticism), Peng had earlier emphasized that "if we don't support him who can we support?"[14] Other leaders, including Deng Xiaoping, went well beyond this to fulsome praise of the Chairman. The most egregious cheerleader for the Chairman was another long-term Mao favorite, Lin Biao, the PLA marshal who had replaced Peng Dehuai as minister of defense after Lushan and who would come to play a crucial role in the Cultural Revolution.

The most important speech to the conference was the official report by Liu Shaoqi. Liu also sought to protect Mao by assuming overall responsibility as the top leader on the "first front." Liu's report was approved by Mao, who, in addition, encouraged Liu to supplement the report with oral remarks. But the report and especially the oral remarks were a particularly systematic critique of the Great Leap, and included a reference to the claims of peasants in some areas that disasters were 70 percent manmade. In sharp contrast to his appreciation of Lin Biao's fawning speech, Mao seemingly took umbrage at the bluntness of Liu's assessment, claiming a number of years later that Liu's performance during the "rightist deviation" of 1962 gave him "food for thought" concerning the reliability of his successor. In the context of the moment, given the severity of the problems facing the PRC, Mao had little immediate recourse and retreated further onto the "second front." He departed from Beijing, leaving Liu to organize further measures to overcome the crisis.

This task was undertaken at another February work conference that concluded the situation was even more dire than previously believed, with the economy "on the verge of collapse." A series of measures followed: on Liu's recommendation Chen Yun was once again placed in charge of the economy; new sharp cutbacks in construction and investment were enforced; and most importantly, with Chen, Deng Zihui, and Deng Xiaoping arguing for concessions to small-scale farming, production quotas were assigned to individual households rather than collective units, and beyond that, even full-fledged private farming was tolerated in extensive areas of the country. Mao had given ambiguous support to this approach at the start of this process. But its underlying spirit, as captured by Deng Xiaoping's comment in a July 1962 speech on restoring agricultural production that "it does not matter if it is a white cat or a black cat, as long as it catches mice" was inevitably too much for the Chairman. This became clear in July as Mao, regarding the measures taken since February as a sign of panic, began to criticize a wide range of policies, starting with the retreat from collective agriculture, and the leaders who had backed them.

The Chairman's undiminished authority was clear. He not only reversed policies by rescinding **household responsibility systems** in the countryside and calling a stop to other concessions, he branded Chen Yun as "always a rightist" and removed Chen from any real power, a situation that would last until 1978. Mao's awesome power extended beyond demoting individuals: he not only dismissed Deng Zihui but also disbanded the party center's Rural Work Department. Even higher figures were chastened as well, with Mao criticizing Liu Shaoqi for paying too much attention to Chen Yun and establishing an "independent kingdom." In this context Liu suddenly and drastically changed course to back Mao's view, while Deng Xiaoping hastily removed his "**cat theory**" from the record and emphasized the collective economy.

Although Mao had halted the retreat, he did not provide a clear direction for future policy. One thing was clear, though: while not disowning the Great Leap, neither was he calling for a return to the radicalism of the Leap program; the collective sector in the rural economy would be boosted, but only in its most moderate form. Mao's lack of clarity about the future was most strikingly reflected in his attempt at the September 1962 Central Committee **plenum**[*] to reorient the overall ideological guideline of the regime with the clarion call, "Never forget class struggle."

While Mao urged party leaders to talk of class struggle every day, this was not much of a guide to concrete action. As he himself put it, work and class struggle were "two different kinds of problems [and] our work must not be jeopardized just because of class struggle."[15] The inherent uncertainty that this indicates was reflected in various ways as the economy and society gradually recovered over the next three years. In the reconstruction of a more regular institutional order as the mobilization approach was abandoned, the government's role in the economy was enhanced, but it did not assume the same dominant role it held in the modern sector under the centralized Soviet model. Ad hoc economic arrangements prevailed as no truly comprehensive plan emerged; significantly, in December 1964, Zhou Enlai observed that "there are still large unknown areas and a great many unfamiliar phenomena [in our understanding of socialist construction]."[16]

The major mass mobilization movement of the period, the rural **Socialist Education Movement** of 1962–1966, which was aimed at ideologically reinvigorating village cadres and combating corruption and other backward phenomena, was not implemented universally but instead only reached about one-third of China's villages. And the overall party line was unclear, with various pragmatic and experimental economic programs implemented, but with more radical political themes, as reflected in the ongoing national campaign to study Mao's Thought proceeding on a parallel if sometimes intersecting track.

---

[*] A plenum, or plenary session, is a meeting of the Central Committee, normally held annually between the elections to that body by the National Party Congress, which now convenes every five years. No plenum was convened between fall 1962 and August 1966, however.

The net result in 1963–1965 was a politics of ambiguity, and at the core of this ambiguity was the relationship of Mao to his colleagues on the "first front." As demonstrated by his actions in the summer of 1962, Mao was all-powerful, but he remained on the "second front" and, his complaints and reservations concerning Liu Shaoqi notwithstanding, left his putative successor in charge of the daily running of the party and state. Mao was now more remote from his colleagues, often outside the capital, but still able to intervene decisively at any point. The real problem for the collective leadership on the "first front" was the Chairman's ambiguous attitudes, and how to be sure that they were in accord with his wishes. Their response was overwhelmingly collegial—rather than compete for Mao's favor by exaggerating differences among themselves, Liu and other leaders sought to come to a consensus position that they believed was acceptable to Mao, and then present it to him. This apparently worked in the overwhelming majority of cases, with the Chairman signing off on even those policies that would be denounced as "revisionist"—a betrayal of Marxism-Leninism—during the Cultural Revolution. But on occasion Mao astonished his colleagues by rejecting their carefully constructed proposals.

The most dramatic case concerned the drafting of a new Five-Year Plan for the economy in 1964. After carefully reviewing and adjusting the draft plan in accord with their perception of Mao's wishes, Liu, Zhou Enlai and the planners were dumbfounded by his angry reaction that labeled their efforts as "practicing [Kuomintang ideology]," in a disparaging reference to the political party of the CCP's archenemy, Chiang Kai-shek. In a display of raw power, the Chairman not only forced changes in the document, but also sidelined the State Planning Commission, creating a "small planning commission" of more junior officials to take over the planning function.

A related aspect of the politics of ambiguity affecting top leaders and subordinate officials alike was that the Chairman periodically expressed unhappiness with some policy or situation and demanded action. The bureaucracies always responded, sometimes drawing Mao's explicit approval, sometimes his tart comments about the inadequacy of the response. There was no certainty that any of these responses indicated a completely satisfied or totally disapproving Chairman, however.

A case in point was education, an area where substantial shifts to the left were made in terms of politicizing the curriculum, increasing the access of workers and peasants to tertiary education, and reforming teaching methods. Still, a major requirement of "work" in education, meeting China's needs for advanced human capital, also had to be addressed. Liu Shaoqi took personal control of the issue and came up with a "two track" solution that supported regular academic education, but at the same time vastly expanded vocational training. While Mao appeared well disposed to the approach at the time, during the Cultural Revolution it was attacked as a typical example of Liu's **revisionism** that condemned the masses to inferior education while training a new bourgeois elite.

A final ambiguous aspect of the period concerned the increasing prominence of the People's Liberation Army. The army, which maintained a strong program of political indoctrination under the slogan of "politics in command," became a model for emulation throughout society with the "learn from the PLA" campaign in 1964. A feature of the PLA's political approach was lavish praise of Mao's Thought, with Defense Minister Lin Biao pushing an early version of the little red book of Mao quotations that would become ubiquitous during the Cultural Revolution.

Other signs of increased military prominence were a more active role in cultural affairs and the transfer of a significant number of PLA officers to staff new military-style political departments in civilian institutions. Yet there is little evidence that any of this involved a significant redistribution in institutional power. The scope and role of the transferred officers is unclear, but the limited evidence available suggests that they were absorbed into their new civilian organizations and began to adopt the perspectives of those organizations. More fundamentally, there is little evidence that the PLA was interested in assuming a civilian role, with Lin himself warning against usurping the power of civilian party committees. The explanation and significance of the army's enhanced status lay with Mao—his appreciation of the PLA's virtues as a politicized army and Lin's promotion of the Mao Zedong Thought, and his unhappiness with what he saw in the rest of the party-state and society as a whole.

Mao's unhappiness went beyond dissatisfaction with bureaucratic responses to his concerns or doubts about the performance of his top colleagues. Looking at the society around him that had been so deeply traumatized by the failures of the Great Leap, Mao saw signs of a possibly degenerating revolution: widespread corruption and self-seeking behavior, significant social inequality, and the emergence of what he called a "new bourgeois" privileged stratum that benefited disproportionately from China's socialist system. In focusing on these developments Mao was profoundly influenced by developments in the Soviet Union. Relations with Moscow had continued to deteriorate since the late 1950s: international disagreements and an escalating ideological polemic drove the relationship to the brink of a split, while the Soviets retaliated to Chinese provocations by reneging on the promised nuclear weapons assistance in 1959, and by withdrawing their experts who had long played such an important role in the PRC's modern sector during the economic crisis in 1960. With the split on the verge of being formalized, Mao went beyond an analysis of Moscow's revisionist foreign policies, which preached peaceful coexistence with the United States, to ask how a communist party could author such policies.

The answer was that the Soviet Union had degenerated internally, due to its party leadership being usurped by a revisionist leading clique, first under Stalin's successor, Nikita Khrushchev, and then Leonid Brezhnev. Mao authorized a detailed polemic in 1963–1964 (in which Deng Xiaoping played a leading role in drafting) making the point that, in fact, capitalism had been restored in the Soviet Union. For Mao, the emergence of Soviet revisionism raised the fear that if the first socialist state could degenerate, what would prevent China from following suit? Mao could only offer some orthodox prescriptions—for example, maintaining the **dictatorship of the proletariat** by which the party-state actively suppressed class enemies, affirming and enforcing party leadership, unfolding mass movements, and conducting repeated socialist education campaigns. But what if the CCP's own leading core was ideologically suspect?

By the start of 1965, Mao harbored growing doubts about Liu Shaoqi, subsequently claiming that he had decided in January that Liu had to go. The immediate factor, according to Mao, concerned differences over the conduct of the Socialist Education movement, something he linked to his earlier "food for thought" over Liu's performance in 1962. In fact, their differences over socialist education were relatively limited and reflected more Mao's shifting position than any major confrontation. One can only speculate about Mao's "real" motives: hitherto repressed resentment over Liu's speech to the 7,000 cadres conference, a paranoid fear that he was somehow losing power to Liu, who was exerting dynamic leadership on the "first front," or a latent distrust of someone who was a rough contemporary, but had never been personally close to him.

It is ironic that Mao turned on Liu; of all top leaders in this period, Liu was most prone to adopting left-leaning tendencies, something that distinguished him from the ever-favored Deng Xiaoping, who subtly distanced himself from the more radical of Mao's interventions, yet who would be treated much better during the Cultural Revolution. In any case, by 1965, Liu, ranking vice-chairman of the CCP, chairman (president) of the PRC, and for more than a decade, the communist leader regarded certain to be Mao's successor, was a marked man. The main reason may have been that Mao perceived Liu as a threat, believed he was promoting or allowing revisionist policies to take hold, or had simply decided that, as the man in charge on the "first front," Liu had to take responsibility for the negative trends in the regime and society. Liu's fate would be sealed in the early stages of the Cultural Revolution.

Great Disorder and Harsh Retribution, 1966–1971

The Great Proletarian Cultural Revolution Begins

The Cultural Revolution, which began with secretive, obscure preparations in 1965, in reality only lasted for two years, from mid-1966 to summer 1968, despite post-Mao claims of a "Cultural Revolution decade" from 1966 to 1976.[17] Throughout this period and into its aftermath, Mao had a clearer idea of what he was against than what he expected to emerge from the tumult. He also demonstrated a deep misunderstanding of the forces he had unleashed. While ostensibly seeking revolutionary purity with such Delphic instructions as "fight self," "make revolution," and "destroy the old and establish the new," Mao's destruction of predictable authority structures left many people, notably rebel activists who supported him, struggling to maintain their own self-interests in fluid and threatening circumstances. Through it all, Mao was central and aloof. He could change the direction of the movement at any point, but he operated from Olympian heights and set no comprehensive or coherent overall policy line.

One of the first signs of the impending storm that was to become the Cultural Revolution was a late 1965 critique of a historical play about an intemperate emperor, written by a leading cultural figure close to Beijing mayor Peng Zhen, and soon attacked as a thinly-veiled criticism of Mao. By the spring of 1966, Peng had been implicated in this alleged smear against the Chairman and purged, followed soon after by the formal launching of the movement with the issuing of the "Circular of the Central Committee of the Communist Party of China on the Great Proletarian Cultural Revolution" on May 16, 1966. This document, known as the "**May 16 Directive**," declared an all out struggle against "those representatives of the **bourgeoisie** who have sneaked into the party, the government, the army, and various cultural circles" and were "counterrevolutionary revisionists" whose aim was to "seize political power and turn the dictatorship of the proletariat into a dictatorship of the bourgeoisie."

A central feature of this new movement was the rupturing of the remaining leadership unity, the "Yan'an roundtable" that, even after the demise of Gao Gang and the ouster of Peng Dehuai, still left the overwhelming proportion of the 1945 leadership in key positions in 1965. By 1965, moreover, Mao increasingly focused on what he saw as the revisionist tendencies of Chinese society, and felt the need for some kind of new revolutionary experience, especially for the generation of young "revolutionary successors" who had not experienced the real thing. He further contemplated new methods to shake up the system, something reflected in Liu Shaoqi's June 1966 remark that "I [have never] in the past come across our party using this form of rectification."[18]

Most fundamentally, as the movement unfolded it became clear that, at least temporarily, in order to achieve his revolutionary goals, the Chairman was willing to destroy the party organization that had been the glue of the system and the vehicle of his past successes. Perceptively characterized by Stuart Schram as a "natural Leninist" for most of his career,[19] Mao now cast aside tight organizational control for the "great disorder" that he envisioned as leading to a revolutionized regime and society. During these years, the movement oscillated through a number of phases, alternately more radical or more constrained, shifts ultimately reflecting Mao's judgment that disruption had gotten out of hand and had to be dampened down, or that efforts to control the chaos were undermining the very purpose of the Cultural Revolution, thus requiring a new upsurge of radicalism.

The Red Guards

The first manifestation of the breakdown of Leninist order was the emergence of the **Red Guards** in Beijing high schools and universities beginning in June 1966 (see Box, **The Red Guard Movement**). Initially guided by **work teams** sent by the central authorities (see below), student Red Guard groups formed and harshly criticized preexisting school and university authorities. Adopting Mao's rebellious spirit, various Red Guards exercised considerable autonomy, in some cases clashing with the work teams. By mid-summer, with the work teams withdrawn, Red Guards became the leading force on campuses. Red Guard behavior included writing **big character posters** pasted on walls attacking campus officials and national figures, ransacking homes to destroy traditional and "bourgeois" property, and abusing, beating, and even killing teachers. After million-strong rallies in Beijing's **Tiananmen Square**, in the fall Red Guards from the capital and other cities began to "exchange revolutionary experiences" by traveling throughout China, thus placing great strain on the country's transportation system. At the same time, factional conflicts developed among Red Guard organizations, reaching violent dimensions in 1967–1968 that Mao would call "civil wars."

Throughout 1966–1968, various forms of violence surfaced, whether Red Guard beatings and killings of suspect teachers or individuals of bad class origin in the community, armed clashes of opposing Red Guard and rebel groups, or the revenge of the authorities when given license to crack down on disruption (something that became even more ferocious after mid-1968). The total number of deaths from this orgy of violence is unknown, but a figure in excess of one million is plausible, with the inevitable damage to social interaction and disruption of the economy immense.

During these two years there were also critical shifts in institutional authority—notably the destruction of the party-state apparatus, but these did not involve an unambiguous investiture of power in alternative institutions. Rather, all remained fluid, uncertainty existed throughout, and Mao stood above everything, even when he refused to give clear orders.

In the earliest period, the so-called Fifty Days of June–July 1966, overall authority for conducting the Cultural Revolution remained with the Politburo leadership of Liu Shaoqi and Deng Xiaoping, but the waters were muddied by Mao's creation in May of the **Central Cultural Revolution Group (CCRG)** with special responsibility for the movement. The CCRG was effectively, if not formally, led by Mao's wife, Jiang Qing,[20] who had been called from the political sidelines by her husband in the early 1960s to counter bourgeois influences in the arts. Most of the other members of the CCRG were, like Jiang Qing, ideological radicals who had been on the margins of the elite, although several figures of Politburo rank, notably Yan'an security chief Kang Sheng and Mao's former secretary Chen Boda, also played important roles. Who better to mount a challenge to the party establishment?

Clearly, while new Cultural Revolution organizations like the CCRG played their roles, institutional power was now thoroughly eclipsed by Mao's personal authority. This was enhanced by Mao's personality cult, something dating from his consolidation of power in

THE RED GUARD MOVEMENT

The Red Guard movement was one of the best known but inadequately understood aspects of the Cultural Revolution. With the campaign beginning in the educational sphere, high school and university students became the movement's first activists, later copied by "revolutionary rebels" in government institutions and factories. These students provided some of the Cultural Revolution's most riveting images, for example, excited adoration of Mao during the summer of 1966 rallies at Tiananmen Square, and the cruel abuse of campus authorities, including professors, and leading party-state officials paraded through the streets in dunce hats. By 1967 the violence let loose by significant numbers of Red Guards against such targets and "bad class elements" in society had been overtaken by brutal clashes among Red Guard factions. Understanding the sources of factionalism and the larger politics of the Red Guard movement is not easy; for a nationwide phenomenon, involving millions of students, remarkably little is known for the vast majority of the country. Existing studies largely focus on high schools in the southern city of Guangzhou, and on the campaign in Beijing's universities.

Two broad explanations have been advanced for Red Guard factionalism: a sociological approach arguing that interests based on status and political networks in the pre-1966 academic structure and broader society determined factional affiliation, and a more political interpretation emphasizing conflicts emerging during the course of the movement itself. Reflecting the tendency for two opposing factions or factional alliances to appear in organizations and localities, the sociological explanation (most clearly documented for Guangzhou high schools) portrays a conflict of "rebel" Red Guards from middling class family backgrounds involving neither exploiters nor the exploited (e.g., intellectuals, professionals) who were disadvantaged by CCP policies, and as a consequence attacked party leaders, *versus* "conservative" Red Guards from "red" class backgrounds (e.g., party officials, factory workers) who both benefited from party policies and formed part of the school political structure as Communist Youth League members, and were thus more supportive of the establishment. Of course, no Red Guard organization labeled itself "conservative," and pro-establishment attitudes had to be tempered by the radical ethos of the Cultural Revolution. But, according to these studies, students joined Red Guard factions on the basis of interests that were present before the movement began.

The political interpretation, which takes into account charismatic student leaders and the ideas and passions of Red Guard activists seeking to interpret and realize Mao's objectives, focuses on the interests created as Red Guards interacted with the environment of the Cultural Revolution. This explanation is largely based on events in Beijing's elite universities, events necessarily unique because of the role of leading CCP figures in the unfolding of the movement there. This raises the question of to what extent the movement was, as many Red Guards bitterly came to believe, simply the result of manipulation by elite politicians. The short answer is that the CCRG was deeply involved and sometimes determined the outcome of factional fights, but the Red Guard movement also had a dynamic of its own and spun out of control.

Contrary to Mao's claim that work teams sent by the central authorities to the universities (on the order of Liu Shaoqi) had suppressed the Cultural Revolution during the so-called "Fifty Days" in June–July 1966, most teams implemented their understanding of Mao's wishes through harsh attacks on university authorities that gained Red Guard support regardless of social status. The work teams, however, clashed with militant students, not over Cultural Revolution aims, but over the teams' efforts to tightly control the movement.

When the teams were withdrawn, the majority of Red Guards who had cooperated with them ironically became the leading force on campus, but the militant minority demanded

(continued)

THE RED GUARD MOVEMENT (continued)

reversals of the negative political labels they received from the work teams during the "Fifty Days." As tensions escalated, the CCRG backed the militants and undercut the power of the conservative majority.

Then, as the Cultural Revolution extended into government organizations in January 1967, the victorious militant Red Guards linked up with "revolutionary rebels" in ministries responsible for their universities before 1966. In the confusion that followed during the struggle to "seize power" in ministries, opposing city-wide Red Guard alliances formed. This was a struggle for political advantage and to avoid losing to bitter enemies, not over different views of the movement's direction or reflecting contrasting class backgrounds. As internecine violence unfolded after January in much of China, the Red Guards played no further useful role for Mao, eventually leading to his dismantling the movement in summer 1968 and the sending of more than 20 million urban youth to temper themselves in the countryside.

the 1940s, but eased at the Chairman's own initiative in the early 1950s, before being taken to new heights during the Great Leap Forward. Now, however, a virulent cult emerged that greatly surpassed all previous manifestations, with loyalty dances and many other quasi-religious phenomena deeply penetrating everyday life.

A key feature of the period was that all leaders were in the dark concerning the Chairman's ultimate intentions, as seen in Liu's lament, cited above, concerning his bewilderment over Mao's new form of rectification. Liu had attempted to conduct the movement with the traditional rectification method of sending work teams to Beijing's high schools and universities to guide the Cultural Revolution as it unfolded on campuses, and this gained Mao's approval, albeit somewhat elusively. The uncertainty was not limited to the established inner circle of leaders; the radical members of the CCRG also defended the work teams in June, although they changed their tune in July, arguably because of a clearer understanding of Mao's intentions. In any case, when Mao returned to Beijing after an extended period outside the capital in late July 1966 and criticized the work teams as suppressing the Cultural Revolution rather than furthering it, a new stage was set. The work teams were withdrawn; Liu and Deng, as the central sponsors of the work teams, were in trouble; and the authority of the party as a whole had been damaged.

A Central Committee plenum in August 1966 laid down a set of guidelines for the Cultural Revolution that were inherently contradictory, both asserting overall party authority and encouraging student rebellion. Moreover, change in the top leadership inevitably contributed to uncertainty. The disgraced Liu was replaced by the loyal Lin Biao as Mao's designated successor. The Politburo **Standing Committee** was significantly enlarged and its internal pecking order revamped, and most provocatively, Mao authored a big character poster that clearly attacked Liu for adopting "the reactionary stand of the bourgeoisie." Yet the future extent of the Cultural Revolution's destruction could not have been imagined. The movement was to steer clear of the productive sectors of the state and society, and Mao indicated it would be wound up in about three months. But following several months of increasing strife on campuses and student incursions into the community, as well as escalating attacks on individual leaders, in the late fall of 1966, the fateful decision was taken to extend the movement into factories and the countryside. This placed extra stress on provincial, municipal, and ministerial authorities that now came under intensified rebel attack. Soon the entire party structure collapsed.

Power Seizures and Revolutionary Committees

The next stage of the Cultural Revolution began with the seizure of power by rebel forces in the so-called January [1967] revolution in Shanghai. In fact, this was a largely peaceful seizure by the leading radical figures of the emerging Shanghai power structure who significantly were also members of the CCRG. The venture thus carried Mao's authority from the outset, something rare in the power seizures by radicals that followed in other parts of the country. After a brief experiment with a radically decentralized power structure called the "Shanghai commune" that Mao rejected as lacking sufficient authority to suppress counterrevolution, **Revolutionary Committees** emerged as the new government in Shanghai and elsewhere, and in the absence of a viable party structure became the organ of local power.

While the unusual circumstances in Shanghai meant that civilian leadership prevailed, the Revolutionary Committee model established in other municipalities, provinces, lower-level jurisdictions, and institutions of various kinds, including schools and factories, promoted a "three way alliance" of PLA representatives, "revolutionary cadres" (experienced officials from the previous regime who possessed necessary administrative skills and were judged sufficiently reformed), and "mass representatives" reflecting the contending rebel factions in the area or organization concerned, with the military generally dominant. The process of forming the Revolutionary Committees was drawn out, intensely contested, with top leaders—notably Zhou Enlai—engaged in efforts to negotiate agreements among sharply opposed, and in some cases intractable factions. Indeed, the final provincial Revolutionary Committees were only established in September 1968 after Mao had called a halt to the Cultural Revolution.

From the outset, the disruption accompanying power seizures was resisted by top leaders who had not been toppled in 1966. The most famous instance was the so-called February [1967] adverse current, a conflict involving seven Politburo-level vice premiers and PLA marshals who, apparently seeing an opening in Mao's recent criticism of the radical excesses of the early Cultural Revolution, confronted leading members of the CCRG over the accelerating chaos. After a sharp argument, Mao sided with the radicals, warning the vice premiers and marshals that "whoever opposes the CCRG will meet my resolute opposition."[21] Mao then suspended the Politburo as a policy-making body, leaving the CCRG, an organization that was growing rapidly from a small group of radical party intellectuals into a substantial bureaucracy, as one of the two authoritative bodies at the party center.

The other body, established at the same time as the CCRG in May 1966, was the arguably even more powerful **Central Special Case Examination Group**. Similar to its sister institution, it grew from a small group investigating the Peng Zhen case to a large bureaucratic organization with a nationwide network seeking incriminating evidence of traitorous activity by high-level figures. It thus became the organ of an inner-party inquisition that directed the ferreting out, arrest, and torture of suspect Central Committee members and other officials. While leading radical figures Jiang Qing and Kang Sheng played particularly notorious roles, many other leaders were drawn in, the ever reliable Zhou Enlai performed the penultimate supervisory role, and Mao of course had the ultimate power to focus or curb the group's activities.

The institution whose domestic power grew markedly during the Cultural Revolution was the PLA. The army was not only the leading force in most of the newly established Revolutionary Committees, it was also the authority responsible for maintaining law and order before and after the committees were set up. But the result was not a true military takeover, or something the army itself welcomed. In 1967–1968 responsible PLA commanders, who were often attacked and their armories raided by rebels, found themselves engaged in bloody struggles with disruptive groups without clear authority from above, and were sometimes rebuked or ousted as a result. Most army leaders wanted the military to disengage from politics and return to national defense duties. Willing or not, the PLA remained at the center of the political structures that evolved from the summer of 1968 after Mao, disappointed by the petty but violent factionalism of the Red Guards, effectively called a halt to the Cultural Revolution by ordering a crackdown on disruptive rebel groups and the dispersal of troublesome Red Guards to the countryside, with perhaps 20 million urban-bred young rebels "sent down to the villages and up to the mountains" to live, work, and learn among the peasants. Emphasis had thus further shifted to the restoration of order, a task that was mainly the responsibility of the PLA.

The Aftermath of the Cultural Revolution

In addition to achieving unprecedented representation on the Politburo and Central Committee at the Ninth Party Congress in April 1969 (the first full party congress since 1956), the military had an even firmer grip on provincial Revolutionary Committees as prominent rebels from 1966–1968 were removed from power or marginalized, and it equally dominated the new party committees that were restored during institutional rebuilding in the provinces and lower administrative levels in 1970–1971. Meanwhile, PLA representatives had played a key stabilizing role in government ministries during factional fighting in 1967–1968, and a substantial number of military officers now became leaders of party core groups as the state structure reemerged as functioning organizations in 1970–1973.

This period also saw harsh, indeed murderous campaigns targeting troublesome rebel elements or others who had earned the displeasure of local authorities during the Cultural Revolution, as well as ordinary criminals, imaginary counterrevolutionaries, and the usual suspects with bad class backgrounds. The **"cleansing of class ranks" campaign** in 1968–1969, together with subsequent suppressions in 1970–1972, probably killed at least 1.5 million people. These campaigns were clearly authorized by Mao, although his available statements advocated a degree of restraint. The PLA, as the ultimate source of local authority in most places during this time, actively participated in the bloodletting or stood by and watched. Overall, since 1966 more deaths resulted from suppression by the authorities than from Red Guard violence, with its scope increasing dramatically from the second half of 1968.

Somewhat paradoxically, this period also saw a moderation of radical Cultural Revolution policy trends. These policy adjustments were modest, and mostly aimed at restoring order and predictability in the economy and administration—and there was no questioning of the central concept of the Cultural Revolution.

In addition, there was a significant change in PRC foreign policy that had domestic political implications. In August 1968, the Soviet Union invaded Czechoslovakia to crush yet another democratic movement, proclaiming the Brezhnev doctrine asserting Moscow's right to intervene in other socialist states. This led to escalating tensions on the Sino-Soviet border in early 1969, a result of which was that Mao not only undertook feverish war preparations, but also began the process of rapprochement with the United States as a way to protect China from the Soviets. The PLA still could not escape its unwanted political tasks, but the focus of the institution was turning back to its basic defense function.

All of this took place in the context of the emergence of an unusual political lineup at the top of the CCP, one marked by peculiarities that went well beyond dismantling the Yan'an roundtable. The new Politburo, consisting of twenty-one full members elected at the Ninth Party Congress in April 1969, contained less than half of the full 1956 members, and of that half nearly half again were elderly leaders without any real function. Liu Shaoqi had been declared a counterrevolutionary in 1968, expelled from the party, and subsequently died from physical abuse. Deng Xiaoping had been labeled a "**capitalist roader**," removed from all his party and government posts, but, with Mao's protection, he was not expelled from the party as the radicals undoubtedly wanted, and was sent to work in a farm machinery repair shop on a rural people's commune.

Meanwhile, the new Politburo was filled out by CCRG radicals with marginal political qualifications led by Jiang Qing, regional military commanders, and central military leaders close to Lin Biao, including Lin's wife. A key figure in the new line-up was Zhou Enlai, valued (but not particularly respected) by Mao as a skilled administrator, reliable political surrogate, and diplomatic negotiator, a role that became especially important in the new post-1968 foreign policy context. In short, with this diverse group, whatever capacity that previously existed for collective influence on Mao had totally dissipated. Yet the election of a new Politburo and Central Committee, together with the subsequent piecemeal reconstruction of a central party apparatus, marked a step toward institutional regularity, and the CCRG, the de facto power center of the last three years, suspended operations in September 1969.

The Lin Biao Affair

The strangest aspect of the new leadership equation was the role of Lin Biao. Although long a Mao favorite and arguably the CCP's greatest general, and widely accepted within the elite as a top Politburo leader, Lin was a curious choice as Mao's successor in that he was in poor health and, crucially, had little interest in power or domestic affairs. He sought to avoid political elevation but could not refuse Mao's designation. Once installed as the successor, Lin played as minimal a role as possible, generally invisible in public after the massive Red Guard rallies in the summer of 1966, and avoiding strong advocacy within the leadership. Moreover, his actual views were comparatively moderate, as indicated to staff and family in private, and as reflected on the rare occasions when he expressed a personal preference in leadership exchanges. Nevertheless, to the public he was a staunch supporter of the Cultural Revolution as befit his position as the Chairman's successor, a position written into the new 1969 party constitution.

Mao's motives in selecting Lin are unclear, but probably involve some combination of having the Minister of Defense at his side to guarantee PLA support, long-standing favoritism toward Lin and appreciation for his role in promoting the Mao cult, and the fact that of all the members of the Politburo Standing Committee, Lin was the only one not tarnished by the perceived revisionist tendencies of domestic policy. In any case, Lin's *modus operandi* was simply to endorse whatever position Mao took and avoid any personal initiative.

Unfortunately for Lin, this was not sufficient, in part because his ambitious wife, Ye Qun, and central military subordinates became involved in disputes with Jiang Qing and other civilian radicals. Lin was dragged into the conflict during a confrontation at the Lushan Central Committee plenum in the summer of 1970, Mao decided in favor of Jiang Qing, and over the next year Mao applied pressure to Lin's "camp," demanding self-criticisms of Lin's associates, which were invariably judged inadequate. Mao did not openly disown Lin, but he denied him a personal audience, and eventually in the summer of 1971 indicated he wanted some kind of (unspecified) showdown with his successor.

Meanwhile, Lin's twenty-six-year-old son, a high-ranking air force officer despite his age, engaged in discussions with other young officers that may have included wild ideas concerning a military coup, and possibly an assassination attempt against Mao, but which do not appear to have involved Lin Biao himself (see Box, **The Lin Biao Affair**). With

THE LIN BIAO AFFAIR

The Lin Biao affair, also known as the September 13 [1971] incident, after the date Lin's plane crashed while fleeing China, remains the CCP's most mysterious leadership conflict. Unlike virtually all other leaders who suffered during Mao's last two decades, there has been no serious official effort to reexamine Lin's case, much less "reverse the verdict" on him. This is probably due to the fact that, unlike other victims of the "Cultural Revolution decade" who were attacked as revisionists, Lin was a major beneficiary of the Cultural Revolution, despite his reluctance to play the role of Mao's chosen successor and his doubts about the movement, and thus he became a symbol of the excesses rejected by the post-Mao leadership. Beyond that, the sheer bizarreness of the claims made about what happened to Lin, the likelihood that key "evidence" was fabricated, and the difficulty of presenting a clear good *vs.* evil narrative arguably contributed to a decision to ignore the case, leaving the story concocted in 1972 as the official version.

There is little to suggest significant reservations on Mao's part concerning succession arrangements in the year following the Ninth Congress in 1969. In the spring of 1970, however, with a new state constitution on the agenda, Mao declared he did not want to serve as state chairman (a position equivalent to that of PRC president), which had been vacant since the purge of Liu Shaoqi. But Lin Biao and other leaders, including Zhou Enlai, continued to advocate that Mao take the post, presumably pandering to Mao's vanity (something also apparent in Lin's claim that Mao was a genius). Bizarrely, these issues fed into tensions between Lin's followers in the central PLA command, and Jiang Qing's civilian radicals who had meddled in military matters. A confrontation erupted at the August–September 1970 Lushan plenum. With radical leader Zhang Chunqiao singled out as a target by Lin's supporters, intense criticism directed at Zhang came from well outside Lin's group. Although it was not Lin's intent, by venting their spleen at one of the Cultural Revolution's main protagonists, many participants were undoubtedly expressing their true feelings about the movement. This was certainly Mao's perception: he sided with Zhang and Jiang Qing, equating opposition to Zhang Chunqiao with opposition to himself, that is, to *his* Cultural Revolution.

Over the next year Mao brought increasing pressure to bear on Lin's followers, notably Chen Boda, Mao's former secretary and CCRG leader who had clashed with Jiang and Zhang before aligning with Lin's "camp," and the "four generals" who led the PLA's service arms. Mao took organizational measures to dilute Lin's military authority, launched a criticism campaign against Chen, labeling him a "phony Marxist" who had pushed the genius issue, and subjected the generals to extended criticism. But Mao's intentions were unclear, and Lin seemed uneasy but resigned to his political fate in summer 1971 when news came that Mao wanted to deal with him upon the Chairman's return to Beijing.

Earlier in March, Lin's son, Lin Liguo, an air force officer himself, had discussed his father's situation with other young officers, discussions later represented as planning for a military coup aimed at Mao. In the official version, this was Lin Biao's plot, something doubtful given its amateurish nature, and post-Mao investigations determined that none of the "four generals" had any knowledge of it. Finally, with Mao's return imminent, panic seized Lin's household, Lin Liguo may have initiated new wild discussions about assassinating Mao, and just before midnight on September 12, Lin, his wife (Ye Qun), and son fled by plane toward the Soviet Union. According to Lin's surviving daughter, her father, drowsy from sleeping tablets, was virtually kidnapped by Ye Qun and Lin Liquo. Whatever the truth, Mao reportedly stopped preparations to shoot down Lin's aircraft, commenting that "Rain has to fall, girls have to marry, these things are immutable, let them go."

Mao returning to Beijing from the south for the showdown, Lin, his wife, and son fled toward the Soviet Union in September under still mysterious circumstances, their plane crashing in the Mongolian desert, killing all aboard. Contrary to what would be expected following the demise of a threatening opponent, Mao went into a physical and emotional tailspin, seemingly unable to accept that a favored colleague, even one facing criticism and uncertainty, would desert him.

Mao's Last Stand, 1972–1976

The Lin Biao affair was a critical turning point in Chinese politics during the Maoist era. Despite Lin's private skepticism about the movement, he was identified with the Cultural Revolution and with Mao as the Chairman's personally chosen and constitutionally mandated successor. When Lin was publicly denounced as a traitor, doubts about the Cultural Revolution that had grown both within the populace and the party elite during the increasingly destructive course of the movement inevitably intensified. Mao was acutely aware of widespread dissatisfaction with the movement, whether by people who saw it as a reign of terror, by officials bent on revenge after being attacked by rebels, or even by those who felt its objectives were good, but that it did not have to be carried out in such a violent and chaotic manner.

On several occasions from 1972 to 1976 the Chairman observed that he had "[only] accomplished two things in my life, [and while few would have reservations concerning the defeat of Chiang Kai-shek], the other matter . . . was to launch the Cultural Revolution [that] few support [and] many oppose."[22] In countering such attitudes Mao would not accept criticism of the concept of the Cultural Revolution, but he acknowledged that much had gone wrong in practice: "the overall assessment [of the Cultural Revolution is] basically correct, [but] some shortcomings. Now we must consider the deficient aspects. It is a 70/30 distinction, 70 percent achievements, 30 percent mistakes."[23] During the last years of his life Mao made concerted efforts to correct the "30 percent mistakes" so that the movement could be consolidated, but the Cultural Revolution per se remained sacrosanct.

The Chairman's fragile health (he turned 80 in December 1973) and even greater remoteness from his leading colleagues after the death of Lin Biao affected the politics of the period. Mao's health was extremely poor in 1972, only improved somewhat in 1973–1974, and began to decline sharply in 1975, finally leaving him in a virtual coma in the summer of 1976. He was out of Beijing for nine months from July 1974 to April 1975, but even when in the capital access to him was highly restricted, resulting in considerable authority for those leaders who did see him and could convey his views. In this regard, remarkable influence was exercised by relatives who had access, for most of the period his niece (together with his interpreter—the "two ladies"), and much more significantly his nephew, Mao Yuanxin, from the fall of 1975, figures who both conveyed information about the highest leadership to Mao, and carried back his orders, which were reflexively obeyed. As before, Mao's ambiguous views complicated the lives of those entrusted with running the state, but the difficulty was magnified by his deteriorating condition and isolation.

Reflecting his contradictory objectives of both correcting and defending the Cultural Revolution, Mao placed contending forces on the Politburo. On the one hand, there were key pre-1966 leaders, most notably Premier Zhou Enlai and Deng Xiaoping, who, after submitting a self-criticism to Mao, had been recalled from internal exile in 1973 and reinstated in his position as vice-premier, and subsequently in January 1975 as vice-chairman of the CCP and effective leader of the "first front." On the other hand, Mao gave Politburo positions to leading Cultural Revolution radicals, including Jiang Qing and her CCRG associates, Shanghai propaganda officials Zhang Chunqiao and Yao Wenyuan; they were joined in 1973 by the young Shanghai factory cadre and Cultural Revolution rebel Wang Hongwen. While much of the history of this period has been written in terms of conflict between this so-called **Gang of Four** (a term bestowed by Mao during one of his periods of displeasure with the radicals) and the old guard headed by Zhou and Deng, this distorts the reality in several ways.

Most fundamentally, this interpretation paints the dynamics of the period as determined by the struggle between these ideologically opposed groups, with Mao doing little more than intervening periodically in the conflict to tip the scale in one direction or the other. In fact, Mao determined *every* turning point during the period according to his own goals, and placed major restrictions on Politburo conflict by demanding party unity. While the Chairman was delusional if he believed these contentious forces could cooperate on a lasting basis to carry out his intention of rescuing key aspects of the Cultural Revolution—and he did at one point envisage a leadership team of Wang Hongwen and Deng Xiaoping—Mao was able to enforce periods of cooperation or at least quiescent relations between the groups.

Finally, by the time of the Lin Biao affair, Mao had also introduced into the higher echelons of the party elite a number of younger leaders who had served in the provinces before the Cultural Revolution. Those he promoted had been beneficiaries of the Cultural Revolution in the sense of attaining higher office than would have been possible without the movement, but they were drawn from the party apparatus and acculturated in its ways. Rather than being a third force between the old guard and radicals, as is often assumed, this group of new younger central leaders were sympathetic to Zhou and Deng in political and in policy terms, most fundamentally because of their respect for party seniority—one of the strongest factors holding the system together before 1966, but one shattered by the Cultural Revolution. The problem was that this group, like both the radicals and old guard, had to tailor their advocacy and actions in accord with Mao's views of the moment.

Over the 1972–1976 period, Chinese politics went through a number of alternating phases, phases that were longer and more coherent than those during 1966–1968, and crucially occurring in a more stable if still volatile and developing organizational context. In 1972, while attempting to blame the excesses of the Cultural Revolution on Lin Biao, Mao authorized a critique of "ultra-left" practices that had disrupted the economy, culture, education, and science, and initiated a new round of rehabilitations of leaders dismissed during the Cultural Revolution. While these moderating measures have been identified with Zhou Enlai, who indeed played the leading role in managing the process, the political decision came from Mao, as reflected in the fact that until late in the year the radicals were largely silent concerning this trend.

Moreover, in the delicate area of leadership rehabilitations, Mao's direct personal imprint was clear on a case-by-case basis—most notably the return to office of Deng Xiaoping in early 1973. This critique of "ultra-leftism" was an extension of the policy drift away from Cultural Revolution excesses over the previous two to three years. But the measures themselves were quite limited, and no overall ideological justification was provided. When the radicals felt the need to speak out against this policy drift toward the end of 1972, their advocacy was tentative. And even after Mao signaled in December 1972 that the critique had gone too far by declaring in a 180-degree ideological turn that Lin Biao was in fact an "ultra-rightist" and a "swindler like Liu Shaoqi," official policy largely continued in the new moderate direction well into 1973.

In any case, Mao concluded that the ideals of the Cultural Revolution had been diluted, and he moved to reassert them at the Tenth CCP Congress in the summer of 1973. This could be seen in the rhetoric of the new party constitution that, among other things, praised the rebellious spirit of the Cultural Revolution by inserting Mao's observation that "going against the tide is a Marxist-Leninist principle," and in the astonishing elevation of model rebel Wang Hongwen as Mao's successor.

By the start of 1974, abetted by his growing unhappiness with Zhou Enlai ostensibly over foreign affairs issues (see below) and concerns with the PLA's political reliability, Mao intensified his effort to reemphasize the essence of 1966–1968 by launching a "second Cultural Revolution," which was formally called the "**Criticize Lin Biao and Confucius**" (i.e., oppose ultra-rightism) campaign. This campaign targeted Zhou (indirectly) and the PLA and produced considerable economic, social, and organizational disruption over the first eight months of the year, but nowhere near the scale of the real Cultural Revolution.

Even though Zhou was under severe stress as he battled cancer, he was able to contain the movement's damage to a limited degree, including tentative moves to repair economic damage. Moreover, independent of the Premier, leading generals were reshuffled and criticized, but not purged, while overall very few important officials were actually removed from office. Much more quickly than in 1966–1968, Mao called a halt to the campaign in August 1974: "The Cultural Revolution has already lasted eight years. It is now time to establish stability. The entire Party and the army should unite."[24]

Mao had now created a new turning point that set in motion the most serious effort during this period to consolidate the Cultural Revolution by dealing with what he had acknowledged were the "30 percent mistakes" of the movement. Several measures showed clearly Mao's intention. One was his directive on stability and unity cited above, plus a second on the priority of developing the national economy. He also appointed Deng as de facto head of government replacing the ill Zhou in the fall of 1974, and aimed several pointed criticisms at the radicals in 1974–1975. The State Council was reorganized in January 1975, which further restored the machinery of government and placed it in a decisive position to implement the consolidation effort. By mid-1975, Mao had vested full authority in Deng that allowed for a much more comprehensive approach to rectifying Cultural Revolution problems.

Yet throughout this time, Deng was dependent on Mao's continuing favor, something indicated by the careful attention that some of Deng's key advisors paid to Mao's works—and indeed by Deng's own study of those works at a time when he was deeply engaged on a wide range of policy issues. Deng was able to dominate the Politburo in this period because he had access to Mao and gained the Chairman's approval of his efforts. This support left Deng all the more dumbfounded when in fall 1975, he suddenly learned of Mao's discontent with his actions.

The central figure in turning Mao against Deng was not any member of the Gang of Four, but rather his thirty-four-year-old nephew, Mao Yuanxin. A leading official in Liaoning, one of the most radical provinces, Mao Yuanxin complained to his uncle about various aspects of Deng's policies, but the core complaint was that Deng fundamentally showed little support for goals of the Cultural Revolution. Following a series of meetings mandated by Mao in November that criticized some of Deng's closest collaborators in the consolidation effort, a campaign to "beat back the right deviationist wind to reverse correct verdicts" of the Cultural Revolution in education unfolded, and Deng was gradually stripped of authority, despite three self-criticisms. Like Lin Biao before him, Deng's pleas for an audience with the Chairman fell on deaf ears.

The Death of Zhou Enlai

Deng had already been effectively removed from power before the death of Zhou Enlai, who had been premier of the PRC since its founding, in January 1976, but the new leadership alignment was only confirmed at the start of February. At that time, to everyone's surprise, one of the relatively young and little known leaders elevated by Mao to the Politburo in 1973, Hua Guofeng, was named acting premier and placed in charge of the party center, meaning he had Mao's support and confidence. Now the campaign against "right deviationist winds" spread to other spheres, ministry leaders were attacked and sidelined, and rebel activities spread in the localities. But, as in 1974, despite significant economic and social disruption, this was again a pale reflection of 1966–1968, with Mao advocating keeping the movement under party control and Hua managing to curb the more threatening developments.

It was against this background in early April 1976 that an incident occurred that reflected the volatile political situation (see Box, **The Tiananmen Incident, 1976**). Hundreds of thousands of Chinese citizens took the occasion of the annual festival to pay respects to

THE TIANANMEN INCIDENT, 1976

The death of Premier Zhou Enlai on January 8, 1976, produced genuine grief within the Chinese population. Of all Chinese leaders, Zhou had the image of a caring figure concerned with the well-being of the people, an image enhanced by his perceived moderation since the outbreak of the Cultural Revolution. If Mao was god, Zhou was the people's friend. Although Zhou received official honors following his passing, they in no way matched popular feelings. Moreover, mourning activities were restricted, the mourning period was curtailed, and the media shifted its emphasis to attacking "right deviationist winds," code words for the policies of Zhou and Deng Xiaoping.

While the Gang of Four was prominent in these measures, Mao was responsible for the relative denigration of the Premier. Mao declined to attend any memorial events despite appeals from top leaders, denied Zhou the accolade of "great Marxist," and as a result inhibited inclinations within the political elite to expand praise of the dead Premier. Apart from his long-standing low opinion of Zhou's political-ideological merits and jealousy over the Premier's high domestic and international reputation, Mao believed Zhou never truly supported the Cultural Revolution, and that the push for mourning activities represented disapproval of the movement.

Over the next two and a half months, resentment simmered over Zhou's treatment, resentment amplified by the upsurge of anti-rightism, which was also perceived as involving esoteric attacks on the Premier. In late March, a series of demonstrations that featured attacks on the Politburo radicals took place in Nanjing. News of this development reached Beijing and fed into the underlying pressure that had been growing since mid-March with the approach on April 4 of *Qingming*, the festival for honoring the dead, an occasion that allowed the public to express respect for Zhou and resentment over his treatment.

From April 1 to *Qingming*, hundreds of thousands of people visited Tiananmen Square, exceeding one million on the day itself. Large numbers of wreaths honoring Zhou were brought to the Square, and beyond that posters, poems, and impromptu speeches lauded the Premier, but many attacked the radicals, with some targeting the regime and Mao, although not by name.

The Politburo was thus in a quandary, facing the conflicting pressures of managing a volatile situation on the Square, allowing appropriate homage to the Premier, and protecting Mao's prestige and the sanctity of his line. Moreover, as a consequence of Mao's rapidly deteriorating health, more key decisions were taken by the Politburo independent of Mao than was ever the case in previous crises. The crucial decision, pushed through by Jiang Qing following reports of how strongly she was being attacked by protestors, was to remove the wreaths despite an informal understanding that they could stay for several days. This occurred overnight following *Qingming*, but as news of the removal spread on April 5, several tens of thousands of outraged people gathered on the Square. With the situation deteriorating, the Politburo turned to Mao for instructions. As conveyed by his nephew, Mao called for persuasion to get people to leave the Square, but force if that failed. In sharp contrast to Deng Xiaoping's solution to the second Tiananmen incident on June 4, 1989, however, this was to be non-lethal force (fists and clubs), and the actual violence on the night of April 5 was limited in scope, duration, and bodily harm.

deceased ancestors to gather in Tiananmen Square for a remarkable and spontaneous demonstration of their affection for the recently departed Zhou Enlai. The Premier had a rather mythologized reputation as a truly honest and selfless leader who stood with the people. The Tiananmen gathering turned into a protest that reflected the popular sentiment at the failure of the party-state to properly honor Zhou Enlai following his death, something for which Mao bore primary responsibility, as well as expressing deep undercurrents of dismay at the latest resurfacing of Cultural Revolution radicalism.

The Politburo was particularly distressed when they learned about thinly veiled criticisms of Mao himself that appeared in the poems and posters of the masses who had gathered at Tiananmen Square. Due to a clumsy decision driven by Jiang Qing to remove the wreaths that honored Zhou, people rebelled, overturned a police vehicle, and burned an official command post on the edge of the Square. The Square was finally emptied with a brief spasm of violence, but, despite popular belief, relatively few people were injured and no one died, and by the end of the year most of those imprisoned had been released.

In retrospect, the overall restraint of the authorities in the face of, what was up to then, the largest spontaneous mass protest in the history of the PRC, is striking. Moreover, the degree of initiative taken by the Politburo in handling the situation was unusual as a result of Mao's fragile health, but even in this situation the leadership absolutely accepted his directives when conveyed by Mao Yuanxin.

Two significant consequences resulted from the **Tiananmen Incident** of April 1976. First, Hua Guofeng was promoted to premier of the State Council (the "acting" part of title was removed) and the unprecedented position of CCP first vice chairman, unambiguously becoming Mao's successor, thereby removing any lingering claims of worker rebel Wang Hongwen. Second, Deng Xiaoping was blamed for instigating what was labeled as a "counterrevolutionary incident," formally stripped of all his posts, and placed under house arrest. Yet, as he did during the Cultural Revolution, Mao again protected Deng, shielding him from physical threat and stipulating the retention of his party membership. Arguably the most telling aspect of the entire affair was the preoccupation of the leadership with sustaining Mao's prestige within the party and among the people in general. Even as he lay in a coma a few months later, and despite real fears that the radicals would somehow use the Chairman's legacy to seize power after his death, Mao's Cultural Revolution remained sacrosanct, even among the more moderate leaders, until his death. Such was the fealty owed to the founder of the regime.

Paradoxically, during Mao's last years the institutions of the party-state were gradually strengthened, but politics was overwhelmingly shaped by the interactions of a small number of leaders looking to an increasingly frail Mao. Indeed, the progress Deng made in developing the consolidation program in 1975 before he lost Mao's favor was not based on gathering a range of institutional or interest group backing, as is sometimes argued, but on Mao's indications of support for his efforts. Despite their clear preferences and pressing circumstances, the leaders of the central economic and planning bodies moved with ultra caution until receiving some sign from Mao. Also, the PLA not only went back to the barracks, as was undoubtedly the military's preference, but when ordered by the Chairman in December 1973 to rotate to different regions with virtually no personal staff, and then facing sharp criticism over the following months, regional commanders who had ruled their areas since 1967 meekly complied.

The key power relationships at the Center were again determined by Mao's preferences, requirements, and personal attitudes. The Chairman's choice of the worker rebel Wang Hongwen as his initial successor, following the demise of Lin Biao, was particularly odd, based not on close knowledge of Wang but apparently because Wang fit Mao's conception of a "revolutionary successor": a Cultural Revolution activist, young, and with a back-ground combining worker, peasant, and soldier experiences. It would be a choice that Mao came to regret in the cold hard light of actual performance, and Wang eventually lost his successor status to Hua Guofeng after Zhou Enlai's death in January 1976.

Much more personal, and reflecting forty-five to fifty years of sustained personal inter-action, were Mao's sharply different attitudes to Zhou Enlai and Deng Xiaoping. Zhou was never ousted by Mao, and he was valued by the Chairman for his skills, loyalty, and utter reliability. But Mao had long looked down on Zhou's political and ideological credentials, and arguably felt uneasy with Zhou's approximate equality in age and party seniority. Also, in the last period of their lives, Mao resented the high regard in which Zhou was held, both domestically for his policy moderation and especially internationally where Zhou was widely hailed for his role in U.S.-China rapprochement. Thus in 1973 Mao twice launched rhetorical attacks on Zhou for foreign policy errors that were at best exaggerated, at worst bogus. Most cruelly, in November–December of that year, Mao demanded intense Politburo criticism of the seriously ill Premier, attacks that all leaders dutifully participated in, Deng included.

In contrast, although twice removed from office for alleged ideological mistakes, the younger Deng had always been one of Mao's favorites, received his highest praise, and was protected when out of power. Mao's behavior of being "bad to Premier Zhou but nice to Deng Xiaoping" was graphically reflected in late 1973 when Deng, as required, joined in the harsh criticism of the Premier. When informed of this, an excited Chairman happily exclaimed "I knew he would speak," and wanted Deng brought to him immediately.[25]

An even more intense relationship concerned Mao and his wife, Jiang Qing, although they had not lived together for many years and she had limited access to him during this last period. On the one hand, Jiang Qing faithfully carried out the radical edge of Mao's Cultural Revolution line. In addition, she was entwined in his personal prestige because of their relationship that dated back to Yan'an. On the other hand, Jiang Qing's abrasive personality and policy excesses undermined her effectiveness as a member of the central leadership, causing the kind of disunity that Mao repeatedly railed against in these years. There are also many indications of marital tensions between the two.

Thus a peculiar dynamic existed: when criticizing the Gang of Four, Mao's barbs were overwhelmingly directed at his wife for matters of her personal style rather than her political orientation, which he shared to a considerable extent. She was strongly protected politically by Mao—a condition of Deng's return to work in 1973 was that he would not oppose Jiang Qing. Even when the Chairman's own criticisms of Jiang Qing created an opportunity to attack her, other leaders held back. Clearly Jiang's special status as Mao's wife shaped and distorted leadership politics.

In this setting of peculiar personal judgments, shifting policy preferences, and a basic incompatibility between trying to save the Cultural Revolution by correcting its excesses while affirming the rebellious essence of the movement, Mao left a seriously weakened regime when he died on September 9, 1976. The Chinese communist party-state he had founded was contending with a new upsurge of disruption, a long list of ignored national needs, mounting tensions among the masses, and sharply divided leadership councils.

Nevertheless, Mao had also left the elements that would quickly right the ship, including a battered but still coherent cadre force that desired order and respected discipline. Most crucial was that, virtually by accident, Mao had designated as his final, if transient successor, Hua Guofeng, someone who both had the legitimate authority to act by virtue of the Chairman's selection and, against some expectations, was prepared to take the decisive action of arresting the Gang of Four in October 1976, a bold step that paved the way for the restoration of the pre-Cultural Revolution political system (see Box, **The Arrest of the Gang of Four**). But the larger story of the dramatic and unexpected developments of the post-Mao period is a matter for the next chapter.

THE ARREST OF THE GANG OF FOUR

The bitter divisions between the radical Gang of Four and the moderate forces led by Hua Guofeng in mid-1976 deepened as the Chairman's life slipped away following the Tiananmen incident. To a large extent, the regime was paralyzed with no one willing to challenge Mao's anti-rightist political line: the Gang pushed radical ideological themes, but had limited impact on concrete policies; the senior revolutionaries, who had largely been relegated to the sidelines, fretted about possible dangers to the country and themselves personally if the radicals seized power once Mao passed away, but they essentially took no action; while Hua deflected radical initiatives without challenging the anti-rightist rhetoric. The deep distrust and fear intensified further following the Chairman's death in early September.

Among moderates, including those like Hua, holding active posts, and the old revolutionaries who mostly lacked formal power, there was a palpable fear that the Gang would indeed attempt to seize power, with their administrative proposals, ideological slogans, and a couple of (wrongly understood or imagined) troop movements seen as evidence of possible planning for a coup. In reality, the radicals undertook no concrete planning for a coup, either in the months before Mao's death or throughout September. The radicals essentially had no political strategy except to continue to push the Cultural Revolution line, seek to maintain a radicalized political environment, and wait and see how Hua as the designated successor would perform. In truth, this fit the larger pattern of the Gang of Four's political performance during Mao's last years: they never had a coherent strategy for power, as their position was totally dependent on the Chairman's inconstant blessing, and there were sufficient suspicions and animosities among the four to prevent a serious coordinated effort.

(continued)

THE ARREST OF THE GANG OF FOUR (continued)

Nevertheless, a possible power seizure was deeply feared by moderate leaders, so they were faced with "solving the Gang of Four problem." Even if there were no coup attempt, Hua realized there was a real question of how the system could function efficiently if leadership councils were engaged in an ongoing bitter ideological dispute. In the end, it was Hua Guofeng who decided the Gang had to be dealt with and played the decisive role throughout.

The old revolutionaries, Marshal Ye Jianying and Vice Premier Li Xiannian, were brought into the planning by Hua, with Ye in particular playing a Mafia-like *consigliore* role as key adviser and serving as a conduit to other elders on the sidelines, more to reassure them that things were under control than to secure any active participation in measures to foil the radicals.

The issue became how to eliminate the radicals' political influence, and while the legal method of calling a Central Committee meeting to vote them off the Politburo was canvassed, it was considered too unpredictable, given the stacking of the body with political unknowns at its last election in 1973. Instead, the four were summarily arrested on the night of October 6, 1976. There had been a coup, but one implemented by Hua Guofeng and his moderate associates, not the radicals.

This outcome was enormously popular within the remaining leadership, causing excited celebrations well into the night following the arrest and for weeks afterward. It also gained broad popular support, with the masses for once genuinely enthusiastic about a sudden change in leadership fortunes. And it provided great support for Hua's temporary legitimacy as Mao's successor. While Hua's contribution was progressively obscured after 1981, in the official summary of his life upon his death in 2008, the CCP ultimately acknowledged that Hua Guofeng had been the "decisive leader" in crushing the Gang of Four, thus making possible the political resurrection of Deng Xiaoping and the launching of the era of reform that led to China's spectacular economic growth.

Mao in Power: An Assessment

In 1981, the CCP released a "**Resolution on Certain Questions in the History of Our Party Since the Founding of the People's Republic of China**" as the authoritative (and still largely upheld) assessment by the post-Mao leadership of the party's achievements and shortcomings since 1949. The resolution declared that "Comrade Mao Zedong was a great...proletarian revolutionary...[who] made gross mistakes during the 'Cultural Revolution,' but [on the whole] his contributions...far outweigh his mistakes." Even his mistakes during that chaotic period were allegedly those of a tragic figure who sought to advance the revolutionary cause, but "confused right and wrong and the people with the enemy."[26]

Although this official assessment is grotesque (given that Mao's personal policy excesses cost anywhere from 20 to 50 million lives, particularly as a result of the Great Leap Forward for which he was also assigned some blame), stripped of rhetoric and the need to make excuses for the founder of the regime, in some respects it has a certain validity. In particular, the resolution presents a chronology not dissimilar from that provided in this chapter: an initial period through 1956 of solid achievement in the regime's own terms, the pre-Cultural Revolution decade where, notwithstanding some economic achievements, serious "leftist" errors affected politics and the economy, and Mao's final decade of chaos and inadequate efforts to repair the damage.

What were the causes of the major turning points during the Maoist era, and what do they tell us about Mao's rule?

From early on in his career Mao was a visionary, a strategic genius, a realistic revolutionary, a nationalist, and a dedicated Marxist. From early days he also saw himself as a leader of great destiny, and he was always acutely attentive to his personal power, but it was power for great purposes. Mao could also capture the popular and elite imagination, whether for the universally approved "standing up" to foreign imperialists and national unification, or, before everything went wrong, the Great Leap's pursuit of unprecedented economic growth.

For all his talent, Mao's successes before 1949 owed much to circumstances, notably the Japanese invasion and incompetence of Chiang Kai-shek's Nationalists. He also built successfully on Marxist ideology and the organizational backbone of a Leninist party. After 1949, Mao initially benefited from an already tested program for state-building on the Soviet model. Mao's great achievement was to enlarge upon these circumstances by developing broad-based party unity, a form of quasi-collective leadership allowing significant leadership discussion, and a pragmatic, often cautious approach to policy. Together this produced the unimaginable victory of 1949, and also sustained the party's further successes to the mid-1950s.

Paradoxically, the seeds of later disasters can be found in the victory of 1949. Most fundamentally, Mao's power, while uncontested within the party as long as successes continued during the struggle for national power, became unchallengeable upon coming to power and would remain so for rest of his life. His emperor-like authority was unmistakable in the Gao Gang case and the handling of agricultural cooperativization, even as he maintained the semblance of collective leadership. In many senses, leadership politics under the Chairman was like the highly personalistic court politics of imperial China that could be altered into more arbitrary forms at any time of the emperor's choosing. For much of the initial period up to 1956, Mao left alone certain areas (notably the economy) where he recognized his limitations, but his ability to intervene was clear.

In addition, the fact of virtual nationwide success during the CCP's first period in power subtly diluted the need for pragmatism, although this developed slowly, given the Korean War and the residual threat from the Nationalists on Taiwan. Without the threats of stronger enemies inside China, by the early 1950s caution was less necessary in the pursuit of ideologically prescribed social change, and overly ambitious policies surfaced. Moreover, the accomplishments of these years created a sense of infinite optimism in Mao about the capacity to shape the national landscape, something that by 1958, in the words of the CCP's official 1981 Resolution on Party History, fed Mao's "smug and impatient" arrogance as he launched the Great Leap Forward.

The Great Leap reflected a serious erosion of the factors that had underpinned Mao's earlier successes—a loss of pragmatism in demanding ever more impractical objectives, personally taking over the economy despite his lack of understanding, and creating so much political pressure and raising the stakes so high that no one dared "say him nay." This shift can be seen as a product of Mao's ambition for China's rapid advance toward development and prosperity. It was also a product of failure, particularly that of the Hundred Flowers movement in 1957 from which Mao concluded that fulfilling his ambitions would require a new strategy. The Hundred Flowers was also Mao's first significant setback in two decades, and the new strategy for development, the Great Leap Forward, held out the promise of escaping the shadow of that setback.

But the new strategy failed, too, and with even more terrible consequences. The collapse of the Great Leap created a novel situation for Mao, one in which he had no clear idea of what to do. He relinquished day-to-day control of the party-state, but retained ultimate power while searching for explanations and scapegoats for what had gone wrong. By the early 1960s Mao was increasingly focused on class struggle against enemies of his revolution, and he began to worry that the revisionism he saw in the Soviet Union might be China's future. Again, he could not develop a coherent response to this danger and approved various pragmatic proposals from his colleagues to repair the damage caused by the Great Leap. He also upheld the fundamental principle of party leadership, and despite reservations about certain individuals left most of the Yan'an roundtable leaders in place—until 1966.

The Cultural Revolution was the result of a complex mix of policy dissatisfaction, paranoia and personal vindictiveness, and a genuine desire to somehow re-revolutionize society that led Mao into totally uncharted waters. While the Great Leap had been a disaster, it was based on a program, carried out by the party organization and the established leadership, and sought objectives that were at least comprehensible to the public. None of this applied to the Cultural Revolution, with the party dismantled as an institution, leadership unity in ruins, and an approach that did not simply lack pragmatism, but barely had any coherent objectives beyond managing the chaos it had created. Through all this Mao was prepared to accept enormous social, economic and human costs in pursuit of a revolutionary purity he could hardly define. Even when he attempted, in his last years, to save the Cultural Revolution by correcting its shortcomings and introducing realistic policy objectives, he refused to give up the implausible dream of a modernizing state that was both authoritarian and allowed rebellion against any signs of revisionism.

Moreover, during the entire decade from the start of the Cultural Revolution until his death, Mao broke with the principle of party seniority that had underpinned CCP rule, instead introducing in idiosyncratic manner marginal figures like Wang Hongwen and Jiang Qing into the highest leading bodies, a situation that could not outlast his life. Indeed, Mao's actions during his final decade did not simply create havoc for the lives of the Chinese people, they fundamentally attacked the interests of the vast majority of the communist party elite that had come to power with him in 1949. By doing this, Mao created the conditions that would lead those members of that elite who survived him to thoroughly reject both the means and the ends of his Cultural Revolution, even though they could not bring themselves to repudiate the Chairman himself.

While it is tempting to conclude with Lord Acton's famous observation that "power tends to corrupt, and absolute power corrupts absolutely," Mao's case is more complex. Although having many of the accoutrements and vices of an emperor, and engaging in personal vindictiveness, even in his last decade Mao indicated (however selectively) some personal remorse and protected individual old comrades, none more significantly than Deng Xiaoping, who would, with some irony, ultimately emerge as Mao's successor as China's most powerful leader.

Mao's sin was less corruption than hubris, his belief that he was "alone with the masses" and had a special understanding of the needs of the revolution and the Chinese people. No one and no costs should stand in the way of his pursuit of those visions, and he could not accept responsibility when that pursuit led to disastrous consequences, which, in his view, were ultimately someone else's fault. Mao Zedong was only able to do this because of the absolute power he had accumulated through the combination of his record of revolutionary success, the centralizing forces of the Leninist party organization that he built, and the authoritarian strain in traditional Chinese political culture.

In speaking of the mistakes of the Great Leap Forward, the 1981 Resolution on the History of the CCP since 1949 said, "Although Comrade Mao Zedong must be held chiefly responsible, we cannot lay the blame on him alone for all those errors." In other words, the entire party leadership let him do it. More broadly, we can conclude that Mao's failures and their catastrophic consequences during the entire period of his rule were uniquely personal, but they were also the failure of the CCP regime.

Notes

1. At the time of his dismissal in 1959, Minister of Defense Peng Dehuai referred to Mao by noting that "the first emperor of any dynasty was always severe and brilliant." "Peng Teh-huai's Speech at the 8th Plenum of the 8th CCP Central Committee (Excerpts)" (August 1959), in *The Case of Peng Teh-huai, 1959–1968* (Kowloon: Union Research Institute, 1968), 36, 427.

2. See *Selected Works of Mao Tse-tung*, Vol. III (Peking: Foreign Languages Press, 1965), 208–210.

3. *Selected Works of Mao Tse-tung*, Vol. IV (Peking: Foreign Languages Press, 1961), 422.

4. *Eighth National Congress of the Communist Party of China*, Volume I: *Documents* (Peking: Foreign Languages Press, 1956), 7.

5. "Talk at Expanded Central Committee Meeting" (January 1962), in *Joint Publications Research Service*, no. 52029, 13.

6. *Selected Works of Mao Tse-tung*, Vol. II (Peking: Foreign Languages Press, 1965), 224.

7. The only exception was PLA Marshal Chen Yi, who served as foreign minister from 1958 to the Cultural Revolution.

8. *Selected Works of Mao Tsetung*, Vol. V (Peking: Foreign Languages Press, 1977), 93–4.

9. See Frederick C. Teiwes and Warren Sun, eds., *The Politics of Agricultural Cooperativization in China: Mao, Deng Zihui, and the "High Tide" of 1955* (Armonk, NY: M. E. Sharpe, 1993), 13.

10. *Selected Works of Mao Tsetung*, Vol. V, 395.

11. "On the Ten Major Relationships" (April 1956), in *Selected Works of Mao Tsetung*, Vol. V, 284–307.

12. See Frederick C. Teiwes with Warren Sun, *China's Road to Disaster: Mao, Central Politicians, and Provincial Leaders in the Unfolding of the Great Leap Forward, 1955–1959* (Armonk, NY: M. E. Sharpe, 1999), 149.

13. See Frederick C. Teiwes, *Politics and Purges in China: Rectification and the Decline of Party Norms 1950–1965*, 2nd ed. (Armonk, NY: M. E. Sharpe, 1993), lviii, 370–71.

14. See Teiwes, *Politics and Purges*, xxxvi; and Roderick MacFarquhar, *The Origins of the Cultural Revolution 3: The Coming of the Cataclysm 1961–66* (New York: Columbia University Press, 1997), 157–158.

15. See Teiwes, *Politics and Purges*, 385.

16. *Main Documents of the First Session of the Third National People's Congress of the People's Republic of China* (Peking: Foreign Languages Press, 1965), 15.

17. For a critical discussion of the appropriate periodization of the Cultural Revolution, see Jonathan Unger, "The Cultural Revolution at the Grass Roots," *The China Journal* 57 (2007): 113–117. While the issue has been whether "Cultural Revolution" should apply to 1966–68/69 or to the entire 1966–1976 decade, as in official PRC usage, three periods can be distinguished: (1) 1966–1968, when party control collapsed in the face of popular turmoil; (2) 1969–1971, which saw severe state repression in an effort to restore order; and (3) 1972–1976, when political trends alternated between moderate and radical phases, but at all times with considerably less violence and/or disruption compared to the preceding periods.

18. See Roderick MacFarquhar and Michael Schoenhals, *Mao's Last Revolution* (Cambridge: Belknap Press, 2006), 63.

19. Stuart R. Schram, *The Political Thought of Mao Tse-tung*, rev. ed. (New York: Praeger Publishers, 1969), 55.

20. For more on Jiang Qing, see Ross Terrill, *Madame Mao: The White-Boned Demon*, rev. ed. (Stanford, CA: Stanford University Press, 1999).

21. See Frederick C. Teiwes and Warren Sun, *The Tragedy of Lin Biao: Riding the Tiger during the Cultural Revolution, 1966–1971* (London: C. Hurst & Co., 1996), 76.

22. See Frederick C. Teiwes and Warren Sun, *The End of the Maoist Era: Chinese Politics during the Twilight of the Cultural Revolution, 1972–1976* (Armonk, NY: M. E. Sharpe, 2007), 595.

23. Teiwes and Sun, *The End of the Maoist Era*, 3.

24. Teiwes and Sun, *The End of the Maoist Era*, 186. Here Mao rhetorically extends the Cultural Revolution from 1966 to the present, but as we have seen the movement was over in mid-1968.

25. Teiwes and Sun, *The End of the Maoist Era*, 20, 110. The statement concerning being bad to Zhou and good to Deng by Politburo member Li Xiannian was applied to the "two ladies" who served as Mao's liaison to the leadership, but clearly they were simply carrying out his wishes.

26. "Resolution on Questions in Party History Since 1949," *Beijing Review* 27 (1981): 29, 23.

Suggested Readings

Bachman, David M. *Bureaucracy, Economy, and Leadership in China: The Institutional Origins of the Great Leap Forward*. New York: Cambridge University Press, 1991.

Cheek, Timothy, ed. *The Cambridge Critical Introduction to Mao*. New York: Cambridge University Press, 2010.

Domenach, Jean-Luc. *The Origins of the Great Leap Forward: The Case of One Chinese Province*. Boulder, CO: Westview Press, 1995.

Esherick, Joseph W., Paul G Pickowicz, and Andrew G Walder, eds. *China's Cultural Revolution as History*. Stanford, CA: Stanford University Press, 2006.

Gao, Wenqian. *Zhou Enlai: The Last Perfect Revolutionary*. New York: Public Affairs, 2010.

Gao, Yuan. *Born Red: A Chronicle of the Cultural Revolution*. Stanford, CA: Stanford University Press, 1987.

Forster, Keith. *Rebellion and Factionalism in a Chinese Province: Zhejiang, 1966–1976*. Armonk, NY: M. E. Sharpe, 1990.

Li, Zhisui. *The Private Life of Chairman Mao: The Memoirs of Mao's Personal Physician*. London: Chatto & Windus, 1994.

Lubell, Pamela. *The Chinese Communist Party and the Cultural Revolution: The Case of the Sixty-One Renegades*. New York: Palgrave, 2002.

MacFarquhar, Roderick. *The Origins of the Cultural Revolution*. 3 vols. New York: Columbia University Press: vol. 1, *Contradictions among the People 1956–1957* (1974); vol. 2, *The Great Leap Forward 1958–1960* (1983); vol. 3, *The Coming of the Cataclysm 1961–1966* (1997).

MacFarquhar, Roderick, Timothy Cheek, and Eugene Wu, eds. *The Secret Speeches of Chairman Mao: From the Hundred Flowers to the Great Leap Forward*. Cambridge, MA: Harvard Council on East Asian Studies, 1989.

MacFarquhar, Roderick, and Michael Schoenhals. *Mao's Last Revolution*. Cambridge, MA: Belknap Press of Harvard University Press, 2006.

Perry, Elizabeth J., and Li Xun. *Proletarian Power: Shanghai in the Cultural Revolution*. Boulder, CO: Westview Press, 1997.

Qiu, Jin. *The Culture of Power: The Lin Biao Incident in the Cultural Revolution*. Stanford, CA: Stanford University Press, 1999.

Spence, Jonathan. *Mao Zedong: A Penguin Life*. New York: Viking, 1999.

Short, Philip. *Mao: A Life*. New York: Henry Holt, 2000.

Teiwes, Frederick C. *Politics at Mao's Court: Gao Gang and Party Factionalism in the Early 1950s*. Armonk, NY: M. E. Sharpe, 1990.

Teiwes, Frederick C. *Politics and Purges in China: Rectification and the Decline of Party Norms 1950–1965*. 2nd ed. Armonk, NY: M. E. Sharpe, 1993.

Teiwes, Frederick C., and Warren Sun. *The End of the Maoist Era: Chinese Politics during the Twilight of the Cultural Revolution, 1972–1976*. Armonk, NY: M. E. Sharpe, 2007.

Teiwes, Frederick C., and Warren Sun. *The Tragedy of Lin Biao: Riding the Tiger during the Cultural Revolution, 1966–1971*. London: C. Hurst & Co., 1996.

Teiwes, Frederick C., with Warren Sun. *China's Road to Disaster: Mao, Central Politicians, and Provincial Leaders in the Unfolding of the Great Leap Forward, 1955–1959*. Armonk, NY: M. E. Sharpe, 1999.

Teiwes, Frederick C., with Warren Sun. *The Formation of the Maoist Leadership: From the Return of Wang Ming to the Seventh Party Congress*. London: Contemporary China Institute Research Notes and Studies, 1994.

Thaxton, Ralph G. *Catastrophe and Contention in Rural China: Mao's Great Leap Forward Famine and the Origins of Righteous Resistance in Da Fo Village*. New York: Cambridge University Press, 2008.

Walder, Andrew G. *Fractured Rebellion: The Beijing Red Guard Movement*. Cambridge MA: Harvard University Press, 2009.

4

Deng Xiaoping and His Successors (1976 to the Present)

Bruce Gilley

Introduction to the Reform Era

The period of Chinese political history since 1976 represents China's return to its century-long project of domestic modernization and international resurgence. In this period of reform, China has picked up the pieces from the disastrous consequences of the Mao era and resumed a trajectory of development that had been abandoned in the early-1950s. China remains an authoritarian regime, but it has become a more institutionalized and regularized one, and one that no longer deserves the label "totalitarian." The CCP remains committed to the preservation of its power, but it has abandoned the aim of totally controlling and transforming China's society.

Yet it is easy to draw too sharp a distinction between the reform era and the pre-reform era. Many things have changed in the reform era, but many others have not. China's official ideology retains its references to Mao Zedong Thought, and Mao's portrait remains ubiquitous in the country—on the currency, in trinket shops, and most notably over Tiananmen Square in Beijing, the large space that dominates the seat of government. Party leadership remains the central and unchallengeable principle of political life in the PRC. And, despite extensive privatization, the party continues to view state ownership of strategic sectors of the economy—airlines, banks, energy suppliers, and even automobiles—as essential. Revolutionary mass mobilization politics continues to be practiced by the CCP periodically—for example, as in the implementation of the country's stringent population policy (see chapter 13) and the post-1999 crackdown on the **Falun Gong** religious group. And most of all, the sometimes xenophobic nationalism that characterized China's relations with the West and, to a lesser extent with Japan, under Mao remains central to China's foreign policy.

Beyond these longitudinal comparisons with China's own history, two sets of cross-country comparisons are useful for understanding China's era of "opening and reform" (*gaige kaifang*) that began under the leadership of Deng Xiaoping and continued with his successors, Jiang Zemin and Hu Jintao.

The first is comparison with rapid industrialization in other Asian countries. Japan's Meiji-era (1868–1912) period of "wealthy country and strong arms" (*fukoku-kyōhei*) is perhaps the earliest example of this. Yet parallels can also be found with the post-1949 Republic of China regime on Taiwan under the Nationalist Party (see chapter 16). There, a Leninist state was transformed through economic liberalization and rapid growth that eventually resulted in a political opening for democracy. From the perspective of culture,

Table 4.1 Top Leaders of China since 1976

Name	Key Titles and Dates	Comments
Hua Guofeng (1921–2008)	CCP Chairman (1976–1981) PRC Premier (1976–1980) Central Military Commission Chair (1976–1981)	Mao's designated successor, Hua was instrumental in the arrest of the Gang of Four, unintentionally paving the way for the rise of reformers led by Deng Xiaoping. Out of respect for Mao, Hua retained a seat on the CCP's Central Committee until 2002.
Deng Xiaoping (1904–1997)	CCP Vice Chairman (1977–1982) PRC Vice Premier (1977–1980) Central Military Commission Chairman (1981–1989)	Long March veteran who overthrew the weak Hua Guofeng and launched China's reform movement. "Core" of the "Second Generation" (after Mao). Deng is widely revered in China for his role in steering economic reforms, but his legacy is clouded by his role in ordering the 1989 Tiananmen Massacre.
Chen Yun (1905–1995)	CCP Vice Chairman (1956–1969; 1977–1982) PRC Vice-Premier (1954–1980)	Long March veteran who became one of China's leading economic planners after 1949. Regarded as an economic conservative who often tried to slow Deng Xiaoping's reforms, he nevertheless played an important role in launching the reform era in the early 1980s.
Hu Yaobang (1915–1989)	CCP Chairman (1981–1982) CCP General Secretary (1982–1987)	Protégé of Deng Xiaoping. Played a key role in rehabilitating Cultural Revolution victims, promoting political reforms, and arguing for liberal policies in Tibet. His death sparked the 1989 Tiananmen Square movement. Officially rehabilitated in 2005.
Zhao Ziyang (1919–2005)	PRC Premier (1980–1987) CCP General Secretary (1987–1989)	Protégé of Deng Xiaoping. Pioneer of market-oriented economic reforms and proponent of democratizing political reforms. Purged after the Beijing Massacre in June 1989, Zhao became even more pro-democratic in his long period under house arrest.
Jiang Zemin (b. 1926)	CCP General Secretary (1989–2002) PRC President (1993–2003) Central Military Commission Chairman (1989–2004)	Jiang oversaw China's recovery from Tiananmen by promoting economic reforms and rebuilding ties to the United States. "Core" of the "Third Generation," Jiang was the first PRC leader to step down voluntarily and peacefully when he handed over power to Hu Jintao in 2002.
Hu Jintao (b. 1942)	CCP General Secretary (2002–) PRC President (2003–) Central Military Commission Chairman (2004–)	Hu has sought to address issues of social justice, redistribution, and welfare. But without major political reforms, those efforts have faced stiff opposition. "Core" of the "Fourth Generation," Hu has displayed little of the personal charisma of his predecessors as head of the CCP, inspiring comparisons with the succession of dull leaders in the late Soviet Union.
Xi Jinping (b. 1953)	CCP Standing Committee Member (2007–) PRC Vice President (2008–)	Xi is an economic reformer and competent administrator widely liked in the places he has served. Expected to become CCP General Secretary in 2012; "Core" of the "Fifth Generation."

East Asian economic success has been deeply rooted in the work ethic associated with the region's entrepreneurial spirit. What was missing on the Chinese mainland before the reform era was an efficient, stable, and market-friendly government to unleash that spirit. There is today a great debate on how well China's experience fits with the developmental trajectories of other East Asian states.[1]

The second comparative perspective is with other communist and post-communist states. In Eastern Europe and the Soviet Union, communist party-states began experimenting with decentralization, market prices, and expanded foreign trade in the 1950s and 1960s in response to the clear failures of highly centralized Stalinist economic policy. But those changes did not save such regimes from collapse in the late 1980s and early 1990s after the threat of Soviet intervention against anti-party movements was lifted. In some places, such as Azerbaijan or Russia, authoritarianism resurfaced after the collapse of communism, often with strong nationalist dimensions. Closer to home, Vietnam's communist party launched a successful program of economic reform called *doi moi* (economic renewal) in 1986, just eight years after attempting to collectivize industry and agriculture. From the perspective of comparative communism, China is an important case of a communist party that successfully carried out and then adapted to market reforms.[2]

Thus, China's reform era, fascinating in its own terms, can be even more richly studied as a case of comparative development and comparative politics. The key to understanding contemporary China can be found in the dramatic divergence between its rapid economic transition but stalled political transition.

The Origins of the Reform Era

At the time of Mao's death in September 1976, the damaging effects of his rule were palpable in nearly every aspect of life in China. Society was so weakened and fractured by Mao's repeated campaigns that the party-state remained de facto totalitarian in spite of lessened repression in the early 1970s. Government institutions had been broken or suspended. For example, the **National People's Congress** had not met in full since 1964. The economy was literally stagnant. Economic growth had barely kept pace with population growth for much of the Mao era, despite a brief recovery in the early 1960s. An estimated 74 percent of China's population lived in poverty in 1976, using the $1 per day standard and purchasing-power parity exchange rates. Beijing's streets were nearly as empty as those of modern-day Pyongyang, North Korea's capital.

The period in Chinese political history from the fall of the **Gang of Four** in October 1976 to the party meeting in December 1978 that has been officially declared the start of economic reforms is easy to see retrospectively as a mere interlude. Indeed, some look back earlier and see the 1970 North China Agricultural Conference, which emphasized technical (seeds, fertilizers, mechanization, electrification) rather than political pathways to agricultural success or Deng's efforts to push modernization rather than revolution and to reintroduce meritocratic education in the 1975–1976 period as signs of what was to come. But it was by no means inevitable that economic and political reforms would result automatically from Mao's death and the arrest of the Gang of Four. Hua Guofeng, as party chairman, had vowed to do "whatever" Mao had said, and done, and the guardians of Maoism, known as the **"whateverist" faction**, remained vigilant. The global environment was not friendly either: the Cold War was only partly unfrozen, and China's relations with its immediate neighbors—in particular Taiwan, India, and Vietnam—remained tense.

Yet movement away from the Cultural Revolution ethos was underway. In 1977, there were some telling signs of liberalization, particularly in culture and education. A ban on the works of Beethoven was lifted to mark the 150th anniversary of the composer's death, allowing the Central Symphony Orchestra to perform his works for the first time since 1959. University entrance examinations were held for the first time since 1965. In October, the first example of a genre of writing that would come to be known as "wound literature" and dealt with the sufferings under Mao appeared in the official periodical *People's Litera-ture*. Yugoslavian president and communist party leader Josip Tito visited Beijing in a sign of the early post-Mao leadership's interest in his decentralized type of "market socialism" that had led Yugoslavia to be excommunicated for the world communist camp by Moscow in 1948. Shortly after Tito's visit, the influential *Guangming Daily* newspaper ran an edito-rial arguing that workers should be paid bonuses for higher output or better work, while a meeting of provincial agriculture heads made similar arguments for rural labor. However, politics remained unsettled in this period and there was every chance that Hua Guofeng's "kinder, gentler" Maoism would remain dominant.

The key event, which had profound and lasting consequences for China, was the politi-cal resurrection of Deng Xiaoping, who had been purged just the previous spring by Mao for his alleged role in the April 1976 "Tiananmen Incident" (see chapter 3) and for showing again that he was an unrepentant capitalist roader. Deng resumed his posts as PRC vice premier and CCP vice chair in mid-1977 as a part of a deal brokered between the party's "whateverist" and "pragmatist" factions. Deng's return was needed to show that it was the developmental policies of the "good Mao," not those of the destructive "bad Mao" of the Cultural Revolution that would prevail. This gave the **pragmatist faction,** led by Long March veteran Chen Yun, the chance to press its case without fear of retribution since Deng was known to sympathize with that group.

Throughout 1978, the two factions engaged in arcane debates about rural labor manage-ment and commune accounting policies. While the two sides agreed with Hua Guofeng's suggestion to make economic development rather than class struggle the primary task of the party, they differed on how to go about it. Borrowing from the experiences of reform communism in Eastern Europe, Chen Yun's faction worked hard to discredit the blind adherence to Mao's Stalinist economic policies. Drawing upon a thirty-year repertoire of policies, ideological concepts, and institutions that had been used to limit the ravages of Mao, Chen effectively isolated and discredited Hua's hopes of continuing Mao's economic policies. . It was Chen who revived the Sichuanese adage first used by Deng to justify mod-est market reforms in rural areas in 1962 and that got him into political trouble with Mao: "It doesn't matter whether a cat is black or white as long as it catches mice."

At a month-long CCP Central Work Meeting in November–December 1978, Chen warned that "commune party secretaries will lead the peasants into the cities demanding food" if the party did not reform rural policies to boost production. Deng, who missed the opening of the conference while on a state visit to Southeast Asia, returned to find that Chen Yun's withering attacks on the "whateverists," led by Hua Guofeng, had already carried the day. Indeed, Chen had expanded his attack on the whateverists from purely economic issues to their lack of sympathies for the political victims of Maoism. The issue that divided the early post-Mao leadership was not whether there should be a return to the radicalism of the Cultural Revolution. Indeed, Hua Guofeng had declared in 1976 that the arrest of the Gang had marked "the triumphant conclusion" of the movement. Rather, the cutting issue was whether the party would break with Mao's Stalinist approaches to eco-nomic development, which decried incentives, efficiency, and local decision-making.

At an anticlimatic party plenum of December 1978 (later hailed in party propaganda as a critical turning point), the agreed emphasis on economic development was reiterated, while rural **communes** were given greater autonomy and the right to experiment with incentive pay. A new pragmatism, not "whatever" Mao had said, would henceforth guide decision-making under the slogan "practice is the sole criterion of truth." Political institutions were to be rebuilt. Mass movements were to be abandoned. Many prominent victims of Maoism were to be rehabilitated, and the April 1976 "Tiananmen Incident" was declared patriotic rather than counterrevolutionary. Yet for all its reformist aspects, the 1978 plenum still reflected a kind of reform Maoism. The single most important rural innovation being carried out by some brave local cadres in provinces like Anhui and Sichuan—dividing collective land among private households and contracting with them for output quotas—was explicitly *forbidden* by the plenum, although experiments at some sites in Anhui were later sanctioned. Nor was there any mention of other economic reforms, much less of opening to the outside world.

What ultimately tipped the balance was Chen Yun's withering attacks in 1979 on Hua Guofeng's overly ambitious ten-year plan (1976–1985) of economic modernization, which already showed signs in 1978–1979 of being a repeat of the Great Leap mentality of setting unreasonably high production targets. Under pressure to produce more oil, for instance, a newly bought Japanese oil rig sank while being hastily towed into position in China's Bohai sea in November 1979 with a loss of seventy-two lives. Chen's earlier counterproposal for "readjustment, reform, correction, and improvement" sounded a decisively cautious and pragmatic tone that by late 1979 had become the slogan summary of the party's official policy. Hua finally lost his leadership in economic areas. Chen was helped on the outside by an eruption of political posters along a 200-meter stretch of wall on Chang'an Boulevard, west of Tiananmen Square, later known as **Democracy Wall**, where the mistakes of Mao and the dangers of the "whateverist" faction were widely debated by Chinese intellectuals.[3]

Hua was gradually eased out of power, first being removed from the position of PRC premier in 1980 and as party chairman in 1981. Out of respect for Mao's legacy, Hua—now referred to simply as "Comrade Hua" rather than as "wise leader Chairman Hua"—retained a seat on the Central Committee until 2002. He did not play any significant role in politics, but he came to symbolize the not-quite-eliminated Maoism in the institutions, ideology, and policies of China's politics in the period between Mao's death and Deng's consolidation of power. Still, Hua had supported the arrest of the Gang of Four and endorsed the shift to economic development—aspects of this life officially recognized when he died in 2008. The handful of other party leaders who were seen as Hua's political and ideological allies were also sent into retirement, and the balance of power in the top party organizations came to rest firmly in the hands of Deng Xiaoping, Chen Yun, and others strongly committed to abandoning Stalinist economics.

The origins of the reforms, then, can be linked to fears of popular uprising and illegal experiments in rural areas, coupled with the deft maneuvering of Chen Yun to discredit Hua Guofeng's reform Maoism. While the sharp-tongued Deng would be officially proclaimed the "architect" of economic reforms, and while his imprimatur was essential for the reforms to take root, the doughty Chen Yun arguably has as great a claim to being the architect of China's reforms.[4]

Beginning with Political Reforms

Conventional views that China reformed its economy first and its political system second are mistaken. Indeed, in many ways political changes preceded and were the necessary condition for important economic ones. The party's repudiation of "class struggle" as its primary objective in late 1978 opened the door for many important political changes. During the 1980s, nearly 5 million people wrongfully accused and persecuted since the founding of the PRC, including 1.6 million intellectuals, were politically exonerated. A law passed in 1979 expanded the direct popular election of people's congress delegates from the **township** to the **county** level. Voting was reinstituted within the party, and cadres were allowed to see the text of policies before being asked to approve them. Village government also became more accountable with the passage of a law in 1987 allowing villages to elect their own leaders, who would enjoy wide autonomy in village affairs. Within a decade, most of the country's nearly one million villages would elect their own leaders (see chapter 8).

The term "political reform" was formally introduced into the modern lexicon of the PRC in a speech given by Deng in 1980. Deng slammed "bureaucracy, over-concentration of power, patriarchal methods, life tenure in leading posts, and privileges of various kinds" within the party leadership. Mao's name came up frequently in examples. The repudiation of the Maoist era was made most clear with the passage in 1981 of a resolution on the mistakes made by Mao and the party since the leftward turn of 1957—a much kinder but similar rebuke to Khrushchev's denunciation of Stalin in 1956. It accused the chairman of smugness, impatience, bad judgment, and being out of touch, although it said his merits exceeded his faults. Earlier drafts had been more scathing, but Deng had to trample carefully on the PRC's founder and its founding mythology.

As part of efforts to reinvigorate the ranks of the CCP, between 1982 and 1992, Deng set up a **Central Advisory Commission**, as an organization with little power to ease elderly senior leaders into retirement. He also launched a program of fast-tracking promising young cadres who had college educations and good administrative skills. Among the beneficiaries of this program were an obscure foreign trade official named Jiang Zemin, who was promoted to vice minister of electronic industry and a Central Committee member in 1982, and an engineer working in the hinterlands, Hu Jintao, who was made second secretary of the Communist Youth League and an alternate (non-voting) member of the Central Committee the same year. These two would go on to become the successors to Deng as top leaders of China.

Courts were revived as semi-independent bodies, although party committees continued to make the final decision on major cases and the party retained its control of judicial appointments. The role of the legal system in the PRC political system was boosted with the passage in 1989 of the Administrative Litigation Law, which for the first time allowed citizens to sue the government. While China's courts still did not have the power of judicial review of laws to determine their legality, they could, in some ways, challenge their implementation.[5]

Deng also cut the ranks of the People's Liberation Army from 4 million to 3 million. The PLA was still the largest standing army in the world, but henceforth it would be a professional military clearly under civilian authority and with only marginal participation in politics, with the exception of policy toward Taiwan. At the top level, military members of the Politburo fell from 57 percent in 1977 to 10 percent by 1992.

With the political obstacles cleared, China entered upon a new era of "reform of the economy and opening to the world" in the early 1980s (see chapter 7). In essence, this boiled down to increasing the role of market forces while reducing government planning in the economy and inserting China more fully in the global economy. Ideologically, this was conceived of, not as an abandonment of socialism, but as a better pathway toward achieving it. The party declared that China was in the **primary stage of socialism** (see chapter 5) under which a flourishing capitalist economy was a prerequisite for a later move to total state ownership. Mao was said to have tried to skip or compress this inevitable stage of historical development by jumping too quickly to the collectivization of agriculture and the nationalization of industry in the early to mid-1950s. In a sense, the was a case of "back to the future," as many of the policies and the ideological justification for them were similar to those of the "New Democracy" period that immediately followed the "Liberation" of 1949 and the recovery interlude of the early 1960s between the end of the Great Leap Forward and the beginning of the Cultural Revolution. Not surprisingly, then, many worried that the reforms would be reversed.

Formally, the reforms of the 1980s were under the leadership of two relatively young protégés of Deng Xiaoping. Zhao Ziyang, who had overseen market-oriented rural experiments as party leader of Deng's native Sichuan province, replaced Hua Guofeng as premier of the State Council in 1980. Hu Yaobang, who had been head of the Communist Youth League prior to the Cultural Revolution, succeeded Hua Guofeng as the chairman of the CCP, with the title of the party leader being changed shortly thereafter to "general secretary" in order to disassociate the position from Chairman Mao's abuses of power. But Deng was clearly the power behind the throne, or as he was called, China's "paramount leader." The one top formal position that he did keep for himself was a chair of the Central Military Commission (CMC), which made him the commander-in-chief of China's armed forces. He was also vice premier of the State Council and, of course, a member of the party top leadership body, the Standing Committee of the Politburo.

China was fortunate in seeking to unravel a planned command economy that had fewer political and bureaucratic supporters than in the Soviet Union and other communist states. A full 69 percent of China's labor force in 1978 was engaged in agriculture (versus just 22 percent of the Soviet Union's labor force in 1975 when party leaders there were attempting unsuccessfully to loosen the powers and perquisites of industrial bureaucrats). This mattered because it was Chinese farmers who hated Soviet-style collective agriculture most of all.[6] This made it easy for China to rapidly introduce household contracting in place of communes, which were virtually eliminated by the end of 1982. Real per capita incomes in rural areas doubled between 1978 and 1983. The 1980s was the "golden era" for China's agricultural sector. The success of China's economic reforms are often credited to Deng's policy of **gradualism**, or "stepping across the river one stone at a time" in contrast to the Soviet "**big bang**" approach to economic reform. In fact, reform of agriculture was the first of many instances in which China's economic reforms were the result of a bold "big bang" rather than patient gradualism.

One of the key innovations in this period was the spread of "**township and village enterprises**"—rural factories owned and operated by local governments that competed head-on in the opening market economy with inefficient state factories. The proportion of China's industrial output from TVEs, as they were called, rose from 9 percent to 23 percent between 1978 and 1991. Yu Zuomin, the party secretary and corporate president of China's "richest village," the steel-producing hamlet of Daqiuzhuang near Tianjin, was celebrated as a national "peasant" hero for much of the decade before being jailed for corruption and obstruction of justice in 1993.[7]

Urban and industrial reforms were a tougher nut to crack—as the leaders of Eastern Europe's disappointing attempts at "market socialism" had discovered. The CCP leadership was particularly wary of a repeat of the worker protests in Poland in 1980 that had led to the resignation of the head of the Polish communist party and to the recognition of a new autonomous workers movement, Solidarity, and ultimately to the collapse of Poland's communist party-state. A CCP plenum decision of 1984 provided for more autonomy for state enterprises in the areas of production, marketing, hiring and firing, and supplies, while endorsing profit-based instead of fixed taxation from the enterprises. Small-scale private enterprise, meanwhile, was given a formal blessing. China's strategy with **state-owned enterprises** was to gradually let the small and medium-sized ones sink or swim—no "big bang" here—hoping that laid off or underpaid workers would find jobs in a growing private sector. The state-owned sector's share of national industrial output fell from 78 percent in 1978 to 55 percent by 1990, bringing China to the brink of an era in which the state sector would be an archipelago of strategically controlled large state enterprises in a sea of private business.

The results were remarkable. Annual GDP growth between 1979 and 1988 was 9 percent, double the average of the previous quarter century. That meant per capita income doubled in a decade, a remarkable feat for any country. But this amazing economic progress and the social and cultural liberalization that came along with it also prompted some sharp political divisions within the party leadership.

First, Deng's choice for party general secretary, Hu Yaobang, was ousted in 1986 by his mentor for being a little too soft on political reform (see below). He was replaced by Zhao Ziyang, Deng's protégé premier, while the premiership passed to Li Peng, the adopted son of the late Premier Zhou Enlai, who held an ultra-cautious attitude toward economic and political reforms. Also, by the late 1980s, Chen Yun had himself became an economic conservative, arguing for caution in proceeding with the next steps of economic reform against those who advocated faster liberalization, more decentralization of economic decision-making, and accelerated inflows of foreign investment. It is ironic that one of the early heroes of post-Mao economic reform would later become a hindrance to further change. Chen, allied with Li Peng, sought to deal with three ills of marketization that were rapidly emerging as political problems: inflation, corruption, and unemployment.

After decades of virtually state-fixed prices, China's consumer prices began creeping upwards as price reforms took hold and as the central government, facing a declining tax base from state enterprises, printed more money to finance its investments. Urban consumer prices rose by 83 percent in the five years from 1985 to 1989. This was a new experience for many Chinese since there had been little to no inflation during the Mao years, but then again there had also been little to no rise in living standards either. Panic buying and foot shortages ensued. Corruption, meanwhile, which had been widespread but petty and mostly invisible in the Mao era, became more lucrative and more visible with market reforms. Deng's own son, Deng Pufang, established the Kanghua Development Company (whose Hong Kong subsidiary was memorably called the Bring Fast Company). It signed lucrative **joint ventures** and property deals until it was closed by the government in 1991 over allegations of corruption.

As for unemployment, as **state-owned enterprise** reforms began to take hold, workers lost their jobs in growing numbers—especially in the industrial heartland of the three Northeastern provinces that had been industrialized under Japanese colonialism. Chinese officials struggled to invent euphemisms to describe the plight of laid-off workers—"awaiting assignment" (*daiye*) was the most popular. Unemployment insurance was launched in 1985, but it was a pittance compared to the perquisites of the "**iron rice bowl**" of state socialism, which included cradle-to-grave benefits as well as guaranteed lifetime employment. The official *People's Daily* proclaimed in 1988 that unemployment was normal and beneficial during the "primary stage of socialism," noting that tens of millions of state employees had spent their work days getting paid for "playing poker or chess, watching television, or racing on bicycles." Deng's reforms were clearly cracking the "iron rice bowl" (see chapter 9). The question was how the party would deal with the political consequences of these dramatic changes.

Political Challenges and the Beijing Massacre

From the very beginning, Deng was careful to make clear that there were limits to political reform. In response to the 1979 "Democracy Wall" protests, Deng had articulated something he called the **Four Cardinal Principles** (see chapter 5). These entailed a commitment to socialism, to the dictatorship of the proletariat, to CCP leadership, and to Marxism-Leninism and Mao Zedong Thought. In other words, the CCP was determined to remain in charge: "What kind of democracy do the Chinese people need today? It can only be socialist democracy, people's democracy, not bourgeois democracy, individualist democracy," Deng said. This theme of a more codified, legal, and rules-based dictatorship but not a democracy was put into writing in the revised PRC constitution of 1982. The constitution reinstated the notions of equality before the law, along with basic rights including religious belief, speech, press, assembly, and demonstration. But it also introduced several reversals. Rights were contingent on a duty to uphold the "the security, honor and interests of the motherland." The rights to free movement and to strike were not included, as they had been in earlier PRC constitutions, and the radically participatory **"Four Big" rights**—speaking out freely, airing views fully, holding great debates and writing big-character posters—that were part of the 1975 Cultural Revolution constitution were removed.

Yet economic reforms, political reforms, and international opening launched under Deng Xiaoping's leadership in the 1980s emboldened Chinese society. Graphic novels, rock music, and action films flooded into the hands of consumers in the 1980s. The "father of Chinese rock and roll," Cui Jian, became the songster to this generation with his 1986 song "Nothing to My Name" (*Yi Wu Suo You*), which would inspire youth with its antimaterialistic message. Increased openness to the outside world, along with looser controls on domestic publications, gave birth to a generation of youth enamored with the West and with studying abroad. Between 1978 and 2007, more than one million Chinese students would go abroad to study, only 30 percent of whom ever returned.[8]

Alongside the growth of pop culture and consumerism were some serious critiques of the party-state especially in the realm of literature. Author Bai Hua's screenplay *Unrequited Love (Ku lian)* was a scathing portrayal of how intellectuals and artists had been treated by the Chinese Communist Party; in one scene, the daughter of an artist, who like Bai Hua was persecuted during the Anti-Rightist Campaign and the Cultural Revolution, asks her father, "Dad, you love our country, but does this country love you?"

Such pointed questions were too much for Deng and other top party leaders. Bai Hua and his screenplay were denounced, and campaigns were launched, first against the "**spiritual pollution**" (1983–1984) caused by certain, mostly foreign, influences and then against "**bourgeois liberalization**," (1986–1987), which was a way of saying that some people had taken the reforms too far and crossed into the forbidden zone of challenging the principle of party leadership. It seemed as if the CCP had once again invoked the strict definition of socialist art that Mao had first articulated at Yan'an in 1942 (see chapter 10).

The anti-"bourgeois liberalization" campaign had a particularly important impact on the course of Chinese politics. The campaign had been instituted as part of a crackdown on peaceful protests in 1985 and 1986, mainly by students, calling for faster political reform, particularly in terms of intellectual freedom. Deng Xiaoping considered that party General Secretary Hu Yaobang had not dealt firmly enough with the dissent and had, in fact, shown some sympathy for the protesters' demands. In a Mao-like move, Deng ousted his own chosen successor as CCP leader for insufficient loyalty, though the fallen leader did not suffer the kind of physical persecution experienced by those who had crossed the Chairman, and he remained a member of the Politburo Standing Committee.

Deng Xiaoping chose Zhao Ziyang, his protégé premier, to move over from the government side of the party-state structure and assume the position of general secretary of the CCP. Zhao had been given much of the credit for the successful implementation of the economic reforms and, up to that point, had toed the correct political line, even chiming in loudly in denouncing the dangers of bourgeois liberalization. However, Zhao's interest in political reforms went far beyond what Deng envisaged. Working through a number of new think tanks in Beijing universities and research institutes, and more directly through an official Central Research and Discussion Group on Political Reform, Zhao gave his blessing to studies of bold political reforms.

Thus, despite the ouster of Hu, China's citizens continued to consider political liberalization and the critique of CCP autocracy as valid topics for public discussion. As inflation soared in late 1988 due to leadership paralysis over price reforms, the stage was set for the biggest demonstration of citizen demands in post-Mao China.

In the spring of 1989, intellectuals in China published three open letters calling for the release of political prisoners who had been jailed following the "Democracy Wall" movement. This was the first time since 1986 that intellectuals and other activists had come forward with organized political demands. The airing of the letters helped to create a mood of free expression and party vulnerability, a mood already rising as a result of the clear split in the leadership between reformers led by Zhao and hard-liners led by Premier Li Peng. What lit this tinderbox was the sudden death during a Politburo meeting of Hu Yaobang in April. Within hours of the death's announcement, students from several Beijing universities began to converge on Tiananmen Square with flower wreaths and poems of condolence—just as students had done at the death of Zhou Enlai in 1976. In the following two months, China was shaken by the largest mass protest against the state since 1949. The **Tiananmen Movement** spread to 341 of China's cities (three-quarters of the total) and was joined by 100 million people, a third of the urban population at the time. In Beijing, staff associations from the NPC, CCTV, the PLA Navy joined in with their own banners. As the movement dragged on through the end of May 1989, the Beijing Autonomous Workers Federation was established with the tacit support of the official All-China Federation of Trade Unions. About the only groups that did *not* take part in the 1989 protest were top CCP leaders and the peasants.

Zhao was tolerant of the movement, commenting in internal meetings that it reflected reasonable demands for stronger anticorruption measures and faster democratization. But party "elders" like Deng and his fellow **"Eight Immortals"** (including Chen Yun) who had fought in the civil war for CCP rule and who were imbued with its claims to historical legitimation, were uncompromising. As the protests dragged on into late May, party elders and hard-liners allied against Zhao, now accused of the same ideological and political mistakes as Hu Yaobang.

When PLA soldiers were brought into Beijing to clear the streets of protestors on the night of June 3–4, 1989, they were reenacting the very civil war against "foreign humiliation," enemy agents, bourgeois and reactionary forces, and internal party enemies that Deng and his comrades had fought forty years before, and ever since. Estimates of the number of civilians killed by the PLA on that night range from a few hundred to several thousand (see Box, **Why Did Tiananmen Fail?**). The exact toll is unknown since the Chinese authorities have never given an accounting. Party rhetoric in the months following the massacre, justifying the suppression of what was (and still is) called counterrevolutionary political turmoil, was redolent of the high communism that China had supposedly left behind.[9]

The party would long be divided about the student movements of the 1980s. The depth of popular outrage was reflected everywhere: the official logo for the Asian Games in Beijing in 1990, when looked at from the back, was a blood-splattered "6–4" (the shorthand for the June 4 massacre), while the words "Down With Li Peng, End People's Rage" were embedded diagonally in a poem carried in the *People's Daily* in 1991. Whatever the regime says about the protestors of the 1980s, they continue to be remembered with sympathy both inside and outside the party.

WHY DID TIANANMEN FAIL?

Why did the Tiananmen protests of 1989 fail to overthrow the Chinese Communist Party? Many answers have been offered. One is that the movement did not intend to overthrow the party in the first place, advocating only tougher anti-corruption measures, better living standards for students, and other bread-and-butter issues. Yet virtually every democracy movement starts in this way before the logic of its own protests against an authoritarian system leads willy-nilly to democracy. China's 1989 protests were no different, and indeed party leaders in their own discussions appeared well aware of the systemic implications of the protests.

Another explanation is bad luck. Unlike other postwar authoritarian states, for example, several of communist China's "founding fathers" were still alive in the form of the "Eight Immortals" of the CCP who usurped power during the crisis. Had they already died off, Zhao Ziyang might have retained power and been allowed to initiate a process of real democratization (which he would later tell a friend was his intention). Also, the liberal chairman of the National People's Congress, Wan Li, happened to be out of the country when the protests erupted, making it easier for the Immortals to neutralize that body's sympathies with the protests. Yet the protests also enjoyed a lot of good luck, not least the international media coverage from journalists who arrived to cover a state visit by Mikhail Gorbachev in May and then stayed on to cover the protests. Luck and contingency seem to have acted both ways.

Some have argued that the protests leaders misplayed their hand. To some, the student leaders were too extreme. They openly humiliated Premier Li Peng during a televised meeting on May 18, for instance. Others, ironically, have argued that they were too deferent. Three students kneeled in Confucian obeisance on the steps of the Great Hall of the People to present a petition on April 22, for instance. Students gathered in the center of Tiananmen Square on the fateful night of June 3–4 sang the communist anthem, *The Internationale*. Others have said the students displayed too much disdain for the nascent worker movements that sought to join them, confining them to security duties in the square and ignoring their livelihood issues in favor of political ones.

Similar arguments have been made about Zhao. For some, his tacit admission of a leadership split on the movement when expressing sympathy for its aims in a speech to Asian Development Bank governors in Beijing on May 4 was an imprudent move that rankled a party that might have been more tolerant otherwise. To others, Zhao was too timorous. Unlike Boris Yeltsin, who faced down an attempted hard-line backlash in 1991 by mounting tanks and standing with the protestors outside the Russian parliament, Zhao simply bid a teary farewell to the students in Tiananmen Square on May 19 and then sheepishly went home to live out his life in silence.

Given that such arguments seem to work both ways, more recent analysis has focused on *structural* explanations. Only a decade into post-Mao reforms, China's society remained relatively poor and disorganized, while the state retained a hard edge of Leninist intolerance and military might, not to mention organizational effectiveness. Moreover, China remained largely immune to the sorts of foreign pressures that, for instance, had encouraged democratization in Taiwan and South Korea. In this view, the cards were stacked heavily against the movement's success. It would have taken nearly miraculous luck and leadership to overcome those obstacles. In the event, Zhao and the protestors of 1989 were not up to that task.

Yet still another answer can be offered: the Tiananmen protests did *not* entirely fail. Tiananmen was followed by even faster economic and social liberalization and continued

(*continued*)

> ### WHY DID TIANANMEN FAIL? (continued)
>
> incremental political changes. The scars of 1989 inside the party led to a new search for popular support, especially in the wake of the collapse of the Soviet Union in 1991. When alleged transcripts of the leadership were published as *The Tiananmen Papers* in 2001, it caused a sensation in China, a reminder of the lingering widespread sympathies with the movement. As acclaimed China filmmaker Jia Zhangke, who was graduating from high school in 1989, told *The New Yorker* magazine in 2009: "Although it failed, it didn't really fail because it took freedom and democracy, individualism, individual rights, all these concepts, and disseminated them to many people, including me."
>
> Tiananmen was a protest against an unaccountable, repressive, and illegitimate party. The party took those lessons to heart after 1989, seeking to avoid the fate of the Soviet Union. Those legacies powerfully shaped the development of China to come.

Hu Yaobang was officially rehabilitated on the ninetieth anniversary of his birth in 2005 and his mausoleum in China Youth League City (*Gongqingcheng*) in Jiangxi province was spruced up. Zhao, meanwhile, who unlike Hu lost all his official positions for his tolerance of protestors, was confined to a traditional courtyard house in central Beijing until his death in 2005. His eventual rehabilitation is probably only a matter of time, with the proviso that his actions in 1989 remain classified as "very serious mistakes."

The fate of Zhao Ziyang and Tiananmen continue to be unhealed wounds of the first decade of reforms in China. A second generation of "wound literature" arose about this era— captured in Cui Jian's aching 1991 ballad *Piece of Red Cloth (Yi Kuai Hong Bu)*, which he usually sung blindfolded by a red bandanna. In 2009, a soldier who took part in the massacre, Zhang Shijun, issued a public letter regretting his role and demanding that the party speed up political liberalization and "return power to the people." While there is ample speculation about why the 1989 protests failed (see Why Did Tiananmen Fail?), one thing was clear: in launching economic reforms in the late 1970s and early 1980s, the CCP had set China on a course of social and political liberalization that would be very difficult to reverse.

Economic Reform after Tiananmen

The person that Deng tapped to fill the post of party general secretary, Jiang Zemin, was a bona fide economic reformer, but, unlike Hu or Zhao, without politically liberal instincts. After being promoted to the fringes of the central leadership during Deng's youth drive in the early 1980s. Jiang went on to become mayor and then party chief of Shanghai, where he was credited with doing a good job on both the economic and political front. During both the 1986 and 1989 student protests, he had deployed massive but nonviolent police and military force to keep demonstrators in the city in check and had engaged the students in dialogue. In 1989 he shuttered the city's leading liberal newspaper, the *World Economic Herald*, winning accolades in Beijing. Plucked suddenly from his perch in Shanghai in June 1989 to take on the top formal position in the party hierarchy, Jiang said he felt like he was standing "at the brink of a large precipice" as he assumed control over a country suffering from the trauma of Tiananmen.[10]

Deng hoped that the Tiananmen crackdown would not slow down economic reforms. But the purge of Zhao Ziyang and those said to sympathize with him—plus the sudden collapse of communist regimes in Europe in the 1989–1991 period—led to the reascendance of hard-liners under Premier Li Peng (known abroad as "the butcher of Beijing" since he was seen as taking a lead in the decision to crush the Tiananmen protests), who sought to roll back political and economic reforms. In 1989–1990, they engineered a wrenching reversal of the trend of economic reform through a combination of austerity (tightening up on wages and prices as well as on investment and credit funds for business expansion), recentralization (all investment decisions reverted back to the provincial or central level), and subsidies to bail out state enterprises. Economic growth slowed to 4 percent in both years.

Coupled with rising bankruptcies for township-village and private enterprises and resurgent unemployment, the hard-liners faced mounting criticism from other leaders and grumbling from the masses. In particular, provincial and local leaders complained mightily about the slowdown, most notably in the editorial pages of the Shanghai party committee's *Liberation Daily* newspaper, which enjoyed the protection of Jiang. They were also supported by reform-minded "retired" party elders in Beijing. Growth rebounded to 9 percent in 1991 as central controls loosened, but the debate within the top leadership about how far to go with reviving the reform effort remained unsettled.

What finally turned the tables was Deng's dramatic 1992 **Southern Inspection Tour** (*Nanxun*) in which he decamped from Beijing for central and southern China, where the country's most notable economic progress had taken place.[11] During his tour, he gave a series of speeches with ringing endorsements of the bold and successful economic reforms in the areas he visited, including a barely concealed threat that "those who do not support reforms should quit." Party conservatives, particularly Premier Li Peng, fearing being deposed by Deng, began frantically issuing documents in support of reform. The signal given to provincial and local leaders was *invest, invest, invest*. Growth and foreign investment surged. At the national congress held in October 1992, the party formally committed itself to building a "**socialist market economy**," replacing the "socialist planned commodity economy" that had been touted as the official aim of economic reform since 1984—a slight change in wording with momentous significance for the economic miracle to come because of the use of the word "market."

Like his speech to the December 1978 plenum launching the reform era, Deng's Southern Inspection Tour was more the culmination than the beginning of a policy battle. But the very public imprimatur of his remarks had a galvanizing effect on economic actors throughout the country. The 1990s became the boom years for China's economy, and the economic proceeds allowed party leaders still steeped in Stalinist traditions to launch a series of gargantuan new projects like the Shanghai Pudong economic zone, the **Three Gorges Dam** along the Yangtze River, and the Qinghai-Tibet Railway. The state sector's share of urban employment plummeted from 60 percent in 1990 to 35 percent by the year 2000 as hurried privatizations were arranged. In signs of just how far reform and opening up went in the 1990s, stock exchanges—the epitome of a market economy—were established. A new social group of "shareholders (*gumin*) was created, grew rapidly, and even rioted on several occasions in the 1990s to protest what they saw as corruption in the selling of shares and other aspects of management of the stock exchange. In 1992, official diplomatic relations were established with booming capitalist South Korea, China's sworn enemy from the Korean War. South Korea quickly became one of the PRC's major trading partners.

Provincial governments enjoyed a degree of autonomy unprecedented in the history of the PRC. Many provincial **people's congresses** in 1993 rejected candidates for governor proposed by the central government. Vice Premier Zhu Rongji complained that he lost 15 pounds hammering out a tax reform package with the provinces in 1994. China also tied its fate to the future global trading system by joining the **World Trade Organization** in 2001 after fifteen years of negotiations; as a result, the PRC agreed to open its economy even more widely to international business. It also began a rapid sell-off of public housing in urban areas—another example of "big bang" tactics in China's economic reforms.

As has historically been the case during the takeoff stage of a country's economic modernization, including the industrial revolutions in Europe and the United States, China's 1990s boom created losers as well as winners. As the initial gains of decollectivization wore off, agricultural incomes stagnated. Anti-tax riots by 10,000 farmers in Sichuan's Renshou county in 1993 were the first indicator of a malaise spreading in the countryside—a malaise later documented by a number of pessimistic books written by scholars (*China along the Yellow River*, 2000), former rural cadres (*I Told the Premier the Truth*, 2002), and crusading journalists (*An Investigation of China's Peasants*, 2004).

Unemployment among former state sector workers rose dramatically—Western economists estimated that China's urban unemployment rate was 11.5 percent in 2000, compared to the official rate of 3 percent, meaning that about 30 million unemployed people languished in cities. A popular joke went that "Mao asked us to plunge into the countryside, Deng asked us to plunge into business, and Jiang asked us to plunge into the ranks of the unemployed." Annual deaths in coal mines soared from around 1,000 in 1993 to over 6,000 in 2004. Coupled with a continued erosion of the country's education, health, and social security systems, caused in part by the weakening of local government revenues due to 1994 tax reforms, China's levels of inequality rose dramatically, a serious dilemma for a ruling party still committed to the egalitarian goals of communism.

Between 1994 and 1997, a series of four **"Ten Thousand Character Letters"** (*wanyanshu*) critical of the direction reform was taking were issued in the form of underground pamphlets like the *samizdat* used by dissidents in the Soviet Union. The authors of the letters, CCP writers associated with the party ideological magazine *Mainstream (Zhongliu)*, complained of the decline in the state sector, rising foreign and private investment, and the declining hold of socialist ideology over society. This group of critics was referred to as China's "New Left," and Jiang Zemin, in a speech in 1997, complained of "interference from a wave of leftist thinking."

Jiang Zemin successfully beat back these attacks, including by shutting down *Mainstream* in 2001 (Jiang thus ironically came to power in part by shutting down a reformist publication, the *World Economic Herald*, and then stayed there by shutting down an antireformist one). During his final year in office, Jiang codified the ideological rationale for his economic program. His so-called **Three Represents** (*sange daibiao*) theory became the party's newest guiding slogan and was inserted into the party constitution in 2002. In claiming that the CCP should represent the advanced forces of the economy, modern culture, and the vast majority of the Chinese people, the "Three Represents" legitimized the party's shift away from its proletarian constituency and aims (see chapter 5).

The result of the "Three Represents" was that the CCP was no longer challenged mainly by the middle class, the educated, nationalistic youths, and intellectuals, as it had been in the 1980s. These groups flourished under Jiang's rule and, for the most part, became staunch supporters of the regime and the party's main de facto constituency. Instead, it was the poor—the urban proletariat and the rural masses—who became increasingly dissatisfied with the communist party-state.

Political Reform in the 1990s

Jiang Zemin was widely dismissed as a weak transitional figure when he came to power in the wake of the Tiananmen crisis of 1989. But he more than proved his mettle in the following decade. After the deaths of Chen Yun (1995), Deng Xiaoping (1997), and other party elders, Jiang gradually asserted his authority through personnel reshuffles and a few outright purges (notably of Beijing party chief Chen Xitong in 1995 and of NPC chairman Qiao Shi in 1997). Before his death, Deng had designated Jiang as the "core" of a "third generation" leadership of the PRC, following the generations of Mao and Deng himself. This gave Jiang an official status that few dared challenge directly.

Jiang's most decisive act against protestors came in 1999. The CCP's loss of moral authority among its traditional constituents, briefly revived in the 1980s, was dramatically highlighted by a protest that year around the **Zhongnanhai** leadership compound near Tiananmen by an estimated 10,000 adherents of a hitherto obscure Buddhist meditation organization, called Falun Gong (literally, "Dharma Wheel Practice"). Complaining about the persecution and disparagement of the group in the nearby port city of Tianjin, the protestors dispersed after just a day. But the event unsettled a leadership with its eerie parallels to the religiously inspired and hugely destructive Taiping Rebellion of 1850–1864 that had taken over half of China and was often cited as a critical factor leading to the collapse of the Qing dynasty in 1911.

Jiang Zemin took the lead in getting a bare majority of the other top leaders to vote to ban the group, leading to a decade-long suppression movement, one of whose unintended consequences was to create by far the best-organized and most committed source of opposition to CCP rule outside China itself. But inside China, the Falun Gong crackdown was thorough and effective.[12] China's middle classes rallied around the regime's persecution of the group, just as China's nineteenth-century gentry (along with Western governments) had supported the Qing army's crushing of the Taiping Rebellion.

Jiang's survival also owed to his steering through important economic and political changes in a mostly consensual manner. Indeed, Jiang's rule can be seen as ushering in the era of relatively consensual elite politics in China after the volatile strongman rule of Mao and Deng. Under Jiang, each leadership faction, defined more by geographical base, personal ties, and institutional affiliation than by policy or ideological differences, got its fair share of appointments (described by a new slang word, *baiping*, or "to arrange evenly"), and policy-making became more institutionalized.

The role of the military in politics, already on the decline in the 1980s, was further reduced under Jiang. In 1992–1993, with Deng's consent, Jiang purged PLA General Yang Baibing and his cousin, PRC President Yang Shangkun, after they had attempted to rebuild the military's role in politics. The last military member of the party's top level Standing Committee retired in 1997, after which just two military delegates would remain as regular members of the next leadership level down, the Politburo, to consult on military matters. In 1998 Jiang banned the very lucrative business activities of the PLA, which ran the gamut from selling weapons to running brothels, shutting off this source of independent income and forcing it, in the words of a classical stratagem of rule in imperial China, to "rely on the emperor's grain."

Jiang's era also accelerated the era of "socialist legality" in China's politics. In 1997, the state constitution was amended to say the PRC "is governed according to the law and aims to build a socialist country under the rule of law." The "legalization" of the CCP party-state under Jiang was an important part of the transition from the charismatic dictatorships under Mao and Deng in which the wishes and whims of the leaders had more authority than the law. The PRC government promulgated one law or regulation after another that sought to create a legal framework for both its expanding market economy, but also for its most repressive policies. Examples of the legalization of repression included a state security law to deal with peaceful dissent (1993), a **martial law** act to deal with mass protests (1996), regulations to limit and control NGOs (1998), an antisecession law to threaten Taiwan about any moves toward independence (2005), and regulations preventing Tibetans from recognizing their own living Buddhas (2007). But legalization also created openings for social pushback, in particular with the emergence of defense lawyers to represent aggrieved citizens. In 2008, activists in the 19,000-member Beijing Lawyers Association, a normally docile state-controlled group, unsuccessfully sought the right to elect their own leaders. The fracas within the association over the challenge was widely discussed within China.

Just as economic reforms in the 1990s gave rise to a New Left in the PRC, political reforms gave birth to a New Right political current that borrowed from traditional Chinese tenets of meritocracy, legalism, and hierarchy to advocate a new form of party dictatorship called **neo-authoritarianism**. The New Right, to which Jiang Zemin was quite sympathetic, argued for more elite and **technocratic** rule, a strong military, and continued market economics mixed with national corporate champions. A typical representative was Beijing University professor Pan Wei, a University of California at Berkeley PhD graduate, who argued for a "consultative rule of law" system modeled on British-colonial Hong Kong and Singapore. Singapore's ruling People's Action Party was a model for emulation—a ruling party that tolerated a symbolic opposition, promoted a market economy, and ruled by legal edicts enforced by pliant courts. For outsiders, the New Right represented something that looked more likely to result in a polarized "bureaucratic-authoritarian" regime such as those of Latin America in the 1960s and 1970s.[13]

Within this main trend of legalized, bureaucratic authoritarianism, there were some democratizing pressures that challenged it. In 1998, a **China Democracy Party** was established as an official and open opposition party by Tiananmen-era activists and, remarkably, was initially given permission to register as an NGO in Zhejiang province. By March 1999, the CDP boasted twenty-nine nationwide branches and eighty-three core leaders. But Beijing's tolerance ended as the CDP started to spread, and by the end of the year, the organization was banned and twenty-six of its leaders were behind bars.

Activists at the local level also continued to press for political change. In 1998, Buyun township (the lowest level of formal government above the village in the hierarchy of rural administration), in Sichuan province, held the first direct popular election for its township governor, a position that was legally supposed to be appointed by the township people's congress. This "illegal" direct township election was an effort to move direct electoral processes up a notch in rural China and triggered a dozen copycat experiments in the following decade (see chapter 8). The political reformers of Buyun consciously styled themselves after the "illegal" peasant economic activists of the early to mid-1970s who had led the way to the dismantling of the communes and the official acceptance of the household responsibility system. They hoped that their experiments would also eventually be endorsed by the party center and spread nation-wide. However, the CCP has remained wary of the experiments and maintained a cautious attitude towards them. After officials in Honghe prefecture in Yunnan province held **direct elections** for ten township governors in 2004, the central government forced them to recall the winners and replace them with party appointees.

Overall, Jiang Zemin could fairly claim to have steered China from a period of threatened re-Stalinization after Tiananmen to irreversible economic liberalization. His achievements in the political realm are more mixed. U.S. President Bill Clinton bluntly told Jiang during a visit to the United States in 1997 that his policies with respect to human rights and democracy were "on the wrong side of history." Yet more than a decade later, the regime that Jiang rescued would remain.

Opening to the World in the 1990s

China developed a somewhat more confrontational relationship with the West during the Jiang Zemin era. The 1980s had been a honeymoon period between China and the West. Deng had toured the United States in 1979, even donning a ten-gallon hat at a Texas rodeo. Western countries began selling small amounts of military equipment to China—a revival of the Cold War alliance of the two against the Soviet Union. A 1988 documentary that aired on China Central Television (CCTV), **River Elegy**, had been scathing about China's cultural chauvinism and insularity (characterized as "yellow culture," reflecting the dull yellow color of the Loess Plateau in northwestern China where Chinese civilization began) and admiring of its cosmopolitan and overseas influences (called "blue culture" in reference to the seafaring and diasporic nature of this side of Chinese culture). The protestors in Tiananmen in 1989 had erected a statue called the Goddess of Democracy that strongly resembled the Statue of Liberty, which, while certainly not sitting well with the party leadership, reflected the esteem in which the United States was held by many at the time.

But after Tiananmen, Western nations imposed sanctions on China, including a ban on military sales. The Tiananmen generation was effectively besmirched at home as stooges of foreign forces intent on weakening China. The party, fearing that the "blue culture" was the road to perdition, consciously began promoting the "yellow culture" as a source of national pride and identity (since socialist culture was now a non-starter). The writings of Confucius were officially promoted again in 1994, and the PRC attempted to expand its influence overseas through **soft power** by the launching of cultural promotion agencies located in host universities called Confucius Institutes in 2004 (of which there were over 350 by 2009). In a highly symbolic gesture in 1995, a member of the Politburo attended the recently sanctioned annual rites at the tomb of the Yellow Emperor (mythical founder of Chinese civilization) in Shaanxi province.

Rising cultural nationalism in China, coupled with post–Cold War American global hegemony, created the conditions for rising tensions between China and the West, particularly the United States. A series of run-ins—the inspection in Saudi Arabia of the Chinese cargo ship *Yinhe* in 1993, following U.S. allegations that it was shipping chemical weapon components to Iran, Western politicking in 1993 to deny China the 2000 Olympic Games (China eventually won the 2008 games), the U.S. dispatch of an aircraft carrier battle group in response to PLA missile tests off Taiwan in 1995–1996, the NATO bombing of the Chinese embassy in Belgrade in 1999, the collision between an American spy plane and a Chinese fighter jet off the south coast of China in 2001, and harassment by Chinese boats of a U.S. Navy submarine detection ship in waters off the PRC island province of Hainan in 2009—brought nationalist emotions to the fore among the Chinese public. A book published in 1996 called *China Can Say No* argued for a get-tough approach to the West, echoing the title of a similar book published in Japan in 1989.[14]

Nonetheless, in the end, Jiang, who certainly was part of China's "blue culture," took the strategic view that Beijing's road to great power status ran through Washington D.C. He paid an official state visit to the United States in 1997, and President Bill Clinton did likewise to China the following year. Jiang and Clinton were attempting to build a "constructive strategic partnership" between the two nations. But the CCP found that it could not simultaneously encourage nationalism at home as the basis of regime legitimacy while at the same time aligning itself with the United States. This led to a cooling down of Sino-American relations and, in the view of some, the beginning of a period of U.S.-China rivalry that would shape world politics for much of the twenty-first century.

The Era of Hu Jintao

Hu Jintao, like Jiang Zemin, had been one of the beneficiaries of Deng's plan to fast-track the promotion of educated and competent young cadres in the early 1980s. During that decade, Hu served successively as party secretary of two poor western regions—Guizhou and Tibet. He accomplished little in either place, but his willingness to accept the tough assignments and to maintain order when protests erupted in Tibet in early 1989 stood him in good stead with his mentor, party elder and left-conservative Song Ping, one of the elders whom Deng put in charge of choosing the new Politburo that would be installed at the party congress in 1992.

Aware of the dangers of a botched succession to the party leadership after Jiang, particularly if Deng had died by then (as turned out to be the case), Song convinced Deng to anoint a presumptive successor to Jiang at the congress. This would settle the post-Jiang succession in advance. Hu Jintao was the one who got the nod because of his fealty to party orders. In the years after his 1992 appointment to the Politburo Standing Committee, Hu was showered in titles to indicate his status as the successor-in-waiting: vice president of the PRC, vice chairman of the Central Military Commission, and head of the **Central Party School**, the highest-level institution for training CCP leaders. He was designated as the "core" of the fourth generation of party leadership, although this term was rarely used after he took over. His elevation in 2002 to the position of party general secretary (and in 2003 to PRC president and in 2004 to chair of the military commission) was thus known a decade in advance.

Perhaps the single most important fact about Hu Jintao was that he was the only top leader of reform China who did *not* suffer under Mao. Deng Xiaoping, Hu Yaobang, Zhao Ziyang, and Jiang Zemin (as well as Hu's designated successor Xi Jinping—see **Box, Who Is Xi Jinping?**) all did to one degree or another. Indeed, as a graduate student and political instructor at Beijing's Tsinghua University from 1964 to 1968, Hu may well have taken part in some Red Guard activities (Tsinghua Red Guards sacked the British Embassy in 1967). The fact that he was given a cushy government engineering job in remote Gansu province in 1968 shows at the very least that he was not seen as an enemy of the Red Guards during those ruinous times.

What difference did this make during Hu's years in office after 2002 (scheduled to end in 2012)? While far from being a Maoist, Hu was clearly more romantic about the party's orthodoxies than the other leaders of the reform era. He was a "Leninist romantic" who believed in firmly upholding the principle of party leadership. He was sympathetic to the ideological critiques of the New Left, favoring more redistribution of the fruits of development through expanded welfare programs.

Under Hu's leadership, China began a serious attempt to redress the questions of social justice and sustainable development that arose during the Jiang era with its emphasis on sheer growth as the measure of success and progress. Hu's conception of a "**harmonious socialist society**" and commitment to "putting the people first" (*yiren weiben*) were

WHO IS XI JINPING?

If everything goes according to plan, Xi Jinping (born in 1953) will take over as head of the Chinese Communist Party in 2012. The party's survival may well depend on Xi's leadership in a period when China is expected to face daunting domestic and international challenges.

Xi is the son of a guerrilla organizer of communist armies in China in the 1930s, Xi Zhongxun (1913–2002). The elder Xi went on to join China's post-1949 leadership. But like many, he was purged by the paranoid Mao, enduring various forms of hard labor and house arrest between 1962 and 1977. As a result, Xi Jinping was sent to do hard labor on a commune at the tender age of sixteen, where he was known as a "black gang child" because of his father.

When the elder Xi was rehabilitated after Mao's death, Xi Jinping's career took off. He graduated in chemical engineering from Beijing's Tsinghua University, China's premiere institution of science and technology, in 1979, and took a series of assignments in local governments beginning in 1982. There he won high marks as an economic reformer with a personal touch. His father was again purged from the Politburo in 1986 for defending Hu Yaobang's tolerant attitude toward student protestors, yet Xi Jinping's career was unaffected. Rising rapidly through the ranks, he became governor of prosperous Fujian province in 2000 and was already on track for a top post in Beijing.

By mid-2007, after ten years of deliberations among China's top leaders, a consensus had developed around Xi as the "core" of the "fifth generation" leadership that would replace Hu Jintao's "fourth generation" in 2012. Xi was appointed to the CCP Politburo Standing Committee and later made PRC vice president, a largely ceremonial post used to signal his future accession. Former party chief Jiang Zemin is a key backer of Xi. If Xi is dutiful and obedient to Hu Jintao and no major scandals arise involving him, he will become party general secretary in 2012, and will assume the state presidency and chairmanship of the Central Military Commission in the following years. He will be the first CCP leader who was not chosen by an "elder" (*yuan lao*) of the party, a term that refers to those who joined before 1949 and later rose to prominent positions in the Mao era, virtually all of whom are now dead. Xi, in other words, will sink or swim on his own merits, without any senior leader to protect him.

While it is hazardous to predict where Xi will lead China, it is clear that he is an avid economic reformer (he was in charge of the regime's celebrations of the thirtieth anniversary of the launching of the reforms in 2008), an opponent of hard-line ideological campaigns, and a relatively cosmopolitan figure who mixes easily in international business and government circles.

But Xi's views on political reform are cautious, perhaps a legacy of his father's suffering as a "liberal" on political issues. He believes that cadres should be popular, but has not gone beyond official doctrine in advocating any changes to the way they are chosen. He was tolerant of mass citizen protests against development projects that erupted during his brief tenures as party chief of Zhejiang province and Shanghai. But he did not initiate new forms of public consultation. His administration is likely to be more populated by economists and lawyers than the engineers and ideologues who dominated the Hu and Jiang eras.

Xi Jinping is also a genuine nationalist who believes that China needs to cut a course distinctly different from other nations. On a visit to Mexico in 2009, he warned that "some well-fed foreigners, with nothing else to do, keep pointing fingers at us." China, he said, had ceased exporting revolution as it had in the Maoist era, conquered poverty at home, and refrained from interfering in the affairs of other countries in the reform era. "What is there to criticize?" he wondered.

written into the party constitution in 2007 as part of his so-called **scientific outlook on development** which emphasizes a shift toward more equitable and sustainable growth (see chapter 5). Tough new rules on industrial safety were introduced, which cut annual coal mine deaths in half to 3,200 in 2008. As a sign of a new seriousness in the crackdown on official graft, Chen Liangyu, the party chief of Shanghai, Jiang Zemin's political base, was jailed for eighteen years for corruption involving property deals and investment funds. A new National Bureau of Corruption Prevention was established with greater autonomy and authority—at least on paper—than its ineffective predecessor body.

Hu Jintao made increased support for agriculture a priority of his administration. In 2006, a forty-eight-year-old head tax on peasant families with land under cultivation was abolished. The loosening of the household registration, or *hukou* system—which had failed to prevent rural to urban migration, as the "floating population" rose to more than 100 million migrants in the 1990s—begun under Jiang Zemin, was accelerated. Some of the efforts to improve rural life faltered on local government opposition, and on limits imposed on peasants to organize effectively to promote their interests. Proposals by scholars and government advisors for the establishment of national or local farmers's organizations, or *nonghui*, were rejected. The party is still wary of the formation of any truly autonomous interest groups.

The harmonious society concept also extends to environmental problems, which impose huge economic costs on China and has become a major source of social unrest (see chapter 11). In the first years of Hu's rule, sixty-one environmental groups in Yunnan province sought to block the planned construction of thirteen small dams along the Salween (Nu) river and a large one at the confluence of three rivers at Hutiaoxia Gorge.[15] Urban protests—against an ethylene plant in Chengdu, against a paraxylene plant in Xiamen, and against the extension of a high-speed train in Shanghai—also gathered steam under Hu's tolerant new approach. Hu was trying to put a stop to the gargantuan projects of the 1990s and put in their place a more sustainable approach to development. The central government's environmental watchdog was upgraded to ministerial status as the new Ministry of Environmental Protection in 2008.

The Jiang era had seen some progress toward the "rule of law," meaning a state whose power was in some degree constrained and guided by formal laws. A new amendment was added to the PRC constitution that read, "The state respects and preserves human rights," although the emphasis continued to be on economic and social rights. Some observers thought that this reflected Hu's populism, which could have more democratic implications than Jiang's more elitist orientation. A World Bank Institute measurement of the quality of rule of law in 212 countries for 2007 found that China did slightly better than other lower middle income countries in maintaining a rule of law system.

One of the key documents of the Hu era was the 2004 resolution issued by a party plenum on strengthening the "governing capacity" of the party. For the first time, the CCP admitted that the 1949 revolution was no longer a sufficient basis on which the party could claim to be the legitimate ruler of China. "The party's governing status is not congenital, nor is it something settled once and for all," read the preamble to the document. By officially raising the question of CCP legitimacy as a present-day task rather than a historically established fact, the resolution stirred an outpouring of discussion among political elites about how the CCP can continue to earn the support of China's people. The party's rapid and relatively successful response to the global economic recession that began in 2008 helped it to avert what might have been a serious challenge to its legitimacy.

Hu also introduced more openness in government and party workings. All government agencies were directed to have public affairs offices, and the official news agency, **Xinhua**, was ordered to issue reports every time the Politburo met. He even abolished the opaque informal summer meetings of China's political elite, previously held from late-July to mid-August at the Beidaihe beach resort in Hebei province.

But in all these areas, Hu's attempts to develop a more sustainable and equitable model of Chinese development foundered on the lack of serious efforts to disperse political power from local party groups. Hu's populism has not extended to democratic elections. True to his Leninist sympathies, Hu has emphasized an improvement in "**inner-party democracy**" instead, in which party members would vote on such things as policies and appointments. When a group of 300 intellectuals, activists, and scholars in China issued a blueprint for democratic reforms under the title **Charter 08** in 2008 (mimicking the ultimately successful Charter 77 democratic movement in the former Czechoslovakia), its leading signatories were detained and sometimes jailed.

Hu has shown less concern than his predecessor with boosting China's place in the world—even though that place has expanded considerably on his watch. As befits a politician with a populist streak, his focus has been on internal problems. China's diplomacy has become less U.S.-centered and more focused on relations with other Asian and developing countries, including a major diplomatic and economic aid, trade, and investment initiative in Africa. Hu has even broached the sensitive issue of relations with Japan, which Jiang had driven to rock bottom by encouraging nationalist emotions in China and by infamously lecturing his Japanese hosts on the lessons of World War II during a state visit in 1998. Hu set up a joint commission of scholars from both sides to look into historical issues, and made a priority of patching up bilateral ties.

What will be Hu Jintao's legacy at the end of his second and final term in office in 2012, when he is expected to be succeeded by fifth-generation leader, Xi Jinping? Hu seems well aware of the urgency of correcting some of the imbalances of development that marked the Jiang era. He has also shown a recognition of the growing challenges of governance that China's leaders face—in particular, the continuing inability of the political system to respond effectively to the country's rapidly changing society and economy. However, his pathway to power—selected for obedience and a firm hand and then groomed over a long period in which caution and consensus were key—left him ill-equipped for the challenges of reform. While Jiang can claim to have rescued China, Hu inherited a China that needed more than mere stability. He will leave behind a long agenda of unfinished business.

Summary and Evaluation

In 2008 the CCP celebrated 30 years since the momentous plenum of 1978 that began to shut the door on the Maoist era and put the official blessing on economic and political reforms. China's economy grew by 9.5 percent a year from 1976 to 2007, which meant that it became a middle income country in the space of just a generation. Real per capita income in purchasing-power equivalent terms rose to $6,000 by 2008 (one-eighth that of the U.S.). Infant mortality, probably the most reliable indicator of material progress, fell from 85 per 1,000 live births in 1970 to 20 by 2008, roughly twice as fast as the global average decline in that same indicator over the same period.

The reform era has brought a long period of relative stability and growth (with the exception of the Tiananmen setback) to China. Chinese politics seems to have passed beyond the cycles of crisis and recovery that characterized the Mao era. Still, it is remarkable that the Chinese Communist Party remains so firmly in power after the traumas it has been through as an organization—and the traumas it has caused the country. The resilience of the party—its ability to reinvent itself—in the reform era has been impressive.

What are the broader implications of the reform era for the study of modern China? As noted in chapter 1, during the Mao era, many scholars felt that politics in China was best analyzed by the use of highly state-centered models. For example, the theory of totalitarianism saw China as the kind of state that attempted to control all aspects of society, indeed as a country where the separation of society from the state barely existed. Or there was Beijingology, the China Watchers version of analyzing Soviet politics known as Kremlinology, a focus on trying to decipher what goes on in the highly secretive top levels of leadership—a more nuanced and informed version of which is still used today to study Chinese politics.

Thirty years into the reform era, these extreme versions of state-centered theory are no longer appropriate to explain political processes or outcomes in China. At the very least, the state had become multifaceted, if not pluralistic, and its various constitutive parts—including local governments, people's congresses, judges and lawyers, the military, **mass organizations**, state enterprises, bureaucrats, journalists, public intellectuals, and party members—more openly contest for political influence. Beyond the boundaries of the state, new forms of civil associations have emerged in China—such as homeowners associations, independent business associations, and environmental groups—with the potential to shape political outcomes. As a result, state-society models that focus on the interactions between state and society can now be usefully applied to some questions about politics in China.

Yet the ability of independent social forces to influence policy is still deeply constrained in a system where communist party leadership remains an unchallengeable principle of political life. Comparative analyses of China's politics continue to stress what has not changed in the political system, especially in a world where many states have been moving in a more democratic direction in the same period.

China in the reform era, then, is a stirring lesson in the autonomy of politics—why politics cannot be reduced to economic conditions or changes. The party created China's economic miracle with early political reforms, managed the consequences of that miracle with a judicious mixture of repression and accommodation, and rebuilt its institutions and ideologies to ensure they would remain compatible with rapid socioeconomic development for a long time to come. Mao's political theory of socioeconomic change—"politics in command" as he called it—is the one part of his legacy that remained firmly embedded in China's politics in the reform era.

Notes

1. See, for example, Jeffrey Henderson, *The Political Economy of East Asian Development: Against the Orthodoxy* (New York: Routledge, 2010).

2. For a comparison of economic reforms in China, Vietnam, Laos, and North Korea, see Peter Ferdinand and Martin Gainsborough, eds., *Enterprise and Welfare Reform in Communist Asia* (New York: Taylor & Francis, 2003).

3. See Merle Goldman, "The Reassertion of Political Citizenship in the Post-Mao Era: The Democracy Wall Movement," in *Changing Meanings of Citizenship in Modern China,* eds. Merle Goldman and Elizabeth J. Perry (Cambridge, MA: Harvard University Press, 2002), 159–186.

4. For more on Chen Yun, see David M. Bachman, *Chen Yun and the Chinese Political System* (Berkeley: University of California Institute of East Asian Studies, 1985), and Nicholas R. Lardy and Kenneth Lieberthal, eds., *Chen Yün's Strategy for China's Development: A Non-Maoist Alternative* (Armonk, NY: M. E. Sharpe, 1983).

5. See, for example, Randall Peerenboom, *China's Long March Toward Rule of Law* (New York: Cambridge University Press, 2002).

6. See Kate Xiao Zhou, *How the Farmers Changed China: Power of the People* (Boulder, CO: Westview Press, 1996).

7. See Bruce Gilley, *Model Rebels: The Rise and Fall of China's Richest Village* (Berkeley: University of California Press, 2001).

8. See David S. Zweig, *China's Brain Drain to the United States* (Berkeley, CA: East Asian Institute, China Research Monograph, 1995).

9. There is a large body of scholarly and popular literature about the Tiananmen Movement and the Beijing Massacre. See the "Suggested Readings" at the end of this chapter for a few recommended titles. Two books, based on materials smuggled out of China, reveal the inner-workings of the party leadership during the crisis. One, *The Tiananmen Papers* (New York: Public Affairs, 2002) are largely the minutes of meetings of the top leaders, while *Prisoner of the State: The Secret Journal of Premier Zhao Ziyang* (New York: Simon & Schuster, 2009) contains transcripts of recordings made by the ousted party general secretary.

10. See Bruce Gilley, *Tiger on the Brink: Jiang Zemin and China's New Elite* (Berkeley: University of California Press, 1998).

11. See Suisheng Zhao, "Deng Xiaoping's Southern Tour: Elite Politics in Post-Tiananmen China," *Asian Survey* 33, no. 8 (August 1993): 739–756.

12. See James Tong, *Revenge of the Forbidden City: The Suppression of the Falungong in China, 1999–2008* (New York: Oxford University Press, 2009); and David Ownby, *Falun Gong and the Future of China* (New York: Oxford University Press, 2008).

13. See, for example, Guillermo A. O'Donnell and David E. Apter, *Modernization and Bureaucratic-Authoritarianism: Studies in South American Politics* (Berkeley: University of California Press, 1979).

14. On the role of nationalism in Chinese politics, see Peter Hayes Gries, *China's New Nationalism: Pride, Politics, and Diplomacy* (Berkeley: University of California Press, 2004).

15. See Andrew C. Mertha, *China's Water Warriors: Citizen Action And Policy Change* (Ithaca, NY: Cornell University Press, 2008).

Suggesting Readings

Baum, Richard. *Burying Mao: Chinese Politics in the Age of Deng Xiaoping*. Princeton, NJ: Princeton University Press, 1994.

Brooke, Timothy. *Quelling the People: The Military Suppression of the Beijing Democracy Movement*. New York: Oxford University Press, 1998.

Dittmer, Lowell, ed. *China's Deep Reform: Domestic Politics in Transition*. Lanham, MD: Rowman & Littlefield, 2006.

Fewsmith, Joseph. *China since Tiananmen: From Deng Xiaoping to Hu Jintao*. New York: Cambridge University Press, 2008.

Goldman, Merle. *From Comrade to Citizen: The Struggle for Political Rights in China*. Cambridge, MA: Harvard University Press, 2007.

Goodman, David S. G. *Deng Xiaoping and the Chinese Revolution: A Political Biography, Routledge in Asia*. London and New York: Routledge, 1994.

Gries, Peter Hayes, and Stanley Rosen. *State and Society in 21st Century China*. New York: Routledge Curzon, 2004.

Harding, Harry. *China's Second Revolution: Reform after Mao*. Washington, DC: Brookings Institution, 1987.

Lam, Willy Wo-Lap. *Chinese Politics in the Hu Jintao Era: New Leaders, New Challenges*. Armonk, NY: M. E. Sharpe, 2006.

Nathan, Andrew J., and Bruce Gilley. *China's New Rulers: The Secret Files*. 2nd rev. ed. New York: New York Review of Books, 2003.

Shen, Tong. *Almost a Revolution: The Story of a Chinese Student's Journey from Boyhood to Leadership in Tiananmen Square*. Ann Arbor: University of Michigan Press, 1998.

Zhao, Dingxin. *The Power of Tiananmen: State-Society Relations and the 1989 Beijing Student Movement*. Chicago: University of Chicago Press, 2004.

II IDEOLOGY, GOVERNANCE, AND POLITICAL ECONOMY

5

Ideology and Chinese Politics

William A. Joseph

What Is Ideology and Why Is It Important?

One of the most influential pre–Cultural Revolution studies of politics in the People's Republic of China was Franz Schurmann's *Ideology and Organization in Communist China*.[1] As the title suggests, Schurmann identified ideology and organization—and the relationship between them—as the keys to understanding what was both unique and comparative (especially with the Soviet Union) about China's political system as it had evolved in the first decade and a half of communist rule. Schurmann's observation is still valid, despite how much has changed about Chinese politics. This chapter will focus on ideology, specifically what can generically be called "Chinese communism," while the next chapter will describe and analyze the organization of the Chinese communist party-state.

What is ideology, and why is it still important in the study of Chinese politics? Ideology is one of the most hotly contested concepts in the social sciences. For our purposes, a simple definition will do. An ideology is a systematic or comprehensive set of values and beliefs ("ideas") that provide a way of looking at and understanding the world or some aspect of it. Our concern is with *political* ideology, which consists of ideas about power and how it should be distributed, organized, and used, including the goals to which it is directed. Furthermore, ideology has action consequences by shaping political behavior, particularly of leaders who have the power to translate ideology into policy. In this sense, ideology shapes what is sometimes referred to as the "**operational code**" of decision-making elites.[2]

The word "ideology" took on a rather negative connotation during World War II and the Cold War: it came to be seen as something "they" (our enemies) have and "we" don't. The fact is that ideology is woven into the political fabric of every society. To be sure, in some cases, including democratic capitalist countries, ideology is relatively latent; that is, it is less publicly visible and less formally proclaimed, and contestation among ideologies is permitted or even encouraged (although there are always limits). In other systems, ideology is a much more overt part of political life. As noted in chapter 1, the existence

A note to instructors and readers: Some might find it useful to read parts of this chapter in conjunction with other chapters in this book with which they coincide in terms of topics or the period in Chinese political history being discussed, as follows: "Introduction" with chapter 1; "Communism" and "Marxism-Leninism Comes to China" with the latter sections of chapter 2; "Mao Zedong Thought" with chapter 3; and "Chinese Communism after Mao" and "Conclusion" with chapter 4.

and enforcement of an official ideology based on Marxism-Leninism is one of the defining characteristics of a communist party-state like the PRC: the ruling party bases its claim to power largely on its role as the only rightful interpreter of the values and the beliefs that will guide the nation to its ideologically determined goals. Serious challenges to the ruling ideology are proscribed and suppressed as threats to the security of the nation and the well-being of the "people."

Ideology has figured very visibly in Chinese politics throughout the history of the Chinese Communist Party, both before and after it came to power in 1949. It motivated the formation and shaped the victory of the revolutionary movement, fueled power struggles, large and small, within the party from the 1920s to the present, and guided leaders in making policies and taking initiatives that have brought both progress and disaster to the country. For all the profound transformations that have taken place in China over the last three decades, including the move toward a market economy, the CCP still swears allegiance to Marxism-Leninism and reaffirms its commitment to the building of socialism with the ultimate goal of reaching the truly egalitarian communist stage of human society. Indeed, it is the ideological adaptability and its political manifestations that help explain the remarkable longevity of the PRC as one of the world's few remaining communist party-states.[3]

The first two sections of this chapter discuss Marxism and Leninism, the ideological foundations of all forms of communism, including that of the Chinese Communist Party. Following a brief transitional discussion of how Marxism-Leninism first came to China in the early twentieth century, the longest section of this chapter is devoted to an analysis of the ideology of Mao Zedong and the ways in which it is a distinctive variation of communist ideology. Not only did Maoist communism have a profound impact on China's political development during the era of his rule in the PRC (1949–1976), but China's post-Mao leaders still swear fealty to certain core principles of Maoism, regardless of how un-Maoist many of their policy initiatives have been. The chapter concludes with an examination of ideology in China after Mao: the CCP's assessment of Maoist ideology; the contributions of Deng Xiaoping, Jiang Zemin, and Hu Jintao to Chinese communism; and some of the ideologies that are supplementing or contending with communism in the People's Republic today.

Communism

Marxism

Marxism is one of the most complex, controversial, and consequential philosophies in human history. The purpose here is only to highlight those points of Marxism that are most relevant for understanding the development of Chinese Communism from Mao Zedong to Hu Jintao. In fact, these points can be considered as common ground for all "Marxists" or "communists," although they may disagree—sometimes violently—over what these ideas mean in practice.

The essence of Marxism is *class analysis*. Marxists see the world—past, present, and future—through the lens of social classes and the economic systems that give rise to them. In particular, they emphasize the struggle between the rich and the poor, the exploiters and the exploited, and the dominant and the subordinate classes. As Karl Marx (1818–1883) and his close collaborator, Friedrich Engels (1820–1895) wrote for the opening line of *The Communist Manifesto* (1848), "The history of all hitherto existing society is the history of class struggle."[4]

Marx believed that from ancient times to his lifetime and beyond, the truly major turning points in history were revolutions in which a ruling class that was hindering further human progress—particularly economic progress—was overthrown by a rising class that would take the lead in moving humankind forward to the next, higher stage of its destined development. According to Marxism, history unfolds in a series of stages marked by increasing levels of economic development made possible by class struggle and revolution. From the Marxist perspective, this path to progress is scientific and inevitable.

For example, feudalism in England was followed by capitalism when the lords of the manor were displaced as the ruling class by the owners of industries and businesses (capitalists) in a revolutionary process that began to unfold in the sixteenth and seventeenth centuries. The same process turned peasant serfs into the industrial working class, or the proletariat.

The timing of revolutions in any particular society is determined largely by its level of economic development and class struggle. Marx concluded that the time and place in which he lived—mid-nineteenth-century Western Europe—was ripe for revolution. Capitalism had been a magnificent achievement in terms of economic development and other areas of human advancement. But it was also a brutally exploitative system in which the capitalist owners of private property (also referred to in Marxism as the "bourgeoisie") literally profited from the labor of the proletariat. Capitalism, in fact, depended on the complete domination and subjugation, including political and cultural, as well as economic, of the proletariat.

Marx identified the proletariat as the most oppressed class in all of human history—and therefore the most revolutionary. History had come down to a final life-and-death class struggle between the proletariat and the bourgeoisie. Revolution was inevitable, as was the triumph of the proletariat. In this sense, Marxism is *a theory of proletarian revolution*.

For Marx, this was the *final* class struggle of history because, once they came to power, the proletariat would abolish private property, and the capitalist class would cease to exist. Indeed, when all property was public property, classes would cease to exist, and the history of all *thereafter* existing society would be a history without class struggle. *Communism*—a truly classless utopia—would be achieved and humankind would enter into an era of *equality, cooperation, and abundance*. These are the essential elements of the communist society that Marxist revolutionaries have envisioned as the ultimate goal of their actions.

This revolutionary transformation from capitalism to communism would not be completed in a short period of time. After the political overthrow of the bourgeoisie and the capitalist system, there would have to be a transitional stage of undetermined length. Marx called this transition stage the "lower stage of communism," but it is more commonly referred to as *socialism*. During the transition from capitalism to socialism, proletarian political power would be used to create the conditions for moving on to the "higher stage" of communism. But unlike any of history's previous transformations, this would be an evolutionary, rather than a revolutionary, process. The progress of evolution from socialism to communism would be measured by the increasing material wealth of society and the deepening of communist values, such as selflessness and devotion to the common good, among the people.

Marxism became a political ideology when it was adapted as the basis of the guiding principles and program of self-proclaimed revolutionary movements. The first of these was the Communist League founded in 1847, by Marx and Engels, among others. It was for the Communist League that Marx and Engels wrote *The Communist Manifesto* as an accessible distillation of the Marxist analysis of historical development and a call for the "workers of the world" to launch the proletarian revolution that would destroy capitalism and begin the transition to socialism.

Marx's ideas were strongly challenged in his lifetime, not only by those who feared his call for communism, but by many who proclaimed themselves to be revolutionaries as well. His radical writings and political activities got him expelled from France (twice) and Belgium before he settled in London in 1849. The strongest challenge to him came from another anti-capitalist revolutionary came from Mikhail Bakunin (1814–1876), the Russian theorist who advocated a radical version of egalitarian self-governance called anarchism and criticized Marx for being too authoritarian in his leadership of the communist movement in Europe.

Marx did not live to see a proletarian revolution under the banner of Marxism come to power. That wouldn't happen until the 1917 Russian Revolution, and its leader, V. I. Lenin, would not only preside (if briefly before his death) over the first government committed to the realization of socialism and communism; his theories would also become the foundation of the second, and in some ways, more politically influential, branch of Marxism known as Leninism.

Leninism

Marxism is a *theory of history* that establishes the claim that the proletariat is destined to lead humankind in a revolution to overthrown capitalism and create a socialist and then as communist society. Leninism is, in essence, a *theory of revolutionary organization*. It builds on Marxism, but it also adds a new, more practical dimension that deals with the actual seizure and exercise of power by a revolutionary communist organization.

Lenin (1872–1924) was set on the path to becoming a revolutionary following the execution of his elder brother in 1887 for involvement in a plot to kill the czar of Russia. He later became a lawyer and was introduced to Marxist theory during his student years. He joined a small Marxist group in the mid-1890s, and his political activism got him exiled to Siberia for a few years. He subsequently traveled widely in Russia and Europe. He rose to a position of leadership in the Russian Social Democratic Labor Party, which was the most important Marxist organization in Russia at the end of the nineteenth century. In 1903, Lenin led the party's more radical "Bolshevik" ("Majority") faction in taking control of the organization.

After a failed attempt at revolution in 1905, Lenin spent the years until 1917 in Europe, mostly in Geneva, but remained an influential leader of the Bolshevik movement in Russia. He returned to Russia a few months after the revolution that overthrew the czar in February 1917. In October, the Bolsheviks seized power from a noncommunist provisional government that had been set up after the ouster of the czar. From then until his death in 1924, Lenin was the head of the government of the country that was renamed the Union of Soviet Socialist Republics (USSR), or Soviet Union, and the organization that became the Communist Party of the Soviet Union (CPSU).

This brief review of Lenin's life as a revolutionary is important to understanding the context of his writings that form the foundation of Leninism. "Leninism" was not a term that Lenin used himself (the same with Marx and "Marxism"), but was coined posthumously by one of his communist comrades when his theories were elevated to join Marxism as the guiding ideology of the Soviet Union. In fact, what is generally described as "Leninism" derives as much, if not more, from how revolutionaries that followed him, including Stalin and Mao, expropriated and adapted his ideas rather than from what Lenin actually did or wrote.[5]

Lenin wrote at length on the issue of how a communist party could best be organized to achieve its political objectives, especially in his 1902 essay, *What Is to Be Done?* He criticized those who favored an open organization that would recruit members widely, particularly among the proletariat. This approach, Lenin argued, was dangerous for two reasons: First, it would make the party highly vulnerable to infiltration and repression by the Czarist authorities. Second, it would dilute the ideological integrity of the party by admitting people who did not fully grasp Marxist theory or were not fully committed to the revolution.

Lenin's solution to this dilemma was to insist that the communist organization be a *vanguard* party, that is, one composed only of professional revolutionaries, many of whom would be intellectuals who had embraced Marxism. It would be the *vanguard*—the leading edge—of the proletarian revolution with the mission to mobilize and lead the working class to seize political power.

To survive, the communist organization not only had to be highly selective in its membership, but also secretive and disciplined. The party would operate according to the principle of **democratic centralism**: debate and the free exchange of ideas would be encouraged while a matter was up for discussion (democracy); but once a decision had been reached by the leadership, discussion stopped and all members were bound to follow without hesitation or dissent (centralism). Lower levels of the organization had to follow the orders of higher levels, and the minority had to follow the majority.

The Leninist theory (and practice) of a vanguard party of the proletariat is an adaptation of (or departure from) Marxism in at least two major ways. First, it substitutes a *political party* claiming to represent the interests of the proletariat for the *proletariat* itself as the leading force of the revolution. Marx and Engels had more faith that the proletariat would rise up in revolution on their own when the time was right.

Second, Leninism reflects the idea that a largely agrarian country with relatively little industry and a small proletariat, such as Russia in the late nineteenth century, could, in fact, begin the process of a communist revolution through the agency of a vanguard party. Both of these Leninist adaptations of Marxism would have great appeal to aspiring revolutionaries in nonindustrialized countries, including China.

Lenin saw the vanguard communist party as the best type of revolutionary organization to *seize* power. But it also became the standard model for all communist organizations *after* the seizure of power when they became the *ruling* party. In his book *State and Revolution* (1917), Lenin expanded significantly on an important idea put forth by Marx: the **dictatorship of the proletariat**. This was to be the form of the political system to be put in place after the communist party took power in the country and that would prevail during at least the early stages of the transition to socialism. "The proletariat," Lenin declared, "needs state power, a centralized organization of force, an organization of violence, both to crush the resistance of the exploiters and to lead the enormous mass of the population...in the work of organizing a socialist economy." It was the communist party that was to be this "centralized organization of force" that would exercise the dictatorship of the proletariat.

Lenin stressed the need for a ruling communist party to remain vigilant against the possibility of a counterrevolution, especially at a time when capitalist enemies surrounded the country. Lenin, like Marx, believed that the state would "wither away" once communism was achieved; but before that time came, the power of the state (and the communist party) would have to increase in order to protect and promote the interests of the proletariat. It is this model of a vanguard party based on the principle of democratic centralism and exercising some variation of the dictatorship of the proletariat that is being conveyed when a communist party, such as the CCP, is referred to as a *Leninist* party, or the PRC as having a *Leninist* political system.

The other main ingredient of Leninism that we should take note of is its theory of imperialism. Basically, Lenin's thesis on imperialism was that the most advanced capitalist countries had been able to avert proletarian revolution at home in the late nineteenth century, at least temporarily, by exploiting their colonies and other less developed parts of the world that were in the pre-capitalist stage of history. These areas, in turn, became the weakest link in the global capitalist chain because of the extreme exploitation they suffered. Communists could find fertile ground for a revolution led by a vanguard party in these weak links, even though they were far from the level of economic and class development that Marx had said was a prerequisite for building socialism. Lenin had in mind Russia as the weak link most ready for revolution in the first decades of the twentieth century, but his ideas on imperialism were one of the main factors in drawing nationalist leaders and intellectuals in the Third World to Marxism-Leninism, including the founders of the CCP and Vietnam's communist leader, Ho Chi Minh. After coming to power, the vanguard communist party would use its centralized authority to promote rapid economic development that would allow the country to achieve industrialization without capitalism.

As Lenin said in 1920, "Communism is Soviet power plus the electrification of the whole country" (Collected Works, Vol. 31, 496–518). In this sense, Lenin's vanguard communist party not only substitutes itself and does the historical work for a weak proletariat class in making revolution, but also for a weak capitalist class in achieving industrialization. Leninism allowed for the acceleration of the Marxist trajectory of history. With the right degree of revolutionary consciousness and the right kind of revolutionary organization, communist power and socialist society became possible for a country without having to wait for and experience the long, painful stage of capitalism to unfold. This, too, was a powerful message to would-be communist revolutionaries in the less developed parts of the world.

In some ways, these theoretical and organizational innovations by Lenin more or less turned Marxism on its head. But they also became foundational pillars of Marxism-Leninism as the guiding ideology of communist movements in China and elsewhere during the twentieth century.

Marxism-Leninism Comes to China

Chapter 2 described the May Fourth Movement of 1919 and the founding of the Chinese Communist Party in 1921. It was these two events that paved the way for the introduction of Marxism-Leninism into China and its emergence as the country's dominant revolutionary ideology.

Socialist ideas had been influential among many Chinese intellectuals since early in the twentieth century, including not only Marxism, but also "non-Marxist socialisms."[6] These schools of thought shared common ground with Marxism in the belief that society would be better if it were organized according to egalitarian principles of collective, rather than private, property, cooperation rather than competition, and power, both economic and political, in the hands of the producers rather than exploiters. But they differed from Marxism (and particularly later with Leninism) over how these lofty goals were to be achieved and what forms they would take when put into practice.

The May Fourth Movement steered some Chinese intellectuals toward more radical variations of socialism in their desperate search for solutions to China's internal and external crises. A few, inspired by the success of the Russian Revolution in 1917 and the anti-imperialist stand of the new Soviet government, began to look more seriously at the ideological and organizational model offered by Marxism-Leninism. These newly converted Marxist-Leninists were guided in establishing the CCP by agents of the Moscow-based Comintern (Communist International) who had been sent to China to help promote revolution. The CCP organization was, from the beginning, structured as a vanguard party along Leninist (or Bolshevik) lines. As the party grew, it enforced both ideological and political discipline on its members that soon squeezed out those advocating alternative non–Marxist-Leninist versions of socialism.

Mao Zedong Thought

Chapters 2 and 3 discussed the gradual rise of Mao Zedong in the hierarchy of CCP leaders during the civil war against Chiang Kai-shek's Nationalist Party and his emergence as the undisputed head of the party during the Yan'an period. It was in Yan'an that Mao also consolidated his ideological domination of the Chinese communist movement.

The Chinese Communist Party first formally proclaimed "Mao Zedong Thought" as its guiding ideology in the party constitution of 1945, which was promulgated in Yan'an toward the end of World War II. The process of enshrining and giving official primacy to Mao's theories had begun a couple of years before. The Rectification Campaign of 1942 had eliminated Mao's major opponents, and in the spring of 1943, he was elected chairman of the party Politburo, a position he held literally until his last breath on September 9, 1976.

It was a conscious decision of the party leadership in 1945 to use the term "Mao Zedong Thought" (*Mao Zedong sixiang*) as the designation for Mao's contribution to communist ideology.[7] They could have chosen—and did consider—other terms, including what would be translated as "Maoism" (*Mao Zedong zhuyi*), but that particular rendition had a foreign connotation, as in the Chinese translation for "Marxism-Leninism" (*Makesi zhuyi, Liening zhuyi*). "Mao Zedong Thought" was chosen as an unmistakable statement that Mao's thinking was neither derivative of nor subordinate to Marxism-Leninism, but embodied the successful "**Sinification**" of Marxism-Leninism. "Sinification" refers to the process of being absorbed or deeply influenced by Chinese culture,society, or thought. In 1931, Mao had cited adapting the European ideology of Marxism-Leninism to China's particular situation as a critical step in the revolutionary process.

After the founding of the People's Republic in 1949, the relationship of Mao Zedong Thought to Marxism-Leninism—and the "true" meaning of Mao Zedong Thought itself—would become a matter of both spirited ideological contention and ferocious, even violent political struggles within the Chinese Communist Party. But the general formulation that Mao Zedong Thought is the integration of the "universal truth" of Marxism-Leninism with the "concrete practice" of the Chinese revolution became the CCP's standard formulation early in the Maoist era and remains so today.

The "universal truth" of Marxism refers to class struggle as the key to understanding the development of human history and the belief in the inevitable downfall of capitalism and the triumph of socialism-communism. For Leninism, it is the theory of the building of a vanguard proletarian party to lead the revolution and the nation. It is Mao's adaptation and enrichment of these universal truths to Chinese circumstances that form the essence of Mao Zedong Thought. As Schurmann put it, Marxism-Leninism is the "pure ideology" part of Chinese Communism, while Mao Zedong Thought is the "practical ideology."[8]

There has been a very vigorous academic debate among China scholars about the extent to which Mao Zedong Thought is based on Marxism-Leninism. One side argues that the core of Maoism is faithful to the fundamental principles of that ideology. The other side concludes that Mao's Thought, while employing communist terminology and rhetoric, deviates so sharply from Marxism-Leninism that it should be considered as an entirely different school of political thought, one more deeply influenced by other sources, such as Chinese philosophy and culture. Some see Mao Zedong Thought as an innovative amalgamation of Marxist-Leninist and Chinese characteristics. Others see it as an utter betrayal or perversion of Marxist ideas. Then there are those who portray Mao as having no ideology or guiding principles other than the pursuit of personal power at any cost.[9]

What are the distinguishing features of Mao Zedong Thought, which is still often referred to outside of China as "Maoism." and how has it influenced China's political development?

The Role of the Peasant Class in the Revolution

First, and most fundamentally, what is distinctive about Maoist Marxism is its designation of the peasants as a leading force in advancing China's revolution. As noted above, Marx saw socialism and communism as the result of a *proletarian* revolution that would take root in and spring from the factories and cities of advanced industrial capitalist societies. Marx had little positive to say about peasants and rural society. He regarded the peasantry as among the most exploited classes in capitalist society, but one that history had passed by on its march toward industrialization and urbanization—and socialism.

Marx once called the peasantry "a class of barbarians standing halfway outside of society, a class combining all the crudeness of primitive forms of society with the anguish and misery of civilized countries" (*Capital*, Vol. III, Part VI, Chapter 47) and compared peasant society to "a sack of potatoes" (*The Eighteenth Brumaire of Louis Bonaparte*, 1852) because of its lack of cohesion and class consciousness, both of which he saw as prerequisites for revolutionary action. *The Communist Manifesto* (1848) actually applauds capitalism for having "subjected the country to the rule of the towns. It has created enormous cities, has greatly increased the urban population as compared with the rural, and has thus rescued a considerable part of the population from the idiocy of rural life."

Lenin was somewhat more optimistic about the revolutionary potential of the peasantry in Russia. He thought rural dwellers—particularly the poorest peasants—could be a valuable ally of the proletariat in seizing power. But, like Marx, he was skeptical that they could see beyond their desire for "freedom and land" to the ultimate goals of socialism, including the abolition of private property (*The Proletariat and the Peasantry*, 1905).

Mao, drawing on his own rural roots, went quite a bit further by identifying the peasantry as a playing a leading role in bringing the revolutionary movement to power, concluding from his own investigations in his home province of Hunan in early 1927 that

> In a very short time, in China's central, southern and northern provinces, several hundred million peasants will rise like a mighty storm, like a hurricane, a force so swift and violent that no power, however great, will be able to hold it back. They will smash all the trammels that bind them and rush forward along the road to liberation. They will sweep all the imperialists, warlords, corrupt officials, local tyrants and evil gentry into their graves. Every revolutionary party and every revolutionary comrade will be put to the test, to be accepted or rejected as they decide. There are three alternatives. To march at their head and lead them? To trail behind them, gesticulating and criticizing? Or to stand in their way and oppose them? Every Chinese is free to choose, but events will force you to make the choice quickly. ("Report on an Investigation of the Peasant Movement in Hunan," March 1927)

Mao went on to make the case that the poorest peasants, which he estimated at 70 percent of the rural population, were "the most revolutionary group" and "the vanguard in the overthrow of the feudal forces," by which he meant the landlord class that had dominated rural society for millennia. He then put the center of gravity of China's struggle squarely in the countryside by claiming that to "overthrow these feudal forces is the real objective of the national revolution."

Mao's rural strategy of "surrounding the cities from the countryside" gradually became the dominant approach of the CCP after Chiang Kai-shek's attacks against the party in the late 1920s drove them out of the urban areas into the countryside and then forced them to undertake the Long March to the hinterlands of Yan'an in the mid-1930s.

But this strategy was not without opposition both from within the CCP, especially from party leaders who had been trained in more orthodox Marxism in Moscow and by Stalin, who had become head of the Soviet Communist Party and the Comintern following Lenin's death in 1924. Although Stalin eventually gave Mao crucial support in his bid to lead the CCP, the Soviet leader was skeptical of a communist revolution based on mobilizing the rural masses. He ordered the Chinese Communists to stay in the urban-based united front with the KMT in 1927 even when it became apparent to many that Chiang Kai-shek was preparing a bloody purge of the communists. He later referred to Mao as a "cave Marxist" who hid in the countryside of Yan'an rather than fighting in the cities.[10]

China scholars have reached very different conclusions, and argued with great intensity, about whether Mao's views of the role of the peasantry in China's revolution constitute a profound break with orthodox Marxism or merely an adjustment in strategy to accommodate circumstances that left him and the communist party no real choice. There is no dispute that Mao exhibited a certain kind of political genius in recognizing that peasants would, out of necessity, be the leading *force* in the struggle to gain power. But he never abandoned the orthodox Marxist assumption that the industrial proletariat was the leading *class* and the peasants a subordinate partner in the revolutionary coalition whose ultimate goal was to bring socialism and modernization to China. Nevertheless, Maoism is a distinctive variant of Marxism in the degree to which it puts a positive emphasis on the rural factor in influencing the revolution both before and after the acquisition of power.

Peasants and the Building of Socialism

After the founding of the People's Republic, Mao, at many times and in various ways, continued to express and act on his ideological view that the peasantry had a special role in bringing about revolutionary change. The most dramatic—and ultimately tragic—example was his decision to launch the Great Leap Forward in 1958. As discussed in chapter 3, the purpose of the Leap was to recalibrate China's approach to building socialism away from the Soviet-style five-year-plan model, with its strong urban bias to a strategy of economic development that would "walk on two legs" in benefiting both city and countryside and promoting both industry and agriculture. Furthermore, the vanguard of the Leap into communism would again be the peasants, and its most revolutionary thrust would be in the rural areas with the founding of the radically egalitarian people's communes. It was also among the peasantry that the Leap took its most terrible toll in the tens of millions who perished because of famine, illness, and mistreatment.

The Cultural Revolution, although it was to be a "great *proletarian*" movement and was a largely urban phenomenon in its first phases, had roots in Mao's concerns in the early 1960s about the growing inequality and cadre corruption in the rural areas that had resulted from the policies sponsored by Liu Shaoqi and Deng Xiaoping to promote recovery from the ravages of the Great Leap Forward. And in the late 1960s, when the Chairman became disenchanted with the factionalism and violence of the urban youth who made up the Red Guards, he sent more than 20 million of them "down to the countryside and up to the mountains" where they could be reeducated by the peasants about what it really meant to make revolution.

Yet, to a certain extent, Mao was ambivalent about the role of the peasantry in the building of socialism. He retained a somewhat utopian view about the revolutionary enthusiasm of the rural folk and the political purity of the countryside. He was also concerned about the corrupting influences of city life. But his vision of the socialist (and communist) future was not a pastoral one. He wanted the rural areas to modernize with the goal of overcoming what he called the "Three Great Differences" between industry and agriculture, town and country, mental and manual labor. Like Marx and Lenin, he believed that the ultimate objective of seizing political power and building socialism was to unleash the productive forces and usher in an era of modernization that would lead to unprecedented bounty. But Mao Zedong Thought does ascribe to the rural peasants a much more vital role as a revolutionary force in achieving those ends.

Leninist Populism—or Populist Leninism?

The Leninist theory of revolution is based on the assumption that the masses cannot lead the revolution on their own, but must be mobilized and directed by a vanguard communist party. Mao was, at bottom, a faithful Leninist, but throughout his political life, both his thinking and his action also reflected a a deep populist streak. "Populism" is an approach to politics (one could say, a kind of ideology) that claims to represent the interests of ordinary people, particularly against predatory elites whose own wealth and power depends on a status quo that disadvantages the vast majority.[11]

One of Mao's first important political essays, written while he was just beginning to learn about Marxism-Leninism, was called, "The Great Union of the Popular Masses" (1919). This essay resounds with populist themes in its call to action against all the woes that plagued China in the tumultuous decade after the fall of the Qing dynasty. After observing that "the decadence of the state, the sufferings of humanity, and the darkness of society have all reached an extreme," he wrote:

> Where is the method of improvement and reform? Education, industrialization, strenuous efforts, rapid progress, destruction and construction are, to be sure, all right, but there is a basic method for carrying out all these undertakings, which is that of the great union of the popular masses. If we look at the course of history as a whole, we find that all the movements which have occurred throughout history, of whatever type they may be, have all without exception resulted from the union of a certain number of people. A greater movement requires a greater union, and the greatest movement requires the greatest union.[12]

Mao rails time and again in this essay against "the union of powerful people" that has caused the abject misery of humankind. At this early time in this pre-Marxist stage of his life, he calls only for "reform and resistance," not revolution, and the perspective is clearly one in which the heretofore powerless masses will, on their own, undertake the struggle for justice without the need for vanguard party.

Once he was a committed Marxist-Leninist, Mao's faith in the masses was tempered, if not tamed, by his belief in the Chinese Communist Party as the vanguard of the revolution. But, he often seemed torn between the two poles of populism and Leninism. During his ascent to power in the 1930s, he reminded his communist colleagues that the party had to "be concerned with the well-being of the masses" if it were to win them over to their side, and that, if they failed in that task, they would fail in making revolution. The party had to think of the masses as more than foot soldiers in the revolution, but as a kind of partner in a mutual cause. The people would not be swayed to join the cause by abstract ideological appeals. Rather, "if we want to win," he said in 1934,

> We must lead the peasants' struggle for land and distribute the land to them, heighten their labor enthusiasm and increase agricultural production, safeguard the interests of the workers, establish co-operatives, develop trade with outside areas, and solve the problems facing the masses—food, shelter and clothing, fuel, rice, cooking oil and salt, sickness and hygiene, and marriage. In short, all the practical problems in the masses' everyday life should claim our attention. If we attend to these problems, solve them and satisfy the needs of the masses, we shall really become organizers of the well-being of the masses, and they will truly rally round us and give us their warm support. Comrades, will we then be able to arouse them to take part in the revolutionary war? Yes, indeed we will! ("Be Concerned with the Well-Being of the Masses," 1934)

The enemy—at that time defined as "imperialism and the Kuomintang"—may have superior weaponry and shield itself in "iron bastions" like military fortifications. But if the revolutionary forces have the people on their side, then the CCP had nothing to fear and victory was assured:

> What is a true bastion of iron? It is the masses, the millions upon millions of people who genuinely and sincerely support the revolution. That is the real iron bastion which no force can smash, no force whatsoever. The counter-revolution cannot smash us; on the contrary, we shall smash it. Rallying millions upon millions of people round the revolutionary government and expanding our revolutionary war we shall wipe out all counter-revolution and take over the whole of China. ("Be Concerned with the Well-Being of the Masses," 1934)

The populist impulse in Maoism often asserted itself after 1949. In the Hundred Flowers movement (1956–1957), Mao called on the people to criticize the party's shortcomings during its first years in power, particularly "bureaucratism" (being out of touch with the masses). At the start of the Great Leap Forward (1958–1960), which was in large measure a turn from an elite-centered model of socialist development to a radically populist one, the Chairman exclaimed that the "most outstanding thing" about China's people was that, for the most part, they were "poor and blank." This gave them "the desire for changes, the desire for action and the desire for revolution." Furthermore, he said, "On a blank sheet of paper free from any mark, the freshest and most beautiful characters can be written; the freshest and most beautiful pictures can be painted." ("Introducing a Co-operative," April 15, 1958).

And in the early stages of the Cultural Revolution (1966–1968) Mao literally unleashed the masses to attack authority in all its personal and institutional manifestations, including the party. Each of these episodes not only resulted in catastrophes that inflicted great suffering on the Chinese people, but also ended with a firm reassertion of Leninist authority., These outcomes reflect both the perils of Maoist radical populism and Mao's deep ambivalence about giving power to the people.

The Mass Line

The tension between populism and Leninism in Mao's thought can clearly be seen in his theory of leadership, which is called the "mass line." Both the theory and practice of the mass line took shape during the years that the CCP spent in rural base areas from 1927 to 1945. It is a method of leadership—or "**work style**"—emphasizing that those with authority ("cadres") must always remain in close touch with those they lead. It rejects both leaderless, spontaneous action by the masses and leadership that is aloof or divorced from the masses. As Mao wrote in 1943:

> However active the leading group may be, its activity will amount to fruitless effort by a handful of people unless combined with the activity of the masses. On the other hand, if the masses alone are active without a strong leading group to organize their activity properly, such activity cannot be sustained for long, or carried forward in the right direction, or raised to a high level. ("Some Questions Concerning Methods of Leadership," 1943)

In other words, cadres have to talk and listen to the people, spend time among them, not live at a level too high above them, share their weal and woe, and avoid arrogance of any kind. In making decisions, cadres have to put into practice the key concept of "from the masses, to the masses":

> This means: take the ideas of the masses (scattered and unsystematic ideas) and concentrate them (through study turn them into concentrated and systematic ideas), then go to the masses and propagate and explain these ideas until the masses embrace them as their own, hold fast to them and translate them into action, and test the correctness of these ideas in such action. Then once again concentrate ideas from the masses and once again go to the masses so that the ideas are persevered in and carried through. And so on, over and over again in an endless spiral, with the ideas becoming more correct, more vital and richer each time. ("Some Questions Concerning Methods of Leadership," 1943)

The mass line approach to leadership certainly does not cede all power to the people. Leaders are meant to exercise authority and expect compliance. But such authority is rooted in the masses, not in the liberal democratic sense that the leaders are ultimately accountable to the people: they are not. According to the Leninist system of democratic centralism, cadres are responsible to higher levels in the party's pyramidal chain of command, not to those below them. But the mass line is distinctive in that it does give more emphasis and life to the democratic vein in democratic centralism than does orthodox Leninism, if democratic is understood as connection and consultation by the leaders with the led. In this sense, the mass line might be said to be the basis of a "quasi-democratic" political system.[13]

The Mass Line: Deviation and Innovation

The mass line was the essence of proper cadre "work style," and deviation from it was one of the deadly sins of Maoism. Tendencies toward elitism, bureaucratism, commandism, and other manifestations of a deviant work style were always to be guarded against in a vanguard party, but they became a central and abiding concern to Mao after the CCP had come to power. On the eve of the communist victory in 1949, he warned in a speech to the party leadership that "With victory, certain moods may grow within the Party—arrogance, the airs of a self-styled hero, inertia and unwillingness to make progress, love of pleasure and distaste for continued hard living." He worried that "There may be some Communists, who were not conquered by enemies with guns and were worthy of the name of heroes for standing up to these enemies, but who cannot withstand sugar-coated bullets; they will be defeated by sugar-coated bullets" in the form of the prestige, privileges, and perquisites that power brings. If the party was to achieve its goal of building a new socialist China, then cadres had "to remain modest, prudent and free from arrogance and rashness in their style of work...[and] preserve the style of plain living and hard struggle" that had won them the support of the masses during the civil war ("Report to the Second Plenary Session of the Seventh Central Committee of the Communist Party of China," March 5, 1949).

In the early years following the establishment of the People's Republic, Mao came to believe that his warnings had been ignored. In 1951, the **Three-Anti campaign** (anti-corruption, anti-waste, anti-bureaucracy) was launched primarily to target cadre abuses of the mass line. The Hundred Flowers movement had a similar thrust. The ideological restlessness that Mao exhibited throughout the remainder of his life derived from his worries— ultimately his obsession—that China was in dire danger of veering off the socialist road to communism and might well wind up, instead, in the clutches of capitalism. The only safeguard against this was if the vanguard party remained true to its mission, and that was only possible if its leaders stayed loyal and attuned to the people through the mass line.

One of the institutional innovations of that grew out of the Cultural Revolution was the so-called **May 7th Cadre Schools**, which were designed, in part, to reinforce the mass line. The name of these "schools" was derived from the "May 7th Directive" of 1966, which was a letter from Chairman Mao (to Lin Biao) that called on the army to be a "big school" in which soldiers engaged in labor and studied politics as well as fulfilling their military duties. Applied to state and party cadres, this Directive led to hundreds of thousands of officials being dispatched on a rotational basis from the relative comfort of their urban offices to work and live among the masses, mostly in rural communes, while also engaging in political study and self-criticism.

The May 7th Schools were an artifact of the short-lived period in which some of the radical ideas of the Cultural Revolution were actually put into practice, and, in practice, the reality of the policy frequently fell far short of its ideals. Cadres were often quartered in barracks at some distance from peasant households and worked on separate plots of land (and, in fact, the peasants did not want the soft-handed city slickers mucking up their crops). Nevertheless, at least the idea of the May 7th Schools embodied the centrality of the mass line approach to leadership in Mao Zedong Thought.

Voluntarism

Voluntarism is the belief that human will ("volition") can be decisive in bringing about major historical changes. It express supreme faith in the power of *subjective* factors such as commitment, faith, determination, and perseverance to overcome *objective* conditions or obstacles that stand in the way of solving a problem or achieving a goal. Voluntarism also has a collective aspect in that it sees the power of human will magnified when people work together for a common cause. Many Mao scholars see voluntarism as one of the defining characteristics of Mao Zedong Thought and as a recurring theme in both his writings and political actions.[14]

This voluntarist element in Maoism is also frequently cited as one of the main points separating it from orthodox Marxism, which puts more emphasis on the limits that objective circumstances, notably economic circumstances, place on the scope of human will and activity. For this reason, Marxism is often said to be based on "economic determinism," meaning that it is the economic structure (and the class system that derives from it) of any given historical era that determines politics, culture, philosophy, and nearly every other aspect of human society. The juxtaposition of Mao's voluntarism with Marx's economic determinism (or **materialism**) can be overstated: Marx did not discount altogether the role of human consciousness and action in shaping important events, and Mao was always an authentic Marxist in the centrality he accorded to the economic forces of production.

Nevertheless, any discussion of Mao Zedong Thought and its impact on Chinese politics has to take account of its strong voluntarist thread.

The essay of Mao's that is most voluntarist in its message is also one of his shortest: "The Foolish Old Man Who Removed the Mountains." The essay comes from a speech that the Chairman gave in June 1945 at a national congress of the CCP. World War II was approaching its end and the likelihood that the civil war against Chiang Kai-shek's Nationalists would resume was certainly on the minds of those attending this meeting.

In order to rally his comrades for the struggles ahead, Mao inserted into his speech an ancient Chinese fable. It tells the story of an old man who decided to dig away two huge mountains that were blocking his house (perhaps from access to the nearest market town?). When a neighbor calls him foolish, the old man replies that if he keeps digging, along with his sons, and their sons, and so on, they will eventually be able to remove the mountains since they weren't growing any higher and each shovelful made them lower. Mao brought the fable up to the present by saying that it was the two big mountains of imperialism and feudalism that "lie like a dead weight on the Chinese people." The CCP, he said, was committed to digging them up. "We must persevere and work unceasingly," he noted, and if we "stand up and dig together" with the Chinese people, "why can't these two mountains be cleared away?" ("The Foolish Old Man Who Removed the Mountains," 1945).

Mao's invocation of this fable at that critical moment of the Chinese revolution was meant to be a clarion call to party members to keep faith in their mission and themselves despite the "objective" fact that they would soon be fighting an army much larger, better armed, and supported by the United States. There are also elements of Mao's Leninist populism in his telling of the fable: it is combination of the Chinese people *and* the Chinese Communist Party standing up and digging together than will ensure victory.

Mao's voluntarism is sometimes analyzed as reflecting a kind of peasant utopianism with roots in his fascination with the fabled heroism of characters from ancient Chinese novels. But it can also be traced to the series of seemingly miraculous successes that he and the CCP had during their rise to power: the escape from Chiang's anti-communist 'White Terror" and extermination campaigns of the late 1920s to mid-1930s; their survival of the Long March of 1934–1935; and their ability not only to survive, but also to thrive in Yan'an while fighting both the Nationalists and the Japanese. The lessons that Mao drew from these experiences could certainly have been a voluntarist one, bolstered by the triumphs of the early years of CCP, such as in the land reform campaign and particularly by fighting the United States to a stalemate in the Korean War.

This voluntarist element in Maoism played out most clearly in the Great Leap Forward, in which the Chairman took the lead in a movement that proclaimed China would achieve economic miracles and reach the ranks of the advanced industrial nations in a decade or less. And how would it do this, despite the fact any "objective" assessment of the technology and resources available to China at that time would say that such a claim was foolish? By relying on the willpower, the labor, and the revolutionary enthusiasm of the Chinese people under the leadership of the CCP. It was during the Leap that the slogan, "The spirit of the Foolish Old Man is the spirit that will transform China" first became popular. Mao's "Foolish Old Man" speech of 1945 became one of his "Three Constantly Read Articles" that were emphasized and often memorized during the Cultural Revolution.[15]

Even some of Mao's poetry (yes, he was a poet, and not a bad one, according to many critics) have lines and stanzas that carry a strong voluntarist message, particularly some written on the eve of the Cultural Revolution, when he was pondering his odds of launching an ideological crusade against much of the party-state establishment. Consider the following excerpt from one poem written in 1965:

Wind and thunder are stirring,
Flags and banners are flying
Wherever men live.
Thirty-eight years are fled
With a mere snap of the fingers.
We can clasp the moon in the Ninth Heaven
And seize turtles deep down in the Five Seas:
Nothing is hard in this world
If you dare to scale the heights.
                    —*"Reascending Chingkangshan"*

Contradiction

Stuart Schram, one of the foremost scholars of Mao Zedong Thought, has called "theory of contradictions" the "philosophical core" of Mao's thinking.[16] It is also one of the more complex aspects of Maoism and one that is not easily illustrated by references to fables, poems, or slogans. In fact, the two major essays in which Mao deals most centrally with this topic, "On Contradiction" (1937) and "On the Correct Handling of Contradictions among the People" (1957), are among his longest and densest writings. Mao's ideas about **contradictions** root his ideology firmly in Marxism-Leninism, while at the same time— rather contradictorily—reflecting one of his most important theoretical innovations, and one that had profound consequences for Chinese politics.

Mao wrote in his 1937 essay that "contradiction exists in the process of development of all things" and that "contradiction exists universally and in all processes, whether in the simple or in the complex forms of motion, whether in objective phenomena or ideological phenomena" ("On Contradiction," 1937). What did he mean by "contradiction"? As Mao uses it, contradictions refers to things that are closely connected, but still fundamentally different from each other, or that "contradict each other."

But it is not just the difference, but the connection that makes for a contradiction.

It is the continuous interaction among the aspects of a contradiction that causes the development of everything—of life, nature, knowledge, culture, society. This view of the centrality of contradictions comes from an approach to philosophy called "dialectics," which dates back to ancient Greece and which was adapted by Marx as the heart of his understanding of history. For Marxists, including Mao, the most important contradiction in human society before socialism and communism are reached is that between classes, particularly between exploiting and exploited classes, which itself reflects contradictions in the process of economic development since without exploitation, development would not occur.

Mao, again building on Marxism-Leninism, made the distinction between two kinds of contradictions in society, *non-antagonistic* and *antagonistic*. Non-antagonistic contradictions are those in which the opposing parts have some common ground despite their differences, which may, in fact, be quite big. In such cases, the contradictions can be resolved through discussion, debate, learning, and other nonviolent means.

Mao often pointed to the contradictions between rural peasants and urban workers as parts of the revolutionary movements as an example of a non-antagonistic contradiction: both classes wanted the same fundamental thing—to overthrow their exploiters and have a "better" life—but because of their vastly different circumstances, they are bound to have differences about both the means and ends of the revolution. There could even be—in fact, given the law of contradictions, there *had* to be—contradictions within the communist party itself, but these were also non-antagonistic, for example, over whether the CCP should follow an urban or rural strategy of revolution to reach the common goal of winning national power.

Mao also referred to non-antagonistic contradictions as "contradictions among the people"—the "people" being a broad yet vague category that included all those who were on the side of the revolution. **Antagonistic contradictions**, on the other hand, are between the people and their "enemy," for example, between poor peasants and the landlords who exploit them. There is no common ground for compromise or room for debate. Such contradictions can only be resolved through class struggle, which requires force to defeat and suppress the enemy.

Responding in the late 1920s to those who claimed that the peasants were "going too far" in their actions against landlords, Mao exclaimed,

> A revolution is not a dinner party, or writing an essay, or painting a picture, or doing embroidery; it cannot be so refined, so leisurely and gentle, so temperate, kind, courteous, restrained and magnanimous. A revolution is an insurrection, an act of violence by which one class overthrows another. ("Report on an Investigation of a Peasant Movement," 1927)

Mao noted that, if left unresolved, non-antagonistic contradictions could fester and eventually turn antagonistic. Therefore one of the primary tasks of a communist party leadership was to differentiate between types of contradiction, decide which were the most important to tackle at any given point in time, and use the correct methods in handling them.

Up to this point, what has been presented as Mao's views on contradictions is pretty standard Marxist-Leninist fare. But he went much further, in both theory and practice, beginning in the mid-1950s. Toward the end of his 1937 essay, Mao approvingly quoted Lenin as follows: " 'Antagonism and contradiction are not at all one and the same. Under socialism, the first will disappear, the second will remain.' That is to say, antagonism is one form, but not the only form, of the struggle of opposites; the formula of antagonism cannot be arbitrarily applied everywhere" ("On Contradiction," 1937). In other words, once the communist party had consolidated power and established a socialist system—including the abolition of private property and exploiting classes—there would still be contradictions, but they would be non-antagonistic contradictions "among the people" since the economic (material) basis of antagonism would have been eliminated.

Chairman Mao changed his mind about the validity of Lenin's conclusion, largely as a result of what happened following his call in 1956 "to let a hundred flowers bloom, let a hundred schools of thought contend." As discussed in chapter 3, Mao launched the Hundred Flowers movement in order to shake up the complacent party-state bureaucracy a bit by inviting the "people" to express their thoughts about progress and problems in the first years of the PRC. Because he thought China was well into the transition to socialism, he expected constructive criticism and suggestions—or what he called "fragrant flowers"—to be forthcoming; but he was taken aback by the storm of condemnation of the CCP and even of himself that the movement unleashed. He concluded that these were not a reflection of non-antagonistic contradictions among the people in China's socialist society, but of "poisonous weeds"—antagonistic contradictions—in the form of bourgeois ideas that had to be rooted out by force before they could destroy the revolution. To that end, Mao implemented the Anti-Rightist campaign in 1957. The dire political consequences of this witch-hunt for class enemies ("rightists") are also discussed in chapter 3.

Mao's conclusion that antagonistic contradictions do *not* disappear with the advent of socialism but remain a mortal threat to the revolution, requiring eternal vigilance, was not only an ideological twist on Marxism-Leninism, but also a major turning point in Chinese politics. It would preoccupy him for the rest of his life. Such ideas about contradictions—seemingly abstract, philosophical musings on what makes the world go round—in fact, help us to understand why Mao Zedong became such an impatient revolutionary and why his use of power, once he had it, led to such radicalism and violence.

Class Struggle as the Key Link

By definition, an ideology has to have internal consistency or logic; in other words, the pieces have to fit together to form a coherent view of the world and guide to action. If the theory of contradiction is the "philosophical core" of Mao's ideology, a number of other ideas flow directly from that core. Perhaps none is more crucial in the whole construct of Mao Zedong Thought than the idea of "class struggle." As noted earlier, the most fundamental connection between Marxism and Maoism is the class analysis approach to understanding history and society. But Mao Zedong Thought takes Marxist class analysis in a much more radical direction.

As discussed above, from the mid-1950s on, Mao was centrally concerned with the persistence, even under socialism and after the abolition of private property, of the most important of all antagonistic contradictions: class struggle, most especially that between the proletariat and the bourgeoisie.

In 1953, Mao was already fretting about the corrosive influence of "bourgeois ideas inside the party" ("Combat Bourgeois Ideas in the Party," 1953). His thoughts about the nature of class struggle in socialist society evolved over the next decade, reflecting his experience of the Hundred Flowers movement, the Anti-Rightist campaign, and the Great Leap Forward. Mao's decision to purge defense minister Peng Dehuai as a "right opportunist" for expressing his opinion at the Lushan Conference in mid-1959 that the Great Leap should be slowed down after the first signs of famine became apparent was particularly significant: it injected the specter of class struggle into the highest echelons of the Chinese Communist Party leadership and represented a fundamental shift in inner-party norms for handling leadership disputes. With the deepening of his dissatisfaction about the direction in which China was headed during the post-Leap recovery, and, importantly, the hardening of his conclusions about the restoration of capitalism in the Soviet Union under Khrushchev, Mao's rhetoric about the persistence of class struggle escalated and became more urgent. (See Box, **The Ideological Origins of the Sino-Soviet Split.**)

At a crucial party meeting in September 1962, Mao said, "We can now affirm that classes do exist in socialist countries and that class struggle undoubtedly exists" and told his comrades that "We must raise our vigilance...from now on we must talk about this every year, every month, every day...." Yet he still cautioned them to "take care that the class struggle does not interfere with our work" ("Speech at the Tenth Plenum of the Eighth Central Committee," 1962).

By July 1964, such caution had been jettisoned. Now Mao proclaimed to his nephew, Mao Yuanxin, who would become one his uncle's most ardent radical supporters, that "Everywhere there is class struggle, everywhere there are counter-revolutionary elements" and "We...have cases where political power is in the grip of the bourgeoisie...No matter what guise they have been transformed into, we must now clean them all out" ("Talk with Mao Yuanxin," 1964). When the Cultural Revolution was launched in full force in May 1966, its targets were those "representatives of the bourgeoisie who have sneaked into the party, the government, the army, and all spheres of culture" ("May 16 Circular," 1966).

In the last months of his life, as the power struggle to succeed him as China's top leader began to heat to a feverish pitch, Mao chastised those (including Deng Xiaoping) he thought were trying to keep the country focused on its economic priorities. In the 1976

THE IDEOLOGICAL ORIGINS OF THE SINO-SOVIET SPLIT

The Soviet Union was a strong supporter of the Chinese Communist Party from the time of its founding in 1921 through its first decade or so in power in the People's Republic of China. There certainly were tensions over revolutionary strategy between Soviet and Chinese communists during the course of China's civil war, and Mao Zedong did not feel well-treated or respected by Stalin when he first visited Moscow in 1949. Nevertheless, a Sino-Soviet Treaty of Friendship, Alliance, and Mutual Assistance was signed in 1950 and became the basis of massive assistance from Moscow to the PRC, mostly in the form of industrial designs, machinery, and technical advisors. The Soviets also backed the PRC in the Korean War (1950–1953).

But relations between the two communist powers began to deteriorate in the mid-1950s, after Nikita Khrushchev had succeeded Stalin as Soviet leader; by the end of the decade, they had reached the point of open rupture. There were a number of causes of the **Sino-Soviet split**, including Chinese suspicion on Soviet meddling in its internal politics; Soviet "requests" for a military presence of Chinese soil; differences in foreign policy, particularly between Moscow's efforts to promote "peaceful coexistence" with the United States and Beijing's preference for confrontation with American imperialism.

Mao was also alarmed at Khrushchev's denunciation of Stalin's crimes in 1956, both because it showed disunity in the communist camp and because he feared he might suffer the same fate after his death. In 1959, the Soviets, due to their increasing displeasure with Mao's taunting rhetoric and reckless policies, withdrew all of their equipment and personnel from China, a move that had a severe negative impact on Chinese industry during the disaster of the Great Leap Forward.

When the Sino-Soviet split spilled out in public in the early 1960s, it took the form of an ideological "debate" in which each side accused the other of having betrayed Marxism-Leninism in both theory and practice. These debates—called "polemics"—were carried out in print and in speeches at international meetings and pitted the Communist Party of the Soviet Union (CPSU) against the Chinese Communist Party (CCP) in a struggle for leadership of the communist world.

Soviet polemics denounced Mao as a narrow-minded nationalist and the CCP as being peasant bandits parading under the banner of communism with no understanding of the "scientific" nature of building socialism. The CCP portrayed Khrushchev as a political bully and an ideological lightweight who had committed the ideological crime of "revisionism," or altering some of most fundamental tenets of Marxism-Leninism.

Mao also came to the conclusion that, under Khrushchev, the Soviet Union had actually abandoned socialism and restored capitalism. In July 1964, the CCP issued an "Open Letter" to the CPSU, which was called "On Khrushchev's Phony Communism and Its Historical Lessons for the World." It declared that "The revisionist Khrushchev clique are the political representatives of the Soviet bourgeoisie, and particularly of its privileged stratum.... [that] has gained control of the Party, the government and other important organizations." This "privileged stratum" supported its decadent lifestyle by exploiting the labor of Soviet workers and farmers and was therefore behaving just like a capitalist class. This dire outcome reflected the fact that the Soviets had the wrong ideological perspective on crucial matters such as antagonistic contradictions and the persistence of class struggle in socialist society. Those points are, of course, central hallmarks of Mao Zedong Thought.

For China, the most significant impact of the Sino-Soviet split was the influence it had on Mao's decision to launch the Great Proletarian Cultural Revolution in 1966. The primary purpose of the Cultural Revolution was to forestall the spread of Soviet-style revisionism to China. Mao's main target in this struggle was Liu Shaoqi, President of the PRC, who was labeled as "China's Khrushchev," as well as "the number-one party person in authority taking the capitalist road."

The ideological estrangement between Beijing and Moscow persisted after Khrushchev had been ousted by Leonid Brezhnev in 1964, and even reached the point of military clashes along the far eastern part of the Sino-Soviet border in 1969. In the 1970s, the Sino-Soviet conflict mostly occurred in the context of rivalry for influence in the Third World. It gradually dissipated after Mao's death and was formally ended when Mikhail Gorbachev visited Beijing in 1989. Today, China and (non-communist) Russia have generally friendly relations.

New Year's Day editorial in the CCP's most important publications, he was quoted as warning that "Stability and unity do not mean writing off class struggle; class struggle is the key link and everything else hinges on it."[17]

The ways in which Mao acted on his views about the persistence and intensity of class struggle in socialist society *and within* the communist party had momentous consequences for Chinese politics. Those views also reflect a number of important points where Mao Zedong Thought is at ideological odds with—or is at least a radical elaboration on—central elements of Marxism-Leninism.

First, consider the Maoist conclusion that a "bourgeoisie" could emerge within socialist society when, in fact, there was no longer a material basis for a capitalist class, since no property was privately owned and no one worked for an owner of a private business. For Mao, class—the basis of all Marxist theory—no longer depended on an individual's or group's relations to the means of production, but was more a matter of ideas, values, goals, behavior, and particularly the way in which they exercised authority over others.[18]

This new "bourgeoisie" included those within the communist party who no longer supported the revolution, but used the socialist system to enrich or empower themselves. The Yugoslav dissident Milovan Djilas called such fallen comrades "the New Class," in his classic 1957 critique of the Soviet Union and similar communist-party states.[19] Mao went a little farther: it was not just entrenched bureaucrats and party big-wigs who could fall victim to the bourgeois ideology of selfishness and individualism; everyone was at risk—even poor peasants, factory workers, and other usually stalwart supporters of the revolution.

Similarly, in the Maoist view, the term "proletariat" no longer applied only to industrial workers, but to all those—be they farmers, intellectuals, cadres—who were committed to the revolution in both thought and practice. Thus, the formal name of the Cultural Revolution was the "Great *Proletarian* Cultural Revolution," the goal of which was to rid China of all manifestations of bourgeois ideology and replace it with a truly proletarian culture that all of the people would embrace. To Mao, being "proletarian," reflected more of an ideological standpoint than membership in a specific economic class.

The second of Mao's elaborations on the idea of class struggle was his warning that, if left unchallenged, the newly-emerged bourgeoisie would eventually change China from "red" to "white"—or from socialist to capitalist. This leads to another of Mao's ideological innovations: the idea that socialism, once established, can degenerate and even retrogress back to capitalism. That was, in his view, exactly what had happened in the Soviet Union, and what the Cultural Revolution was designed to prevent from happening in China. The notion that such ideological retrogression was possible is contrary to more conventional Marxism, which saw history as inevitably and irreversibly moving in only one direction, toward socialism and communism.

"Permanent Revolution"

Another component of Mao Zedong Thought that logically derives from his theory of contradiction and his views on class struggle under socialism is his notion of "**permanent revolution**."[20] This is also another aspect of Maoism that many scholars argue distinguishes it from mainstream Marxism. In Mao's view, the process of revolution does not stop when the communist party seizes power, and "continuing the revolution" does not just mean putting into place new institutions and policies that reflect the goals of the revolution. For Mao, permanent revolution meant there would have to be revolutions *within* the revolution if human society was going to continue to make progress. At the outset of the Great Leap Forward, Mao declared,

> I stand for the theory of permanent revolution....In making revolution one must strike while the iron is hot—one revolution must follow another, the revolution must continually advance. The Hunanese often say, "Straw sandals have no pattern—they shape themselves in the making." ("Speech to the Supreme State Conference," 1958)

If the hot iron of revolution is left to cool off, it would harden and become an obstacle to change rather than its instrument. Mao's reference to the saying from Hunan (his native province) about straw sandals meant that although the purpose of the revolution (to build socialism and reach communism) is clear—as is the purpose of sandals (to protect the feet)—the actual process of achieving their purpose must be custom made to fit the circumstances (or the feet of the wearer). The revolution that worked at one historical moment will not fit the next, so the revolution must be continually remade.[21]

Much of Mao's rule over China can be seen as an application of his theory of permanent revolution: for example, the full-steam-ahead, don't-stop-to-consolidate approach to the collectivization of agriculture culminating in the formation of the radically egalitarian people's communes in 1958; and the all-out class warfare against the "representatives" of the bourgeoisie in the party during the Cultural Revolution.

But, in theory, Mao went even further with his views on permanent revolution. Not only would it be a feature of socialist society, but it would even continue into the era of communism: "Will there be revolutions in the future when all imperialists in the world are overthrown and all classes eliminated?...In my view, there will still be a need for revolution. The social system will still need to be changed and the term 'revolution' will still be in use" ("Speech at the Second Plenary Session of the Eighth Central Committee of the CCP," 1956). In 1962, he wrote, "The transition from socialism to communism is revolutionary....The transition from one stage of communism to another is also revolutionary...Communism will surely have to pass through many stages and many revolutions" ("A Critique of Soviet Economic," 1962).

Mao conceded that revolutions in the communist era "will not be of the same nature as those in the era of class struggle" ("Speech at the Second Plenary Session," 1956). How could they, since communism is, by definition, a classless society? But there would be scientific, technological, cultural revolutions—and even, he suggests, the need to "overthrow" many aspects of communist society when they impede further progress.

Communism will be an era of "uninterrupted development," which will be the new form of permanent revolution ("A Critique of Soviet Economic," 1962).

In a very un-Marxist mode, Mao several times even mused that communism would not be the ultimate destination of human social development. He did not speculate on what might lie beyond communism, but said that it, too, at some point "would come to an end." Even as he was preparing in March 1958 to launch China on the Great Leap Forward with the goal of reaching communism as its objective, Mao noted that "There is nothing in the world that does not arise, develop, and disappear. Monkeys turned into humans; human-kind arose; in the end, the whole human race will disappear, it will turn into something else; at that time the earth itself will also cease to exist. The earth must certainly be extinguished, the sun too will grow cold.... All things must have a beginning and an end." ("Talks at the Chengtu Conference," 1958).

"Seek Truth from Facts"

It may seem rather strange that a revolutionary best known for his utopian ideas and radical polices would also have a pragmatic side. But that is very much the case with Mao Zedong. Mao's pragmatism was a key part of his operational code.

One of Mao's most important essays is called "On Practice," written in 1939, and in which he explores at great length the Marxist-Leninist theory of knowledge (epistemology), or how it is that human beings come to learn about the world around them and determine truth from falsehood. Mao adamantly affirms that "social practice alone is the criterion of the truth" and that only by constant reengagement with concrete reality can a person claim to have true knowledge of anything. As he colorfully put it, "If you want to know the taste of a pear, you must change the pear by eating it yourself." He goes on to say, "If you want to know the theory and methods of revolution, you must take part in revolution" ("On Practice," 1939).

Not only was this one of Mao's guiding principles in developing his revolutionary strat-egy (including **guerrilla warfare**), but in the mid-1960s, it would also become part of his rationale for the Cultural Revolution. One of Mao's goals for that movement was to give the youth of China, born after Liberation and accustomed to a relatively easy life, an opportunity to "taste" revolution so that they would become worthy successors to the Maoist cause.

Mao was, of course, a strong believer in Lenin's point that "without revolutionary theory there can be no revolutionary movement" (*What Is to Be Done?*, 1905). But, in the Chairman's view, the only way to develop a *correct* theory was on the basis of practice, and the only way to make sure that it continued to be correct was to constantly subject it to practice, and, if need be, adjust the theory so that it more correctly reflected reality. Marxism, Mao said,

> emphasizes the importance of theory precisely and only because it can guide action. If we have a correct theory but merely prate about it, pigeonhole it and do not put it into practice, then that theory, however good, is of no significance. Knowledge begins with practice, and theoretical knowledge is acquired through practice and must then return to practice. ("On Practice," 1939)

Or, in another context, he pronounced simply that "No investigation, no right to speak!" ("Oppose Book Worship," 1930).

In stressing the importance of practice, experience, and investigation, Mao was arguing against those in the party leadership who approached any problem with an absolutely
fixed theory and refused to bend even if it was not working or proved counterproduc-
tive. Such people were called "dogmatists" because they treated *their interpretation of*
Marxism-Leninism as "dogma," or as absolutely authoritative and not to be disputed or
diverged from under any circumstances. He was also refuting the "empiricists" in the
party who thought theory was of no great importance in guiding practice but only looked
to their own experiences and the empirical facts of the immediate situation in deciding
policy.

How then, according to Mao, can one strike the right balance between theory and practice? Not surprisingly, the right balance comes from the *contradiction* between the two—
the unity of opposites that is the source of the development of all things.

During the period of the civil and anti-Japanese wars (1927–1949), Mao seemed to
come down on the side of practice being the most decisive factor. In two essays, written
in the 1940s, he used the phrase "seek truth from facts" (*shi shi qiu shi*) as a capsule summary of how communists are supposed to evaluate the correctness of their theories, and
that phrase was adopted as the motto for the school to train party leaders in Yan'an.[22] Mao
did point out that communists must be "guided by the general principles of Marxism-
Leninism" when deciding what conclusions to draw from the facts" ("Reform Our Study,"
1941). But in "On Practice," he makes the rather bold statement that "Marxism-Leninism
has in no way exhausted truth, but ceaselessly opens up roads to the knowledge of truth in
the course of practice." This quote from Mao and the slogan "seek truth from facts," not
surprisingly, were cited extensively during the early Deng Xiaoping era as guiding principles for the reform era.

Both chapters 2 and 3 note that one key source of Mao's success in the struggle for
national power was his willingness to modify policies, such as land reform in the communist base areas, that were not working, even if that meant adjusting the way in which
ideology was applied. In chapter 3, Frederick C. Teiwes discusses the "two broad tendencies" of Mao's approach to policy: "the 'revolutionary romantic' and the pragmatic." In his
view, it was pragmatism that characterized *most* of Mao's career as a revolutionary, but that
after the Hundred Flowers and particularly with the onset of the Great Leap Forward, the
romanticism took over.

But, even on the eve of the Cultural Revolution, the pragmatic Mao wrote: "Where do
correct ideas come from? Do they drop from the skies? No. Are they innate in the mind?
No. They come from social practice, and from it alone" ("Where Do Correct Ideas Come
From?," 1963). One could conclude that the latter Mao lost touch with his own good
advice to "seek truth from facts" as he became more isolated and detached from reality—
in fact, as will be discussed below, that is exactly what his successors, beginning with
Deng Xiaoping, did say about him.

Chinese Communism after Mao

Did Mao's death and the coming to power of Deng Xiaoping bring "the end of ideology"
in the PRC and a complete renunciation of Maoism? After all, Deng and his successors,
Jiang Zemin and Hu Jintao, have taken the country a long way down the "capitalist road"
that the Chairman decried ideologically and fought so hard to prevent. China is certainly
less ideological than it was in the Maoist era, but the Chinese Communist Party still swears
allegiance to "Marxism-Leninism-Mao Zedong Thought," and that ideology—although

having been reformulated in major ways—still provides the foundation of the operational code of China's leaders and defines the boundaries of what is permissible in Chinese politics.

Maoism after Mao

In 1956, Nikita Khrushchev, the leader of the Communist Party of the Soviet Union, gave a "Secret Speech" that depicted in great detail the crimes of his predecessor, Joseph Stalin. The speech sent shockwaves throughout the world, particularly the communist world. It set in motion the process of "de-Stalinization" during which Stalin was literally erased from the formal history of the USSR. It culminated in the removal of Stalin's embalmed corpse from the Mausoleum in Moscow's Red Square, where it had been on display next to that of Lenin (which is still there), and its burial in a grave near the wall of the Kremlin.

Nothing so drastic has happened to Mao in post-Mao China. Too much of the history of the Chinese Communist Party is bound up with the legacy of Mao Zedong for his successors, no matter how far they deviate from his ideology and policies, to repudiate him or his ideas completely. It has been remarked that Mao was Lenin and Stalin wrapped into one—meaning that he not only led the communist party to power, but that he also ruled the country for a long period. (Lenin died about six years after coming to power, while Stalin ruled the Soviet Union for nearly thirty years.) The CCP cannot totally disassociate itself from the legacy of Mao without seriously undermining its legitimacy and its claim to be China's rightful ruling party.

This was particularly true for Deng Xiaoping. Not only was he a veteran of the Long March, but he also was among the top leaders at the founding of the regime and backed some of Mao's most disastrous campaigns, including the Anti-Rightist movement and the Great Leap Forward. As chapter 3 notes, Deng was for a long time one of Mao's favorites among the top party leadership, and Mao protected him from suffering even worse harm when he was purged for ideological mistakes in both 1966 and 1976.

Yet it was politically critical for Deng to separate himself from Mao's most radical ideas and particularly from the Cultural Revolution as he undertook his program of market reform and opening the Chinese economy to the world. To that end, he engineered a nuanced reevaluation of Mao that criticized the Chairman's errors and praised his accomplishments. This reevaluation never became a "de-Maoification" campaign. As Deng put it: "We will not do to Chairman Mao what Khrushchev did to Stalin" ("Answers to the Italian Journalist Oriana Fallaci," 1980). The Chairman's embalmed remains are on solemn public display—and still attract huge crowds—in a Memorial Hall in the center of Tiananmen Square, behind which is a souvenir store selling all sorts of Mao trinkets. (See Box, **Maoism Outside of China.**)

In 1981, the CCP issued a lengthy document called "Resolution on Certain Questions in the History of Our Party since the Founding of the People's Republic of China." Chapters 3 and 4 both note the political significance of the Resolution. The Resolution concluded that Mao's achievements were much greater than his mistakes, and it also spends many pages providing an assessment of Mao Zedong Thought. It reaffirms that his ideology remains "the valuable spiritual asset of our party" and that "it will be our guide to action for a long time to come." The document presents an extensive catalog of the ways in which Mao "enriched and developed Marxism-Leninism, including his ideas about a rural based revolution that involved "encircling the cities from the countryside and finally winning countrywide victory"; his contributions to military theory, particularly guerrilla warfare

MAOISM OUTSIDE OF CHINA

In the 1960s, many student activists in the United States and Western Europe were enamored with Maoism. The Cultural Revolution, and the ideology that guided it, seemed tied to a worldwide struggle against oppressive authority, crass materialism, and imperialism—including the American war in Vietnam. They saw the Red Guards as kindred spirits in rebellion against stuffy professors, uptight administrators, and out-of-touch elders in general. After all, Chairman Mao had said things like "There are teachers who ramble on and on when they lecture; they should let their students doze off. If your lecture is no good, why insist on others listening to you? Rather than keeping your eyes open and listening to boring lectures, it is better to get some refreshing sleep. You don't have to listen to nonsense, you can rest your brain instead" ("Remarks at the Spring Festival," 1964).

Little did Mao's foreign admirers know of the terror being unleashed by the Red Guards against alleged "class enemies," many of whom were physically or psychologically brutalized, or the scale of cultural destruction that the young rebels caused.

A few Maoist organizations emerged outside of China from the tumult of the 1960s. Most of these have remained on the fringes of politics in their respective countries, including the Revolutionary Communist Party, USA, which was founded in 1975, or are now defunct. In a handful of countries, self-proclaimed Maoists have engaged in armed struggle against the government, the most active being in India, Nepal, and Peru.

The Communist Party of India (Maoist) and its People's Liberation Guerrilla Army have been waging an insurgency for more than twenty-five years and have recently become very active, mostly in the eastern part of the country. This organization is often called the "Naxalites" after the region in the state of West Bengal where it was founded in 1967. It occasionally carries out assassinations of politicians, attacks police offices to gain weapons, and robs banks. It is estimated to have 20,000 members, with bases in nearly half of India's twenty-eight states where it effectively controls large parts of the countryside. They draw supporters largely from among the *adivasis* (Sanskrit meaning, "original people") who are descendents of the first inhabitants of the Indian subcontinent. The *adivasis* live mostly in densely forested areas and are among the most impoverished and discriminated against groups in India—which makes them, particularly the young, receptive to the call to revolution of the Naxalites. Although India's Maoists have never seriously contended for power, they remain a source of considerable worry for the government, especially in the states where their operations are expanding.

In neighboring Nepal, a tiny nation in the Himalayan Mountains, a Maoist party actually won the most seats in parliamentary elections in April 2008. A coalition arrangement with two other parties gave the head of Communist Party of Nepal (Maoist) enough votes to be elected as the country's prime minister.

The Maoists had been fighting a violent "people's war" against Nepal's monarchy for ten years until signing a peace agreement in 2006. During the war, which claimed an estimated 13,000 lives, the rebels gained widespread support in the rural areas of Nepal, which is one of the world's poorest countries. The party's founder is Pushpa Kumal Dahal, a school teacher turned guerrilla fighter better known by his revolutionary name of Prachanda ("Fierce One"). Its ideology is officially called "Marxism-Leninism-Maoism-Prachanda Path," which reflects its leader's adaptation of communist theory, notably Mao Zedong's ideas about peasant revolution, to Nepal's particular situation, such as the combination of class and caste oppression. The Chinese Communist Party did not support the Maoist insurrection in Nepal because, from China's perspective, it was a destabilizing force in that part of the world.

Once the Nepali Maoists gave up armed struggle in order to participate in the democratic process, they had to tone down some of their most radical demands, but the party remains committed to pursuing social and economic justice. They also achieved one of their most important political aims: the abolition of the monarchy. In May 2008, the Kingdom of Nepal was renamed the Democratic Federal Republic of Nepal. Prachanda served as Nepal's prime minister for about a year before resigning in a dispute with the country's president over who had the power to appoint the army chief of staff.

Prachanda drew inspiration not only from the Chinese revolution, but also from another communist movement that claimed a Maoist ideological lineage: the Shining Path (*Sendero Luminoso*) in Peru. The Shining Path was established in the early 1980s, declaring that all of the world's ruling communist parties at the time, including China under Deng Xiaoping and the Soviet Union under Gorbachev, had become revisionist counter-revolutionary organizations. Shining Path remained loyal to the most radical variation of Maoist thought and practice, as developed by its founder-leader, philosophy professor Abimael Guzmán, known as Gonzalo. "Gonzalo Thought" had its roots in the writings of earlier twentieth century Peruvian revolutionaries and embodied elements based on the country's Indian heritage and culture. The Shining Path gained some support among poor peasants, but its extremely violent, often brutal, tactics, eroded its popularity. Guzmán and other top leaders of the movement were captured in the 1990s. The organization dwindled dramatically in size, but remains sporadically active in remote areas of the country.

and the need to develop a people's army; and *some* of his thoughts about guiding China through the transition to socialism.

The Resolution then focuses on "three basic points" that it says constitute "the living soul of Mao Zedong Thought" that are particularly of continuing relevance to the CCP in how it legitimizes its rule in China. The first is "seek truth from facts," which, as noted above, conveys the pragmatic side of Maoism. The second is the "mass line" as the guiding principle of the party in "all its work":

> As the vanguard of the proletariat, the party exists and fights for the interests of the people. But it always constitutes only a small part of the people, so that isolation from the people will render all the party's struggles and ideals devoid of content as well as impossible of success. To persevere in the revolution and advance the socialist cause, our party must uphold the mass line.

The final basic point of the "living soul" of Maoism is "independence and self-reliance." This encompasses the idea that China must chart it own way and must always "maintain our own national dignity and confidence and there must be no slavishness or submissiveness in any form in dealing with big, powerful or rich countries." This may sound somewhat ironic, given the depth of China's current integration in the international economy and its rise to great power status. But the idea of self-reliance persists in the PRC's contemporary statements on the overall orientation of its foreign policy.

The Resolution also warns against adopting "a dogmatic attitude towards the sayings of comrade Mao Zedong, to regard whatever he said as the unalterable truth which must be mechanically applied everywhere." It stresses that the CCP must acknowledge that Mao made serious blunders, especially in his later years, and that some of these were guided by parts of his ideology that simply were wrong. Mao is chastised for "enlarging the scope of class struggle and of impetuosity and rashness in economic construction." These errors were, of course, the basis of the three great tragedies of Maoist China from which the post-Mao leadership wants to cut the ideological cord: the Anti-Rightist campaign, the Great Leap Forward, and the Cultural Revolution.

Finally, as a way to depersonalize even the positive components of Mao Zedong Thought, the Resolution declares that the ideology of the CCP is "a crystallization of the collective wisdom" of the Chinese communist party, not the product of one person. "Many outstanding leaders of our party" made "important contributions" to "the scientific works of comrade Mao Zedong." Mao's problem was that he deviated from his own "scientific" ideas, as well as from the "collective wisdom" of the party leadership. In other words, we will all take credit for what has gone right since the founding of the PRC and the Chairman's good ideas; what went wrong, well, that was *his* fault and the result of *his* faulty ideas. This is still the official evaluation of Mao Zedong Thought in China. By establishing the principle that the guiding ideology of the CCP is the result of collective wisdom rather than the product of any single individual, the party was partly dethroning Mao, but also opening up the possibilities for further "important contributions" to Chinese communism.

Deng Xiaoping Theory

If Mao Zedong is often seen as a "revolutionary romantic" guided by a radical ideology and impervious to practical concerns, then Deng Xiaoping is, in contrast, viewed as the ultimate pragmatist who had little use for communist theory. Both are exaggerations that distort any thorough understanding of what made these two towering figures in modern Chinese history tick. As pointed out previously, Maoism has a significant pragmatic element, and the Chairman's dictum to "seek truth from facts" became an early watchword of the Deng regime and remains so today. Likewise, Deng Xiaoping did have a distinctive ideology that shaped his political choices and the way that he used his power.

Although he never took for himself the formal top positions in either the party or the state, Deng Xiaoping was often referred to in the Chinese media while he was alive as China's "paramount leader" and as the "architect of China's reform and opening up." After his death in 1997, "**Deng Xiaoping Theory**" was added into the CCP constitution, along with Marxism-Leninism and Mao Zedong Thought, as the party's guiding ideology. Deng Xiaoping Theory was said to be

> the outcome of the integration of the basic tenets of Marxism-Leninism with the practice of contemporary China and the features of the times, a continuation and development of Mao Zedong Thought under new historical conditions; it represents a new stage of development of Marxism in China, it is Marxism of contemporary China and it is the crystallized, collective wisdom of the Communist Party of China. It is guiding the socialist modernization of China from victory to victory. (General Program of the Constitution of the Communist Party of China)

Some of the central features of Deng's ideological contribution to the CCP are conveyed under the general rubric of "**Building Socialism with Chinese Characteristics**." Mao, it was inferred, had successfully led a Marxist-Leninist revolution with Chinese characteristics to power from the 1920s and leading China through the mid-1950s, when he started to make mistakes. Deng picked up not where Mao had *left off* when he died in 1976, but where he had *gone wrong*, beginning in the mid-1950s. He provided the CCP with the theory that correctly addressed the "basic questions concerning the building, consolidation and development of socialism in China," which is precisely where Mao failed.

Deng Xiaoping Theory gives absolute priority to economic development—"economic development is the center of party work" (under party leadership, of course)—while Mao Zedong Thought, though certainly not shunning that as a goal, put "politics in command." As Deng noted in 1984, in an off-handed slap at Mao, "What is socialism and what is Marxism? *We were not quite clear about this in the past.* Marxism attaches utmost importance to developing the productive forces.... One of our shortcomings after the founding of the People's Republic was that we didn't pay enough attention to developing the productive forces. Socialism means eliminating poverty. Pauperism is not socialism, still less communism" ("Build Socialism with Chinese Characteristics," 1984; emphasis added).

"Building Socialism with Chinese Characteristics" is the party's way of explaining in ideological terms the introduction of market reforms into China's economy and for letting aspects of capitalism (such as the profit motive and private ownership of businesses) be the driving force for the country's economic development. It is, in essence, the updated version of Deng's "cat theory," first expounded in 1962 when he said: "It doesn't matter if a cat is white or black, as long as it catches mice" as a way of advocating the use of any kind of economic policy in order to restore agricultural production after the Great Leap Famine. That sentiment got Deng into big political trouble with Mao (and branded as a capitalist roader) during the Cultural Revolution. Once he had returned to power in the late 1970s, Deng really let the capitalist cat loose and transformed the PRC's centrally planned economy into a mix of socialism and capitalism that since the 1990s has been called a "socialist market economy." The nature of that transformation and the extent of the marketization of China's economy is discussed in both chapters 4 and 7.

Deng Xiaoping Theory rationalizes the "socialist market economy" by saying that China is in the "primary," or "initial stage" of socialism. Based on an orthodox Marxist view that history inevitably passes through a sequence of stages of development, the *primary* stage of socialism is that which follows immediately after the political overthrow of the capitalist system. For some period of time, it would be unavoidable, in fact, absolutely necessary, to use many aspects of capitalism while building socialism. And this, it is implied, is where Mao Zedong (and his Thought) got it wrong. Although in the early 1950s, during the first period of communist rule in China, Mao said the PRC would have a mixed economy, he came to believe that the transition to socialism could happen much faster and all aspects of capitalism done away with much sooner (a reflection of his voluntarism) and began the country's full socialist transformation in 1954. In contrast, Deng is credited with correctly recognizing that socialist China, even in the late twentieth century and beyond, would have to use capitalist means to become developed enough to move on to the next stages of the socialist transition. Even more un-Maoist are some of the slogans often associated with Deng Xiaoping Theory, such as "Let some people get rich first" and "To get rich is glorious" (although he never used those exact words).

Deng was adamant that China would not become capitalist even if it used many aspects of a capitalist market economy to promote development. Rather, he insisted that "we can develop a market economy under socialism.... Developing a market economy does not mean practicing capitalism" ("We Can Develop a Market Economy under Socialism," 1979).

The critical difference between a socialist market economy and a capitalist market economy seems largely to be a matter of who has political power in the country. In Deng's view, in a capitalist country, the wealthy capitalists (owners of private property) dominate both the economic and political systems. In a socialist system, political power is in the hands of the vanguard communist party that represents the interests of the "people." It is the party that will make sure that the socialist market economy does not lead to the kind of exploitation and inequalities that mar a truly capitalist system and that the market part of the economy ultimately serves the goal of building socialism and achieving communism.

The Four Cardinal Principles

If "Building Socialism with Chinese Characteristics" conveys the economic heart of Deng Xiaoping Theory, the "Four Cardinal Principles" express its political essence.[23] The phrase "Four Cardinal Principles" comes from a lengthy speech that Deng gave in March 1979 at a forum on the Party's theoretical work very soon after he had consolidated his position as China's undisputed leader. In this context, "cardinal" means essential or fundamental.

The speech did not gather much attention outside of China at the time because most of the world was focused on the economic changes Deng was bringing to China. He had been named *Time* magazine's "Man of the Year" for 1978 (in the January 1, 1979, issue) and was grandly feted in an official visit to the United States in late January–early February of 1979. In retrospect, the speech was one of the most important Deng ever gave, and the "Four Cardinal Principles" are as essential as "Building Socialism with Chinese Characteristics" is to understanding Deng Xiaoping Theory.

The purpose of the forum at which Deng gave this speech was to set the ideological and political guidelines for the Party's shift in the focus of its work from the class struggle of the Cultural Revolution and late Maoist era to economic development. In that speech, Deng reiterated that modernization would be the Party's "main task for the present and for some time to come." He then laid out what he called the Four Cardinal Principles that were "the basic prerequisite for achieving modernization":

1. Upholding the socialist road.
2. Upholding the dictatorship of the proletariat.
3. Upholding the leadership of the Communist Party.
4. Upholding Marxism-Leninism and Mao Zedong Thought.

Deng asserted that only by following these principles in carrying out economic reform could the party be sure that it was fostering *socialist* modernization rather than promoting capitalism, as some in the party were contending would happen if China followed Deng's path. Deng also stressed that ideological reinforcement was urgently needed at that particular time, which coincided with the "Democracy Wall" movement of the late 1970s (see chapter 4). Deng warned in this speech of certain "incidents" incited by "bad elements" who raised slogans like "Give us human rights!" and set up organizations such as the "Democracy Forum." "Can we tolerate this kind of freedom of speech?" Deng asked. "No Party member…must ever waver in the slightest on this basic stand. To undermine any of the Four Cardinal Principles is to undermine the whole cause of socialism in China, the whole cause of modernization."

Deng went into great detail about the meaning and importance of each of the four principles. But they really all boil down to the principle of upholding the leadership of the communist party. It is the party that will keep China on the socialist road; it is the party that enforces the dictatorship of the proletariat; it is the party that interprets the current meaning of Marxism-Leninism–Mao Zedong Thought. And about party leadership, Deng declared:

> In the China of today we can never dispense with leadership by the Party and extol the spontaneity of the masses. Party leadership, of course, is not infallible, and the problem of how the Party can maintain close links with the masses and exercise correct and effective leadership is still one that we must seriously study and try to solve. But this can never be made a pretext for demanding the weakening or liquidation of the Party's leadership.

The Four Cardinal Principles do not reflect the kind of sharp break with Mao Zedong Thought that the make-way-for-capitalism emphasis of the "Building Socialism with Chinese Characteristics" does. In fact, the principles represent one of the clearer ideological continuities between the two leaders.

The Four Cardinal Principles are very similar to the "six criteria" that Mao laid out in the *revised* version of his 1957 speech, "On the Correct Handling of Contradictions among the People" during the Hundred Flowers movement. Mao said that these criteria should be used to distinguish between "fragrant flowers" (non-antagonistic contradictions) and "poisonous weeds" (antagonistic contradictions) when judging how to treat criticism of China's political system and leaders. The key distinction was whether the criticism was helpful or hurtful to six indisputable aspects of politics in the PRC, including the unity of "the people of all our nationalities"; the goal of "socialist transformation and socialist construction"; the people's democratic dictatorship; "democratic centralism"; "the leadership of the Communist Party," and "international socialist unity and the unity of the peace-loving people of the world." The Four Cardinal Principles is certainly a variation on a Maoist theme, and as Mao emphasized, "Of these six criteria, the most important are the two about the socialist path and the leadership of the Party."

During the era of his rule, Deng Xiaoping often invoked the Four Cardinal Principles, including in the aftermath of the Beijing Massacre in June 1989. In his "Address to Officers at the Rank of General and Above in Command of the Troops Enforcing Martial Law in Beijing," (June 9, 1989), Deng commented that

> It is not wrong to keep to the Four Cardinal Principles. If we have made a mistake, it is that we have not kept to them consistently enough and inculcated them as basic ideas in the people, the students and all cadres and Party members.... True, we have talked about keeping to those principles, conducting ideological and political work and combating bourgeois liberalization and mental pollution. But we have not talked about those things consistently.... The mistake was not in the principles themselves, but in the failure to keep to them consistently enough and to do a good job in education and in ideological and political work.

The Four Cardinal Principles were written into the CCP constitution in 1992 at the same time "Building Socialism with Chinese Characteristics" was added, which was a prelude to the formal inclusion of Deng Xiaoping Theory as part of the CCP's guiding ideology in 1999. The principles themselves, though not the phrase "Four Cardinal Principles," were incorporated into the Preamble of the constitution of the PRC in 1993, which gave them the force of law.[24] They remain today part of the Chinese Communist Party's core doctrine. As China's current leader, Hu Jintao, succinctly put it in his major report to the CCP's Seventeenth National Congress in October 2007, "The Four Cardinal Principles are the very foundation for building our country and the political cornerstone for the survival and development of the Party and the nation."

Understanding these two aspects of Deng Xiaoping Theory—"Building Socialism with Chinese Characteristics" and the "Four Cardinal Principles"—reveals the operational code of China's communist leaders as they continue to navigate the delicate balance between promoting an increasingly open economy and keeping a firm grip on power.

Jiang Zemin and the Theory of the "Three Represents"

Deng Xiaoping seems to have set, intentionally or otherwise, the precedent that the top leader of the Chinese Communist Party has the right to make an "original contribution" to the CCP's guiding ideology that conveys the theory behind major policy initiatives of that leader's administration. Both Jiang Zemin and Hu Jintao have done this, each praising and building on the contributions of his predecessors while adapting them to the priorities of the times.

Jiang's ideological innovation is called the "Three Represents," which he first expressed during an inspection tour of Guangdong province in February 2000. He noted at the time that CCP should always represent "the development trend of China's advanced productive forces, the orientation of China's advanced culture, and the fundamental interests of the overwhelming majority of the Chinese people."

What this boiled down to was a reaffirmation of Deng's modernization program and economic reforms. But there was also an important element of innovation that was made clear only through further explication and other formulations of the "Three Represents" and how it was actually put into practice. During his last term in office (1997–2003), Jiang took the bold step of leading the CCP to recognize the crucial role of the so-called **new social strata** as the most dynamic force in China's economic development. The new social strata includes groups that had been created during the process of market reform and internationalization, most importantly private entrepreneurs, managers and technical staff who work for foreign enterprises, as well as professionals, intellectuals, and others who are self-employed or work outside the public sector of the economy. The Three Represents theory was an ideological rationalization for allowing members of these strata to join the CCP. In other words, in a truly innovative and ironic adaptation of Marxism-Leninism: capitalists—as representatives of China's "most advanced productive forces"—were welcome in the communist party!

At a broader ideological level, Jiang's Three Represents implied that the CCP was moving to cast itself as the representative, not just of the working classes, but also of "the overwhelming majority of the Chinese people." Some scholars see this as reflecting an even more profound transformation of the CCP's self-image role from being a "revolutionary party" committed and empowered to lead the nation toward socialism and communism to that of a "governing party," which implies a less ideological claim about its purpose and possibly a greater sense of accountability to all citizens of the PRC.[25]

As discussed in chapter 4, when Jiang Zemin began to put forth the ideas of the Three Represents, he ran into significant political opposition from conservative party leaders who were particularly unhappy with such an open embrace of private entrepreneurs (they are never officially referred to as "capitalists") by the CCP. But in the end, he and his supporters prevailed. Jiang's theoretical contributions were inscribed in the party (2002) and state (2003) constitutions and the CCP's guiding ideology was formally dubbed "Marxism-Leninism, Mao Zedong Thought, Deng Xiaoping Theory, and the important thought of the Three Represents."

Hu Jintao's "Harmonious Socialist Society"

The constitutional enshrinement of the Three Represents took place at party and state congresses that were also the moments of transition in leadership from Jiang Zemin to Hu Jintao. Although there had been clear signs of political rivalry between Jiang and Hu, Hu has generally been effusive in his praise of his predecessor and his ideological contributions. The three-volume collection of *The Selected Works of Jiang Zemin* was published with great propaganda fanfare in 2006, followed by a national campaign to study Jiang's writings, aimed largely at party cadres.

While paying due respect to the "important thought of the Three Represents," Hu has also carved out an ideological niche of his own.[26] Soon after he had become CCP general secretary (2002) and PRC president (2003), Hu began to enunciate slogans and signal policy priorities with a definite populist tinge. Hu's brand of populism is very different from Mao's, which was mostly a matter of mobilizing the masses to take action in support of his agenda. In contrast, Hu is a populist in the sense of advocating policies that address some of the socio-economic downsides of China's three decades of spectacular growth: inequitable income distribution among people and regions; unemployment; and inadequate public services, particularly health care. Special emphasis is placed on combating rural poverty and narrowing the vast rural-urban gap. The country's very serious environmental problems and the necessity for sustainable development are also high on Hu's agenda.

The overall goal of these policy priorities is said to be to create a "harmonious socialist society." The underlying assumption is that unless these issues are addressed, social and political instability will increase and lead to disharmony. The extent of protests by displaced workers and discontented farmers in recent years has certainly influenced Hu's thinking.

The idea of a "harmonious socialist society" with its calls for "social justice" and "putting people first" is an implicit critique of Jiang Zemin's growth-at-any-cost and rather elitist economic strategy (and Deng Xiaoping's, as well). Hu has faced some resistance to his effort to shift the focus of the party's work in a more populist direction from those leaders who do not want resources diverted away from the more prosperous coastal areas and modern sectors of the economy.

Nevertheless, Hu Jintao's policy and ideological initiatives were formally endorsed at the 17th CCP Congress in late 2007. They were written into the party constitution with statements such as "The Communist Party of China leads the people in building a harmonious socialist society" added to the preamble. The more general formulation of Hu's contribution to the CCP ideology was presented as a "Scientific Outlook on Development" that "calls for comprehensive, balanced and sustainable development." The constitution goes as far as saying this is "a scientific theory that is in the same line as Marxism-Leninism, Mao Zedong Thought, Deng Xiaoping Theory and the important thought of Three Represents and keeps up with the times."

But it has not yet been appended by hyphen to the CCP's official pantheon of guiding theories. It would be unseemly while he is still in office to give Hu's ideological contribution to Chinese communism the same status as that of Marx, Lenin, Mao, Deng, and Jiang; for the same reason, Hu's name does not appear in association with the "Scientific Outlook on Development." Perhaps that will come with his retirement in 2012. Nonetheless, it is quite a political accomplishment for him to get his ideas planted in the party's governing document after just five years as leader.

Conclusion: Ideology in a Changing China

Much has been written about the increasing irrelevance of communist ideology in the People's Republic of China. Yet the ruling party (with about 76 million members) still assigns a high priority to Marxism-Leninism and its Chinese adaptations. There is a Central Party School in Beijing, which all mid- and high-ranking party cadres must attend for a few months to a few years to study a variety of subjects, including ideology. The CCP often convenes "theoretical work" conferences, especially when its ideology has been given a new wrinkle like the "Three Represents."

In the Maoist era, the CCP published a monthly ideological journal called *Red Flag* (*Hong Qi*). The party still has a monthly publication devoted to ideology, but the journal's title, *Seek Facts* (*Qiu Shi*), is more appropriate to the times.

And there are campaigns to publicize ideology among the population as a whole, often in a less direct Marxist-Leninist guise, such as the campaigns to promote various types of "civilization" that the CCP says it is trying to create, including "material civilization" (modernization and economic reform) and "spiritual civilization" (cultural pride, patriotism, ethical behavior, abiding by the law).[27] The party is cast as the vanguard in the building of these civilizations and the only party that can lead the entire people of China toward the bright future they hold. Not exactly the same as building socialism and reaching communism under the party's wise leadership, but the idea is very similar, just packaged for broader appeal.

The CCP has also injected a strong element of nationalism into the legitimizing ideology of the party-state. Many scholars have pointed to the CCP's efforts to portray itself not only as the manager of China's great economic success (and the only thing standing between prosperity and great chaos), but also as the guardian of the nation's sovereignty and the promoter of its international image.[28] At the founding of the PRC in 1949, Chairman Mao proclaimed, "The Chinese people have stood up!" after more than a century of humiliation and exploitation by foreign powers. And whatever one can say about the terrible costs of Mao's rule, he did found a nation that has stood on its own and greatly elevated its stature in the world. The CCP can still draw on that deep reservoir of legitimacy.

But it also can, and does, point to more contemporary triumphs of the Chinese nation, such as the hosting of the 2008 Beijing Olympics and the 2010 World Expo in Shanghai. At times, the party-state has fanned (and controlled) anti-Japanese or anti-American sentiment to arouse the patriotic spirit of the Chinese people. The message is clear: the CCP was the savior of the nation, and remains the protector of its interests. This message is supplemented by official presentations of the greatness, uniqueness, and antiquity of Chinese culture and civilization.

Appeals to patriotism, nationalism, and cultural pride as a way to enhance legitimacy and generate popular support are by no means unique to the CCP as a political party. But the part it plays in sustaining the power of the ruling party in a one-party state is particularly noteworthy. There are also those who worry that the reliance of the CCP on nationalist appeals might lead the PRC to a more aggressive foreign or military policy in order to enhance its image among its citizens.

There are also important ideological debates within the Chinese Communist Party. "**Inner-party democracy**"—meaning tolerance and even encouragement of the expression of diverse points of view—has become much more substantive in the post-Mao era and increasingly so in recent years. As chapter 7 highlights, there is a measure of pluralism *within* the framework of communist party rule when it comes to exploring different political and economic priorities. The trend toward a more collective leadership versus one-person rule (as was the situation in the Mao and Deng eras) has institutionalized (limited) ideological diversity within the CCP.

Party leaders on the so-called New Left take the position that the CCP has strayed too far from its socialist ideals, particularly egalitarianism. They find some comfort in Hu Jintao's priority to create a "harmonious" society. Other leaders (the "New Right") staunchly defend the Chinese version of "**neoliberalism**" that favors free market–friendly policies and decries most state interventions in the economy even to ensure more equitable outcomes. Then there are the "conservatives" who emphasize social stability, morality, political order, and economic growth.[29] If this sounds similar to ideological debates in the United States, that is, indeed, the case—except for the most important fact that, in China, this debate occurs within a context that excludes democratic political competition. The "Four Cardinal Principles" and the sanctity of communist party leadership are still very much in effect as limits to whatever pluralism and democracy may be emerging with in the CCP.

Some scholars have argued the CCP is not really a communist party anymore, except in name. They say that the party has moved so far from Marxism-Leninism in practice that it is more accurate to analyze its ideology in an entirely different framework. The case has been made, for example, that the prevailing ideology of the leadership in China is **fascism**,[30] an extreme right-wing ideology based on assertive (even aggressive) nationalism, the glorification of national culture, a strong state with a highly centralized leadership, one dominant political party that "represents" all the people, and a partnership between the government and the private sector to enhance the country's economic and military power. Italy under Mussolini was a fascist state; the ideology of Nazi Germany (national socialism) was a variant of fascism with a virulent strain of racism at its core.

The focus of this chapter has been on the *official* ideology of the Chinese Communist Party and how that ideology has both shaped and reflected different stages in the political development of the CCP and the PRC. But there are multiple other ideological influences that are also much in evidence in the PRC, and some of them should be noted, at least in passing, as they are likely to play an increasingly important role in the politics of a rapidly changing China.

The most potent and pervasive contending ideology is probably "consumerism." Can the preoccupation with buying and acquiring things of value (and increasing value) really be considered an ideology? Yes, to the extent that many people take it as a guide to action and a measure of their own value. Contrary as this is to any standard of Marxism, it is hard to deny that this is the most prevalent ideology in China today. As one scholar of Chinese culture noted, the philosophical essence of contemporary China could be conveyed as "I shop, therefore, I am."[31] A slew of other analyses of China from the 1990s to the present convey the same conclusion in catch-all phrases such as the PRC meaning the "People's Republic of Capitalism," or other characterizations like "From Communism to Consumerism," "Cashing in on Communism," "From MAOsim to MEism," and the "Great Mall of China"[32] to describe life and values in the PRC today.

But is consumerism a *political* ideology? Not directly, but it certainly has political implications. If many of the Chinese people, and especially the growing middle class, are fixated on improving their material lives (and who can blame them after decades of deprivation?), then that is a message the ruling party has to pay heed to in order to maintain popular support, which it seems to have done. Opinion polls show that private entrepreneurs, in general, are strong supporters of the CCP and the status quo.[33]

Religion is also remerging in China as a central focus in the lives of many citizens. Religion is not a political ideology *per se*, but, as is evident in the world today, it can become highly politicized. For most of the Mao era, religious organizations were severely repressed or closely controlled by the party-state. The constraints on religion have been gradually loosened during the reform era. The PRC constitution has long affirmed freedom of religion, but with restrictive clauses such as the state only "protects *normal* religious activities" (emphasis added). In 2007, the Chinese Communist Party constitution was amended to mention religion for the first time. Although the party remains officially atheist, the General Program of the CCP as laid out in the constitution now states "The Party strives to fully implement its basic principle for its work related to religious affairs, and rallies religious believers in making contributions to economic and social development."[34] This amendment may reflect the CCP's increasing tolerance of religion; it may also be an effort to co-opt believers into supporting the party. If a communist party can embrace capitalists, why not Christians as well?

Estimates of the number of religious believers in China varies widely. Officially, it is given as 100 million, including Buddhists, Muslims, Christians, and Taoists. Other sources claim that there are more than 130 million Christians alone, which would be almost twice the size of the membership of the communist party.[35] In any case, religion is growing in China, and has already become an ideological rival of the CCP. The fierce repression of the quasi-religious movement, Falun Gong, that began in 1999 (see chapter 4) clearly showed the limits of the party's tolerance for alternative belief systems that become too popular and too-well organized. Religious identities also pose a challenge to the regime in Tibet and Xinjiang (see chapters 14 and 17).

Then there's democracy. This is the one ideology that it would be hard for the communist party to incorporate or co-opt without changing its very essence. To acknowledge the rights of citizens, the accountability of leaders, the rule of law, and the political competition that are the core values of democracy are inconsistent with the CCP's claim to be *the* ruling party and to exercise the "leading role" in all aspects of Chinese society.

Organized public expressions of demands for democratization have been nearly non-existent since the Tiananmen crackdown in June 1989. The one notable exception was the effort to establish a China Democracy Party in 1999: although they followed the rules for registering a new organization, the leaders of the party were arrested and sent to prison for endangering state security. But in recent years, advocates of democracy, particularly intellectuals, have been increasingly active in print and at conferences, and are allowed to do so as long as their musings remain theoretical. Given the deepening of the PRC's interdependence with the global community and the rise in the living standards and educational level of its people, it is quite likely that the time will come when the leadership of the communist party will again have to decide how to respond to the challenge of the "democratic idea."[36]

Notes

1. Franz Schurmann, *Ideology and Organization in Communist China* (Berkeley: University of California Press, 1966).

2. Alexander L. George, *"The "Operational Code": A Neglected Approach to the Study of Political Leaders and Decision-Making* (Santa Monica, CA: The Rand Corporation, 1967).

3. See John W. Lewis and Xue Litai, "Social Change and Political Reform in China: Meeting the Challenge of Success," *China Quarterly* 176 (December 2003): 926–942.

4. All quotations from the works of Marx, Engels, Lenin, Mao, Deng, et al., will be cited by title and date in the text or parenthetically rather than in a reference note. All of these works are easily accessible online via such web sites as "The Marxist Internet Archive" (http://www.marxists.org/).

5. See Lars T. Lih, *Lenin Rediscovered: What Is to Be Done? In Context* (Boston: Brill, 2006).

6. Arif Dirlik, *The Origins of Chinese Communism* (New York: Oxford University Press, 1989), chap. 1.

7. Raymond F. Wylie, *The Emergence of Maoism: Mao Tse-tung, Ch'en Po-ta, and the Search for Chinese Theory, 1935–1945* (Stanford, CA: Stanford University Press, 1980).

8. Schurmann, *Ideology and Organization*, 21.

9. See, for example, Jung Chang and Jon Halliday, *Mao: The Unknown Story* (New York: Knopf, 2005).

10. Sergeï Khrushchev, ed., trans. by George Shriver, *Memoirs of Nikita Khrushchev*, Vol. 3, *Statesman (1953–54)* (College Park: Pennsylvania State University Press, 2007), 405.

11. See, for example, Daniele Albertazzi and Duncan McDonnell, *Twenty-first Century Populism: The Spectre of Western European Democracy* (New York and London: Palgrave Macmillan, 2007).

12. As cited in Stuart R. Schram, *China Quarterly* 49 (Jan.–Mar. 1972): 76–78.

13. Brantly Womack, "The Party and the People: Revolutionary and Post-Revolutionary Politics in China and Vietnam," *World Politics* 39, no. 4 (July 1987): 479–507.

14. See, for example, Maurice J. Meisner, *Marxism, Maoism, and Utopianism: Eight Essays* (Madison: University of Wisconsin Press, 1982).

15. Besides "The Foolish Old Man," the other two constantly read articles were "Serve the People," in which Mao lauds the sacrifice for the revolutionary cause of a common soldier, and "In Memory of Norman Bethune," in which Mao praises a Canadian doctor who came to China to aid the revolution (and died there) as a example of proletarian internationalism.

16. Stuart R. Schram, *The Thought of Mao Tse-tung* (New York: Cambridge University Press, 1989), 84.

17. Cited in Tang Tsou, "Mao Tse-tung Thought, the Last Struggle for Succession, and the Post-Mao Era," *China Quarterly*, no. 70 (1977): 518.

18. See Franz Schurmann, "On Revolutionary Conflict," *Journal of International Affairs* 23, no. 1 (1969): 36–53.

19. Milovan Djilas, *The New Class: An Analysis of the Communist System* (New York: Praeger, 1957).

20. For excellent discussions of this topic, see Nick Knight, *Rethinking Mao: Explorations in Mao Zedong Thought* (Lanham, MD: Lexington Book, 2007), 225ff; and Stuart R. Schram, "Mao Tse-tung and the Theory of the Permanent Revolution, 1958–69," *China Quarterly* 46 (June 1971): 221–244.

21. Schram, "Mao Tse-tung and the Theory of the Permanent Revolution".

22. "On the New Democracy," 1940, and "Reform Our Study," 1941; see Deng Xiaoping, "Hold High The Banner of Mao Zedong Thought and Adhere to the Principle of Seeking Truth from Facts," September 16, 1978.

23. In yet another twist of ideological phrasing, Deng Xiaoping Theory is often summed up as consisting of "one central task, two basic points," the one central task being economic development, and the two basic points of upholding the Four Cardinal Principles and the policy of market reform and opening to the outside world.

24. The PRC Constitution uses the phrase, "**people's democratic dictatorship,**" rather than "dictatorship of the proletariat." This is more than semantics, but, essentially, the two terms imply the same thing: that there are those in society over whom dictatorship needs to be exercised.

25. Joseph Fewsmith, "Studying the Three Represents," *China Leadership Monitor* 8 (Fall 2003).

26. Heike Holbig, "Remaking the CCP's Ideology: Determinants, Progress, and Limits under Hu Jintao," *Journal of Current Chinese Affairs*, 38, no. 3 (2009): 35–61.

27. Nicholas Dynon, " 'Four Civilizations' and the Evolution of Post-Mao Chinese Socialist Ideology," *The China Journal* 60 (July 2008): 83–110.

28. See, for example, Peter Hayes Gries, *China's New Nationalism: Pride, Politics, and Diplomacy*. (Berkeley: The University of California Press, 2004).

29. Peter Moody, *Conservative Thought in Contemporary China* (Lanham, MD: Lexington Books, 2007).

30. Michael Ledeen, "Beijing Embraces Classical Fascism," *Far Eastern Economic Review* (May 2008); A. James Gregor, *A Place in the Sun: Marxism and Fascism in China's Long Revolution* (Boulder, CO: Westview Press, 2000).

31. Geremie Barmé, "Soft Porn, Packaged Dissent and Nationalism: Notes on Chinese Culture in the 1990's," *Current History* (September 1993): 584–558.

32. See, for example, the Discovery Channel TV series "The People's Republic of Capitalism" (2008).

33. Jie Chen and Bruce J. Dickson, "Allies of the State: Democratic Support and Regime Support among China's Private Entrepreneurs," *The China Quarterly* 196 (December 2008): 780–804.

34. This was added to the Constitution of the Communist Party of China in October 2007.

35. "Sons of Heaven: Christianity in China," *The Economist*, October 2, 2008.

36. See William A. Joseph, "China," in *Introduction to Comparative Politics*, 5th ed. (Boston: Wadsworth Cengage Learning, 2009).

Suggested Readings

Brugger, Bill. *Chinese Marxism in Flux, 1978–84: Essays on Epistemology, Ideology, and Political Economy*. Armonk, NY: M. E. Sharpe, 1985.

Chun, Lin. *The Transformation of Chinese Socialism*. Durham, NC: Duke University Press, 2006.

Dirlik, Arif, Healy, Paul Michael, and Nick Knight, eds. *Critical Perspectives on Mao Zedong's Thought*. 2nd ed. Amherst, NY: Humanity Books, 1997.

Joseph, William A. *The Critique of Ultra-Leftism in China, 1958–1981*. Stanford, CA: Stanford University Press, 1984.

Knight, Nick. *Rethinking Mao: Explorations in Mao Zedong's Thought*. Lanham, MD: Lexington Books, 2007.

Meisner, Maurice. *Mao Zedong: A Political and Intellectual Portrait*. New York: Polity, 2007.

Misra, Kalpana. *From Post-Maoism to Post-Marxism: The Erosion of Official Ideology in Deng's China*. New York: Routledge, 1998.

Schram, Stuart R. *The Thought of Mao Tse-tung*. New York: Cambridge University Press, 1989.

Sun, Yan. *The Chinese Reassessment of Socialism, 1976–1992*. Princeton, NJ: Princeton University Press, 1995.

Wakeman, Frederic, Jr. *History and Will: Philosophical Perspectives of Mao Tse-tung's Thought*. Berkeley, CA: University of California Press, 1973.

Womack, Brantly. *Foundations of Mao Zedong's Political Thought, 1917–1935*. Honolulu, HI: The University Press of Hawaii, 1982.

Wylie, Raymond F. *The Emergence of Maoism: Mao Tse-tung. Ch'en Po-ta, and the Search for Chinese Theory, 1935–1945*. Stanford, CA: Stanford University Press, 1980.

6

China's Communist Party-State: The Structure and Dynamics of Power

Cheng Li

Ever since the founding of the People's Republic of China (PRC) in 1949, the Chinese Communist Party (CCP) has been the country's ruling party. With the exception of a few tumultuous years during the early phases of the Cultural Revolution, the ultimate source of political power in China has always been the Communist Party. Indeed, for the past six decades, power struggles within the CCP leadership have been the only serious instances of political contention in the country. With more than 76 million members, the CCP is currently the world's largest ruling political party, and only the Korean Workers' Party of North Korea has held on to power for longer.

The CCP is not willing to give up its monopoly on political power to experiment with multi-party democracy, nor do Party leaders appear interested in moving toward a Western-style system based on a separation of power between the executive, legislative, and judicial branches of government. This does not mean, however, that the Chinese Communist Party is a stagnant institution that has been completely resistant to political change. On the contrary, the CCP has experienced a number of profound transformations in terms of the recruitment of party elites, institutional reforms, and ideological changes. It would also be an oversimplification to assert that there is a complete absence of checks and balances in the Chinese political system. The CCP leadership today is by no means a monolithic group whose members all share the same ideology, political background, and policy preferences.

This chapter argues that two main political factions or coalitions within the CCP leadership are currently competing for power, influence, and control over policy initiatives. These two coalitions represent the interests of different socioeconomic classes as well as different geographical regions, thus creating something approximating a mechanism of checks and balances in the decision-making process. This development reflects an important transition away from the political system that existed throughout the first four decades of the PRC, one that relied on the arbitrary decision-making power of an individual leader, notably Mao Zedong, then Deng Xiaoping. Today, Chinese politics are characterized by a system of collective leadership, or what the Chinese call "inner-party democracy," which functions according to commonly accepted rules and norms such as term limits and regional representation. This experiment provides only limited political choices for the party establishment. However, the gradual evolution of this new system of inner-party bipartisanship may pave the way for greater transformations within the Chinese political system in the years to come.

This chapter aims to highlight both the sources of continuity in China's long-standing party-state system and some of the more recent and profound changes in the PRC's political landscape. An analysis of the structure and dynamics of power in China will not only reveal how the world's most populous country is governed, but will also provide valuable assessments concerning the future political trajectory of this emerging world power.

The Structure of China's Party-State

The Chinese Communist Party describes the history of its leadership in terms of generations. Mao Zedong was the core of the first generation of PRC leaders, Deng Xiaoping the core of the second, and Jiang Zemin the core of the third. Current CCP General Secretary Hu Jintao is a prominent member of the fourth generation. Despite the dramatic changes in ideology and policy over the course of these generations, the CCP has always explicitly maintained that it plays the "leading role" in the state and society and therefore has the power to command the government, the media, the legal system, and the military.

By design, the top leaders of the Chinese Communist Party have always held the most important positions in the state (or government) concurrently, including president of the PRC, premier (or prime minister) of the State Council (the government cabinet), the chair of the National People's Congress (NPC, the legislature of the PRC), and chair of the Central Military Commission (CMC). Leading party cadres at various levels—provincial, municipal, county, and township—concurrently serve as officials in local government organizations, and usually occupy the highest posts in the government or local People's Congress. The top party leader—called the secretary—is the real "boss" at both the national and local levels of leadership.

In a very real sense, the institutions of party and state are intimately intertwined, which is why political systems such as the PRC (and previously, the Soviet Union) are referred to as communist party-states. The constitution of the People's Republic of China is rather ambiguous about where supreme political power truly lies, but in practice the communist party is unequivocally in charge at all levels. The state—or government—operates merely as the executor of decisions made by the party.[*]

Although high-ranking Chinese leaders have sporadically called for a greater separation between the party and the state, the overwhelming trend of the last two decades has been to consolidate and revitalize the party rather than fundamentally change the communist party-state system. The new catchphrase of the Chinese leadership under Hu Jintao is "enhance the governing capacity of the ruling party." This means that party officials, especially young rising stars at various levels of the leadership, often simultaneously serve in important positions within both the party and the government (including the People's Congress).

Two important observations can be made regarding the party-state structure in present-day China. First, the party has the power to make all of the state's most important personnel and policy decisions. Second, notwithstanding the party's leading decision-making role,

---

[*] The PRC does have eight political parties other than the CCP, which are often collectively referred to as the "democratic parties." They include: the Revolutionary Committee of the Chinese Nationalist Party; the China Democratic League; the China National Democratic Construction Association; the China Association for Promoting Democracy; the Chinese Peasants' and Workers' Democratic Party; the China Zhi Gong Dang; the Jiu San Society; and the Taiwan Democratic Self-Government League. These parties are too small to compete with or challenge the CCP in any meaningful way, with membership ranging from 2,100 (Taiwan Democratic Self-Government League) to 181,000 (China Democratic League) as of 2007.

many important policy discussions, as well as most activities relating to policy implementation, take place in or through *government* institutions, not CCP organizations. In order to understand the complex relationship existing between the CCP and the PRC government, it is essential to grasp the basic structure of both the party and the state.

The National Congress of the CCP

The organizational structure of the Chinese Communist Party at the national level is presented in Figure 6.1. The **National Congress of the CCP**, which convenes for about two weeks once every five years, is the most important political convention in the country. There were two types of delegates to the most recent party congress, which met in October 2007: regular and invited. The 2,213 regular delegates came from thirty-eight constituencies. This group included delegates from China's thirty-one province-level administrations, a delegation of ethnic Taiwanese, a delegation from the central departments of the party, a delegation from the ministries and commissions of the central government, a delegation from the major state-owned enterprises, a delegation comprised of representatives from China's large banks and other financial institutions, a delegation from the People's Liberation Army (PLA), and a delegation from the **People's Armed Police**. The fifty-seven invited delegates, who are also eligible to vote, are usually retired party elders and can be considered China's equivalent of the "superdelegates" of the Democratic Party in the United States.

The party congress elects the Central Committee (currently 371 members) and the **Central Commission for Discipline Inspection** (127 members). In *theory*, the Central

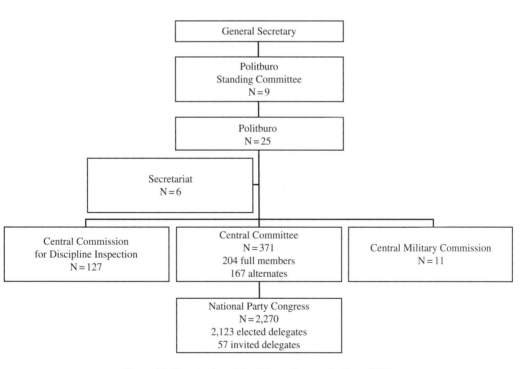

Figure 6.1 Organization of the Chinese Communist Party (2007)

Committee then elects the Politburo (25 members), the Politburo Standing Committee (9 members), the general secretary of the CCP, and the Central Military Commission (11 members). In *practice*, however, the process is top down rather than bottom up: members of these leading organs of the party guide the selection of members to the lower-level leadership bodies such as the Central Committee, which then "approves" the slate of candidates for higher-level positions such as the next Politburo and its Standing Committee.

According to the CCP Constitution, the Central Committee should convene at least once per year in meetings called plenums or plenary sessions. Generally, all full members and alternate members attend these sessions. Top officials in CCP central organs, government ministries, provincial administrations, and the military who are not members of the Central Committee are also invited to attend the plenary sessions as nonvoting participants. Plenary sessions provide an opportunity for the announcement of new policy initiatives and major personnel appointments. For example, the Central Committee Plenum held in December 1978 adopted Deng Xiaoping's reform and opening proposals, and this landmark meeting is often considered the turning point in CCP history from an emphasis on revolution to reform. Also of special importance was the 4th Plenary of the 16th Central Committee, held in September 2004, where Hu Jintao was appointed to replace Jiang Zemin as the chair of the Central Military Commission, signifying the completion of a power transition from the third generation to the fourth.

As suggested above, to call the Central Committee's selection of the Politburo an election is something of a misnomer, since they are actually selected by either the outgoing Politburo Standing Committee or, in the recent past, by powerful political figures known as "strongmen" or paramount leaders, such as Deng Xiaoping. Nevertheless, it would be wrong to assert that there is no intra-party competition for Central Committee seats. Since the 1982 National Congress of the CCP, the Party has followed the method of "more candidates than available seats" (*cha'e xuanju*) for the election of the Central Committee. For example, if the top leaders plan to have a 300-member Central Committee, they may place 310 names on the ballot. The ten candidates who receive the lowest number of votes will be eliminated. Party leaders claim that there will be an increasing number of candidates in future elections to the Central Committee. It is possible that this method will also be applied to the selection of the Politburo, the next organization up in the party's power structure, in the near future. These inner-party elections are important components of the CCP's broader political reform strategy to gradually make China's party-state system more open, competitive, and representative, without weakening its "leading role."

The Central Commission for Discipline Inspection, while less important than the Central Committee, can play a crucial role in monitoring and punishing abuses of power, corruption and other wrongdoings committed by party officials. Lower level party organizations, including provincial, municipal, and county-level bodies, also have discipline inspection commissions that report directly to the commission one level above them. The chiefs of the local discipline inspection commissions are usually not selected from the localities that they serve, but are transferred in from elsewhere. This practice is in accordance with traditional Chinese custom of the "**law of avoidance**" that prohibited imperial officials from being stationed in their home provinces in order to reduce the possibility of favoritism and region-based factionalism.

The Secretariat

The **Secretariat** is an important leadership body that handles the Party's routine business and administrative matters. Secretariat members meet daily and are responsible for coordinating the country's major events and important meetings as well as top leaders' foreign and domestic travel. The more powerful Politburo and Standing Committee, by comparison, meet only once a month and once a week, respectively. Members of the Secretariat, like members of the Standing Committee, all live in Beijing. Some Politburo members reside in other cities, where they serve as provincial or municipal party chiefs. The current Secretariat has six members, three of whom also serve as members of the Politburo, with one serving concurrently on the Standing Committee.

The Secretariat supervises the work of the General Office of the CCP (its administrative coordinating body) as well as the party's four central departments—the **Organization Department**, the Publicity (or Propaganda) Department, the United Front Work Department, and the International Liaison Department. The current directors of the General Office, the Organization Department, and the Publicity Department also serve on the Secretariat. The Organization Department determines the personnel appointments of several thousand high-ranking leadership (or cadre) positions in the party, government, and military, as well as in large business firms, key universities, and other institutions. These positions are part of the *nomenklaturā* ("name list") system that was adopted from the Soviet communist party. Control of the cadre appointment process is one of the CCP's most important sources of power. The Publicity Department is primarily responsible for propaganda and controlling the media. The United Front Work Department deals with issues concerning Taiwan, Hong Kong, and Macau, as well as ethnic and religious issues such as Tibetan affairs. The mission of the International Liaison Department is to establish contacts with foreign political parties; it was more important and active when there were more communist parties in the world.

The Politburo and the Standing Committee

Among the twenty-five members of the current Politburo (or Political Bureau), seven primarily represent Party organizations, ten come from government organizations, two from the military, and six from province-level administrative units. Table 6.1 lists the backgrounds of the nine members of the Politburo who were elected to the country's most powerful leadership body, the Standing Committee, in 2007. These individuals hold, concurrently with their positions on the Standing Committee and Politburo, the most important offices in the party-state, including the presidency and premiership of the PRC, the chair of the National People's Congress, and other important posts in the offices responsible for propaganda, party discipline, and domestic law enforcement. Party General Secretary Hu Jintao serves simultaneously as President of the PRC and Chairman of the CMC.

An analysis of the composition of the Central Committee formed in 2007, especially the Secretariat, Politburo, and its Standing Committee, reveals two important trends. The first has to do with relations between the central and local governments and the second concerns the role of the military in domestic politics.

The Rise in Local Representation

An overwhelming majority of China's top national leaders have advanced their careers through experience in provincial leadership posts. All nine members of the Standing Committee, save Premier Wen Jiabao, served as provincial party secretaries and/or governors prior to their ascent to the supreme decision-making body. Since the reform era began in 1978 the most important political credential for a top leadership position has been experience as a provincial-level party secretary. Former party leader Jiang Zemin was promoted to general secretary of the CCP in 1989 from the post of party secretary of Shanghai (where he had been credited with the "successful" handling of pro-democracy demonstrations). Hu Jintao had served as party secretary in both Guizhou and Tibet before being promoted to the

Table 6.1 The Politburo Standing Committee elected by the 2007 National Party Congress

Name	Concurrent Main Posts	Year Born	Birthplace	Educational Background	Provincial Leadership Experience
Hu Jintao	CCP Secretary General, PRC President, Chairman of Central Military Commission	1942	Anhui	B.A. Engineering Tsinghua Univ.	Party Secretary of Guizhou, Tibet
Wu Bangguo	Chairman of National People's Congress	1941	Anhui	B.A. Engineering Tsinghua Univ.	Party Secretary of Shanghai
Wen Jiabao	Premier	1942	Tianjin	M.A. Engineering Beijing Institute of Geology	None
Jia Qinglin	Chairman of the Chinese People's Political Consultative Conference	1940	Hebei	B.A. Engineering Hebei Institute of Engineering	Party Secretary and Mayor of Beijing, Governor of Fujian
Li Changchun	Secretary of Central Committee of Ethical and Cultural Construction	1944	Liaoning	B.A. Engineering Harbin Institute of Technology	Governor of Liaoning, Party Sec. and Governor of Henan, Party Sec. of Guangdong
Xi Jinping	PRC Vice President, Executive Member of the Secretariat	1953	Shaanxi	Ph.D. Law Tsinghua University	Governor of Fujian, Governor and Party Sec. of Zhejiang, Party Sec. of Shanghai
Li Keqiang	Executive Vice Premier	1956	Anhui	Ph.D. Economics Beijing University	Governor and Party Secretary of Henan, Party Secretary of Liaoning
He Guoqiang	Secretary of Central Committee for Discipline Inspection	1943	Hunan	B.A. Engineering Beijing Institute of Chemical Engineering	Governor of Fujian, Party Secretary of Chongqing
Zhou Yongkang	Secretary of Central Commission of Political Science and Law	1942	Jiangsu	B.A. Engineering Beijing Institute of Petroleum	Party Secretary of Sichuan

Standing Committee in 1992. The two youngest members—and rising stars—of the Standing Committee at present, Xi Jinping and Li Keqiang, both served as party secretaries in two province-level administrations.

The increase in the percentage of members with experience as provincial leaders in the Politburo over the past fifteen years is shown in Figure 6.2. The fact that over three-fourths of current Politburo members have leadership experience as provincial chiefs speaks to the importance of this path to the pinnacle of power. The large representation of leaders with provincial experience in the Politburo and its Standing Committee not only reflects the growing power and influence of the politicians who run the country's thirty-one province-level administrative units, but also illustrates how the central authorities try to contain economic localism and region-based factionalism through the promotion and reshuffling of provincial leaders.

Top CCP officials seem to be seriously concerned with ensuring regional balance in the national leadership. Each of China's five major geographic regions—the northeast, the east, the southern-southwest, the center, and the northern-northwest—is represented by at least one current leader who was elected to the Politburo in 2007. In addition, there are the Politburo members who had previously served as province-level party secretaries in the four major cities directly under central government control: Beijing, Shanghai, Tianjin, and Chongqing. Similarly, five provincial leaders served on the Membership Qualification Committee of the 2007 National Congress of the CCP, each representing a different geographic region.

This concern for equal regional representation in the CCP's leadership organizations is even more evident in the distribution of full membership seats on the 2007 Central Committee. A strong political norm in Chinese elite recruitment since the 1997 Central Committee has been that each province-level administration has two full membership seats on the Central Committee, the exception being the minority regions of Tibet and Xinjiang (see chapters 14 and 17), whose representation is not limited by such norms. In the 2007 Central

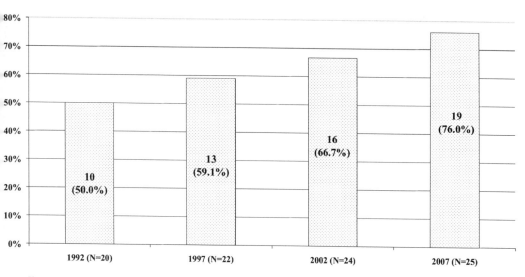

Figure 6.2 The Increase of Politburo Members with Experience as Provincial Chiefs (Year Refers to Date of Election by CCP Central Committee)
Source: Based on the author's own research. For more detail, see Cheng Li, "A Landslide Victory for Provincial Leaders," *China Leadership Monitor*, Winter 2003.

Committee, these two full membership seats were occupied by each province's party secretary and governor, without exception. Although provincial chiefs are sometimes promoted to the central government or transferred to other provinces, this distributional norm was strictly applied at the time the Central Committee was initially elected. Local demands for an even distribution of membership seats across provinces and regions in both the Central Committee and the Politburo have become increasingly accommodated and institutionalized by the party leadership.[1]

Fairly equal regional representation in the CCP Central Committee has created new dynamics and tensions in the complicated relationship between central and local government in the PRC. The fact that provincial leaders' career prospects depend on their superiors in Beijing speaks unambiguously to the enormous power the central party-state has over local administrations in China's still highly hierarchical, authoritarian system.

At the same time, top national leaders still need to accumulate political capital through close ties with some of the country's most important regions. The priority that top party elites place on leadership experience as a party secretary in major provinces and cities serves to make such posts pivotal stepping-stones for aspiring entrants into the top national leadership. This factor further enhances the political weight of local power in present-day China. The large number of Politburo members with backgrounds as provincial chiefs and the even distribution of full membership seats in the Central Committee may potentially contribute to a more pluralistic Chinese leadership in the years to come.

The Military and Chinese Politics

The second important trend in the formation of the national leadership bodies of the CCP is the relative decline of the People's Liberation Army (PLA), China's combined armed forces. The party's control over the military has been an important principle in the long history of the CCP. On a few occasions, however, the PLA has intervened in Chinese politics, such as the 1971 "Lin Biao incident," when Minister of Defense Lin Biao pursued a failed military coup (see chapter 3), and in the two years immediately following the 1989 Tiananmen crisis, when the generals of the so-called Yang family clique gained enormous power, only to be outmaneuvered by Deng Xiaoping (see chapter 4).

But over the past decade, China's military has steadily moved away from active involvement in domestic politics. The chance that a military figure might serve as a "king-maker" has become increasingly remote. In each of the last three Politburos (1997–2007) there were only two representatives of the military, and none served on the Politburo Standing Committee. Furthermore, no member of the military elite serves on the current Secretariat, which signals the further retreat of the PLA from domestic affairs and foreign policy and toward a more narrow focus on military affairs.

The most important organizations for deciding military policy are the CCP Central Military Commission and the PRC Central Military Commission. Although technically the former is a party organization and the latter is part of the state structure, they are in fact different names for the same institution with identical membership. This arrangement reflects the CCP's desire to exercise its power and authority, at least formally, through the PRC's constitutional framework. In reality, however, the Central Military Commission reports to the Politburo and its Standing Committee, not to the State Council (the government cabinet). In other words, China's armed forces are under the command of the Chinese Communist Party, not the government of the People's Republic of China.

Since 1992, only two civilian leaders, Jiang Zemin and Hu Jintao, have served on the CMC. It should be noted that both Deng Xiaoping and Jiang Zemin delayed turning over the CMC chairmanship to a relatively untested successor by holding onto the seat for a few more years, even after they had stepped down from their party or government posts. This rather strange transition strategy in which the civilian commander-in-chief of China's armed forces does not hold any other position in the party or the government reflects the political importance of the CMC.

The current CMC has eleven members. CCP General Secretary and PRC President Hu Jintao is the chairman, which effectively makes him commander-in-chief of China's armed forces. The two military leaders who are on the Politburo serve as CMC vice chairmen. Other members include the minister of defense and the heads of the PLA's four general departments (staff headquarters, political, logistics, and armament) and three services (Navy, Air Force, and Second Artillery Corps, which is China's strategic missile force). Hu Jintao will likely appoint at least one of the younger "fifth generation" of CCP leaders to the CMC, probably to the post of vice chair, a move that might well indicate who the party leaders have settled on to be Hu's successor as general secretary. Moreover, like Deng and Jiang before him, Hu may seek to retain the CMC chairmanship for a short while, even after he retires from his posts as CCP general secretary (in 2012) and PRC president (in 2013). In any case, the norm that a civilian party leader is in charge of military affairs seems to be well accepted by the PLA. The organization of China's military is presented in Figure 6.3.

In addition to these formal leadership institutions, the CCP also has a number of informal decision-making bodies focused on major functional issue areas, which are called "**leading small groups**." They are also regarded as interagency executive committees for functional issues. Some of these leading small groups are more or less permanent and some are temporary and currently include the following organizations at the national level: "Leading Small Group on Foreign Affairs," "Leading Small Group on National Security," "Leading Small Group on Taiwan Affairs," "Leading Small Group on Hong Kong–Macao Affairs," "Leading Small Group on Propaganda and Ideology," "Leading Small Group on Party Building," "Leading Small Group on Finance and the Economy," "Leading Small Group on Rural Work," and "Leading Small Group on Politics."

The main purpose of these leading small groups is to coordinate the implementation of policies across top decision-making bodies such the Politburo, the State Council, the CMC, and the Ministry of Foreign Affairs. Leading small groups report directly to the Politburo and its Standing Committee, and they are normally headed by a member of the Standing Committee. At present, for example, Hu Jintao heads the leading groups on national security, foreign affairs, and Taiwan affairs. Xi Jinping heads the leading groups on party-building and Hong Kong–Macao affairs.[2]

The Major State Institutions: The NPC and the State Council

The structure of PRC state institutions is presented in Figure 6.4. Each of the five administrative levels—township, county, municipal, provincial, and national (see Figure 1.1)—has its own people's congress. Deputies to the National People's Congress are allocated according to the population of a given province. The NPC recently equalized the representation of urban and rural areas. Prior to this reform, every 960,000 rural residents and every 240,000 urban residents were represented by one NPC deputy. The province with the smallest population is guaranteed at least 15 deputies. Special administrative regions such as Hong Kong and Macau have a set quota of delegates, as does the PLA. The current NPC, formed in 2008, has nearly 3,000 deputies elected to five-year terms.

Deputies to the lowest level people's congresses at the township level are *directly* elected by all eligible citizens. Only at the township and the village levels do direct elections take

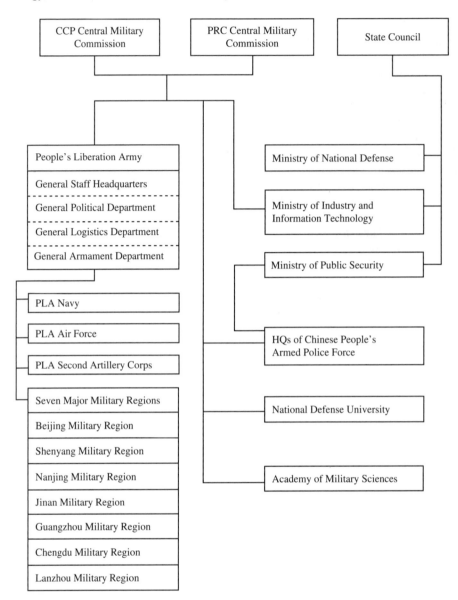

Figure 6.3 Organizational Chart of the Chinese Military
Source: *China Directory*. Tokyo: Radio Press, Inc., 2005, 178. Updated and modified by the author.

place in China (see chapter 8 for more on rural elections). Elections at all higher levels are *indirect*. For example, county-level congresses are elected by township congress deputies, not by all the "voters" in the county, and deputies to the National People's Congress are elected by the people's congresses at the provincial level.

Just as the National Congress of the CCP elects party leaders every five years, the National People's Congress elects a new state leadership at a meeting, usually held in the spring of the year following the party congress. The NPC convenes in its entirety every March for a two-week session during which deputies discuss the reports by the premier and other government leaders and approve laws and legislative regulations. The NPC has increasingly served as a venue for policy debates. The work of the NPC has become more substantive in terms of drafting laws and regulations and providing a venue for policy discourse, even though it still largely remains under CCP control.

When the NPC is not in session, the **Standing Committee of the National People's Congress** (not to be confused with the CCP's Politburo Standing Committee) takes responsibility for any issues that require congressional consideration. The Standing Committee of the NPC generally convenes every two months, with each meeting lasting about one week. The NPC also appoints nine special committees to draft legislation in various areas such as economics, education, energy, and the environment.

In theory, NPC delegates are not only supposed to elect the members of the Standing Committee of the NPC, but are also constitutionally entitled to elect the president and vice president of the PRC, the chairman of the CMC, the chief justice of the Supreme People's Court, and the chief of the **Supreme People's Procuratorate** (the PRC's top law enforcement official, roughly equivalent to the attorney general of the United States). The body is also empowered to approve the premier, who is appointed by the president, as well as the other members of the State Council and CMC. In reality, however, all of these candidates are nominated by the NPC's top leadership (the **Presidium**), which simply passes along to the People's Congress the list of nominees that the Central Committee had designated for appointment. This formal process is hardly competitive. When Hu Jintao was elected to his second term as PRC president in 2008, the vote was 2,956 for, 3 against, and 5 abstentions.

This lack of competitiveness notwithstanding, it is an interesting and fairly recent phenomenon that NPC delegates sometimes vote against top leaders and cabinet ministers in the confirmation process, particularly when voicing their dissent about political nepotism or favoritism by certain senior leaders or factions. For example, the "Shanghai Gang," a group of leaders mostly from Shanghai that advanced largely as a result of their patron-client ties with Jiang Zemin, have often scored very poorly in these confirmation votes. To cite one such case, in the confirmation for the post of PRC vice president in 2003, Zeng Qinghong, Jiang's protégé from Shanghai, received only 87.5 percent of "yes" votes—of the 2,945 valid votes, 177 were "no" votes and 190 were abstentions.

The State Council is China's cabinet. Headed by the premier, the Executive Committee of the State Council consists of four vice premiers and five state councilors, who are senior government leaders with broad responsibilities. The secretary-general (not the same as the general secretary of the CCP) manages the day-to-day business of the Council, which currently includes 28 ministers or commissioners, each of whom heads a functional department such as the Ministry of Foreign Affairs or the National Population and Family Planning Commission. At present, all but two of these individuals belong to the CCP (the exceptions being the minister of science and technology and the minister of health). These two recent appointments of non-CCP leaders to ministerial positions are largely symbolic, since all of the major decisions are still made by the party leadership.

The CCP does not take a hands-off approach when it comes to the work of the Supreme People's Court and the Supreme People's Procuratorate of the People's Republic. The party, through the *nomenklatura* system and other means of control, keeps a close watch on all aspects of China's legal system. Some Chinese intellectuals who believe that the PRC should move toward a true rule of law system have spoken out against party interference. In 2006, for example, the well-known professor of law He Weifang criticized then Politburo member and Minister of Public Security (and now CCP Standing Committee member) Zhou Yongkang for his heavy-handed "oversight" of the Supreme People's Court. To Professor He, Zhou's actions exemplified the lack of a genuinely independent judicial system

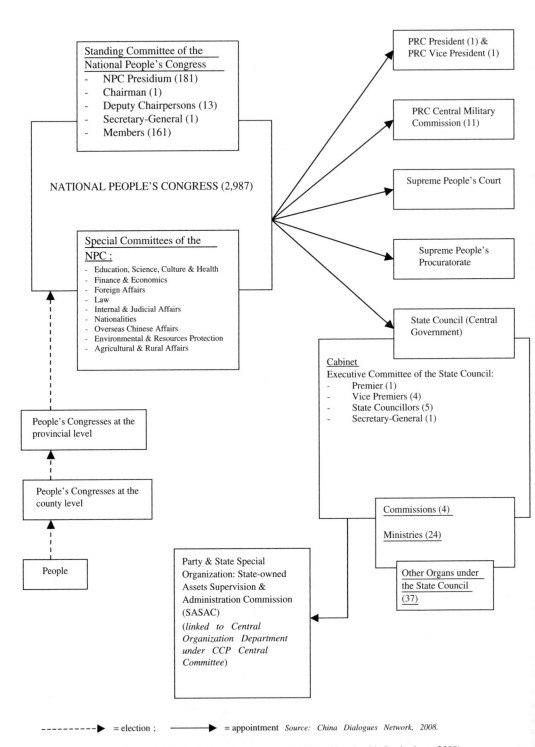

Standing Committee of the
National People's Congress
- NPC Presidium (181)
- Chairman (1)
- Deputy Chairpersons (13)
- Secretary-General (1)
- Members (161)

NATIONAL PEOPLE'S CONGRESS (2,987)

Special Committees of the
NPC :
- Education, Science, Culture & Health
- Finance & Economics
- Foreign Affairs
- Law
- Internal & Judicial Affairs
- Nationalities
- Overseas Chinese Affairs
- Environmental & Resources Protection
- Agricultural & Rural Affairs

PRC President (1) &
PRC Vice President (1)

PRC Central Military
Commission (11)

Supreme People's Court

Supreme People's
Procuratorate

State Council (Central
Government)

Cabinet
Executive Committee of the State Council:
- Premier (1)
- Vice Premiers (4)
- State Councillors (5)
- Secretary-General (1)

People's Congresses at the
provincial level

People's Congresses at the
county level

People

Party & State Special
Organization: State-owned
Assets Supervision &
Administration Commission
(SASAC)
(*linked to Central
Organization Department
under CCP Central
Committee*)

Commissions (4)

Ministries (24)

Other Organs under
the State Council
(37)

- - - - - - - - ▶ = election ; ──────▶ = appointment *Source: China Dialogues Network, 2008.*

Figure 6.4 China's State Structure: National Level Leadership Institutions (2008)
Source: China Dialogues Network, 2008.

in the country. As he stated bluntly at a conference in Beijing in 2006, "there is no other country in the world in which the chief justice reports to the chief of police."[3]

It remains to be seen whether the CCP's supremacy over the judicial system will be further challenged by Chinese public intellectuals, and if so, what impact this will have on the rule of law in China. Although Professor He was harassed by the political establishment after his bold remarks, he has continued to advocate for political reforms and constitutionalism in China. In fact, Professor He is one of the most respected legal scholars in China. In a way, this episode bodes well for the emergence of a more pluralistic and tolerant political atmosphere in the country. A related trend is that lawyers are becoming more numerous and influential in China, even within the CCP.

The Changing Composition of the CCP and Its Leadership

While the Chinese party-state structure has remained more or less the same over the past six decades, the composition of the CCP, especially in terms of the educational and occupational backgrounds of its leadership, has changed profoundly. The CCP has been transformed from a revolutionary party consisting primarily of peasants, soldiers, and urban workers to a ruling party that includes an increasing number of professionals and business entrepreneurs. Since the mid-1980s, party elites known as **technocrats** who were trained as engineers and natural scientists before beginning their political careers have become a dominant component of the CCP leadership. More recently, leaders with formal training in economics, other social sciences, and law have also increased their presence in the national and provincial leadership.

The Changing Pattern of Elite Recruitment

In the three decades after the establishment of the PRC, elite recruitment—bringing in new leaders—was mostly based on family background (the preferred categories being peasant or worker), ideological loyalty, and political activism, rather than on educational credentials and/or managerial skills. This politicized pattern of recruitment was expressed by the idea that it was better to be "red" than "expert" during the Mao years. "Reds" were cadres who advanced their careers on the strength of their revolutionary pedigree and ideological purity, while "experts" were members of the elite who distinguished themselves by their educational credentials and technical skills.

When it came to elite recruitment and promotion, reds almost always prevailed over experts. Thus, from 1949 through the early 1980s, the educational attainment of party cadres and members was extremely low. In 1955, for example, only 5 percent of national leaders had a junior high school education or above.[4] Even in 1982, according to the Chinese census, only 4 percent of CCP members were educated beyond the high school level, and a majority (52.3 percent) had received only a primary school education or were illiterate. These numbers reflect the low value placed on educational accomplishments and technical know-how within the CCP before the reform era.

Over the past half century, CCP membership has increased enormously. Figure 6.5 shows the growth of CCP membership as reported in the ten National Congresses of the CCP held since the founding of the PRC. CCP membership increased from 10.7 million in 1956 to 74.2 million in 2007. This being said, this number still constitutes a small proportion (about 8 percent) of the total age-eligible (over 18) population in the most populous country in the world.

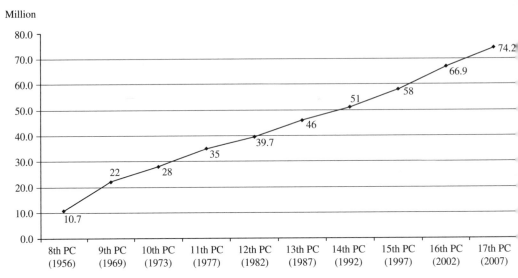

Figure 6.5 The Growth in Membership of the CCP, 1956–2007
PC: Party Congress. Source: http://www.xinhuanews.net.

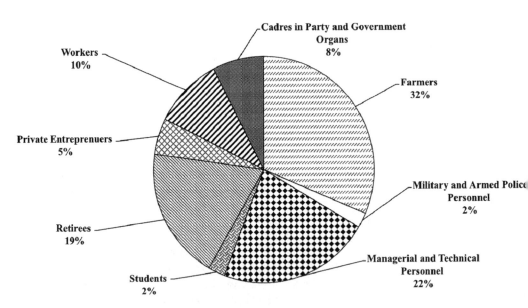

Figure 6.6 The Occupational Composition of CCP Members (2007)
Source: http://news.xinhuanet.com/newscenter/2008–07/01/content_8471350.htm. July 1, 2008.

Not only has the CCP grown enormously in size, but its occupational composition has also changed in dramatic ways over the past three decades. Figure 6.6 displays the occupational composition of CCP members in 2007. Although farmers continue to constitute the largest single group in the CCP, other groups, including managerial and technical personnel, retirees, workers, cadres in party and government organs, and even private entrepreneurs (a fairly recent addition), also comprise significant percentages of the CCP's membership.

The Rapid Increase in College-Educated Elites and the Technocrats' Dominance

The educational level of CCP members has gone up significantly in the past three decades, now that "expertise" is much more valued than "redness" in the recruitment process. In 1998, among the 61 million CCP members, over 11 million were college graduates (17.8 percent), about 4.5 times more than the general population average in the 1982 census.[5] By 2007, about 24 million CCP members held, at minimum, a two-year college degree, constituting 32.4 percent of the total membership.[6]

The growth in the percentage of national-level party leaders with higher education has been particularly dramatic. For example, the percentage of college-educated members of the Politburo has increased from 23 percent in 1978 to 100 percent today and, for the Central Committee, from 26 percent to 99 percent. The percentage of college-educated top provincial leaders (party secretaries, governors, and their deputies) increased from 20 percent in 1982 to 98 percent in 2002.[7]

This change in the educational level of China's leaders was initially due in part to the fact that many of them attended training programs in party cadre schools, which means that the substance of their education was largely political and ideological.[8] But in the late 1980s and the early 1990s, most of the college-educated elites recruited had received a regular education, with many majoring in engineering or the natural sciences.

Indeed, this period was a time of "technocratic turnover" within China's party-state leadership. In 1982, technocrats—cadres with a university-level technical education—constituted just two percent of the Central Committee, but by 1987 they made up 25 percent of the Central Committee. By 1997 they made up over half. The nine members of the Politburo Standing Committee elected in 2002 were *all* engineers, including the three top leaders, General Secretary Jiang Zemin (electrical engineer), Chairman of the NPC Li Peng (civil engineer) and Premier Zhu Rongji (electrical engineer). This is also true of the current leadership's top three: General Secretary Hu Jintao (hydraulic engineer), Chairman of the NPC Wu Bangguo (electrical engineer), and Premier Wen Jiabao (geological engineer). The representation of technocrats has also risen dramatically in other high-level leadership categories such as State Council ministers, provincial party secretaries, and governors (see Figure 6.7).

The dominance of technocrats in the Chinese leadership over the past two decades is striking if we consider the following three facts. First, the proportion of college graduates in the Chinese labor force in the 1980s was only 0.8 percent. Second, although China was traditionally a meritocratic society in which status was largely determined by success in the imperial exams, scientific knowledge and technical competence, which have for centuries been esteemed in the West, were always subordinate to literary and cultural achievements in the Confucian worldview.[9] Third, China's meritocratic tradition underwent an extreme reversal during the Mao era, especially during the Cultural Revolution, when professionals or "experts" were repeatedly targeted as enemies of the people.

The New Players in the CCP: Entrepreneurs and Lawyers

Technocrats, however, are not the only new players in Chinese politics. In fact, in recent years, the technocrats' dominance in Chinese leadership has eroded as the sociological backgrounds of CCP members and cadres have become increasingly diverse. Figure 6.7 not only shows the rapid rise of technocrats between 1982 and 1997, but also their rapid

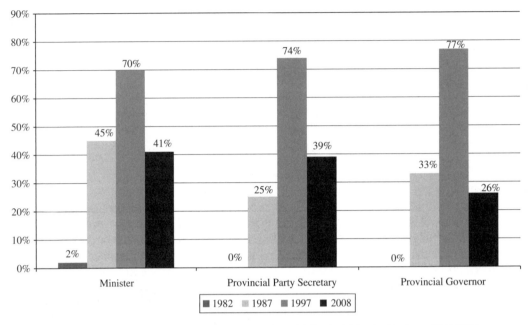

Figure 6.7 Changes in Technocrats' Representation in Ministerial/Provincial Leadership Posts, 1982–2008
Source: The data for the years of 1982, 1987, and 1997 are based on Hong Yung Lee, *From Revolutionary Cadres to Party Technocrats: The Changing Cadre System in Socialist China* (Berkeley: University of California Press, 1991), 268; Kenneth Lieberthal, *Governing China: From Revolution through Reform* (New York: W.W. Norton, 1995), 236; and Li and White, "The Fifteenth Central Committee of the Chinese Communist Party: Full-Fledged Technocratic Leadership with Partial Control by Jiang Zemin," *Asian Survey* 38, no. 3 (March 1998): 251.

decline over the last decade or so. Two distinct elite groups, entrepreneurs and lawyers, have recently emerged as new and important players in both the socioeconomic and political life of the country.

Like the rise of the technocrats, the upward social mobility of entrepreneurs—owners and managers of private businesses—represents a momentous change in Chinese society. Traditional Chinese society, which was dominated by the scholar-gentry class, tended to devalue merchants because they lived by making profits off others rather than through "honest" mental or manual labor. The anti-capitalist bias reached its extreme during the first few decades of the PRC. The four million private firms and stores that had existed in China prior to 1949 had all but disappeared by the mid-1950s as part of the transition to socialism.[10] During the Cultural Revolution anything to do with capitalism was branded poisonous, and top leaders such as Liu Shaoqi and Deng Xiaoping were purged for allegedly taking China down "the capitalist road."

Several factors have contributed to the reemergence of entrepreneurs in the PRC. Among them are the rapid development of rural industries, rural-urban migration, urban private enterprises, foreign joint ventures, the adoption of a stock market and land lease, and the technological revolution, especially the birth of the Internet. Private enterprises that could employ a large number of laborers did not exist in China until the late 1980s. During the past two decades, the number of private firms has greatly increased, from some 90,000 in 1989 to 5,210,000 in 2007 (see Figure 6.8). Today, such private firms account for 60 percent of the total number of enterprises in the country.[11] In 2007 they had at least

53 million employees. In addition, roughly 26 million people ran their own small businesses without hiring outside employees.[12]

Chinese entrepreneurs are, of course, a diverse lot. There are three distinct subgroups: (1) self-made entrepreneurs—peasants-turned-industrialists in rural areas and owners of business firms of varying size in cities; (2) bureaucratic entrepreneurs—corrupt officials and their relatives who made their fortunes by abusing power in various ways throughout the process of market reform; and (3) technical entrepreneurs—computer and Internet specialists who became wealthy as a result of rapid technological development. Self-made entrepreneurs usually come from humble family backgrounds and received relatively little education. In contrast, a large number of bureaucratic entrepreneurs received undergraduate degrees in economics and even master's degrees in business administration, usually in part-time mid-career programs. Furthermore, most of them were already CCP members or officials when they began to engage in private business. Technical entrepreneurs may or may not have strong family ties. They are often seen as China's "yuppie corps," and some received training abroad.

The rise of the entrepreneurs in terms of political influence can be traced to July 2001, when then CCP General Secretary Jiang Zemin gave an important speech on the eightieth anniversary of the Party's founding. In his speech Jiang claimed that the party should be representative of three components of society: the advanced social productive forces, advanced culture, and the interests of the overwhelming majority. As discussed in chapters 4 and 5, Jiang's so-called Theory of the Three Represents was an ideological justification for the priority given to the private sector in China's economic development and for allowing entrepreneurs to be members of the communist party (the CCP still shies away from calling them "capitalists").

A 2004 official study by the United Front Department of the CCP Central Committee found that 34 percent of the owners of private enterprises were members of the Chinese Communist Party, up from just 13 percent in 1993. Of them, however, only 9.4 percent had joined *after* Jiang's 2001 speech,[13] which reflects the fact that Jiang's ideological embrace

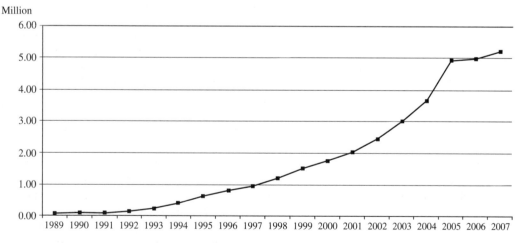

Figure 6.8 The Growth of Private Firms in China, 1989–2007
Sources: *China Statistics Year Book* (various years). For the data on 2007, see *Renmin Ribao* (*People's Daily*), August 16, 2007, 1.

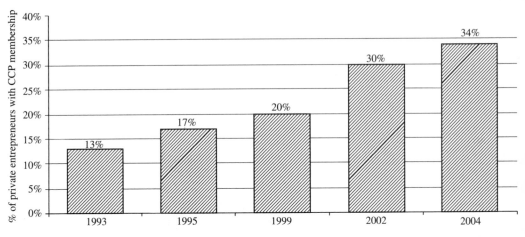

Figure 6.9 Percentage of Private Entrepreneurs with CCP Membership
Source: The United Front Department of the CCP Central Committee, "2005 nian Zhongguo siying qiye diaocha baogao" (A survey of private enterprises in 2005). See also http://www.southcn.com/finance/gdmqgc/gdmqyyrl/200502030218.htm and *Xingdao ribao*, December 13, 2004, 1.

was mostly just formal acknowledgement that a large number of party members were already engaged in private business (see Figure 6.9). In 2006 *Forbes* magazine revealed that 35 percent of the 500 richest people in China—all of them multimillionaires or even billionaires—are CCP members.[14]

Entrepreneurs have just begun to acquire positions in the national and provincial political leadership. The heads of some of China's largest business firms—both private and state-owned—currently serve on the CCP Central Committee as full or alternate members. A few former CEOs currently hold posts as provincial party secretaries or governors. However, most of these entrepreneurs-turned-political leaders worked in state-owned enterprises; very few have come from private firms or firms jointly owned by foreigners and Chinese. It is worth noting that the children of many of the top Chinese leaders are now pursuing careers in the business sector, with most working in foreign joint ventures such as investment banks, rather than climbing the ladder of the CCP political hierarchy as their technocrat fathers did. If, as is likely, some of them aspire to political careers, it would represent a very different path to power, with important implications for the future of the Chinese communist party-state.

Along with the economic and political rise of entrepreneurs, there has also been an increase in the power and prevalence of lawyers in China. The Maoist system was hostile to both the legal profession and the legal system. At the start of the reform era in the early 1980s, there were only 3,000 lawyers in a country of over one billion people. Since then, the number of registered lawyers and law school students has increased significantly.[15] In 2004, China had a total of 114,000 lawyers in 11,691 registered law firms. This is still a tiny legal profession (especially on a per capita basis!) when compared to the more than one million lawyers in the United States. It was reported that during his visit to China in 1998, President Bill Clinton said to his Chinese hosts: "You have too many engineers and we have too many lawyers; let's trade with each other." But the number of lawyers in China will probably increase dramatically in the next few years.[16] Today, China has 620 law schools and departments that produce roughly 100,000 law graduates per year.[17] The number of enrolled students at the Law School of Beijing University in 2004, including those studying part-time, equaled the total number of law students trained at the institution over the previous fifty years.[18]

Some of China's lawyers work outside the political establishment to challenge abuses of power, including rampant official corruption, and seek to promote the rule of law at the grassroots level. While activist lawyers are an emerging factor in Chinese politics, they are still subject to regulation and persecution by the party-state. All lawyers must be licensed by the government, and the authorities often refuse to renew these licenses if the lawyer in question has been regarded as a troublemaker. Among the lawyers recently subjected to harassment are those representing the families whose children were killed in poorly constructed schools during the earthquake that struck Sichuan province in May 2008 or were injured by drinking contaminated milk. They have also represented Tibetans detained as a result of the anti-government uprising in March 2008 and followers of the Falun Gong sect, which the government labeled a "dangerous religious cult" and banned in 1999.[19]

Other lawyers work within the political or intellectual establishment and may become political leaders. The rapid rise of younger leaders with legal training is an important trend in Chinese politics. Three of the top contenders in the fifth generation to ascend to the CCP's highest leadership positions, Vice President Xi Jinping, Executive Vice Premier Li Keqiang, and Director of the CCP Organization Department Li Yuanchao, all received their academic degrees in law from prestigious educational institutions in China.

An important theoretical proposition in Western studies of political elites is that the occupational identity of the leaders in a given country correlates with—and sometimes has a determining effect on—the nature of the political system.[20] Political elites often want to leave their leadership legacy in the area in which they have a personal or professional interest. Technocrats, for example, are often particularly interested in economic growth and technological development due to their own backgrounds in these subjects. It is not difficult to imagine that the growing presence of lawyers and social scientists in the upcoming fifth generation will cause these leaders to have an impact on the fields of political and legal reform. Indeed, they already appear to be more interested in these subjects than the preceding generations of communist ideologues, revolutionary veterans, and engineer technocrats ever were.

The emergence of technocrats, entrepreneurs, and lawyers in the CCP during the reform era not only reflects a profound change in the occupational and educational backgrounds of the Chinese ruling elite, but also indicates the changing nature of upward mobility in Chinese society and the growing diversity of the CCP leadership. To a great extent, such diversity is also evident within each of these new elite groups. Although China remains a one–party state and the communist party still lays claim to its leading role, the composition, power base, and political priorities of the CCP's leadership have all fundamentally changed.

New Dynamics in the Chinese Political System

Perhaps even more important than Chinese political leaders' growing diversity in educational and occupational experiences is the trend, within the upper reaches of the CCP, toward checks and balances. The Chinese Communist Party leadership is now structured around two informal coalitions or factions that have come to check and balance each other's power. This is not the kind of institutionalized system of checks and balances that operates with the executive, legislative, and judicial branches of the American government, an essential element of a truly democratic system. But it is an important development in how Chinese politics works and may have far-reaching implications for the future.

The two groups can be labeled the "**populist coalition**," led by President Hu Jintao and Premier Wen Jiabao, and the "**elitist coalition**," which was born in the Jiang era and is currently led by Wu Bangguo, chairman of national legislature, and Jia Qinglin, head of a national political advisory body.[*] These four individuals are currently China's top four leaders. The populist coalition wants to shift China's policy priorities to address some of the serious problems, such as vast economic inequalities and environmental degradation, that resulted from the growth-at-any-cost strategy of development pursued by Jiang Zemin and the elitist coalition when they were in charge. Both coalitions have strong representation in the party leadership, and they rotated the driver's seat in the previous succession from Jiang to Hu and will likely do so again in the expected succession from Hu to Xi Jinping. This current situation is sometimes referred to as the "one-party, two-coalitions" political mechanism.

Factional politics is, of course, not new in China. Major events during the Mao era, such as the Anti-Rightist campaign, the Cultural Revolution, and the 1989 Tiananmen crisis, were all related to factional infighting in the CCP leadership. But factional politics is no longer a vicious power struggle and zero-sum game in which winner takes all and those on the losing end are likely to be purged or worse. Neither the elitist nor the populist coalition is capable of, nor really wants to, totally defeat the other. Each coalition has its own strengths, including different constituencies, which the other does not possess. Their relationship, when it comes to policy-making, is one of both competition and cooperation.

Inner-party bipartisanship in the CCP has not come about simply as a result of the ideas of China's top leaders. Rather, this remarkable development in Chinese elite politics reflects important trends in the nature of party leadership, the institutionalization of party rules and procedures, and the relationship between the central party-state and local authorities.

The first trend is a gradual transformation in Chinese politics from an all-powerful, god-like, and charismatic single leader to a system of collective leadership. Mao Zedong wielded enormous, almost unchallengeable, personal power (see chapter 3). He treated succession as if it were his own private matter; discussion of the transition of power after Mao was taboo. The omnipresent slogan "Long Live Chairman Mao" reinforced the illusion of Mao's "immortality." The Chairman literally held on to power until he had exhaled his dying breath in September 1976. The result was a cataclysmic succession struggle that led, ironically, to Deng Xiaoping's rise to power.

During the Deng era, political succession and generational change in the Chinese leadership became a matter of public concern (see chapter 4). Yet, because of his legendary political career, no leader dared to challenge Deng's authority. Even when he did not hold any important leadership positions following the Tiananmen crisis, Deng was still regarded as China's "paramount leader." For many years during the 1990s, people in China and Sinologists abroad speculated about when the elderly and ailing Deng would die, often causing stock markets in Hong Kong and China to fluctuate wildly. Like Mao, Deng thought who took over after him was pretty much his choice alone. But unlike Mao, Deng importantly and effectively handed over the reins of power to Jiang well before he died in 1997.

---

[*] That advisory body is the Chinese People's Political Consultative Conference (CPPCC), which consists of over 2,000 members who represent a wide range of constituencies, including the CCP, China's non-communist "democratic parties," official mass organizations (such as the All-China Women's Federation), various occupational "circles" (such as artists and writers, educators, medical personnel, and farmers), ethnic minorities, and religions. Although the majority of members of the CPPCC are non-communists, the organization is bound by its charter to accept the leadership of the CCP, and it has always been headed by a high-ranking party leader (e.g. Mao Zedong, Zhou Enlai, and Deng Xiaoping). The Conference meets each year for about two weeks, concurrent with the annual session of the National People's Congress, but its function is only to advise the Congress; it has no legislative power of its own.

Jiang Zemin had neither the charisma nor the revolutionary experience possessed by Mao or Deng. To a large extent, Jiang exercised power primarily through coalition building and political compromise. Hu Jintao's generation of leaders relies even more on power sharing and finding consensus. Hu is known for his low-profile personality, compared to his predecessors, as party leader. During the past few years some foreign observers have even wondered whether Hu is in charge. To a certain extent, Hu is not fully in charge, but the "first among equals" in his generation of leaders. As result of this shift toward collective leadership in the CCP, negotiation and compromise among competing factions is now playing a far more prominent role in Chinese elite politics than ever before.

The second trend is the movement toward increasing institutional restraints on the exercise of power within the Chinese party-state. Nepotism of various forms (e.g., blood ties, school ties, regional identities, bureaucratic affiliations, or patron-client ties) continues to play an important role in the selection of leaders. At the same time, however, institutional mechanisms, including formal regulations and informal norms, have been more effectively implemented to curtail various forms of favoritism and abuse of power. These institutional developments include:

- *Inner-party election and decision by vote.* The CCP has adopted some election methods to choose the members of the Central Committee and other high-ranking leaders. Major personnel and policy decisions are now often decided by votes in various committees, rather than solely by the committee's party chief.
- *Term limits.* With few exceptions, a term limit of five years has been established for top posts in both the party and the government. An individual leader cannot hold the same position for more than two terms.
- *Age limits for retirement.* Based on CCP regulations or norms, leaders above a certain level cannot exceed a set age limit. For example, all of the members who were born before 1940 retired from the Central Committee at the Party Congress in 2007. This is quite a change from the past; even during the Deng era, China's political system was said to be a "gerontocracy," or "rule by the elderly."
- *"Law of avoidance" in selection of local top leaders.* For example, provincial party secretaries, secretaries of the discipline commissions, and police chiefs are often nonnative outsiders who were transferred from another province or the central administration.

These institutional rules and norms not only generate a sense of consistency and fairness in the selection of leaders, but also make the circulation of the Chinese political elite very fast. The turnover rate of the CCP Central Committee membership, for example, has been remarkably high over the past twenty-five years, with newcomers constituting an average of 62 percent at each of the five Party Congresses held during that period (see Figure 6.10). As a result of the fluidity of membership in this crucial leadership body of the CCP, no individual, faction, institution, or region can dominate the power structure. These developments have reinforced the norm of checks and balances in the Chinese leadership and have affected elite behavior. Leaders are now far more interested in establishing their legitimacy through institutional channels than were their predecessors, who relied only on personal power and connections.

The third trend that is having a profound effect on Chinese politics is the changing relationship between the central party-state and local authorities. This shift has been hastened by the emergence of local interests politically and economically empowered by the decentralization stemming from China's market reforms (see chapter 7). The renewed regulations in terms of the law of avoidance, however, can have only limited efficacy in restraining growing localism. The many inequalities (e.g., between urban and rural, coast and inland, the prosperous and the poor) that have also been a product of a quarter-century

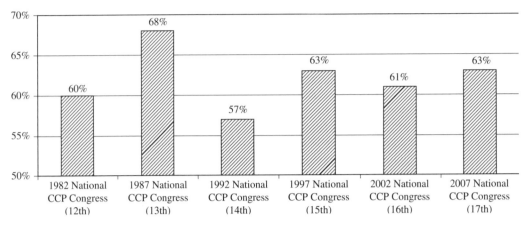

Figure 6.10 Turnover Rate of the CCP Central Committee, 1982–2007
Source: Cheng Li and Lynn White, "The Sixteenth Central Committee of the Chinese Communist Party: Hu Gets What?" *Asian Survey* 43, no. 4 (July/August 2002): 560. The data on the 17th Central Committee are updated by the author.

of economic reform have transformed center-local relations into one of the country's most daunting challenges.

Understandably, local leaders (mainly provincial and municipal leaders) tend to side with the top national leaders who will protect or advance their interests. Politicians in areas that have benefited from the reforms want to keep the policy orientation that favors their interests, while those in disadvantaged regions favor members of the central leadership who represent a change in direction. Whichever "side" they are on, local leaders in China have a much bigger stake in—and a bigger opportunity to influence—elite politics than ever before in the history of the People's Republic.

This trend also explains important policy differences between Jiang Zemin's elitist coalition and Hu Jintao's populist coalition, and the role they now play in China's new bipartisan politics. Upon his ascension to the post of general secretary of the Party in 2002, Hu quickly sensed that his mandate was to fix the economic disparities associated with Jiang's leadership. As a result, Hu has spent the last few years outlining his populist strategy under new catchphrases such as "scientific development" and "harmonious society" (see chapters 4 and 5). To a great extent, he has already altered China's course of development in two important ways: (1) from an obsession with GDP growth to greater concern with social justice; and (2) from the single-minded emphasis on coastal development to a more balanced regional development strategy.

The Dynamics of China's New Bipartisan Factional Politics

China's new factional dynamics have three main features. First, the two coalitions not only compete for power for their own sake, but also represent different socioeconomic and geographical constituencies. Second, these two competing coalitions are almost equally powerful, partly because they have an equal number of seats in the top leadership organizations, and partly because their leadership skills and credentials naturally complement each other. Third, while they compete with each other on certain issues, they are willing to, and sometimes must, cooperate on others.

Socioeconomic and Geographical Contrasts.   The elitist coalition represents the interest of the entrepreneurs and the emerging middle class, while the populists often voice the concerns of vulnerable social groups such as farmers, migrant workers, and the urban poor. Geographically, the former advances the needs of the coastal region and the latter protects the interests of the inland region.

These differences are usually reflected in their leaders' distinct personal careers and political associations. Most of the top leaders in the elitist coalition are children of revolutionary heroes or high-ranking officials. This group of so-called **princelings** includes Jiang Zemin, whose adoptive father (his uncle) was a CCP martyr killed in 1939 during the anti-Japanese war. The elitists advanced their political careers primarily in Shanghai or other major cities or coastal provinces. By contrast, most of the leading figures in the populist coalition, for example, General Secretary–President Hu Jintao and Premier Wen Jiabao, come from more humble or less-privileged families. They usually had substantial leadership experience in less-developed inland provinces. For example, Hu Jintao spent most of his working life in some of the poorest provinces of China's inland region, including fourteen years in Gansu, three years in Guizhou, and four years in Tibet. Similarly, Premier Wen Jiabao spent fifteen years after graduating from college working in extremely arduous conditions (also mainly in Gansu). Many of the prominent populist leaders also advanced their political careers through the ranks of the **Chinese Communist Youth League** (CCYL) and have therefore garnered the label *tuanpai*, literally, "league faction" (see Box, **The "Princelings" and the *Tuanpai* in China's Elite Politics**).

An Equal Allocation of Seats in High Offices.   The factional power and influence of both princelings and *tuanpai* is not new, but has been a factor in Chinese politics for the last twenty years or so. It was only with Hu Jintao's rise to the top leadership, however, that the *tuanpai* really came of age in terms of power, and these groups have only recently established themselves as equally dominant forces in the CCP.

Even more significantly, these two factions, as part of their bipartisan relations, have allocated to themselves an equal number of seats in the top leadership organizations. In the current twenty-five-member Politburo, the princelings occupy seven positions (28 percent), while the *tuanpai* occupy eight (32 percent). The factions have even arranged a near-perfect balance of power among the next generation of rising stars (the fifth generation) in all of the important decision-making bodies in both the party and state. For example, there is one member of each faction's fifth generation on the CCP Standing Committee: Xi Jinping, representing the princelings, who is expected to become party general secretary in 2012; and, Li Keqiang, representing the *tuanpai*, who is likely to become premier of the State Council in the same year.

The one high-level organization where there is an imbalance is the 371-member Central Committee. There the *tuanpai* holds 86 seats (23.2 percent) to the princelings' 32 (8.6 percent). Both the *tuanpai* and princelings serve as a core group in the larger competing political coalitions—populists and elitists, respectively. The relatively small number of Central Committee seats held by princelings is due, in part, to the fact that they usually perform very poorly in elections where the voters have a choice—a reflection of the elitist coalition's association with some of China's most serious problems, including inequality and corruption.

Interdependence and Cooperation between the Two Coalitions.   To a great extent, the relationship between these two informal coalitions is both conflictual

THE "PRINCELINGS" AND THE *TUANPAI* IN CHINA'S ELITE POLITICS

The elitist and populist factions that now share in a balance of power within the Chinese Communist Party leadership each have at their core a group of members with very different career paths. The term "princelings" is often used to refer to those among the rising fifth generation of CCP leaders in the elitist faction who come from families of former high-ranking officials (vice minister level or above).

Princelings share a strong political identity. Without exception, all of the prominent leaders with princeling backgrounds greatly benefited from their family ties early in their careers. They were "born red"—a large number born during the late 1940s and 1950s as their parents' generation won civil war victories and became the new rulers of the communist regime. They typically received the best education available when they were young, and often had a "short-cut" or "helicopter-like promotion" in their political career advancement. Several of the top leaders in the fifth generation of the CCP are princelings whose fathers or fathers-in-law were vice premiers, including Xi Jinping (Politburo Standing Committee member and PRC Vice President), Wang Qishan (Politburo member and PRC Vice Premier), Bo Xilai (Politburo member and Chongqing Party Secretary).

The princelings are not a monolithic group or a formal network, and thus they usually do not have strong personal ties among themselves. As an elite group, the princelings are far less cohesive than any of the other political networks that were once dominant or are still powerful in the Chinese leadership, including their "rivals," the Chinese Communist Youth League faction (*tuanpai*), who are the core of the fifth generation of the populist faction.

The Chinese Communist Youth League (CCYL) is a membership organization for people aged fourteen to twenty-eight. Its main function is to identify and foster new Communist Party leaders. In 2008, the CCYL had 75 million members and a staff of 191,000 full-time cadres (many of whom are older than the age limit for ordinary members). The CCYL's mission statement refers to the organization as the "reserve army" for the party. In addition to providing ideological training, the league runs a variety of social service programs and operates several prominent media outlets, notably the *China Youth Daily* newspaper.

The current CCP General Secretary, Hu Jintao, worked for several years at the provincial and national levels of the CCYL and served as the head of the organization in the mid-1980s. Several members of the upcoming generation of Chinese leaders were Hu's junior colleagues in the Youth League. Although it is difficult to trace each young leader's precise associations with General Secretary Hu, one can reasonably assume that they have known one another, through CCYL work and other connections, for over two decades. President Hu's closest associates in the CCYL network, or *tuanpai*, are believed to be Li Keqiang (Politburo Standing Committee member and PRC executive Vice Premier), Li Yuanchao (Politburo member and Director of the CCP Organization Department), Wang Yang (Politburo member and Guangdong Party Secretary), Ling Jihua (member of the Secretariat and director of the CCP General Office), Wu Aiying (Minister of Justice), Cai Wu (Minister of Culture), Zhang Baoshun (Shanxi Party Secretary), and Liu Qibao (Sichuan Party Secretary).

and cooperative. It is very important to note that both factions share fundamental goals: to ensure China's socioeconomic stability and the survival of CCP rule at home, and to enhance China's status as a major international player. These common goals often push the two factions to compromise and cooperate with each other. They also make "bipartisanship with Chinese characteristics" a sustainable proposition for the near- to medium-term future.[21] As mentioned above, Hu Jintao has made some major policy shifts in a populist direction since he took the post of general secretary of the party in 2002. To a degree, leaders of the elitist coalition also recognize the need to allocate more resources to inland regions and help vulnerable social groups, just as the populists understand the importance of maintaining rapid economic growth to meet the rising expectations of China's urban middle class.

Furthermore, because the leaders of the factions differ in expertise, credentials, and experiences, they understand that they need to find common ground to coexist and govern effectively. The *tuanpai* are masters in terms of organization and propaganda and have often had experience in rural administration, especially in poor inland regions, but they generally lack experience and credentials in some of the most important administrative areas and are short on skills related to the handling of foreign trade, foreign investment, banking, and other crucial aspects of economic policy-making. Therefore, they have to cooperate with the elitist leaders, who have strong backgrounds in economic and financial administration and have spent most of their careers in the developed coastal cities.

The interaction between populists and elitists in the leadership—between the *tuanpai* and princeling factions—reflects a new dynamic of interdependence and power-sharing through checks and balances in Chinese politics. Make no mistake, the CCP is determined to protect its political prerogatives, and there is an absence of serious effort to make ordinary people and officials "equal under the law." But inner-party checks and balances can undermine the degree of "legal impunity" of corrupt officials in high offices. This bipartisan collective leadership also entails a more pluralistic decision-making process through which political leaders can represent various social and geographic constituencies. It is hard to overemphasize what a dramatic change this marks in the "rules of the game" for the Chinese Communist Party's leadership politics.

Conclusion: The Limits of Inner-Party "Bipartisanship" and the Future of Chinese Politics

Despite its important implications for how China is governed, the CCP's new inner-party "bipartisanship" has significant limitations in terms of further political reform. The People's Republic of China is still an authoritarian communist party-state that can be brutal in repressing dissent and opposition. Factional politics within the CCP, although not nearly as opaque to the public as in the Mao era, are not transparent. The lack of an independent press means that the public mostly knows only what the party leadership wants them to know about the policy-making process and the contenders for power. The seats in the most powerful bodies in the party-state are still decided by a very small number of top leaders through deal-making, not through open competition.

The CCP's bipartisan factional politics may provide a semblance of checks and balances that helps to keep the party leadership resilient and adaptable to changing circumstances, but it also presents a major challenge to the CCP's status as the ruling party in two important respects. Conflicting interests and competing policy initiatives may make the decision-making process lengthier and more complicated, perhaps leading to deadlock. At a time when China confronts many tough choices, the "bipartisan" leadership may find it increasingly difficult to reach a consensus on how to deal with crucial issues such as the regional redistribution of resources, an inadequate public health system, failing environmental protection, ethnic tensions in Tibet and Xinjiang, relations with Taiwan, reform of the banking system, and disputes with the United States over foreign trade.

On the political front, the diverse educational, occupational, administrative and political backgrounds of China's leaders, especially in the emerging fifth generation, are often considered as positive developments that may contribute to political pluralism. But it remains to be seen whether Chinese leaders will overcome their deep-rooted obsession with political stability and introduce a more competitive process to choose members of the Central Committee, the Politburo, and the Standing Committee in the near future. If not, bipartisanship could quickly dissolve into ruthless factional power struggles—perhaps even involving the military.

But even if bipartisan political competition continues to develop within the CCP leadership, the broader pubic in China may come to ask why only the party elite are entitled to have democracy. If so, the country may soon witness an even more dynamic and more "bipartisan" phase in China's political transformation. China's emerging bipartisanship is crucial to our understanding of China's party-state not only because it sheds light on the often ambiguous concept of inner-party democracy, but also because it reveals how the governance of the most populous country in the world is evolving.

Notes

1. For more discussion of this development, see Zhiyue Bo, "China's New Provincial Leaders: Major Reshuffling before the 17th National Party Congress," *China: An International Journal* 5, no. 1 (March 2007): 1–25; and Cheng Li, "Pivotal Stepping-Stone: Local Leaders' Representation on the 17th Central Committee," *China Leadership Monitor* 23 (Winter 2008): 1–13.

2. For more discussion of the leading small groups, see Alice L. Miller, "The CCP Central Committee's Leading Small Groups." *China Leadership Monitor* 26 (Fall 2008).

3. See *China Economic History Forum*, May 3, 2006, http://economy.guoxue.com/article. php/8291/2.

4. See *Xinhua banyüe kan* (Xinhua bimonthly), January 2, 1957, 89; Franz Schurmann, *Ideology and Organization in Communist China*, 2nd ed. (Berkeley: University of California Press, 1968), 283.

5. *Shijie ribao* (World Journal), June 28, 1999, A9.

6. See http://news.xinhuanet.com/newscenter/2008–07/01/content_8471350.htm. July 1, 2008.

7. The 1978 and 1982 data are from Cheng Li, *China's Leaders: The New Generation* (Lanham, MD: Rowman & Littlefield, 2001), 38. And 2008 data are from Xinhua Agency, http://www.xinhuanet.com. August 1, 2008.

8. Cheng Li and Lynn White, "The Fifteenth Central Committee of the Chinese Communist Party: Hu Gets What?" *Asian Survey* 43, no. 4 (July–August 2003): 248.

9. Ho Ping-ti, *The Ladder of Success in Imperial China: Aspects of Social Mobility, 1368–1911* (New York: Columbia University Press, 1962), 259.

10. *China News Analysis* 1501 (January 1, 1994), 2.

11. *Renmin ribao* (People's Daily), August 16, 2007, 1.

12. *Ibid.*

13. The United Front Department of the CCP Central Committee, *2005 nian Zhongguo siying qiye diaocha baogao* (A survey of private enterprises in 2005). See also http://www.southcn.com/finance/gdmqgc/gdmqyyrl/200502030218.htm.

14. See "Hu Run's List of the 500 Richest People in China in 2006," http://news.xinhuanet.com. Accessed on October 11, 2006. Also, see Bruce Dickson, *Wealth into Power: The Communist Party's Embrace of China's Private Sector* (New York: Cambridge University Press, 2008).

15. Ji Shuoming and Wang Jianming, "*Zhongguo weiquan lushi fazhixianfeng*" (China's lawyers for human rights protection: Vanguards of the Rule of Law), *Yazhou zhoukan* (Asia Week), December 19, 2005.

16. Jean-Pierre Cabestan, "*Zhongguo de sifa gaige*" (China's Judicial Reform), news.bbc.co.uk/hi/chinese/china_news/newsid_2149000/21492061.stm. July 27, 2002.

17. Jerome Cohen, "Can, and Should, the Rule of Law be Transplanted Outside the West?" Paper presented at the Annual Meeting of the Association of American Law Schools, Washington, D.C., January 4, 2007.

18. *Renmin ribao* (People's Daily), May 19, 2004, 15.

19. Michael Hines, "China Said to Harass Rights Lawyers," *New York Times*, June 27, 2009, A12.

20. For more discussion of the elite theory, see Vilfredo Pareto, *The Rise and Fall of the Elites: An Application of Theoretical Sociology* (Totowa, NJ: Bedminster, 1968); and Robert D. Putnam, *The Comparative Study of Political Elites* (Englewood Cliffs, NJ: Prentice-Hall, 1976).

21. For a detailed discussion of emerging Chinese bipartisanship, see Cheng Li, "The New Bipartisanship within the Chinese Communist Party." *Orbis* (Summer 2005): 387–400.

Suggested Readings

Brown, Kerry. *Friends and Enemies: The Past, Present and Future of the Communist Party of China*. New York: Anthem Press, 2009.

Dickson, Bruce. *Red Capitalists in China: The Party, Private Entrepreneurs, and Prospects for Political Change*. New York: Cambridge University Press, 2003.

Dickson, Bruce. *Wealth into Power: The Communist Party's Embrace of China's Private Sector*. New York: Cambridge University Press, 2008.

Li, Cheng, ed. *China's Changing Political Landscape: Prospects for Democracy*. Washington, DC: The Brookings Institution Press, 2008.

Li, Cheng. *China's Leaders: The New Generation*. Lanham, MD: Rowman & Littlefield, 2001.

Lu, Xiaobo. *Cadres and Corruption: The Organizational Involution of the Chinese Communist Party*. Stanford, CA: Stanford University Press, 2000.

Pei, Minxin. *From Reform to Revolution: The Demise of Communism in China and the Soviet Union*. Cambridge, MA: Harvard University Press, 1998.

Pei, Minxin. *China's Trapped Transition: The Limits of Developmental Autocracy*. Cambridge, MA: Harvard University Press, 2008.

Peerenboom, Randall. *China's Long March toward the Rule of Law*. New York: Cambridge University Press, 2002.

Shambaugh, David. *China's Communist Party: Atrophy and Adaptation*. Berkeley: University of California Press, 2008.

Shirk, Susan L. *China: Fragile Superpower: How China's Internal Politics Could Derail Its Peaceful Rise*. New York: Oxford University Press, 2007.

Tsai, Kellee. *Capitalism without Democracy: The Private Sector in Contemporary China*. Ithaca, NY: Cornell University Press, 2007.

Yang, Dali L. *Remaking the Chinese Leviathan: Market Transition and the Politics of Governance in China*. Stanford, CA: Stanford University Press, 2004.

Yu, Keping. *Democracy Is a Good Thing: Essays on Politics, Society and Culture in Contemporary China*. Washington, DC: The Brookings Institution Press, 2009.

Zheng, Yongnian. *Will China Become Democratic? Elite, Class and Regime Transition*. Singapore: Time Academic Press, 2004.

Zhao, Suisheng, ed. *Debating Political Reform in China: Rule of Law vs. Democratization*. Armonk, NY: M. E. Sharpe, 2006.

7

China's Political Economy

David Zweig

Few modern societies have as "political" an economy as China. Even after thirty years of market reform, bureaucrats, local and national leaders, as well as new and old government regulations, still have remarkable influence over the allocation of goods and services. Similarly, because the legitimacy of the Chinese Communist Party (CCP) depends so heavily on continuing economic growth; because expanding inequalities threaten social stability; and because corruption has seeped deeply into the political system, economics has enormous political significance in China.

China's national leaders make a huge difference in the country's economic fortunes, as their preferences for different developmental strategies and policies have shaped China's trajectory. And leaders use their power to press their preferences. Every leadership change in China, including subtle shifts of power from one leader or faction to another, influences public policy. Without Mao's death in 1976, Deng Xiaoping would have been unable to introduce the reform era. Similarly, after coming to power in 2002, Hu Jintao and Wen Jiabao established a more balanced development strategy than their predecessors to ameliorate the inequality that had emerged in the 1990s. Conversely, economic problems undermine the authority of factions or leaders. When price reforms in the summer of 1988 triggered popular fears of inflation, the resulting run on Shanghai banks allowed conservative party leaders to attack one of the key supporters of reform, then CCP General Secretary Zhao Ziyang, who was ousted from office as part of the Tiananmen turmoil in 1989.

A second component of China's "political" economy is that economic deregulation threatens the power of bureaucrats who struggle to maintain their influence. Decades of economic planning and regulations empowered millions of bureaucrats from Beijing down to the villages, giving them control over the allocation of wealth, resources, jobs, and people's right to participate in the economy. Reforms that decentralized control over the economy left local officials, not the market, in control over many resources. No doubt, decades of reform and deregulation, in particular, the requirement for joining the WTO that all laws be transparent and open to public scrutiny, have severely undermined bureaucratic authority. Yet today, despite a booming private sector, central and local bureaucrats still control 33 percent of China's gross domestic product (GDP).

A final aspect of state power is to determine a country's relationship to the global economy. How tightly should economic interactions with the outside world be regulated? What balance between imports, exports and trade regulations is most likely to enhance national power and the pace of economic development? As states open their economies to the world, their leaders discover that a predetermined set of international rules, norms, international organizations, trading structures, transportation networks, and pricing mechanisms constrain their choices. The study of these issues, which falls under the purview of political economy, form a key part of China's transition from a relatively isolated state with a stagnant or, at best, slowly growing economy in the Maoist era to the economic dynamo and trading giant it is today.

Political Economy in the Mao Era

The CCP came to power in 1949 planning a moderate program of economic change, but with several pressing issues on the agenda. In 1950–1952, land reform redistributed 42 percent of arable land from richer farmers to poorer villagers. The goal was to weaken the landlord class, which had supported the Kuomintang (KMT), and repay China's peasants who fought and died on behalf of the CCP. Hyperinflation, which had undermined KMT support in the cities during the civil war, was tamed. Under the slogan of "thirty years without change," the CCP promised to leave the private economy alone in the hope that China's small capitalist class would continue to invest in their own firms, which they did.

Beginning in 1953, the state promoted rapid industrialization, largely by copying the Soviet model of economic development. Twenty million peasants were moved into the cities to provide workers for an enormous number of new factories; urbanization expanded, and industrial production grew. With direct Soviet assistance, 156 major projects were begun, including 24 electric power plants, 63 machinery plants, and 7 iron and steel plants. Many of China's key state-owned enterprises (SOEs), such as the Luoyang tractor factory, new steel plants in Wuhan and Baotou (Inner Mongolia), and Changchun's First Auto Works (FAW), were all started in this period.[1]

At the same time, the CCP also began to extend its reach over other parts of the economy. In the countryside, the state took control of the rural grain markets in 1953, prohibiting private trading in grain. After Land Reform, some peasants had sold their land to local officials and former landlords; Mao saw a new, rural ruling class emerging. To stop this trend, in the summer of 1955, Mao urged local officials to press villagers to join rural cooperatives in which the land would be owned and farmed collectively. By the end of 1956, 98 percent of villagers had turned their land, oxen, and tools over to the cooperatives and were drawing their income based largely on the work they performed for the collective. Property transfer accelerated in the cities, as in the waning weeks of 1955 and the early part of 1956, all capitalists, small shopkeepers, and professionals running their own businesses turned their firms over to state.

In the fall of 1957, China entered the Great Leap Forward, a period of euphoric anticipation of the advent of the communist utopia. Mao and other leaders argued that larger collective farms, filled with peasants possessing heightened ideological fervor, would dramatically increase economic production. So, local officials lied, reporting dramatic, but impossible, rises in agricultural output. Central leaders, deep in the throes of self-deception, demanded that localities remit their "surplus grain" to the state, leaving little food in the villages. When the weather soured in 1959, famine struck rural China, claiming tens of millions of lives in the poorer parts of the country.

The famine led Mao Zedong to withdraw from day-to-day management of the economy, allowing more pragmatic leaders, especially Liu Shaoqi and Deng Xiaoping, to introduce reforms that undid the extremism of the Great Leap. Between 1962 and 1966, China's economy grew at a stable pace. But trouble was looming. Mao, convinced that the CCP was becoming a new capitalist class, launched the disastrous Cultural Revolution in 1966 to keep the party and the country on what he considered to be the correct revolutionary road. The scope of private economic activity was greatly restricted in both city and countryside. Under these policies, rural production did not make much progress in the decade from 1966–1976.

In retrospect, the Mao era rapidly industrialized an impoverished China. It limited inequalities, raised health and education standards, and improved agricultural infrastructure. But alternative policies might have been even more successful, bringing more rapid economic development. Surely, the Great Leap was an unmitigated disaster. Collective agriculture lacked sufficient incentives to generate rapid growth. Also, Mao's misguided belief that China's global strength would be enhanced with a larger population led to a baby boom in the 1960s that has created population pressures on the economy, which even today have national and global repercussions.

Political Economy in the Reform Era

Since 1978, China has gone through five waves of reform that have literally changed every aspect of both domestic and foreign economic policy. These waves of reform began formally with the crucial meeting of the Central Committee in December 1978, which redirected national policy from the Cultural Revolution's emphasis on politics and ideology to improving the Chinese economy and the people's livelihood. The Third Plenum, as it is known, introduced rural reforms, established official diplomatic relations with the United States, opened the economy to the outside world, and ended "class labels" that had divided citizens into "friends and enemies" of the state. It also heralded the return of Deng Xiaoping and other reformers into the top leadership.

The takeoff of the Chinese economy and the subsequent three decades of unheralded economic growth actually began in the countryside in 1978. De-collectivization, which returned land *management* to each household, while maintaining **collective** *ownership* of land, linked the amount of work that villagers performed with their financial rewards. Families, not the collective, decided what crops to plant, how to allocate labor, and how to dispose of the agricultural output; combined with a 25 percent jump in the price paid by the state for agricultural produce, newly energized villagers dramatically increased rural output and incomes. Grain production soared. And as cash-rich peasants demanded home building materials and consumer goods, urban manufacturing boomed as well.

In the early 1980s, the first major step toward opening the Chinese economy to the outside world was the establishment of four **Special Economic Zones (SEZs)** in coastal areas that had links to Chinese communities overseas. The SEZs—Shenzhen, Zhuhai, Xiamen, and Shantou—were given special privileges in terms of imports, exports, labor policy, and the management of foreign direct investment (FDI).

The second wave of reforms emerged in 1984–1985. Fourteen more coastal cities were opened to foreign trade. Scientific institutions and universities were encouraged to work with enterprises and keep the profits. Universities were allowed to link directly with universities overseas. Foreign trade controls were decentralized to city governments. In the cities, efforts were made to invigorate state-owned enterprises, which were responsible for most industrial output in China. Central planning was curtailed; as long as firms fulfilled their yearly targets which stipulated what goods they had to sell to the state and at what prices, they could produce more goods that they could sell at market prices. This "dual price system" expanded output and efficiency; but it was also wide open to corruption: people who could buy goods produced at planned prices and sell them on the free market made a killing.

In 1987–1988, the third wave of reform opened all of coastal China to the global economy. This "Coastal Development Strategy," including the establishment of over 6,000 foreign trade companies (FTCs), really marks the beginning of China's export-led economic growth, which continues today.[2] China's rural industry—which had expanded significantly after 1984—became a driver of China's export boom. For the next seven years, China's export growth came largely from these small- and medium-sized rural enterprises along the coast.

But in the summer of 1988, the reforms ran into trouble. The further lifting of price controls on many items, which had begun in 1985, triggered a run on the banks, as people, frightened that the cost of goods would soar, withdrew their cash and bought everything off the shelves. The panic had political repercussions, undermining CCP General Secretary Zhao Ziyang, who was directing the reform movement with Deng Xiaoping's support. The power struggle, pitting conservative leaders who felt that reform should be slowed down against Zhao and other committed reformers, would play out over the next year and form the political background to the crisis in Tiananmen Square that shook China to the core in May–June 1989.

The military assault on Beijing on June 4 had economic repercussions, leading to negative growth in the fall of 1989 and a general economic slowdown that lasted until 1992. In late 1989, the CCP watched with horror as communist party-states across Eastern Europe tumbled down, along with the Berlin Wall. Further shock followed the collapse of the Soviet Union in August 1991, as Mikhail Gorbachev's reforms led to the dismantling of the Soviet empire.

Yet, Deng Xiaoping learned his own lesson from communism's demise in Europe. While fear paralyzed most Chinese leaders, Deng understood that the CCP's political survival was wedded to economic growth; Gorbachev's mistake was promoting political reform without putting more food on the table of the Soviet citizens. So, in January 1992, Deng, then well into his eighties, embarked on his "Southern Journey" to Shenzhen, one of China's fasting-growing cities next to capitalist Hong Kong, where he called on the people and local governments to "move faster and take greater risks" in reform. Though conservative opponents in Beijing stifled his words for almost two months, his exhortation to return to a path of reform struck a chord with the Chinese people along the coast, triggering a new phase in China's reform. In the fall of 1992, the 14th Party Congress of the CCP announced that henceforth, China would establish a "socialist market economy," ending once and for all the ideological debate about whether China would remain a fully socialist economy or move more rapidly toward capitalism.[3] This was the start of the fourth wave of reform.

Foreign and domestic investment boomed, following the liberalization of trade and investment (see Table 7.1 at the end of this chapter). Whereas most foreign investment in the 1980s involved overseas Chinese investors in small enterprises, between 1993 and 1995, larger firms from Europe, the United States, and Japan poured into China, and, along with Taiwanese investment, triggered a foreign direct investment (FDI) boom. Local governments, too, dusted off plans drafted in 1987–1988, but tabled in 1989, and began many new local projects.

In the following years, China privatized all but the largest state-owned enterprises (SOEs), including tens of thousands of collectively owned enterprises in the countryside, so that by 2003, the share of workers in the public sector, including rural labor, was down to 4 percent. When the fifth wave of reform began in 1998, Jiang Zemin had already succeeded Deng Xiaoping (who died in 1997) as China's top leader. During this wave, the leadership cut the number of state bureaucrats in half and promoted the private ownership of apartments—triggering a nationwide housing boom.[4] Final plans were made to join the World Trade Organization (WTO) in 2001, which entailed removing regulations that limited foreign access to China's domestic market, deepening China's integration into the international economy.

The themes raised above, and discussed in greater depth below, reflect core aspects of the dramatic transformation of China's economy since the founding of the People's Republic: (1) its transformation from a state-run economy, dominated by public property, with an "iron rice bowl" for its working class (i.e., no layoffs), to one characterized by a thriving private sector, unemployment, and a weak, social safety net; (2), a shift from autarky to interdependence, as China became a trading powerhouse and a major member of the WTO; (3) the initial granting of property rights over land to peasants during Land Reform, then forcing them into collectives, and a return to household-based farming (although without private ownership of land); (4) from radical egalitarianism under Mao, in which cities still did benefit more than the countryside, to an initial narrowing of the urban-rural gap in the early reform era as decollectivization spurred a jump in agriculture production, followed by the growth of dramatic urban-rural, interpersonal, and interregional inequalities in the 1990s; and, (5) from a country with a generally low standard of living to one with a fast-growing middle class seeking to become Western style consumers, which, in turn, is driving China's global search for energy and resources.

The Political Economy of Rural Reform

To set the context for understanding the dramatic changes in the rural political economy in the reform era, one needs some detail about Maoist era rural policy. Although peasants were the base of power for the communist revolution, the CCP turned on the peasantry in the mid-1950s, freezing rural to urban migration through the introduction of a "household registration system" (*hukou*) that legally consigned every citizen of the PRC to residence in either city or countryside. At that time, about 80 percent of Chinese were rural residents. Pittman Potter has equated the *hukou* system to a Chinese form of apartheid (see chapters 8 and 9).

Why employ such harsh language? Because the state gave enormous benefits to urban residents that it denied to its rural-based citizens. This "urban bias"[5] included subsidized grain, food, and housing, retirement benefits or pensions, better-quality urban schools, health care coverage, and many social amenities that turned large SOEs into welfare units. Rural residents, on the other hand, had to sell grain to the state at relatively low prices, build their own homes, finance low-quality schools, fund their own cooperative medical program, and rely on their sons to support them in their old age. Under the slogan of "self-reliance," the state invested little in rural China; less than 8 percent of total government financial expenditure in the 1950s went into agriculture, although the vast majority of China's citizens relied on that sector for their livelihood.[6]

Rural collectives were forced to sell what was called "surplus" grain—which, in fact, was just a part of the harvest—to the state at below cost. Also the gap between the low prices paid to farmers for agricultural products and the high sales prices for urban industrial goods—what is called a "price scissors"—may have shifted some wealth from the countryside to the cities. But while Chinese economists who speak for the peasants have pushed this viewpoint, empirical studies suggest that the rural-urban gap grew largely due to direct state investment in industry in the cities, rather than because of any large-scale transfer of wealth from the countryside to the cities.

During most of the Mao era, ideological constraints undermined villagers' efforts to enhance their income through private economic activity. Village officials were often pressured to limit "the tail of capitalism"—that is, private economic activity that might lead to the reemergence of capitalism in the countryside. Between 1966 and 1978, under policies of "agrarian radicalism," rural markets were closed and household sideline production (such as raising pigs and chickens for sale or consumption) was frowned upon and, in some places, even prohibited.[7] Private plots, comprising 5 to 7 percent of collective land, which had been allocated during collectivization to villagers for their own production, were sometimes banned or placed under collective controls. Under a policy called "taking grain as the key link" (*yi liang wei gang*), the state forced collectives to forgo producing higher valued "economic crops," such as fruit orchards, horticulture, oil-bearing crops, bamboo, forestry, or fish ponds, in order to ensure local (and national) grain self-sufficiency.

In sum, the Maoist legacy in the rural economy is a mixed one. On the positive side, under Mao, village health cooperatives significantly improved rural health care and life expectancy, bringing "developing" China to the level of "developed" Western societies on these indicators. Rural capital construction projects undertaken by the people's communes improved irrigation in much of rural China, and this "embedded investment" may have contributed to the dramatic growth in rural output that followed de-collectivization after 1977.

On the other hand, both production and living standards in the countryside stagnated or improved very little from the mid-1950s through the mid-1970s. And the terrible human cost of the Great Leap Forward has to tilt the balance sheet sharply toward the negative. The Great Leap left a deep reservoir of bitterness among farmers toward the regime, making the countryside ripe for reform once Mao's death in 1976 and Deng Xiaoping's consolidation of power in 1978 changed the political context entirely.[8]

Decollectivization

Rural reform occurred in two stages. Between 1977 and 1983, agricultural production was decollectivized. The people's communes were dismantled and replaced with a household-based farming system. A second phase began in 1984, which promoted industrialization, commercialization, specialization, and marketization of the rural economy.

The story of de-collectivization is the stuff of novels, reflecting the audacity of China's peasants to challenge the state. Dismantling of the people's communes began in a small village in Fengyang District, Anhui Province, a region rocked by very high death rates during the Great Famine of 1960–1962. Faced with starvation at that time, peasants had divided the collective land and farmed independently. While many lives had been saved by this action, Mao sacked the provincial leader for undermining collective agriculture, admonishing the CCP to "never forget class struggle."

In 1977, about a year after Mao's death, peasants in Anhui and Sichuan provinces again faced famine. Fengyang's cadres and villagers signed a secret document, in blood, saying that they would again farm the land as families, but this time not tell higher-level officials. Deng Xiaoping was back in power in Beijing, and the two provinces were under the authority of party leaders committed to reform who did learn of the spontaneous de-collectivization. So, when Wan Li, Anhui's party secretary, told Deng that spontaneous de-collectivization was underway, Deng reportedly told Wan to let the policy unfold. By the December 1978 Central Committee's Third Plenum, which heralded the official beginning of the reform era, de-collectivization became the official policy. The decision to dismantle the people's communes faced policy-makers with two big questions: First, should groups of peasants continue to farm together in some collective arrangement, or was the individual household an ideologically acceptable farming unit? For some leaders, household-based production equaled private farming, which they saw as incompatible with the party's commitment to socialism. The second question was: Should villagers keep most of their output—turning over only a small grain tax to the state—and sell the surplus on the free market? Or should most of the distribution and sale of the output be kept under collective control?

By the spring of 1983, rural China had adopted a system in which individual households were contracted "use rights" to the land, which was still owned by the village. In this so-called household responsibility system, families, not the collective, decided about crops, investment, savings, labor allocation, and marketing. They paid only a small tax in grain. The state increased its price for most crops by an average of 25 percent, stimulating growth in output and significantly increasing incomes in the countryside. Households switched to higher value cash crops, further enhancing their incomes, while "specialized households" engaged in larger-scale farming, animal husbandry, fishery and other forms of agricultural specialization.

The rural economy boomed during the first wave of reform. While average annual increase of the gross value of agricultural output (GVAO) between 1952 and 1978 had been 4.2 percent, the growth rate of GVAO in 1979–1984 was 7.4 percent (see Figure 7.1). The annual output of grain had risen by only 2.3 percent a year between 1952 and 1978, but this went up to 5.1 percent a year between 1979 and 1984. This increase was even more impressive on a per capita basis, because rural population growth also dropped during this period.

With more money, China's peasants demanded more durable consumer goods; while 31 percent of rural households owned a bicycle in 1978, by 1985, 81 percent of households

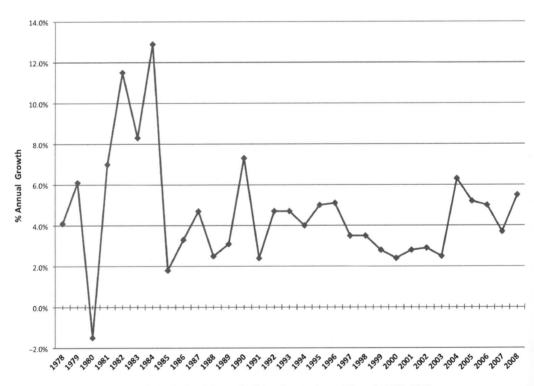

Figure 7.1 Agricultural Output in China, Percent Annual Growth, 1978–2008
Source: World Bank World Development Indicators.

did. Only 20 percent owned a sewing machine in 1978; by 1985, over 43 percent had one. Flush with cash, as many as 80 percent of rural Chinese families renovated their homes in the 1980s, replacing mud walls with brick ones, thatched roofs with tiled ones, and dirt floors with concrete ones. With rural Chinese comprising approximately 18 percent of the world's population, and with 80 percent of them significantly upgrading their homes, rural reform helped 16 percent (18 percent × 80 percent) of the world's inhabitants significantly upgrade their homes—the largest housing boom in world history!

Between 1978 and 1984, de-collectivization, higher prices for farm products, more off-farm business activity, and clearer incentives shrunk the urban-rural income gap precipitously. Between 1978 and 1984, rural household income grew by 12.4 percent annually, while urban incomes grew 6.8 percent. The quality of food in the cities, not just in the countryside, improved enormously because of the rural reforms: to give just one example, *tofu* and soya milk *(doujiang)*, former staples of Chinese breakfasts that had disappeared due to China's "grain first policy," returned to urban food markets. The stunning successes of the first stage of rural reform led to an upsurge of support for the Chinese Communist Party and its reform wing that laid a very strong base for the reform of the entire economy.

But the rural areas fell behind again after 1984, as the state turned its attention to urban industrial reform and allowed the prices of consumer and industrial goods to rise to stimulate the urban economy. By 1994, the urban-rural income gap was even greater than it had been on the eve of rural reform in 1978 (see Box, **The Problem of Inequality in China**).

A 1994 tax reform introduced by Premier Zhu Rongji compounded the problems of the rural areas. In the 1980s, the central government's share of GDP and total investment had dropped precipitously due to decentralization and de-collectivization. The provinces and localities had become rich, while the central government had grown poor, complicating any redistribution of wealth among regions of the country; the central government also lacked the funds to have a significant impact on the direction of development across the country. In response, Zhu increased the taxes that provinces and local governments paid to the central government, leaving most rural counties without the finances to help the areas under their administrative authority. Moreover, the central government imposed new tasks on local officials, such as running schools, reestablishing health care programs, and building new roads, without giving them adequate funds to do so.[9] To pay for these projects, local cadres imposed "arbitrary" taxes and illegal fees on peasants for all kinds of activities, such as slaughtering pigs or chickens or building new schools or roads. These financial burdens were among the leading cause of the upsurge in rural protests in the decade after 1994 (see chapter 8).

China's current leaders, Hu Jintao and Wen Jiabao, have raised the slogan of creating a "new socialist countryside" as a priority for their administration. To that end, the state has increased investment in rural China. All rural children are now guaranteed free education through the end of junior middle school, as the central government has taken responsibility for teachers' salaries. The state also ended all agricultural taxes, increasing rural incomes by about 5 percent. Figure 7.1 shows the volatility in the growth of China's agricultural output during the reform era. Current government policy aims to establish a more stable and sustained pattern of growth for agriculture, even as more people move out of that line of work and agriculture continues to decline as a percentage of China's GDP.

Township and Village Enterprises

The second stage of reform in the Chinese countryside began in 1984 with a rapid expansion of rural industrialization. Much of the increase in rural incomes in China in the 1980s and the 1990s was because of the growth of township and village enterprises

(TVEs). These rural industries were not part of the state **planned economy**. Many were funded by local governments or received loans from local credit cooperatives, where peasants had put some of their newly gained disposable income, while others operated under contracts with urban state-owned enterprises that sought to expand outside of the state-controlled sector of the economy. In the Yangtze River Delta of central China, particularly in southern Jiangsu and northern Zhejiang provinces, SOE engineers spent weekends upgrading production in these rural firms. Much of the surplus agricultural labor released by de-collectivization, as well as rural youths entering the working force for the first time, found work in TVEs.

Initially, TVEs competed very effectively with SOEs. They were unburdened by welfare costs—workers' housing, medical benefits, subsidized meals, schooling, and retirement benefits—that saddled SOEs, so their products were cheaper. Suddenly, China's "urban bias," that had endowed urban residents with so many more perquisites than their rural cousins, became a liability in a competitive market. As a result, TVEs took the production of many household appliances away from SOEs.

TVEs also had an advantage in cheap labor relative to Taiwan, Japan, Hong Kong, and other rapidly developing regions of East Asia, leading the government to see TVEs as the basis of an "export-led" strategy for China. As part of the 1984 urban reform, the government had pushed SOEs to enter the global marketplace. But they proved inflexible and unwilling to meet foreign expectations. In 1987, under his "Coastal Development Strategy," then Premier Zhao Ziyang gave TVEs incentives to look for markets overseas, including the right to keep more of the foreign currency that they earned through exports.

By 1994, over 50 percent of all products purchased in China by state-run foreign trade companies for export came from TVEs.[10] Rural joint ventures with overseas investment also boomed, as Hong Kong and Taiwanese firms moved into the Pearl River Delta in southern China, the Min River region in Fujian across from Taiwan, and the lower reaches of the Yangtze River. In the mid-1990s, TVEs were the fastest growing sector of the Chinese economy, expanding at rates of nearly 30 percent annually and accounting for more than two-thirds of China's increased foreign trade.[11]

While most TVEs had been owned by local governments, a wave of privatization hit the sector beginning in 1994. TVE managers, who were part of the local power elite, often engaged in "manager buyouts" (MBOs), taking ownership over their firms. Township and village governments supported this wave of privatization because private firms generated more profits and taxes than collectively owned ones, while TVEs that proved unable to make the transition from collective to private ownership were closed.[12]

Today, collectively owned TVEs have largely disappeared from China's economy, replaced by private enterprises in the more prosperous parts of the country. Eastern China now has an industrialized countryside that covers much of the Pearl River Delta bordering Hong Kong in the south, the Yangtze River Delta west of Shanghai, as well as suburban communities all along the coast.

The Struggle over Rural Land

Land has long been a source of conflict between the state and the peasants and between urban and rural China. After giving land to poorer villagers during Land Reform (1950–1952), the CCP reasserted control over all rural land and its products beginning in 1956, when it transferred ownership rights from individuals to the collective economy run by local officials, culminating in the creation of the people's communes during the Great Leap

Forward. Once land became "collective property," it became unclear who actually owned it, which allowed cadres to grab land for their collective unit whenever they could. In fact, almost every new policy or campaign focusing on the countryside since the 1950s has become an opportunity for a new wave of land expropriations.

The Great Leap Forward (1958–1960) involved a huge land grab by the government even beyond the creation of the communes, when it took land for **state farms** run by the central administration and for massive irrigations projects and reservoirs.[13] During the Cultural Revolution, local officials at the county and commune level expropriated land for rural industries and new office buildings, under the slogan of "building socialism in a big way" (*da gan shehuizhuyi*). In fact, the opening shot of Deng Xiaoping's rural reforms in the summer of 1978 targeted officials in a county in Hunan Province who had taken control of large amounts of land owned by the villages in their area.

Land grabs persisted into the reform era. In 1982, to prevent rural surplus labor freed up by decollectivization from flooding into the large cities, the central government called for the establishment of "rural small towns" (*xiao cheng zhen*). Suddenly, in one locality outside Nanjing, township leaders confiscated land owned by village collectives around the township center and let officials and friends from more distant villages move into the town. In the early 1990s, urban areas across China designated large swaths of suburban land that belonged to villages for building "development zones" dedicated to industrialization, and particularly export production. The massive land grab that ensued—communities around China quickly set up over 8,000 development zones—transferred control of large amounts of suburban village land to urban officials. The most recent wave of land grabs began with the building boom that followed the decision to allow private ownership of apartments in 1998.

A huge gap exists between the compensation that villagers receive for giving up their use rights to the land (they still cannot sell it outright) and the profits earned by local officials and development companies from new projects built on that land, including housing estates, apartment buildings, shopping malls, and even golf courses.[14] As the last public good in China, whose value is revealed only as it is put up for sale on the market, land is a battleground among citizens (urban and rural residents), local officials, and private entrepreneurs.

In late 2008, the CCP explored the idea that villagers should sell or subcontract their "use rights" to the land to agribusinesses, which would benefit from economies of scale by combining small plots of land into large farms. This step could increase overall agricultural production, and the businesses could hire peasants at salaries far greater than what they could earn from farming as individual families. It was also proposed that a more institutionalized process be set up to ensure that the farmers are getting a fair deal when they give up their land rights and that rural residents be given urban *hukou* (residence permits) as part of the compensation for their land.

If the peasants gained legal title to the land as part of this process, they could also use it as collateral for bank loans, something they have been unable to do. With this money, they could start businesses, generating new jobs and economic growth in poorer regions of the country. Estimates are that this policy could create over 2 trillion *renminbi** (RMB)—more than US\$290 billion—of wealth.

---

* *Renminbi*, literally "people's currency," is the name of China's currency. It is abbreviated as RMB. Chinese currency is also referred to as *yuan*, which is the basic unit of the RMB (as the dollar is the basic unit of U.S. currency. In fact, the official international designation of China's currency is *yuan renminbi* (CNY).

But some in the government worried that if villagers sold their land, they would lose their safety net. Jobs in cities or factories are nice, but should peasants lose those jobs, and not have land to which they can return, the state will need to help them or face social unrest. At that point, it will be of little benefit to the state to remind them that they should never have sold their land. Also, for leaders who remain committed to communist ideals, allowing private ownership of the land is ideologically unpalatable and politically unacceptable.

In any case, this new "land reform" policy has not been implemented, and the CCP seems to have moved away from plans for privatizing rural land. This was probably fortuitous. As a result of the financial global financial crisis that began in late 2008, approximately 25 million migrant workers lost their jobs in China's export factories, and most returned to their villages to farm the land that they had not sold.

China's Changing Economic Structure

The economies of developing countries are dominated by the primary and extractive sectors—agriculture, raw materials, and natural resources. Most laborers work in these sectors, where returns on investment are low. Economic modernization expands industry, services, transportation, and utilities; it transfers labor from low-skilled to high-skilled jobs; and it directs investment into science, technology, and education. While the shift from agriculture to industry forms the first stage of development, the growth of the service sector, such as banking or insurance, often heralds the next step in modernization of the economy. These changes occur through domestic investment and government policy, as well as by opening to the global economy in search of capital, technology, and markets for manufactured goods. In general, China has followed this pattern, although with some of its own unique characteristics.

In the early 1950s, agriculture dominated the PRC's economy. But following the Soviet model of development, China rapidly urbanized and industrialized. Millions of rural residents were brought to the cities and suburban factories, triggering what Andrew Walder has called the "making of the Chinese working class."[15] In the "largest example of technology transfer in world history,"[16] the Soviet Union in the 1950s helped China build 156 major infrastructure and industrial projects, sent over 11,000 engineers and scientists to China, and trained over 28,000 Chinese technical personnel. Almost half of China's industrial investment in the first half of the decade went to support these projects. As a result, the Chinese economy recovered swiftly from the devastation of the Japanese invasion and the civil war and began down the road to industrialization.

Nevertheless, by the end of the Maoist era in the late 1970s, China still relied heavily on agriculture. An overemphasis on heavy industrial development—such as chemical or steel plants—and too little investment in light industry, such as textiles, not only led to a scarcity of consumer goods, but also failed to create enough new jobs to move more people off the land. Light industry is labor intensive, so it creates many more jobs for each unit of input than capital intensive, heavy industry. Therefore, a developing country, with a growing population, seeking rapid industrialization and increased labor productivity, must expand light industry. Exports, particularly of light industrial goods, can also facilitate rapid economic growth. But this was not the model of development adopted under Mao.

One hallmark of the reform era in China has been the accelerated transition of labor from agriculture to light industry, with much of that industrial labor becoming a key part of the country's export-led growth (ELG) strategy. Under ELG, exports produced by new (and comparatively cheap) labor pay for technology imports that fuel modernization and shift the composition of GDP, first from agriculture to industry, and then to services (see Figure 7.2).

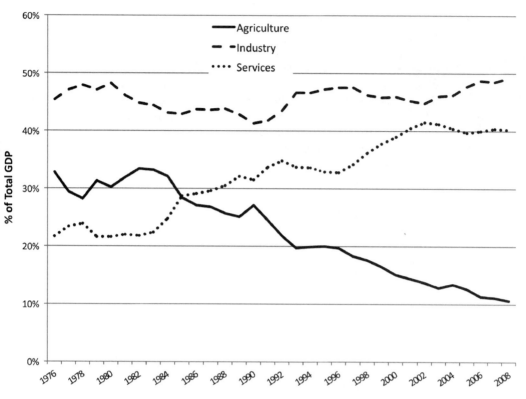

Figure 7.2 China's GDP by Sector of the Economy, 1976–2008
Source: World Bank World Development Indicators.

In transitional economies, entrenched interests that benefited from preexisting patterns of government investment often resist efforts to shift investment from one sector to another. Political economists call this resistance "**path dependence**," which means that decisions by policy-makers are often shaped or even limited by past decisions that were made under very different circumstances. For example, under the reforms, after SOEs cut their work-force to enhance efficiency, they still had to pay not only the pensions of retired workers, but also for the retirees' housing, health care, and even their children's education, which had been guaranteed to them as part of the Maoist "iron rice bowl" system. SOE leaders and their allies in the party-state battled to keep state resources flowing into their coffers, or they diverted funds intended to promote modernization to pay the retired workers.

Nevertheless, national leaders, committed to restructuring government investment from heavy to light industry—Dorothy Solinger calls this a shift from "lathes to looms"[17] in China's economy—laid the groundwork for the export-led growth strategy in the 1980s by investing in harbors and roads in coastal regions that linked China to the global economy.

Political economists and politicians also debate which level of government should keep what share of taxes in order to best promote national development. National governments need to invest in public goods and services, education, welfare, or transfer wealth from richer to poorer regions. Such transfers often hold countries with significant regional varia-tions together. But which level of government—central, provincial (or state), municipal, or county—is best able to address citizens' needs, all the while granting the central government enough funds to ensure some modicum of regional equity?

Early in the reform era (circa 1984), the central government established a "financial responsibility system" (*caizheng baogan*), where each level of government was given a fixed level of taxes to remit to the level immediately above it in the administrative hierarchy. The amount to be remitted was set for three years and was based on the average tax revenues of the previous three years. Surplus taxes that were collected remained with the government that collected them. Given that at this time governments at various levels still owned most enterprises in China, this strategy gave local governments strong incentives to promote economic development and exhibit entrepreneurship. After all, the amount they had to give up to the higher level of government was fixed; so increased profits allowed them to keep more money at their own level.

Within seventeen years, however, central government revenue as a share of GDP had dropped from 33.8 percent in 1978 to 10.8 percent in 1995.[18] In response, in 1994, then Vice Premier Zhu Rongji committed provincial-level governments to turn over more revenue to the central government. The provinces, however, extracted more revenue from governments at the level below, including the rural county. This policy bankrupted many counties who were unable to fund their payrolls, public services, and particularly, schools and teachers' salaries. Rural education suffered terribly.

Yet in the long run, extracting more local wealth has improved the central government's ability to invest in infrastructure—railroads, harbors and other public facilities—that are critical for a modern economy. As note above, the Hu-Wen administration increased the allocation of state funds to the countryside. The PRC government is also using a big chunk of the 4 trillion RMB (US$585 billion) stimulus package implemented to deal with the 2008–2009 global financial meltdown to promote economic growth in the rural areas.

The Decline of the Public Sector

The reform era has seen a dramatic decline in the role of the public sector in the economy and a rise of the private sector. Industrial profits as a percentage of GDP accounted for by publicly owned enterprises (SOEs and TVEs) shrunk from 14 percent in 1978 to 6 percent in 1987 and less than one percent in 1996. But the public sector remained burdened by overemployment, as well as by welfare responsibilities for millions of retirees. To deal with this huge drain on China's economy, the leadership decided in 1997 to privatize some **small and medium enterprises (SMEs)**.

The subsequent pace of privatization was so rapid that the government tried to slow it down. Particularly worrying was the pervasive tendency toward "asset stripping," whereby new owners (mostly former state-employed managers) sold the equipment and pocketed the cash, often leaving the workers without jobs or any share of the enterprise's value. The central government's call for "gradualism"—a hallmark of China's economic reforms—conflicted with a hunger among local officials to pillage the public sector as it was being dismantled. But in 1999, the National People's Congress seemed to legitimize this process by passing a law that announced that the private sector was no longer simply a "supplement to the public sector" but was now a "core component" of the national economy.

Commenting on the rush to privatization in the 1990s, Barry Naughton, in reference to Russia's post-communist economic reforms, which sought fast results through rapid fundamental changes, has written: "if anything in China's transition counts as a 'big bang,' this was it."[19] Between 1993 and 2003, more than 30 million SOE workers were laid off.

Including layoffs from collective enterprises and the state bureaucracy, urban China lost 50 million jobs in 10 years! By 1999, the privatization or closing of TVEs created another 35 million unemployed rural workers.

The decline in the share of public sector workers was huge and swift: from 24 percent of the labor force in 1996 to 7 percent by 2003. By 2007, over 80 percent of Chinese workers, including the 47 percent of farmers who work on land contracted from the village, were in the private sector or relying on their own labor for their income.

Layoffs and the creation of a more mobile employment system has had enormous social and political implications. China's working classes face great insecurity in terms of jobs and retirement benefits and now confront three great fears: finding affordable housing; managing the medical costs of a serious illness; and educating their children so that they can improve their social standing. The change from a state-owned industrial structure and an overpopulated agricultural sector to an economy driven by an urban white collar and capitalist class has had dramatic political implications for party membership, the CCP's base of power, and the political status of the laboring classes of China. As discussed in several previous chapters, the CCP has shifted its base of class power, away from its historic "worker, peasant, soldier alliance" to an urban, middle-class foundation.

Between Plan and Market: Dilemmas of Partial Reform

China's transition from plan to market has been fraught with difficulties. Although the above discussion emphasized the decline of the public sector in the Chinese economy, by no means has it disappeared. Key industrial enterprises remain under state control and most are now managed through the **State Asset Supervision and Administration Commission (SASAC)**. SASAC covers five sectors of the economy—telecommunications, petroleum and refining, metallurgy (steel and other metals), electricity and military industry—leaving it in control of 33 percent of total industrial assets nationwide.

One very serious problem in this partially reformed economy has been the widespread tendency toward what social scientists call "**rent seeking**." Simply put, this means the introduction of regulations that, in various ways, create conditions where officials can gain economic advantages for themselves or their organization that would not occur in an open market situation (see Box, **Rent Seeking and Corruption**).

Rent seeking became a problem early in China's economic reform process. In 1984, a "dual price system" (*shuang jiage*) was introduced to limit the negative impact of sudden price increases as the economy was deregulated. This system compelled firms to sell products produced according to the state plan at fixed prices; but goods produced *beyond* the plan could be sold at market prices, and the firms could retain the profits. The intention was to allow the real cost of goods to determine the market price through a gradual process while also continuing to make sure SOEs had access to the goods they needed at a price they could afford.

But the distributors who purchased goods at the lower fixed prices often resold them on the market for higher prices. These distributors thus earned "rents" in the form of the profits that they pocketed by taking advantage of the price differential. As a result, goods allocated to state firms on the plan often did not arrive because they had been sold off for a better market price. In order to get the goods they needed for production, the firms had to pay intermediaries a higher price (a kind of bribe) or turn to the private market, which also meant paying more than the fixed price would have been. Since a planned economy depends on knowing precisely the availability and the price of "inputs," rent seeking made

RENT SEEKING AND CORRUPTION

"Rent seeking" is often equated with corruption, but it is not quite the same thing. The idea of rent seeking has its roots in the study of how bureaucrats in the United States manipulate regulations to their own advantage. Regulations can limit which firms can engage in business or stop firms from producing the amount of goods that the society wants, creating shortages in the marketplace. If the demand for a good exceeds its supply, the price of that good or service rises above what economists call "the market clearing price," that is, the price that the good would fetch in the marketplace under conditions of full and open market competition when supply and demand are balanced. The difference between the higher price created by regulation-induced shortage and the "market clearing price" is called a "rent."

"Rents" can be captured by manufacturers or suppliers whose selling price is increased by the impact of the regulation, or by bureaucrats who may get a payoff from the manufacturers for introducing the regulation that creates the higher price. Bureaucrats can also charge firms fees for the right to enter a regulated marketplace that has these higher prices, because the firms can earn large profits, which give them the money to share with the bureaucrats. While the higher price is called a "rent," any payoff to the bureaucrats is simply corruption.

"Rents" are prevalent in international trade, as bureaucrats use regulations to keep competitive foreign firms, or lower-priced or better-quality goods, out of the domestic market. These regulations involve tariffs (which increase the cost of foreign goods to consumers), quotas (which prevent the importation of foreign goods), or non-tariff barriers (which increase the cost for foreign firms of doing business in the domestic market.) In the 1980s, a foreign firm investing in China had to get dozens of approvals before it could establish a joint venture, increasing the time needed and therefore the cost of opening the company. Chinese firms, that could sell their goods at a higher price because foreigners were unable to compete, benefited from the regulations imposed on a foreign competitor and could be said to have profited from rent seeking. If the bureaucrats who made or enforced these regulations shared in these rents through payoffs, bribes, or other means, they were engaging in corruption.

life very difficult, if not impossible, for many state-owned enterprises. In one case, the difference between planned and market prices for coal was so high that it became more profitable for a steel factory to take coal received under the plan and resell it on the market, rather than use it to make and sell steel.

There have been several attempts to rein in bureaucratic rent seeking. But bureaucrats have responded to these efforts through various evasive means. For example, in the 1980s there was an explosion of so-called briefcase companies—meaning firms with few assets or employees—mainly set up by bureaucrats or ex-bureaucrats in order to use their connections to buy state goods and resell them at market prices. Many of today's millionaires in China made their first big pot of cash in this early transition period through such maneuvers.

Ironically, in some sectors, China may actually suffer from too little, not too much, regulation of the market.[20] For example, as new drugs enter the market, or the number of food producers grows, firms often produce low-quality products, even to the point of endangering the public. In one case, China's State Food and Drug Administration proved completely ineffectual, as its director succumbed to bribes and kickbacks for approving low-quality drugs. After 10 patients in a Shanghai hospital died from bad drugs, the director was found guilty of corruption and executed.

In 2008, the Sanlu Dairy Group was discovered to have put the poisonous chemical melamine in its milk, in order to falsify its protein levels. As of November 2008, 290,000 Chinese children had developed kidney stones and eleven had died because of the tainted milk powder. Chinese exports of milk powder, pet foods, toothpaste, dumplings, and other products have also caused illness and death worldwide. Growing public outcry in China and abroad has prompted the PRC government to promise stricter regulation and enforcement of consumer safety standards.

Internationalization of the Chinese Economy

China's overall economic strategy since 1978 is called "reform and opening up," meaning first, market reform, and second, opening the economy to the world, which is generally referred to as the "open policy." Since this strategy began, China's economy has become increasingly internationalized. For example, China's foreign trade has increased from US$20 billion in 1978 to over US$2 trillion by 2007 (see Figure 7.3). China invested in harbors, export-oriented high-tech parks, new roads and airports, so that as of 2008, over 60 percent of China's gross domestic product (GDP) came from the country's imports and exports (see Figure 7.4).

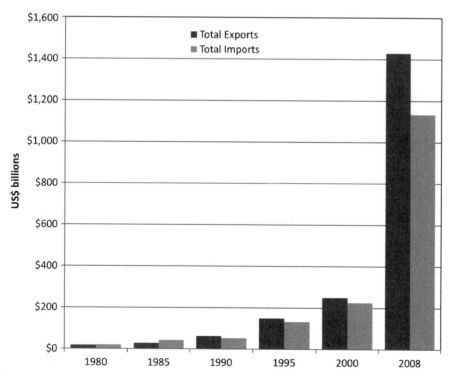

Figure 7.3 China's Foreign Trade, 1980–2008
Source: U.S.–China Business Council.

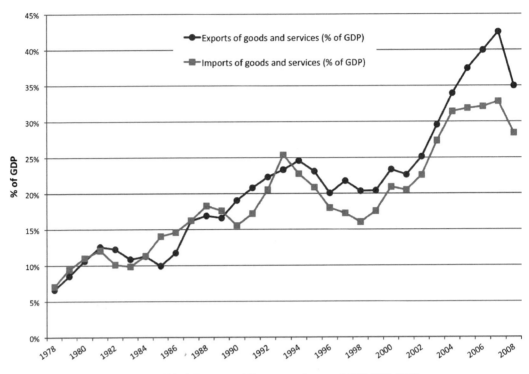

Figure 7.4 China's Imports and Exports as a Percent of GDP, 1978–2008
Source: U.S.–China Business Council.

The depth of China's integration into the global economy since 1978 is breathtaking. For centuries, China tried to limit foreign influences. Before the Opium War, foreign traders had to reside in Canton or other border towns and could deal only with trade officials and intermediaries designated by the imperial government. From 1949 and well into the 1980s, foreign traders could only buy a very limited range of Chinese products at the twice annual Canton Fair. But since 1978, China has opened its door to the world, as reflected in the variety of indicators presented in Table 7.1 at the end of this chapter.

But, as involvement with the international system deepened, so, too, has the impact of the world on China, as states who choose to join the global economy must negotiate the terms of their engagement with international organizations and countries that dominate the world's economy. States may prefer to limit external influences through quotas, tariffs and other barriers on imports, manipulate the value of their currency to affect their trade relations, or even subsidize their exports. But trading partners want reciprocity—fair trade, prices that reflect the real cost of production, free access to domestic markets, and rules that prevent copying of their products. Thus, states entering the global economy need to conform to international rules, such as those set by the Berne Convention for the Protection of Literary and Artistic Works and by the World Trade Organization, which are enforced by international tribunals or courts.

Opening to the World.   China opened to the outside world under an approach called "**segmented deregulation**," where rules controlling cross-border exchanges were lifted (or deregulated), but only for specific localities—Special Economic Zones (SEZs) or Export

Processing Zones (EPZs)—at a time when business relations between the world and the rest of China remained under tighter bureaucratic control.[21] For example, in 1984, China granted special status to fourteen newly declared "open coastal cities," cutting their production, export, import, and land taxes, and liberalizing their labor markets. Twelve of those cities were also allowed to open "economic and technical development zones" (ETDZs), with further tax advantages, but only for foreign and Chinese enterprises situated in those city's zones. Outside the ETDZs and the "open cities," the planned or regulated economy still reigned.

Not surprisingly, nationwide, city and provincial leaders lobbied the central government for such privileges, which the Chinese call "preferential policies." Concessions to more and more regions by the central government led to a "zone fever," which, as noted above, led to the creation of thousands of local export processing zones in the 1990s. Although the fever has been brought under control, development zones of various kinds remain an important feature of China's internationalized economy.

Foreign Direct Investment (FDI).   In its first efforts to attract foreign investment, the PRC turned to "Diaspora Capitalism"—Overseas Chinese in Hong Kong, Macau, Taiwan, and Southeast Asia—who were eager to invest their enormous wealth in the newly opened China. They liked China's cheap labor, cheap land, low taxes, and huge domestic market. They also wanted to establish projects in their home towns which would enhance their social status. Thus, most firms entering China in the 1980s were ethnic Chinese, family-run firms, investing under US$500,000 in joint ventures with local governments.

For the first twenty years of the open policy, China forced all foreign companies that wanted to invest in the country to form joint ventures with local firms—usually run by local government—that could control the foreign investor's behavior. Foreign investors were also limited to a less than majority share in joint ventures. But, after 1999, many new entrants to the Chinese market were totally foreign owned, with no domestic partner. In 2001, China joined the World Trade Organization, and after that, further lowered external and internal barriers to foreign investment; today foreign firms compete on a relatively level playing field in many sectors of the Chinese economy, drawing market share away from domestic firms. Ninety percent of the Fortune 500 firms have established a presence in China.

By 2007, 60 percent of exports from China came from firms with some foreign capital in them. Still, as discussed below, opening the domestic economy to FDI, under the terms stipulated by China's WTO accession, has put Chinese firms at enormous risk, as powerful multinational corporations will challenge newly emerging Chinese firms for a share of the domestic market.

A significant amount of FDI flowing into China comes from mainland Chinese firms whose overseas offices invest in China as "foreign entities" in a process referred to as "round tripping." In other words, funds are sent out of China to an (often fake) overseas company, which then reinvests the money back in China in order to benefit from the "preferential policies" that are available only to foreign firms. Two common localities for such companies are the Cayman Islands and the British Virgin Islands, which, despite the small size of their economies, are important centers of FDI into China, as well as being among the international tax havens used by many firms and individuals around the world. Taiwanese firms, too, seeking to evade the Taiwan government's restrictions on investment in the mainland, invest in China from these locations or from the United States.

Joining WTO.   No single act better reflects China's global economic integration than joining the World Trade Organization (WTO) in November 2001. After World War II, leaders in the West believed that the world would get richer if each country produced more of the goods in which it had a "comparative advantage"—that is, what it made best and most efficiently—and then traded these goods to other states, buying in turn what they made best. But free trade was necessary if this idea were to work, so the United States and its allies created the General Agreement on Tariffs and Trade (GATT), whose goal was to stop countries from using tariffs and quotas on imports to protect their local markets. This way, countries producing most efficiently would have larger markets.

But many countries still used protectionist strategies such as domestic rules or regulations that favored local firms over foreign firms in competing in the domestic market. These restrictions are particularly troublesome for the service sector, such as banking, insurance, accounting and the retail sector, in which the West had a comparative advantage. In 1995, the GATT was replaced by the WTO, which targets domestic or internal regulations that harm foreign competitors *within* countries, not just "at the border" tariffs and quotas that countries introduce to limit imports.

China applied to join the GATT in 1986, but its numerous regulations that constrained foreign economic activity and the crackdown in Tiananmen Square in 1989 led to long delays. The United States demanded enormous concessions from China, even though China cut its tariffs dramatically throughout the 1990s. According to Nicholas Lardy, to meet the rigorous terms set by the United States, the European Union, Japan, and Canada, China made greater compromises to enter the WTO than any other country in history.[22]

Joining the WTO was not an easy decision for China's leaders. Yielding to the West on these issues weakened China's sovereignty in the eyes of strongly nationalistic intellectual circles,[23] while the WTO's prohibition on discrimination by any member country against firms from any other member country (under the concept of "most favored nation status"), its insistence that all economic regulations be made public (under the concept of "transparency"), and the rule that foreign firms must be treated like any local firm (under the concept of "national treatment") challenged the PRC government's control over the economy. Rising nationalism in China in the mid-1990s made such compromises politically risky for any leader. In the spring of 1999, when the concessions that Premier Zhu Rongji made to U.S. trade negotiators to enter the WTO became public, he was pilloried on Chinese blogs and attacked by domestic opponents.[24]

But China's top leaders agreed to the terms and China officially became a member of the WTO in November 2001. Joining the WTO has had enormous implications for China's emerging industries. Well-funded high-tech, foreign firms entering China's economy challenge such "sunrise" enterprises for domestic market shares, threatening their survival, even before they develop the wings to fly.[25] Similarly, the entry of multinational corporations (MNCs) into China's domestic market could destroy "sunset firms"—those with older technologies that have difficulty adjusting to global competition—causing further job losses.

But overall, WTO entry has had positive implications for China's political economy. Under the WTO, trade disputes are resolved by an impartial tribunal—the "dispute resolution mechanism"—and not by pressure from individual countries. Second, by joining the WTO, China traded easier access to its market for similar access by Chinese firms to the rest of the world's domestic markets. Third, the demand for "transparency," which forces national governments to publish all rules regarding trade, severely undermines bureaucratic authority. No longer can bureaucrats stop foreign or domestic firms from opening new companies, or charge high fees for approving licenses, based on secret rules or regulations. This way, the "rule of law" replaces the whim of bureaucrats as the guide to business practice and may, therefore, serve as a check on rent seeking. Similarly, lower barriers to trade have decreased the amount of smuggling and closed many rent-seeking opportunities for bureaucrats. In fact, corruption seems to have become a minor issue in China's foreign trade sector compared to other parts of the economy.

China as a "Trading State."   Before the global economic crisis of 2008–09, China had become the quintessential "**trading state**,"[26] whose international commerce dramatically increased its national power. China's trade grew at an annual rate of 15 to 17 percent for almost thirty years, well above the 7 percent growth rate for world trade over the same period.[27] Following its entry into the WTO, China's trade became an even more important source of growth for its overall economy, supplying one-third of the annual increase in GDP between 2004 and 2007.

Some people assert that trade has contributed to the technological upgrading of goods produced in China, as indicated by a change in the structure of exports from labor-intensive goods to higher value-added ones. The share of machinery and equipment (capital goods) in China's exports rose from 27.3 percent to 46.2 percent between 1998 and 2005, while the share of light industrial (consumption) goods declined from 38.2 percent to 25.5 percent.

Similarly, internationalization has helped China's exports shift from low-tech to high-tech products. For example, all of China's major auto manufacturers in cities such as Shanghai, Wuhan, Guangzhou, Tianjin, Changchun, and others have established joint ventures with leading foreign car manufacturers, and the foreign partner has significantly improved the quality of Chinese cars. Thus, while the initial Chinese-produced Santana car, manufactured jointly by Volkswagen and the Shanghai Automotive Industrial Works (SAIW), cost 180,000 RMB (US$26,000) and was of poor quality, its quality has much improved and the cost is under 100,000 RMB (US$14,000), making it much more affordable to China's growing middle-class consumers. Japanese carmakers are the leaders in China—Honda has a huge plant outside Guangzhou—but General Motors transferred a state-of-the-art design center to its Shanghai partner, which allowed for significant industrial upgrading. As a result, in 2003, less than two years after joining the WTO, China ranked fourth in the world in terms of automobile production, and Chinese cars are moving onto the world stage as inexpensive exports.

However, while China is exporting more electronics, appliances, transportation equipment and machinery, and fewer agricultural products, textiles, and apparel, much of the growth in machinery exports has been due to "processing trade"—assembling equipment whose various parts are manufactured in other countries. The share of exports based on processing was 47 percent in 1999, 57 percent in 2002, and 55 percent from 2003 through 2005. The parts that are assembled originate in the United States, Japan, and Southeast Asia. So while it looks as if China is producing more sophisticated products, it still relies heavily on its cheap labor to assemble increasingly sophisticated products that are still made elsewhere.

Similarly, between 1997 and 2005, most of China's export growth was based on selling more of the products they had already been manufacturing, rather than expanding exports of new, more technologically advanced, products. Moreover, by manufacturing and exporting more of the same product, China forced down the international price of its own exports, benefiting importers, who were mostly developed economies. Between 1997 and 2005, the average price of exports from China to the United States fell on average 1.5 percent per year, while the prices of these same products from the rest of the world to the United States increased on average by 0.4 percent per year.[28] Therefore, even as China expanded its global market share, this deeper level of global integration did not significantly modernize its economy.

THE BEIJING CONSENSUS: A NEW CHINESE MODEL OF DEVELOPMENT?

Chapter 1 briefly noted that the People's Republic of China, during the latter part of the Maoist era and again now, has been viewed by many as providing an economic model for other developing countries. The current Chinese model is sometimes referred to as the **Beijing Consensus**. This name emerged from a comparison with the **Washington Consensus**, which became the dominant model of international development starting in the early 1980s and particularly after the end of the Cold War. Both the Beijing and Washington Consensus are informal sets of ideas and policies, rather than a formal organization in any sense. Neither reflects a firm consensus; both the Washington and the Beijing variant have lots of critics at home and abroad.

The Washington Consensus, a term coined by economist John Williamson, are policies promoted primarily by the United States, the World Bank, and the International Monetary Fund (IMF), that prescribe a **neo-liberal** approach to economic development that includes reducing the role of the state in the economy and maximizing that of the free market, eliminating government subsides, privatizing government industries and public utilities, and removing barriers to free trade and foreign investment. The Washington Consensus was criticized for promoting economic growth over social welfare and for the stringent economic and political conditions that its proponents attached to giving aid and loans to developing countries. For example, under pressure from the IMF, Egypt cut its food subsidies, which in 1977 triggered massive urban riots. But this view of economic development really took a hit with the global financial crisis that began in late 2008, which many people blamed on the lack of effective government regulation of a get-rich-at-any-cost market economy.

China's spectacular economic performance had certainly been gaining attention as a model of development well before the 2008 meltdown. The term "Beijing Consensus" was popularized by author Joshua Cooper Ramo in 2004, and embodied three main guidelines for development: a commitment to innovation and experimentation; sustained growth based on sustainable and equitable development; and global integration with national self-determination. The environmental and social part of these guidelines seem to embody the yet-to-be-realized agenda of the Hu Jintao administration since ecological degradation and gross inequalities are two of the most obvious downsides of the Chinese economic miracle to-date. When the PRC talks about its development model, it emphasizes guidelines such as strong government orientation, prudence in market reforms and growth with stability—each of which are obvious knocks on the Washington Consensus. Furthermore, one commentary in *People's Daily* said:

> In foreign relations, China never politicizes economic issues, makes empty threats, or forms a small clique and confederate with others, instead always considers the feelings of citizens of other countries as far as possible. With the international arena accustomed to the Cold War mentality, China's sober and pragmatic diplomatic style with Confucian features is a breath of fresh air.[*]

Critics of the Beijing Consensus say that it does ignore some of the deep problems in the Chinese economy, such as China's record on human rights and labor abuses; moreover, its policies are not that different in certain fundamental ways from the Washington Consensus, including spawning cut-throat capitalism and crass commercialism. Finally, other developing countries use the Beijing Consensus (and Beijing's economic success) to justify political repression, protective tariffs, and government intervention in the market.

[*] "Analysis: Why Does the China Model Fascinate the World?," *People's Daily* Online English, June 30, 2009, http://english.peopledaily.com.cn/90001/90780/91345/6689725.html.

Still, the introduction of foreign manufacturers, particularly joint ventures, where the Chinese partner is a significant participant and new technologies are actually transferred, can play a major role in modernizing the Chinese economy and truly upgrading the nation's indigenous industrial capacity.

In any case, changes in the global economy have compelled China's leaders to think seriously about shifting the country's engine of growth from exports to domestic consumption. China's savings rate (the percentage of a person's disposable income devoted to savings rather than consumption) is between 30 and 40 percent—very high in comparison to, say, the United States, where for several decades personal savings ranged at around nine percent before tumbling to below zero (in other words, debt) in the run-up to the financial meltdown in 2008–2009. Confucian culture is traditionally frugal, and the experience of great economic uncertainty, especially during the Mao years, has made many PRC citizens prone to save money when they have it. Moreover, despite being a so-called socialist state, the weakness of China's welfare system, in terms of hospitalization and retirement, forces most Chinese to put away money for a rainy day. The Chinese government is trying to encourage its citizens to spend more and save less (the opposite of America's problem), so that Chinese companies do not have to depend so much on selling their goods in a volatile international economy. Managing this shift from an export-led growth strategy of development, that served it so well for decades, to one more based on domestic consumption is a major challenge facing the government of the People's Republic.

China's "Going Out" Strategy

As part of its economic development strategy, China is purchasing overseas firms, mines, and resources, locating its own companies overseas, and listing Chinese firms on global stock markets to acquire foreign capital. This "going out" strategy (*zou qu chu*) began in the mid-1990s when the State Economic and Trade Commission selected 120 "national champions" to lead China's engagement with the world. As China edged toward joining the WTO, large Chinese firms needed new technology, internationally recognized brand names, large injections of capital, and modern management teams to compete in the international marketplace. Also, under China's WTO accession agreement, MNCs would enter the Chinese market.[29] Many Chinese firms were listed on Nasdaq and the NYSE, and the number and proportion listed on the Hang Seng Exchange in Hong Kong rose from 182/1882 (10 percent of all overseas Chinese firms) in 1995 to 2336/7470 (40 percent) at the end of 2003.[30] By 2007, there were more than 10,000 Chinese firms with investments abroad.

According to the *World Investment Report 2007*, China's outbound non-financial (i.e. in businesses, manufacturing, mining, etc.) FDI in 1990–2000 averaged US$2.2 billion per year, but leaped to over US$25 billion in 2008 (see Figure 7.5). As a share of total state investment, China's own FDI remains relatively low at 1.9 percent in 2006; however, that level has doubled from 1.0 percent in 2003.

"Corporate China's" sudden buying spree shocked the world. In 2005, when the China National Offshore Oil Corporation tried to buy the U.S. oil company Unocal, the U.S. Congress blocked the sale, arguing that the PRC government was subsidizing the (US$18 billion) purchase. Since then, China's leading computer company, Lenovo, bought the personal computer arm of IBM, making China an instant global competitor in the industry. Still, integrating two firms with distinct business cultures has not proven easy, as many foreign employees of IBM chose to move on after the deal was struck, leaving Lenovo dependent on less globally experienced leadership. In mid-2009, a bankrupt General Motors sold its Hummer division to a little

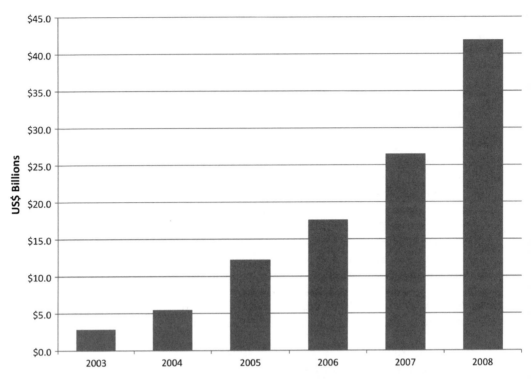

Figure 7.5 China's Nonfinancial Outbound Investment, 2003–2008
Source: PRC Ministry of Commerce.

known Chinese equipment parts manufacturer, Sichuan Tengzhong Heavy Industrial Machinery Company, which said it planned to keep producing and selling the vehicles in the United States.

Many observers see such investment abroad by Chinese corporations as positive, not only for China but also, for the world economy.[31] Increased Chinese investment overseas boosts the global economy and lets China recycle its massive foreign exchange holdings (and its massive domestic savings). Shifting Chinese manufacturing to countries with cheaper labor than China, such as Cambodia or Bangladesh, promotes the economies of the world's poorer countries. Finally, stiff competition will force Chinese firms to conform to global standards (rather than change those standards, as others worry). Thus, Geoff Dyer and Richard McGregor see a "quiet revolution under way in the Chinese state sector, which has produced a new generation of confident companies with global ambitions."[32]

But, because Chinese firms often do not conform to global norms of corporate responsibility, they sometimes get into trouble with overseas trade unions. They also pursue opportunities in countries where Western firms have chosen not to compete for political reasons, such as Sudan, Iran, or Burma, creating problems for China with the United States and the European Union, which seek sanctions against these "rogue" states. One Chinese scholar, Zhu Feng, at Beijing University's Centre for International and Strategic Studies, has written that some of the PRC's SOEs, such as the oil company, Petro-China, have become very powerful interest groups. "They even hijacked China's foreign policy in Sudan."[33] Zhai Kun, of the China Institute of Contemporary International Relations in Beijing, said that while large state companies are driven by "economic considerations... more and more regulations should now be created by the government to constrain their behavior overseas."[34]

THE PROBLEM OF INEQUALITY IN CHINA

The Maoist model of development promoted egalitarianism as one of its major goals. Although significant gaps in income, services, and welfare persisted throughout the Maoist period, particularly between the urban and rural areas, there were significant achievements in promoting equality within China through land reform, the collectivization of agriculture, the nationalization of industry and commerce, the expansion of literacy and education, public health campaigns, and other policies that were part of the PRC's socialist agenda. Of course, economic growth was quite slow from the mid-1950s until Mao's death in 1976, so the Chinese people were both relatively poor and relatively equal by the end of the Maoist era.

China's economic boom that began in the late 1970s has led to a spectacular growth in national wealth and improvement in the standards of living for the large majority of the population. But particularly in this century, it has also led to the appearance of multiple and deep inequalities in the country. Several of the chapters in this book touch on this problem of inequality in the contemporary People's Republic.

There are various ways to measure inequality within China and to compare levels of inequality with that in other countries. One measure of national inequality used by economists in called the **Gini Index**. It measures the distribution of family income within a population and comes up with a composite number between 0 (perfect equality) and 1 (perfect inequality). In other words, the higher the number, the greater the level of inequality. The most recent measure of China's GINI Index (2007) was .47, which put it in the range of countries such as Nepal (.472), Rwanda (.468), and the United States (.45). For comparison, some of the world's most unequal countries are South Africa (.65) and Brazil (.567), while the most equal are Sweden (.23), Slovenia (.24), and Denmark (.24).

To measure inequality within China, you might consider, for example, the range in gross domestic product (GDP) per capita among the PRC's administrative divisions. While national GDP per capita (at purchasing power parity) for the whole country was about $6,000 in 2008, regionally it varied from near $20,000 in Shanghai to about $2,300 in the far western province of Guizhou.

Or consider the urban-rural gap, which is discussed in this chapter and others. As the following graph shows, incomes in both city and countryside have grown dramatically since the economic reforms began three decades ago. But so has urban-rural inequality (see Figure 7.6). Dealing with this urban-rural gap and other forms of inequality is one of the biggest political economy challenges facing China's leaders in the early decades of the twenty-first century.

Finally, "going out" involves the search for resources, particularly energy. In 1993, China became a net importer of oil, and since 2007, despite abundant quantities of coal, it began importing that energy source as well. In 2007, China was the number three importer of oil and the number two consumer of oil in the world. Much of its oil consumption has followed the rapid expansion of the auto industry; yet, as China's urban middle class grows, and if more and more foreign enterprises continue to manufacture on the mainland, China's energy hunger will likely rise rapidly. The result is increased dependence on imported energy and a proliferation of bilateral trading relationships, as China's national oil companies (NOCs) move out into the world to get China the energy it needs.[35]

In 2008, the *Economist* reported that from Canada to Indonesia and Kazakhstan, Chinese firms were gobbling up oil, gas, coal, and metals, paying for the right to explore for them, or buying up firms that produce them.[36] In June 2007, 79 ships were lined up off Australia's biggest coal port, Newcastle, to load cargoes destined for China; African and Latin American economies grew at their fastest pace in decades, thanks to Chinese demand for their resources.

According to Credit Lyonnais Securities of Asia's aptly named report, "*China Eats the World*,"[37] the PRC's combined share of world consumption of aluminum, copper, nickel, and iron ore doubled from 1990 (7 percent) to 2000 (15 percent), and by 2004 was about 20 percent. Chinese demand for these commodities was expected to double again by 2010. According to Barbara Stallings, because the Chinese economy relies so much on manufacturing, as compared to the service sector, China remains excessively hungry for resources, making it more dependent on the world economy than most large economies.[38]

A close link exists between China as a trading state, its hunger for resources, and its need for a "going out" strategy. According to the International Crisis Group's 2008 report, "*China's Thirst for Oil*," heavy industry makes up over 2/3 of China's energy demand, which "is mostly driven by the manufacturing of goods sold on global markets, not least in the U.S. Much energy in China is dedicated to the creation of infrastructure—factories, roads, and ports—that makes possible an economy that supports overseas consumption."[39] Thus, while many Westerners criticize China's high rate of energy consumption, much of that demand arises because China is meeting the needs of Western consumers.

Current and Future Dilemmas

What dilemmas does China's political economy face in the coming decades? Even before the economic crisis of 2008–2009, the list of problems was already quite long. China can no longer accept highly polluting enterprises, as the pea soup fog that has settled over small towns around the country shows the high price China is paying for industrialization (see chapter 11). According to a 2006 report by the State Environmental Protection Administration, air, water, and solid-waste pollution caused US$64 billion in damages across China in 2004, accounting for 3.05 percent of the year's GDP.[40] Pollution is a major source of popular protests that challenge CCP authority. Yet, industrialization and the manufacturing sector remain the main source of new jobs for China's growing population.

The pace of land expropriation for development within China has become so intense that the PRC is now looking overseas for food and farmland. Growing gaps between rich and poor people, among regions, and between the cities and the countryside have reached dangerous levels. A lack of social welfare policies means that most citizens fear medical bills that could bankrupt their families, while workers fear retirement. Finally, a property bubble has priced new apartments out of the reach of China's rapidly growing middle class, which could undermine some support for the CCP. And even the collapse in prices resulting from the recession has not helped the average Chinese citizen buy an apartment, as the stimulus policy introduced by the government quickly led to a new bubble in property prices.

Internationally, the cost of Chinese labor has increased significantly, leading many manufacturers to relocate to Vietnam, Bangladesh, Cambodia, India, and other lower cost countries. China must strengthen its product regulations, particularly food, medicine, and toys, as China's exports of these items make its poorly regulated markets the world's headache as well. China's need for foreign oil and gas grows daily, but if the world has indeed moved to the point where few new supplies are to be found—what is called "peak oil"—the cost of driving China's economic engine will grow significantly. Should China contest the United States and other advanced countries for oil and gas, its foreign relations could become far more complicated and even conflictual. Finally, the PRC's accumulation of foreign exchange holdings has become excessive, while China's trade imbalances with the United States and

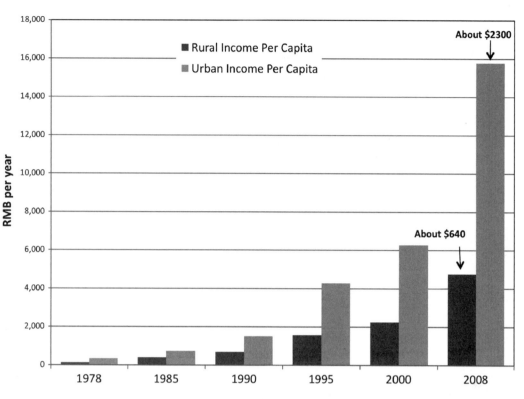

Figure 7.6 Urban and Rural Incomes in China, 1978–2008
Source: U.S.–China Business Council.

the European Union are becoming politically unsustainable. Protectionism could emerge in both of these continental economies aimed at Chinese products. Should this occur, China would be hard pressed to maintain its growth rates, unless it significantly increases the role of internal trade and domestic consumption in its economic development.

China's "export-led" development strategy is facing enormous problems. The financial "tsunami" has collapsed U.S. and EU demand for China's exports, which decreased in the last quarter of 2008 to their lowest level in seven years. The export sector shed approximately 25 million jobs (mostly rural migrant workers) at the end of 2008. Like many other governments around the world, the PRC hopes that its stimulus package will create a lot of new jobs.

Yet it is clear that the structure of the world's political economy, not just China's, must be adjusted. There particularly needs to be an adjustment in Sino-American economic relations. By buying hundreds of billions of dollars in U.S. Treasury bills with its foreign exchange reserves, earned through its export-led growth, China supplied American consumers with cheap capital and low-interest loans that allowed them to buy China's manufactured good and obtain mortgages that in the end, they could not afford. But the United States cannot run such huge fiscal and trade deficits indefinitely, and the PRC cannot run such huge fiscal and trade surpluses. China must begin to transfer its engine of growth from exports to domestic consumption. Whether China will be able to make this transition, how long such a transition will take, and whether Americans can wean themselves from their high consumption, low savings mentality will have enormous significance for China and the world in the coming decades.

Table 7.1 Selected Indicators of China's Global Integration, 1978—2008

	1978	1980	1984	1988	1990	1992	1994	1998	2000	2002	2004	2006	2008
Total Foreign Trade ($US bil.)	20.6	38.1	53.5	99.8	115	165.5	236.6	324.0	474.3	620.8	1,155	1,760	2,561.6
Foreign trade as % of GDP (current prices)	n.a.	12.6	17.3	24.7	29.6	33.9	42.3	31.8	39.6	42.7	59.8	66.6	63.4
Total Exports ($US billions)	9.8	18.1	26.1	47.5	62.1	84.9	121.0	183.7	249.2	325.6	593.3	968.9	1,428.5
Exports by Foreign-Invested Firms ($US bil.)	n.a.	n.a.	n.a.	2.46	7.80	17.4	34.7	80.9	119.4	169.9	338.6	563.8	790.4
Exports by foreign-invested firms (% of total exports)	n.a.	n.a.	n.a.	5.2	12.6	20.5	28.7	44.0	48.0	54.8	57.1	58.2	55.3
Inbound Foreign Direct Investment ($US bil.)	n.a.	n.a.	1.4	3.2	3.5	11.0	33.8	45.5	40.7	52.7	60.6	63.0	92.4
Foreign Exchange Reserves ($US bil.)	n.a.	-1.3	8.2	3.4	11.1	19.4	52.0	145.0	165.6	286.4	609.9	1,066.3	1,946
Cargo Handled in Major Coastal Ports (mil. tons)	198	217	275	438	483	603	744	922	1,256	1,666	2,461	3,422	4,296
Deep-Water Berths in Major Ports (10,000 tons)	85	n.a.	173*	226	282	314	359	468	518	547	687	883	1,076
Number of Foreign Tourists (1,000s)**	230	529	1,134	1,842	1,747	4,006	5182	7,108	10,160	13,440	16,933	22,210	24,325
International Air Routes	n.a.	n.a.	24	40	44	58	84	131	133	161	244	268	297
Number of Foreign-Invested Star-rated Hotels	n.a.	n.a.	n.a.	n.a.	n.a.	9	529	694	833	686	531	585	n.a.

*This is for 1985.
**Excluding overseas Chinese and Chinese from Hong Kong and Macau.
Sources: China Statistical Yearbook; Ministry of Commerce of China; US-China Business Council; World Bank World Development Indicators.

Notes

1. Nicholas R. Lardy, "Economic Recovery and the First Five-Year Plan," in Roderick MacFarquhar, John King Fairbank, and Dennis Crispen Twitchett, ed., *The Cambridge History of China*, Vol. 14 (Cambridge: Cambridge University Press, 1987), 177.

2. Foreign trade companies (FTCs) were owned by various levels of the government, from the center to the county. They carried out trade for the state but also monitored imports and exports for the state. Before the mid-1980s, twelve centrally managed FTCs had a monopoly on all aspects of China's foreign trade.

3. Fan Yongming, "Reform Is the Driving Force of China's Integration into the International Community," in *Globalization and China's Reforms*, ed. Chen Zhimin and David Zweig. (London: Routledge, 2007).

4. David Zweig, "The Stalled 'Fifth Wave:' Zhu Rongji's Reform Package of 1998–2000," *Asian Survey* (March–April 2001): 231–247.

5. Michael Lipton shows that this urban bias is a universal phenomenon in most of the developing world. See Michael Lipton, *Why Poor People Stay Poor: Urban Bias in World Development* (Cambridge, MA: Harvard University Press, 1976).

6. David Zweig, *Freeing China's Farmers: Rural Restructuring in the Reform Era* (Armonk, NY: M. E. Sharpe, 1997), 347.

7. David Zweig, *Agrarian Radicalism in China, 1968–1981* (Cambridge, MA: Harvard University Press, 1989).

8. Dali Yang, *Calamity and Reform in China: State, Rural Society and Institutional Change since the Great Leap Famine* (Stanford, CA: Stanford University Press, 1996).

9. Thomas Bernstein and Xiaobo Lü, *Taxation without Representation in Contemporary Rural China* (Cambridge, UK: Cambridge University Press, 2003).

10. In Jiangsu Province, by 1995, two-thirds of all foreign trade was still dominated by official foreign trade companies at various levels, and by 1996, 47.8 percent of all of China's foreign exchange earnings came from TVE export earnings. David Zweig, *Internationalizing China: Domestic Interests and Global Linkages* (Ithaca, NY: Cornell University Press, 2002), 116–118.

11. Zweig, *Internationalizing China*, 122–123.

12. James Kai-sing Kung and Yi-min Lin, "The Decline of Township-and-Village Enterprises in China's Economic Transition," *World Development* 35, no. 4 (2007): 569–584.

13. Zweig, *Freeing China's Farmers*, 130–150.

14. For reports about the current struggles over land, see Peter Ho, "Contesting Rural Spaces: Land Disputes, Customary Tenure and the State," and David Zweig, "To the Courts or to the Barricades: Can New Political Institutions Manage Rural Conflict?" in *Chinese Society*, 2nd ed., Elizabeth J. Perry and Mark Selden (London and New York: RoutledgeCurzon, 2003), 93–112 and 113–135, respectively.

15. Andrew G. Walder, *Communist Neo-traditionalism: Work and Authority in Chinese Industry* (Berkeley: University of California Press, 1986).

16. Barry J. Naughton, "The Pattern and Legacy of Economic Growth in the Mao Era," in *Perspectives on Modern China: Four Anniversaries,* ed. Kenneth Lieberthal. et al. (Armonk, NY: M. E. Sharpe, 1991), 226–254.

17. Dorothy J. Solinger, *From Lathes to Looms: China's Industrial Policy in Comparative Perspective, 1979–1982* (Stanford, CA: Stanford University Press, 1991), 136.

18. Barry Naughton, *The Chinese Economy: Transitions and Growth* (Cambridge, MA: MIT Press, 2007), 101.

19. Nasughton, *The Chinese Economy*, 184.

20. Margaret M. Pearson, "The Business of Governing Business in China: Institutions and Norms of the Emerging Regulatory State," *World Politics* 57, no. 2 (January 2005): 296–322.

21. See George T. Crane, *The Political Economy of China's Special Economic Zones* (Armonk, NY: M. E. Sharpe, 1997).

22. Nicholas R. Lardy, *Integrating China into the Global Economy* (Washington, DC: Brookings Institution Press, 2002).

23. Di Yingqing and Zheng Gang, "What Does China's Joining the WTO Actually Imply with Regard to China's Long-term Interests? An Analysis of the Question of China's Joining the WTO," *Gaige neican* (Internal Reference Material on Reform) 9 (May 5, 1999): 34–38, translated in *The Chinese Economy: China and the WTO, Part II*, 33, no. 2 (March–April 2000): 19.

24. Margaret M. Pearson, "The Case of China's Accession to GATT/WTO," in *The Making of Chinese Foreign and Security Policy in the Era of Reform, 1978–2000*, ed. David M. Lampton (Stanford, CA: Stanford University Press, 2001), 337–370.

25. Peter Nolan, *China and the Global Economy: National Champions, Industrial Policy, and the Big Business Revolution* (New York: Palgrave, 2001).

26. Richard N. Rosecrance, *The Rise of the Trading State: Commerce and Conquest in the Modern World* (New York: Basic Books, 1986).

27. Eswar Prasad, ed., *China's Growth and Integration into the World Economy* (Washington, DC: Occasional Paper No. 232, International Monetary Fund, 2004).

28. Mary Amiti and Caroline Freund, *An Anatomy of China's Export Growth* (Washington, DC: National Bureau of Economic Research, January 31, 2008).

29. Nolan, *China and the Global Economy*.

30. Friedrich Wu, "The Globalization of Corporate China," *NBR Analysis* 16, no. 3, December 2005.

31. Wu, "The Globalization of Corporate China."

32. Geoff Dyer and Richard McGregor, "China's Champions: Why State Ownership Is No Longer Proving a Dead Hand," *The Wall Street Journal*, March 16, 2008.

33. Richard McGregor, "Chinese Diplomacy 'Hijacked' by Companies," *Financial Times*, March 17, 2008.

34. McGregor, "Chinese Diplomacy 'Hijacked' by Companies."

35. David Zweig and Bi Jianhai, "China's Global Hunt for Energy," *Foreign Affairs* 84, no. 5 (September–October 2005): 25–38.

36. "A Ravenous Dragon," *The Economist*, March 15, 2008, 4.

37. Andy Rothman, "China Eats the World: The Sustainability of Chinese Commodities Demand," *Credit Lyonnais Securities Asia*, March 2005.

38. Barbara Stallings, "China's Economic Relations with Developing Countries," Brown University, December 12, 2007, unpublished paper.

39. International Crisis Group, *China's Thirst for Oil*, Asia Report no. 153, 9 June 2008, 3.

40. Mark Leonard, *What Does China Think?* (New York: Public Affairs Books, 2008), 42.

Suggested Readings

Benewick, Robert, and Stephanie Hemelryk Donald. *The State of China Atlas: Mapping the World's Fastest-Growing Economy,* 2nd ed. Berkeley: University of California Press, 2009.

Bernstein, Thomas P and Xiaobo Lü. *Taxation without Representation in Contemporary Rural China.* New York: Cambridge University Press, 2003.

Bongiorni, Sara. *A Year without "Made in China": One Family's True Life Adventure in the Global Economy.* New York: Wiley, 2007.

Chen, Calvin. *Some Assembly Required Work, Community, and Politics in China's Rural Enterprises.* Cambridge, MA: Harvard University Press, 2008.

Huang, Yasheng. *Capitalism with Chinese Characteristics: Entrepreneurship and the State.* New York: Cambridge University Press, 2008.

Lardy, Nicholas R. *Integrating China into the Global Economy.* Washington, DC: Brookings Institution Press, 2002.

Li, Lanqing. *Breaking Through: The Birth of China's Opening-up Policy.* New York: Oxford University Press, 2010.

Naughton, Barry. *The Chinese Economy: Transitions and Growth.* Cambridge, MA: MIT Press, 2007.

Nolan, Peter. *Integrating China: Transition into the Global Economy.* New York, Anthem Press, 2008.

Oi, Jean C. *Rural China takes off: The Institutional Foundations of Economic Reform.* Berkeley, CA: University of California Press, 1999.

Steinfeld, Edward S., *Forging Reform in China: The Fate of State Industry.* New York and Cambridge: Cambridge University Press, 1998.

Steinfeld, Edward S. *Playing Our Game: Why China's Rise Doesn't Threaten the West.* New York: Oxford University Press, 2010.

Whiting, Susan H. *Power and Wealth in Rural China: The Political Economy of Institutional Change.* New York: Cambridge University Press, 2000.

Zweig, David. *Internationalizing China: Domestic Interests and Global Linkages*. Ithaca, NY: Cornell University Press, 2002.

Zweig, David. Freeing *China's Farmers: Rural Restructuring in the Reform Era*. Armonk, NY: M. E. Sharpe, 1997.

Zweig, David and Jianhai Bi, "China's Global Hunt for Energy," *Foreign Affairs*, Volume 84, No. 5 (September–October 2005): 25–38.

III POLITICS AND POLICY IN ACTION

8

Rural China: Reform and Resistance

John James Kennedy

From spreading grassroots democracy to rising incidents of unrest, rural China has witnessed dramatic political change over the last quarter century. New political opportunities for rural residents began with the introduction of economic reforms in the early 1980s. Market reforms and the abolition of the people's commune system eroded the political authority of local cadres, who, in the Maoist era, had control over the rural economic and social life, and fundamentally altered cadre-villager relations. While the leaders' control over basic resources and activities has diminished, villagers' participation in political affairs has increased. With the introduction of the **Organic Law of Villagers Committees** in 1987 (revised in 1998), villagers could directly elect and recall their local leaders. The quality of village elections varies across rural China, but cadre accountability by their village constituents has improved. The next step was experiments of direct elections for high authorities at the town level in 1998. However, the central leadership quickly ended these experiments and scaled back the direct elections for town government heads with more inclusive, but less direct selection mechanisms.

At the same time, throughout the 1990s and beyond 2000, reported incidences of rural unrest have dramatically increased. The modes of resistance range from legal petitions to massive demonstrations that sometimes turn violent. Yet, these social disturbances do *not* threaten the central government or the Chinese Communist Party (CCP). Most incidents of rural resistance tend to be directed toward local government officials rather than the central authorities. Indeed, many of these resisters use national laws, such as the Organic Law, to protect themselves from local abusive cadres. This has created a contradiction of rural unrest that has a relatively high level of support for the central leadership.

Still, unrest reflects villagers' discontent, as well as demands for greater participation in the local decision-making process. Thus, in order to maintain popular support from the rural population, the CCP leadership continues to slowly expand political reforms. The question is whether the gradual introduction of reforms is enough to satisfy rural political demands before the incidents of rural unrest become unmanageable for the central party-state.

This chapter is divided into seven parts. The first section is a brief introduction to the rural administration that comprises counties and town governments. Part two focuses on villagers and village cadres concerns, such as: land management, local economy, taxes, and environmental protection. This includes the change in cadre-villager relations from the 1980s to the present. The third section introduces the town and township officials and how the *nomenklatura* system of cadre management shapes their incentives to fully implement central policies. The chief question for students studying the politics of rural China and political reform is this: Does the central government lack the political *will* or *capacity* to influence county and town officials? Part four focuses on the development of village elections. This section will address the introduction of the Organic Law of Villagers Committees and the uneven implementation of the law. The fifth part addresses several experiments with direct elections for town mayors and more accountable local People's Congresses. While the central leadership quickly ended early attempts at direct elections for government heads, there have been a number of less direct election methods that broaden the public participation in the cadre selection method. The sixth section focuses on rural resistance. This section will look at the various methods of rural resistance: legal means, semi-legal (**rightful resistance**), and illegal actions. One key observation is that resistance and protest is associated with the uneven implementation of rural political reforms. Indeed, many large illegal protests started out as local legal attempts to get specific reforms, such as a fee reduction regulation or village election law, fully enforced in their village. The final part addresses the prospects of future political reform in rural China.

Rural Administrative Divisions

As discussed in greater detail in the next chapter, China has experienced extensive urbanization in recent decades. In 1980, about 81 percent of China's population lived in the rural areas. By 2008, that percentage was down to 55 percent. Nevertheless, that means over 700 million people are still classified as rural residents, which is more than twice the total population of the United States. Moreover, there is an enormous diversity in the countryside that makes it difficult to generalize about the rural population, especially in terms of geography. From abject poverty in remote mountainous villages to industrialized villages near larger cities, the levels of wealth, access to health care, and educational opportunities vary by proximity to urban centers.

The definition of rural residents is associated with the administrative hierarchy that dramatically changed with decollectivization and the end of the communes in the 1980s. From 1958 to 1982, the administrative division below the county was the commune, and its subordinate units, the production brigade and production team. Rural residents were citizens who lived and worked in the communes. As a result of restructuring, after 1982, communes were renamed town or townships, brigades were villages, and production teams became small groups. In essence, this was going back to the traditional, pre-communist names for these levels of social organization.

Currently, the formal administrative hierarchy of the PRC includes the national, provincial, municipal (or city), county, and the town or township levels of government. Technically, rural residents are those citizens who live below the county level and whose registration (*hukou*) is in a town, township, or village. The town or township is the lowest formal administrative level of state authority in China. Villages are not part of the formal administrative structure of the state, but, according to the 1982 PRC constitution, are self-governing units.

The difference between a town and a township is the percentage of registered urban population who live in a particular locale. A town has over 10 percent of the population registered as non-agricultural (urban), while a township has over 90 percent of the population registered as agricultural (rural). Reflecting the trend toward urbanization, the number of towns surpassed the number of townships in 2002.[*]

Figure 8.1 displays the administrative hierarchy of the People's Republic below the provincial level. Within every municipality there are a number of counties; within every county, there are towns; and below the towns are villages; and within every village there are a number of small groups. According to the *2008 China Statistical Yearbook*, there are 283 large municipalities that typically have over one million people; these are called "cities at the prefecture level." The population of these municipalities can range from 9.2 million in Shijiazhuang city, Hebei province, to 1.8 million in Xining city, Qinghai province. Within every municipality there are about 5 to 15 counties. There are over 2,800 counties in China, and their population varies from approximately 200,000 to 500,000. County population size can vary widely even within one province. According to the 2000 Census for Shaanxi province, Hu county near the provincial capital of Xian municipality has over 250,000 residents, while the geographically larger, but more remote Ganquan county has only 30,000. Under each county, there are about 10 to 20 towns, and the population is usually about 20,000, but can be as large as 70,000 or as low as 7,000. There are over 34,000 towns, and within every town there are about 15 to 20 villages. Rural China has over 600,000 villages, formally called **administrative villages**. Village population is typically around 1,000 to 2,000 residents. Finally, within every village there are two to seven small groups or "**natural villages**." While some small groups in densely populated villages near urban centers can be as large as a typical village (2,000 residents), in the more remote mountainous areas, they may have no more than a dozen widely dispersed households.

In order to maintain CCP influence in the large and varied rural areas, each town, county, and village has a party secretary as well as a government head. The party secretary has the most political power and makes the final policy decision at his or her respective level. Party secretaries connect higher authorities with the lower levels to ensure that policies are carried out and laws are enforced. Therefore, although the Chinese communist-party state is *not* a monolithic regime that can enforce its will at all times and in all places, the CCP still retains significant authority to carry out priority policies and maintain at least a minimum level of control down to the village level.

Villagers and Cadres: Changing Social and Political Relationships

Villagers

China's villagers have a keen sense of justice. Whether it is the distribution of collective land or investment of public funds, villagers expect a fair decision from their local leaders. For example, villagers *do not* own the land they cultivate and live on. It remains collectively owned and managed by village cadres. Villagers lease land, and cadres decide how to allocate the collective land among households. For most villagers, this is *the* most crucial cadre decision because of the variation in land quality and location. Each household is allocated two to four separate plots of land, and the location of the plot can be a few yards from the their back door or several miles away. Moreover, arable land is scarce. Currently less than 15 percent of land in China is cultivated. In villages where arable land is less than 50 percent, the local leaders tend to give every household a small portion of the good

---

[*] To simplify the discussion of rural governance in this chapter, the term "town" will be used to refer to both towns and townships.

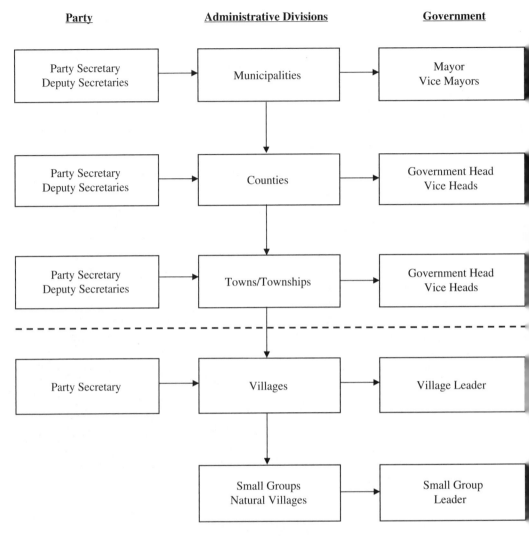

Figure 8.1 Party/Government Officials and Administrative Divisions Below the Provincial Level
Note: The dashed line represents the lowest official administrative level (the town).

land. This is because villagers prefer an allocation decision based on fairness rather than efficiency (the relationship between labor and output), which would dictate that the land be allocated in larger, contiguous pieces rather than in smaller, dispersed segments. Portions of village land are still readjusted every five to ten years due to demographic changes such as births, deaths and marriages. Village cadres can also lease land to people outside the village. Rapid industrialization and urbanization have made land a very valuable commodity and the source of profit. Villagers expect leaders to protect the arable land or at least to receive fair compensation for leased land. But this situation has created enormous opportunities for corruption and has been on the major causes of growing rural unrest (see chapter 7).

Villagers also expect fair and transparent management of public funds especially in the area of rural education. For villagers, the local elementary school is vital for the education of their children and grandchildren, and local cadres are responsible for construction and maintenance. Villagers rely on the local cadres to spend education funds in an efficient and honest manner that will to ensure quality schooling and the safety of their children. Neglecting the maintenance or cutting corners during school construction can be disastrous. For example, the May 2008 earthquake in Sichuan province occurred in the middle of a school day, and many rural elementary and junior high schools collapsed, killing thousands of children. Grieving parents asked why local government buildings remained standing while most of the schools collapsed. Thus the quality of education and the safety of their children remains a vital concern for villagers.

Villagers can also be proactive when their expectations of fairness are not met. Many rural people are unafraid to meet or even confront local cadres and town officials. Villager action can be as simple as an individual walking over to the leader's home to discuss a problem such as road maintenance or a land lease issue. It may also be more complex, when villagers take legal action to recall an elected leader or sue a town government official in the local courts for attempting to extract excessive fees. If legal action does not resolve the problem, then some rural residents may turn to public demonstrations such as a roadblock or sit-in. Of course, not all villagers take political action, but most retain a sense of justice and support resistance when expectations of fairness are not met.

Village Cadres

Village cadres are community members who have leadership positions and are responsible to both villagers and higher authorities. Residents are very familiar with local cadres since they are from families who have long lived in the village. Of course, this familiarity does not always reduce friction between cadres and villagers, nor does it increase cadre authority. Whether they are popularly elected or appointed from above, village cadres are caught in the middle between villagers and town officials, and therefore have a delicate balancing act in carrying out their jobs. Town officials depend on them to carry out national policies and local regulations. Many of these are unpopular policies, such as tax and fee collection or family planning. In the 1980s and 1990s, villagers called town and village officials the "three wanting cadres": they want your money, grain, and unborn children. The last is in reference to the role that cadres play in carrying out China's strict "one-child policy" (see chapter 13).

Village committees were officially established as the governing body on the village level with the enactment of the 1982 state constitution. The constitution does not provide great detail regarding the composition and functions of the village committee. In fact, the language combines both the rural village and urban residents' committees. According to Article 111 of the constitution, "the residents' committees and villagers' committees established among urban and rural residents on the basis of their place of residence are mass organizations of self-management at the grass-roots level. The chairman, vice-chairmen and members of each residents' or villagers' committee are elected by the residents." A village committee consists of three to seven members, including the chair of the committee or village leader, vice chairs, an accountant, a female member who deals with family planning and women's affairs, and finally, a person in change of public security. "Grass-roots level" means that the village committee is not an official administrative division of the party-state; nevertheless, committee members are still responsible for carrying out national policies.

Below the village committee are small groups or natural villages. Each small group has an elected leader, but no party secretary (see Figure 8.1). The village committee assigns small group leaders with specific duties, and in some cases they manage the small group's collective land.

Villages also have a communist party branch that is made up of a party secretary and two or three deputy party secretaries. According to Article 32 of the CCP constitution, "The primary Party committees in communities, townships and towns and village Party branches provide leadership for the work in their localities and assist administrative departments, economic institutions and self-governing mass organizations in fully exercising their functions and powers." The village party secretary is the most powerful political figure in the village. In many cases, one person serves as both the party secretary and the village head. The village committee is responsible for carrying out policies, but major public affairs are first approved by the party secretary. This includes finical matters and village collective enterprises.

During the Maoist era (1949–1976) and into the 1980s, local cadres had considerable control over the economic, social, and political life for most villagers. In the economic arena, village cadres managed the collective land, and they also had administrative control over access to subsidized agricultural necessities, such as chemical fertilizers and hybrid seeds. Village cadres managed collective industries, including small factories and shops; they alone decided who had access to these lucrative jobs. After the implementation of the one-child policy in 1980, local cadres were responsible for reproduction education, introducing contraceptive methods, and birth planning in their village. The village and party leaders also often act as the mediators dealing with family disputes from marriage problems to clashes between households over land.

In the 1970s and even into the mid-1980s, political campaigns were still a central part of rural life, and CCP cadres were responsible for disseminating party propaganda and educating villagers about specific policies and laws. The methods for spreading CCP information were through a village-wide public address (PA) system, village assemblies, and political study sessions. Cadres used their considerable authority over the local economy to get villagers to attend these political meetings.

The 1982 constitution refers to the election of village committee leaders. However, town government officials had the last word in selecting the village leaders and committee members throughout the 1980s, and for some villages even into the 1990s. Likewise, the town party committee had the power to appoint village party secretaries. The main reason that town party and government cadres intervened in village affairs was that they relied on village cadres to carry out national mandated policies and local regulations. While village cadres in the early to mid-1980s had significant authority, they also owed their position to the town officials. As a result, both the village leader and the party secretary were more accountable to the town officials than to the villagers. This does not mean that village cadres were unresponsive to villagers. Indeed, for village cadres, improving the general welfare of the entire village could satisfy the community as well as the town officials.

By the late 1980s and the 1990s, market reforms had eroded village cadres' traditional economic and political authority. As villagers gained access to the open market, they became less dependent on village cadres for agricultural necessities such as fertilizer and farming equipment. Moreover, there were significant changes in off-farm employment. The rise in private enterprises meant that local factories producing everything from clothing for export to small electronic goods for local retailers were built in or near the village. Rural residents could get local industrial jobs without relying solely on their personal relations (*guanxi*) with the village cadre. Also urban industrialization and construction meant greater employment opportunities outside the village.

Political campaigns and study sessions became less frequent. After cadres lost most of their authority over economic opportunities, they also lost their leverage to get villagers to attend political meetings. In fact, cadres frequently complained that villagers displayed little interest in village assemblies and study sessions and begrudgingly admitted that the only reason people came to village assemblies was to vote in village elections once every three years. The PA system is now used for mundane matters such as announcing a missing goat or found shoes.

Despite their reduced authority, village cadres still retain a number of vital duties including land management, family planning, economic development, maintenance of village schools, dispute mediation, and, until recent reforms, tax and fee collection. The collection of taxes and fees, also called "villager's burdens" has been one of the most contentious duties for village cadres.[1] Some of these fees were arbitrarily imposed on villagers by corrupt officials. But others resulted when central government told town and village cadres that they were responsible for implementing certain policies and projects, without providing them with adequate funds to implement these mandates. Therefore local cadres had to collect fees from villagers in order pay for projects, including family planning programs, school and village road maintenance, and irrigation works. The list of taxes and fees could be long and consisted of ten to twenty different items, such as payments to support the family members of revolutionary martyrs, village militia, family planning, and electricity. By the late 1990s, in some places, villagers were paying anywhere from 20 to 50 percent of their annual income on taxes and fees.[2] While most of the fees were legitimate, villagers worried about how and where the money was spent. For example, in one village, residents pointed out that their village road maintenance fee increased every year, but their dirt road remained in very poor condition and impassable during the rainy season.

In an attempt to reduce villager's burdens, the central government enacted the tax-for-fee reform in 2002 that eliminated all local fees at the village and town levels. All fees were abolished in favor of a single agricultural tax, and in 2004, the agricultural taxes were removed altogether. While villager's financial burdens have been dramatically reduced, village committees and the town governments have become heavily dependent on funds from the county, and it has become more difficult for local cadres to provide public services, such as maintenance of local schools, health clinics, and irrigation projects.

Town Leading Cadres

Town governments are responsible for local economic development, including agricultural and rural industries, and public services such as health, education, family planning, water and land management, and security. Throughout the 1980s, 1990s, and after 2000, town staff ranged from twenty to eighty officials, depending on the number of villages and villagers under their jurisdiction.

The most politically powerful individuals at the town level are the party secretary, the government head, and their several deputies (see Figure 8.1). For these town cadres, promotion to higher administrative levels depends on fulfilling policy obligations passed down from county government offices, which have, in turn, received them from higher-level provincial authorities. All personnel matters are handled through the *nomenklatura* system of cadre management (see chapter 6), which means that the appointment and promotion of "leading cadres" must be approved by the CCP organization department at the next level up the administrative hierarchy. For example, town officials are managed by the county organization department (see Figure 8.2).

Higher authorities at the county levels therefore have a direct influence the behavior of town leading cadres.[3] In fact, town party secretaries and government heads are generally

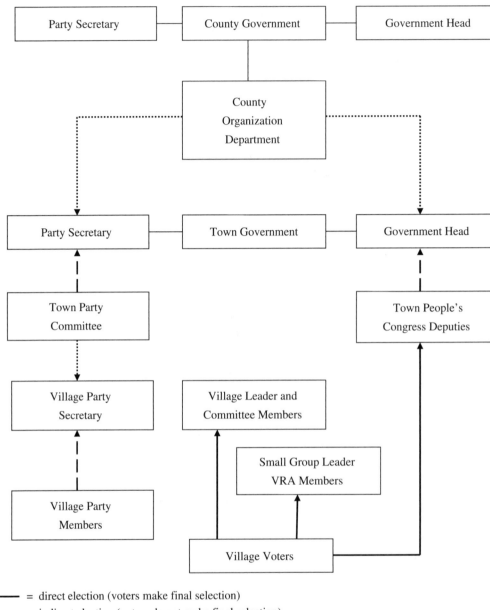

Figure 8.2 Selection of Village Cadres and Town Officials

more responsive to higher officials one administrative level above them, rather than to central government directives or villagers under their authority. The mechanisms that these higher authorities use to control lower level officials are the **one-level-down management system** and the **cadre exchange system**. In the one-level-down management system, officials at each level have the authority to appoint their own subordinates. For example, the head of a county government can appoint the head of the town government without seeking approval from higher authorities at the municipal or provincial levels; the same is true of party secretaries at the county and town levels. The implication of this system is that promotion or reassignment depends on the ability of the subordinate to carry out policies of his or her immediate superior. This can create highly personalized politics whereby the decision of the county officials can have direct influence on a town leading cadre's career.

In the cadre exchange system, leading town cadres are transferred to a different locality every three to six years. Cadre exchange does not apply to the average town bureaucrats, only to leading cadres, such as the CCP secretary and the town head. By limiting leading cadres to a short fixed term of office, this system is meant to prevent cadres from developing local networks that might dilute their allegiance to higher-level authorities or provide opportunities for corruption. The cadre exchange system can have a strong influence on a leading cadre's direction of accountability. For instance, if a town party secretary or government head does not fulfill his or her policy obligations to the county government after a fixed time, he or she may receive a lateral transfer to another town rather than be promoted. On the other hand, leading town cadres who successfully complete their policy obligations may be promoted to the county government. Under this system, the direction of accountability leads upward to the individual cadre one administrative level above, rather than downward toward villagers.

This combination of the one-level-down management and the cadre exchange system ensures tight control over immediate subordinates, which leads to selective policy implementation.[4] Subordinates selectively implement the policies that enhance their career opportunities while ignoring policies that have little influence over their prospects for promotion or transfer. This partly explains the variation in local policy implementation in rural China, especially with political reforms such as village elections.

Village Elections: Grassroots Democracy?

Organic Law of Villagers Committees

The Organic Law of Villagers Committees was enacted on a trial basis in 1987 and then made into a permanent law in 1998. The Organic Law allows villagers to select three to seven village committee members and the village leader in a competitive election (see Figure 8.2). Elected cadres serve three-year terms, and there is no term limit. Villagers can recall elected leaders if over one-fifth of the eligible voters file a case to the town government for impeachment. The Organic Law also covers more than elections. It spells out village committee duties in greater detail than the 1982 constitution, including transparency in village financial affairs and public investments. Why would top leaders of a single-party authoritarian regime introduce local democratic institutions and processes?

The central government first introduced village elections as a mechanism for citizens to monitor the performance of village leaders and committee members, and to replace those who were incompetent or corrupt.[5] At the time, leading cadres in the villages were appointed by higher-level town officials. In the 1980s, one of the greatest supporters for the Organic Law was the veteran party leader and former mayor of Beijing, Peng Zhen, who was the chairman of the Standing Committee of the National People's Congress from 1983 to 1988. Peng believed that relations between villagers and cadres were deteriorating and that rural discontent was rising. Elections were seen as a way to improve cadre-villager relations and policy implementation at the grassroots level. Indeed, direct elections for village leaders have more to do with administrative efficiency than with democracy. In 1985, China had over 940,000 village committees, and it was nearly impossible for authorities to keep tabs on all village cadres.[6] According to Peng, top-down monitoring of local cadres was not enough: "Who supervises rural cadres? Can we supervise them? No, not even if we had 48 hours a day."[7] Elections were designed to shift basic responsibility for cadre supervision from higher authorities to the villagers. Despite support from some top leaders, there was still opposition to direct village elections within the CCP and the National People's Congress (NPC). A number of NPC deputies expressed their concerns that villagers were not ready to govern themselves and they did not have the "democratic consciousness" to manage elections. Other opponents said that village elections would weaken town officials by removing their authority to select village leaders. But both the supporters and the opponents agreed that some form of elections was needed to improve the political conditions in the countryside.

While Peng made a good case for village elections, he and his supporters still had to compromise. In 1987, the NPC passed the Organic Law of Villager Committees on a trial basis, which meant that the policy could be reversed before the Organic Law became official. In 1988, the Ministry of Civil Affairs was put in charge of carrying out the Organic Law throughout rural China, and by 1993, most villages had held at least one round of village elections. By 2008 most villages have had at least five rounds of elections.[8] Yet, from the start the Organic Law has been unevenly implemented, which means that the quality of village elections has varied significantly across China.

The trial version of the Organic Law allowed villagers to select leaders and committee members in a competitive election, but the regulation did not specify how candidates were to be chosen. This left a large legal loophole for county and town officials to manipulate the election law to their advantage. In the first round, most elections were not truly competitive. For example, many elections had just one candidate for village leader. Consequently, some people referred to these elections as "old wine in a new bottle," meaning that the newly "elected" cadres were no different from the previously appointed ones.

One of the main reasons for the slow and uneven implementation of the Organic Law was the resistance of town officials, who had a strong incentive to manipulate the election process. This is not because town officials are inherently anti-democratic, but rather, as noted above, their promotion depends on the fulfillment of mandated policies set forth by the county government. Thus, in order to ensure that village committee members can be trusted to fully implement policies, especially unpopular policies such as family planning and tax collection (before 2002), town officials feel they must either appoint leaders or at least be involved in the candidate selection process. Competitive elections generally occurred only in villages where county authorities pressured town officials to fully implement the Organic Law.

Nominations and Voting

In 1998 the trial law became an official law and was revised to include a clause that ensures a villager nomination process. According to Article 14 of the Organic Law (1998), "candidates shall be directly nominated by villagers." However, the nomination process, which is one measure of election quality, still varies greatly among villages across China. In general, an open nomination process means villagers can freely nominate candidates without town or village party branch interference. That is, election outcomes are uncertain (i.e., not predetermined). The highest-quality election process is one in which villagers nominate the candidates in a village assembly (see below). These are called "open sea" nominations. Lower-quality elections involve a nomination process in which the village party secretary or town officials select or exercise the power to approve the candidates,[9] even if these elections are competitive. In a village where the town official selected the candidates, one villager bemoaned, "Why even bother to vote? The outcome is a foregone conclusion." Nevertheless, a growing number of villages have an open sea nomination process, and there has been tremendous progress in the quality of elections since 1998.

These improvements include increasing use of secret voting booths and limited use of proxy votes and roving ballot boxes. Secret balloting is an important aspect of democratic elections, and Article 14 of the Organic Law guarantees access to secret voting booths on election day. In the early rounds of elections, few villages employed secret ballots, but since 1998 more villages have adopted the practice. A 2005 Ministry of Civil Affairs national survey found that 49 percent of villages made secret balloting boxes available to voters.[10]

Proxy voting allows a single voter to cast a ballot for someone else or even for a few other people. This was an adjustment to the large-scale temporary migration that has led to a large number of people (mostly men) to leave the village to work in the city. However, this practice can corrupt the electoral process if proxy voters are dishonest in casting the ballots entrusted to them. While the Organic Law does not prohibit the use of proxy votes, several provinces have banned the practice, and new restrictions are now in place, such as limiting the number of proxy votes or requiring written authorization from the absentee voter.

Roving ballot boxes are exactly what they suggest. On election day, village cadres take a ballot box in hand and go door to door to collect votes, instead of having villagers attend an election assembly with secret voting booths. The idea was to accommodate rural residents who live in more remote natural villages and the elderly. But, the potential for stuffing ballot boxes and intimidating voters is obvious. As one villager in Shaanxi complained, "They collect the ballots and count them in secret then they announce the winners days later. Who knows who really won?"[11] As with proxy voting, provinces are starting to restrict the use of roving ballots.

Accountability and Relations with the Party Secretary

The evidence suggests that elected leaders are more accountable to villagers then previously appointed cadres. In fact, popular elections have changed the behavior of village cadres. Rather than looking upward to the town authorities in order to secure their position, elected cadres are more responsive to their village constituents. Some studies show that even imperfect elections can curb corrupt behavior and misuse of public funds because villagers can more easily remove elected cadres.[12] Other studies demonstrate that land management decisions of elected leaders reflect villagers' preferences for a fair allocation.[13]

At times, elected leaders may also place villager preferences over the demand set by town officials. Indeed, a noted researcher on village elections states that, "Much to the concern of township authorities, some village heads put the villager's will before that of the township authorities when they have to make a choice."[14] For example, in Ningxia province, an elected village leader refused to collect a town-wide irrigation maintenance fee for the town officials because their village had no irrigation. In an interview, the town party secretary bemoaned, "I miss the days when we could just fire the guys who do not listen to us, now we have to wait until the next election."[15] His comment expressed not only his frustration with non-compliant village cadres, but also the hope that he would be able to influence the outcome of the next round of village elections.

Nevertheless, elected village leaders still have to implement policies mandated by higher levels and remain dependent on the town government for investment funds. Furthermore, in order to best serve the village, an elected leader must work well with town authorities. For instance, elected leaders can work with the town officials to help farmers get low-interest loans to build a greenhouse or buy agricultural equipment.

The Organic Law is also changing the relationship between popularly elected village leaders and the appointed (or elected only by CCP members) village party secretary in those cases where one individual does not hold both offices. Of course, party secretaries are also village residents, but their direct constituents are the minority of villagers who are members of the town party branch, even though their authority extends over the whole village.

The role of village party organization is not spelled out in the Organic Law, which leads to imprecise and overlapping areas of jurisdiction between the party secretary and the village leader. The CCP's policy is that the "party manages cadres," and according to Article 3 of the Organic Law (1998), the party organization assumes the core leadership role in the village. Therefore, the party secretary is considered the "number one hand" in the village, and elected cadres must accept party leadership. Yet, it is well documented that many popularly elected village leaders are acting in the interest of their constituents, even if it means going head-to-head with the party secretary. A number of elected leaders are attempting to create an equal rather than subordinate relationship between the village committee and the party branch.

Villager Representative Assembly

According to Article 21 of the Organic Law, residents may establish a **villager representative assembly (VRA)** to which every five to fifteen households elect one representative (see Figure 8.2). The function of the VRAs is to monitor the work of the village committee. The Organic Law does not provide a list of specific VRA responsibilities, but counties, towns, and even villages can write up documents that detail VRA duties. For example, in some localities, the VRA is in charge of reviewing annual village budgets, investment plans, and implementation of national policies. During VRA meetings, representatives can raise questions about village-wide problems or specific constituent issues.

In some cases, the VRA will challenge a village leader's decision and even make motions to dismiss the leader or village committee members. For example, in Shaanxi province, one VRA led the fight to recall the elected village leader because they believed he misappropriated funds meant to improve and remodel the outdoor toilets for the elementary school. The leader said the accusations were baseless, but he ended up quitting over the "toilet scandal." Finally, the VRA can serve as a deliberative body, participating fully in policy-implementation decisions.

Although there are some reported cases in which VRAs seem to exert significant village authority, many scholars find that VRAs are generally less effective. The main criticism is that the VRAs, like the people's congresses at the town and county levels, are little more than rubber stamp agencies for party-state policies. One scholar who examined a number of surveys on VRAs concluded that they are "largely ceremonial and not signs of the villager's increased decision-making power."[16] The variation in VRA authority may depend on how well the Organic Law is implemented and whether the town or county officials believe that a strong VRA is necessary. Some town officials view strong VRAs as an efficient mechanism to keep the village committee and elected leader in line, while others may prefer to keep the VRAs weak and ineffective. Nevertheless, whether they are strong or weak, VRAs have become a part of village political life.

Women in Village Politics

Few women are elected as village committee members and even fewer are village leaders. Women are participating in elections, and in many villages there are more women voters than men. However, the female vote does not translate into more women elected to village committees. As a result, women are left underrepresented and at a political disadvantage in rural China.

Article 9 of the Organic Law states that, "Female members shall take a proper portion in the composition of villager's committees." Yet, the law does not make it clear what the proper portion of women should be on any given village committee. According to the State Statistical Bureau of China, in 2004, only 15 percent of elected village committee members nationwide are women.[17] Less than one percent of elected village leaders nationwide are female.[18] Even at higher administrative levels, women seem to be hitting a "bamboo ceiling." According to a 2000 **All China Women's Federation (ACWF)** report, the proportion of women holding official government positions at or above the county level was 15 percent. The irony is that as the election process becomes more open, with less interference from higher authorities, the portion of women elected to committees declines.

Elected female village committee members are usually confined to roles that are considered "women's work" or are just plain ignored. Women's work includes checking birth quotas and disseminating contraception material, such as condoms and pamphlets on available types of contraception. Indeed, in many cases, the work of female cadres is limited to family planning duties and not much else. Many elected women feel ineffective and overpowered by the men in the village committee. For example, in an interview, one elected female committee member said that she was proud to be elected, but felt ignored at committee meetings when she demanded more funds to improve family planning duties. She eventually quit before her three-year term was up.[19] Without adequate representation in the village committee, serious women's issues, such as domestic violence, the high elementary and middle school dropout rates of girls, and mental health, are not addressed (see Box, **Suicide among Women in Rural China: The Silent Epidemic**).

Traditional attitudes held by rural men and women prevent females from getting nominated and elected to leading cadre position. Although the economic and political reforms have altered the relationship between male cadres and villagers, political and social relations between men and women remain unequal. At issue is the pervasive belief that politics and public affairs is a man's job. A traditional saying that is still widely repeated in rural China is, "women live inside and men live outside." In many respects, rural China is still a male-dominated society, both politically and culturally. For example, the burden of family planning has fallen on rural women for contraception, sterilization, and most importantly, the pressure to give birth to sons.

Nevertheless, government agencies and nongovernment organizations (NGOs) are breaking the impasse and promoting greater local representation for women (see Box, **Quotas for Women in Local Government**). In 2004, the Ministry of Civil Affairs published and widely disseminated the pamphlet entitled "Guidebook on Women's Participation in Villagers' Self-Governance." The pamphlet educates women about the Organic Law as well as realistic strategies on how to get elected and participate in villager committees. The ACWF has been working to improve women's social and political standing by providing them with agricultural technology training and programs to reduce the female dropout rates in rural middle and high schools. In addition, a number of NGOs are playing a role in improving rural women's political participation. The most prominent NGO that is active in this area publishes the magazine called *Rural Women*. The

SUICIDE AMONG WOMEN IN RURAL CHINA: THE SILENT EPIDEMIC

China is the only country in the world where the suicide rates of women outnumber that of men. The global suicide rate in 2000 was 16 per 100,000 people and for women 7.5. In China the suicide rate is 23 per 100,000 people, and for rural women, it is 30 per 100,000, which is among the highest rates in the world. According the Chinese Ministry of Health, suicide is one of the leading causes of death among rural women between the ages of fifteen and thirty-four.[1]

While depression and other mental disorders are the main causes for over 90 percent of suicides in Western countries, the majority of suicides in rural China are due to acute stress from life events just prior to the suicide or suicide attempt. In fact, researchers suggest that the majority of the rural women who commit or attempt suicide do *not* have mental illness.[2] One of the principal reasons for suicidal behavior among young rural women is family conflict and martial problems such as abusive mother-in-laws or violent husbands. For many rural women with little education or independent sources of income, suicide seems to be the only way out of a seemingly hopeless situation. Indeed, some Chinese psychologists suggest that women who sense that they have been wronged and feel powerless in life may believe that taking their own life is the best revenge or act of rebellion. While the stress and suffering due to domestic violence and abusive in-laws can last for years, most suicides tend to be impulsive actions based on the emotions at the time.

The most common method of suicide among rural women is pesticide ingestion. One national study in 2000 found that pesticide ingestion accounted for 79 percent of young rural women who died from suicide.[3] Pesticides are readily available and widely used in agriculture throughout rural China. The death rate from the use of pesticides is higher in countryside due to inadequate training of rural doctors and poor medical facilities that are unable to handle severe poisonings. In urban areas, doctors are better trained and hospitals are more equipped to resuscitate the victims of pesticide ingestion.

The high suicide rates of young rural Chinese women have not gone unnoticed by the local authorities or the central leadership. The attempts at reducing suicide deaths include increasing the training of medical personnel, improving rural medical services, and regulating the use of pesticides. However, the root of the problem is still the emotional stress that leads to suicide attempts. There is no single solution to the problem, but providing young women with alternatives to suicide means developing social support networks outside the family to help women cope with emotional stress. This includes training cadres at the village-level women's associations and increasing community awareness of psychological problems associated with family conflict and domestic violence.

1. Shan Juan, "Suicide Remains Shadowy Subject," *China Daily*, August 24, 2007, http://www.chinadaily.com.cn/china/2007–08/24/content_6038855.htm, accessed August 11, 2008.

2. Liu Meng, "Rebellion and Revenge: The Meaning of Suicide of Women in Rural China," *International Journal of Social Welfare* 11 (Winter 2002): 300–309.

3. Gong-Huan Yang, Michael R. Phillips, Mai-Geng Zhou, Li-Jun Wang, Yan-Ping Zhang, and Dong Xu, "Understanding the Unique Characteristics of Suicide in China: National Psychological Autopsy Study," *Biomedical and Environmental Sciences* 18, no. 6 (December 2005): 379–389.

goal of *Rural Women* is to share information, stories, and coping strategies. This is vital for many rural women, who have limited or no access to computers or the Internet.

Vote Buying and Family Clans

Villages that have an "open sea" nomination process and competitive elections may be free from town government and village party branch interference, but there are also non-party and non-government community forces that can influence local elections and political life more broadly. The two common issues are vote buying and the influence of village family clans (kinship ties).

When town officials or village party secretaries manipulate the elections process candidates must curry favor with the officials in order to get elected. In this case, the election outcome is decided by officials, and villagers' votes are not worth buying. However, when the election process is free from official interference, voters determine the outcome. Then the value of the vote increases. Thus, candidates who are out to win at any cost will attempt to influence voters, and buying votes is one way to sway the election. The price of a vote can range from 7 RMB (US$1.00) to 20,000 RMB (US$2,898.00), and candidates have offered t-shirts, pens, and even appliances in exchange for votes. Given the fact that village leaders' authority has eroded over the last two decades as the scope of the private economy has widened, why would a candidate spend so much money to be a village leader?

The reason is land. Leasing village land to developers can be hugely profitable for a village leader (see chapter 7). In an interview, one village committee member in Shaanxi admitted, "While a candidate may spend a ridiculously large sum of money to get elected, he can easily get the money back after a post-election land deal." Land, which is still managed by local cadres, is a scarce resource in rural China, particularly in areas close to a city. Developers are eager to acquire land for factories, housing developments, shopping malls, golf courses, and other ventures that promise to yield high profits. As the demand increases, so does the leasing price.

Land management is one of the most contentious issues between cadres and villagers. Due to villagers' concerns over land, vote buying can backfire. In one southern village, the incumbent leader offered about 2,000 RMB (about one-third of the average annual per capita rural income) for each vote just before the election. He won. However, soon after the election, villagers discovered that the leader leased portions of the village land to local developers without giving villagers legal compensation. The compensation should have been 7,000 RMB per villager. Upon hearing the news, a group of villagers went to the leader's home and proceeded to beat him. Recognizing the corrupt behavior of the incumbent leader and wanting to ease tensions, town government officials paid the villagers 7,000 RMB each and nullified the election results.[20]

In the wake of post-Mao economic reforms, some areas of rural China have experienced a resurgence in the role of village kinship groups. Kinship groups or family clans can complicate the election process or even highjack village committees. In some villages with two or more competing organized kinship groups, town officials have intentionally appointed one representative of a clan as party secretary and the other as village leader in order to strike a balance. However, an open election process can upset the balance. Moreover, in villages with only one dominant kinship group, elections may just be a formality in which the traditional clan leadership assumes authority over the village committee as well as the party branch. While some reported cases suggest that strong kinship organizations can subvert village elections and the authority of the village committee, it is still unclear how family clans will influence the future development of grassroots democracy at the village level

QUOTAS FOR WOMEN IN LOCAL GOVERNMENT: A MODEL FOR CHINA?

It is difficult for women to get elected to local governing bodies in countries with a male dominated political culture, such as Muslim nations or countries with a large rural population and a long history of traditional practices that exclude women from positions of power, such as China. In these countries, an open election system with limited government interference can result in few or no women elected in local assemblies. Two countries, Pakistan and India, have adopted election quotas for women at the local level to deal with this problem.

In Pakistan, quotas for women, or "reservations," in local and national government are not new.[1] From 1956 to 1988, the constitutions (there were five during this period) reserved seats for women at most levels of government, but only 5 to 10 percent of elected seats were provided for women. By the 1990s, the situation had not changed and women made up less than 10 percent of the local and national governing bodies.

In 2000, the military government adopted a 33 percent quota for all three levels of local government: the district council, the *tehsil* (county) council, and the union council. Since 2000, women candidates have filled the quota at all three levels and continue to run for local councils. Although many cultural barriers persist, Pakistani women have used their position to advance female education and health issues.

In 1992, India passed the 73rd Amendment to the constitution that provided more power to the village councils and mandated wider representation for historically marginalized groups such as scheduled castes and women.[2] Quotas or reservations for castes were in place before the amendment, but quotas for women were new. Indian local government has three tiers: district councils that have 1,000 villages, block councils with 100 villages, and village councils. The amendment requires that 33 percent of elected council members are women, and one-third of all village council chairpersons (i.e., village leaders) are also women.

Women have enthusiastically run for these positions, and in some Indian states, women represent 40 percent of the elected village chairpersons and council members. Increased presence in these local governing bodies has allowed women to address issues such as women's land rights and health care. Moreover, villagers are observing that elected women leaders are just as competent as men. As a result, both male and female voters are electing local women leaders in greater numbers. Mandating quotas for women will not bring an immediate end to traditional practices and attitudes, but these laws can bring about significant changes for women.

1. Socorro L. Reyes, "Quotas in Pakistan: A Case Study," International Institute for Democracy and Electoral Assistance (September, 2002), http://www.quotaproject.org/CS/CS_Pakistan.pdf, accessed May 25, 2008.

2. Vasanthi Ramon, "The Implementation of Quotas for Women: The Indian Experience," International Institute for Democracy and Electoral Assistance (September 2002), http://www.quotaproject.org/CS/CS_India.pdf, Accessed May 25, 2008.

or even possible elections for town government heads. A recent study of several villages in east central China showed that kinship and religious groups are more important than elections in holding local cadres accountable for providing the kinds of public goods, such as paved roads and running water, that villagers want and expect from their government.[21]

Town Direct Elections for Government Head: The Next Step?

Although direct, competitive elections have become commonplace at the village level in China, party-state leaders have been much more cautious in extending such democratic practices to the next level of rural administration, the town. Town people's congresses are directly elected, but not the town head or other leaders. They are still mostly appointed from above (see Figure 8.2). During the National Party Congress in late 1997, then PRC president and CCP general secretary Jiang Zemin pledged to "extend the scope of democracy at the grassroots level." This was viewed by many as an official nod to expand the direct elections for village leaders to the town level.

The first push for a more inclusive selection process for town government heads came from party leaders in Shizhong district, part of Chengdu municipality in Sichuan province.[22] The leading reformer was a female party secretary of Shizhong district, Zhang Jinming. The Shizhong party committee was having problems with town government heads, and saw more open elections as a way to improve relations between villagers and town officials.

One particularly troubled spot was Baoshi town, where the government head was dismissed for embezzling public funds. Moreover, the local economy was stagnant. Shizhong officials knew that villagers were growing dissatisfied, and the local leadership was losing political legitimacy. In an attempt to regain public confidence, the Shizhong party and government leaders, led by Zhang Jinming, implemented a breakthrough political reform in Baoshi town. They adopted a new system known as **open recommendation and selection** in May 1998.

The process began with an objective written civil service exam for all aspirants to town offices. Then the district CCP organizational department screened potential nominees who passed the exam. The second stage was a limited vote to select the final nominees. This was not a direct election in the sense that all eligible voters in the town and villages cast ballots. But it did provide greater representation than purely **indirect elections** by allowing town people's congress deputies, village leaders and party secretaries, and village small group leaders to vote. The balloting, vote count, and announcement of the winners occurred on the same day. Once candidates were chosen, town people's congress deputies voted for the town government head and other leading cadres, in accordance with the constitution.

In response to positive comments about the Baoshi elections from both central leaders and villagers, the Shizhong party and government leaders decided to move forward with direct elections for the government head of Buyun town. Thus, the combination of cues from the central leadership and villager demands from below convinced Shizhong leaders that the time was right to hold direct elections for town heads.

On December 30, 1998, residents of villages in Buyun town went to the polls to elect the head of the town government. This was the first publicized direct election for town government head in China, and it attracted considerable domestic and international media attention because such positions had previously always been appointed and subject to approval by the CCP organization department.

However, the central and provincial governments swiftly put an end the **Buyun experiment** with town-level democracy. They denounced the direct election of town heads as unconstitutional, but their political reason behind their alarm was because such elections reduced the authority of county party leaders to manage town cadres. In 2001, the CCP Central Committee issued Document Number 12, which officially put the development of direct elections for town leading officials on hold. The document stated that direct elections for town heads, "does not accord with the constitution and the Organic Law of People's Congress and Local Governments."

According to Article 9 of the Organic Law of Local People's Congresses and Local People's Governments and Article 101 of the state constitution, the town people's congress deputies elect the town government head and deputy heads. The county party committee has strict control over the selection of candidates for these positions. Town government heads and party secretaries are leading cadres, and they are managed through the county CCP organizational department. Typically the selection of candidates via the *nomenklatura* system occurs behind closed doors and only includes top party leaders in the county.

Town People's Congresses

As noted above, although town government heads are not directly elected, deputies to town people's congresses are chosen by all the voters in the area (see Figure 8.2). Elected representatives to the local congress serve a three-year term. According to the Electoral Law of the People's Republic of China on the National People's Congress and the Local People's Congresses, the minimum number of deputies to a town people's congress is 40 and the maximum is 130. The town people's congress convenes at least once a year for two or three days to approve policy initiatives put forward by the town government and ratify the budget. They are also responsible for approving government decisions regarding matters, such as education, economic development and public health. Between meetings, people's congress deputies may also meet individually with town officials to discuss issues of concern to their constituents. Despite the formidable powers and functions described on paper, town congresses still play a minor role in shaping and affecting government decisions.

Consultative Elections

The end of the Buyun experiment with direct town head elections did not spell the end of the open recommendation and selection process or popular participation in selecting town officials. Since 2001, a process similar to that first used in Baoshi has been adopted in other towns in Sichuan, as well as other provinces. Local officials have made the process more inclusive, but still within the framework of the constitutional provision that town heads be elected by the local people's congress.

One particular recent innovation has moved beyond the open recommendation and selection process, and it was initiated by the same reformer who led the Buyun elections, Zhang Jinming. Even though the party-state had denounced the direct election of town government heads in 1998, Zhang received positive recognition for her innovation. In 2002, she was appointed as the party organizational department head (i.e., managing the *nomenklatura* system) in Ya'an municipality south of Chengdu, Sichuan. In 2004, Zhang was promoted to deputy party secretary and that same year she received the "Chinese Government Trailblazer Award."

In 2006, Zhang introduced a selection method that includes a popular vote for nominees to the positions of town head and even the party secretary.[23] Dubbed the Ya'an experiment, it is a four-stage process. First, nominees must meet qualifications that include a college education, being below the age of fifty, and having at least three years of cadre experience. Second, all nominees, including incumbent leaders, are subject to a popular vote. Third, the county party committee screens the nominees and makes the final selection list. Then the town people's congress elects candidates from the final list for town head, and the town party congress selects the party secretary. The last step ensures that the process remains within constitutional boundaries. The Buyun experiment crossed the line by allowing direct election of town government heads.

The current system is called a **consultative election** because the popular vote is only one consideration when the county party committee makes the final candidate list for the town people's and party congresses.[24] The voters do not make the final decision in the election of leaders. The popular vote has two functions in this system. First, it expands popular participation in the direct nomination process. Second, villager participation helps the county party committee spot unpopular town officials. As a result, the popular vote is also an efficient tool for county party leaders to monitor town leading officials.

Rural Unrest and Rightful Resistance: Social Instability or Exercising Legal Rights?

Since the 1990s, researchers and journalists have closely followed reports of mounting unrest in rural China. In July 2005, the Minister of Public Security, Zhou Yongkang, said that incidences of social disturbances, such as riots and demonstrations, had risen from 58,000 in 2003 to 74,000 in 2004. By the end of 2005, the number of reported social disturbances increased another 6.6 percent to 87,000 incidences.[25] Over 40 percent of these disturbances are in response to abusive local cadres and corrupt local government practices.

These numbers suggest that protest and discontent may put support for the Chinese Communist Party (CCP) at risk. However, rural unrest and villagers' disapproval is directed toward village cadres or town officials, not the national government of the CCP; many demonstrations that end in violent clashes between villagers and the local police began as legitimate claims against local governments and then escalated into riots. Thus, so far, rural unrest does not threaten the central leadership.

Rightful Resisters

Some villagers appeal to the central government and invoke national laws when they seek redress for abuses by local cadres. This is type of protest, in which villagers claim that local officials are breaking the law, is called **rightful resistance**.[26] Rightful resisters believe that the legal system and the national leadership are on their side. The central government usually permits this kind of protest, but some rightful resistance pushes the legal limits and sometimes goes beyond. While many resisters take to the streets to press their claims, others use the courts to sue local officials and government agencies to protect their interests.

Rightful resisters tend to be well informed about specific national polices or laws when they take action. They learn about specific laws and policies in various ways. Of course, the most prevalent source is from watching television news, listening to the radio, and reading newspapers and magazines. The central government also provides large print, easy-to-read legal pamphlets for specific laws, such as Organic Law of Villager Committees. These can be bought at most book stores in smaller cities such as county seats. The great increase in rural to urban migration has also contributed to the flow of information.

Sometimes villager activists stumble across a copy of a law. In one case from Hebei province, a villager activist, who went to the town government office to lodge a complaint against a village cadre, noticed a copy of the Organic Law. After reading the law and sharing the information with other villagers, he lodged a compliant against the town government for failing to allow democratic elections.[27] Thus, resisters not only obtain information, but they make the crucial connection between the published law and administrative misconduct.

Rightful resisters use their knowledge about specific laws and local officials' unlawful activity to inform the village community and grab the attention of higher authorities. They may take advantage of a public event such as a Spring Festival gathering or a public performance at a village fair. Sometimes, resisters will literally use a soapbox and loud speakers at rural markets to denounce illegal actions of local officials. In order to gain a wider audience, village activists may work with local or even national journalists to publicize their discovery of official misdeeds.

The central party-state tolerates rightful resisters because they provide information about local corruption and illegal administrative acts. Corruption reflects uneven implementation of laws and weakened political capacity of the central leadership to control officials at the county and town governments. The national leadership cannot monitor all mid-level officials all the time; rightful resisters act as fire alarms so that higher authorities can identify misconduct. Still, while national leaders allow villager activists to point out fires, they do not tolerate rightful resisters putting them out.

There are several legal and semi-legal modes of resistance that activists can employ. These include petitions, lawsuits, noncompliance, and demonstrations. While many reports from the Western media about rural unrest focus on relatively large demonstrations that result in violent clashes with local police, most acts of rural resistance take place within the legal system.

Legal Modes of Resistance

The most common mode of legal resistance is petitioning higher authorities. This involves visiting a county government office or above to submit a letter of complaint against a local cadre or organization, such as the town government or village committee. The reasons for petitioning range from complaints about exorbitant elementary school fees and excessive irrigation charges to cadres who beat and extort villagers.[28]

Many counties and municipalities have **Letters and Visits Offices** where villagers can officially lodge a complaint. Rather than going through the formal court system, petitioners are seeking official mediation through the Letters and Visits Offices to resolve issues involving local cadre abuse. Successful mediation occurs when the higher officials directly address the complaint and confront local cadres to resolve the problem. However, sometimes mediators do not mediate. According to Kevin O'Brien and Lianjiang Li, villagers and small delegations can "languish for weeks waiting for an appointment with leaders who never emerge."[29] Other unsuccessful attempts at mediation include complaints being treated politely at the office, then ignored once the petitioners return home, or authorities making decisions that are not enforced.

Individuals and even whole villages can register a specific grievance to these offices. The State Council's Regulation Concerning Letters and Visits (1995, revised 2005) allow citizens to petition as a group, but the number of representatives a group can send to the office is limited to five people. If an individual or group is dissatisfied with the ruling of the mediation at the municipal level, they can take their case to higher levels. The highest level is the Letters and Visits Office in Beijing, and a large number of citizens have taken their grievances all the way to the top. In fact, there are "petitioner's camps" where individuals or group representatives wait to be heard.

While petitioning is the most common form of legal resistance, it can be costly for villagers in term of money and their physical well-being. For many villagers, it is time-consuming and expensive to travel to the Letters and Visits offices, especially when the wait to be seen can take days or weeks. Back in the village, petitioners may be faced with threats of violence from the village cadres or town officials. Thus rightful resistors take a huge risk to get higher authorities to hear their grievances. Nevertheless, the numbers of legal complaints have been on the rise since the 1990s. In 1995, about 5 million petitions were received by county-level and above Letters and Visits Offices nationwide. In 2005, the number was over 11 million.[30] This increase caught the attention of President Hu Jintao, and in 2005, the 1995 State Council Regulation Concerning Letters and Visits was revised to include a clause that forbids any individual or organization from retaliating against petitioners.

Another form of rightful resistance is lawsuits filed against local officials or government offices. The Administrative Litigation Law (ALL) allows citizens to sue local governments for unlawful acts such as the misuse of public funds. However, the law does not allow citizens to sue any party committee or party secretary. (The party has its own Central Discipline Inspection Commission that is supposed to investigate wrongdoing by party members or organizations. See chapter 6.) Moreover, between 1998 and 2002, less than 5 percent of the cases resulted in full compensation. Despite this limitation, the number of citizens using the ALL to sue local officials continues to increase. In 2003, Chinese courts accepted 87,919 new administrative cases that citizens brought against government officials. In 2004, the number of new cases increased another 5.7 percent to 92,613. In 2005, it was over 97,000.

In many instances, whole villages bring cases against a town government. For example, in 1999, 5,000 villagers from Shaanxi province sued the leading cadres of the Zizhou county government for imposing unfair fees and beating a number of villagers. They asked for compensation and took their case to the municipal court in Yulin City. But the local government officials arrested the lawyer representing the villagers on the grounds that he was "disturbing social order" and they did not receive compensation.[31] Nevertheless, people continue to use ALL to get their cases heard.

Semi-Legal and Illegal Modes of Resistance: Noncompliance and Demonstrations

Noncompliance is one mode of resistance that can easily go beyond the accepted limits of the law. For example, the 1993 Agricultural Law grants villagers the right to refuse to pay illegal fees. Legal fees and taxes before 2002 were authorized and posted by the town people's congresses. Any fees that are not sanctioned by the local people's congress are considered illegal, and villagers have the right to refuse payment of these illegal fees. However, villagers are not allowed to actively resist fee collectors; they are supposed to leave resolution of their complaints to the government. And they are still obligated to pay sanctioned taxes and fees. Nevertheless, some villagers invoked the law to justify "tax strikes" where they refused to pay any taxes or fees until illegal fees were eliminated. In this case, villagers' use of the 1993 Agricultural Law went beyond the legal limits in order to stop cadres' illegal actions. However, these tax strikes are not without consequence. In some cases, village cadres will try to negotiate with the resistant villagers. Cadres may go door to door to cajole villagers to pay or forcibly take items from the home, such as television sets and even beds, as payment. There are also incidents that ended in violent clashes with police.

Villager demonstrations and violent unrest are often the result of failed legal attempts to resolve grievances. In 2004, a prominent researcher for the State Council made a clear connection between petitions and unrest; "villagers start by lodging complaints at the county level or higher, and doing so at the province or in Beijing is also fairly common. If the petition fails, they often turn to 'direct' resistance." On paper, demonstrations are legal. Article 35 of the PRC constitution grants Chinese citizens "freedom of speech, of the press, of assembly, of association, of procession and of demonstration." However, the October 1989 Law on Assembly, Procession and Demonstration (promulgated in the aftermath of the Tiananmen protests) requires that all citizens who wish to demonstrate must first obtain police approval in advance. Of course, even in the United States, large demonstrations require a permit. But, in China, local police rarely grant these permits. Therefore, many of the demonstrations, road blocks, or sit-ins that begin as peaceful are broken up by police, and these confrontations between protesters and police can become violent.

Two publicized accounts provide examples of how lawful protests can end in violent clashes with local police. In 2005, residents from Taishi village, Guangdong province attempted to use the Organic Law to recall the incumbent village leader, who they accused of misusing public funds and creating secret land deals with local developers.[32] Villager activists collected the necessary signatures for a recall motion, and they tried to obtain the village financial records as evidence of misappropriations. This led to a stand-off between cadres and villagers. Unfortunately for the villagers, the town government backed the incumbent leader, and the confrontation ended with a violent clash between 500 town and county police and 1,500 villagers. There were several arrests and injuries of villagers, but no recall election.

Another example occurred in Zhejiang province when, in 2005, over 3,000 police clashed with 20,000 villagers who were protesting against an industrial park built next to their villages that housed thirteen chemical factories.[33] Ever since the industrial park had opened in 2001, villagers complained of factory chemical waste that spilled into the local streams and fields. It also polluted the irrigation and drinking water. After several years of petitioning the municipal, provincial, and even central authorities without satisfactory results, thousands of villagers and village cadres blocked the entrance to the industrial park. Then police were ordered to disperse the demonstration. Dozens of police and villagers were injured. However, in the end, some of the villager demands were eventually met, and six of the most polluting factories were relocated.

These examples of protests and demonstrations paint a picture of widespread rural discontent, but the vast majority of villagers do not protest. In 2004, about 3 million rural residents took part in legal petitioning and lawsuits, as well as in large and small demonstrations. That is only 0.4 percent of the rural population.

Why aren't more villagers protesting? One reason may be fear. Another may be poverty. The economic and physical costs of resistance can be high. However, even if villagers do not take to the streets, they still have a strong sense of justice and an expectation of fairness. Thus, another possible explanation is that most disputes are being resolved at the village level. For instance, if village elections are making elected leaders more accountable to villagers, then there may be greater transparency in village financial accounts and a relatively fair management of collective land. This means that political reforms in China's countryside are helping to maintain social stability, which is one major reason they were implemented by the central government in the first place.

The Future of Political Reform in Rural China

Political reform in rural China has made significant progress since the 1980s, but it is still unclear whether the current reforms are enough to deal with villagers' expectations for fairness and growing demands for greater participation in the local decision-making process. Village elections have been a relative success, but they may also contribute to rising demands for direct elections at the town level. This success has even emboldened some reform minded mid-level officials at the county and municipal levels to introduce semi-direct elections of town government heads. Nevertheless, uneven implementation and the resulting rural unrest still pose serious problems for the CCP.

In his political report at the National Party Congress in October 2007, CCP General Secretary Hu Jintao said, "We need to improve institutions for democracy, diversify its forms and expand its channels, and we need to carry out democratic elections, decision-making, administration and oversight in accordance with the law to guarantee the people's rights to be informed, to participate, to be heard, and to oversee."[34] As Jiang Zemin's statements spurred reformers in 1997, it is possible that reformers working at the municipal and county levels may also take Hu's words as encouragement to move forward with their efforts to democratize rural politics, trying again to win approval for the direct election of town government heads. Rural activists may also try to increase their influence by working through the local people's congresses. In recent years, more rural activists have taken advantage of the legal opportunity for self-nomination in local people's congress elections, and a number have actually won seats. Nevertheless, continuing dominant role of the cadre management system and the authority of the party secretary over town government heads and the local people's congresses stand in the way of further democratization and accountability.

Therefore, the question remains whether the gradual introduction of reforms is enough to satisfy rural political demands before the incidents of rural unrest become unmanageable for the central government. The relative success of limited reforms suggests that the central leadership has adapted to some of the growing demands from the rural population, but the pace and depth of political change will need to speed up if the CCP is to maintain political legitimacy and social stability and in the countryside.

Notes

1. See Thomas Bernstein and Xiaobo Lü, *Taxation Without Representation in Contemporary Rural China* (New York: Cambridge University Press, 2003).

2. Ray Yep, "Can 'Tax-for-Fee' Reform Reduce Rural Tension in China? The Process, Progress, and Limitations," *The China Quarterly* 177 (2004): 42–70.

3. Kevin J. O'Brien and Lianjiang Li, "Selective Policy Implementation in Rural China," *Comparative Politics* 31, no. 2 (1999): 167; Maria Edin, "State Capacity and Local Agents Control in China: CCP Cadre Management from a Township Perspective," *The China Quarterly* 173 (2003): 35–52.

4. Kevin J. O'Brien and Li Lianjiang, "Selective Policy Implementation in Rural China."

5. Kevin J. O'Brien and Lianjiang Li, "Accommodating 'Democracy' in a One-Party State: Introducing Village Elections in China," *China Quarterly* 162 (2000): 465.

6. According to the 1986 *China Statistical Yearbook* from China Data Online (http://chinadataonline .org/), the number of village committees was 940,617, but by 2005 (2006 *China Statistical Yearbook*) the number has decreased to 640,000. This was due to urbanization and administrative changes such as combining villages and changes from townships to towns and towns to counties (see 1986 *China Yearbook*, 2, General Survey, Number of Grassroots Units by Department).

7. Kevin J. O'Brien and Li Lianjiang, "Accommodating 'Democracy' in a One-Party State: Introducing Village Elections in China."

8. "The 'Normalization' of China's Village Elections" (*Zhongguo cunguan xuanju'changtaihua'*), *People's Daily (Renmin Ribao)*, January 9, 2008, http://www. chinaelections.org/NewsInfo. asp?NewsID=121299, accessed April 23, 2008.

9. John J. Kennedy, "The Face of 'Grassroots Democracy': The Substantive Difference between Real and Cosmetic Elections in Rural China," *Asian Survey* 42, no. 3 (May–June 2002).

10. Baogang He, *Rural Democracy in China: The Role of Village Elections* (New York: Palgrave, 2007).

11. Author interview, March 2001.

12. Loren Brandt and Matthew A. Turner, "The Usefulness of Imperfect Elections: The Case of Village Elections in Rural China," *Economics and Politics* 19, no. 3 (November 2007), 453–479.

13. John J. Kennedy, Scott Rozelle, and Yaojiang Shi, "Elected Leaders and Collective Land: Farmers' Evaluation of Village Leader's Performance in Rural China," *Journal of Chinese Political Science* 9, no. 1 (Spring 2004).

14. Baogang He, *Rural Democracy in China: The Role of Village Elections*, 110.

15. Author interview, March 2001.16. Björn Alpermann, "The Post-Election Administration of Chinese Villages," *The China Journal* 46 (July 2001): 45–67. See also Sylvia Chan, "Villagers' Representative Assemblies: Towards Democracy or Centralism?," *China: An International Journal* 1, no. 2 (September 2003): 179–199.

17. Department of Population, Society, Science and Technology of the State Statistical Bureau of China, ed., *Women and Men in China*, 83; also see Xiajuan Guo and Yongnian Zheng, "Women's Participation in China," Briefing Series, no. 134 (2008), University of Nothingham, China Policy Institute, http://www .nottingham.ac.uk/shared/shared_cpi/documents/policy_papers/Briefing_34_Women_Political_ Participation.pdf, accessed April 20, 2008.

18. Fan Yu, *Cunweihui Xuanju: Nongcun funu fazhande jiyu yu tiaozhan* (Village Committee Elections: Opportunities and Challenges for Rural Women's Development), Chinese Center for Rural Studies (CCRS) 2000, http://www.ccrs.org.cn/cunminzz.htm, accessed June 2003; also see Asian Development Bank, *County Gender Assessment: People's Republic of China 2006*, http://www.adb.org/Documents/ Reports/Country-Gender-Assessments/cga-prc.pdf, accessed April 20, 2008.

19. Baogang He, *Rural Democracy in China: The Role of Village Elections*, 129.

20. Minnie Chan, "Local Polls Put off After Corruption Charges" *South China Morning Post*, June 7, 2008, http://archive.scmcom/results.php, accessed June 10, 2008.

21. Lily T. Tsai, *Accountability Without Democracy: Solidary Groups and Public Goods Provision in Rural China* (New York: Cambridge University Press, 2007).

22. Lianjiang Li, "The Politics of Introducing Direct Township Elections in China," *China Quarterly* 171 (2002): 704–723.

23. According to Thøgersen, Elklit, and Lisheng (see note 24), the 2006 election experiment, "involved all voters in four townships in the election of the entire township leadership, including the township party secretary (68)." This is the second stage.

24. Stig Thøgersen, Jørgen Elklit and Dong Lisheng, "Consultative Elections of Township Leaders: The Case of an Experiment in Ya'an, Sichuan," *China Information* 22, no. 1 (2008): 67–89.

25. Thomas Lum, "Social Unrest in China" *CRS Report for Congress* (May 8th); Ni Ching-Ching (2006) "Officials Report 39,000 Protests in the First Half of 2006, Down from '05 but Still a Key Concern." *Los Angeles Times* (August 10); Tony Saich, "China in 2005: Hu's in Charge," *Asian Survey* 46, no. 1 (2006): 37–48.

26. Kevin O'Brien and Lianjiang Li, *Rightful Resistance in Rural China* (Cambridge: Cambridge University Press, 2006).

27. Kevin O'Brien and Lianjiang Li, *Rightful Resistance in Rural China*, 39.

28. For an informative and entertaining depiction of one young rural woman's efforts to take legal action against a village cadre for injuring her husband, see the 1992 Chinese film *Qiu Ju Goes to Court* (or *The Story of Qiu Ju*). See also Jerome Alan Cohen and Joan Lepold Cohen, "Did Qiu Jiu Get Good Legal Advice?" in Corey K. Creekmur and Mark Sidel, eds., *Cinema, Law and State in Asia* (New York: Palgrave Macmillan, 2007), 161–174.

29. Kevin O'Brien and Lianjiang Li, *Rightful Resistance in Rural China*, 81.

30. Kevin O'Brien and Lianjiang Li, *Rightful Resistance in Rural China*, footnote, 124.

31. Yuen Yuen Tang, "When Peasants Sue En Masse: Large-scale Collective ALL Suits in Rural China," *China: An International Journal* 3, no. 1 (March 2005): 24–49.

32. Tim Luard, "China Village Democracy Skin Deep," BBC (October 10, 2005), http://news.bbc .co.uk/hi/asia-pacific/4319954.stm, accessed May 2, 2008.

33. Edward Cody, "For Chinese, Peasant Revolt Is Rare Victory: Farmers Beat Back Police in Battle over Pollution," *Washington Post* (June 13, 2005), http://www.washingtonpost.com/wp-dyn/content/ article/2005/06/12/AR2005061201531.html, accessed May 2, 2008.

34. "Hu Jintao's Report at 17th Party Congress," *China Daily*, October 25, 2007, http://www.china-daily.com.cn/china/2007–10/25/content_6204667_6.htm, accessed May 2, 2008.

Suggested Readings

Chan, Anita, Richard Madsen, and Jonathan Unger. *Chen Village: Revolution to Globalization*. 3rd ed. Berkeley: University of California Press, 2009.

Chen Guidi and Wu Chuntao. *Will the Boat Sink the Water?: The Life of China's Peasants*. New York: Public Affairs, 2007.

Goldman, Merle and Elizabeth J Perry, eds. *Grassroots Political Reform in Contemporary China*. Cambridge, MA: Harvard University Press, 2007.

Guldin, Gregory Eliyu. *What's a Peasant to Do? Village Becoming Town in Southern China*. Boulder, CO: Westview Press, 2001.

Friedman, Edward, Paul G. Pickowicz, Mark Selden, and Kay Ann Johnson. *Chinese Village, Socialist State*. New Haven: CT: Yale University Press, 1993.

Friedman, Edward, Paul G. Pickowicz, and Mark Selden. *Revolution, Resistance, and Reform in Village China*. New Haven: CT: Yale University Press, 2006.

He, Baogang. *Rural Democracy in China: The Role of Village Elections*. New York: Palgrave, 2007.

Hessler, Peter. "China's Instant Cities," *National Geographic*, June 2007. http://ngm.nationalgeographic. com/ngm/0706/feature4/index.html.

Huang, Shu-min. *The Spiral Road: Change in a Chinese Village Through the Eyes of a Communist*. Boulder, CO: Westview Press, 1998.

O'Brien, Kevin J., and Lianjiang Li. *Rightful Resistance in Rural China*. Cambridge: Cambridge University Press, 2006.

Yan, Yunxiang. *Private Life under Socialism: Love, Intimacy, and Family Change in a Chinese Village, 1949–1999*. Stanford, CA: Stanford University Press, 2003.

Tsai, Lily T. *Accountability Without Democracy: Solidary Groups and Public Goods Provision in Rural China*. New York: Cambridge University Press, 2007.

Unger, Jonathan. *The Transformation of Rural China*. Armonk, M. E. Sharpe, 2002.

Zhang, Yang. *Local Government and Politics in China: Challenges from Below*. Armonk, NY: M. E. Sharpe, 2003.

9

Urban China: Change and Contention

William Hurst

China is the world's largest and most important agrarian society, with about 55 percent of its population residing in its vast countryside. Despite this, it also has the largest urban population in the world, and more people live in its cities than in the entire United States. China is also, by many measures, the world's most rapidly urbanizing country. As such, there are many important issues in urban Chinese politics and society. Understanding these is key to comprehending what drives Chinese politics as a whole.

This chapter will cover several facets of urban Chinese social and political life in eight sections. These will focus on: (1) historical background of the idiosyncrasies of Chinese cities; (2) administrative reform of urban governance in the post-Mao era; (3) rural-to-urban migration and the shifting boundaries between urban and rural China; (4) reform of the state-owned economy and the massive unemployment it has caused; (5) the rising middle class and the new rich; (6) the political and social life of urban youth; (7) new concerns such as environmental protection and urban planning; and (8) the likely dynamics and trajectories of future reform.

Sections 1 and 2 will discuss the impact of reform on the functioning of the state and shape of society. Sections 3 through 7 will do this as well, but with added attention to axes of contention or confrontation where new wedges have been driven between state and society or between social groups. Section 8 will go back to the institutional focus of the early sections, but with an eye to what things might look like going forward. The conclusion will recap the main points of the preceding sections and offer some suggestions for further reading or study.

Historical Background

Chinese cities have been among the biggest in the world since the time of the Han Dynasty (206 BCE–220 CE) and Roman Empire (27 BCE–476 CE), and several cities in China were larger than almost any in Europe during the Middle Ages. During the Qing Dynasty (1644–1911), China experienced unprecedented urbanization and industrialization, producing a number of "megacities" to rival the industrial hubs of Western Europe and North America. Despite massive damage and destruction from World War II and the Chinese civil war, China's urban centers recovered quickly after 1949. Today, at least seven of the world's forty largest cities are in China.

Though most Chinese cities were traditionally not especially well-planned and extremely crowded, the Chinese Communist Party (CCP) imposed its particular brand of order on them after 1949.[1] There were three key elements of the CCP's early program for urban areas: the reorganization of housing and transportation; the **work unit** (*danwei*) system; and the household registration (*hukou*) system. Almost immediately upon coming to power, the CCP set about remaking the urban landscape, erecting new housing blocks to replace packed tenements, corralling commercial activities into regulated zones, closing many markets and street stalls, widening and straightening roads, and building new highways and transit corridors. These moves were made with the goal of following the model laid down earlier in the Soviet Union. Soviet cities, and by extension, socialist cities the world over, were to be rational, modern, functional, and grand.

Though the physical environment of Chinese cities changed much throughout the 1950s and beyond, the social landscape saw an even greater transformation. After 1949, and especially after the nationalization of private business in 1956, most urbanites were employed in state-owned enterprises (SOEs) or smaller urban collectives. These, along with government bureaus and state agencies, operated as work units (*danwei*) that provided not simply jobs, but also housing, health care, education, day care, pensions, restaurants, shopping, and vacation resorts, for their members. These benefits, along with permanent employment, made up the "iron rice bowl" that was a feature of urban (and to an extent rural) life in Maoist China. Work units became truly all-encompassing social institutions to the extent that many came to resemble cities within cities that their residents quite literally never had to leave. Though it has undergone quite fundamental change in the reform era, this form of organization continues to exert an influence on Chinese urban life in the twenty-first century.

Finally, the household registration (*hukou*) system was established in order to keep rural residents out of cities in the 1950s. The primary goal was to avoid the development of unmanageable shantytowns or slums and to ensure that villagers and city dwellers alike could be accounted for and monitored in their places of residence. Another purpose was to facilitate the expropriation of the agricultural surplus by the state to finance urban construction and industrialization. Under the system, all families were assigned a registration, either "agricultural" or "nonagricultural," tied to their specific place of residence. Moving anywhere, especially from rural to urban areas, was extremely difficult and often impossible.

These three aspects of the Maoist order altered the social and political dynamics of Chinese cities tremendously.[2] They became rather rigid and unchanging, largely self-sufficient, well-managed metropolises. In such an environment, urbanites lived stable, well protected, if somewhat restricted, lives. This placed city dwellers at a substantial advantage over their rural counterparts, for whom life was still precarious and fraught with shortage and deprivation.

What Is a City? Administrative Reform and Continuity

More so than in many countries, the question of just what a city in China is comes up with astonishing regularity. Some places classified as rural county towns have nearly one million residents, with traffic congestion and tall buildings that would rival some of America's larger cities. Cities like Chongqing can formally include vast hinterlands larger than some European countries, with many more farmers than there are residents in the urban core. Including those rural areas, Chongqing has a total population of over 30 million, which would make it, by far, the world's largest city; but only about 6 million live in its urban districts.

Prior to the late 1980s, defining urban areas as those districts where residents were allocated non-agricultural registrations was simple enough. Now, for a variety of reasons, including large-scale rural-to-urban migration, it has become harder. Still, there are three basic levels of city in China: county (*xian*), prefecture (*diqu*), and province (*sheng*) (see Figure 1.1 in chapter 1). County-level cities have a status equivalent to rural counties and generally tend to be small and under the jurisdiction of a larger city nearby. Prefecture-level cities are not true cities, but rather large regions encompassing a major city and a significant rural hinterland. In fact, since the late 1990s, nearly all of China has been organized into such "cities" that have become the dominant organizational unit between province and county. Finally, Beijing, Chongqing, Shanghai, and Tianjin are "**directly administered municipalities**" (*zhixiashi*) that have the status of provinces, with no intermediary institution between them and the central government.

Each class of city faces distinct issues, in part because each is governed differently in terms of its relationship to higher levels of authority. Provincial-level directly administered municipalities have mayors and communist party secretaries of provincial rank who are among the most important political figures in the country. They have direct links to the central government in Beijing and all the spending and revenue powers of provinces. Prefecture-level cities fall one level down the chain of governance and must bargain for resources and access doled out by provincial governments. County-level cities are at the bottom of the pile when it comes to status, resources, and access and often have to contend with local rural areas for attention even from prefectural governments.

Over the past twenty years, a number of changes have shaken up the administrative hierarchy. Chongqing was split off from Sichuan Province to form a new directly administered municipality in 1997. There has been talk of something similar happening to Guangzhou

HOW CHINA'S CITIES ARE GOVERNED

Like all other administrative levels in the PRC, cities in China have both a state (or government) structure and a communist party structure. The two most powerful officials in a city are the mayor, who presides over the municipal administration, called the "**people's government**," and the party secretary, who is the head of the municipal party committee and is the real "boss." In most cases, the mayor serves concurrently as the deputy secretary of the city's CCP committee.

As noted in chapter 1, China has a unitary political system in which sub-national levels of administration are subordinate to the central government. The mayor and other important city officials are appointed by higher levels and must be approved by the CCP organization department as part of the PRC's *nomenklatura* system.

The mayors and party secretaries of major cities are important national political figures who frequently rise to key positions in the party-state system. Former Shanghai mayor (and party secretary) Jiang Zemin became general secretary of the CCP in 1989 and president of China in 1993. Xi Jinping, a member of the CCP Politburo Standing Committee and widely expected to become general secretary of the CCP when Hu Jintao retires in 2012, once served as party secretary in Shanghai.

Cities are divided into districts (Shanghai has, for example, 19), some of which are suburban or even rural. Districts are, in turn, divided into "**Street Offices**" (Shanghai has about 100), which is the lowest level of formal administration in a city. However, there is another level of urban organization, the **Residents' Committee** (Shanghai has around 3,000), at the grassroots (like a village in the rural areas). As discussed below, a relatively new kind of urban organization, the *shequ* ("community") is being implemented around the country. All these various sub-levels of urban administration combine service to constituents and surveillance/security functions.

Municipal people's governments have a variety of agencies such as education commissions and health bureaus. The chief law enforcement agency in Chinese cities is the Public Security Bureau (PSB), which has offices at the municipal and district levels. Municipal PSBs are subordinate to the central government's Ministry of Public Security. This arrangement might be compared to a situation in which city police departments in the United States were under the authority of the FBI.

China's cities also have people's congresses, which are constitutionally empowered to supervise the work of the people's government, but, in fact, have very little authority. The city-wide people's congress is *indirectly* elected by members of the district-level people's congresses. Elections to the district congress are *direct*, which means that all eligible citizens who live in the district are entitled to vote for their representatives. These elections have become more competitive and lively in recent years, although they are always carried out under the watchful eye of the CCP.

---

in Guangdong province or Qingdao in Shandong. Such splits change the makeup and economic, political, and social geography of some of China's most important provinces and therefore encounter considerable resistance. Overall, the trend toward increasing central power at the expense of provinces seems to be continuing, with the effect that all cities, but especially those directly administered from Beijing, are being drawn closer into the central government's orbit.

The second important change has been the rising importance of the nearly 300 prefecture-level cities as compared to other forms of sub-provincial organization. This trend has privileged urban areas locally, even as it saddles cities with obligations to engage directly with and be responsible for the well-being of rural districts under their administrative control. It also contributes to a further blurring of boundaries between city and countryside that has been underway since the 1980s.

Finally, even at the local level, the past fifteen years have seen an increasing emphasis on building state capacity—that is, the ability of the central government to exercise its authority—and increasing hierarchical control. The central government apparatus has been taking a growing role in the local urban economy, fine-tuning its regulatory and enforcement bureaus, and trying to integrate itself more deeply into urban daily life, even as citizens grow more savvy about using state actors and agencies to their own ends.[3]

Rural-to-Urban Migration: China's "Floating Population"

Since the early 1980s, at least 100 million, and likely 150 to 200 million, villagers have streamed into Chinese cities. Though it is hard to pinpoint just who is moving where, what kind of life they lead in cities, and with what effects, a few general trends within this so-called floating population are apparent. First, most migrants are young and travel short-to-moderate distances to find work, often returning to their villages on a weekly or even daily basis. Second, having reached the city, migrants face significant bias and discrimination in their daily activities and mostly end up in certain low-end jobs. Third, many of the problems migrants encounter can be tied to the persistence of the *hukou* system. Fourth and finally, migration and the remittances that migrants send home have had significant effects, positive and negative, on village life.

Though there are exceptions, the floating population is generally young and works in jobs that are largely segregated by age and gender. For example, young women often work in service jobs, including as domestics, or in "sweatshop" factories, while men tend to find jobs in construction and building trades.[4] This is true to such a degree that in many cities virtually all workers employed in certain jobs are migrants. Networks have also developed to recruit migrants in their home villages for specific jobs in their destination cities, and migrants from particular regions have cornered the market in certain sectors. For instance, there are scores of laundries in Beijing run by people from Chongqing's Rongchang County.

Though much publicity is attracted by the millions of migrants who travel hundreds of miles across China to work in the teeming metropolises of Beijing, Shanghai, and the Pearl River Delta (near Hong Kong), most stay closer to home. Many even commute on a daily or weekly basis from village to city. Working in the nearest—or a neighboring—prefecture-level city has certain advantages. But it also limits migrants' earnings potential and job prospects. Traveling farther afield opens up more possibilities but also carries greater costs and risks.

When they do travel to major urban centers, migrants are often shunted into particular jobs. Sometimes they will even have been recruited for a specific position. Work in restaurants, retail, and construction is common for migrants throughout China. In certain cities, migrant labor is also heavily represented in other sectors. Perhaps the most well-known are the export manufacturing contractor firms in the Pearl River Delta that employ millions of migrant workers from various parts of China. In other cities, though, sectors like transportation draw largely on migrants. Most of their jobs, regardless of sector, come without comprehensive benefits or most forms of security and protection common to state sector or other "regular" urban jobs. A new labor law implemented in 2008 was meant to address some of these problems. It required written contracts for all employment, demanded that "informal" employees be granted at least minimal benefits previously only afforded their "formal" counterparts with urban household registrations, and empowered wronged employees to sue errant employers more easily. At the time of this writing, it is still too soon to evaluate the full impact of the law, but its passage shows that the Chinese government had at least become acutely concerned about the issues migrants confronted.

The floating population also must overcome systematic disadvantages when working in the city. These stem from lingering elements of the old *hukou* system. Most important, migrants do not have legal rights to work in permanent or formal urban jobs, or even to live in the city. Rather, they are almost always hired "off the books" in a manner similar to illegal immigrants in the United States and with a similar pattern of low wages and lack of protections. They also are unable to access subsidized urban health care systems and must pay very high out-of-pocket costs for treatment of illness or injury (even for work-related injuries in some cases). Preventive care or other routine medicine is mostly unavailable. Finally, migrants' children are unable to enroll in urban schools without a local *hukou*. This effectively forces migrants to leave their children behind, where they attend village schools, or to allow their children to grow up without the benefits of an education. Even though some informal schools have been established for migrants' children, these are generally not accredited and cannot provide the educational credentials needed to advance to the next level in China.

The social bias and difficult working conditions migrants encounter are worthy of special mention. Many urbanites actively discriminate against the floating population in their cities. Local officials often blame spikes in criminal activity or problems of public health or sanitation squarely on migrants who usually have nothing to do with them. One researcher uncovered a particularly sharp articulation of this bias in a Beijing newspaper commentary praising proposals to segregate members of the floating population into separate areas of the Qingdao City public transit network because urban residents allegedly could not stand their foul smell.[5] In terms of their working environment, migrants usually must do the most difficult or dangerous jobs while enjoying the weakest protections and lowest compensation.

On a more human scale, Pun Ngai's interviewees at a fairly typical factory in the Pearl River Delta described the day-to-day health risks of their long hours working with toxic chemicals in poor conditions as: "headache, sore throat, flu and coughs, stomach problems, backache, nausea, eye strain, dizziness and weakness, and aggravated menstrual pain." As one worker explained, "The room is stuffy, and the smells are worse than the smells in the hospital. Those acids make me feel dizzy all the time and I can't make my mind concentrate. Recently I find my head is too painful to describe." Another coworker added that, "we all know our eyesight is becoming weaker and weaker. Sometimes when I leave the factory, I do not dare to glance at the sunlight. I find my vision blurred, and I can't walk a straight line."[6] These young women and millions of other migrants like them suffered direct repercussions of the maltreatment of the floating population in their daily lives and long-term health.

Migration changes not only cities, but also the villages left behind. There are three main effects on village economic and social life from out-migration, particularly in poorer, more densely populated parts of China like Sichuan and Jiangxi. First, population pressure and the village labor pool are both reduced. Depopulation can have both positive and negative effects, but the effects are substantial. There are now many villages where only children, elderly people, and a very few others remain. In some of these, farms are mostly worked by hired hands recruited from even poorer, more remote settings. Second, remittances sent home by migrants have helped fuel a house-building boom in many rural areas, along with general improvements in living conditions. But there are additional social effects that are harder to measure. Exposure to life in the city gives returned migrants a new perspective previously unknown in most rural areas. Many migrants also form links and social ties to people from far-flung regions while in the city, connecting villages with one another to a much greater degree than had been imaginable previously.

In the long term, it is difficult to say exactly what political effect such large-scale rural-to-urban migration will have. But it is clear that the once impregnable ramparts separating city and countryside in China have been broken down. They will no doubt continue to erode until Chinese rural residents at last enjoy the freedom of movement promised them since 1949. The final demise of the *hukou* system may well cause those hallmarks of third world urbanization most feared by the CCP—shanty towns, poor hygiene, high crime rates, severe environmental pollution, and extreme inequality—to become ensconced in the social fabric of Chinese cities. But it would also have a leveling effect on Chinese society that few other reforms, on their own, could achieve. While there has been talk on and off for some years about formally scrapping the *hukou* system, those charged with implementing any such reform steadfastly reject any suggestion that the already strained urban education and health care systems be opened to migrants.[7]

State Enterprise Reform and Unemployment

For the first twenty years of reform, state-owned enterprises (SOEs) remained largely unchanged from the Mao era. Only at the National Party Congress in 1997 did the CCP leadership decide to implement thoroughgoing reform of the state sector and *danwei* system. Between 1997 and 2002, China moved to close insolvent SOEs, merge successful ones to create multinational corporations, and "reduce staff to increase efficiency" (*jian yuan zeng xiao*) in underperformers. The results have been mixed economically but intensely disruptive in social and political terms. Figure 9.1 shows the sharp drop in employment in state-owned and urban collective enterprises and the sharp rise in urban disposable incomes since 1993. As discussed below, the new urban middle class has been the main beneficiary of the income rise, while laid-off workers are a large part of the urban poor.

SOE reform is a complex and ongoing process (see chapter 7). But the gist of it can be summed up in a few key points. First, SOEs did not change their basic structure or practices very much from the years after the Cultural Revolution in the mid-1970s until the late 1990s. Second, SOEs ran up tremendous debts in the 1990s as they struggled to survive in a changing economic environment. Third, when change did come, it came quickly and harshly. Fourth and finally, the Chinese party-state is unwilling to give up the state sector entirely, necessitating the maintenance of a large state economy even as subsidies decline and competition increases.

By 1997, SOE debts and business losses convinced the top leadership that decisive action was needed to reform the state sector. From that year, SOEs were largely cut off from additional credit or lending, many were closed or merged, and all were strongly encouraged to reduce their workforces as a way of cutting costs and stemming losses. Little more than ten years later, China's remaining state companies are indeed in better financial shape, but they also employ far fewer workers and provide much more limited benefit to urban society and the broader economy.

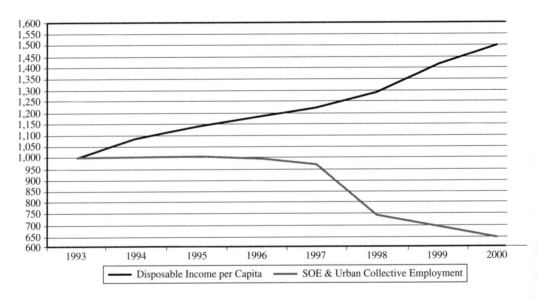

Figure 9.1 Urban Disposable Income per Capita and On-Post Employment in State-Owned and Urban Collective Enterprises, 1993–2000

The greatest social impact came from the massive layoffs that SOEs implemented after 1997. Between 1993 and 2008, more than 60 million state sector jobs were lost, the majority to layoffs, the rest to attrition or voluntary departure. Considering that the overall SOE labor force in 1993 was roughly 140 million, this represented a more than 40 percent reduction in fifteen years, pushing a population of workers out of their jobs that was larger than the combined total population of Texas and California. More than any other event, SOE layoffs have sealed the demise of the *danwei* system.[8]

With nearly half of all SOE workers being forced out of their work units, and those that remained being offered much reduced services and benefits, little remained of "work unit socialism." Without a comprehensive state welfare system in place, millions of workers who had formerly been assured a stable if Spartan livelihood suddenly found themselves in poverty without any meaningful social safety net or security. Though the government tried to help, its assistance programs were not always effective.

There have been three broad types of policies put forward to assist laid-off workers. The first, which lasted from about 1997 to 2003, was a system under which laid-off workers were termed "off post" (*xiagang*) rather than unemployed, and were shunted to re-employment service centers (RSCs) rather than directly into the labor market. The idea was that enterprises would continue to provide for downsized workers through RSCs for at least several years, before workers moved into new private sector jobs or retired. The problem was that many SOEs lacked the resources to establish RSCs or to provide adequately for their workers once they were enrolled in them. Workers, in turn, did not find new jobs at nearly the rates the government had hoped, and so chose to remain in the RSCs as long as possible.

Sensing that it was unrealistic to expect SOEs to keep up welfare elements of the *danwei* system after subsidies and planning aspects had faded away, the government offered two programs to replace the old work unit-based system. The first, known as the *dibao* or "minimum livelihood protection" was meant to provide subsidies to all individuals with incomes below locally determined poverty lines. This theoretically egalitarian program was in fact implemented in such divergent ways across regions and localities that it exacerbated existing inequalities. In nearly all cities, the *dibao* failed to provide sufficient security to keep many workers out of desperate poverty.

Second, a new organization called the *shequ*, or community, is being developed as the most basic level institutions of urban governance in an effort to capture laid-off workers in a new formal state embrace. These have had limited success so far in re-employing and taking care of the unemployed but, with increased funding, could perhaps prove more effective than RSCs or the *dibao*. Most often, however, workers have been left to rely on informal personal connections, both to ensure their daily survival and to search for new work, after losing their jobs in SOEs.

Not all workers start on an equal footing, however. Those from more privileged backgrounds, who are Party members, or who had previously held managerial positions have been in a much stronger position when seeking new work or informal living assistance through their personal networks. Results in terms of re-employment and basic welfare have also varied substantially across regions, with workers along the central coast faring much better than their counterparts in northeastern, central, or western regions. Overall, a significant proportion of laid-off workers have remained in a sort of limbo that has proved fertile ground for collective action against the local state.

Workers have indeed often engaged in contention against local authorities. The form, frequency, and severity all vary by region, but there are three basic styles. In Shanghai and other central coast cities, laid-off workers protest only rarely, when welfare benefits go

After 1949, the CCP put into place a strictly hierarchical system of urban governance. Below the province came prefecture-level cities that were in turn divided into districts. Districts then were broken into neighborhoods managed by street committees (or sub-districts) that each presided over several residents' committees at the very lowest level of governance (see Figure 1.1). State-owned work units, though not official organs of government, frequently assumed many of the functions otherwise performed by street committees, residents' committees, or even districts—including sanitation, basic social services, and even some elements of policing. With the disintegration of China's work unit system and the fraying of vertical ties that had bound grassroots governmental organizations, this framework became less workable.

Since the late 1990s, China has made a concerted effort to craft a new institution of local governance at the most basic level of urban society—the "community" or *shequ*. These grassroots units were explicitly intended to take over many of the political and social functions of the work unit and other institutions of street-level governance. They were staffed and funded directly by city and district governments, often recruiting personnel and appropriating funds that had previously been channeled to neighborhood level organs. The implication was that the *shequ* would become a new all-encompassing social institution. Individuals would be associated with their *shequ*, as they once were with their work unit or neighborhood.

Three *shequ* models have been developed: (1) a weak "Shenyang model" under which the authority of both the new community and older organizations (both work unit and street and residents' committees) was limited; (2) a hierarchical "Shanghai model" under which the community was essentially co-opted by increasingly powerful local street committees; and (3) a "Jianghan model" that sought to use broadly autonomous and consultative *shequ* to shore up faltering local state capacity to deliver basic social services such as day care and elder care.

As of early 2009, *shequ* had directly replaced work units as neighborhood-level organizations in some cities. *Shequ* have also steadily assumed increased responsibility for reemploying laid-off workers. Nationwide, by the end of 2004, *shequ* directly employed over 2 million workers in various positions ranging from office staff to sanitation workers and through outright featherbedding. Such *shequ*-based programs have been touted as more successful in promoting reemployment than city government labor bureaus or work units.

Some national level mass organizations, like the All China Women's Federation, that had earlier run informal reemployment programs have worked through the *shequ* as a mechanism not only for that purpose, but also for many other functions, ranging from providing legal aid to implementing birth planning policies on the local level. This has helped both to establish the new *shequ* model of governance and to breathe new life into tired mass organizations like the Women's Federation.

Finally, the *shequ* has become a mechanism of social control by the party-state that may help fill the void left by the decrepit work unit system. This was especially true under the Shanghai model, which had social control as one of its primary goals. But every model of *shequ* has sought to enhance the declining capacity of local governments to head off popular discontent before it turns into contention.

By 2009, it was clear that government's primary goal of the *shequ* policy was to create a new institutional basis for social welfare and control in China's cities to replace the *danwei* system. If it is successful, this organizational transition could preserve or even reinvigorate many important aspects of pre-reform urban China.

unpaid or when working conditions in their new jobs are unbearably poor. Generally, central coast workers frame their grievances in contractual terms and call upon local authorities to ensure that employers and former employers pay workers what they are legally entitled. The local government most often appeases or accommodates workers, either by issuing one-time payments to them or by leaning on firms to give workers their due.

In north-central and southwestern areas, the situation is quite different. There, workers are often not provided with benefits or new jobs. Managers and local officials are often palpably corrupt, and malfeasance is frequently the root cause of job losses and other difficulties. Despite this, there are many informal avenues to subsistence for workers in these regions. Markets are large and demands for many types of goods and services often go unmet. Workers, therefore, tend to target the allegedly corrupt officials they believe are either preventing them from finding their own way in the informal economy or flagrantly abusing them in other ways. The state, lacking either desire or capacity to accommodate them, nearly always responds to workers' protests with harsh repression, as evinced for example in the government's violent response to workers' protests surrounding the bankruptcy of the Chongqing Special Steel Plant in the summer and fall of 2005.

Finally, in the Northeast—the first region of China to industrialize and the heartland of its socialist development in the Maoist period, but now often referred to as China's "rust belt"—has seen the highest frequency of protests. In Benxi, a city roughly the size of San Francisco in Liaoning Province, morning traffic reports on local radio in the early 2000s used to advise drivers of which intersections were being blocked by protesting workers. Many cities in the region have so many workers' protests every day that manifestations have taken on a quotidian aspect—no one pays much attention anymore. Workers grievances are legion, but usually relate to their inability to provide for their most basic necessities like food and housing. Local officials are often sympathetic but are rarely able to offer much to restive workers. Instead, they sometimes highlight ongoing contention in their pleas to higher authorities to release special funds to assist displaced workers. By showcasing their cities' troubles, rather than covering them up, they sometimes manage to convince their superiors in provincial or even central government offices of their dire need for more resources than allocated under the budget.

Overall, there is hope for SOE workers as a group, in that the new generation is not likely to face the layoffs their parents have endured. There are not enough jobs to replace those lost from the state sector in many regions, however. Though Shanghai should fare better than most other cities, with eventually even the children of today's laid-off workers likely finding decent and stable employment, places like Benxi or most other cities outside the central coast face a much more uncertain future. Given the continuing lack of geographic mobility for most Chinese urbanities, this could consign multiple generations to poverty and desperation. Interregional and local inequalities will likely grow far worse before they get better. While the state has prioritized the issue, SOE reform and its negative effects have shaken the foundations of urban social life and threaten the stability of Chinese urban politics.

The Rising Middle Class

The foreign media have been enthralled by the rapid development of a Chinese middle class. But who are these tens of millions of new consumers? How large a force are they in urban China? These are just some of the questions that arise as a segment of China's urban public the size of Japan's entire population (about 125 million) emerges as a new middle-income market community. To assess their role in politics, it is necessary to understand a bit about the new urban rich in China—where they have come from, and what they want for themselves.

Broadly speaking, there are three subgroups among the urban middle class: (1) young professionals working for foreign firms or domestic private sector start-ups or high-flyers; (2) former SOE managers who have converted their companies or professional contacts into private-sector successes; and (3) entrepreneurs from rural or working class backgrounds who "made it big" in the classic sense depicted in American popular "rags to riches" discourse. Each subgroup has particular features that make it hard to lump all three together.

Young professionals, as will be discussed further below, suffer from a degree of insecurity and uncertainty that imbues many of them with strong measures of cynicism and a focus on short-term horizons. This leads many to have little loyalty to their employers, jumping from job to job, several times a year in many cases. As one young professional in Beijing explained, "I don't know if I'll have any job a year from now, so I'll change jobs after only three months if the new one pays RMB 500 (US$60) more per month."[9] Some observers also point to the fact that more and more rising professionals were raised in one-child families to explain their allegedly self-centered focus.

Those new rich who come from the ranks of former SOE managers, on the other hand, while less numerous than young professionals in cities like Beijing or Shanghai, form the main body of the middle class in most other cities. These are mostly older, usually male, ex-bureaucrats who found a pathway to wealth that led from SOEs to the private sector. Often, this involved taking possession of privatized (or stripped) state assets (see chapter 7). Other times, this entailed leveraging political clout or status into capital to launch private ventures. Nearly always, success rested on connections (*guanxi*) or privileged access to information, capital, or opportunities.

The smallest but most inspiring segment of the new working class are those workers and farmers who have managed to make their own way in the new market economy, becoming wealthy businesspeople through hard work and perseverance. Many of these individuals are in trades in which state managers and yuppies take little interest—for example, recycling, taxi service, waste removal, food service, religious statuary and incense production, and retail. In one widely publicized example, a man laid off from a furniture factory in Jiangsu Province used his severance pay to build fish ponds in several villages, transforming himself into a "goldfish king" and becoming very wealthy in the process.[10] These self-made success stories inspire many to believe in the opportunities available in the new market economy. But most realize that they are extremely rare.

A second question is how the new rich live their lives. Many reports have stressed the tendency of wealthy Chinese urbanites to consume conspicuously in a manner similar to post-Soviet Russian "oligarchs" or turn of the twentieth century American "robber barons." Such a tendency is real. But for every tycoon buying frivolous and overpriced luxuries, there are many yuppies—sometimes even called by the grating epithet "Chuppies"[11]—buying their first house or car. Because personal consumption was depressed so severely for so long in China, many people view big-ticket purchases (in the early to mid-2000s, a car and a condominium; in the 1980s and early 1990s, a television and refrigerator) as markers of improved living standards.

The growth in the ranks of the middle class has contributed to a number of new phenomena in urban China. Air pollution, traffic congestion, and rapidly rising home prices are some consequences of this expansion. There are also now some cities, notably Shanghai, Beijing, and Guangzhou, where the middle class has attained critical mass, becoming an important force in urban society even if its numbers still pale in comparison to the working class. The overall long-term trend, however, is toward growth of the middle class, even as millions of destitute migrants continue to enter the city and many SOE workers slip into poverty upon being laid off. Nevertheless, it would take several more decades at the current pace of change before urban China became a truly middle-class society.

Finally, most of the new rich have not been particularly politically active—at least not in ways that have challenged the CCP or local governments. Though this may be changing somewhat as issues like the environment come more to the fore, it is hardly surprising in an authoritarian context such as China's. The new rich have benefited from recent policy and development strategies. They also have the most to lose from instability, whether political or macroeconomic. Considering the close ties between many members of the new middle class and the state and Party apparatus, their quiescence is even less surprising and looks set to continue for the foreseeable future. As previous chapters note, former CCP leader, Jiang Zemin, made an effort under his "Three Represents" ideology to reach out to the private sector entrepreneurs and employees and even encourage them to join the communist party.

Urban Youth Politics

Dating back to the 1989 Tiananmen protests, the Cultural Revolution, and the May Fourth Movement, urban youth have been a key constituency for Chinese governments. But young people in Chinese cities today do not appear as politicized as in the recent past. They are still an important group, however, since even their apathy or self-centeredness will influence future trends in political, economic, and social life.

Perhaps the biggest change in young people's lives since the 1980s (and least intuitive one for students outside China) has been the end of the **job assignment**, system or *fenpei* system; in other words, they are *pleased* with the fact that they are no longer guaranteed a job when they graduate. From the 1950s into the 1990s, university students were assigned state-sector jobs upon graduation, in much the same way that Chinese workers were assigned to factories, which they were obliged to remain in for at least several years. This was in exchange for the free university tuition and housing they had received. Students had little choice over what jobs they were assigned or even where they were located. They could be sent more than a thousand miles away from where they wanted to be, to take up a job in which they were uninterested and for which they were unqualified, but they had no rights to appeal or complain. In practice, given the rigidities of the *danwei* system, initial job assignments often shaped the entire future careers of university graduates. While this system prevented unemployment, it stifled students' prospects and detracted from their dignity and autonomy.

One, perhaps unintended, effect of the *fenpei* system was that students were heavily politicized. This sprung not so much from some idealistic sense of civic engagement as from their desire to have more control over the course of their own lives and careers. Reform of the *fenpei* system was a major goal of the Tiananmen protesters and their allies in 1989, and it was in the aftermath of that conflagration that the CCP leadership decided to dismantle the system.

What has emerged in the past fifteen years is a China that requires university degrees for decent employment, but in which university admission has become even more intensely competitive (only 3 out of 5 pass the required national university entrance exam) and vastly more costly, and where even top-ranked students from leading universities often cannot find a job when they graduate. But young people at last have mastery of their own fates, at least in the sense that no one compels them to take particular jobs. The other major change is that the most lucrative and promising careers are now most often found in private or even foreign companies, rather than SOEs or government bureaus. These shifts have dramatically reoriented political and social life for urban Chinese people under the age of thirty.

The phenomenal success of books and periodicals purporting to be guides to financial and social success is a sign of this transformation. One of the most popular routes to success has been studying abroad. Parents are desperate to give their children every advantage in attaining this type of success. A book titled *Harvard Girl*, written by the parents of a young Chinese woman who actually went to Harvard, detailed how to raise successful, academic-star children from birth; it became a huge best seller in China.[12] Such parents' guides to helping their children win the new rat race are a new phenomenon in urban China (though they have been around for decades in Taiwan and Hong Kong) and foretell a sea change in attitudes affecting several generations.

While most urban youth today are best described as apathetic toward politics, they are intensely concerned about their own career and life prospects. Most undergraduates at Beijing University, China's most prestigious institution of higher education, know little and care less about the events of Tiananmen in 1989 or the Cultural Revolution, both of which played out in important ways on their campus, but they are palpably fearful of graduating and not landing a job. Worse, those not from Beijing are often concerned that they might lose their right to reside in Beijing if they are unable to get a job with an employer capable of sponsoring them for a Beijing *hukou*—no small feat. At the same time, though, in part related to pressures to get ahead in the job market, students have become much more internationalized and cosmopolitan than prior generations.

With so many plum jobs in foreign companies and with English as a mandatory examination field, Chinese urban youth and students are almost compelled to take an interest in international affairs. Many read foreign media sources and literature. Those who work in foreign firms interact regularly with foreign coworkers. In addition, studying abroad has become extremely popular. Those who return with advanced degrees frequently move on fast tracks into leadership positions in many sectors. They also usually retain networks of contacts and friends outside China. These both help them succeed in their work and ensure that they keep an eye focused on developments beyond China's borders. The experience of living abroad inevitably also broadens their perspectives.

Knowledge of and interaction with the outside world, combined with extreme insecurity and wrenching change at home, help produce two negative currents among contemporary urban youth—deep cynicism and anti-foreign nationalism. The tendency to become cynical about contemporary society is widespread across all walks of life in Chinese cities, but for those with the best understanding of the outside world and the most precarious positions in urban society, the trend is overwhelming. One antidote for many is nationalism. Nationalist sentiment is sometimes regarded as the last pure political viewpoint. Nationalism is also the least risky position from which to criticize the government or the CCP.[13] The 2005 protests against Japanese attempts to become a permanent member of the United Nations Security Council and the riots after China's defeat by Japan in the 2004 Asian Cup soccer final are recent examples.

The dangers of a new generation succumbing to either nationalist fervor or cynical anomie are not to be underestimated. But all is far from lost for today's urban youth. For those who do succeed, opportunities abound that earlier generations could not even imagine. If China's leaders can manage ongoing change reasonably smoothly, there is reason to hope that the rising cohort of young urban professionals might have a more comfortable and less tumultuous life than even those who came of age ten years ago. If this leads to decreased political activism, it would mark another milestone in the transformation of China into a country more closely approximating many in the West, where political and social mobilization has generally been on the wane since the 1970s.

New Concerns

Several new issues are beginning to come to the fore that are reshaping debates and conflicts in urban Chinese politics. The most obvious such issues are environmental protection and social inequality. Recently, there have been many news stories in the foreign press about "AIDS villages" (where large numbers of farmers were infected by tainted blood donation equipment and poor practices), lead in exported toys, and air quality in Beijing. But environmental issues in urban China go well beyond this list. Many people are only slowly becoming aware of the problems, and some are growing angry at what they regard as a lack of attention, or worse, from government.

For example, Datong, a city of roughly one million people in Shanxi Province, is home to China's most productive coal mines; but the ever-present visible coal dust and soot in Datong's air makes many visitors choke and would seem linked to the fact that Datong has what is said to be the highest rate of lung cancer in China. At one point the government presented residents with "evidence" that the prevalence of lung cancer was due to local residents' penchant for consumption of pickled vegetables. Many people in Datong have expressed outrage at the government's lack of concern about their air and water quality, even as they worry that enforcement of environmental standards could put additional pressure on mining jobs. The government seems to have begun to take occupational health and safety issues, especially for miners, more seriously, which has opened the door for a nascent environmental movement in Datong and elsewhere (see chapter 11 for a fuller discussion of environmental politics and policy in China).

Social inequality is another major issue in China's cities—indeed, in all of China. Over the last two decades, the PRC has moved from being one of the most egalitarian societies in the developing world to being one of the most unequal (see Box in chapter 7, **The Problem of Inequality in China**). A prominent sociologist at Qinghua University in Beijing, Sun Liping, has made much of his career writing about China's "fractured" society and the negative social implications of excessively sharp cleavages and rigid stratification.[14]

Much of China's inequality is interregional: for example, Shanghai is much richer than Xining, the capital of the far western province of Qinghai. A respected Chinese sociologist observed that, just as many used to speak of first, second, and third worlds, within China there are actually four "worlds": Hong Kong; Beijing, Shanghai, and Guangzhou; all other cities; and rural areas.[15] There are also still grinding disparities within cities (see Box, **Inequalities in Chinese Cities**).

Just within Beijing, for example, there are by many estimations at least one million middle class citizens, but there are about 5 million migrant workers living on the edge of subsistence. Such extreme gaps between rich and poor are both new and highly incongruous with the CCP's publicly proclaimed ideology and principles. They concern policy-makers and ordinary citizens alike. But their ultimate impact is not yet clear. Many societies, notably across much of Latin America, have lived with even sharper levels of inequality for decades without constant or overly disruptive political upheaval. But, counter to Chinese long-term trends and current global tendencies, the distribution of wealth in China is becoming more, rather than less, skewed and its current level of inequality is unprecedented for a self-proclaimed socialist society led by a communist party. It seems likely that social injustice will continue to spark popular discontent and worry Chinese leaders for some time to come.

There are three main divisions of inequality in Chinese cities: (1) the urban core of the city versus its incorporated rural areas; (2) well-functioning units of the state or collective sector versus poorly functioning ones; and (3) state sector versus new private sector. Each of these three divisions is more nuanced than it may appear on the surface, and each is closely linked to idiosyncratic aspects of Chinese politics and political history.

Urban-rural divides have always been the most salient axes of inequality in post-1949 China. These divisions existed before the revolution, but were rendered considerably more severe and permanent by the imposition of the *hukou* (household registration) system in the 1950s. Even today, the gap between urban and rural living standards and incomes is wide (see Figure 7.6). Rural residents lack access to health care, social security, pension, and other benefits routinely enjoyed by their urban counterparts. Workers migrating from countryside to city also face blatant discrimination and are paid dramatically lower wages than urbanites.

Most of the benefits urban resident enjoyed have historically been rooted in the *danwei* (work unit) system. Rather than providing general public goods to all citizens through state agencies, individual work units administered and funded health insurance, pensions, and other social protection measures. This created two types of inequality between units: the gap between categories of units favored by the government and those neglected by it, and the divide between well-off and poorer units within each category.

Broadly speaking, workers in defense plants, heavy industrial and resource-extraction (such oil field and coal mines) firms, and branches of the state or Party bureaucracy or apparatus enjoyed higher living standards and better benefits than those who worked for light industrial plants, service providers, or retail outlets. There was also a division between those employed in state-owned enterprises and urban collective firms. Employers in the former category were directly responsible to and cared for by the government, whereas those in the latter, which were mostly smaller subsidiaries set up by SOEs, were dependent upon, but often not well taken care of by, the state.

Beyond these structural divisions, firms performing well could offer employees better benefits than those that were foundering. For example, someone who works today for Baoshan Steel in Shanghai is much better compensated and cared for than his or her counterpart in Baotou Iron and Steel in Inner Mongolia, both of which are state-owned. Even within the same city, employees of failing textile mills receive fewer benefits and enjoy less security than workers in a successful appliance factory or auto plant across town.

Then there is the glaring divide between state work units and private firms. SOE workers often lack security and have limited upward mobility, but they have at least a basic income and usually some benefits while they remain on the job. Private sector workers, on the other hand, tend to be concentrated more at the extremes, both high and low, of the income scale in Chinese cities. On the one hand, most high-flying executives and yuppies work in private companies. But, on the other hand, sweatshop production of low-end export goods is also almost exclusively in the non-state sector. Private firms employ more migrants under worse conditions *and* more advanced degree holders with generous pay packages than SOEs do.

Together these three dimensions make urban China one of the most glaringly unequal environments in the world. As the gap between rich and poor continues to grow wider and more of the population becomes concentrated toward the extremes, inequality will remain a top concern of Chinese officials and students of Chinese urban politics alike for many years to come.

Beyond these two marquee issues of environmental problems and growing inequality are two other concerns that should be highlighted—urbanization and city planning. China is urbanizing faster and more thoroughly than almost any other society in the world today. Roughly 20 percent of China's population was urban in the 1980s, about 45 percent is today. By 2015, the United Nations predicts that more than half of all Chinese people will live in cities. This is a sea change in Chinese politics and society, one that would stretch any country's ability to cope. China must balance a desire to avoid an unmanageable explosion of urban areas with the necessity of accommodating people's inexorable drive to leave the land and look for work outside the agricultural sector.

So far, China has kept pace with urbanization in the most basic sense of providing sufficient infrastructure to withstand the deluge. But in the years ahead, other areas of urban politics will all be affected by massive increases in urban population. The job market, both for downsized state workers and newly graduated students, will tighten. Environmental goals will be harder to achieve, rather than easier, and will often be pitted against the demands of bursting new cities. Inequality will likely be exacerbated before it can be curtailed. While the government cannot stop urbanization, it must continue to search for integrated responses.

One such response is a new emphasis on urban planning. Remaking the urban landscape has been a hallmark of CCP rule since 1949. But in recent years, several new focal points have emerged. Building subway systems and other rapid transit networks is one new focus of urban planning. New attention to the creation or preservation of green space and parks, as well as to aspects of zoning, has also been notable. Finally, debates have begun about the relative value of historic preservation versus urban renewal. These debates and others will, no doubt, continue. But the crucial new focus on careful planning of new urban development or renewal is encouraging as China moves forward. Only through consensual and holistic deliberation does China have hope to ward off the strongest threats to stability and prosperity from the ongoing growth of its cities.

Future Trajectories for Urban China

Four broad trajectories are important to emphasize as Chinese cities move into the second decade of the twenty-first century. First, they will continue to grow. The rapidly expanding population of Chinese cities, as noted above, will shape decision-making in all other areas. Indeed, there have been few examples in history of successful management of urbanization on a scale such as China is now experiencing. Yet everything, including the CCP's survival in power, is contingent upon the government's ability to meet this challenge.

Second, problems related to employment and the urban job market will not disappear. Rather, they appear poised to intensify and draw in increasingly broad swaths of the population, from laid-off SOE workers to yuppies and migrants. How the Chinese government addresses these issues will be key in determining whether it has the breathing space to cope with newer challenges and opportunities. If it cannot help urbanites adjust fast enough, it will be forever putting out fires of discord and resistance when it could otherwise be charting a new course in other policy realms.

Third, environmental and public health issues are likely to become primary concerns for both leaders and citizens for at least the next fifteen to twenty years. The 2003 outbreak of Severe Acute Respiratory Syndrome (SARS) and international concerns over Beijing's air quality for the 2008 Olympic Games were harbingers of much larger arguments and higher-stakes contests to come. These problems are not just new areas of special concern for Chinese urban residents, but also for the world. SARS spread to every continent within weeks of its initial detection in Guangzhou (see chapter 12). Traces of the mixture of sand and loess particles that chokes Beijing's air during spring windstorms can be detected soon afterward in California and Oregon. And the emissions of urban China's burgeoning fleet of automobiles and growing stable of manufacturing plants have become even larger contributors to global warming than their U.S. counterparts (see chapter 11). If China's responses to employment and urban population growth are linchpins of its success in other domestic policy areas, how it deals with public health and environmental problems will affect profoundly the rest of the world as well as China.

Fourth, there is a great opportunity for at least some key urban areas in China to join the ranks of "global cities." Sociologist Saskia Sassen has put forward the idea of the "global city" to describe metropolises that serve as critical nodes of interaction in the world economy.[16] The interchange of ideas, capital, people, and goods at these commercial and financial centers is often seen as *the* key to advancing the agenda of international integration and globalization.

Hong Kong is considered a global city (see chapter 16). Its tourism slogan, "Asia's World City," even echoes this theme. But many say it is losing its place at the lead among Chinese cities. Others, notably Shanghai—but also Beijing and Guangzhou—are beginning to catch up. By the very rough measure of how many times they are mentioned in advertisements in the globally influential *Economist* magazine over a nine-month period in 2000–2001, however, they have a way to go. Hong Kong was advertised twenty-three times, the same total as New York, though still short of London's forty mentions. Beijing, on the other hand, was cited only five times, Shanghai seven.[17]

Still, few would dispute that Mainland Chinese cities are internationalizing at a prodigious rate with significant effects on domestic politics.[18] If critical obstacles (such as barriers to immigration and free flows of information and capital) are removed, urban China may become one of the most globalized societies in the world within the next two to three decades. If this happens, it will still remain to be seen whether Shanghai, Beijing, and Guangzhou catch up to or even supplant New York, London, and Tokyo as global cities, but on some level it does not matter. If these cities become focal points of the global economy, there is no doubt that China's role in the world will have become much more consequential.

Conclusion

To sum up, five major areas of change have shaped new social and political dynamics in urban China. Administrative reform has redefined what a city is, and changed the way cities relate to higher levels of government. Rural-to-urban migration has increased the population of Chinese cities dramatically and injected a new reserve army of unskilled labor into the cities' mix.

Massive layoffs from state-owned enterprises, which had been the core of urban employment until very recently, have jolted the working class out of any sense of complacency in the face of market reforms. Just as millions have been forced to search for new work, millions of others are entering cities willing to accept below-subsistence wages, while yet millions more thrive and live in hitherto unimagined luxury in the new economy. As the new middle class has become increasingly economically powerful, however, it has remained politically quiescent and dependent upon the state and Party hierarchy for its position.

Finally, Chinese urban youth are far different from previous generations. Those who have come of age since 1990 have not been imbued with the deprivation and upheaval that affected their counterparts who grew up before 1949, during the Great Leap Forward or Cultural Revolution, or against the backdrop of the 1989 Tiananmen demonstrations. As the young people of today develop their lives and careers in new directions and as barriers between city and countryside and between China and the rest of the world gradually break down, the dynamics of Chinese urban politics and society are sure to continue evolving.

Notes

1. That said, certain important cities, like Beijing, were planned during the pre-modern era around *feng shui* (geomancy) principles.

2. For more on Chinese cities during the Maoist era, see John Wilson Lewis, ed., *The City in Communist China* (Stanford, CA: Stanford University Press, 1971).

3. Jane Duckett, *The Entrepreneurial State in China* (London: Routledge, 1998); Kenneth Foster "Embedded within State Agencies: Business Associations in Yantai" *The China Journal* 47 (2002): 41–66; Benjamin L. Read "Democratizing the Neighborhood? New Private Housing and Home Owner Self-Organization in Urban China" *The China Journal* 49 (2003): 31–59.

4. Pun Ngai, *Made in China: Women Factory Workers in a Global Workplace* (Durham, NC: Duke University Press, 2005).

5. Stanley Rosen, "The State of Youth/Youth and the State in Early 21st Century China: The Triumph of the Urban Rich?" in *State and Society in 21st Century China,* ed. Peter Hays Gries and Stanley Rosen (London: Routledge, 2004), 171.

6. Pun Ngai, *Made in China*, 169–170, 172.

7. Personal communication with the communist party secretary of a prefecture-level city in Jiangsu Province, 2005.

8. Lu, Xiaobo and Perry, Elizabeth J., eds. *Danwei: The Changing Chinese Workplace in Historical and Comparative Perspectives* (Armonk, NY: M. E. Sharpe, 1997).

9. Personal communication with advertising company junior executive, Beijing 2001.

10. Chen Tao, "Cong Xiagang Zhigong Dao 'Jinyu Wang' " (From Laid-off Worker to 'Goldfish King') *Yuye Zhifu Zhinan* 3 (2003): 14.

11. See, for example, Bay Fang, "China's Next Generation of Yuppies," *US News and World Report*, April 21, 2006.

12. Rosen, "The State of Youth/Youth and the State," 164.

13. Peter Hays Gries, *China's New Nationalism: Pride, Politics, and Diplomacy* (Berkeley: University of California Press, 2005).

14. See, for example: Sun Liping, *Zhuanxing yu Duanlie: Gaige yilai Zhongguo Shehui Jiegou de Biangan* (Transition and Cleavage: Change in China's Social Institutions under Reform) (Beijing: Qingghua Daxue Chubanshe, 2004).

15. Personal communication with a sociologist from the Beijing Academy of Social Sciences, 1998.

16. Saskia Sassen, *The Global City: New York, London, Tokyo* (Princeton, NJ: Princeton University Press, 1991).

17. J. Taylor, "Cities Mentioned in Advertisements in *The Economist* (May 2000 to January 2001). http://www.lboro.ac.uk/gawc/datasets/da9.html, accessed June 24, 2008.

18. David Zweig, *Internationalizing China: Domestic Interests and Global Linkages* (Ithaca, NY: Cornell University Press, 2002).

Suggested Readings

Cai, Yongshun, *State and Laid-off Workers in Reform China: The Silence and Collective Action of the Retrenched.* London: Routledge, 2006.

Chan, Anita. *China's Workers under Assault: The Exploitation of Labor in a Globalizing Economy.* Armonk, NY: M.E. Sharpe, 2001.

Chang, Leslie T. *Factory Girls: From Village to City in a Changing China*. New York: Spiegel & Grau, 2008.

Gallagher, Mary E. *Contagious Capitalism: Globalization and the Politics of Labor in China*. Princeton, NJ: Princeton University Press, 2005.

Gries, Peter Hays, and Stanley Rosen, eds. *State and Society in 21st Century China: Crisis, Contention, and Legitimation*. London: Routledge, 2004.

Gold, Thomas B., William J. Hurst, Jaeyoun Won, and Qiang, Li. *Laid-Off Workers in a Workers' State: Unemployment with Chinese Characteristics*. New York: Palgrave Macmillan, 2009.

Hurst, William. "The City as the Focus: the Analysis of Contemporary Chinese Urban Politics" *China Information* 20, no. 3 (November 2006): 457–79.

Hurst, William. *The Chinese Worker after Socialism* New York: Cambridge University Press, 2009.

Lee, Ching Kwan. *Against the Law: Labor Protests in China's Rustbelt and Sunbelt*. Berkeley: University of California Press, 2007.

Lewis, John Wilson. *The City in Communist China*. Stanford, CA: Stanford University Press, 1971.

Lin, Yi-min. *Between Politics and Markets: Firms, Competition, and Institutional Change in Post-Mao China*. New York: Cambridge University Press, 2001.

Murphy, Rachel. *How Migrant Labor Is Changing Rural China*. New York: Cambridge University Press, 2002.

Solinger, Dorothy J. *Contesting Citizenship in Urban China: Peasant Migrants, the State, and the Logic of the Market*. Berkeley: University of California Press, 1999.

Tang, Wenfang, and William L.Parish. *Chinese Urban Life under Reform: The Changing Social Contract*. New York: Cambridge University Press, 2000.

Wank, David L. *Commodifying Communism: Business, Trust, and Politics in a Chinese City*. New York: Cambridge University Press, 1999.

Yusuf, Shahid, and Tony Saich. *China Urbanizes: Consequences, Strategies, and Policies*. Washington, D.C.: World Bank Publications, 2008.

Zhou, Xueguang. *The State and Life Chances in Urban China: Redistribution and Stratification, 1949–1994*. New York: Cambridge University Press, 2004.

10

Policy Case Study: The Arts

Richard Curt Kraus

China's arts and their political context have changed dramatically since the Maoist period. The arts constitute one of the most open and dynamic aspects of civil society in the PRC, although the cultural arena remains under political scrutiny by the party-state. The arts are near the frontlines of political change in China, and how they fare is a measure for future progress in other areas of public discourse. This section will first introduce the background for the current arts scene, then discuss three topics: the new relationship between art and politics, the declining effectiveness of party-state censorship, and the party-state's new vigor in promoting culture as a symbol of Chinese nationalism.

Background for Arts Reform

China's recent arts policies have been fashioned by and against two great inheritances. One of these is the tradition of Confucian learning and statecraft. Modern leaders look to a past in which the state was an important arbiter of defining what was art, and in which great political figures were often significant poets, calligraphers, or connoisseurs. The bond between art and power was intensified by a second legacy, the communist revolution. Mao and other party leaders won power by force of arms, but also by harnessing the arts to mobilize mass support. The victories of the Red Army were accompanied by Party-sponsored songs, novels, dance, ballads, woodcuts, and film.

During three decades of revolution, the Chinese Communist Party (CCP) learned to use the arts as a political weapon. As discussed in chapter 3, a critical moment was the 1942 party "rectification" in Yan'an. Many sophisticated urban writers, painters, and musicians had joined the party in its Northwest China base. Mao Zedong spoke to an arts conference, demanding that these newcomers to Yan'an learn new skills to produce art that would inspire an uneducated and largely rural audience. Mao charged that they would remain "heroes without a battlefield," as long as they imagined they were producing works for Shanghai intellectuals and were unfamiliar with the needs of their new audience.[1] "If the professional writers and artists regard themselves as masters of the masses, as aristocrats on a superior level to the 'lower classes,' then no matter how talented they may be, they are completely useless as far as the masses are concerned and there is no future for their work."[2]

By the time the party came to power in 1949, it had learned to organize and discipline its arts workers. No civil libertarian heritage held back party leaders from "interfering" with artists;

WHAT WAS "CULTURAL" ABOUT THE CULTURAL REVOLUTION?

Political Scientists typically treat the Cultural Revolution as a power struggle over China's future. It is seen primarily as a time when Mao mobilized radical youth, the Red Guards, to attack those among his fellow senior leaders he judged to have betrayed him and who were leading China down the "capitalist road." But over the course of the "decade of chaos" from 1966–1976, as the Chinese officially date the Cultural Revolution, political conflict spilled over into nearly every aspect of life in China, including every facet of the arts. Literature, music, painting, drama, film, architecture, and even fashion became ideological battlegrounds that had an impact on all citizens.

Why did Mao and his supporters think a Cultural Revolution in the arts was necessary? Maoists believed that the 1949 seizure of political power and subsequent control of the economy had not truly empowered the working class. They concluded that once-stalwart veteran revolutionaries had been seduced by the attractive yet corrupting culture from China's feudal past or from foreign bourgeois nations. The Maoist prescription was to limit these "sugar-coated bullets" while fostering a new and potent culture that was truly proletarian in form and content.

Schools were closed in the early period of the movement, both to choke off the flow of bourgeois ideology to students, and also to provide a source of Red Guard activists to serve as the shock force of Mao's crusade. When rebels toppled party leaders from power, they typically included among their charges such aesthetic misdeeds as patronizing feudal operas from China's imperial past, supporting capitalist reforms in the arts, or showing an interest in foreign arts.

The Maoist approach to revolutionizing culture encountered several problems in implementation:

- In the course of opposing the "four olds" (old customs, culture, habits, and ideas), Red Guards destroyed many priceless artifacts of traditional Chinese culture. In many cases, the state, and in some cases, local people, such as in the birthplace of Confucius, intervened to protect major monuments. Nevertheless, not only was the scale of the destruction of national treasures caused by the young rebels incalculable, but many personal items, including family genealogies, paintings, books, phonograph records, and religious images, were also lost forever.
- Maoist leaders enforced Cultural Revolution guidelines for the arts hypocritically. While traditional operas were banned, Mao Zedong watched a set of specially filmed performances in his private residence. Lower level party leaders could watch foreign movies barred to public view. Kang Sheng, a leading Mao ally, was also an arts connoisseur, and he added thousands of paintings, seal carvings, and books to his personal collection that had been seized by Red Guards from "bourgeois" and "feudal" owners.
- Radical leaders were slow to develop new and revolutionary art. Mao's wife, Jiang Qing, a one-time actress before she met Mao in the 1930s, made the radical reform of Chinese opera a personal project. She commissioned new stage works with revolutionary themes, such as *The Red Lantern, The Red Detachment of Women, and Taking Tiger Mountain by Strategy*. These works had some successes, but the development of new pieces progressed slowly, in part because artists feared to cross her. As a result, only **"eight model operas"** and a few other artistic works gained official approval. For the Chinese people, it was truly a time of cultural famine.
- Other arts reform projects only flourished late in the Cultural Revolution, such as peasant painting, which again went slowly, in part because of the awkward need to use formally trained (but ideologically discredited) experts to train new peasant artists.

- The downfall of the pre-Cultural Revolution arts leadership in the CCP shifted influence to new centers of power. One was the army, whose performing arts groups gained new prestige. Even non-military units, such as the Central Philharmonic Orchestra, began to perform in army uniforms as a sign of political allegiance. This afforded some political protection to the musicians, but it was also a sign of the loss of any artistic independence.

Older artists and their children often became targets of the Cultural Revolution as it unfolded on the local level. Many of these came from highly educated families who had initially supported the CCP when it came to power in 1949. But the double blows of the 1957 Anti-Rightist campaign and the Cultural Revolution made it difficult for the Party to draw upon their training and enthusiasm. After Mao's death, Deng Xiaoping was able to tap into the deep cultural resentments of such families as he launched his effort to turn China away from the Maoism in every way, including the arts.

both the Confucian and revolutionary traditions regarded energetic cultural intervention as the responsibility of wise leadership. Only a less frequently invoked **Daoist** ideal suggested that the best government was achieved by inaction.

The new government's statist inclinations were reinforced through its first decade by influence from the Soviet Union. China's new cultural institutions, like its political system in general, resembled the Union of Soviet Socialist Republics, its socialist "elder brother." Russian oil painters lectured in Chinese arts academies, as Chinese pianists trained at the Moscow Conservatory.

The peak of centralized control over the arts in China came during the Cultural Revolution and its aftermath (1966–1976). During this protracted political struggle, some arts were dismissed as feudal (such as calligraphy) or bourgeois (such as oil painting), while others were recrafted for a new era of Chinese revolution (see Box, **What Was "Cultural" about the Cultural Revolution?**).[3]

After Mao's s death and the arrest of the Gang of Four in the fall of 1976, China's leaders sought initially to restore the system of the early 1950s, which featured a more tolerant and looser party leadership, paying China's intellectuals proper respect as both arts producers and consumers. This initial reform period (which lasted until 1989) was especially influenced by expanded exposure to foreign trade and competition in arts products, and by the party's decision to reduce subsidies to arts organizations, which were called upon to earn more of their own income. The 1980s were filled with cultural controversies, as artists pressed the limits of the post-Mao order, and as citizens reveled in new tastes that had earlier been banned, such as public dancing, more variety in clothing, imported television shows, and recorded music.

The 1989 Tiananmen political crisis stalled momentum for change. Many artists participated in the spring demonstrations and were shocked by the Beijing massacre of June 4. Many who were abroad at the time chose not to return to China; others became cautious in their work, as the harsh climate emboldened leaders who favored heavy-handed tactics in disciplining the arts.

A New Balance between Party-State and Market

After suppressing the 1989 demonstrations, Deng Xiaoping's solution for the political mess he had made was to push more boldly toward marketization of the economy. His

1992 initiative intensified economic changes underway in the 1980s, and resulted in the dramatic remaking of China's cities, transportation system, and consumption habits, as well as reuniting Hong Kong and Macao with China. In contrast to Maoist policies, which explicitly focused on the arts, Deng's economic reforms affected the arts indirectly, yet profoundly.

The economic reforms launched by Deng liberalized Chinese culture by weakening the grasp of party-state patronage, encouraging artists and arts organizations to turn to the marketplace instead of relying upon automatic government subsidies. In addition, a new array of cultural products was introduced in the PRC, not only from across China but also around the world.

However, the reforms have had significant costs, both to artists and art consumers. Some prominent writers, singers, and painters have literally profited enormously from these changes, which also removed limits on individual income. Other artists have fared less well, especially folk musicians, dancers, puppeteers, and traditional landscape painters. Many have found the process of change to be unnerving and disorienting. Although there are still many government subsidies for the arts, most artists have had to learn to find employment outside official circles, give up subsidized housing and other benefits, purchase their own arts materials, and, in general, fend for themselves.

A broader critique of the market reforms in culture is that they have rewarded coarseness, sensationalism, and vulgarity, at the expense of higher artistic principles. In the past, the Chinese communist party-state may have set political limits for what artists could produce, but typically interfered little with the pursuit of artistic techniques. The exception was during political campaigns such as the Cultural Revolution when the arts were not only totally controlled by the party-state, but were also actively used as a propaganda tool to mobilize the masses and send not-so-subtle messages about proper communist attitudes and behavior.

Artists are often quick to protest the cultural destruction associated with a three-decade construction boom that began in the late 1970s. Old architecture is vanishing to make way for new housing, shopping malls, and even Olympic venues. Cultural traditions are also collapsing before economic growth. Chinese opera, a national icon of traditional culture, is losing its audience, especially in urban areas, where it cannot face the competition from more modern forms of entertainment, such as video games, television, and pop music.

These trends have elicited some serious interest in cultural protection. By the mid-1990s, some began to attempt at least to slow the replacement of distinctively Chinese buildings by new structures of no national character. This has been accompanied by a broader interest in signs of older Chinese culture and art, precisely as it is being destroyed. Corrupt officials in cahoots with real estate speculators make preservation difficult. However, it would be unfair to blame the housing transformation on corrupt officials: Chinese citizens want new, clean, and well-insulated homes with adequate plumbing. The politically motivated destruction of the Cultural Revolution had mostly ended by 1968. In contrast, the present era's economically driven destruction has had few checks since Deng Xiaoping reignited the market reforms in 1992.

It would be a mistake to view these changes as a simple triumph of the marketplace over the party-state, instead of a reconfiguration of the party-state's visible role in producing art. The party-state still maintains a role in overseeing and financing cultural affairs. Indeed, there is a whiff of the ancient Roman strategy of "bread and circuses" in its conscious use of the market to provide greater cultural opportunities, entertainment, and distraction from political controversy.

A Weakened Censorship

The distractions of popular culture are one way the CCP protects its rule. The strong hand of censorship is another. Yet current Chinese censorship is very different from its Maoist predecessor.

Arts censorship began to loosen in the 1980s, gradually becoming more of a recurring annoyance than a central feature of cultural life. Censorship of news is more pervasive, although it too is much looser than in the past. For the arts, control mechanisms and party-state interest vary by genre. Music is probably the least controlled, and film and television the most supervised. Fiction and painting are only loosely monitored. Except for broadcasting and film, China practices a post-publication censorship, which means that a painting might be withdrawn after a show opens, or a book might be cancelled, but not until tens of thousands of copies have been distributed. So writers and painters calculate the prevailing political climate as shrewdly as they know how, self-censor when necessary, and plunge ahead when the country is in a relatively open period.

The decline of censorship has been uneven, in cycles of loosening and tightening, but generally leaving the censors with less power in the end. This is in part a result of economic change, as there are too many cultural products on the market for anyone to monitor them all. Also, China has never had a Soviet-style corps of professional censors (with the important exception of television and film). In the Maoist years, cultural controversies often began when a local activist or zealous official decided to make a fuss about a particular work. As political life in China became less intense, many people decided that censorship was not worth the trouble or even a bad idea.

Generational change has also consolidated the process, with the retirements, then deaths of the old revolutionaries who founded the People's Republic and had held on to more conservative views of the limits of artistic freedom. In the 1970s and even 1980s, debates over individual songs, or scenes in films, would bubble up to the top of the system, requiring the top party leadership to determine whether a particular work of art was permissible. In the twenty-first century, the scope of censorship is much narrower, and is handled at lower political levels. Even so, the opening ceremony of the 2008 Olympics was judged to be so important to China's national image that a top leader is said to have intervened to substitute a prettier child for the little girl whose voice was actually heard singing a prominent song.[4]

The erratic weakening of censorship often assumes forms that Westerners may not expect. For example, one battleground was paintings of nude figures. Figure painting is not an important theme in Chinese painting, and Confucian propriety reinforced communist prudery to suppress naked images for much of the twentieth century. Liu Haisu, an oil painting master, fled to Japan in the 1920s to escape a warlord who was outraged by his use of naked models in teaching.

After 1949, communist patronage of oil painting as a "modern" art form led again to nude modeling, and to renewed attacks on the painters, the models, and the people who viewed the art. In 1965 Mao Zedong intervened on this subject:

> Fundamental training in drawing and sculpture requires models—male, female, old and young; they are indispensable. The prohibitions of feudal ideology are inappropriate. It is unimportant if a few bad things emerge. For the sake of art and science, we must put up with some small sacrifices.[5]

No one dared pursue his encouragement in the ensuing Cultural Revolution. Yet in the post Mao relaxation of cultural controls, a wave of nude painting spread over the nation in the

1980s, this time with success. The nudes were almost all young women, as the fight over gender equality was another matter. In one case, a painter pulled an abstract oil from his closet and labeled it a "nude" in order to enter it into a hastily arranged exhibition of nude art. The breakthrough of this restricted zone also produced profits for the institutions that organized the shows. Conservative critics denounced the new work as pornographic, but over the course of the 1990s, it became another fallen aesthetic barrier, and no longer inspired controversy.

What gets censored now? In politics, lots of things, such as critical views of China's control of Tibet; it is also taboo to talk in public about the 1989 Beijing protests and massacre. In the arts, no one will satirize living political leaders. But you can certainly mock corrupt or sanctimonious officials, if they are suitably local and not famous. Academy Award winner (*Brokeback Mountain*) Ang Lee's imported movie, *Lust, Caution* (2007), had some steamy moments clipped before its mainland release. Twenty Chinese writers were instructed not to attend a 2007 Hong Kong conference of PEN, an international human rights organization that focuses on support for freedom of artistic expression. A recent book of biographical sketches of Beijing Opera stars was "blocked," apparently because its author was the daughter of a particularly controversial critic of Mao in the 1950s, even though it had already been published and sold in stores. A 2000 Chinese film, *Devils at the Doorstep*, was banned because it showed too nuanced a view of the Japanese occupation. But the ban only applied to theatrical distribution, so the film was available on DVD, and its director, Jiang Wen, continued to work on and act in other movies.

China maintains some limits on foreign culture, although with less success and zeal than in the past. Visiting musical groups need to have their programs vetted before going on stage. The party-state restricts the number of Hollywood movies that can be shown, although this is more to protect China's film industry than to block American ideology.

Efforts to control Internet access are contentious, and China's government is certainly more activist in directly controlling unfavorable news than most Western governments. But the "great firewall of China" is erratic and porous. Like many forms of Chinese censorship, control of the Internet is reasonably effective toward the masses, and less so toward educated or politically connected elites. The party worries less about the elites, who long enjoyed books, performances, films, and news that ordinary people could not access. Computer restrictions are most easily evaded by technically savvy citizens who slip around the firewall, and by bloggers who employ circumlocutions to beat censoring software.

Other countries attempt to create national firewalls (for example, Singapore, Malaysia, and several Middle Eastern countries). In the West, arts controls tend to be private, enforced by the state through intellectual property lawsuits. The main state interest in the West seems to be restricting pornography, terrorist information, and criminal access to computers.

China has far less efficient censorship than Westerners want to believe. Many artists have boosted their celebrity by playing the system, while assuming the pose of the dissident to Westerners. Books sales in the West can soar if ads claim that the text has been "Banned in China!" even if the volume had in fact been sold to a million Chinese readers before being withdrawn.

Many Chinese artists sell "dissident" paintings that mock Mao Zedong to foreign collectors, understanding full well that making fun of Mao is no longer very controversial, and that the CCP backs their success in the international art market. Artist and architect Ai Weiwei, an extremely well-connected cultural leader and entrepreneur, celebrated for his "birds-nest" conception for the Beijing Olympic Stadium, tweaked the party-state with his criticism of the Olympics, encouraging Western journalists to publicize him as a dissident flirting with political danger. A subsequent beating showed this to be true.

Westerners also imagine China to be much more repressive toward its artists than is the case. As China has become more prosperous, less Maoist, and more like "ordinary" countries, its censorship issues have also become more ordinary.

A National Quest for Global Cultural Respect

While the post-Mao Chinese party-state leads cultural policy with a lighter hand, it uses cultural symbols for its political purposes. The party continues to invoke the memory of revolution, but recognizes that this is no longer an adequate claim to political legitimacy. Instead, the party substitutes a continuously expanding economy, but adds to this a sometimes deft, sometimes heavy-handed manipulation of nationalist cultural symbols.

One sees this in the restoration of once disfavored heroes of Chinese culture such as Confucius or Sun Yat-sen, who can appeal across region and class. China's new prosperity has permitted an astonishing growth in public works, not just railroads, highways, and airports, but also prominent cultural infrastructure, such as concert halls and museums in nearly all provincial capitals. The impact of these shining new temples of culture is probably analogous to the wave of cultural construction that swept late-nineteenth-century Europe, where nationalist politics were mixed with a desire to bind citizens together in the consciousness of a newly shared national culture.

China wants its culture to impress not only residents of Wuhan or Shanghai, but foreigners as well. This desire stems in part from the tradition of Confucian statecraft, by which China awed lesser nations with its arts and inventions. It also flows from the sense that China has left behind the period of national humiliation, when it was unable to prevent imperialist armies from plundering its temples, homes, and palaces.

In the Maoist era, China enjoyed extensive artistic ties to Eastern Europe until the eve of the Cultural Revolution. China then sought cultural ties with "third world" nations, such as Algeria or Indonesia (with whom China planned a counter-Olympics—the "Games of the New Emerging Forces"—in the early 1960s). But by the end of the Cultural Revolution, China was so culturally isolated that screening Albanian or North Korean films was a major act of artistic exchange.

Maoist leaders viewed foreign culture with suspicion, as uncontrolled, or controlled by outsiders. Even foreign artists sympathetic to the revolution were treated with paranoia. China invited Italian director Michelangelo Antonioni to China to make a three hour film, *Zhongguo* (China, 1972), which the leftist filmmaker certainly intended to be sympathetic to the PRC. But Antonioni's fondness for filming the picturesque, the old, and the human-powered was misunderstood by Cultural Revolutionaries as an imperialist belittling of China's backwardness. Few Chinese saw the movie, although it was the subject of a fierce nationwide campaign of criticism in 1974. *Zhongguo* was not shown to a Chinese audience until 2004.

Now Chinese filmgoers have experienced decades of post-Mao Western and Japanese cultural imports, and Chinese citizens have increasingly become world travelers. The sustained economic growth of the past two decades has inspired a new level of national confidence, so the nation's leaders are less likely to bristle at foreign criticism.

At the same time, China wants to promote its art and artists abroad. Chinese media report with special joy the accomplishments of ethnically Chinese performers and artists such as architect I.M. Pei (American), cellist Yo-Yo Ma (American), pianist Lang Lang (Chinese), film directors Zhang Yimou (Chinese) and Ang Lee (Taiwanese), and actors Bruce Lee (Hong Kong), and Jackie Chan (Hong Kong), whether or not they are citizens of the People's Republic of China. There was great pride in China when the renowned Italian tenor, Placido Domingo, sang the lead role of Qin Shihuangdi, founder of the Chinese empire in 221 BCE, at New York's Metropolitan Opera in Tan Dun's *The First Emperor*. The fact that works by several contemporary Chinese artists are now in great demand by Western collectors and command some of the highest prices in the global arts market is another source of satisfaction.

These artistic accomplishments were often achieved without party-state support Nonetheless, most of the recent Chinese stars in the international art market have enjoyed free training in Chinese arts academies. And some of their breakthrough works have been subsidized by the state. This is true, for instance, of Xu Bing's celebrated *Book of the Sky*, a massive installation of "nonsense" Chinese characters, printed from thousands of blocks carved by Xu.[6] The hugely successful new art district in Beijing, the 798 Factory, enables artists to exhibit to Chinese and foreign visitors, yet part of its charm is that it is reconfigured from a one-time military electronics factory, a foreign aid project of East Germany.[7]

Less glamorous, but economically more important, is the low-end art exemplified by the painting sweatshop village of Dafen, Guangdong, which exports millions of cheap oil paintings. Here, the arts harness low-cost labor for export product, much like the shoe industry.

Conclusion

China's rulers have adopted a new approach to cultural policy, withdrawing from micromanagement of the arts, and only intervening in what they regard as key matters. These include limiting the flow of news critical of the PRC, protecting China's film industry against foreign competition, and promoting cultural achievements with nationalist pride. They are managing culture less, but better.

Nevertheless, the arts in the PRC remain more political than in the United States, which, unlike most nations, has no ministry of culture to promote or oversee the arts. China's approach to the arts would still seem intrusive to many Americans, but it works reasonably well in China, with its inherited practice of government responsibility for the arts.

Notes

1. Bonnie S McDougall, ed., *Mao Zedong's "Talks at the Yan'an Conference on Literature and Art": A Translation of the 1943 Text with Commentary* (Ann Arbor: University of Michigan Center for Chinese Studies, 1980), 61.

2. McDougall, 73.

3. Richard Curt Kraus, "Art Policies of the Cultural Revolution," in *New Perspectives on the Cultural Revolution*, ed. William A. Joseph, Christine Wong, and David Zweig, et al., eds., (Cambridge, MA: Harvard University Council on East Asian Studies, 1991), 219–249.

4. Jim Yardley, "In Grand Olympic Show, Some Sleight of Voice," *New York Times*, August 12, 2008.

5. "*Lu Xun Meishu Xueyuan huifu yong 'mote'er' jinxing renti xiesheng jiaoxue*" (Lu Xun Fine Arts Academy resumes use of "models" for classes in life drawing), *Meishu* (Fine Arts) 16 (May 1978): 46.

6. See Jerome Silbergeld and Dora C.Y. Ching, eds., *Persistence-transformation: Text as Image in the Art of Xu Bing* (Princeton, NJ: Princeton University Press, 2006).

7. Huang Rui, ed., *Beijing 798: Reflections on Art, Architecture and Society in China* (Beijing: timezone 8 + Thinking Hands, 2004).

Suggested Readings

Andrews, Julia F. *Painters and Politics in the People's Republic of China, 1949–1979*. Berkeley: University of California Press, 1994.

Barmé, Geremie. *In the Red: On Contemporary Chinese Culture*. New York: Columbia University Press, 1999.

Clark, Paul. *The Chinese Cultural Revolution: A History*. Cambridge: Cambridge University Press, 2008.

Curtin, Michael. *Playing to the World's Biggest Audience: The Globalization of Chinese Film and TV*. Berkeley: University of California Press, 2007.

Huot, Claire. *China's New Cultural Scene*. Durham, NC: Duke University Press, 2000.

Kraus, Richard Curt. *The Party and the Arty: China's New Politics of Culture*. Lanham, MD: Rowman & Littlefield, 2004.

Link, Perry. *The Uses of Literature: Life in the Socialist Chinese Literary System*. Princeton, NJ: Princeton University Press, 2000.

Lovell, Julia. *The Politics of Cultural Capital: China's Quest for a Nobel Prize in Literature*. Honolulu: University of Hawai'i Press, 2006.

Silbergeld, Jerome. *Contradictions: An Artistic Life, the Socialist State, and the Chinese Painter Li Huasheng*. Seattle: University of Washington Press, 1993.

Wang, Jing. *Brand New China: Advertising, Media, and Commercial Culture*. Cambridge, MA: Harvard University Press, 2008.

Zha, Jianying. *China Pop: How Soap Operas, Tabloids, and Bestsellers Are Transforming a Culture*. New York: New Press, 1995.

11

Policy Case Study: The Environment

Katherine Morton

In traditional Chinese philosophy, wise leadership was based on achieving a balanced approach to the human-nature relationship known as *tian ren he yi*—harmony between heaven and humankind. The values of moderation and adaptation meant that sustainable forms of agriculture, forestry management, and the protection of biodiversity were in evidence centuries ago. Such practices, however, did not prevent environmental mismanagement. Over time, China's ecological balance became disrupted by excessive land cultivation and the extraction of natural resources in the pursuit of state industrial and military power. This reached a peak during the Mao era when *ren ding sheng tian*—humans must conquer nature—became the new metaphor for understanding the relationship between humans and nature, with devastating environmental consequences.

More recently, thirty years of rapid economic growth have placed further pressures on the natural environment. The People's Republic of China (PRC) is now home to some of the most polluted cities in the world, over 70 percent of its rivers and lakes are seriously polluted, and ecological degradation is widespread. The scale and severity of China's environmental problems threaten the sustainability of its modernization drive. Many commentators have warned of impending economic collapse, rising social conflicts, and political breakdown. The critical question that arises is whether China can adapt and make a transition toward a more sustainable path of development. The stakes are high. Over the next decade, the direction that China takes in responding to environmental challenges will have considerable implications for its own future as well as that of the rest of the world. At a broader level, China's pattern of development inevitably affects the international distribution of resources and the global environment.

This case study will discuss China's contemporary environmental challenges within a broader global perspective. It begins with an overview of the current environmental crisis and its spillover effects beyond borders. This is followed by a brief review of evolving government responses and civil society initiatives at the grassroots. Attention then turns to identifying the core challenges that remain, especially in the poorer and more ecologically fragile regions. The final part of the case study discusses the potential for a more sustainable future that takes into account the importance of leadership at both the domestic and global levels.

China's Environmental Crisis in the Making

Problems of landslides, flooding, deforestation, and increased silt loads in rivers have existed in China for centuries. The uniqueness of the current environmental crisis lies in its scale, severity, and interdependence with the outside world. Most visible to the outside observer are the rising levels of pollution. China is now the world's leading emitter of sulphur dioxide (SO_2) emissions—in many cities exceeding World Health Organization recommendations by two to five times.[1] SO_2 pollution is a precursor of acid rain, which now covers roughly 30 percent of the total land area of China. In the major cities of Shanghai, Beijing, and Guangzhou, nitrogen oxide (NOx) emissions have also risen dramatically. As a result of heavy traffic pollution, these cities are experiencing Los Angeles–style photochemical smog on a regular basis. The rapid rise in car ownership means that air pollution is likely to get far worse before it gets better. Between 2000 and 2008, the number of cars on the roads in Beijing tripled to around 3.5 million. On a significant number of days in the year, breathing the air in Beijing is now equivalent to smoking two packs of cigarettes per day. One year after the Olympic Games, air quality in Beijing has improved but airborne particulates (TSP) are still dangerously high with serious implications for human health.

Water pollution is also reaching record levels. The industrial discharge of toxic substances, such as mercury, phenol, chromium, and cyanide, is largely to blame, together with untreated municipal wastewater and fertilizer runoff. Over half of the monitored urban river sections in northern China do not meet the lowest ambient standard (grade 5)—the water is officially classified as unfit even for irrigation. Despite efforts to enforce regulatory controls, an estimated 300 million people (almost a quarter of the Chinese population) still do not have access to clean water.

The trends relating to ecological degradation in China are just as sobering. According to official statistics, 90 percent of China's grasslands have become degraded, and desertification—the gradual transformation of habitable land into desert—now covers one-third of China's land base. Forest resources are scarce (18 percent of the total land area, compared to 33 percent in the United States) and wetlands have been reduced by 60 percent. In addition, almost 40 percent of the nation suffers from soil erosion as deforestation and unsustainable farming practices cause 10,000 square kilometers (about 3,900 sq. mi.) of lost soil per annum. The sediment discharge from soil erosion is filling up rivers and lakes, thus contributing to the frequency of flooding. At the same time, water scarcity is reaching a critical threshold. China holds the fourth-largest freshwater reserves in the world, but they are unevenly distributed, and per capita water use is only a quarter of the world average. Most of the water supply to major cities depends upon groundwater pumped from aquifers (geological formations that store water underground). But these are drying up, or becoming depleted due to the accumulation of salts in the soil.

Transboundary Effects

The spillover effects of China's environmental problems began to attract attention in the early 1990s, when it became apparent that a significant proportion of acid rain in Korea and Japan had its origins in China. Dust and aerial pollutants are now transported as far as the United States, and high levels of toxic pollution in China's Bohai Sea and Pearl River Delta are having a serious impact on regional fish stocks. In 2005, the explosion of a state-owned petrochemical plant in Jilin province, which released tons of toxic benzene into the Songhua River, affecting water supply in Harbin as well as the Russian city of Khabarovsky, placed a spotlight on the need for significant improvements in information disclosure as well as monitoring systems across the Sino-Russian border.

In an era of global interdependence, it is becoming increasingly difficult to apportion blame for transboundary environmental problems. Foreign firms generate a significant portion of pollutants in China; and an estimated 40 percent of China's total energy demand ends up in exported manufactured goods. Thus consumers in other parts of the world benefit considerably from China's status as a global factory, and it is fair to say they are also one source of the PRC's increasing demand for energy and natural resources, which, in turn, has an impact on the regional and global environment. At the regional level, it is widely known that the cascade of dams built on the Mekong River in Yunnan province poses serious risks for countries downstream (Laos, Burma, Thailand, Vietnam, and Cambodia). Equally worrying is the destruction of Burma's northern frontier forests by Chinese loggers. Following a logging ban imposed by the Chinese government in 1998, the importation of illegal logs from across the China-Burma border has increased exponentially to meet the huge demand for timber that comes largely from the almost uncontrolled building boom in the PRC.

Consequences of Climate Change

At the global level, China's rising contribution to global CO_2 (carbon dioxide) emissions from fossil fuel combustion is attracting significant attention. The burning of coal, in particular, pumps millions of tons of chemicals into the atmosphere. China is dependent upon coal to meet 70 percent of its total energy needs. Efforts are now under way to invest in alternative sources, and China is becoming a world leader in developing both cleaner coal burning technology and wind turbines,[2] but energy demand is outpacing reforms; thus highly polluting coal will remain the primary source of China's energy supply for the foreseeable future. As a consequence, in 2007 China overtook the United States (with 25 percent of the world's total CO_2 emissions) to become the world's biggest emitter.[3] Although per capita emissions are still relatively low (in 2005 China emitted 3.9 tons of CO_2 per capita, compared with 25.6 tons in Australia and 24.5 tons in the United States), they already exceed the world average.

Not surprisingly, at the international level, the Chinese government remains committed to the principle of common but differentiated responsibilities based on historic cumulative emissions. It points out that the developed countries did not sacrifice growth for environmental concerns during their "industrial revolutions" and insists that it is the responsibility of richer countries to take the lead in cutting emissions. In the lead up to the Climate Summit in Copenhagen in 2009, China's stance has softened to some degree. It now supports nationally appropriate mitigation actions (NAMs) contingent upon the transfer of enabling finance and technology from industrialized states. However, it continues to refuse to commit to binding targets.

Closer to home, attitudes are changing more quickly. It is increasingly recognized that the consequences of climate change demand an immediate response. In China's first National Climate Change Assessment Report published in late 2006, it was predicted that the average annual temperature could increase between 1.3 and 2.1 degrees by 2020 and as much as 3.3 degrees by 2050. Major cities in coastal areas will face serious challenges due to rising sea levels, and extreme weather patterns are likely to increase.

The impact of climate change on the Qinghai-Tibetan Plateau in China's far west is particularly worrying both for China and the Asia region. As the largest freshwater reserve outside the polar ice caps, the Plateau is also known as Asia's water tower, or the "Third Pole." For climate change, the Plateau is the equivalent of the proverbial canary in the

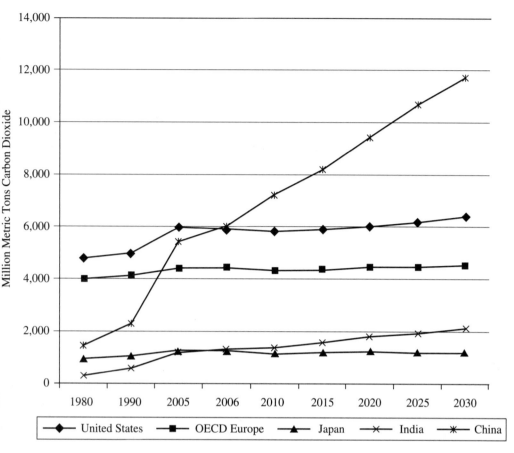

Figure 11.1 World Carbon Dioxide Emissions, 1980–2030
Source: *International Energy Outlook* 2009, Energy Information Administration, U.S. Department of Energy.

coalmine that stopped singing (or died) as a warning to miners of dangerous methane gas buildup. The glaciers that feed Asia's great rivers—the Yellow, Yangtze, Mekong, Salween, Indus, Ganges, and Brahmaputra—have shrunk by at least 17 percent over the past decade. Data from the United Nations Environment Programme and the World Glacier Monitoring Service reveal that the Himalayan glaciers are shrinking faster than anywhere else and could totally disappear by 2050. Glacial melt has dramatic adverse effects on biodiversity, people, and livelihoods, with long-term implications for water, food, and energy security. Over the longer term, higher temperatures will increase flooding in the rainy season and reduce water in the dry season, thus affecting food production in the provinces downstream as well as the livelihoods of over a billion people in China, South and Southeast Asia. Eventually, water shortages will occur on a massive scale. This is particularly troubling given that Asia already has less freshwater—about 3,920 cubic meters (about 5,130 cu. yd.) per person—than any other continent outside Antarctica.

In effect, China's current development trajectory represents a fragile balance between human and environmental needs that cannot be sustained over time. Is an environmental catastrophe inevitable, or does the potential exist to shift toward a more sustainable pattern of development? Clearly, much will depend upon China's capacity to adapt. How is the

Chinese government responding to the crisis? And to what extent can citizen participation help to alleviate environmental problems?

Taking Action: Government Responses

Over the past decade, the Chinese government has expressed a growing commitment toward environmental protection: the regulatory and legal frameworks have expanded, with a stronger emphasis upon ecological protection as well as pollution control. Environmental priorities have been fully integrated into the state five-year plans for development; and investment in environmental protection as a percentage of gross national product (GNP) has risen from 0.67 percent during the seventh five-year plan (1986–1990) to a planned 1.4 percent during the eleventh five-year plan (2006–2010), which is equal to the average investment ratios of the industrialized OECD (Organisation for Economic Co-operation and Development) countries.

The most important change to have taken place is at the attitudinal level. During the early stage of economic reforms in the 1980s and early 1990s, environmental issues remained low on the political agenda. Rising pollution and other forms of environmental degradation were seen as an inevitable consequence of modernization. Environmental protection became a fundamental state policy (*jiben guoce*) in 1993, opening the way for further environmental laws and regulations. There now exists a realization within elite policy circles in Beijing that the pursuit of economic growth at all costs is no longer environmentally or socially sustainable.

As in the case of most other countries, China lacks a centralized regulatory authority capable of mainstreaming environmental concerns into development policy-making. It also experiences the familiar problem of poor interagency coordination. The upgrading of the State Environmental Protection Administration to a cabinet-level Ministry of Environmental Protection in March 2008 may help to strengthen its authority at the central level, but it is unlikely to make a difference to the political status of environmental agencies working at the local level, which generally have little power to enforce regulations.

Despite these problems, governing the environment from above has had some positive impacts. For example, a nationwide campaign has helped to promote cleaner production methods in Chinese factories, strict vehicle emissions standards have been imposed in major cities, and reforestation programs are beginning to reap rewards. According to official estimates, by the end of 2003 almost 80,000 square kilometers (about 31,000 sq. mi.) of cropland had been reforested or reverted back to grassland. Policies promoting energy conservation and the adoption of new technologies have also led to significant improvements in energy efficiency. The government has now set an ambitious target of reducing China's energy intensity (energy consumption per dollar of GDP) by 20 percent by 2010. Given that a few highly inefficient industries, such as paper and pulp production, copper smelting, and cement production, account for a large proportion of carbon emissions, this approach may well make a difference to China's overall emissions trajectory.

Coinciding with the shift toward a market-based economy, top-down command and control measures are no longer seen as the only means of protecting the environment. To reduce pollution, market incentives are being used to internalize environmental costs. For example, an environmentally informative labeling plan is now in place to promote green consumerism; a quota system for regulating sulphur dioxide (SO_2) emissions has been set up in some provinces and cities; and new proposals have been introduced to place a monetary value on scarce resources such as water and coal.

Environmentalism from Below

Citizen involvement in environmental protection is also expanding. The Chinese print and television media play a critical role in channeling public opinion; and new forms of "electronic government" have provided an alternative virtual means of soliciting citizen ideas for environmental improvement.[4] Public participation is demonstrated most clearly in the emergence of environmental nongovernmental organizations (NGOs) that are seeking to bring about changes at the local level.

According to official statistics, over 3,000 environmental NGOs are now operating across China.[5] They vary greatly in the scope of their activities, the degree of government autonomy, and access to resources. What they tend to share in common is a strong desire for environmental reforms. To this end, many prioritize the importance of environmental education, including training for government officials. Others focus on advocating alternative solutions for restoring degraded ecosystems, or improving the effectiveness of pollution control mechanisms. At the community level, small initiatives can gain momentum. A group of environmentalists in Gansu have helped to protect the habitat of the wild camel, leading to the construction of a new nature reserve; a small NGO advocating the reduction of pesticide use in Yunnan has facilitated a revival in organic farming; in Qinghai a grassroots organization has successfully campaigned against the use of plastic bags in areas on the **Tibetan Plateau**, thus preempting a nationwide ban that came into effect on June 1, 2008; and in Beijing many groups are working to advance energy conservation at the community level.[6]

The problem is that these kinds of initiatives often generate considerable resistance from local vested interests, including bureaucrats and business owners who do no want to do anything that may limit economic growth or lessen profits. This is exacerbated by the fact that the political status of NGOs in China remains unclear. Government regulations on social organizations—first promulgated by the State Council following the student led pro-democracy movement in 1989—are highly restrictive. The party-state is largely supportive of NGOs whose agenda coincides with its own, which is the case with many aspects of environmental protection. That said, the Chinese authorities are intolerant of any social movement or organization that is perceived to pose a direct threat to the regime or national stability. Consequently, self-censorship remains a unique characteristic of Chinese environmental activism. Although this does not necessarily impede effective action, it does restrict the ability of NGOs to fulfill their creative potential as advocates of environmental protection. In effect, bringing about reforms from below remains limited by the refusal to relinquish control from above.

The extent to which state controls can continue to subdue public grievances over the longer term is less certain. Citizen action on environmental issues is by no means limited to formal organizations. Spontaneous protests against polluting industries are now commonplace across China. According to the conservative estimates of the Ministry of Civil Affairs, there were more than 60,000 environmental protests in 2006 alone. The majority of protests are highly localized and limited to rural areas. However, more recently, large-scale demonstrations have taken place in urban areas, facilitated by the spread of mobile communications. In June 2007 up to 20,000 people took to the streets in the coastal resort city of Xiamen in protest over the construction of a chemical factory close to residential areas. Massive public opposition caught the attention of the central authorities in Beijing, and the project was suspended pending an environmental review.

For those living with the consequences of environmental pollution, the potential exists to seek compensation through legal means. The Chinese media have reported a growing number of cases in which citizens have filed lawsuits against polluting enterprises, often with the support of legal aid centers. For example, in October 2000, fishermen from Laoting county in Hebei took their case to court after losing the majority of their stock when a paper mill upstream in Qian'an county had discharged wastewater into their aquaculture farms. Little information exists on the success rate of these cases, but the fact that ordinary citizens are pursing a legal means of redress suggests a rise in public confidence in China's legal system. Equally promising is the fact that polluters are facing more serious punitive action. In the wake of a rising tide of environmental disasters, special environmental courts have been set up in Wuxi, Guiyang, and Yunnan. In a high-profile case in Yancheng, Jiangsu, the chairman of a chemical company that had discharged toxic chemicals into the city's water supply received an 11-year sentence.[7]

Limits to Environmental Reform

Taking into account China's level of economic development, the new initiatives described above provide grounds for optimism. In seeking a sense of perspective, however, it is important to bear in mind that the overall strategy for economic development in China is still one of pro-growth, with the aim of quadrupling per capita income by 2020. In addition, current efforts toward protecting the environment are limited by three key constraints: weak implementation at the local level; an over-reliance upon large-scale engineering solutions; and a highly centralized decision-making process.

The Implementation Deficit

It is now widely recognized that environmental policies are extremely difficult to implement in China because of weak compliance at the local level. The basic problem is that self-serving officials collude with local enterprises to pursue profits at a cost to the environment. The situation is made worse by the fact that dirty factories are relocating away from large urban cities and into rural areas, where regulatory control is weaker. A sobering example is the village of Xinsi in Gansu province, where more than 250 children are reported to be suffering from lead poisoning—with up to five times the blood-lead levels considered safe by the World Health Organization. Local villagers were unaware of the significant health risks involved in living next to a lead factory, and their children now live with the consequences of severe intellectual impairment.[8]

It is already clear that uneven development is leading to a situation in which the richer regions can more easily adapt. Given that China's poorest regions—including Tibet and Xinjiang—are also the most ecologically fragile, a fundamental challenge for the Chinese government is to ensure that the burden of responsibility for environmental protection does not fall on the shoulders of those who are least able to carry it. Over the longer term, the risk is that sustainability will become the preserve of the rich thus exacerbating pre-existing inequities.

The Engineering Fix

A second major constraint on environmental protection is the continuing reliance on large-scale engineering projects that offset the benefits of alternative solutions. The highly controversial Three Gorges Dam (*Sanxia*) on the Yangtze River, which is expected to generate 18 gigawatts of electricity (equivalent to 7 percent of total production) and in the process lead to significant ecological disruption and the displacement of more than 1.5 million people, is a good example of this trend.[9] Equally problematic is the south-north water transfer program (*nanshui beidiao*) that aims to alleviate flooding in the south and water scarcity in the north by diverting water from the Yangtze to the North China Plain. Three planned routes have been designed to connect the Yangtze with the Huang, Huai, and Hai rivers. Construction is now under way. Potential problems include large-scale soil salinization, polluted sewage water intrusion, and adverse effects upon aquatic life along the route.

China has the highest number of large dams (above 15 meters [49 ft.] high) in the world—22,000 or almost half of the world's total. With the new policy of relying on renewable energy for up to 10 percent of total energy demand by 2010, hydropower will expand dramatically in the coming years. As noted by Vaclav Smil, it is not the emphasis upon dam building per se that is the problem. What is of concern is the obsession with scale and the inability to approach the harnessing of natural resources with an appreciation of the environmental and social costs involved.[10] In the case of the Three Gorges Dam, the costs are already apparent. The huge weight of water behind the dam is causing erosion of the riverbank, leading to landslides; the quality of water in the tributaries of the Yangtze has severely deteriorated, and sediment accumulation is greatly reducing the dam's future capacity for power generation and flood control.[11] It is not surprising that China relies so heavily on such large-scale projects to deal with environment issues, given that the top leadership of the CCP is dominated by technocrats with a background in engineering (see chapter 6).

A Lack of Openness

A third constraint relates to China's highly centralized decision-making process. The relevance of public accountability in the Chinese context lies in its potential to act as a vital check against political excess, as well as a safeguard against social inertia that resists change. At a minimum, accountability can only happen within the context of an open society supported by the rule of law. The free flow of information is essential for effective policy-making to take place. The implementation of a national sustainability agenda relies upon "learning by doing" that requires high levels of transparency across the policy-making system. An open public debate also plays a central role in the negotiation of the difficult trade-offs between individual concerns and social and environmental needs, as perceived by the Chinese people, who are, understandably, mostly concerned about raising the living standards for themselves and their family. Above all, a balanced assessment of the complex relationships between poverty alleviation, energy security, and environmental protection cannot be made if decision-making power is highly concentrated; this inevitably increases the risk that powerful vested interests will hold sway over broader public concerns.

The new measures on open environmental information, introduced in the PRC in May 2008, are a positive step in the right direction. Under these guidelines, environmental agencies are required to disclose information on enterprises exceeding discharge quotas. For their part, corporations are under the obligation to disclose discharge data within a certain period of time or pay a fine of up to 100,000 RMB (roughly US$14,500). Over time, these measures may help to improve regulatory compliance in China, but they are unlikely to provide a substitute for active public participation.

Is a More Sustainable Future Possible?

Overall, China's approach to environmental governance is a story of continuity and change. A strong preference for top-down decision-making still remains, but it coexists with new forms of non-state activism that reflect greater pluralism within Chinese society. In the early twenty-first century, Chinese leaders are caught between a continuing desire to control nature via large-scale engineering projects, and a new aspiration to chart an alternative development path that reconciles human and environmental needs.

"**Ecological civilization**" is the most recent metaphor employed by the Chinese party-state for understanding the relationship between humans and nature that promises to transform the processes of industrialization and, in turn, reconnect Chinese civilization with its environmental genesis. It is a key part of PRC President and CCP General Secretary Hu Jintao's so-called scientific outlook on development and his commitment to creating a harmonious socialist society, which have become at least the rhetorical focus of his administration (see chapters 4 and 5). How this translates into action remains to be seen. This new thinking reflects a deeper cultural aspiration that has yet to permeate through the domestic agenda. For this to happen, further reforms are required to support public participation in environmental efforts. Ultimately, redressing the balance between human and environmental needs is not simply a question of improving efficiency and taking corrective measures; it can only be achieved if the Chinese people who stand to benefit—both rich and poor—are central to the process.

Tipping the balance in favour of sustainability will also require greater cooperation at the international level. A fundamental problem with current Chinese practice is that efforts to protect environmental and human welfare are largely concentrated within territorial boundaries. This is not to suggest that China has failed to participate in relevant international treaties and regimes. Rather, it is to make the point that, given the transboundary nature of environmental problems, China's growing demands for resources from other nations (see chapter 7), and its emerging role as an international donor of aid to less developed countries, much more needs to be done to enhance environmental cooperation at the international level.

Clearly, leadership by the more developed countries is imperative if China is to strengthen its role in multilateral efforts to address climate change. Transfers of knowledge, funds, and clean technologies will also remain important in the short to medium term. At the same time, a strong case can be made for a parallel transfer of experience and resources from the PRC to other developing countries that look to China as a model of development. This kind of cooperation is long overdue, and it may well help to break the unsustainable pattern of economic development that exists globally. In the coming years, the touchstone of the success of China's transition toward a sustainable model of development will be the extent to which it is able to reverse negative environmental trends and demonstrate an alternative vision both within and beyond territorial boundaries.

Notes

1. Unless otherwise stated, the statistics used in this case study are taken from the official Chinese environmental yearbooks and the web site of the Ministry of Environmental Protection http://www.mep.gov.cn.

2. See Keith Bradsher, "Green Power Takes Root in China," *New York Times*, July 3, 2009; and Keith Bradsher, "China Outpaces U.S. in Cleaner Coal-Fired Plants," *New York Times*, May 10, 2009.

3. Between 1950 and 2002, China's cumulative CO_2 emissions totaled only 9.3 percent of the world total. Up until the turn of the twenty-first century, the Chinese economy grew without placing a significant burden on energy resources. This has recently changed as a consequence of an investment-led shift back to heavy industry, together with higher levels of consumption growth. Hence, the rapid growth in carbon emissions is a fairly new phenomenon.

4. For example, in the planning stage of the tenth five-year plan (2001–2006), the National Development and Reform Commission is reported to have received over 10,000 suggestions from citizens, many of which were environment-related. FBIS Beijing Xinhua, Hong Kong Service in Chinese.

5. Xinhua News Agency, 30 October 2006, http://www.china.org.cn/english/environment/186754. htm.

6. To date, much of the literature on environmental activism in China has tended to focus on a small number of relatively independent organizations in Beijing such as Friends of Nature or Global Village. Many organizations are also working below the radar screen in diverse regions of China, as noted in these examples.

7. Lucy Hornby, "Chinese executives sentenced for polluting lake," *Reuters*, 2 June 2009, www.reuters.com/article/environmentNews/idUSTRE5513G820090602.

8. Shai Oster and Jane Spencer, "A Poison Spreads Amid China's Boom," September 30, 2006, http://online.wsj.com/article/

9. Other concerns include silt buildup behind the dam, which is highly likely to place it in jeopardy, blocking downstream regions of vital nutrients as well as stalling power generation, and the destruction of much of China's finest scenery and wetlands habitat.

10. Vaclav Smil, *China's Past, China's Future: Energy, Food, Environment* (London: Routledge Curzon, 2004).

11. Serious silt buildup in the Three Gorges reservoir is encouraging further dam building in the tributaries of the Yangtze, thus leading to a vicious cycle of ecological degradation without significantly improving energy security.

Suggested Readings

Economy, Elizabeth C. *The River Runs Black: The Environmental Challenge to China's Future*. Ithaca, NY: Cornell University Press, 2004.

Edmonds, Richard Louis. *Patterns of China's Lost Harmony: A Survey of the Country's Environmental Degradation and Protection*. London: Routledge, 1994.

Liu, Jianguo and Jared Diamond. "China's Environment in a Globalizing World: How China and the Rest of the World Affect Each Other," *Nature* 435 (June 2005).

Ma, Jun. *China's Water Crisis*. Translated by Nancy Yang Lin and Lawrence R. Sullivan. Norwalk, CT: EastBridge, 2004).

Mertha, Andrew C. *China's Water Warriors: Citizen Action and Policy Change*. Ithaca, NY: Cornell University Press, 2008.

Morton, Katherine. *International Aid and China's Environment: Taming the Yellow Dragon*. London: Routledge, 2005.

Shapiro, Judith. *Mao's War against Nature: Politics and the Environment in Revolutionary China*. Cambridge: Cambridge University Press, 2001.

Smil, Vaclav. *China's Environmental Crisis: An Inquiry into the Limits of National Development* Armonk, NY: M. E. Sharpe, 1993.

12

Policy Case Study: Public Health

Joan Kaufman

Health care provision and health care policy are important themes in China's modern history and contemporary politics. From the late nineteenth and early twentieth centuries up to the time of the founding of the People's Republic, China was known as the "sick man of Asia" with high rates of death from infectious and preventable diseases. In fact, the blatant neglect of the public's health was a rallying cry for change at the end of the republican era. One appeal of communism to China's vast rural population was the promise of equitable social welfare investment, especially for health and education.

During the early years of the new regime, attention to health and other social issues began to pay off. Deaths, including infant deaths, began to rapidly decline, contributing to a booming population increase along with one of the highest life expectancies in the developing world. Infant mortality declined from 200 to 23 per 1,000 live births between 1949 and 2005, and life expectancy rose during the same period from thirty-five to seventy-two years.

But in the 1980s and 1990s, the attention to primary care and equitable access to health care that had been given priority during the Maoist era, all but disappeared, one casualty of the breaking of the "iron rice bowl" that had guaranteed most Chinese with free or inexpensive social services and the shift to a marketized economy and fiscal decentralization. By the end of the 1990s, medical expenses topped the list of reasons that rural families gave for falling into poverty.[1] In more recent years, China's response to emerging epidemics like Severe Acute Respiratory Syndrome (SARS), AIDS, and avian flu have been windows into understanding how bureaucratic governance can adversely affect the control of emerging infectious diseases. But top-down policy making can also contribute to positive change: China's current leaders have made medical care financing and reform a key part of their equity-oriented political agenda under the rubric of creating a "harmonious socialist society." Changes under way in the health governance arena may become models for more flexible policies in other domains, especially with respect to partnerships with a growing civil society movement, including nongovernmental organizations (NGOs). This case study reviews the main phases of public health policy in China since 1949 and highlights achievements, challenges, and future prospects. The government's response to HIV/AIDS from 1985 to 2008 will be used as a window into how health policy is made and revised in the People's Republic of China (PRC).

The Maoist Approach to Public Health

Control of infectious diseases, rampant in China before 1949, was an initial priority for the communist government. Preventable infectious diseases such as plague and cholera, vaccine preventable childhood diseases, and vector-borne diseases such as schistosomiasis (snail fever) and intestinal parasites (worms) sickened and killed millions in the pre-communist era.[2] A campaign approach to public health, utilizing propaganda and mass mobilization, was developed during these early years of the regime, and "the patriotic health campaigns" has been a hallmark of China's political system ever since. Even as recently as the SARS epidemic in 2003, the patriotic health campaign approach was used to mobilize the population to self-quarantine, report fellow citizens with fevers, and glorify medical personnel.

One of the first actions of the new regime after 1949 was the launching of a massive campaign to eradicate sexually transmitted diseases that involved both political and health service approaches.[3] Prostitutes were arrested and sent for rehabilitation and job training, while medical workers diagnosed and treated their sexually transmitted diseases. For other infectious diseases, a combination of political mobilization and public spending on public works (sanitation, snail eradication from rice fields, killing of insects) and the training and deployment of a corps of primary health care workers and the setting up of subsidized (essentially free) health stations at local levels, along with nutritional improvements through grain rationing and subsidies, set in motion a dramatic "epidemiological transition" during the 1960s and 1970s.

As a result, death rates fell to levels only seen in developed countries with higher per capita incomes. Maternal mortality (death in childbirth) and infant mortality improved, at least in part from the reduction in the number of births per woman (from over 6 in the 1960s to less than 3 by the early 1980s) brought about by China's birth planning program, launched in the 1970s. Building on this basis, China today still has generally excellent basic health statistics when compared with other developing countries. For example, in 2005, China maternal mortality rate was 46 per 100,000 births, while India's was 450 per 100,000 live births; for infant mortality, China's rate was 21 per 1,000 live births, India's 58 per 1,000.

From 1949 to the late 1970s, social investments in health and education were prioritized in China, as they were in many socialist countries. But China's primary health care system became a target of the Cultural Revolution after Mao had proclaimed in 1965, "The Ministry of Public Health is not a Ministry of Public Health for the people, so why not change its name to the Ministry of Urban Health, the Ministry of Gentlemen's Health, or even to Ministry of Urban Gentlemen's Health?.... In medical and health work put the emphasis on the countryside!"[4]

Reflecting a historical tension in China (as in many other countries) about the balance between investing in the urban hospital system versus a rural public health system, the PRC's health spending pendulum shifted strongly toward the construction of an equity-oriented public health approach for the rural poor during the Cultural Revolution and its aftermath. Because the rural economy was organized into large agricultural production units, the "people's communes," it was possible to allocate a portion of the commune funds to support such an approach, including a rudimentary health insurance system. With basic services provided at the village level by minimally trained community health workers called "**barefoot doctors**" and a network of clinics and better health facilities and hospitals at higher levels of administration, most rural citizens had access to medical care.[5]

In the late 1970s, over 90 percent of rural citizens were covered by a health insurance system called the **Cooperative Medical Scheme (CMS)**. Since rural mobility was restricted and insurance coverage dependant on referral up the chain, access to higher and more expensive levels of health care were controlled. The local level curative health system of basic care was supported by investments in preventive health through the "patriotic health campaigns" that carried out public projects such as mosquito control and improving access to clean water and also educated the public about disease prevention through means like hand-washing, prenatal care, and immunizations.

While few rural Chinese wish for a return to the restrictions and shared poverty of the commune system, which was dismantled in the early 1980s as the country returned to family farming and a market economy, and few would glorify the quality of China's rural medical care system in the Maoist era, many long for a return to its equity and emphasis on prevention, and these themes have permeated the current debates on health reform and are reflected in some of the new reform initiatives.

Market Reforms and Health Care

After the breakup of the commune system, the rural CMS was dismantled, and health care financing was delegated to provinces and local areas, which turned to the market economy to provide the necessary funds by privatizing much of the health care system. As public financing of health care decreased, the unregulated market (especially for drugs and medical tests) steadily increased the price of care. Limited public finances were diverted to cover staff salaries at county- and township-level facilities. Health care stations at the local level were supported by village governments, but medical staff salary had to be earned from fees for service and drug sales. Rural citizens who could afford to do so bypassed township facilities for the better county-level care, undermining the tiered referral chain and distorting the value of manpower investments and training for the township level health facilities. By 1993, only 13 percent of rural residents were still covered by rural health insurance.[6]

The current health care system, with its focus on fee-based financing of curative rather than preventive care, has shifted attention and investments away from vital public health education and public works that reduce both chronic and infectious diseases, like the protection of clean drinking water sources, pest eradication, and health education.

In recent years, the level of curative care in rural China has greatly improved, and most essential drugs are available, even in remote parts of the country, with staff trained in their use. But the cost of that care and the breakdown in the government's preventive public health functions have created serious inequities in the rural health system and threaten

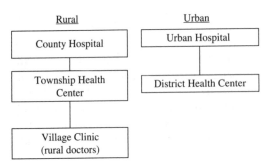

Figure 12.1 China's Three-tiered Medical System

the ability to control new emerging and common infectious diseases. An official national survey in 2003 showed that nearly 49 percent of patients needing treatment did not go to a doctor and nearly 30 percent of patients needing hospitalization did not receive it because of cost. Government contributions to hospital running costs have decreased from about 30 percent in the 1970s to less than 8 percent in 2000, with the difference made up by patient fees.[7]

There are also numerous indicators of the reemergence of sharp urban-rural inequalities in the distribution of health care resources and access. In 1999, of total government health spending, a full 25 percent occurred in just four of China's wealthiest cities and provinces, Beijing, Shanghai, Zhejiang, and Jiangsu. In 2002, 50 percent of all hospital beds and personnel were in urban areas and 80 percent of medical resources were spent in cities, although the large majority of China's population lived in the rural areas.[8] It was precisely this inequitable investment and urban focus of the medical system that was the rallying cry for Mao during the Cultural Revolution. While health reform is now back on the government's policy agenda, reconstructing an equitable health system will not be easy.

The SARS Crisis

The outbreak of SARS in 2003 was a major wake-up call for China's leadership and is a major reason that the government is now giving higher priority to health care.

China's SARS epidemic in 2003 signaled a new chapter in infectious disease challenges for China and the world. Since animals, especially pigs and chickens, live in close proximity to humans, southern China with its dense backyard farming practices has been a breeding ground for new viruses. There has been a huge increase in China's animal population in the last forty years—from 5.2 to 508 million pigs between 1968 and 2005, and from 12.3 to 13 billion poultry.[9] Recently, several new strains of flu have emerged from the area and have moved quickly from southern China to Hong Kong with the massive movements of people across relaxed borders.

SARS began in Guangdong in November 2002, but provincial authorities concealed the gravity of the early epidemic. Between November and January 2003, the outbreak gained momentum in Guangdong, but the epidemic was only reported to the World Health Organization (WHO) on February 11, 2003, and only after the organization initiated an inquiry, based upon reports received from Hong Kong's Global Outbreak Alert and Response Network (GOARN). A WHO team was dispatched from Geneva to investigate the outbreak on February 19, but was stonewalled in Beijing. The team was not granted permission to travel to Guangdong until April. These failures in early acknowledgment and appropriate response during March and April set the stage for China's massive SARS epidemic in the following months and allowed the outbreak to spread to Hong Kong and from there to the world. Through a combination of luck (virus seasonality) and effective person-to-person control measures, the epidemic subsided by the summer of 2003. Toward the end of the worldwide epidemic, of the 8,422 cases and 916 deaths in thirty countries and Hong Kong, 5,327 cases and 349 deaths were in China, or a full 63 percent of all worldwide SARS cases.[10]

Only when SARS became a political issue, an embarrassment for Beijing, did the central government impose its authority on Guangdong. In a dramatic move, the Chinese government fired the minister of health and changed course, instituting a rarely seen transparency and honesty in reporting, and allocating 2 billion Chinese RMB (over US$250 million) in emergency funding for national SARS control. The international loss of "face" and the resulting policy reversal set in motion the actions that brought SARS under control. This was an example of how political will and national mobilization are required for tackling serious threats to public health in China, and provided lessons for China's response to its AIDS epidemic and other newly emerging infectious diseases like avian influenza.

The SARS epidemic was also a wake-up call for China's government on the deterioration of the public health capacity of China's rural health system. However, the extensive but weakened health infrastructure was still able to rise to the occasion once national leadership provided the mandate for action, along with adequate funding. It is important to note that few countries in the world have the capacity for national mobilization that extends to the most remote corners of a large and increasingly independent nation. China was able to fall back on traditions of public health mobilization from the 1960s and 1970s. The mobilization was precisely what was required to put in place the series of preventive measures that broke the chain of SARS transmission.

During the SARS epidemic, the patriotic health campaign approach was resurrected to mobilize the population to self-quarantine, report fellow citizens with fevers, and glorify medical personnel, especially nurses, who were at the forefront of the control effort and played an important role in keeping the epidemic from spreading in China's rural areas.[11]

China's AIDS Policy

The lessons China learned from the SARS response had lasting benefits for the control of infectious disease threats in China. China learned a hard lesson from its belated SARS response that not responding to infectious disease threats can undermine economic growth and tarnish its global image. Waiting in the wings after the SARS crisis died down, China's AIDS advocates from government, civil society, academia, and their international partners grabbed the opportunity to push forward greater action on AIDS, highlighting similarities in issues of transparency, media control, concealment, government leadership, and the accountability of public officials.

AIDS is an infectious disease, albeit spread less easily than SARS. However, the stigma and embarrassment associated with its two main routes of transmission, sex and drugs, makes AIDS much harder to openly discuss and address, especially in China's morally conservative society. However, there is no question that if not controlled, AIDS will have serious economic and social impacts in China, as tragically evidenced by several sub-Saharan African countries.

China's AIDS epidemic began in the early 1980s as a localized epidemic among needle-sharing intravenous drug users along the southern border with Myanmar (Burma), where the opium poppies that are the source of heroin is an abundant crop. At that time the disease was viewed by the Chinese authorities as a foreign illness associated with illicit behavior, which could be controlled by testing all foreigners who entered the country. In contrast, China now has an AIDS prevention and treatment policy that endorses many best practices and is promoted by the country's top leadership and praised by international observers. While many factors contributed to this turnaround, the major impetus for change resulted from the SARS epidemic and response in 2003, as discussed above.

The government of the PRC now estimates 700,000 HIV infections in the country, and the disease is found in all of China's thirty-seven provinces, municipalities, and autonomous regions, with new infections growing at an alarming rate, for example, by 45 percent in 2007.[12]

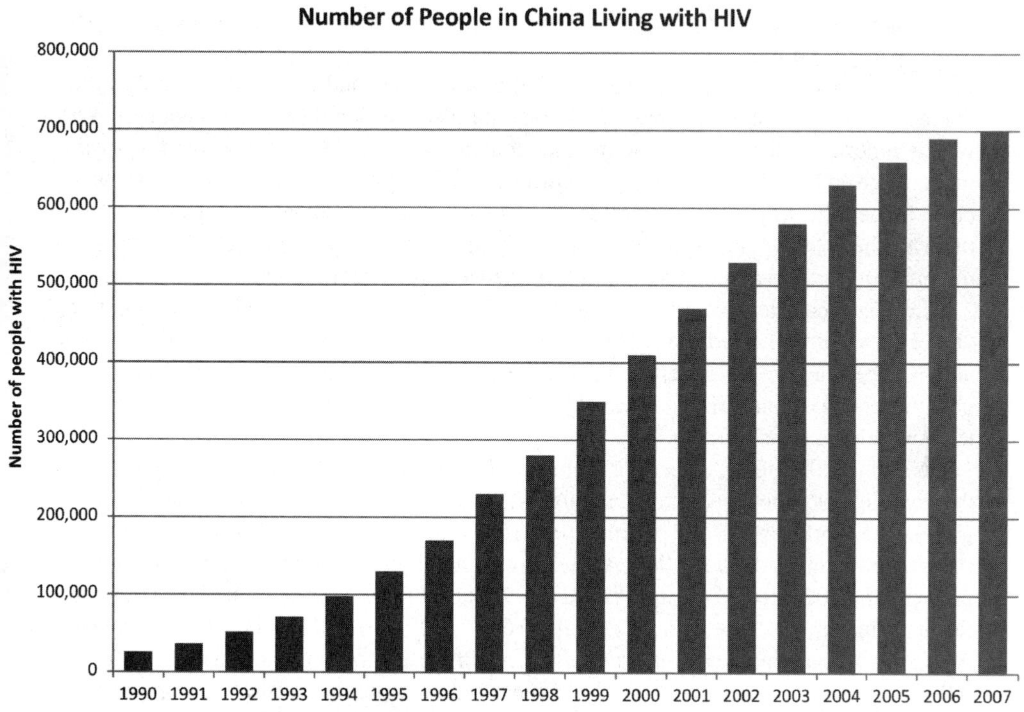

Number of People in China Living with HIV

Figure 12.2 Number of People in China Living with HIV, 1990–2007
Source: *2008 Report on the Global AIDS epidemic,* UNAIDS/WHO, July 2008.

While infections from shared needles by injecting heroin users still account for 42 percent of new infections, more than half are now heterosexually sexually transmitted (44.7 percent), mainly among commercial sex workers and their clients and among sexual partners of injecting drug users; new infections are also increasing among men who have sex with men (12.2 percent). The proportion of infections in women is also increasing: from 19.4 percent in 2000 to 27.8 percent in 2006.[13] The epidemic continues to expand, and some of the challenges to control it include the size of China's young sexually active population, changing sexual behaviors and norms, massive internal migration, low knowledge about AIDS and perception of risk among the general population, and the expanding epidemic among hard-to-reach gay men.

A separate epidemic among paid blood plasma donors in central China accounts for a large proportion of current AIDS cases. Intravenous drug users traveling through Henan province in central China, a major transportation crossroads, have been identified as the source of tainted blood that resulted in the epidemic in the region that began in the mid-1990s. These addicts would earn money by selling their blood at semi-official plasma collection stations run by so-called **blood heads**—often with the collusion of local officials—who stood to make a nice profit by selling what they had collected to medical firms and hospitals that needed the blood for transfusions or manufacture of drugs derived from blood products. At the same time, many poor farmers in Henan and bordering provinces (Anhui, Hunan, Shanxi, Hubei, Hunan) also sold blood at these stations, where blood samples were pooled and red blood cells re-injected into donors. The result was widespread

HIV infections, which were then transmitted to sexual partners and through pregnancy and delivery to newborns.

A retired doctor, Gao Yaojie, was the first to investigate and expose the severity of the epidemic caused by these tainted blood donation practices. Dr. Gao's investigations were widely reported in the Chinese and international press and led to the exposure of a government cover-up by Henan provincial authorities.[14] As the plight of rural farmers was publicized in the following years, it created a flood of sympathy by China's citizens. Previously, there had been little public sympathy for the victims of AIDS, mainly injecting heroin users or commercial sex workers, both highly stigmatized and illegal groups.

The facts that Henan's farmers and their affected children and elderly parents were "innocent victims" helped the AIDS crisis gain public awareness and led to a demand for action. The pressure on government to respond, along with existing concern about the potential for a political crisis generated by demands for justice by infected farmers, pushed the government to take action.[15]

To address the plight of central China's AIDS infected farmers, in September 2003, the government announced a free national AIDS treatment program, one of the few countries in the world to do so. This important (and expensive) act was the first of many to move China out of denial in its response to its AIDS epidemic. Mainly focused on the predicted 80,000 infected persons, mostly in central China, requiring immediate treatment, the program entitled "The Four Frees and the One Care" provided free HIV treatment using domestically manufactured generic drugs (some imported drugs are now also used) for the AIDS treatment cocktail for all rural residents and poor people in cities. It also provided free HIV counseling and testing services, free testing and treatment for pregnant women and their offspring to prevent transmission of the virus to their newborns, free school fees for children affected by HIV and AIDS, and financial support for affected families.[16] With this policy, the government squarely recognized the need for treatment and care, not only as a means of improving the lives of people and functioning of communities affected by HIV and AIDS but also as a way to protect social stability in affected communities.

The government's response to AIDS has continued to become more aggressive and open. These actions, and the greater transparency that has accompanied them, come from the administration of Hu Jintao and Wen Jiabao, which is defining itself as more willing to prioritize the poor and more concerned with both equity and social development. A State Council AIDS Working Committee (SCAWCO) was established in early 2004, chaired by Vice Premier Wu Yi (who also successfully steered the SARS response in 2003), elevating the importance of the AIDS issue at the national level. Following similar moves put in place during the SARS epidemic, the government clearly stated its intention to hold all government officials accountable for their honesty in dealing with AIDS and for ensuring heightened attention, surveillance, and resources for infectious disease control. A strong five-year action plan for dealing with AIDS was published in 2006, and the State Council issued a decree the same year signaling its determination to fight AIDS. Prime Minister Wen Jiabao has publicly met AIDS patients and orphans, including in Henan villages affected by the blood scandal.

However, even with this newfound national will to tackle AIDS, the changes wrought by nearly three decades of fiscal and political decentralization have made the provincial governments increasingly independent of Beijing, even within the context of China's unitary political system. China's national ministries may set policy and program guidelines, but real control over decisions and budgets rests with provincial and local governments. As an example, even as China's response to its escalating AIDS epidemic has improved, officials in Henan Province, where the blood head scandal occurred, have blocked accurate reporting, and some research and prevention efforts. Despite pressure from Beijing, Henan officials have engaged in a cover-up for years and remained in their jobs.[17]

However, there are many positive developments. Chinese leaders have made several well-publicized visits to AIDS patients, including Premier Wen Jiabao, who visited some of the most stricken villages in Henan just before World AIDS Day in 2007. As part of both outside funding requirements and donor calls for greater participation of people living with AIDS in the global AIDS response, some urban hospitals have set up patient groups that routinely participate in meetings and workshops on AIDS. Some national Chinese leaders have also acknowledged that there is a need for NGOs in China's AIDS response, particularly to reach groups that avoid government service programs, such as sex workers, drug users, and gay men. As a result, there has been a proliferation of AIDS orphan relief charities and volunteer groups, patient support groups, and groups working with gay men. For example, in Chengdu, a mostly volunteer group of gay men, the Chengdu Gay Community Care Organization, provides AIDS education outreach and condoms in bars and bathhouses and has been collaborating with the provincial and municipal health bureaus and foreign donors in their efforts. Homosexuality was only decriminalized in China a few years ago, and the growing tolerance for gays may make it easier to involve that community in the fight against HIV/AIDs.

The development of China's AIDS policy has been shaped by a combination of both internal and external events. Domestic advocacy from within government and from NGO activists, medical professionals, and academic scholars have spurred government action following the SARS crisis. But external pressure from the international community has also been an important factor in pushing for greater attention to AIDS in China. As with many other issues, the international perception of denial, inaction, human rights abuses, and cover-up have threatened China's self-image and spurred internal debate and response, which has often been positive. Combined with a realization that economic growth and participation in the fruits of globalization depend on good global citizenship, these forces have propelled an uncustomary government accountability on the AIDS issue. This overdue and more proactive government AIDS response also points out clearly, however, that the mustering of the party-state's high-level political commitment is the essential requirement in China for implementing responsive national policies and mobilizing local-level action.

As the AIDS and SARS responses illustrate, national-level solutions to health crises are hard to carry out without the political will to overcome bureaucratic and financial barriers. The Health Ministry is an especially weak player on the national, provincial, and local stage, where other priorities, especially economic, are of greater perceived importance.

The leadership's newfound pragmatic approach to dealing with AIDS has helped push China's government toward increasing tolerance and support for the role of civil society and is an important public policy development. But this tolerance has not always extended to the local level, where officials often distrust or feel threatened by nongovernmental actors and limit their actions. And it is ultimately at the local level where access to the most at risk populations is needed, that the success or failure of China's response to AIDS response will be determined.

Conclusion

China's leadership is now engaged in a massive new health reform effort. Thirty years of privatization, decentralization, and benign neglect of the rural health system, coupled with new threats from emerging or resurgent infectious diseases, finally pushed the central government to begin the arduous process of fixing a very broken health care system, albeit one that has achieved high levels of population health on par with more developed countries. Moreover, with economic development and increased wealth has come the challenge of addressing chronic disease problems and improving health behaviors such as smoking, traffic accidents, and diet.

The government has committed $130 billion to the reform effort that will include a new and more generous medical insurance program, an effort to reign in the overuse of drugs and tests as money-earning, regulate drug costs and institute rational drug prescribing, and revitalization of a basic public health prevention approach to population health. The SARS epidemic was the wake-up call for the problems of an inequitable and poorly functioning health care system. This led first to greater transparency, better international cooperation on infectious disease reporting, then to a strengthened and more open response to HIV/AIDS, and now to a major overhaul of the entire health care system. However, the government will likely need to embrace some outsourcing of services to both private sector and NGO agencies, following more efficient approaches from the rest of the world. The next few years will be a crucial test for the reform effort, and China may soon be again a model to the world on how to achieve "health for all."

Notes

1. Li Changming, "China's Rural Health in Economic Transition," power point presentation prepared for the Consultative Meeting of the China Health Development Forum, April 2002, Beijing, www.ids.ac.uk/ids/health/chdf.presentation.ppt, accessed August 15, 2005; and Tony Saich and Joan Kaufman, "Financial Reform, Poverty and the Impact on Reproductive Health Provision: Evidence from Three Rural Townships," in *Financial Sector Reform in China*, ed. Yasheng Huang. Anthony Saich, Edward Steinfeld (Cambridge, MA: Harvard Asia Center Publications, 2005).

2. Wang Longde, et al., "Emergence and control of infectious diseases in China," *Lancet* 372, no. 9649 (2008): 1598–1605; and Victor Sidel and Ruth Sidel, *Serve the People: Observations on Medicine in the People's Republic of China* (Boston: Beacon Press, 1974).

3. Henderson Cohen and Aiello Zheng, "Successful Eradication of Sexually Transmitted Diseases in the People's Republic of China," *Journal of Infectious Diseases*, 174, supp. 2 (October 1996): s223–229.

4. "Directive On Public Health," June 26, 1965, http://www.marxists.org/reference/archive/mao/selected-works/volume-9/mswv9_41.htm.

5. Victor W. Sidel, "The Barefoot Doctors of the People's Republic of China," *New England Journal of Medicine* 286, no. 24 (June 15, 1972): 1292–1300; and W. C. Hsiao, "Transformation of Health Care in China," *New England Journal of Medicine* 310 (1984): 932–936.

6. Yuanli Liu and Keqin Rao, "Providing Health Insurance in Rural China: From Research to Policy," *Journal of Health Politics, Policy and Law* 31, no. 1 (2006): 71–92.

7. "Minister: Health System in Poor State," *China Daily*, August 7, 2005.

8. Ministry of Health, *China Health Yearbook*, 1999 (in Chinese) (Beijing: Peoples Health Publishers, 1999); Li Changming, "China's Rural Health in Economic Transition."

9. Michael T Osterholm, "Preparing for the Next Pandemic," *New England Journal of Medicine* 352, no. 18 (May 5, 2005): 1839–1842.

10. Joan Kaufman, "Infectious Disease Challenges in China," in Xiaoqing Lu, ed., *China's Capacity to Manage Infectious Diseases: Global Implications* (Washington, DC: Center for Strategic and International Studies, 2009).

11. Joan Kaufman, "SARS and China's Health Care Response: Better to Be both Red and Expert!" and Anthony Saich, "Is SARS China's Chernobyl or Much Ado about Nothing?," in *SARS: Prelude to Pandemic?*, ed. Arthur Kleinman and James L. Waston (Stanford, CA: Stanford University Press, 2006).

12. Xinhua News Agency, *Medical News Today*, March 28, 2008.

13. Xinhua News Agency, "More Women Suffer from HIV/AIDS in China," June 4, 2007.

14. Gao Yaojie has been recognized and won several prestigious awards both abroad and in China for her courageous work on behalf HIV/AIDS. Ironically, she has also been placed under house arrest, harassed by police, and refused permission to travel abroad at various times by Chinese authorities, who worry about her outspokenness. She is now in the U.S. and seeking asylum.

15. Jun Jing, "The Social Origins of AIDS Panics in China," in *AIDS and Social Policy in China,* ed. Joan Kaufman, Arthur Kleinman, Anthony Saich (Cambridge, MA: Harvard University Asia Center Publications, 2006), 152–169.

16. State Council AIDS Working Committee (SCAWCO) and UN Theme Group on HIV/AIDS in China, *A Joint Assessment of HIV/AIDS Prevention, Treatment and Care in China,* December 2004.

17. Joan Kaufman and Jing Jun, "China and AIDS: The Time to Act is Now," *Science* 296 (June 28, 2002): 2339–2340.

Suggested Readings

Henderson, Gail, and Myron Cohen. *The Chinese Hospital: A Socialist Work Unit.* New Haven, CT: Yale University Press, 1984.

Horn, Joshua. *Away with All Pests: An English Surgeon in People's China: 1954–1969. New* York: Monthly Review Press, 1969.

Kaufman, Joan, Arthur Kleinman, and Tony Saich, eds. *AIDS and Social Policy in China* Cambridge, MA: Harvard University Asia Center Publications, 2006.

Kleinman, Arthur, and James L Watson, eds. *SARS in China: Prelude to Pandemic?* Stanford, CA: Stanford University Press, 2006.

Lu, Xiaoqing, ed. *China's Capacity to Manage Infectious Diseases: Global Implications.* Washington, DC: Center for Strategic and International Studies, 2009.

Sidel, Victor, and Ruth Sidel. *Serve the People: Observations on Medicine in the People's Republic of China.* Boston; Beacon Press, 1973.

Wagstaff, Adam, et al. *Reforming China's Rural Health System.* Washington, DC: World Bank Publications, 2009.

13

Policy Case Study: Population

Tyrene White

When the People's Republic was formed in 1949, China's population had climbed to more than 500 million. By way of comparison, that figure was roughly the same as the total population of Europe at that time, and more than three times the population of the United States. By the year 2005, China's population had grown to 1.34 billion, roughly double the population of Europe and 4.5 times the population of the United States. The population increase alone over the last quarter century—approximately 350 million—is a number that exceeds the combined population of the United States and Canada in 2009. Looked at another way, China's primary school enrollment is about the same as the entire population size of Mexico—about 110 million.

It is numbers like these that led Chinese leaders to implement the so-called one-child policy in 1979, and make them reluctant to repeal it more than thirty years later, despite the dramatic changes that have occurred in the interim. The *annual increase* in population has declined, dropping from a peak of around 23 million per year in the 1980s to a low of 12 million in the late 2000s. China's *total population size* continues to climb, however. It will not stop until around 2050, when China's population is forecast to top off at 1.4 to 1.5 billion. Despite its undesirable consequences, then, which include rapid population aging and skewed sex ratios, the one-child policy remains China's official population policy.

How Did They Get Here?

If you ask mainland Chinese how China got into this predicament, they will likely blame Mao Zedong, the revolutionary leader of the Chinese Communist Party (CCP) who ruled the People's Republic from 1949 until his death in 1976. His pro-natalist stance and opposition to family planning, they will say, resulted in high rates of population growth for more than two decades. By the time the post-Mao regime began to enforce a serious birth limitation policy, China's population had grown so much that even a radical program like the one-child birth limit could not prevent its continued increase for decades to come.

There is some validity to this view; Mao's pro-natalist views certainly slowed the implementation of birth control programs and contributed to the more accelerated growth of the population after 1949. China's demographic challenge did not begin in 1949, however, nor was Mao's view as crude and simplistic as it is usually portrayed. When the CCP came to power in 1949, they inherited an empire that had experienced a fivefold increase in population over the previous three centuries. Around 1650, China's population size topped 100 million for the first time. From that point, it only took another 250 years to pass the 400 million mark (circa 1900) and just 50 more to top 500 million.

From the creation of the People's Republic in 1949, then, population pressures received the attention of Chinese Communist party (CCP) leaders. During the first two decades of the Maoist era, however, the proper approach to demographic issues was hotly debated and contested. Initially, the CCP and its leader, Mao Zedong, resisted any suggestion that a large population constituted a problem. They argued that what appeared to be "overpopulation" was actually the result of the exploitative system of capitalism, and would disappear as capitalism was replaced by socialism. It did not take long, however, for top officials in the CCP to begin to worry about the population pressures. Some began to speak in more practical ways about the burden of population growth, and to recommend that China amend its population policy to provide more support for family planning education and allow the import of condoms and other contraceptive supplies.

Before these first steps could yield any meaningful results, however, the radicalization of domestic politics interrupted the effort, and advocates of family planning were branded as "rightists," or enemies of the revolution. At the same, time, however, the second half of the 1950s was a period of intensified state planning. All institutions and bureaucracies were mobilized to put into place annual and five-year performance plans that would help China achieve its goal of becoming an advanced socialist economy and society. In this context, it was Mao who suggested in 1957 that China should attempt to plan reproduction in the same way it aspired to plan material production. At the time, birth planning (*jihua shengyu*), that is, the attempt to regulate population growth so as to keep it in balance with levels of economic production and growth, was only a goal to be reached at some more advanced stage of socialist development.

As China's population continued to grow rapidly in the 1960s, however, key leaders such as Premier Zhou Enlai came to believe that birth planning could no longer be postponed. In 1965, Zhou proposed the first national population control target—reducing the annual rate of population growth to one percent by the end of the century, and by 1972 he had authorized the creation of an extensive family planning bureaucracy to oversee implementation, provide free access to contraceptives, abortions, and sterilizations, and monitor the enforcement of local birth targets. Socialist planning thus came to embrace human reproduction in much the same way that it embraced agricultural and industrial production. Local officials who were responsible for meeting grain and steel production quotas now began to receive quotas for babies.

In the early and mid-1970s, the campaign focus was "later, longer, fewer," that is, promoting later marriage, longer spacing between births (three to five years), and fewer births (a two-child ideal and a three-child limit). By mid-decade, the childbearing norm began to tighten; the new slogan was "one is not too few, two is enough, three is too many." In the cities, young couples began to feel pressure to have only one child. In the countryside, they were urged to have no more than two. In 1979, a group of China's top scientists announced that if China were to achieve its economic goals by the year 2000—a goal that the new Deng regime had expressed as achieving a per capita gross domestic product of $1,000 by the year 2000 (subsequently reduced to $800 per capita), population had to be contained within 1.2 billion. In turn, this meant that the official birth limit had to be lowered to one child per couple (with some exceptions for special circumstances).

In an extraordinary "Open Letter" to CCP members that was published in all newspapers in September 1980, China's leaders defended the new policy and made it clear to the CCP membership the high level of priority they attached to it. They argued that the two-decade delay after 1949 was a fateful mistake. By the time the state began to encourage fertility control, a huge new generation of young people had already been born and were approaching their childbearing age years. As a result, even with declining fertility levels (i.e., the average number of children born to a woman during her reproductive years), demographic momentum meant continued growth of total population size. That growth, which threatened to reach 1.5 billion by century's end if no action was taken, could doom China to poverty and economic backwardness through another generation if urgent action was not taken by this generation.

Implementing the One-Child Policy

The one-child policy was inaugurated just as the Deng regime was about to embark on a far-reaching reform program that gradually transformed China's economy, polity, and society. As previous chapters have described, the collective economy was gradually decollectivized and marketized; politics was de-radicalized and political institutions revived; society was granted relief from the all-intrusive party-state that had permeated every aspect of public and private life. Change came in fits and stops, with periods of dramatic change often followed by a partial retreat to safer political ground. This pattern gave Chinese politics a cyclic or wave pattern, not unlike the high tides and low tides of the mass campaigns of the Mao era.

Through all of these changes and fluctuations in political atmosphere, the insistence on strict birth control never faltered. It was a constant in an otherwise volatile situation. That does not mean, however, that the content and enforcement of the policy were static. On the contrary, officials at all levels struggled to adapt to a rapidly changing situation, to unintended consequences of the policy, and to a lesser degree, international scrutiny and criticism. This translated into several different stages of implementation.

Phase One: Collectivism and Coercion, 1979–1983

In the early years of the program, as the Deng regime fought against the lingering influences of the Cultural Revolution, it was possible to use the tools and institutions of the Maoist era to press for strict enforcement of birth quotas that were handed down to each city, county, neighborhood, and village. Thirty years of Maoism had taught Chinese citizens to be wary of voicing opposition to the latest campaign, taught officials that they could intimidate and coerce anyone who dared to defy them, and taught party leaders at all levels that the failure to meet campaign quotas was one of the most deadly sins of Chinese politics. A poor campaign performance could spell the end of a promising career. All childbearing-age couples, urban and rural, had to receive official birth permits from the state in order to give birth legally. In addition, provinces and local governments drafted regulations offering economic incentives to encourage policy compliance and imposing stiff sanctions on policy violators. All childbearing-age women were required to undergo periodic gynecological exams to ensure they were not carrying an "unplanned" pregnancy, and if they were, they were pressed to undergo an abortion immediately. In addition, all CCP members were urged to "take the lead" in implementing the one-child policy by accepting it themselves, urging family members to do so, and in every respect setting a good example for others to follow.

Gaining compliance from those under their jurisdiction took much more than setting a good example, however. In China's cities and towns, growing acceptance of the small-family norm, free access to contraceptives, and tight administrative control in work-places and neighborhoods had brought the urban total fertility rate down from 3.3 in 1970 to about 1.5 by 1978, a remarkably low level for a developing country. With a large cohort of women about to enter their peak childbearing years, however, the state deemed even this low level inadequate. To further suppress fertility and prevent more second births, state monitoring intensified in workplaces and neighborhoods. Monthly gynecological examinations for childbearing age women, plus a system of marriage and birth permits provided by the work unit, ensured that anyone attempting to have a second child was caught in a tight surveillance net. Those who escaped the net faced severe penalties, including fines, loss of employment, and perhaps even one's coveted urban household registration (*hukou*).

If changing childbearing preferences and strong mechanisms of state control worked together to induce compliance with the one-child policy in urban China, rural China posed a far more difficult challenge. Like rural populations in other places and times, life in the countryside encouraged higher levels of fertility. Agricultural work requires household labor, and unlike their urban counterparts, even very young children can be put to work in the service of family income. Moreover, while many urban couples could rely on a state pension for retirement support, rural families had no such welfare net. Children were the only guarantee of old-age support, and the most destitute villagers were inevitably those who were alone and childless. Only a son could assure a couple that they would be spared such a fate. Daughters usually married out of the village, transportation links were often poor, and upon marriage a daughter's first obligation transferred to her husband's family. Even the most devoted daughter could not be counted on to provide either income or assistance.

In addition to these practical considerations, the traditional emphasis on bearing sons to carry on the ancestral line remained deeply entrenched in the countryside. As a result, although rural fertility levels were cut in half between 1971 and 1979 (declining from approximately 6 to 3), much of rural China remained hostile to a two- or one-child limit, including the rural cadres who would have to enforce the policy. When the rural reforms implemented after 1978 began to relax the state's administrative grip on the peasantry, just the launching of the one-child policy set the stage for a prolonged and intense struggle over the control of childbearing.

The struggle took a variety of forms, and evolved over time as the unfolding rural reforms altered the local context. In some villages, women who refused to abort an unplanned birth were subjected to meetings where they were berated, intimidated, and threatened into cooperation. In others, medical teams and party cadres swooped in unexpectedly, in an effort to catch women who were eluding them. At worst, women were forced onto trucks and taken directly to the township headquarters, where medical personnel would perform abortions and sterilizations and insert intrauterine devices (IUD). The use of some form of birth control after the first or second child became mandatory, and in the countryside the preferred method was the IUD, since it was not easily removed.

Rural villagers responded with a wide variety of resistance strategies. Enraged family members who came home from a day outside the village to discover that the birth control team had swooped in and performed abortions on their wives or daughters sometimes beat or killed those responsible. Others bribed local officials to accept their stories when they returned to the village after an absence with an "adopted" child. Subterfuges of this sort were acceptable to rural officials, as long as they did not need to register the new infant as a birth in their jurisdiction. Others used their standing in the village to avoid compliance; many rural officials, or their family members, expected the compliance of others while flaunting the policy themselves. Other officials colluded with village families to hide unauthorized pregnancies, particularly for couples with no sons.

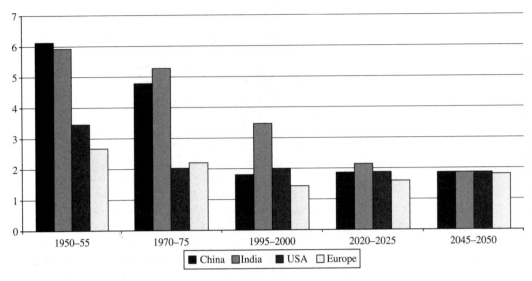

Figure 13.1 Total Fertility Rates for China, India, USA, and Europe, 1950–2050*
Total Fertility Rate (TFR) is the average number of births per woman of childbearing age, 15–49.
*Data for 2020–2025 and 2045–2050 are projections based on the medium variant model.
Source: United Nations Population Division, *World Population Prospects: The 2008 Revision, Population Database*. Data available online at http://www.esa.un.org/unpp/index.asp?panel=2.

Worst of all, the intense pressure to limit births led to many cases of female infanticide. Absent the one-child policy, most families welcomed the arrival of daughters and sons, though a daughter was described as a "small happiness" and a son as a "big happiness." If only one child was to be allowed, however, many villagers—male and female, young and old—felt it was imperative to have a son, so much so that female infanticide was frequently reported.

There were two possible responses to this volatile rural situation. One was to relax the one-child policy, hoping that more education and support for rural women and children would hold birth rates down and improve cadre-mass relations. The other was to intensify enforcement for a short time, but use widespread sterilization to guarantee that those who already had two or more children would never have another. In the short run, the latter option won out, and a massive sterilization campaign was launched. The key campaign target was to eliminate all third and higher order births. Once that problem was solved, more pressure could be brought to bear on those who were having a second child without state permission.

The result of this massive campaign was a fourfold increase in the number of tubal ligations performed in 1983, as compared with the previous years, and large increases across every category of birth control procedures. So severe were the local pressures to meet sterilization targets that many women who had long since completed their intended childbearing, and had been effectively utilizing some form of birth control, were forced to undergo sterilization.

Phase Two: Policy Relaxation, 1984–1989

As the campaign began to play itself out and elite politics took a more "liberal" turn, a decision was made in the mid-1980s to modify the one-child policy to allow for more exceptions. Fearful of a breakdown of authority in the countryside and widespread anger over the one-child limit and the often brutal tactics used to enforce it, leaders in Beijing decided to simply concede the need for a son in the countryside. Henceforth, the rural policy became a one-son or two-child policy. Village couples whose first child was a daughter would be allowed to have a second child, allowed to try again for a son. This concession was made in the hopes of pacifying restless villagers and improving enforcement, but over a period of several years, the net effect of this and other rural reforms was to encourage local governments to unduly relax their enforcement efforts. Village officials who themselves were subject to the birth control policies often colluded with their neighbors to avoid enforcement efforts undertaken by outside teams. As the agricultural reforms destroyed the instruments of control and power that officials had enjoyed in the past, they found it difficult to enforce birth limits, and found it easier to report false numbers than fight with neighbors and kin.

The net effect of this policy "slippage" was to weaken central control over the levers of enforcement and to provide support for experts and birth planning officials who argued that the policy should be more flexible across different regions of China, allowing those in the most impoverished areas with difficult, hilly terrain to have two children, allowing those in average circumstances to have one son or two children, and limiting those in more prosperous areas to only one child. They believed that the same results could be achieved, with less effort and more compliance, than if policy did not respond to the nuances of family need and economic circumstance.

Phase Three: Another Cycle Unfolds, 1989–1995

This more differentiated policy was put into place in the latter half of the 1980s, only to be upset by the events of May–June 1989, which ended in a military crackdown on Tiananmen protesters and their supporters in Beijing and in other cities around the country. The martial atmosphere that returned to Chinese politics for the next two to three years made it possible to once again tighten local enforcement and to carry out another campaign. As in 1982–1983, fear about a poor performance justified the revival of campaign methods. Cadres who had been warned off those methods in the mid-1980s were now instructed to use "crack troops" and "shock attacks" to break through resistance and meet the new goals of the 1991–1995 plan period.

The campaign was justified by the results of the five-year plan that ended in 1990. It showed that China's population control targets had been exceeded by a very substantial margin, giving fuel to those who believed that it was acceptable to use coercion in service of the higher goal of achieving the per capita economic goals that had been set for the year 2000. It was also justified by the preliminary results of the 1990 census, which indicated that China's population had grown more quickly than planned or expected. Even worse, despite the massive effort that went into the census-taking process, it was clear that rural officials were manipulating local data in ways that hid "excess births" that should have been registered in their jurisdiction. They had a strong incentive to do this, since failure on their part would also reflect badly on their immediate superiors. Even when fraud was suspected, therefore, it was rarely investigated by those higher in the political command.

These numbers prompted the conservative leadership to tighten enforcement, returning to a strict formula that limited all urban couples to only one child, and all rural couples to one son or two children. Exceptions were granted only to some of China's smaller minority nationalities and to parents whose first child was mentally or physically handicapped to such a degree that they would be unable to function as a healthy, working adult. Local officials were put on notice that they were liable for strict enforcement, and that failure to achieve their performance targets for birth planning would result in economic penalties, administrative sanctions, and even demotions. They were to assume that meeting population targets was just as important to their future career success as meeting key economic goals.

This success came at a price, however. Evidence of intimidation and coercion was widespread, particularly in areas that had done poorly prior to 1990. Cadres destroyed crops, homes, and property to force compliance or punish policy violators. Relatives, particularly the elder members of the family, were detained indefinitely until they paid their fines, aborted an unplanned pregnancy, or agreed to sterilization. Rural cadres who sided with their fellow villagers did what was necessary to give the appearance of compliance, but also behaved as they had in the past when the work was hard and the campaign targets too ambitious—by lying, exaggerating, and dodging, or finding other ways to manipulate the system.

On the one hand, data for the period between 1990 and 1995 indicate a significant improvement in enforcement, as well as a further reduction of the fertility level. With greater pressure on local officials to report impressive results, however, came greater pressure on grassroots personnel to submit fraudulent data. When official reports based on these data claimed that China's fertility level had dropped to an unusually low 1.4, many Chinese demographers were skeptical, reporting their concerns in scholarly journals and other reports.

Phase Four: Population Control for a New Era

In 1989, when the Deng regime crushed the pro-democracy movement, China still inhabited a world defined by the contours of the Cold War. By 1992, that world had disappeared, and the CCP now faced the problem of how to survive in a post-Leninist, post-socialist world. Responding to the new challenges, the post-Tiananmen politics of conservatism gave way to a new wave of reform and opening that rapidly transformed the political, economic, and social landscape.

It was in this context that many of China's population specialists began again to challenge the wisdom of the administrative and punitive approach to population control that had been relied on since the 1970s. Leading figures in China's new generation of highly trained demographers and sociologists criticized the assumption that "fewer births is everything," arguing that it led to "short-sighted actions (such as surprise raids on big-bellied women)." Frankly acknowledging that China's fertility decline had been induced through the widespread use of coercion, they insisted on the need for a broader and more complex view of population dynamics and a population policy better suited to an overall strategy of "sustainable development." Writing that "the curtain is gradually closing on the era of monolithic population control," these critics went on to discuss the disturbing consequences of that approach (including **sex ratio imbalances** and a rapidly aging population) and the necessity of shifting to a developmental approach that emphasized improvements and investments in the quality of the population.[1] In short, they argued that development was the best route to fertility decline, rejecting in the process the sort of "population determinism" (fewer births is everything) that was so deeply embedded in China's population control strategy.

This open revolt against the theory and practice of birth planning was unprecedented, and it proved to be the leading edge of a push to reform China's program. Like the critique of excess coercion that emerged in 1984, the timely convergence of multiple political developments, both domestic and international, helped to advance the reform agenda in population policy. Domestically, the problem of rural unrest and instability was again pre-occupying the leadership, and one of the major complaints of villagers was the use of coercive birth control tactics to collect burdensome and excessive taxes. Not only did new documents on rural taxation explicitly forbid the use of those measures, a family planning document issued in 1995 codified them as seven types of prohibited behaviors: (1) illegally detaining, beating, or humiliating an offender or a relative; (2) destroying property, crops, or houses; (3) raising mortgages without legal authorization; (4) the imposition of "unreasonable" fines or the confiscation of goods; (5) implicating relatives or neighbors of offenders, or retaliating against those who report cadre misbehavior; (6) prohibiting childbirths permitted by the local plan in order to fulfill population targets; (7) organizing pregnancy checkups for unmarried women.[2]

When China began to implement its one-child policy in 1979, it was widely lauded by leaders in the international family planning community who subscribed to the dominant theory that population growth was a primary, if not *the* primary, impediment to economic growth. By the mid-1990s, another school of thought began to dominate the discourse on population and development. This alternative approach, which focused on women's reproductive health and rights, was crystallized in Cairo at the 1994 United Nations International Conference on Population and Development. It emphasized the organic relationship between the elevation of the status of women (especially through increased education and employment outside the home), the elimination of poverty, and declining fertility levels.

The substance of the conference was reported in some detail in the Chinese media and in population journals, and shortly thereafter, the influence of the new international approach on Chinese policy became clear. In China's "Outline Plan for Family Planning Work in 1995–2000," for example, stress was placed on the impact of the socialist market economy on population control, and on the necessity of linking population control to economic development. In addition, the plan placed special emphasis on the role of education, and urged aggressive efforts to increase women's educational level in order to promote lower fertility.

If the Cairo conference was influential in China, it was because there was a constituency in China ready to seize the opportunity to press home similar views. In the early 1970s, China's leaders, while publicly condemning the orthodox view, had quietly embraced it. Though framed in Marxist terms, the logic of China's policy was the same—that reducing population growth was a prerequisite for socioeconomic development, and that China could not afford to wait for a development-induced **demographic transition** like that which occurred in Europe and North America. In the post-Mao era, this rationale legitimated the regime's insistence that population control was the linchpin of the modernization strategy, even as it came under increased international criticism.

The new language of Cairo—protecting women's rights and taking a more holistic approach to achieving demographic goals—buttressed the position of Chinese population policy reformers. It also provided institutional contacts and resources they could use to experiment with a softer approach to enforcement. The UN's Fourth World Conference on Women, held in Beijing in 1995, strongly reinforced the Cairo message, provoking a new wave of feminist thinking and action, further encouraging State Family Planning Commission[*1] officials to consider a more client-centered approach that gave greater consideration to women's needs and their reproductive health.

---

[*] The name of the State Family Planning Commission was changed to the National Population and Family Planning Commission (NPFPC) in 2003.

Predictably, however, reform came slowly and remained highly controversial. Faced with the reality of a rapidly aging population at one end of the demographic pyramid, a bulging workforce in the middle that even the fast-growing Chinese economy could not absorb, and at the bottom, sex ratios so skewed that they posed a threat to social stability, family planning professionals were persuaded that the costs of China's one-child policy had become too high. Other experts, however, especially economists, placed less import on the costs than on the economic benefits of low fertility.

After some internal debate, China officially reaffirmed its one-child policy in 2000 and in 2001 passed a long-debated Population and Family Planning Law that upheld the existing policy and gave compliance the force of law.[3] Although the law included provisions that echoed the Cairo and Beijing conference agendas, calling for an "informed choice of safe, effective, and appropriate contraceptive methods" and one provision prohibiting officials from infringing on "personal rights, property rights, or other legitimate rights and interests," it reiterated China's basic approach to population control. Nevertheless, after thirty years of a strict birth-planning regime, the chorus for reform appeared to be growing louder.

That chorus was reinforced by several parallel developments in Chinese politics and public policy during the first decade of the twenty-first century. First, the year 2000 had come and gone, and although China's population had exceeded the original target number of 1.2 billion, the rate of economic growth after 1980 had exceeded all expectations, suggesting that population growth was no longer a critical threat to China's continued development. Second, young couples entering their childbearing years in the twenty-first century

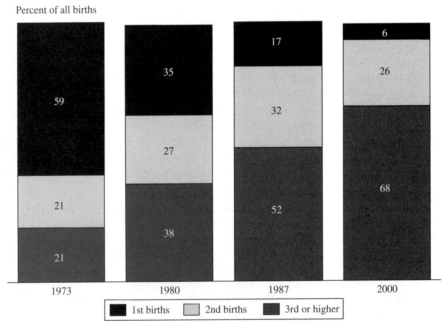

Figure 13.2 Share of First, Second, and Third or Higher Order Births in China, Selected Years, 1973 to 2000
Note: Totals may not equal 100 due to rounding. Sources: From Nancy E. Riley, "China's Population: New Trends and Challenges." *Population Bulletin* 59, no. 2 (June 2004), Washington, DC: Population Reference Bureau, 16.

were far more likely than their predecessors in 1980 to desire only one or two children, to prefer to delay childbirth, or, in the case of some professional women, to forgo childbearing altogether. Traditional norms and expectations regarding marriage and childbirth had been altered by twenty years of rapid economic development and by the relentless education they had received about the individual and societal costs of childbearing.

With acceptance of the one- or two-child norm on the rise, some argued, the regulation of childbirth could be relaxed without fear of a rise in birth rates. And as China began to take a more active role in international institutions after 2000, developing strong links to the global community of nongovernmental organizations (NGOs), the overt use of coercion in enforcing birth planning became an embarrassment to the now highly professionalized state family planning bureaucracy. Many were convinced that it was time for China to shift more decidedly toward a system of education, rewards, and support for those who chose to have no more than two children and who were willing to space those children four or five years apart. To support this softer approach, the United Nations Population Fund (UNFPA) launched projects designed to test this model in many counties around the country.

What the demographic experts were unable to do, however, was to convince China's top leaders that it was "safe" to abandon the one-child policy. Fears of a fertility rebound remained, and the necessity of keeping the numbers of births in check continued to outweigh the opinion of specialists that China's population goals could be better achieved, and at a lower social and economic cost, by moving to a universal two-child policy that gave enduring rewards for compliance rather than penalties for violations.

Costs and Benefits of the One-Child Policy

The internal debate over the merits of continuing the one-child policy is one that weighs the costs of the program against the gains. Some scholars focus on economic data that they insist demonstrate how vital it was that China suppress childbearing when it did. On the other hand, those who argue for some degree of relaxation of the policy point to disturbing side effects that they believe offset or exceed policy benefits. The two side effects they discuss most frequently are the skewed sex ratio that suggests widespread use of sex-selective abortion by those who feel they *must* have a son to continue the family line (or to pacify their elders who demand it of them), and the rapid aging of Chinese society.

Sex-Selective Abortion and Sex Ratio Imbalance

Over time and across many different human populations, sex ratios at birth—that is, the number of males born during a given time period compared to the number of females— hover around 105 boys for every 100 girls. On occasion, for a limited period of time, this ratio may vary naturally, with a few more or a few less boys for each 100 girls. Data from China's 2000 census, however, revealed that the sex ratio at birth was approximately 119 boys for every 100 girls, and a 2005 demographic survey reaffirmed that number. In some provinces and localities, the sex ratio was substantially higher, climbing to over 130 boys per 100 girls.

From the beginning of the one-child policy, there was concern that it might result in an imbalanced sex ratio at birth. In the September 1980 "Open Letter" on the one-child policy, for example, several of the most common objections to the policy were aired, including fears that it would lead to female infanticide and abandonment and, consequently, to an imbalance in the sex ratio. These fears were initially discounted, but they proved to be warranted.

In the early 1980s senior officials became alarmed about the many reports of female infanticide and female abandonment on the part of couples desperate to have a son. The infanticide reports produced a firestorm of controversy at home and abroad, leading the regime to respond in two contradictory ways. First, it denied that there was a widespread problem; census and survey data were used to show that China's sex ratio at birth was well within what was considered to be the normal range. Though conceding that incidents of infanticide and abandonment did occur, it was insisted that such cases were rare, and that they occurred only in the most backward regions of the countryside, where the "feudal mentality" remained entrenched. The solution proposed was an education campaign to uproot such backward ideas, but education alone was of little use, given the social and economic realities that privileged male offspring.

By 1984, as reports of female infanticide multiplied and the All-China Women's Federation (ACWF) began to insist that the problem be faced and addressed, the state changed tack. Rather than address the underlying causes of gender bias, it made concessions to rural sensibilities and adjusted the one-child policy to allow single-daughter households to try again—for a son. In the countryside, the state conceded, women were socially inferior and worth less economically. Sonless couples were disadvantaged, the potential prey of stronger families and kin groups, and they were forever disgraced by their failure to continue the male ancestral line. Single-daughter households should therefore be given special consideration, just as the parents of invalids were given special consideration. They should be allowed to try again for a son.

Although the intent of the 1984 policy change was merely to legitimize what was already the de facto rural policy in many areas, it also had the effect of underscoring the unequal status of males and female, especially in rural China. A woman with a single daughter and no sons might be applauded by local officials, but in the real world of the village she was likely subject to a lifetime of pity, social ridicule, and blame, much of it heaped upon her by other rural women who had themselves endured such pressures.

Faced with intense pressures from the state, on the one hand, and their peers and elders, on the other, some took the desperate course of female infanticide to preserve the chance to have a son. As the 1980s progressed, however, two alternative strategies emerged. The first was infant abandonment, which increased substantially in the late 1980s and 1990s in response to a tightening of the birth control policies. There is no official figure for the number of abandoned children, but it likely exceeded 150,000 annually for several years, and may have been much higher.

Also disturbing is the escalating incidence of sex-selective abortion and its impact on China's sex ratio. By the early 1990s, all county hospitals and clinics and most township clinics and family planning stations had ultrasound equipment capable of fetal sex determination. As private clinics proliferated in the 1990s, they too were equipped with ultrasound technology, providing easy access for a fee.

Despite repeated condemnations of sex-selective abortion and attempts to outlaw the use of ultrasound technology for fetal sex identification, easy access to the technology, combined with the lure of lucrative bribes and consultation fees, made ultrasound use very popular. This was especially true in newly prosperous county towns and rural townships, where higher incomes made ultrasound diagnosis possible, but where modest degrees of upward mobility had done nothing to undermine the cultural prejudice and practical logic that favored male offspring.

The impact of sex-selective abortion on China's sex ratio became increasingly clear in the 1990s. In 1981, the Chinese sex ratio at birth, 108.5 males for every 100 females, was already slightly in excess of the norm. Though this figure raised questions about female infanticide and "**missing girls**," those questions were dismissed by Chinese spokesmen, who argued that the sex ratio was well within normal bounds and in keeping with China's own population history. Over the next twenty years, however, the sex ratio at birth rose dramatically, to approximately 111 in 1985, 116 in 1992, and 119 in 2005.

While the sex ratio for first-born children is badly skewed, the skew is far worse when one looks only at second-born children, or third or higher order children. Since most who have a second child already have a daughter, and since they are risking steep fines or worse by violating the policy, they are determined that a second or third child will be a boy. For example, in 2000, the sex ratio for third births was 160 males per 100 females (see Figure 13.3). India, which does not have strict birth limits imposed by the government, however, also suffers from a skewed sex ratio at birth that gets worse at higher birth orders.[4] Close analyses of both cases have led scholars to conclude that the arrival of increasingly affordable and accessible ultrasound technology in the late 1980s was a key factor in both countries in the sharp rise in sex ratios at birth.

Some of this gap can be accounted for by the underreporting of female births by families and local officials who have incentives to ignore them. Underreporting was certainly widespread, leading to the emergence of a new social category of children whose birth went unregistered and who became known as "black" children (*hei haizi*).

In the early 1990s, Chinese experts attributed most of the skew in the sex ratio to underreporting of female births, implying that the actual sex ratio at birth remained within, or close to, acceptable norms. By the late 1990s, however, more candid assessments concluded that sex-selective abortion was widespread and was the main cause of the distorted sex ratio. Moreover, accumulating data indicated that the phenomenon was not just a rural problem, nor was it concentrated in the least educated segment of the population. In other words, son preference was not confined to the rural or backward elements of society. Instead, the

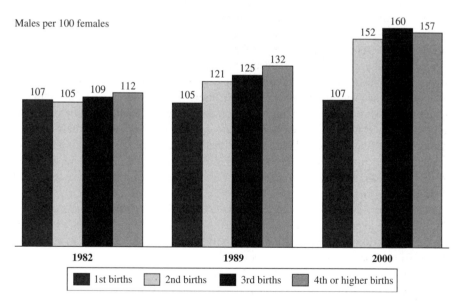

Figure 13.3 Sex Ratio at Birth by Birth Order in China, 1982, 1989, and 2000
Source: From Nancy E. Riley, "China's Population: New Trends and Challenges." *Population Bulletin* 59, no. 2 (June 2004), Washington, DC: Population Reference Bureau, 18.

combined effect of the one-child birth limit, traditional son preference, and easy access to a technology that allowed couples to make sure they had a son was to tempt people from a wide variety of socioeconomic backgrounds to choose sons over daughters.

The resulting skew in the sex ratio has raised alarms over the "army of bachelors," or as they are referred to in Chinese, "bare branches" (*guang gen*), who will be unable to find wives as adults. Although this problem has already begun to appear among those born after 1980, it will get much worse before it gets better. Officials with the Women's Federation, for example, estimate a shortfall of 30 to 40 million females, and worry openly about the unsavory social consequences that may result. Recent studies have warned of the prospect of growing violence, instability, and warfare, noting that historically, societies with large numbers of unemployed, transient, unmarried young men have been prone to these forms of unrest and upheaval.[5] Others link the shortage of women to the disturbing increase in the abduction and sale of women and young girls as brides or prostitutes.

Rapid Population Aging

The second major concern for those who argue for an end to the one-child policy is the problem of population aging. Persons aged sixty or older comprised 8.8 percent of China's population in 1990, and reached 10 percent by the end of the century. Though this figure did not yet place China among those countries with the highest percentages of elderly population, the raw numbers were breathtaking, especially considering China's woefully inadequate pension, welfare, and health care systems. By the year 2008, the elderly population numbered approximately 160 million, on its way up to an estimated 284 million by 2025, and 440 million by 2050.[6]

This trajectory of rapidly increasing numbers of elderly persons as a proportion of the total population results from the very rapid decline in fertility rates after 1970, a decline induced by strict birth limitation policies. As fertility levels declined and average life span increased, even the enormous cohorts of children born after 1970 were not enough to offset a steady rise in the numbers of elderly. As China developed rapidly after 1980, the **dependency ratio**, that is, the size of the working-age population expressed as a proportion of the total population, worked in China's favor. The working-age population was large enough and young enough to ensure an adequate labor force with plenty to spare. Looking ahead, however, that will change rapidly. In 2009 there were thirteen working-age adults for each elderly person; by 2050, there will be only two. This will place tremendous pressure on the working adult population, as their labor will be expected to generate much of the national wealth needed to care for their elders and their children.

Although many countries will face similar challenges, or are already facing them (e.g., Italy and Japan), China's per capita income is also relatively low for a nation with such a rapidly graying population. As *The Economist* put it, China is unusual because it is "getting old before getting rich."[7]

China is also one of the few countries that face the problem of rapid demographic aging while still having to provide for very large cohorts of children. Despite today's low fertility levels, the proportion of the population aged fourteen and under is forecast to decline only modestly, from about 21 percent of the population in 2005 to 18 percent of the population in 2050. This is a very sobering picture of the future: by 2050, there will be on average only one working-age adult to support one elderly person and one child. What this will mean for China's economy and society is unclear, but this looming reality helps to account for the more urgent attention Chinese leaders have given in recent years to the development of a social welfare system that will serve the elderly population.

Conclusion: By the Numbers

China's one-child policy has been lauded for its contribution to slowing world population growth, and its contribution to China's rapid economic development. Given the costs and negative consequences of the policy, however, it is important to ask if a similar result could have been achieved by different means.[8] China's approach to population control was set in motion prior to the era of reform that began in 1978, and while nearly every other policy arena underwent a transformation in the decades that followed, population control policy remained static. The policy was tinkered with, and sometimes relaxed on the margins, but the possibility of changing China's entire approach to population issues never gained traction with China's leaders.

Still, the new conditions China faces in the twenty-first century, combined with growing fears about the social and economic consequences of the sex ratio imbalance and rapid demographic aging, have begun to chip away at the old birth planning regime. Local officials have been given more authority to tailor policy to local needs and conditions, and family planning officials have criticized and sought to punish those who use coercive enforcement techniques. Programs that promote a service-oriented model of enforcement are widespread, and major cities like Shanghai, where the rate of population aging is highest, are offering incentives to couples to bear a second child. But old habits die hard. Media reports of localized use of coercion continue to appear, but the perpetrators are rarely held accountable. Instead, human rights lawyers who defend the victims of coercion are harassed, arrested, and sentenced to jail terms.

The claim made by Chinese authorities is that the birth limitation program has prevented 400 million births since the mid-1970s, but they offer no explanation for how this number is calculated. It appears that it is derived by subtracting China's actual population today from a calculation of what it would have been if the fertility levels of the early 1970s—before the birth limitation program began to be implemented—had remained relatively stable at those levels. The problem with this formula is that it fails to consider the independent impact of reform and modernization on population growth. There is abundant historical evidence that fertility rates drop in response to rapid urbanization, increasing costs of childbearing, the commercialization of agriculture, and improved educational opportunities, especially for women. Changes like these, all of which occurred in China after 1978, may not have been enough to bring down fertility rates as far and as fast as Chinese leaders desired, but it is at best misleading to suggest that the enforcement of birth limits prevented the growth of the population by an additional 400 million.

The impact of the one-child policy on population numbers, then, has most certainly been more modest that what is claimed by the regime. A more sophisticated assessment of its impact must revisit that calculation, and take into consideration the full range of costs and benefits—economic, human, and social—that have accompanied China's one-child policy.

Notes

1. Gu Baochang and Mu Guangzong, "A New Understanding of China's Population Problem," *Renkou yanjiu* (Population Research) 5 (1994): 2–10.

2. The text of Document 138, issued by the Policy and Legislation Department of the SFPC on July 1, 1995, may be found on the UNESCAP Web site, www.unescap.org/pop/database/law_china.

3. For the full text of China's Population and Family Planning Law, see *Population and Development Review* 28, no. 3 (September 2002): 579–85.

4. Carl Haub and O. P. Sharma, "India's Population Reality: Reconciling Change and Tradition," *Population Bulletin* 61, no. 3 (September 2006).

5. Valerie M. Hudson and Andrea M. den Boer, *Bare Branches: The Security Implications of Asia's Surplus Male Population* (Cambridge, MA: MIT Press, 2004).

6. *People's Daily Online*, "China's Population of Over 65's to Reach 109.56 Million," May 26, 2009, http://english.peopledaily.com.cn/90001/90776/90882/6665983.html; UN Data online, "World Population Prospects: The 2008 Revision," United Nations Population Division, http://data.un.org/Data.aspx?q=over +60&d=PopDiv&f=variableID%3a22.

7. "China's Predicament: "Getting Old before Getting Rich," *The Economist*, June 25, 2009.

8. See Amartya Sen, "More Than 100 Million Women Are Missing," *The New York Review of Books* 37, no. 20 (December 20, 1990), available at http://www.nybooks.com/articles/34081; and A. Sen, *Development as Freedom* (New York: Alfred A. Knopf, 1999), 204–26.

Suggested Readings

Banister, Judith. *China's Changing Population*. Stanford, CA: Stanford University Press, 1987.

Chu, Junhong. "Prenatal Sex Determination and Sex-Selective Abortion in Rural Central China," *Population and Development Review* 27, no. 2 (February 2001): 259–282.

Croll, Elisabeth. *Endangered Daughters: Discrimination and Development in Asia*. New York: Routledge, 2000.

das Gupta, Monica. "Explaining Asia's 'Missing Women': A New Look at the Data," *Population and Development Review* 31, no. 3 (September 2005): 529–535.

Greenhalgh, Susan, and Edwin Winckler. *Governing China's Population: From Leninist to Neoliberal Biopolitics*. Berkeley: University of California Press, 2005.

Hudson, Valerie, and Andrea den Boer. *Bare Branches: The Security Implications of Asia's Surplus Male Population*. Cambridge, MA: MIT Press, 2004.

Johnson, Kay Ann. *Wanting a Daughter, Needing a Son: Abandonment, Adoption, and Orphanage Care in China*. St. Paul, MN: Yeong & Yeong, 2004.

Lee, James, and Wang Feng. *One Quarter of Humanity: Malthusian Mythologies and Chinese Realities*. Cambridge, MA: Harvard University Press, 1999.

State Council of the PRC White Paper. *China's Population and Development in the Twenty-first Century*, http://www.cpirc.org.cn/en/whitepaper.htm.

White, Tyrene. *China's Longest Campaign: Birth Planning in the People's Republic, 1949–2005* Ithaca, NY: Cornell University Press, 2006.

Zeng, Yi, Tu Ping, Go Baochang, Xu Yi, Li Bohua, and Li Yongping. "Causes and Implications of the Recent Increase in the Reported Sex Ratio at Birth in China." *Population and Development Review* 19 (June 1993): 283–302.

Zhao, Zhongwei, and Fei Guo. *Transition and Challenge: China's Population at the Beginning of the 21st Century*. New York: Oxford University Press, 2007.

IV POLITICS ON CHINA'S PERIPHERY

14

Tibet

Robert Barnett

The display and pageantry of the Beijing Olympics in 2008 demonstrated a notion common to most nations: that its capital city represents what is most important about that country. The focus on a nations's capital is usually accompanied by a presumption that the actions, decisions, and views of the metropolitan élite define a country's politics and drive its future, while events and opinions in the hinterland diminish in significance according to their distance from the center. From that perspective, Tibetans, a group of about 5.7 million people living on average some 14,000 feet above sea level and up to 2,500 miles from Beijing, with 85 percent of them living in rural areas on semi-arid grassland or in high altitude valleys, are marginal to China's politics. But the most telling challenge to the success of the Beijing Olympics came from Tibet, after over a hundred protests erupted there in the spring of 2008. These did more than capture the attention of the world's media: they led the PRC to cut off one third of its territory from the outside world for several months as troops were put in place and reprisals carried out. Why did the unrest in Tibet have such a dramatic effect, when the thousands of protests known to have occurred in other parts of China during the previous year did not?

The response of the Chinese state is hard to explain if the protests were due to economic opportunism by disgruntled Tibetans or anti-China agitation instigated by foreigners and expatriates, as the Beijing media suggested at the time. Rather, it suggests that Tibetans, who represent about 0.4 percent of China's total population, have a significance as political actors within China that is disproportionate to their numbers. And, indeed, if we set aside the small size of the Tibetan population, the location and history of Tibet should lead us to expect that the area will be politically important. In terms of geography and environment, the 1.1 million square miles of the Tibetan plateau represent 30 percent of current Chinese territory; the areas traditionally inhabited by Uyghurs and Mongols, two other peoples whose histories have also led to a series of pro-independence protests since the early 1980s, cover another third of China. The headwaters of at least seven of Asia's most important rivers flow from the Tibetan plateau, including the Yangtze, the Yellow, the Brahmaputra, the Salween, the Mekong, the Irrawaddy and the Indus. It is the strategic high ground where Central, South and East Asia converge, and it has 2,300 miles of international borders with four countries. Of those borders, the one with India is still disputed and highly militarized, and the border with Bhutan has yet to be settled.

Tibet, in its loosest sense as the Tibetan Plateau, the area traditionally inhabited by Tibetans, has been under Chinese military and political control since at least 1951; in 1965

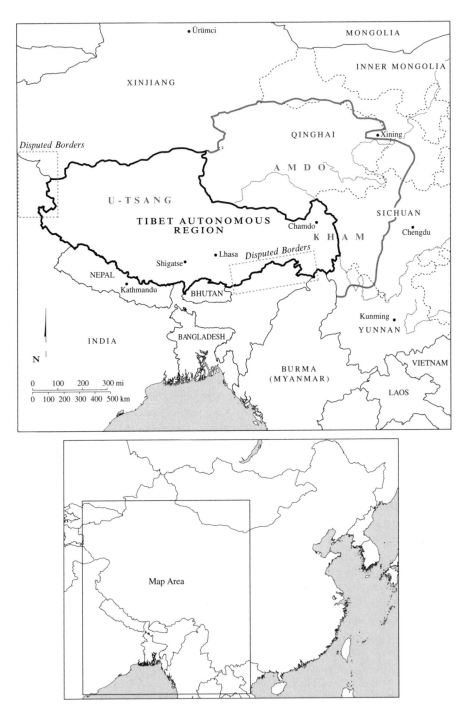

Map 2 Tibet Autonomous Region

the western half of the Plateau, which had been the only area ruled directly by the Lhasa government in the 1940s and which is the only area recognized by China as Tibet, was formally renamed the Tibet Autonomous Region (TAR). The most serious armed challenge that the CCP has faced since it took over China came from Tibetans in the late 1950s. The only sustained guerrilla attacks it has faced since 1949 were those staged by the Tibetan resistance movement from 1956 to 1974. China's only war to have remained unresolved was with India in 1962, a result of the continuing dispute over Tibet's borders. In the last two decades Tibet has become a major feature in international affairs, particularly in U.S.-China relations, and since 1987 Beijing has allowed no nation to open diplomatic relations with it unless that nation states publicly its recognition of China's sovereignty over Tibet, as well as over Taiwan.

The current Chinese leader, Hu Jintao, was promoted to the top position in the nation partly because he had proved his abilities by serving as the party secretary of the TAR* from 1988 to 1992, crushing protests there and overseeing the imposition of martial law in the region for thirteen months from March 1989. The current mayor of Beijing, Guo Jinlong, was also promoted to a position in the capital after working as the party secretary of the TAR, suggesting that Tibet is seen as a proving ground for China's highest leaders. Nor are these the only signs that Tibet is viewed by China's leaders in a different way from other areas. All of the 55 nationalities that are not ethnically Chinese or "Han," to use the word preferred by officials in China (since it implies that Tibetans and other nationalities are also Chinese), are supposed to be governed according to a single policy, but of the 65 official "White Papers" released by the Chinese government since 1992, eight were on Tibet or Tibetans, and only two covered any other specific nationality area. In 2005 Tibetans became the only nationality to have their own bureau (No. 7) within the United Front, the department of the CCP in Beijing that governs all ethnic affairs. The TAR remains the only area of China which foreign tourists are required to have a special permit to enter.

These factors suggest that, although many people both in China and the international community think of Tibet as geographically peripheral and politically marginal, Tibet and Tibetans are central, perhaps even critical, to Chinese politics. They indicate that China's leaders respond to such issues, with their complex historical legacies, and to certain forms of internal pressure much more nervously and with much less success than they do to questions such as economic progress, urban growth, modernization, international relations, or social unrest in China proper. In fact, the standard formulation used by Chinese leaders since 1990 to describe the political significance of China's Tibet policy has long suggested that the Tibet issue is anything but marginal to them: "From a strategic height and an overall point of view," goes the formula, the PRC's policy in Tibet is "crucial to the success of reforms, development, and stability throughout the country."[1] In 2008 Hu Jintao said in his annual statement on Tibet that "the stability in Tibet concerns the stability of the country;"[2] major protests erupted in Lhasa four days later. These statements, repeated in China's major policy documents on Tibet, may well mean exactly what they say: Tibet is a crucial political concern for the PRC.

---

* The CCP party secretary is the most powerful person in Tibet, as in each of the PRC's autonomous regions, provinces, and other administrative units. The autonomous regions also have a chairman, who is the head of the government (similar to a governor of a province). The government chairman by law has to be a member of the traditionally largest ethnic minority in the region. The CCP party secretary in Tibet has never been a Tibetan.

Sino-Tibetan Relations and the Role of the "Gift"

If we look at China's dealings with Tibet over the last sixty years and try to envisage the perspective of Chinese officials and the CCP, what we see for the most part is not an effort to destroy or attack Tibetan culture, as some critics have alleged, but a history of giving gifts. From the Chinese perspective, the state has been involved since the earliest contacts between the CCP and Tibetans in a long series of donations, broken only in its view by what it now describes as the "errors" of the Cultural Revolution. The names of these donations changed according to shifts in political conditions and ideology in China, as did the explanations that went with them. The gift of liberation in 1950 was replaced by the gift of socialism in 1959, regional autonomy in 1965, cultural recovery and modernization in 1980, stability in 1990, the market economy in 1992, and "comfortable housing" in 2006. Thus, in the late 1970s, when socialist goals gave way to the drive for economic growth in China and for "opening up" to the international community, the nature of the gift in Tibet had changed from promoting equality and class struggle to offering people the opportunity to run individual enterprises together with a degree of cultural and political tolerance. With each of the shifts in policy, the principal recipients of the state's donations changed too. Thus, for example, the official definition of "the people," the primary beneficiaries of all state policies until 1979, changed its meaning, so that it no longer referred just to peasants, workers and soldiers, but to almost the whole community, including former aristocrats and landlords. When in 1992 the country shifted from establishing the household economy to promoting the market economy, the gifts became modern infrastructure and a competitive economic system, and entrepreneurs of all kinds were regarded as principal beneficiaries, since they now were hailed as showing other people how to become rich. In Tibet, the main beneficiaries of these changes in the 1990s were local entrepreneurs, officials, and the newly emerging urban middle class; there were some benefits for rural people too, but these were clearly of secondary importance to policy-makers in Lhasa or Beijing.

The many uprisings, rebellions, protests, and other forms of political resistance that have taken place in Tibet over the last sixty years have been interpreted, particularly among foreigners and exiles, as indications that these gifts were seen by many Tibetans as impositions, oppression, manipulation, or, at best, flawed policies. Many Chinese officials and writers, on the other hand, have attributed the negative reception by many Tibetans to these displays of state largesse to backwardness, opportunism, foreign instigation, or, in the final analysis, ingratitude. The latter perspective has shaped how Tibetan responses have been viewed by Beijing. It is this perception of ingratitude, backwardness and opportunism that seems to have scripted the cycles of repeated failure and conflict in China's policies toward Tibet.

Tibetan-Chinese relations have long been governed by gifts. The traditional Tibetan view of China—at least from the mid-seventeenth century, when the Dalai Lamas, spiritual leaders regarded as the reincarnations of a fifteenth century Buddhist master (see Box, **The Dalai Lamas and Panchen Lamas**), came to political power in Tibet and created something like a state—may not have been of China as a country so much as of an Emperor with an army, wealth, and major reservoirs of symbolic capital. The Emperors of the Qing dynasty were not seen as Chinese, but as Manchus and as Buddhists, and the relationship between them and the Dalai Lamas was seen as that between a patron and a lama—the Emperor was seen as the *yon bdag*, or donor, who gave patronage and protection to the Dalai Lama, who was perceived as the *mchod gnas*, the recipient of offerings who gave religious teachings in return. The Emperor's patronage was expressed by material gifts, by his recognition of the Dalai Lama's title, and by military support whenever it was called for. The importance of those gifts can be seen in the autobiography of the

THE DALAI LAMAS AND THE PANCHEN LAMAS

Although all forms of Buddhism recognize reincarnation, only the Tibetans developed a theory that certain highly achieved spiritual masters, or lamas, voluntarily renounce nirvana so that they can be reborn as a human in order to help others. They also developed techniques, such as visions in divination lakes, tests, and prayers, which are believed to enable the previous lama's followers to identify the right child as the reincarnation of that *trulku* or lama. Such children inherit their predecessor's position and estate.

The longest continuous *trulku* lineage is that of the Karmapa, first recognized in the thirteenth century and now in his seventeenth body. There are at least a thousand *trulku*, or lama, lineages, at least four of which are or were composed only of women. The most famous and influential is that of the Dalai Lamas, which began in the late fourteenth century. The Third Dalai Lama (1543–1588) was the most important spiritual master in the Gelugpa school of Tibetan Buddhism and became well-known in Mongolia as the teacher of Altan Khan, ruler of the Tumed Mongols. When a Mongol army invaded Tibet in 1642, its leader appointed the Fifth Dalai Lama (1617–1682) as the ruler of Tibet, with the Potala Palace in Lhasa as his seat. The Great Fifth, as he was called, was able to create a unified nation and a governmental system that was presided over by his successors, or by their Regents when they were young, for the next 300 years. The Panchen Lamas, first recognized as a *trulku* lineage by the Fifth Dalai Lama in the seventeenth century, were based in Tashilhunpo monastery in Tibet's second largest town, Shigatse, and became the second most famous teachers in the Gelugpa school. The Panchen Lamas and the Dalai Lamas were sometimes tutors to each other, depending on who was older at the time.

In Tibetan, the word "lama" is only used to describe a highly regarded spiritual teacher, but in Chinese it is used incorrectly to refer to any Tibetan monk. English terms like "Lamaism," "Living Buddha," "Living God," "God King," or "Soul Boy," have no equivalent in Tibetan (there is no creator God in Buddhism, and no belief in the soul) and are considered derogatory by many Tibetans.

Fifth Dalai Lama (1617–1682), which includes detailed lists of all gifts offered to him by the Emperors and other potentates. Each letter that the Manchu Emperors sent to the Tibetan rulers, even if it contained instructions that to modern readers appear to indicate superiority, was also accompanied by such a list. "With this decree," wrote the Emperor Daoguang to the Tenth Dalai Lama in 1823, "I am presenting you with a 60-*liang* gold-plated silver container for tea-leaves, a gold-plated silver vase, a large goblet, 30 rolls of assorted silk...in addition to a jade figure of Buddha, a set of bells and sticks, a jade *ruyi*, a chaplet of coral beads, a python-patterned robe, two boxes of fragrant cakes and a pair of padded mattresses."[3] These were just half of the 24 offerings listed in the letter, which had no specific content apart from conveying respect and itemizing gifts.

As the anthropologist Marcel Mauss famously pointed out, gifts are social transactions that are always heavily invested with unstated meanings known to the giver and expected of the recipient. "In theory," he wrote, an act of giving is "voluntary, disinterested and spontaneous" and "the form usually taken is that of the gift generously offered." But in fact, he argued, this is a "pretence and social deception," because behind the formal transaction are notions of "obligation and economic self-interest."[4] Whatever we say to others or tell ourselves, according to Mauss, when we give, we expect something in return. This appears to be even more the case with political gifts, and still more so with those given by one nation to another. The Tibetans certainly understood that they should give something in return for the satin and the silk, and so gave religious respect, charismatic status, and limited forms of obedience to the Qing Emperors, such as asking them to confirm the Tibetans' most senior appointments. In particular, the Fifth Dalai Lama declared—though only after first receiving gifts from the new dynasty in Beijing—that the Qing Emperor was an emanation of the Bodhisattva Jampeyang, known in Sanskrit as Manjushri. This recognition was of major symbolic importance to the Manchus, who some scholars believe may have wanted to recall Manjushri when they had chosen the designation "Manchu" as the new term for their people some thirty years earlier. If we use the concept of tribute to describe China's relations with its peripheries and neighbors, we could call what the Tibetans gave in response to the gifts that they received "soft tribute," since it consisted mostly of intangibles like titles, spiritual empowerments, and deference of a sort. But it was of incalculable value to the Manchu Qing dynasty in its quest for legitimacy, especially in their dealings with Buddhist Inner Asia.

Manchu Views of Tibet

When China had been part of the vast land-based empires run by the Mongol Yuan dynasty (1271–1368) or the Manchu Qing dynasty (1644–1912), Tibet had been seen as both a part of those empires and at the same time as a distinct political entity. There had been no flattening of space or persons that conceived of all the people within those empires as coequal or equivalent, as happens with citizens in a modern nation-state. Traditional leaders in Tibet received imperial orders from time to time, mainly confirmations of appointments, but largely were left to rule as they saw fit. Indeed, the Ming Emperors (1368–1644) seem not to have considered Tibet a part of their domain at all and did not include it in their official maps. From 1720, the Manchu Qing Emperors sent *ambans*, or imperial commissioners, with a small detachment of troops to Lhasa, where they were kept informed of certain kinds of local decisions, such as official appointments and some interactions with foreigners. But otherwise there seems to have been little role for these officials from Beijing (who until the twentieth century were always Mongols or Manchus, never Chinese), and there was certainly no idea among Tibetans that Tibet and China were a single country.[5] The Thirteenth Dalai Lama (1876–1933) declared in an official statement in 1913 that the relationship between Tibet and China "had not been based on the subordination of one to the other,"[6] reflecting a Tibetan view that it was in part a personal tie between charismatic leaders of a kind peculiar to Inner Asian cultures rather than a political tie between countries, and that it related to the Mongol or Manchu empires, which were ruled by Buddhists (and in the latter case by Bodhisattvas), not to China as such. Diplomats and historians from other countries, seeking Western legal terms to describe the Tibet-China relationship, have defined it variously as a form of suzerainty or protectorate, legal terms that mean that during these periods Tibet retained its status as a distinct nation and a separate political entity, although generally it was not in practice a fully independent one.[7]

Like the Tibetans, the Manchu rulers in Beijing did not refer to the status of Tibet in modern terms until just before the twentieth century. Instead, they described it as a "barbarian" (*fan*) region that was part of their "outer dominions" and administered it through a special office, the *Lifanyuan* or "Court of Colonial Affairs," as distinct from the "inner" areas that had been part of China under the Ming and which were administered directly as provinces.[8]

This loose terminology was changed after a British army led by Francis Younghusband invaded Tibet in 1903–1904, supposedly to guarantee British trade rights and to respond to reports of a buildup of Russian weapons in Tibet (the reports were largely invented—after massacring some 3–4,000 Tibetans, the British found just three Russian-made rifles). Younghusband forced the Tibetans to sign a humiliating surrender and then returned with his troops to India within six months, but his escapade impelled the Qing court to formalize its relationship with Tibet and to try to integrate it within China, leading Beijing to send an army to invade Lhasa in 1910 in order to turn the region into a Chinese province. That effort failed because the Qing dynasty and the imperial system in Beijing collapsed in 1912, leaving the Chinese soldiers with no money and no supplies, so that the Tibetans were easily able to rout them and reclaim control.

The failure of the Qing attempt at full annexation in turn led the Thirteenth Dalai Lama, having returned to Lhasa from refuge in British India, to redefine Tibet's status in modern terms by declaring that neither he nor Tibet were subordinate to China. "The Chinese intention of colonizing Tibet under the priest [lama]-patron relationship has faded like a rainbow in the sky," he wrote to the Tibetan people in 1913.[9] Tibet, or at least those parts of it that his government controlled, became a de facto independent country, and all remaining Chinese officials and their dependents were expelled.

The government of the Republic of China (1912–1949) continued to assert its claims over Tibet, using modern terms such as sovereignty and ownership, but was unable even to gain entry to the region for its officials until 1934, let alone to exercise authority. From then until 1950, a few Chinese officials were allowed to reside in Lhasa, but only with the same status as the representatives of Nepal, Bhutan, and Britain. When the Chinese Communist Party came to power in China in 1949, it used the same terminology as the Republic of China had done, claiming Tibet as an integral part of China's sovereign territory.

The "Exceptionalist" Agreement in 1951: The First Gift from the CCP

Echoes of the historical gift relationship between China and Tibet can, however, be detected in many of the CCP's statements and policies even before 1949. In its Jiangxi Constitution of 1931, the new party had spelled out its policy toward Tibetans and other non-Chinese nationalities. These peoples had been promised the ultimate gift: the right to "complete separation from China, and the formation of an independent state" once the party had obtained power. This commitment, partly driven by admiration for Lenin's "accomodationist" approach to nationalities in the Soviet Union,[10] was quietly withdrawn some ten years later before it could be implemented. Recollections of this early, undelivered gift had important consequences, particularly among early Tibetan communists like Baba Phuntsog Wanggyal, once the highest placed Tibetan in the CCP, who was to spend eighteen years in prison for having tried to remind his comrades in 1957 of the Jiangxi promise, long after it had been taken back.[11]

In October 1950, exactly one year and a week after the CCP had come to power, some 40,000 troops of the People's Liberation Army (PLA) invaded Tibet, easily overwhelming the 7,000 or so Tibetan forces at Chamdo near the current border with Sichuan province. Beijing then faced the reality of ruling over a people who had had almost no contact with anything Chinese, let alone communist, and yet were being told by their new rulers that they were not only part of China, but were themselves Chinese.

At that moment Mao made a bold decision that reflected the legacy he had inherited from the Qing: he decided to give Tibetans almost everything they wanted, short of independence. In May 1951, the Tibetan government, having been rebuffed in its efforts to obtain concrete support from Britain, India, or the United Nations, signed a surrender document titled "The Agreement Between the Central Government and the Local Government of Tibet on Measures for the Peaceful Liberation of Tibet," known more usually as the **Seventeen Point Agreement**. This agreement stated that, although Tibet was now part of China, "the central authorities will not alter the existing political system in Tibet [or] the established status, functions and powers of the Dalai Lama" (Article 4). As for "reforms in Tibet, there will be no compulsion on the part of the central authorities" (Article 11), Tibetan officials were to remain in position, and "religious beliefs, customs and habits of the Tibetan people would be respected, and the lamaseries shall be protected" (Article 7). The Chinese Communist Party was not mentioned in the Agreement, and its representatives were to take only an advisory role in Tibet.

This was a policy of exceptionalism, according to which Tibet was to be treated quite differently from the rest of China and given a treaty-like document to confirm its status. It was unlike anything else in Communist history until the arrangement with Hong Kong thirty years later. In return, the Tibetans gave China soft tribute in a strong form: recognition for the first time of China's sovereignty over their territory.

Mao had several reasons to treat Tibet so differently from the rest of China—there were no roads to move supplies and troops, no party members or cells in place, few translators, no experience of working with Tibetans or Tibetan Buddhism, and almost no indigenous calls for social reform, let alone for invasion. He was also cautious because of the international dimensions of the Tibetan issue. The British had had a diplomatic presence in Lhasa from 1936 to 1947, along with Nepal, Sikkim, Bhutan and, later, India. American interest in Tibet had begun to increase following a mission sent in 1943 by the Office of Strategic Services, the predecessor of the Central Intelligence Agency (CIA). American offers of military support in 1951 were rejected as too tentative and unreliable by the Fourteenth Dalai Lama, then in his late teens, and his advisers, but from 1956, the CIA gave covert support to Tibetan resistance forces in Eastern Tibet, airlifting munitions into the region and later giving training to 250 Tibetans, first on the Pacific island of Saipan and then in the Colorado Rockies. About 50 of them were dropped into Tibet, and later the agency equipped some 2,000 Tibetan guerrilla fighters who operated from a base in Nepal (reportedly without the knowledge of the Dalai Lama) until 1974. The history of international interest in Tibet was thus one of several practical reasons why the new Chinese rulers of Tibet initially chose to avoid alienating the existing élite and the middle class in Lhasa, and to treat the region much as the Qing had done a half century earlier, demanding respect and offering gifts, but not interfering in internal affairs. At least on the surface, Mao appeared to be following imperial traditions in his approach to ruling Tibet.

1959: The Policy of Exceptionalism Unravels

From the outset, the Tibet annexation was explained by Chinese officials, especially for its domestic audience, not as non-interference but as "liberation." At the time, this referred not to the freeing of Tibetans from feudal serfdom, the phrase the Chinese used after 1959 to describe traditional Tibetan society, but to freeing them from imperialism, by which was meant British or American interference. The CCP's first substantive dealings with Tibet were thus presented as the gift of being freed from threats of foreign domination. The Tibetans had no reason to consider their limited foreign connections as threats—there were just six Westerners in the country in 1950, and no nation had been offering substantive support to the Tibetans at that time. The only significant request from a Tibetan for China to take over Tibet had come from the Panchen Lama, one of the most important Tibetan religious leaders, but he was then living in exile in China, estranged from the Tibetan government, desperate for Chinese support in his dispute with Lhasa, and just eleven years old at the time. Mao's promise was nevertheless important and persuasive for Tibetans, since it meant that their government and religious institutions would remain intact. That promise was not, however, sustainable, coming as it did from a communist party committed to bringing radical change throughout society.[12] The monasteries and the aristocrats that were the foundation of the traditional Tibetan order would be allowed to survive in the short term, but it was only a matter of time before they would be displaced, once the inevitable socialist transformation began.

There was another contradiction within China's 1950s policy toward Tibet. Mao's policy of exceptionalism was not offered to Tibetans, but only to "Tibet," a place name that in Chinese usage refers only to the area formerly administered directly by Lhasa, the 472,000 square miles that constitute the western half of the Tibetan plateau. The majority of Tibetans live in the eastern part of the Tibetan Plateau (referred to by the Chinese as the Qinghai-Tibetan Plateau). Those areas, some 628,000 square miles lying to the east of the upper Yangtze River, are called Kham and Amdo in Tibetan and are now part of the provinces of Qinghai, southern Gansu, western Sichuan, and the northern tip of Yunnan.[13] The Seventeen Point Agreement had never been intended by Mao to apply to Tibetans who lived in those areas, and there were only short delays before the imposition of socialist policies there. By 1955 a land reform campaign—in effect, armed attacks on the landholding classes, including the monasteries—had begun in the eastern Tibetan areas, leading to widespread resistance, uprisings, and military conflict across the eastern plateau, reaching a climax in 1958.

Most of these Tibetan areas had been separate domains or small principalities, some of which had not been directly ruled by the government of the Dalai Lamas for decades, if not centuries. But Tibetans there had strong cultural and religious links to Lhasa, and it was to that city that thousands fled to avoid the fighting and destruction in the east. The refugees brought with them accounts of the suppression of religion and the bombing of major monasteries. This news helped trigger the Lhasa uprising of March 10, 1959. It was an armed rebellion, with huge popular support, but it was suppressed within a few days by the PLA, which had been expecting such a confrontation for several months. The failed uprising led to the flight of the Dalai Lama and some 80,000 refugees to India, where for several years they struggled to survive in appalling conditions until Indian and Western financial support gradually enabled the exile Tibetan administration to set up orphanages, schools, and agricultural settlements.

The Gift of "Democratic Reform"

Inside Tibet, the Party immediately introduced new policies in March 1959 that marked an end to exceptionalism. It renounced the Seventeen Point Agreement (as did the exiles) and began imposing radical social levelling, which it referred to as "democratic reform" (*minzhu gaige*). It seized land from landlords and monasteries, ended all debts, and disbanded the traditional government, as it had done some four years earlier in Kham and Amdo and in the rest of China. It thus shifted its alliance in Tibet from assuaging the concerns of the élite to promoting the interests of the peasantry. This provided it with a much stronger argument to explain its mission in Tibet. Official newsreel footage at the time shows thousands of farmers burning their debt documents and denouncing their former landlords. The mass ceremonies were partly staged, but certainly there were many people who were deeply grateful for the chance to have their own land and to speak out against whatever suffering they had endured under the previous system. This footage, and its reconstruction in popular Chinese films like the 1963 epic, *Nongnu* (The Serf), the story of a Tibetan serf who is freed from his chains, became extremely influential in China and in other communist and developing countries, presenting apparently indisputable evidence that ordinary Tibetans were overwhelmed with gratitude for the gift of democratic reform. The word used in Chinese documents to describe this dispensation was again "liberation," though it now referred not to freedom from imperialism but to the freeing of the Tibetan peasants from the alleged brutality of feudalism and serfdom.

The new gift, land for the farmers and herders and an end to class privilege, had a hard side too: it was combined with punishment for those who had rejected or undermined the previous gifts, namely liberation from foreign threat and tolerance of the traditional Tibetan system. In a campaign called the "Elimination of the Rebellion," the Chinese military began a sweep across Central Tibet (it was already carrying out armed reprisals in Kham and Amdo), killing or imprisoning those suspected of sympathy for the uprisings, the previous system, Tibetan independence, or opposition to socialism. The Chinese military historian Ji Youquan wrote that some 90,000 Tibetans were killed or wounded in the campaign in Central Tibet alone.[14] Thousands of others who had not been able to reach the safety of India and were suspected of dissent were sent to labor camps, where most died of starvation or abuse. Most of those who survived were not released until twenty years later. Years afterwards, the Tenth Panchen Lama (1938–1989), the highest ranking lama to have remained in Tibet after the Dalai Lama fled, who as a child had asked Mao to invade Tibet, said that 10 to 15 percent of the Tibetans in Qinghai province had been imprisoned for involvement in the rebellions there, and half of those had died in prison.[15] Only a handful of these, he said, had had any involvement in the armed resistance of the 1950s.

In towns and villages throughout Tibet, mass struggle sessions were convened to denounce alleged traitors and counterrevolutionaries. In 1962 the Panchen Lama sent an internal petition, 120 pages long, to Chairman Mao and Premier Zhou Enlai begging them to end the extreme abuses that he had witnessed on a tour of the Tibetan plateau the previous winter. In his appeal he described the effects on Tibetans in Qinghai of the famines created by the Great Leap Forward: "There has been an evident and severe reduction in the present-day Tibetan population [presenting] a great threat to the continued existence of the Tibetan nationality, which is sinking into a state close to death," he wrote.[16] He went on to describe local policies that were decimating Tibetan society and religion, so that he doubted they could survive. He noted that 97 percent of the monasteries in the TAR had been shut down, and 93 percent of monks and nuns had been forced to leave their institutions, and probably made to shed their robes.[17] The report was written four years before the Cultural Revolution began, making it impossible that policies of cultural and religious destruction in Tibet could have been limited to the Cultural Revolution, as most accounts in China and elsewhere suggest. The petition led to the Panchen Lama himself being subjected to struggle sessions in Lhasa every day for two and a half months in 1964, and then to fourteen years in prison or under house arrest.

By the early 1960s, the increases in agricultural production that had resulted from the new techniques introduced by the Chinese were being offset by increasing tax demands on the Tibetan farmers, partly a result of China's loss of aid from the Soviet Union, and partly a result of the introduction of the commune system. For some farmers this meant that the gift of land they had received in 1959 now seemed to have been reversed. In this climate Beijing made another gift to Tibetans in 1965: local autonomy. Tibet was renamed as the TAR, much as had already been done with twelve prefectures and counties in the eastern Tibetan areas. This meant that these areas were allowed to appoint a Tibetan as their governor or chairman and to have a local legislature. However, all decisions, policies, and appointments have to be approved by local and national party officials whose ultimate leaders (often even at the prefectural level) are always Chinese, so the gift of autonomy has remained largely nominal.

The Cultural Revolution in Tibet

The Cultural Revolution, which began in May 1966, made relatively little difference to the former élite in Tibet, most of whom had already been in actual or virtual imprisonment since 1959, but it caused further damage to cultural, intellectual, and religious life in the rest of the society. Again, it was presented as a gift to the people, a term which at that time, as we have seen, referred only to peasants, workers, and soldiers. On this occasion, the gift was freedom from the "Four Olds"—old customs, old culture, old habits, and old ideas—that were presented as a form of oppression. This is now seen as having been an explanation for what was in large part a factional attack by Mao's supporters on officials and cadres within the party who were suspected of disloyalty to Mao. It led to a social leveling and equality that is recalled by some as refreshing, but it came at a huge cost: disrobed clerics, who were supposed to be celibate, were forced to marry; disgraced aristocrats and intellectuals were paraded through the streets; the empty monasteries were pillaged and the buildings wrecked; teachers were paraded in the streets and denounced in ritualistic displays of political violence; schools were disbanded; and literature, art and film production all virtually ceased for ten years, except for a short list of ideologically acceptable items. Only thirteen out of more than a thousand monasteries are said to have been left standing in the TAR by the time the violence was over. No-one had the option of remaining uninvolved in these activities and Tibetans also took part in the destruction and violence of this period, under the leadership of Red Guard teams sent to Tibet from different parts of China.

Within a year the situation had deteriorated into civil war between two Red Guard factions, both led by Chinese, known in Tibet as Nyamdrel (the "Cooperative") and Gyenlok (the "Rebels"). Several small rebellions took place in 1969, leading to killings and fighting in at least a quarter of the rural counties in the TAR. The most famous of these was the Nyemo revolt, led by a charismatic village oracle, the nun Thrinley Choedron. The nun, inspired by visions of Tibetan warriors from ancient epics, called on villagers to ransack local government offices in neighboring villages, slaughtering some fifty Chinese officials and soldiers and mutilating Tibetans deemed to be sympathetic to them. Historians disagree over whether the revolt was a nationalist movement against the Chinese presence in Tibet, a dispute over the failure of officials to distribute resources, or a conflict deliberately incited by Chinese leaders in the Gyenlok faction (the last two factors are described in official documents from the time).[18] As in the rest of China, the army had to be brought in to regain control, and thirty-four leaders of the Nyemo rebellion, including Thrinley Choedron, were captured and executed.

During the Cultural Revolution the Chinese promoted a new kind of leadership among Tibetans: former serfs—not so different in their background from Thrinley Choedron, except that they espoused atheism—were promoted to leading positions throughout the region. There were few other Tibetans whose loyalty to Beijing could be relied upon: no one else benefited from the gift of revolutionary violence and cultural destruction then on offer. Although in China as a whole, all leaders of this cohort were replaced in 1978 or shortly afterwards, in Tibet several of these leaders remained in office until 2000.

The Turning Point

The most violent phase of the Cultural Revolution ended in 1969, but many of its radical policies remained in force throughout China until the death of Mao in 1976, and for some three years longer in Tibet. A turning point came on May 23, 1980, when Hu Yaobang, then general secretary of the CCP and an appointee of Deng Xiaoping, gave a speech in Lhasa that was unique in CCP history. Rather than accusing the Tibetans of ingratitude or foreigners of interference, Hu declared that party policy had failed in the TAR. He accused the Chinese cadres stationed there of having thrown the money entrusted to them by Beijing into the Lhasa river and said that Tibetans should be allowed to run their own region and to practice their own cultural traditions. Most of the Chinese living in the TAR at that time—mainly party or government cadres—were told to hand over their positions to local people and leave the region. Former aristocrats and intellectuals were rehabilitated, and local people were encouraged to wear traditional clothes again. Within a few years, people discovered that they were allowed to rebuild monasteries and temples that had been desecrated or destroyed, and by the end of the next decade over a thousand of these had been restored.

Hu delivered his speech on the anniversary of the signing of the Seventeen Point Agreement in 1951, signaling that Beijing wished to return to the exceptionalist policies of the early 1950s, when Central Tibet had been treated as if it were a truly autonomous area. This time the gift from Beijing was cultural tolerance and Tibetan involvement in the government of the TAR. The beneficiaries included almost the entire society: aristocrats were released from prison, the communes were disbanded, private management of land and herds was allowed again, monasteries and temples were gradually reconstructed, and internal travel and pilgrimage became possible. Tibetan language education was reintroduced, at least in primary schools, and for the first time since the Chinese takeover, foreign tourists were allowed to visit the capital and certain other areas. In the summer of 1985 several thousand Tibetans were even permitted to travel to India to attend an important Buddhist ritual known as the *kalachakra*, conducted by the Dalai Lama. No statement of apology was offered to the eastern Tibetans, who had suffered even longer and rebelled more ferociously than those in the TAR, but they benefited from similar policy relaxations, which were implemented with more commitment and continued much longer than in Lhasa.

Even before Hu Yaobang made his historic apology in Lhasa, Deng Xiaoping had opened talks for the first time since 1959 with the Tibetan exiles. He met with the Dalai Lama's elder brother in Beijing in February 1979 and allowed the first of three exile delegations to visit Tibet to see conditions there the following year, leading to formal negotiations between the two sides in 1982 and 1984. The widespread poverty and desperation the delegates saw and filmed were beyond anything outsiders had envisaged, and almost certainly beyond anything that Deng had been told about: Beijing probably had little idea of the real conditions on the periphery, consistently misinformed by local satraps there. But the introduction of the "household responsibility" system and the restoration of some elements of religious freedom meant that the situation improved extremely rapidly across the entire plateau throughout the 1980s—economically, culturally and politically—just as it did in China proper.

The Collapse of the 1980s Exceptionalism

As economic and cultural conditions improved in Tibet, pressure on Beijing to negotiate with the exiles diminished, and the negotiations collapsed in 1984. By the summer of 1987, there had been no sign of any thaw in relations with the exiles, and Sino-Indian relations had also worsened, leading to serious fighting between India and China along the Tibetan border. That September the Dalai Lama turned for the first time to the West for international support, giving his first political speech in the West at the Capitol in Washington, D.C., in which he presented the Tibet issue for the first time as one of human rights rather than as a call for independence. In Lhasa the party responded with anti–Dalai Lama campaigns and a public sentencing rally in which two Tibetans were sentenced to death. This in turn triggered the first street protests by Tibetans to be seen by foreign tourists, with the result that they made headline news around the world. Although the exiled leader was already signaling a decision to accept local autonomy of some kind within China instead of independence, a position he made explicit one year later and has since maintained, the protestors in Tibet called for independence and for the Chinese to leave Tibet.

The official response in China was that these protests had been instigated by the exiles. But some people—including the Tenth Panchen Lama, who had been released from prison in 1978 and was again the most important Tibetan official remaining in Tibet—said that the protests had been provoked by "leftist" policies introduced in Tibet by hard-liners in the CCP who, angered by Hu Yaobang's liberalization in 1980, wanted to see a much tougher policy on religion and nationalities. The death of the Panchen Lama in January 1989 at the age of fifty left Tibetans without any leading figure with the stature to present this case. It also left China without any intermediary who could speak on its behalf to Tibetans or openly challenge hard-liners. In Lhasa street protests and mass arrests continued off and on for nearly a decade, with many of the detainees being tortured in prison. At least 150 street protests calling for independence took place there during those years, most of them broken up by police within five or ten minutes, with participants getting average sentences of six and a half years in prison. Four were major incidents, involving hundreds and sometimes thousands of laypeople, and in March 1989 one of these continued for three days; it was in response to this event that Hu Jintao imposed martial law on the region, the first time this had happened in China since the People's Republic had been established. An estimated 75 to 100 Tibetans were shot dead during these protests, and about three to four thousand were arrested.

From the perspective of a CCP hard-liner, these developments were similar to what had happened in the 1950s: within eight years of a major gift in the form of political and cultural concessions, Tibetans had rejected Beijing's generosity by rising up and calling for independence, again with vocal support from the Western world. This seemed to indicate that cultural and religious concessions to Tibetans, plus foreign instigation, had led on both occasions to an upsurge in nationalism and unrest. The collapse of the Soviet Union in 1991, which was seen in China as connected to the license given to Soviet nationalities during the liberal Gorbachev era, led this perception to become a major force in Chinese nationality policy. In Tibet the result was a systematic effort to reverse the liberalization policies of the 1980s. The earlier gift was withdrawn.

The Gift of Economic Development

In 1992 a new party secretary was appointed to run the TAR and to introduce these new policies—Chen Kuiyuan, formerly a deputy party leader in Inner Mongolia. Besides escalating the usual repression of political criticism or dissent, Chen set out to identify and truncate the parts of Tibetan culture and religion that he thought fueled "splittism," as the Chinese officials termed efforts to separate Tibet from China. In July 1994 new policies were ratified at a meeting in Beijing called the "Third National Forum on Work in Tibet" and chaired by the party secretary of the CCP, Jiang Zemin. In a ninety-six-page document called "A Golden Bridge to the New Era," the Forum confirmed two major shifts. One was the decision to outlaw worship of the Dalai Lama. After the end of Cultural Revolution, he had been attacked repeatedly for his political views, but his religious status and personal standing had not been questioned. Now photographs and images of him were banned, along with any prayers to him. Everyone in the TAR had to learn slogans deriding him and all monks and nuns were required to undergo three months of "patriotic education" that concluded with them denouncing him in writing as a religious leader.

The policy was extended from the TAR to cover all Tibetan areas in China. Some of the new policies in the TAR were conveyed orally rather than written down, probably because some were illegal under China's constitution: *all* forms of religious practice were outlawed for Tibetans in the government, from janitors upward, for their family members, and for all Tibetan students who were Buddhists. Older scholars with traditional training were retired early, university textbooks on Tibetan history were rewritten to reduce references to religion, and Tibetans who had travelled secretly to India for their educations were banned from working as tour guides or in government-owned companies. Tibetan-medium education in middle schools in the TAR was brought to an end within a year of the meeting in Beijing.

The second, much more visible, shift outlined in the "Golden Bridge" was the decision to marketize the economy and to boost central investment to the region. This had already begun in 1992 in response to Deng Xiaoping's call that spring to reinvigorate economic reform after the post-Tiananmen retrenchment. The number of individually run businesses in the TAR had soared from 489 in 1980 to 41,830 in 1993. The 1994 policy further accelerated and confirmed this approach and promised major investment from inland China. There was an explosion of shops, malls, luxury housing developments, leisure zones, and top-rate transportation facilities. Tibet was given large subsidies in order to develop infrastructure and stimulate urban growth. From 1994 to 2001 the Central Government invested 4.86 billion RMB (over US$670 million) in sixty-two projects in the TAR, and other regions of China gave 3.16 billion RMB (over US$450 million). Subsidies from the Central Government as a proportion of Tibet's gross domestic product (GDP) rose from 46.5 percent in 2000 to 71 percent by the close of 2001. Nearly 95 percent of this investment was directed into state-owned enterprises.[19]

Critics of this economic boom argue that this strategy had structural weaknesses because it was subsidy dependent; it therefore expanded but did not strengthen Tibet's economy. It left Tibetans with tourism as their main source of income, and it limited growth mainly to towns rather than concentrating on enhancing local education, capacity or occupational skills. The central government subsidy program certainly led to development, but it was a kind that worked against the 1980s priorities, which had identified Tibetans and Tibetan culture as the primary beneficiaries of development. Instead, the beneficiaries of the new largesse were anyone in China, particularly Han Chinese. From December 1992 onward, all intra-provincial checkpoints on roads leading to the TAR were closed (making migration into the area by job-seekers easier), cheap loans were announced, business licenses were made easily accessible, numerous spaces were opened up to be rented out as stores, and it was announced that the number of towns in the TAR would increase from 31 to 105 by 2010.[20]

All of these were signals designed to encourage would-be entrepreneurs from China to come to the region. The thousands who came lived mainly in towns or along major roads in Tibet and stayed for only five to ten years, unlike the much larger number of permanent, agricultural Chinese settlers who have repopulated Xinjiang and Mongolia. But the economic and cultural impact of these migrants in Tibetan towns was immense. According to the national census in 2000, of the 223,000 registered inhabitants in the inner Lhasa urban area (the *chengguanqu*), 46 percent of those aged between twenty-five and forty and a fifth of those under fifteen were not Tibetan. In 2007 the regional government, though saying officially that there was no migration to the region, announced the construction of a new suburb in Lhasa in 2009 to house 110,000 people, at the least a 25 percent increase in the city's population.[21]

Party secretary Chen Kuiyuan and other hard-line leaders in the TAR used the economic infusion drive for an internal struggle of their own. They moved to marginalize Tibetan moderates in the party, who until then had argued that because Tibet had "special characteristics," it was entitled to introduce local variations of central policies, as was constitutionally allowed for autonomous regions. In May 1994 the national newspaper of the CCP, the *People's Daily*, made it clear that the party's leaders at national level were backing Chen in his crushing of the moderates:

> Can Tibet remain "special" forever and continue to depend on the state's long-term "blood transfusions"? Is Tibet willing to accept the label of "being special" and stand at the rear of reform and opening up? Backwardness is not terrifying. Being geographically closed is not terrifying. What is terrifying is rigid and conservative thinking and the psychology of idleness.[22]

This meant there was to be no discussion of preferential policies for Tibetans in the economic sphere and no discussion of any regulation of non-Tibetan migration to the region.

The 1994 "Golden Bridge" document defined Tibet policy for the following decade and beyond; it was in effect reconfirmed ten years later. Its symbolism was taken for granted: Tibet may have been granted limited autonomy, but its policies were to be made by Chinese leaders in Beijing and implemented by Chinese officials in Lhasa.

In the years between the Third Forum and the unrest of 2008, more huge subsidies were given to the TAR by Beijing. In 1999 the "Great Western Development" drive (also known as the "Open Up the West" campaign) was announced, leading to major construction in western China, including the $4.2 billion Qinghai-Tibetan railway, further integrating the Tibetan economy with that of China. The economic infusion from the center led to double digit GDP growth in the TAR for fifteen consecutive years from 1993, a high level of infrastructure and telecommunications development, and a great improvement in the quantity and quality of consumer goods available in stores. The salaries of government employees in the TAR, most of whom are Tibetans, surged from 3,459 RMB (a little over US$500) a year in 1992 to 20,112 RMB (nearly US$3,000) in 2001 to become the highest of any province or region in China. A new and wealthy urban Tibetan middle class had been created, but there was much less growth in the income of the majority in the countryside.

In 2005, a new party secretary for the TAR, Zhang Qingli, was appointed, with a mandate to carry out large-scale social programs: 250,000 Tibetan villagers were moved to new houses alongside major roads in the following year alone on the presumption that this would improve their access to the modern economy and thus boost their incomes. In Qinghai and Gansu provinces, officials, in order to protect grasslands from being overgrazed, began to settle 100,000 Tibetan nomads permanently in remote villages, with no clear way to generate income in the future. In 2008, the Sichuan government announced that half a million Tibetan nomads would be made to settle in villages, without their animals and again with no clear way to earn a living.

From Beijing's perspective, this was being done to help Tibetans. Their economy was being developed, their environment was being protected, the rural poor were being moved closer to commercial opportunities in towns, and migrants were being encouraged to come to work in Tibet because "the Tibetan people learn the skills to earn money when a hinterlander makes money in Tibet."[23] By learning Chinese earlier, Tibetans were increasing their employment prospects, and the new construction that replaced traditional buildings provided improvements in facilities and appearance. In many cases, these benefits indeed improved material conditions in the region, much like the silk and satin sent by former Chinese emperors to the Dalai Lamas. But the imperial-era gifts to Tibet had indicated China's respect for the Tibetans' religious leader, whereas the more recent gifts from Beijing were sent to teach modernity to a backward people. They were accompanied by attacks on the Tibetans' religious leader and they encouraged Chinese traders to move into Tibet in significant numbers. The party's gifts were thus not likely to be received with unquestioning gratitude.

Tibet Erupts

On March 10, 2008, the anniversary of the 1959 uprising, three to four hundred monks from Drepung monastery near Lhasa set out to stage a march, the first public political protest in the city for nearly a decade. Four days later, amid rumors that some of the monks had been ill-treated in prison, gangs of Tibetans beat up Chinese migrants in the streets of Lhasa and burned down about a thousand Chinese-owned shops, killing nineteen people. Troops with armored vehicles later took over the city, and, according to claims by the exile Tibetan government, strongly denied by China and still not verified, eighty Tibetans were shot dead.

Within a week over a hundred protests had taken place across the Tibetan Plateau. Beijing insisted that these were coordinated by exiles, but it is just as likely that they were a result of people hearing news of events in Lhasa by cell phone or from Tibetan-language radio broadcasts by the U.S.-funded stations Voice of America and Radio Free Asia. Eighteen or so of these incidents after March 14 involved violence by protestors, mostly against Chinese government buildings, with none against civilians. In at least eleven cases, protestors took over villages and hoisted the forbidden Tibetan national flag, suggesting support for independence. In other cases, protestors called for the Dalai Lama to be allowed to return, a more moderate demand since his objective is "genuine autonomy" in Tibet.

The Chinese press focused only on the riot and the anti-Chinese violence in Lhasa on March 14, while the Western media included the other incidents in its coverage, leading to furious condemnation of western bias by many Chinese critics. In the official Chinese version, Tibetans were seen as hooligans who were jealous of migrant wealth and were stirred up by exile and foreign instigators. The counter-view presented Tibetans of various social sectors and regions as protesting against attacks by the state on their culture and religion, against policies of state-encouraged immigration, and against repeated anti–Dalai Lama campaigns by Beijing. Meanwhile, Tibetan territory was closed to foreign tourists and journalists, and armed troops were posted throughout major towns. That spring, in Europe, the United States and other countries, the Olympic torch relay was received by a series of protests against the crackdown in Tibet as it made its way to Beijing for the 2008 games that autumn. This in turn led to a flurry of counterprotests and hypernationalistic postings on Chinese blogs.

By late 2009, eighteen months after the protests had erupted, little had changed on the ground: troops remained in position on every street corner in the Tibetan quarter of Lhasa as well as in many Tibetan towns across the plateau. An unknown number of Tibetans remained in custody, and two had been executed for burning shops in which people had died. Small protests continued to occur, particularly in Tibetan areas of Sichuan. Foreign tourists were allowed entry only in accompanied tour groups, and foreign journalists were permitted access to Tibet only three or four times a year in large groups with fixed itineraries. No alterations were made to existing policies and no officials are known to have been criticized or replaced because of their policies in Tibet, with China's leaders continuing to say that the protests had been instigated by the exiles rather than a response to any policy excesses. In May 2009, an unofficial group of reform lawyers within China issued a detailed study of social and economic factors behind the unrest, a rare acknowledgment from within China of a Tibetan perspective, although the authors later insisted that they were not questioning the government's view that the primary factor was foreign instigation (the organization, the Open Constitution Initiative, was closed down two months later by the government, supposedly for late payment of tax). One important change, however, was clear: in the spring of 2009, China's leaders openly stated that Tibet was as important as Taiwan in China's international relations, and foreign leaders who planned or held meetings with the Dalai Lama came under increasingly pointed and assertive pressure from Beijing, to the extent that in December 2008 Beijing cancelled a planned summit meeting with the EU because of a meeting between the French President and the Dalai Lama later that month. As in every eruption of unrest since 1950, the Tibetan crisis triggered a highly polarized debate outside Tibet. As before, it was a debate in which the voice of Tibetans inside Tibet was hardly heard.

Conclusion: Unresolved Questions, Persisting Tensions

The story of modern China's interactions with Tibetans is threaded through with instances of violence by the state and aggressive policies, but also with traces of Chinese deference to history, exceptionalism, and gifts. The Cultural Revolution, and much of the decade before it, saw an attempt to destroy or suppress cultural identity, tradition, and religion, but the CCP did not otherwise attempt the total assimilation of Tibetans that the Qing modernizers had planned in 1910. The PRC has so far not implemented suggestions by Mao to promote the mass settlement of millions of Chinese in Tibet, as had been done in other autonomous regions: according to official figures, about 96 percent of the registered population of the TAR remains Tibetan, compared to Inner Mongolia, where only 22 percent of the population are Mongolians, and Xinjiang, where 61 percent of the inhabitants are Uyghurs or other minorities.

The uprisings of the 1950s may have made some CCP leaders wary of relying on military force alone to control Tibetans. Successive Communist leaders tried periodically to treat Tibet as politically exceptional. They sought to secure loyalty through beneficence, offering pale imitations of Manchu ways of managing the area, ending up with the notion—many people would say the fiction—of regional autonomy. This pattern of intermittent concessions is an index of the strategic and political importance of the Tibetan areas to modern China, but it comes with an unstated, deep anxiety about the major challenge presented by Tibetans' memories of their separate history from China's state-building project.

China's efforts at winning over its Tibetan subjects seem thus far to have failed, despite a view among many Chinese that their government has been exceptionally generous to Tibetans. The party's gifts were, however, never likely to succeed; unlike those of the Manchus, the new gifts were accompanied by messages of Chinese prowess and Tibetan backwardness rather than respect for religion and traditional local leaders. Each phase of gift giving has been followed by periods of punishment, and at times the two functions have been carried out simultaneously. Since 1996, for example, the state has provided lavish housing and increased salaries for the Tibetan urban middle class whilst at the same time banning many of them from any form of Buddhist practice.

Apart from the Great Leap Forward and the Cultural Revolution, which were China-wide phenomena rather than responses to events in Tibet, most of the punitive campaigns were Tibet-specific. Some were a response to rebellions or street protests in Tibet, but others, such as those of 1994 and 2006, were imposed at times when there were few if any demonstrations. These crackdowns increased during the later 1990s, with some targeting Tibetans in general, others aimed at Tibetan Buddhists in particular, and few if any directed at Chinese citizens as a whole. They may have been partly due to anxieties in Beijing arising from the Soviet collapse and from the democratic movements in Georgia, Ukraine, and elsewhere, and to fears about the impact of successful exile activism abroad, but for the most part they were reactions to an indistinct sense, often without much evidence, that Tibetans harbored "splittist" plans to unsettle the state. Behind these moves can be detected a culture of distrust or resentment among Chinese officials engendered by the perceived refusal of Tibetans to recognize the generosity of China's gifts.

Should China's policy toward Tibet be considered to be a type of colonialism, the term that the Thirteenth Dalai Lama had used in 1913 to describe Qing rule? Some have argued that colonialism only exists where nations are geographically separate, or where the colonizer is a traditional imperial power that has not itself been colonized in the past, or where a nation extracts more resources from a place than it puts in, none of which are known to apply to Tibet. The most frequently encountered view in China is that Tibet, although remote, is a region within the single Chinese state, and so it cannot be a colony. In many cases, it is also claimed that Tibetans are part of the Chinese race or culture, and so linked by blood or history to the Chinese people. From this perspective, the disparities in power and wealth between Tibet and China are seen as accidents of uneven development; China's East is said to have "advanced" earlier and faster than its West, and the East thus compensates the West when possible, so that, over time, the West will "catch up" with the East and enjoy the same benefits and life-style that it has created. Critics of these views argue that China's administration of Tibet has many of the typical features of colonial rule: there is a permanent military garrison in the subject areas with soldiers of one ethnicity ruling subjects of another; restrictions on local religion, culture, and discussion are much stricter than in the homeland areas; rules and practices apply to members of the subject ethnicity that do not apply to those of the ruling nationality; public explanations by the mother-state stress the benefit brought to the local population by its policies; the presence of migrants and officials from the ruling ethnic group is considered beneficial to local people, presumably because they are assumed to be more advanced in some way; local culture and religion are re-assessed, with the mother-state deciding which cultural practices are unacceptable and which should be allowed.

The deep difference between Chinese and Tibetan views of their relationship is also related to a profound divergence over the primary role of the nation-state. The general Chinese view can be described as statist—it is centred on the pre-eminent importance in people's lives of the modern state, viewed as an impersonal, machine-like institution that strives to benefit the majority of its citizens by distributing goods, enforcing security, and maximizing efficiency and production, thus producing what since 2004 is described in China as social harmony. The other view, which is currently found among many Tibetans and foreigners, can be described as a national view. It sees the nation as the primary representative and source of identity for its people, imagining it as an organic, exclusive collectivity that sustains communality through shared culture, language, memory, and religion. In this view, as Ernest Renan put it, "a nation is a soul, a spiritual principle." [24] This view has no necessary relation to ideas of independence or separate statehood; it will only tend to harden into such a position if it is repressed or ignored. The holder of the statist view thinks typically in terms of numbers, things that can be measured, majorities, social norms, and laws, while the national view is aware primarily of intangibles, heritage, perceptions, and specialness or difference. A test of where people place themselves in this spectrum is to ask who should participate in a referendum on the future of Tibet, something the current Dalai Lama has called for unsuccessfully several times. The nationalists would say that participants should be Tibetans, defined by birth, language, culture or a similar shared feature, while the statists will say that all citizens of China should vote, since it concerns a part of the state of which they are all equal members. Which criterion is used to decide participation—ethnicity or citizenship—will largely determine the outcome of any referendum or consultation exercise on this issue.

A six-year series of talks between Beijing and the Tibetan exiles failed in late 2008, in large part because of these clashing perspectives: the nationalists see an entitlement to special treatment for Tibet for largely cultural and religious reasons, while the statists see Tibetans as having finally been brought by China to levels of prosperity not so much below the rest of the country and therefore not needing change. Additionally, the statists are considering the welfare and sustainability of the larger unit, and are fearful of making concessions toward real autonomy in Tibet that could then be claimed by other groups in China, such as the Uyghurs in Xinjiang. Chinese statists also find it hard to reconcile themselves to accommodating Tibetan religion, or at least the Dalai Lama, either because the idea of a religious leader having political influence is inherently abhorrent to them, or perhaps because it recalls threats to the state posed by religiously inspired rebels such as the Taipings and the Boxers in the late Qing era, or supposedly by the Falun Gong in the late 1990s. Tibetan exiles in turn aggravate many Chinese by accusing the Beijing government of "cultural genocide" and by arranging for Western leaders to meet the Dalai Lama, which is seen as humiliating for China, given his public criticisms of Beijing.

The Dalai Lama was born in 1935, and the chances of a negotiated resolution of the Tibetan issue with him will soon run out of time. Since the party has suppressed the emergence of indigenous leadership within Tibet, there will not be a credible Tibetan leader with whom to negotiate for another thirty years or so, when a new Dalai Lama will reach maturity. By that time there will probably be two Dalai Lamas, since China has already said that it will insist on its own candidate, as it did with the Panchen Lama in 1995. We thus are left with a fundamental paradox. On paper, the Tibet situation should be easy to resolve before time runs out: the Dalai Lama publicly gave up calling for independence in the late 1980s, the exiles have no substantive source of power or leverage, and China's policies in the early 1980s had for a while accepted many of the more practical Tibetan demands. Yet the issue has become increasingly difficult to solve. Until its cycles of gift and retribution in its relations with Tibet are reconsidered by China in a way that takes into account the memories and history of a separate Tibetan nation, China is not likely to receive the "soft tribute"—loyalty to the Chinese state—that it wants to obtain from Tibetans. Meanwhile, Beijing's policies in Tibet remain contradictory and inconclusive, fueling the very nationalism that China's leaders had hoped to extinguish.

Notes

1. "Milestone in Tibet's Reform, Development, and Stability," *People's Daily* (*Renmin Ribao*), July 19, 2001, accessed at http://www.chinahouston.org/news/2001719071430.html. At the Third Forum in 1994 "Jiang underscored the region's importance to all of China and observed that maintaining stability in Tibet

was 'crucial to the success of reforms, development, and stability throughout the country'" (Allen Carlson, *Beijing's Tibet Policy: Securing Sovereignty and Legitimacy*, Policy Studies 4, Washington, DC: East-West Center, 2004, citing "Jiang Zemin on Stability in Tibet," *Xinhua*, July 26, 1994).

2. "Chinese President Stresses Stability, Social Harmony in Tibet," *Xinhua*, March 6, 2008, accessed at http://www.nyconsulate.prchina.org/eng/xw/t412955.htm#. The struggle against separatism is also one of the three primary objectives in China's relations with the Central Asian states through the Shanghai Co-operation Organization. Statements on Xinjiang are somewhat similar: "As the country's front line in battling terrorism and separatism, Xinjiang's anti-terrorism fight is of crucial importance to the stability of the whole country" ("No Let-up in Fight against 'Forces of Terror,'" *China Daily*, March 3, 2008).

3. Huang Wenkun, Liu Xiaodai, and the Editorial Committee, eds., *A Collection of Historical Archives of Tibet* (Compiled by the Archives of the Tibet Autonomous Region), (Beijing: Cultural Relics Publishing House, 1995), item 59–5.

4. Marcel Mauss, *The Gift* (New York: Norton, 1967 [1923]), 1.

5. In Tibetan the words "Rgya" (China) and "Bod" (Tibet) have always denoted separate countries. There was no word that described a China that included Tibet, and in 1951 the Chinese translators at the negotiations over the Seventeen Point Agreement invented a new Tibetan word (Krung go, for Chinese *Zhong guo*) to refer to this, the use of which has since been obligatory in Tibetan publications.

6. Melvyn C. Goldstein, *A History of Modern Tibet, 1913–1951: The Demise of the Lamaist State* (Berkeley: University of California Press, 1989), 60.

7. Until it announced unilateral recognition of China's sovereignty claim to Tibet in October 2008, the British government's position was that "Tibet is autonomous and China has a special position there," a variation of its recognition of China's suzerainty (meaning that it did not have absolute sovereignty) over Tibet in the 1914 Simla Convention and other agreements.

8. Evelyn Rawski, "Presidential Address: Re-envisioning the Qing: The Significance of the Qing Period in Chinese History," *Journal of Asian Studies* 55, no. 4 (1996): 829–850.

9. Goldstein, *A History of Modern Tibet*, 60.

10. Minglang Zhou, *Multilingualism in China: The Politics of Writing Reforms for Minority Languages 1949–2002* (Berlin and New York: Mouton de Gruyter, 2003), 37–38.

11. See Melvyn C. Goldstein, Dawei Sherap, and William R. Siebenschuh. *A Tibetan Revolutionary: The Political Life and Times of Bapa Phüntso Wangye* (Berkeley: University of California Press, 2004).

12. See Chen Jian, "The Tibetan Rebellion of 1959 and China's Changing Relations with India and the Soviet Union," *Journal of Cold War Studies* 8, no. 3 (2006): 54–101.

13. The western half of the former Tibetan province of Kham is now in the TAR. The eastern part of Kham, which is now the western part of Sichuan, was recognized by China as a separate province, Xikang, from 1935 to 1955.

14. Ji Youquan, *Xizang pingpan jishi* (Factual Record of Rebellion Suppression in Tibet) (Lhasa: Xizang Renmin Chubanshe, 1993).

15. "The Panchen Lama's Address to the TAR Standing Committee Meeting of the National People's Congress, 28th March 1987" in *The Panchen Lama Speaks* (Dharamsala, India: Department of Information and International Relations [of the Central Tibetan Administration in exile]).

16. Robert Barnett, ed. *A Poisoned Arrow: The Secret Petition of the 10th Panchen Lama.* (London: Tibet Information Network, 1998), 103.

17. Barnett, *A Poisoned Arrow*, 52.

18. See Melvyn C. Goldstein, Ben Jiao, and Tanzen Lhundrup, *On the Cultural Revolution in Tibet: The Nyemo Incident of 1969* (Berkeley: University of California Press, 2009).

19. Andrew Martin Fischer, *State Growth and Social Exclusion in Tibet* (Copenhagen: Nordic Institute of Asian Studies Press, 2005), 59, 71.

20. "Ninth Five-Year Plan," TAR Government, Lhasa, published in English translation by the BBC *Summary of World Broadcasts*, August 5, 1996.

21. "Lhasa Plans Homes for 110,000," *Xinhua*, November 20, 2007. This article gives the 2007 population of "downtown" Lhasa as around 480,000, about four times the figure in the 2000 census for the inner urban area of the city.

22. Liu Wei and He Guanghua, "Looking at Tibet in a New Light," *People's Daily* (*Renmin Ribao*), Beijing, in Chinese, May 16, 1994, 1, published in translation by the BBC *Summary of World Broadcasts*, May 31, 1994.

23. Speech by Chen Kuiyuan, Tibet People's Broadcasting Station, Lhasa, November 28, 1994, published in translation as "Tibet: Chen Kuiyuan in Qamdo Says Prosperity Will Drive Out Religion," BBC *Summary of World Broadcasts*, December 5, 1994.

24. Ernest Renan, "What Is a Nation?" (1882), in Geoff Eley and Ronald Grigor Suny, eds., *Becoming National: A Reader* (New York: Oxford University Press, 1996), 41–55.

Suggested Readings

Barnett, Robert. *Lhasa: Streets with Memories*. New York: Columbia University Press, 2006.

Fischer, Andrew Martin. *State Growth and Social Exclusion in Tibet*. Copenhagen: NIAS (Nordic Institute of Asian Studies) Press, 2005.

Goldstein, Melvyn C. *A History of Modern Tibet, 1913–1951: The Demise of the Lamaist State*. Berkeley: University of California Press, 1989.

Goldstein, Melvyn C., Dawei Sherap, and William R. Siebenschuh. *A Tibetan Revolutionary: The Political Life and Times of Bapa Phüntso Wangye*. Berkeley: University of California Press, 2004.

Goldstein, Melvyn C., and Cynthia M. Beall. *Nomads of Western Tibet: The Survival of a Way of Life*. Berkeley: University of California, 1990.

Gyatso, Janet, and Hanna Havnevik, eds. *Women in Tibet, Past and Present*. New York: Columbia University Press. 2005.

Khétsun, Tubten. *Memories of Life in Lhasa under Chinese Rule: An Autobiography*. Translated by Matthew Akester. New York: Columbia University Press, 2007.

Knaus, John Kenneth. *Orphans of the Cold War: America and the Tibetan Struggle for Survival*. New York: Public Affairs, 1999.

Rabgey, Tashi, and Tseten Wangchuk Sharlo. 2004. *Sino-Tibetan Dialogue in the Post-Mao Era: Lessons and Prospects* (Policy Studies 12). Washington, DC: East-West Center, Washington.

Sautman, Barry, and June Teufel Dreyer. *Contemporary Tibet: Politics, Development, and Society in a Disputed Region*. Armonk, NY: M. E. Sharpe, 2005.

Shakya, Tsering. *The Dragon in the Land of Snows: A History of Modern Tibet since 1947*. New York: Columbia University Press, 1999.

Schwartz, Ronald D. *Circle of Protest: Political Ritual in the Tibetan Uprising*. New York: Columbia University Press, 1994.

Smith, Warren W., Jr. *China's Tibet? Autonomy or Assimilation*. Lanham, MD: Rowman & Littlefield, 2008.

Virtanen, Riika J., ed., trans. *A Blighted Flower and Other Stories: Portraits of Women in Modern Tibetan Literature*. Dharamsala: Library of Tibetan Works and Archives, 2000.

Wang, Lixiong and Tsering Shakya. *The Struggle for Tibet*. London: Verso, 2006.

15

Xinjiang

Gardner Bovingdon

Once all but unknown to outsiders, **Xinjiang** has recently come to be seen by many as China's second Tibet. The ethnic protests and violence of early July 2009 brought the region, located in the far northwestern part of China, bordering on Central Asia, and home to most of China's 11 million Muslim **Uyghurs**, unprecedented coverage in international media. But Xinjiang began to claim international attention nearly two decades earlier. Sympathetic stories about large protests violently suppressed by the government splashed across U.S. newspaper pages in the 1990s. Those stories were followed in the 2000s by news of large-scale Han Chinese immigration into Xinjiang, forced linguistic assimilation, and the razing of Uyghur neighborhoods. A second set of stories focused on a spate of bombings and assassinations beginning in the 1990s, the nearly two dozen Uyghurs imprisoned by the United States government as suspected terrorists in Guantanamo after 9/11, and the **Eastern Turkistan Islamic Movement (ETIM)**, a small Uyghur separatist group supposedly affiliated with Al Qaeda that the US Government declared to be a terrorist organization in August 2002 (see Box, **The Eastern Turkistan Islamic Movement**). A reader of both kinds of coverage could be forgiven puzzlement: Were Uyghurs freedom fighters, like Tibetans but without a Dalai Lama to lead them? Or were they religious extremists and terrorists, participants in a global jihad?

Chinese officials, and most Han people, believe that Xinjiang is part of China and that Uyghurs are part of the Chinese nation. They are confident that Uyghurs struggling for independence constitute a tiny fraction of the population and lack popular support. Uyghur activists abroad, and many inside Xinjiang, believe that most if not all Uyghurs desire independence, and that Uyghurs constitute a nation of their own rather than a part of the Chinese nation. Many see Xinjiang as a colony of China that must, and one day shall, be an independent state.

Geography and Demography

To understand the political economy of Xinjiang since 1949, it is essential to first note the importance of its geography and cultural diversity. The Xinjiang Uyghur Autonomous Region (XUAR), as it has been called since 1955, is the largest provincial-level unit in the PRC, with one-sixth of the country's total land mass (640, 930 square miles), equal to two-thirds of continental Europe and just a bit smaller than Alaska. The region's vastness

The Eastern Turkistan Islamic Movement (ETIM) is a small, militant organization based in Xinjiang that is seeking an independent Uyghur state called East Turkistan. The ETIM was virtually unknown to the outside world before August 2002, when U.S. Deputy Secretary of State Richard Armitage announced in Beijing that Washington had labeled it a terrorist organization. The United Nations quickly followed with a similar designation.

Critics observed that the timing of the designation was strangely convenient, since Washington was, at the time, seeking Beijing's support for, or at least acquiescence to, a military offensive against Iraq as part of the war on terrorism. Furthermore, most of the published information about ETIM seemed to come from Chinese government sources, about which neutral observers raised serious doubts. The U.S. government claimed to have independent information that two ETIM members had plotted to blow up the U.S. embassy in Bishkek, the capital of Kyrgyzstan. Outside experts raised concerns about this claim as well, since the United States appeared to be the Uyghurs' sole hope for outside support of any kind. American officials claimed that some of the twenty-two Uyghurs apprehended in Afghanistan in 2001 and detained in Guantanamo had belonged to ETIM, though the assertion is controversial. (The revelation that the U.S. military had allowed Chinese interrogators into Guantanamo to question the Uyghur detainees raised strong criticism from members of Congress and also elicited fresh doubts about the quality of any information the questioning might have elicited.) Five of the Uyghur detainees were released in 2006 and were accepted by Albania instead of being sent back to China, where they claimed they would face persecution; in mid-2009, four were sent to live in Bermuda and negotiations were underway to relocate others to the Pacific island of Palau.

Journalists later lent credence to the claim by the United States and Chinese governments that ETIM had received support from Al Qaeda in Afghanistan in the mid-90s, and that some members met with Osama Bin Laden in 1997 and 1999. At the same time they reported that Bin Laden and other Al Qaeda fighters had focused attention on the struggles of Muslims in various Middle Eastern countries and Chechnya, saying nothing about Xinjiang. ETIM members reportedly left these meetings chagrined and discouraged.[*]

Soon after the U.S. designation of ETIM, Chinese officials began to imply in domestic media that Washington regarded all groups seeking an independent "Eastern Turkistan" terrorists, despite American officials' insistence that the government was identifying only the one organization. When in December 2003 Beijing promulgated a list of four Uyghur organizations and ten individuals it considered terrorist, other governments declined to designate them as such.

In the same month of 2003, ETIM leader Hasan Makhsum was killed by Pakistani soldiers in Wazirstan, a mountainous region of northwest Pakistan bordering Afghanistan. Internationally verified evidence of the organization's activities dried up after that. Yet when several Uyghurs drove a truck into a phalanx of Han policemen in Kashgar in summer 2008, Beijing claimed that the attack had been orchestrated by ETIM, although that was never proven.

Chinese officials also later asserted that ETIM had plotted several attacks on the Olympics, all thwarted. Some analysts regarded the "(Eastern) Turkistan Islamic Party" (TIP) as a splinter group that had emerged from the moribund ETIM. The self-styled leader of TIP, "Commander Abdullah Mansour," promulgated a video in summer 2008 claiming responsibility for several explosions in China (a claim denied by Beijing), and issued another video in May 2009 warning governments against extraditing TIP members to

(continued)

THE EASTERN TURKISTAN ISLAMIC MOVEMENT (continued)

China. There was no way to establish the origins of the videos, the validity of the threat, or how substantial an organization Abdullah actually represents.

* David S. Cloud and Ian Johnson, "Friend or Foe: In Post-9/11 World, Chinese Dissidents Pose U.S. Dilemma." *The Wall Street Journal*, August 3, 2004, A1.

is compounded by its geological and climatic extremes. It includes two large cold deserts and four mountain ranges. Summer and winter temperatures can vary by more than one hundred degrees, and annual rainfall in much of the region is a scant six inches. Xinjiang's great size, scarce waterways, and rugged terrain have made transportation unusually difficult for most of its history. But the region is rich in natural resources, which includes 25 percent of the national total of oil and natural gas and 38 percent of the country's coal.[1]

Furthermore, the region has strikingly few inhabitants, given China's enormous population. Roughly 21 million people currently inhabit Xinjiang, giving the region a population density of roughly 12 people per square kilometer (about 31 per square mile), one-tenth the density of China as a whole. But just as China's population density differs widely across the country, with some 90 percent of the citizens living on less than 40 percent of the land, human habitation in Xinjiang is very unevenly distributed. Most of the people in southern Xinjiang are crowded into a string of oases ringing the Taklamakan desert, which are as densely peopled as almost any region in China.[2]

Any would-be ruler seeking to control Xinjiang from afar has faced a fundamental political economic challenge: how to generate enough revenue from a region that is huge, largely desert, sparsely populated, encircled and crisscrossed by high mountains, and remote from any coast, to pay for local administration and satisfy the material wants of its inhabitants. The ethnic and cultural characteristics of those inhabitants have compounded the difficulty for Chinese governors from the Qing dynasty to the present.

For centuries prior to the Qing conquest in the mid-eighteenth century, the vast majority of the population of Xinjiang was Turkic-speaking and Muslim. While members of this majority differed among themselves in lifestyles, customary dress, and dialect, they did not divide themselves or others into ethnonational categories; instead, they identified themselves as inhabitants of particular oases, as settled people or as herders, and as Muslims. Hence it is conventional to refer to the settled Turkic-speaking population of the region prior to the twentieth century simply as Turki. As discussed below, the name "Uyghur" did not come into common use until the late nineteenth century to refer to one part of the region's Turkic population.

The Incorporation of Xinjiang into Qing China

The Qing dynasty Emperor Qianlong conquered the region now known as Xinjiang in 1759, at great expense and after a long, bloody campaign. He did so not principally out of territorial ambition, but in order to rid the Qing empire of threatening Mongol neighbors. Ruling the new colony proved costly and difficult, as will be described in more detail below. In the nineteenth century, prominent Chinese intellectuals urged that the Qing government wash its hands of the region, focusing instead on the empire's vulnerable coast. A competing

Map 3 Xinjiang Uyghur Autonomous Region

group of intellectuals persuaded the emperor instead to commit further resources to ruling and colonizing the region, arguing that it was a crucial bulwark against the loss of Mongolia, and in turn the imperial capital, Beijing.

The Qing government began to promote Han migration into the region from the late eighteenth century, to "fill out the borders" of its colony and help sustain the military garrisons needed to rule the vast territory. By the early 1800s, Hans comprised nearly one-third of the total population of half a million, though they were mainly concentrated in the area north of the Tianshan Mountains, while more than 300,000 Turkis lived mainly in the Tarim Basin south of the mountains. Fearing friction between groups, the Qing initially discouraged Han migration to the Tarim Basin, though after a series of uprisings in the south in the 1830s, Qing administrators came to regard the Muslim population with suspicion and reversed the prior policy, actively encouraging Han farmers to move into the Basin. Although they added to the tax rolls and produced crops to feed the garrisons, the Han migrants could not fundamentally alter the region's desert economy. The huge colony with its legions of imperial soldiers and network of administrators required considerable annual subsidies from the central government.

Despite the soldiers and the sustained largesse, Beijing could not maintain a firm grip on the region. In 1864, a warlord named Ya'qub Beg from Kokand, in what today is Uzbekistan, led a Turki uprising that wrested nearly all of the area from Qing control for more than a decade. Russian generals took advantage of the ensuing chaos to occupy and claim for the Russian empire a strategic swath of territory's northwest. Qing General Zuo Zongtang (immortalized in the "General Tso's Chicken" found in many Chinese restaurants) mounted an expensive expedition in the mid-1870s that reconquered most of the territory, but it took several more years of careful diplomacy to persuade the Russians to return the region it had claimed.[3]

In 1884, the Qing government transformed the colony into a formal province, which they named Xinjiang, meaning "New Frontier," with the hope of placing it beyond the claims and aspirations of the Russian empire. Beijing committed to sponsoring new migrants to rebuild the war-torn province and add to its tax base. But the cost of the reconquest and the late Qing's financial difficulties left the court without resources to promote further immigration. Instead, increasing taxes in Xinjiang actually drove some Han immigrants to return to China proper. One unintended and significant consequence was that substantial numbers of Turkis moved into parts of northern Xinjiang, where they had not previously had large settlements.[4]

Xinjiang under the Republic

In the chaos following the fall of the Qing dynasty and the founding of the Republic of China (ROC) in 1912, Tibet lay beyond Chinese influence, and outer Mongolia was "lost" to formal independence that was, in reality, Russian, then Soviet control. Xinjiang fell under the sway of a series of autocratic Han warlords, the last being General Sheng Shicai, who formed much closer ties in the 1930s with the Soviet Union than with the ROC government. During that decade, many Chinese officials and intellectuals alike argued that it was desperately important for China not to lose Xinjiang. With so much of the former Qing territory gone already, they feared the weakening and even the ultimate disappearance of the country, a worry considerably exacerbated by increasing Japanese encroachment.

The Republican government led by Chiang Kai-shek and the Kuomintang (KMT, or Nationalist) party lacked the capacity to stimulate substantial Han immigration to the region, and attempts by several of Xinjiang's Han warlords to lure migrants by forcing Turkis off farmland and offering it tax-free to Han farmers proved both politically explosive and unsuccessful. By 1940 there were only about 190,000 Han Chinese in Xinjiang, scarcely more than the number in the early 1800s. By contrast, the population of Turkis had grown tenfold to around 3 million.

The cultural identity of that population had also grown more politicized in the intervening decades. As an assertion of cultural pride, some Turki intellectuals in the late nineteenth century began to refer to themselves by the traditional term "Uyghur," and in the mid-1930s the government of Sheng Shicai granted the name official recognition, along with different names for other Turkic groups in the province. Sheng's gesture of "recognizing" distinct groups must have seemed magnanimous to many, particularly in contrast to Chiang Kai-shek's assertion that all the peoples of China came from the same root stock, looking and sounding different only because of regional differences in water and soil; but Sheng made the choice under Soviet influence, and clearly intended to avert the emergence of Pan-Turkism, the specter of which had alarmed Russians for decades. It was no coincidence that the names of the major Turkic groups Sheng recognized in Xinjiang had exact counterparts in Soviet Central Asia.[5]

In the decade before the communist victory in China, Uyghurs settled in the Tarim basin in southern Xinjiang and the Ili River valley in the northwest, made up 80 percent of the provincial population; another 400,000 Turkic-speaking pastoralists, now known as Kazakh and Qirghiz (Kyrgyz), roved the grasslands of the Zunghar Basin in the north and the foothills of the Tianshan and Pamirs. Only 5 percent of Xinjiang's inhabitants were Han, still concentrated mostly in the cities of the North.[6]

When Turkis declared an independent Eastern Turkistan Republic (ETR) in northwestern Xinjiang in 1944, it rattled Kuomintang and Communist leaders alike. Chiang Kai-shek sent one of his ablest generals, Zhang Zhizhong, to negotiate a coalition between ETR leaders and the KMT administration in the provincial capital, Dihua (today's Ürümchi, or Urumqi). Five years later, as the civil war was drawing to a close, Mao Zedong dispatched a trusted subordinate to parley with ETR officials; he also sent the First Field Army to occupy strategic points in the huge province and ensure it not evade the grasp of the Chinese Communist Party (CCP) once it had won national power.

Xinjiang in the PRC

Many Uyghurs had reason to hope that they would enjoy political independence in part or all of Xinjiang after the Chinese civil war. In the late 1940s, Xinjiang's last Han governor under the KMT, Zhang Zhizhong, had speculated publicly about its eventual "decolonization," citing the examples of India and the Philippines.[7] Seeking to outbid the Nationalists and win support among non-Hans for the anti-Japanese war, Mao promised Mongols and Muslims several times in the 1930s that they would be able to decide freely whether to join a federal China under the CCP (explicitly modeled on the Soviet Union) or declare independence.[8] Yet Mao stopped speaking about self-determination in the 1940s, and after the founding of the People's Republic, CCP leaders expected Uyghurs to be satisfied with limited regional autonomy under a unitary Chinese state. This proved particularly unpalatable to individuals who had lived in the Eastern Turkistan Republic (ETR) during the latter half of the 1940s.

As the prospect of true autonomy faded, protests in Xinjiang became increasingly strident. At a 1951 conference in Ghulja, the former seat of government of the ETR, a group of Uyghur leaders proposed the establishment of a "Republic of Uyghurstan" with the capacity to regulate all its internal affairs. Local party officials, on instructions from Beijing, hastily convened a meeting to condemn the proposal and ensure that this "incorrect idea" was not spread widely.[9] It gradually became clear that the premise of the system of autonomy proposed by the CCP had never been the protection of regional political rights, but rather maintaining national unity.[10] This fact was amply demonstrated in the organization of the government, the distribution of power, and the nature of the legal system in the Xinjiang Uyghur Autonomous Region, which was officially established on October 1, 1955.

By law, members of local minorities were to hold the top government positions of all autonomous units, from the regional level to the county. Government personnel were to be recruited from the several ethnic nationalities in proportion to their weight in the unit's total population, though generally slightly favoring non-Hans over Hans. In the first decades of the PRC, tens of thousands of Uyghurs and other non-Hans were recruited into Xinjiang's government. But no corresponding laws mandated proportional representation of groups in the party, and the continued appointment of Han to the most powerful position in the CCP organizations (called the first secretary of the party committee) at all levels in the region came to appear over time not as a temporary aberration but as Beijing's long-term plan. As the reality of strong party control and continued Han dominance set in, many Uyghurs became deeply and increasingly dissatisfied with their lack of political power. It seemed to them that the Xinjiang Uyghur Autonomous Region was neither truly Uyghur nor autonomous.

Han Immigration to Xinjiang

The leaders of the People's Republic of China (PRC) clearly intended to increase the Han presence in Xinjiang shortly after the CCP came to power in 1949. But the crowded oases settlements could not easily accommodate new colonists, and there was worry in Beijing that Uyghurs' mistrust of Han Chinese would be exacerbated if the two groups were forced to live side by side. Uyghurs had come to resent the intrusion of outsiders who did not speak their language or share their faith, and who, moreover, regarded them with suspicion or disdain.

Beginning in 1949, on orders from Chairman Mao, the top party and military official in Xinjiang, Wang Zhen, demobilized over 100,000 soldiers and settled them on a network of paramilitary farms and in small-scale industrial projects throughout the province. The demobilized soldiers were still under the command of the PRC's People's Liberation Army, and military training and preparation were important parts of their routine. In 1954, this network was christened the Xinjiang Production and Construction Corps (XPCC), or as it is commonly called, the ***Bingtuan*** (from the transliteration of the Chinese for the XPCC).[11] The *Bingtuan* was charged with both protecting the region from external incursions and guarding against internal "rebellion" by nationalist Uyghurs. As the organization grew, Wang Zhen chose new sites at strategic points throughout Xinjiang, often outside existing cities or on marginal land. The aim was to implant millions of Han Chinese and at the same time avoid arousing suspicion. The immigrants farmed and worked in isolated, overwhelmingly Han communities, so their presence, even in large numbers, did not immediately compound tensions with Turkic groups. But frictions developed despite the geographic isolation of the respective communities. In 1980, a conflict between Han XPCC members and local Uyghurs precipitated a major riot in the city of Aqsu.[12]

The party also openly encouraged urban youths in Shanghai and other major coastal cities to move to Xinjiang and help "build the borderlands." The millions of Hans who answered the party's call flowed not only to the *Bingtuan* but also into the cities of northern Xinjiang, fundamentally altering the region's demography over time. In 2008 the capital city, Ürümchi, was over 75 percent Han, and the 8.2 million Hans in Xingjiang constituted 40 percent of the autonomous region's total population of roughly 21 million, while the 9.6 million Uyghurs were 46 percent of the total.[13]

Xinjiang's Economic Development

Since the founding of the People's Republic, Beijing has consistently directed economic development in Xinjiang with an eye to integrating it more fully into the national territory. Investment or distributive decisions have generally been linked to central goals rather than local needs. In the first decades of the new state, the party steadily weakened Xinjiang's connections with Central Asia, while simultaneously strengthening the region's links to China Proper. The three pillars of Beijing's economic policy for Xinjiang have been industrial development, expansion of agriculture, and sustained support for the large-scale *Bingtuan* farms.

In the Mao era, the central government funded factory construction to give Xinjiang a modest complement of industrial capacities. Yet considering the region "tactically expendable, if strategically useful," the government declined to create anything either too vulnerable or too useful should the region fall under Soviet control. There were reasons to worry that the Soviet Union might covet the region. First, Stalin had supported the Eastern Turkistan Republic in the 1940s, which Mao saw as a plot to make Xinjiang a nominally independent, Soviet client state after the model of outer Mongolia. The doubling of Soviet forces along the Xinjiang border in the 1960s and a series of Red Army incursions over that decade only increased this concern. Second, Chinese scientists were working to build the PRC's first atomic bomb in Lop Nor, a remote area in southwestern Xinjiang, from the early 1960s.[14] Khrushchev had originally offered to help China build a bomb, but later reneged on the offer as relations between Moscow and Beijing soured. There were credible reports in the late 1960s that the Soviets considered launching an air strike against Lop Nor in order to destroy China's nuclear weapons program.[15]

The economic priorities of the Mao era brought considerable benefits to Xinjiang. Boons to the region included significant growth in gross domestic product (GDP), nascent industrialization, and infrastructure improvements. Planners set up factories for vehicle repair, machinery, cement, and textiles, as well as facilities for exploiting the area's rich natural resources, especially oil and coal. Agricultural output, and particularly the production of commercial crops such as cotton, increased as a consequence of land reclamation and investment in irrigation, fertilizer, and mechanization. Moreover, the party placed an emphasis on hiring large numbers of Uyghurs, Kazakhs, and other non-Hans. To integrate Xinjiang more tightly with China proper the government expanded the network of roads, rail, and airports. Economic growth also brought general, if modest, improvement in living standards. **State-owned enterprises** provided industrial and service jobs in unprecedented numbers. Annual GDP per capita rose from 170 *yuan* in 1952 to 314 in 1960, though it had fallen to 229 by the end of the Mao era in the mid-1970s.[16] All of this development was underwritten by enormous subsidies from Beijing.

The drawbacks of Maoist economic policies in Xinjiang included distorted development and the inefficient use of capital, as with the rest of PRC. Ill-planned and breakneck development also caused environmental degradation. This included soil deterioration, desertification that often outpaced land reclamation by the XPCC, and a drop in the water table. There is some evidence that nuclear fallout from the testing at Lop Nor contaminated groundwater. Also, in emphasizing economic integration with China proper and attempting to guard against Soviet aggression by sealing the border, the government kept Xinjiang isolated from natural markets in Central Asia.

In the post-Mao reform era, the PRC government has invested in industrial concerns that directly serve national interests and reflect Xinjiang's comparative advantage in serving the country's needs. In the 1990s, planners began to speak of Xinjiang's economic future in terms of a strategy of "one black, one white": the black stood for oil, the white for cotton. Thus oil production and petroleum processing have received considerable support, with the goal of exporting the resource to parts of the country where economic expansion has generated almost insatiable demand for energy.

Cotton cultivation in Xinjiang has consistently received both policy and financial support from the central government. In 1998, for instance, Beijing extended a subsidy of 5.5 billion *yuan* to the government of the autonomous region to purchase locally grown cotton at below-market prices, which it could then sell for the market price and reap a considerable profit; the 1998 subsidy was equal to Xinjiang's *entire revenue* in 1997.[17] Xinjiang became the largest cotton producer in the country in the 1990s. As part of the ninth five-year Plan (1996–2000), the government sponsored the movement of hundreds of thousands of spindles used in cotton production from cities on the coast such as Shanghai, Guangdong, and Tianjin to Xinjiang, seeking at once to unite cotton production and weaving in China's northwest and help enterprises on the coast to shift to producing more capital-intensive and high-technology goods. At the same time, the focus on cotton production and textile manufacture in Xinjiang suits the government's regional political goals. The "ultimate explanation" for the CCP's emphasis on cotton and the development of commercial agriculture, one expert writes, is that it helps sustain the influx of enormous numbers of Han immigrants to "reinforce territorial consolidation."[18]

Beijing has also continued to support the *Bingtuan*, an organization that simultaneously serves the developmental, military-strategic, and immigration goals of the central government. In the late 1990s, the *Bingtuan* was separated from any supervision by the People's Liberation Army and was formally designated as a corporation directly accountable to the CCP and to Beijing rather than to the government of the Xinjiang Uyghur Autonomous Region.[19] As of mid-2009, there were more than 2.5 million *Bingtuan* "soldiers" in Xinjiang farms, working on nearly 200 farms and running a vast array of industrial and commercial enterprises, as well as media, educational, and medical institutions.[20] The *Bingtuan* has become the single largest producer of cotton in Xinjiang, and the fourth-largest producer of tomato paste in the world.[21] The transformation of this massive Mao-era highly militarized socialist entity into a profit-making business enterprise in recent decades has been nothing short of astonishing.

By maintaining "one face to the outside world and another domestically"—that is, by operating as a commercial business internationally, under the name "China Xinjian Group" (China New Construction Group) while continuing to sustain some armed militias and large farms—the *Bingtuan* has served the twin aims of Han colonization and regional security much less expensively than the operation of separate self-directed farms and fully military units would have. In the unvarnished language of a self-styled "veteran warrior" in the *Bingtuan*, the purpose of the organization is to ensure that "the whole of Xinjiang's territory is forever surnamed 'Zhong'"—meaning that it remains eternally part of *Zhongguo*, the Chinese term for China.[22]

All in all, the reform era has brought mixed benefits to Xinjiang. The region gained an industrial base and basic transportation network, and saw a substantial rise in GDP. Economic growth also brought about a general improvement in living standards. These were underwritten by enormous continuing subsidies from Beijing, which have regularly provided half of Xinjiang's annual expenditures and reached more than eighteen billion *yuan* (about US$2.2 billion) in 2001.[23]

Agricultural reforms have allowed some Uyghurs (and many Hans) to prosper through specialization. Uyghurs in Turpan and nearby regions profited by cultivating melons and grapes. Uyghur traders prospered, first from internal trade, then from transborder activities. Domestic traders traveled to China's major cities to sell fruits, raisins, walnuts, and shish kebabs. After the borders with Central Asia were reopened in the 1980s, many merchants embarked on the shuttle trade, sending textiles and housewares west and importing steel and other industrial commodities in return. Per capita GDP in Xinjiang has been remarkably high, given the region's geographic and climatic disadvantages. In 2000 it was twelfth among the thirty-one provincial-level units, falling behind only the coastal provinces;[24] by 2007 it stood at fifteenth, slightly below the national average, but still far ahead of all of its inland neighbors except heavily industrialized Inner Mongolia.

At the same time, reform policies have exacted costs for Xinjiang. Reforms of state owned enterprises (SOE) eliminated at least 600,000 jobs between 1995 and 2000.[25] In many cases Uyghurs appear to have been fired before Hans in those enterprises. Hiring patterns in key state industries have been at best discriminatory and often exclusionary.[26] The workforce in Xinjiang's booming oil industry is overwhelmingly Han. Uyghurs have long felt intentionally excluded from the industry. In 1993 Xinjiang Party Secretary Wang Lequan dismissed the charge of bias by claiming dubiously that "all" workers came from oil fields elsewhere in the country, so no locals of any sort were hired.[27] The following year an official in the industry said more candidly that non-Han employees were scarce because "most can't meet the basic standards"[28] due to low levels of education.

Though the state sector has continued to contribute a disproportionate share of regional GDP, private enterprise has expanded dramatically. Uyghurs and other non-Hans have much greater difficulty than Hans in finding jobs in the private sector. Preferential policies still officially in effect have no sway over private organizations. In fact, job advertisements convey the message explicitly or tacitly that Uyghurs are not wanted. For example, some ads call for people natively fluent in Chinese, which excludes most Uyghurs. Staff at university job fairs in the early 1990s made clear to Uyghurs they were not welcome with a curt "We don't want Uyghurs." An official told a foreign researcher in the late 1990s that the Law on Regional Autonomy was "no use" because it put no pressure on private firms to hire non-Hans. The ratio of non-Hans among factory workers in Turpan fell as a consequence.[29] Only days before the July 2009 riots in Ürümchi, the Post Office Hotel in Kashgar, still a predominantly Uyghur city, posted a recruitment sign for various jobs from service workers to administrators, all open only to Hans.[30]

No publicly available statistics on unemployment indicate what proportion of the jobless belong to each ethno-national group, but a Chinese study in 1998 found that one in three rural Uyghurs was underemployed and that half of the population had left many villages in search of work. Other evidence suggests urban Uyghurs face even greater problems finding jobs.[31] Uyghur immigrants to Xinjiang's major cities, such as Ürümchi, Kashgar, and Turpan, often live in poverty and great uncertainty. Early reports on the July 2009 riots in Ürümchi suggested that many of the Uyghur participants were migrants from southern Xinjiang.[32]

As in the rest of China, economic growth has been accompanied by growing inequalities in Xinjiang. For example, in 2007 the oil-producing center of Karamay boasted

98,000 *yuan* (about US$14,000) per capita, and the capital city of Ürümchi, 31,000 *yuan* (about US$4,500). The Khotän region in the southwest, however, earned on average only one-ninth of that (Y3,400, just under US$500). The rural-urban divide in Xinjiang is conspicuous as well: in the same year urban dwellers had a per capita disposable income of 10,313 *yuan* (US$1,500), while the disposable income of the rural population stood at only one-third of that, or 3,183 *yuan* (US$467).

Although it is difficult to establish with accurate figures, there are clearly systematic differences in living standards between Hans and Uyghurs. There are shelves full of published statistical works comparing Uyghur, Han, and other populations on urbanization, gender ratios, age profiles, female fertility, birth and death rates, sectoral employment, and educational attainment. There is not a single statistic comparing incomes among groups. This appears to be a premeditated state policy rather than an inadvertent omission.[33] Officials might well be seeking to avoid publicizing "negative" information that could be used to criticize the government and the system of autonomy. While state-sponsored reports do acknowledge that "real inequalities" persist despite the establishment of "absolute legal equality," they studiously avoid putting numbers to those gaps.

On the other hand, it is easy to find statistics on living standards divided by region, and then to correlate them with population distributions. Uyghurs predominate in the south, and are mostly farmers. Hans are the majority population in the north, and a significant proportion of them live in cities—they comprise over 75 percent of Ürümchi's population of about 2 million, and 94 percent of the population in Shihezi, a *Bingtuan* settlement than has been transformed into a city of over 300,000 people. The visitor to Xinjiang can see immediately that Uyghur farmers in the south live much simpler lives than do Han oil workers or agro-industrial combine workers in the north, and several scholars have remarked on the strong correlation of high incomes and high concentrations of Hans, and low incomes and Uyghur predominance.[34]

Despite the lack of official figures, an economist used regression analysis to tease out systematic differences in incomes from a detailed 1998 sample, finding that each one percent increase in Han population in a district added an increment of 44 *yuan* to per capita income. Thus in two localities with the same ratio of agricultural to non-agricultural production, one that was three-quarters Han had a per capita income of roughly Y7,300 (US$1,070), while in one that was only one-quarter Han, the figure fell to Y5,100 (US$748). The overall economic difference is actually greater since areas where non-Hans predominate depend more heavily on agriculture, which generates less income than industry or commerce.[35] Furthermore, the pattern of state investment in energy exploitation and commercial crop production shows a clear orientation to national rather than regional concerns that certainly has ethnic consequences.

The economic priorities set by officials in the last decade, notably the "one white, one black" approach, appear certain to have left Uyghurs, and much of southern Xinjiang, further behind. With state subsidies, growing cotton is profitable for large mechanized *Bingtuan* farms where Hans predominate, while small-scale Uyghur cultivators have ended up worse off. Those farmers confront very high prices for inputs such as seeds, fertilizer, and fuel, and face volatile market demand and prices. In some cases, it costs more to grow cotton than farmers take in from selling it. Furthermore, cotton is an extraordinarily thirsty crop. Xinjiang's water table has already dropped 60 meters (nearly 200 feet) over the last thirty years, and increasing cotton monoculture will almost certainly cause further damage. Farmers have had to dig deeper and deeper wells, and conflicts over water use have increased. Since so many *Bingtuan* units are situated at the sources of the region's major rivers, the organization has "effective control of [Xinjiang's] surface water."[36]

Uyghurs have also complained that Beijing simply carts off the mineral wealth of Xinjiang without adequate compensation, and rumors abound that even a small surtax on the oil sent inland would make every Uyghur rich. It has been suggested that the huge subsidies Beijing has provided Xinjiang for decades are really "a disguised form of payment" for mineral exploitation at below world market rates set by the central government. In any case, it appears that despite the subsidies and other measures, most of the profits from energy and mineral exploitation in Xinjiang enrich Beijing rather than the region.[37]

It is widely recognized that Uyghurs are as a group less educated than Hans, and that this is a serious disadvantage to finding employment in the modernizing economy. There are numerous reasons for the comparatively low rates of educational attainment and high rates of unemployment among Uyghurs. Many Uyghur families who make a living through farming feel compelled by economic necessity to keep school-age children home to work in the fields.[38] As school fees have risen in the reform era, poorer families may be financially unable to keep their children in school. Poorly funded schools in southern Xinjiang often lack adequate equipment and are unable to attract and retain good teachers. The strong and increasing emphasis on Chinese-language instruction, even in schools with non-Han majorities, may also have deterred parents who hoped their children would grow up with a strong basis in Uyghur language and culture, and may also have discouraged students with little or no facility in Chinese. Finally, the high Uyghur unemployment rate has clearly sent the dispiriting message to many students that even if they work hard, their prospects are poor, leading many to question the ultimate value of education. Uyghur families, particularly those in predominantly agrarian southern Xinjiang, may place less emphasis on education than their Han counterparts. In addition, some Uyghurs are by their own account not interested in jobs with long hours and rigid work discipline as required in factories and other sectors of the modern economy.[39] It is important to acknowledge both the systemic factors and the individual choices here because many Uyghur dissidents and international observers attribute all Uyghur problems to discrimination, unfairly suggesting that the Chinese government has the capacity to change everything with a few policy adjustments.

In sum, there is clear evidence that Uyghurs have fallen behind Hans economically in the reform era, and every reason to believe the gap will widen.[40] While publicly billed as a way to reduce regional and intergroup inequalities,[41] the central government's "Open the West" campaign in the 1990s did not close income gaps, and instead of narrowing the differences between Uyghurs (or non-Hans more generally) and Hans, the initiative appears to have directed most of the benefits of Xinjiang's conspicuous economic growth to Hans. One analyst has argued that the developmental policies applied to Xinjiang "can only be seen as Han economic imperialism."[42]

Political Developments in the 1980s and 1990s

When then CCP General Secretary Hu Yaobang visited Tibet in May 1980, he was horrified to find many Tibetans living in dire poverty and profoundly alienated from the government, despite decades of substantial financial support from Beijing. Hu proposed to remedy both problems by enacting "ample autonomy"; as a first step he ordered that two-thirds of the cadre positions there be filled with Tibetans and a large number of Han cadres be retired or transferred to China proper.[43] After convening a meeting with members of the Xinjiang Party Committee in July 1980, Hu approved a proposal along similar lines, mandating that the party appoint non-Hans as first party secretaries at various levels and stipulating that the ratio of minority cadres in Xinjiang be raised to over 60 percent.[44]

Hu pushed these changes through despite ferocious resistance from Han officials.

In Xinjiang, more than 7,000 Han cadres were transferred to China proper in 1981 alone, and in the early part of the decade all top-ranked Han cadres in the villages of southern Xinjiang reportedly moved to cities or other administrative positions. Some 200,000 Hans left Xinjiang between 1979 and 1993, though new immigration more than replaced that number. At the same time, despite the substantial nativization of party and government in Xinjiang and Tibet in the wake of Hu Yaobang's directives, Beijing continued to select only trusted Han officials as first secretaries of the regional party committees, as it had done with very few exceptions in prior decades.

The liberalization of cultural policies and nativization of administrative ranks under Hu Yaobang pleased many Tibetans and Uyghurs, even if those changes did not extinguish criticism of Beijing. A sizable number of Tibetans reportedly said they "had never had it so good," and Uyghur peasants and traders avowed a satisfaction with the party disconcerting to Uyghur nationalist intellectuals. At the same time, Han cadres in both Xinjiang and Tibet deeply resented Hu, feeling that his policies called their political contributions into question, rewarded local anti-Han prejudice, and threatened the very security of Hans living in the regions.[45] One Han official in Xinjiang reportedly fulminated that the author of these proposals was a "traitor" aiming to "create an East Turkestan... surrendering Xinjiang to the Soviet Union and Turkey."[46]

When a series of major protests rocked Xinjiang in the mid-to-late 1980s, Hu's policies were held responsible. Hu was removed in 1987 as general secretary by Chairman Mao, though the unrest in Xinjiang was only one aspect of his liberal approach to politics that got him into trouble. The generally peaceful demonstrations of the 1980s gave way to more violent ones in the following decade, possibly as a consequence of the prior harsh reprisals. Nearly one hundred Uyghurs staged an armed uprising in Baren, southwestern Xinjiang, in April 1990. In 1992 several buses were bombed in one day in Ürümchi; five Uyghurs were executed for the attack. In 1997, large numbers of Uyghurs marched in the streets of Ghulja to protest against religious and political repression, and after the police responded harshly, the protests turned violent and the police, in turn, suppressed them with brutal force. Shortly afterward, more bus bombings occurred in the region's capital. Hard-liners in Beijing and Ürümchi pointed to violent events in the 1990s as further evidence that the liberal policies had been a mistake. Many of those hard-liners, or their successors, maintain the same perspective today—one reason that Beijing has refused to negotiate with external parties or accommodate local demands.

After Hu's ouster, Xinjiang's leaders reversed the nativization initiative and again promoted the recruitment and retention of Han cadres. The party stepped up calls for Han cadres to work in Xinjiang beginning in the late 1990s.[47] In 1996 the CCP promulgated "Document Number 7," a top secret order for authorities in Ürümchi to "...train a number of minority cadres who can determinedly defend the nation.... At the same time... train a large number of Han cadres who love Xinjiang... and then relocate them to Xinjiang." It also instructed the Autonomous Region's Party Committee to place greater restrictions on religious practices, insist that non-Han officials demonstrate loyalty to country and party or face dismissal, and extend the *Bingtuan* (meaning targeted Han immigration) into Xinjiang's south.[48] The document set the tone for policies in the region for following decade, which combined strong support for economic growth with rigorous political control and intolerance for dissent.

The July 2009 Crisis

The frequency of protests fell dramatically in the early 2000s, and the economy continued to grow at a rapid clip. Nevertheless, Xinjiang remained a contentious place and a political headache for Beijing. The most obvious concern for China's leaders has been to avert the emergence of widespread, sustained ethnic violence. A second concern, with the situation of Tibet in mind, has been to prevent the "internationalization" of the "Xinjiang problem." Both of these concerns became a reality with the outbreak of the riots in Ürümchi in July 2009.

The complete story of the riot and its aftermath will take some time to emerge. Nearly every aspect of the events is controversial: whether it was organized or spontaneous; whether it began with a peaceful protest; when and why it turned violent; how many people were killed, wounded, and arrested; whether the government's heavily armed response provoked or followed the violence; and when and why bands of armed Han Chinese took to the streets several days later.

Most observers agree that the riot was touched off by a brawl that took place in late June in Guangdong province, some 2,000 miles distant from Ürümchi.[49] On June 25, responding to a rumor that several Uyghur men had raped two Han women at the Xuri Toy Factory in the city of Shaoguan—a story later repudiated by one of the women supposedly involved— Han workers stormed a dormitory where Uyghur workers lived. Armed with crude weapons such as iron bars and long knives, the Han workers attacked the occupants indiscriminately. Two Uyghurs were killed and hundreds injured, according to official reports.

On July 5, hundreds of Uyghurs took to the streets of Ürümchi to protest the killings and the government's handling of the episode. Party officials in Beijing and Ürümchi responded to the demonstration as they had to previous such protests. They mobilized police with riot gear and paramilitary forces armed with automatic weapons. The police sought to bring the protest to a halt; People's Armed Police (PAP) forces roved the streets, aiming to stop violent attacks. Either they arrived too late to halt the violence or, according to some reports, they waited several hours to take decisive action while awaiting instructions from Beijing. On July 6 the government shut down Internet and cell phone service and continued to bring PAP forces into Ürümchi.

Chinese government officials announced that 140 people had died in the violence. They quickly claimed to have evidence that **Rebiya Kadeer** (Rabiyä Qadir), president of the World Uyghur Congress (WUC), an international organization headquartered in Germany, had organized and triggered the protest via a series of phone calls to relatives in Ürümchi (see Box, **Rebiya Kadeer**). It also asserted that Rebiya and the WUC had ties to the Eastern Turkistan Islamic Movement (ETIM), the group linked to Al-Qaeda by the United States, though this claim faded over time. Officials later asserted that simultaneous eruption of violence in fifty different sites in the city proved it had been premeditated. They also announced that women in "long Islamic robes and head coverings" had directed the rioters, and that one even distributed clubs.[50] On July 7 bands of Han Chinese roaming the streets with homemade weapons carried out revenge killings, though no casualty figures were made available.

In a departure from previous practice, Beijing invited a group of foreign reporters to Ürümchi to investigate and report on events there firsthand. They were all housed in the Hoi Tak Hotel, which reportedly had the only working Internet connection in the XUAR at the time. At one point a group of journalists walking down a street were accosted by roughly 200 women who demanded that the government release their male relatives detained after the protests. International journalists wrote numerous stories from Ürümchi investigating

A shopkeeper turned millionaire; the mother of eleven children; a delegate to a national-level advisory body to the government of the PRC, later imprisoned in China for "revealing state secrets"; a businesswoman and philanthropist turned independence movement leader; a human rights activist accused by Beijing of supporting terrorism. Rebiya Kadeer (Rabiyä Qadir) is a complex and controversial figure.

Born in 1947 into a poor Uyghur family in Altay in northern Xinjiang, Rebiya entered business in the in late 1970s with a single laundromat. Through a series of increasingly bold ventures she managed to build an international trading company that made her one of the richest people in China by the early 1990s. She used some of her wealth to help other Uyghur women get a start in business through her foundation, the 1,000 Families Mothers Project. In recognition of her achievement, she was appointed to the government advisory body in 1993, and in 1995 was a representative of China at the United Nations Conference on Women in Beijing.

Following large-scale Uyghur protests of early February1997, her husband Sidik Rozi Haji, who had emigrated to the United States, heaped criticism on Chinese policies in Xinjiang. The Communist Party subsequently stripped her of her passport and prevented her from conducting international trade. Rabiyä also spoke critically about Beijing's rule in Xinjiang in her capacity as a delegate in the national advisory body, and was summarily removed from her position. She later sent newspaper clippings to Sidik in the United States. As she prepared to hand a file on Uyghur political prisoners to a U.S. congressional delegation in 1999, police took her into custody, and she was subsequently charged with "revealing state secrets." Sentenced to ten years in prison, she was released and deported in 2005 after strong pressure from Washington.

For years Uyghurs in diaspora had lamented the lack of a leader with the charisma or international stature of the Dalai Lama. When Rabiyä arrived in Washington in 2005, she was quickly touted as the Uyghurs' great new hope. Twice nominated for the Nobel Peace Prize, awarded the Norwegian Rafto Prize (often taken as a harbinger of a future Nobel winner) in 2004, energetic and articulate, she has done much to raise the profile of Uyghur organizations and concerns outside Xinjiang. In 2006 she was elected president of the World Uyghur Congress (WUC), an international organization that claims to represent the interests of Uyghurs in Xinjiang and elsewhere. She has also met with many world leaders, including President George W. Bush, the head of the European Parliament, and UN Secretary Kofi Annan.

At the same time, she has made some embarrassing gaffes and leveled exaggerated charges against Beijing that have damaged her credibility and that of the organizations she heads. After the July 2009 riot she held a press conference during which she presented a picture supposedly showing police cracking down on Uyghur demonstrators; within hours it was revealed to have been an image from an unrelated protest in south China.

Given that the Dalai Lama has been unable to wrest political concessions from Beijing in years of trying, despite his fame and international support, it seems unlikely that Rabiyä will have much impact on politics in Xinjiang. However, if China continues to bring her international attention and sympathy, as it did when it tried unsuccessfully to persuade Australia and Japan to refuse her permission to visit in August 2009, it will only enhance her influence among Xinjiang Uyghurs and globally.

the extent of the violence and trying to clarify the causes. These reports praised the government for being more open to journalists, but also produced graphic evidence of police handling unarmed protestors very roughly, kicking them, striking them with batons, and even punching them in the face. The Han vigilantes drew considerable attention; international media reported the vigilantes did not trust Beijing or local police forces to protect Han residents. The government announced new figures of 156 dead, 123 of them Han Chinese and 33 Uyghur, and over 1,000 wounded, and promulgated news of a curfew from 9 P.M. to 8 A.M.

The violence and tension were serious enough that on July 8, President Hu Jintao returned early from Italy, where he had been scheduled to take part in the G-8 summit. By Friday, July 10, the violence had reportedly stopped; but in the name of avoiding further conflict, the government posted placards announcing that all Ürümchi mosques would be closed for Friday prayers and ordering men to pray at home. Groups of Uyghurs gathered angrily before a number of mosques and the government relented, allowing several to open. On the same day a smaller group of Uyghur protestors took to the streets to demand the release of those who had been detained. Though the protestors were marching peacefully, riot police set upon them with truncheons and fists, an episode captured memorably by BBC video cameras.

From July 11 there were no further reports of violence, though the government announced that over 1,400 people had been detained in connection with the events. With the heavy police presence, the city reportedly became quiet, but remained extremely tense. A month later the government announced it would try some 200 suspects in connection with the riots and that there would be a "drastic increase in security" in preparation for the trials.[51]

The Future of Xinjiang

Chinese leaders have several reasons for wanting to keep Xinjiang part of the PRC. First, Xinjiang represents a large piece of Chinese territory, and the government of the PRC worries that the growth of a separatist movement there might encourage similar trends in Tibet or Taiwan. Second, the region has some of the country's largest remaining reserves of coal, oil, and natural gas. Third, Xinjiang provides a vital link to Central Asia and territories beyond. An oil pipeline connects Xinjiang to the even richer deposits of China's neighbor, Kazakhstan, and Beijing has begun construction of a pipeline from Turkmenistan to tap that country's rich natural gas holdings. From the time of Sino-Soviet split of the 1960s and 1970s until 1991, Xinjiang had an additional kind of importance for Beijing, as a buffer protecting China from the Soviet Union. With the collapse of the Soviet Union and Beijing's successful negotiation of friendly relations with the Central Asian successor states, the fear of a military threat from the region disappeared, although given geopolitical realities in that part of the world, Xinjiang remains a strategically important part of the PRC.

In sum, China would not willingly relinquish control of Xinjiang, and the country has developed sufficient economic, political, and military capacity that neither Uyghurs nor any outside power could force it to do so. Nevertheless, despite the central government's overwhelming tactical advantage, it would be unwise to ignore the signs of deep and pervasive discontent among non-Hans in China's West. For even though they have little chance of gaining independence, as events in Tibet in March 2008 and in Xinjiang in July 2009 have demonstrated, these populations can still cause Beijing difficulties. However much party leaders might wish it, economic growth will not eliminate the discontent, nor will more rigorous political control eliminate the ability of Uyghurs or Tibetans to express it.

Unfortunately, there is little evidence that China's current leadership has contemplated alternatives.

Notes

1. "Xinjiang's Natural Resources," http://www.china.org.cn/english/MATERIAL/139230.htm.
2. Stanley W. Toops, "The Demography of Xinjiang," in *Xinjiang: China's Muslim Borderland*, ed. S. Frederick Starr (Armonk, NY: M. E. Sharpe, 2004), 241–263.
3. James A. Millward, *Beyond the Pass: Economy, Ethnicity, and Empire in Qing Central Asia, 1759–1864* (Stanford, CA: Stanford University Press, 1998), 197.
4. James A. Millward and Nabijan Tursun, "Political History and Strategies of Control, 1884–1997," in Starr, *Xinjiang*, 65–67.
5. James A. Millward, *Eurasian Crossroads: A History of Xinjiang* (New York: Columbia University Press, 2007), 206–210.
6. Toops, "The Demography of Xinjiang," 244–245.
7. Gardner Bovingdon, "The History of the History of Xinjiang," *Twentieth Century China* 26, no. 2 (2001): 95–139.
8. Walker Connor, *The National Question in Marxist-Leninist Theory and Strategy* (Princeton, NJ: Princeton University Press, 1984), 80–81 and chap. 4 *passim*.
9. Zhu Peimin, *Ershi shiji Xinjiang shi yanjiu* (Research on the history of Xinjiang in the 20th century) (Urumci: Xinjiang renmin chubanshe, 2000), 335.
10. Baogang He, "Minority Rights with Chinese Characteristics," in *Multiculturalism in Asia*, ed. Will Kymlicka (Oxford: Oxford University Press, 2005), 68.
11. On the XPCC (*Bingtuan*), see Donald H. McMillen, "Xinjiang and the Production and Construction Corps: A Han Organization in a Non-Han Region," *Australian Journal of Chinese Affairs* (1981), 65–96; James D. Seymour, "Xinjiang's Production and Construction Corps, and the Sinification of Eastern Turkestan," *Inner Asia* 2 (2000): 171–193; Nicholas Becquelin, "Xinjiang in the Nineties," in *The China Journal* 44 (2000): 65–90; Thomas Matthew James Cliff, "Neo Oasis: The Xinjiang Bingtuan in the Twenty-first Century," *Asian Studies Review* 33 (2009) 33: 83–106.
12. Michael Dillon, *Xinjiang: China's Muslim Far Northwest* (London: RoutledgeCurzon, 2004).
13. *Xinjiang 2009 Statistical Yearbook*.
14. See John W. Lewis and Xue Litai, *China Builds the Bomb* (Stanford, CA: Stanford University Press, 1991).
15. See various documents at "The Sino-Soviet Border Conflict, 1969: US Reactions and Diplomatic Maneuvers," A National Security Archive Electronic Briefing Book, William Burr, ed., June 12, 2001, http://www.gwu.edu/ percent7Ensarchiv/NSAEBB/NSAEBB49/. Decades later, it also emerged that in 1964 U.S. president John F. Kennedy had proposed to Khrushchev that the U.S. and the USSR send two bombers to Xinjiang and jointly destroy the nuclear outpost; Khrushchev declined; see Gordon H. Chang, "JFK, China, and the Bomb," *The Journal of American History* 74 (1988): 1287–1310.
16. Calla Weimer, "The Economy of Xinjiang," in *Xinjiang: China's Muslim Borderland*, 169.
17. Becquelin, "Xinjiang in the Nineties": 82–83.
18. Becquelin, "Xinjiang in the Nineties": 83.
19. Cliff, "Neo Oasis": 87–89.
20. "XPCC Transforms Future of Northwest," *China Daily Online*, July 6, 2009, http://www.chinadaily.com.cn/bw/2009–07/06/content_8380510.htm.
21. Millward, *Eurasian Crossroads*, 287.
22. Wang Lixiong, *Wode Xiyu, nide Dong Tu* (My Western Regions, your Eastern Turkestan). (Taibei: Dakuai wenhua chuban gu fen you xian gong si, 2007), 21.
23. David Bachman, "Making Xinjiang Safe for the Han? Contradictions and Ironies of Chinese Governance in China's Northwest," in *Governing China's Multiethnic Frontiers*, ed. Morris Rossabi (Seattle: University of Washington Press, 2004), 172; "History and Development of Xinjiang," PRC Government White Paper, May 2003, http://www.china.org.cn/e-white/20030526/index.htm}.
24. Weimer, 164.
25. Weimer, 179.
26. Becquelin, "Xinjiang in the Nineties" 85, 90.
27. Barry Sautman, "Preferential Policies for Ethnic Minorities in China: The Case of Xinjiang," *Nationalism and Ethnic Politics* 4 (1998): 97. The author met a number of workers in the oil industry between 1995 and 2002 who had grown up in Xinjiang.

28. K. Chen, "Muslims in China Hate Beijing a Bit Less—Recent Economic Gains Temper Calls for Revolt," *Wall Street Journal*, October 21, 1994, A10.

29. Sautman, 97. Government and PCC job advertisements have often noted straightforwardly that most positions were reserved for Han Chinese; see, e.g., http://www.cecc.gov/pages/virtualAcad/index.phpd?showsingle=122703/

30. James Fallows, "No Uighurs Need Apply," http://jamesfallows.theatlantic.com/archives/2009/07/no_uighurs_need_apply.php

31. Nicholas Becquelin, "Staged Development in Xinjiang," *The China Quarterly* (2004): 372.

32. Charles Hutzler, "Income Gaps, Corruption Fuel China riots," *Seattle Times*, July 15, 2009.

33. Such statistics are closely guarded, even in the most peaceful and least politicized of the autonomous regions, such as the Guangxi Zhuang Autonomous Region in southern China. Guangxi officials told a foreign researcher in the 1990s that they were forbidden even to study differences in Han and Zhuang incomes, as the topic was "too sensitive"; Katherine Palmer Kaup, *Creating the Zhuang: Ethnic Politics in China* (Boulder, CO: Lynne Rienner, 2000).

34. Toops, "The Demography of Xinjiang," 261–262.

35. Weimer, 177.

36. Cliff, "Neo Oasis": 272–77. Figure on dropping water table from Eric Hagt "China's Water Policies: Implications for Xinjiang and Kazakhstan," *Central Asia—Caucasus Analyst* (2004), http://www.cacianalyst.org/?q=node/1358.

37. Comment on subsidies as "disguised payments" from Minxin Pei, "Self-Administration and Local Autonomy: Reconciling Conflicting Interests in China" in *The Self-Determination of Peoples: Community, Nation, and State in an Interdependent World,* ed. Wolfgang F, Danspeckgruber (Boulder, CO: Lynne Rienner, 2002), 315–332. For analysis of relative benefits to Xinjiang and Beijing, see Weimer, 174.

38. An official government report acknowledged this problem in 2001. See "Guanyu zhengque renshi he chuli xin xingshi xia Xinjiang minzu wenti de diaocha baogao," *Makesi zhuyi yu xianshi* (February 2001), 34–38. Cited in Becquelin, 'Staged Development in Xinjiang": 358–378.

39. Author's field notes 1997, 2002.

40. Hannum and Xie came to the same conclusion by studying the data from the 1982 and 1990 PRC censuses. They found that, compared with Hans, Uyghurs were overrepresented in agriculture and underrepresented in industry and service sectors, and that these imbalances grew more pronounced over the interval. Given the increasing importance of education to financial success and continuing differences in educational levels across the same period, they projected that inequalities would persist. See Emily Hannum and Yu Xie, "Ethnic Stratification in Northwest China: Occupational Differences between Han Chinese and National Minorities in Xinjiang, 1982–1990," *Demography* 35 (1998): 323–333.

41. Qunjian Tian. "China Develops Its West: Motivation, Strategy and Prospect," *Journal of Contemporary China* 13 (2004): 611–636.

42. Bachman, 156.

43. Melyn C. Goldstein, *The Snow Lion and the Dragon: China, Tibet, and the Dalai Lama* (Berkeley: University of California Press, 1997), 65.

44. Zhu Xiaomin, "Jiefang hou zhi 20 shiji 80 niandai Xinjiang Yily fan fenlie douzheng jiaoxun qianxi" (A preliminary analysis of the lessons from the struggle against separatism in Xinjiang's Ili from the Revolution through the 1980s)," *Zhonggong Yili zhou wei dangxiao xuebao* (2006): 61–63.

45. Zhu Xiaomin, 61–63. Information about Tibet from Tsering W. Shakya, *The Dragon in the Land of Snows: A History of Modern Tibet since 1947* (New York: Columbia University Press, 1999) 400, 410.

46. Cited in Dillon, *Xinjiang: China's Muslim Far Northwest*, 36.

47. Deng Liqun, *Deng Liqun zishu: shi'er ge Chunqiu* (Deng Liqun in his own words: twelve seasons) (1975–1987), Hong Kong: Da Feng chubanshe, 2006), 205–208.

48. CCP Central Committee, "Document #7: Record of the Meeting of the Standing Committee of the Politburo of the Chinese Communist Party Concerning the Maintenance of Stability in Xinjiang." English translation published by Human Rights Watch (1996).

49. The chronology below hews closely to that offered on the BBC web site (http://news.bbc.co.uk/2/hi/asia-pacific/8138866.stm), although it incorporates information from numerous other sources.

50. Barbara Demick, "China Says It Has Evidence Deadly Uighur Uprisings Were Coordinated," *Los Angeles Times*, July 21, 2009.

51. Cai Ke and Lei Xiaoxun, "200 to Face Trial for Day of Carnage," *China Daily*, August 24, 2009, available from http://www.chinadaily.com.cn/china/2009xinjiangriot/2009–08/24/content_8605477.htm.

Suggested Readings

Bovingdon, Gardner. *The Uyghurs: Strangers in Their Own Land*. New York: Columbia University Press, 2010.

Dillon, Michael. *Xinjiang: China's Muslim Far Northwest*. London: RoutledgeCurzon, 2004.

Gladney, Dru C. *Dislocating China: Reflections on Muslims, Minorities, and Other Subaltern Subjects*. Chicago: University of Chicago Press, 2005.

Goodman, David S. G. *China's Campaign to "Open up the West": National, Provincial, and Local Perspectives*. New York: Cambridge University Press, 2004.

Kaltman, Brian. *Under the Heel of the Dragon: Islam, Racism, Crime, and the Uighur in China*. Athens, OH: Ohio University Press, 2007.

Lipman, Jonathan N. *Familiar Strangers: A History of Muslims in Northwest China*. Seattle: University of Washington Press, 1997.

Millward, James A. *Eurasian Crossroads: A History of Xinjiang*. New York: Columbia University Press, 2007.

Rossabi, Morris, ed. *Governing China's Multiethnic Frontiers*. Seattle: University of Washington Press, 2005.

Starr, S. Frederick, ed. *Xinjiang: China's Muslim Borderland*. Armonk, NY: M. E. Sharpe, 2004.

16

Hong Kong

Sonny Shiu-hing Lo

From British Crown Colony to Special Administrative Region of China

Hong Kong, with a total area of a little over 420 square miles (less than a quarter the size of Rhode Island) and a population of about 7 million, became a special administrative region (SAR) of the People's Republic of China (PRC) on July 1, 1997. For about 150 years prior to that it was a colony of Great Britain. The territory became a British possession in three phases after the first Opium War between United Kingdom and the Qing dynasty in 1839–1842. The first phase included Hong Kong island (about 50 square miles), which was ceded to Great Britain in perpetuity according to the terms of the Treaty of Nanjing. Britain also took control in perpetuity of Kowloon (18 square miles) in 1860 as part of the Convention of Peking (Beijing) that ended the **Second Opium War**. In 1898, the largest part of Hong Kong, the New Territories (368 square miles) was *leased* for 99 years from Qing China to the United Kingdom in the Second Convention of Peking (The Convention for the Extension of Hong Kong Territory).

For more than a century, the British government directly governed Hong Kong by sending governors and expatriate civil servants from London and indirectly ruled the territory through the co-optation of local elites, in both the urban and rural areas. The co-optation of Hong Kong's local elites took the form of appointing them to various consultative bodies and conferring upon them honors and titles such as the Members of the British Empire (MBE) and Order of the British Empire (OBE). A **Legislative Council (LegCo)** was established in colonial Hong Kong in 1843, but it always played a subordinate role in the executive-dominant system. Prior to 1985, the governor appointed all members of the Legislative Council.

In 1979, when the British governor of Hong Kong, Sir Murray MacLehose, visited Beijing, the Chinese leader Deng Xiaoping told him that the People's Republic of China would take back Hong Kong by 1997, when the lease on the New Territories between the UK and the Qing dynasty would expire. MacLehose did not inform the people of Hong Kong of this message, but he conveyed Deng's remark that the Hong Kong people should put their hearts at ease about their future.

In 1982, British prime minister Margaret Thatcher visited Beijing and began negotiations with the PRC on Hong Kong's sovereignty. The negotiations got off to a rocky start, but eventually Thatcher made an important concession by exchanging sovereignty over Hong Kong for Beijing's promise of a high degree of autonomy for the territory after the

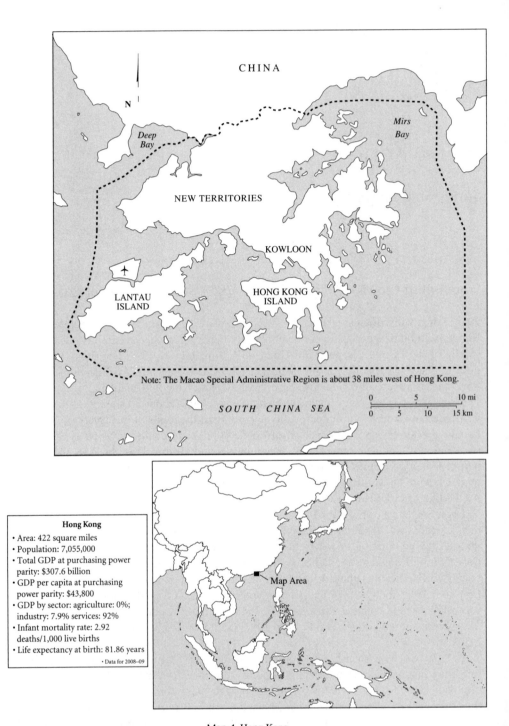

CHINA

N

Deep
Bay

Mirs
Bay

NEW TERRITORIES

KOWLOON

LANTAU
ISLAND

HONG KONG
ISLAND

Note: The Macao Special Administrative Region is about 38 miles west of Hong Kong.

SOUTH CHINA SEA

0	5	10 mi
0	5 10	15 km

Hong Kong

· Area: 422 square miles
· Population: 7,055,000
· Total GDP at purchasing power
  parity: $307.6 billion
· GDP per capita at purchasing
  power parity: $43,800
· GDP by sector: agriculture: 0%;
  industry: 7.9% services: 92%
· Infant mortality rate: 2.92
  deaths/1,000 live births
· Life expectancy at birth: 81.86 years
    · Data for 2008–09

Map Area

Map 4 Hong Kong

British departure. The **Sino-British Joint Declaration** (formally, the Joint Declaration of the Government of the United Kingdom of Great Britain and Northern Ireland and the Government of the People's Republic of China on the Question of Hong Kong) was signed in Beijing in December 1984 and set out the terms for the formal transfer of sovereignty on July 1, 1997.

The Joint Declaration was based on the principle of "**One Country, Two Systems**" for Hong Kong, which was to become a special administrative region (SAR) of the People's Republic of China. This principle meant that, although Chinese sovereignty over Hong Kong would be recognized, Beijing promised that it would not impose socialism or direct communist party-rule on the SAR, and the capitalist system and way of life would not be changed for at least 50 years.

In 1990, the Chinese government promulgated the "**Basic Law**"—a mini-constitution for the Hong Kong Special Administrative Region (HKSAR) based on the "One Country, Two Systems" principle. The Basic Law provided a blueprint for maintaining Hong Kong's legislative, administrative, judicial, social, and economic autonomy under Chinese sovereignty. But it also empowered the Standing Committee of the PRC's National People's Congress to interpret the provisions of the Basic Law, thus giving China final say on all matters related to Hong Kong.

After the British became aware of the Chinese plan to take back the sovereignty of Hong Kong, they decided, rather belatedly in the view of many, to implement political reform in the territory by introducing direct elections to some of the seats in the local advisory bodies called District Boards. In 1985, the British introduced *functional* constituency elections to the Legislative Council. This meant that certain occupational or interest groups, such as business, law, finance, health care, education, labor, and engineering, were to select representatives to the law-making chamber. The main objectives of these elections were to introduce an element of democracy into the Hong Kong legislative process and to encourage political participation by important functional groups.

The British attempted to accelerate democratization in Hong Kong by toying with the idea of introducing directly elected seats from *geographical* constituencies to LegCo in 1987. This would have given all citizens of Hong Kong, not just the members of the designated functional constituencies, at least one vote for a legislator. But because of Beijing's opposition, this was postponed to 1991. As a result of these changes, between 1991 to 1997, more pro-democracy supporters were directly elected to the legislature. Although they did not constitute a majority in LegCo, the PRC government viewed them as a political menace and therefore attempted to apply the brake on democratic reforms in Hong Kong.

However, when the last British governor of Hong Kong, Christopher Patten, arrived in 1992, he was determined to accelerate the pace and scope of democratic reform. Patten also adopted a confrontational approach to dealing with Beijing over political change in Hong Kong. Although his political reform package was approved narrowly by LegCo in 1993, Beijing was determined to thwart his plans. To do so, in 1996, it set up a handpicked Provisional Legislative Council to replace LegCo to handle the transitional matters straddling the period from the July 1, 1997, turnover until new elections were held in 1998.

Despite the efforts of both local supporters of greater democracy and Governor Patten to reform the legislature, the top policy-making body in Hong Kong, the **Executive Council**, was still composed of non-elected elites, including businesspeople and senior civil servants. In the 1980s, the British proposed that some Executive Council members be elected from among LegCo members. This bold idea was, as expected, rejected by the PRC, which wanted to maintain a powerful executive-led government in Hong Kong. Beijing's bottom line was clear: Hong Kong democrats would not be allowed to capture more than half of the seats in LegCo, and LegCo would remain less powerful than the Executive Council.

The judiciary in Hong Kong under British rule was basically independent of any control or interference from the executive, and equality before the law was a strictly observed norm. Moreover, the colonial government was constantly checked by the Independent Commission Against Corruption, which was set up in 1974 to tackle the serious problem of corruption within the bureaucracy and by the Audit Commission, whose findings were often critical of departmental misuse of government funds. Although Hong Kong was not a Western-style democracy where the chief executive was directly elected by citizens through universal suffrage or chosen by a directly elected legislature, it had some of the trappings of a democratic system, including the freedoms of speech, press, and assembly; judicial independence; the rule of law; and internal checks and balances on public maladministration.

Political parties did not emerge in Hong Kong until shortly after the Tiananmen tragedy in China in June 1989. A whole range of political parties, mostly split along pro-Beijing or pro-democracy lines, have been formed since then, but none have been able to capture a majority of seats in the Legislative Council.[1] Since the return of Hong Kong's sovereignty to mainland China in 1997, the major political parties have been the liberal-oriented Democratic Party, the pro-business Liberal Party, the pro-Beijing Democratic Alliance for the Betterment and Progress of Hong Kong (DAB), and the professional-oriented Civic Party.

Traditionally, the Chinese Communist Party (CCP) has operated in Hong Kong in a secretive manner. An underground CCP organization was established in colonial Hong Kong and was under the local supervision of the PRC's New China News Agency (Xinhua), which acted as the public cover for communist activities in the territory. The New China News Agency conducted activities beyond its media functions. It also engaged in intelligence gathering and united front work (i.e., building support for the PRC) targeted at the business, political, professional, grassroots, and religious sectors of Hong Kong society. After sovereignty over Hong Kong reverted to China, an official PRC Liaison Office was established to oversee Beijing's interests in the SAR.

The Basic Law gives responsibility for Hong Kong's defense to the government of the PRC. A 6,000-troop strong garrison of the People's Liberation Army is stationed in the SAR. It plays no active role in local police or security functions, although it does engage in joint exercises and liaison work with the Hong Kong police, for example on matters relating to terrorism. The PLA Hong Kong garrison also has a public relations function for the PRC, and it is generally regarded by Hong Kong people as an important and necessary symbol of national sovereignty.

Hong Kong prospered economically under British rule. It was (and still is) considered to have one of the freest-market economies in the world. In 2008, it had a gross domestic product (GDP) per capita (as purchasing power parity) of $43,800, compared with $47,000 in the United States and $34,200 in Japan. It is one of the world's great financial and commercial centers, and one of the PRC's main concerns in exercising its sovereignty of the HKSAR is to preserve its economic vitality. The population of Hong Kong is about 7 million. (See Box, **Macao: The Other SAR**.)

From Tung to Tsang: The HKSAR's First and Second Chief Executives

The Basic Law of the Hong Kong SAR established the position of **chief executive** to be the head of the government. The chief executive must be a Chinese citizen, at least forty years old, and have lived in Hong Kong for twenty years or more. He or she is elected for a five-year term by an Election Committee that currently consists of 800 members elected or appointed from various sectors of society, such as commerce, finance, labor, the professions, religion, and government. The composition of the Election Committee is closely controlled by Beijing, and the candidate elected has to be approved by the government of the PRC.

The first chief executive of the HKSAR was Tung Chee-Wah, who served from 1997–2005. Tung was a very wealthy shipping industry tycoon with strong ties to the PRC when he was tapped by Beijing to run Hong Kong. Although he was popular when he first took office, his term was quite politically turbulent. Tung's policies included civil service and housing reforms that antagonized many career bureaucrats and the middle class. His civil service reforms included cuts in the number and salaries of civil servants, an increase in the number of principal officials directly appointed by the chief executive, and changes in how government contracts were given to the private sector. Many civil servants who had a vested interest in the status quo inherited from the colonial administration strongly opposed Tung's reform plans.

Tung's housing reforms embraced the idea of expanding the number of residential units built each year, intentionally driving down the sky-high prices on the Hong Kong housing market, but unintentionally affecting the interests of the many in the middle-class who had speculated heavily in the property sector. Tung's reforms also coincided with the start of the Asian financial crisis in 1997–1998, which hit Hong Kong hard and plunged many middle-class citizens into economic difficulties as their assets declined drastically in value.[2]

The controversies stirred by Tung's civil service and housing reforms were compounded by his effort, with Beijing support, in September 2002 to pass and implement a tough anti-subversion law under the terms of **Article 23** of the Basic Law, which deals with the security of the HKSAR. Many SAR citizens felt that security was adequately protected by existing Hong Kong laws governing treason, subversion, and the theft of state secrets; they also feared that the new anti-subversion law, if enacted, would be used to undermine civil liberties in Hong Kong. Many other Hong Kong people believed that additional measures were needed to prevent espionage and subversion aimed against the PRC from occurring in the SAR. Not surprisingly, opposition to the anti-subversion law was strongest among those who identified themselves most closely with Hong Kong, while support for the law was strongest among those who identified with China (see further discussion of the importance of identity in Hong Kong politics below).

The heated political controversy over Article 23 lasted until September 2003, when Tung announced that the so-called National Security (Legislative Provisions) Bill would be withdrawn and not reintroduced until public consultations were held. No timetable for reintroduction of the bill was mentioned. The bill's withdrawal was clearly due to strong public opposition that culminated in protests by half a million citizens on July 1, 2003. Shocked by the massive and unexpected public outcry against the bill, Beijing moved to calm the crisis by setting up a committee led by CCP Politburo member Zeng Qinghong to look into the situation. Nothing further has happened with regard to this matter since then.

To rescue Tung's declining popularity, Beijing decided to introduce two polices that would be beneficial to Hong Kong. One was the Closer Economic Partnership Arrangement (CEPA), which gave preferential treatment to Hong Kong companies that conducted business in the mainland. The other was the Individual Visit Scheme. This allowed individuals from mainland China to visit Hong Kong, whereas previously they had to be part of a tour group. It was hoped that this would stimulate the tourism industry in the HKSAR. Both policies were designed to offset the political alienation toward the PRC that many

Hong Kong people were feeling in the early 2000s. The measures apparently worked well, since public attitudes toward the government and Chief Executive Tung improved after they were implemented.

Nevertheless, in March 2005, Tung tendered his resignation to the central government in Beijing, citing health reasons. Rumors were rife that he had lost the support of China's new leaders, including CCP general secretary and PRC president Hu Jintao and Premier Wen Jiabao. Tung had been supported by the former Chinese leader Jiang Zemin. With the gradual retirement of Jiang from the Chinese political arena in 2002–2003, Tung lost his main patron in Beijing.

Patron-client relations between the Chinese leaders and the HKSAR chief executive persist, and, in fact, are very much a part of Hong Kong's overall political culture. The chief executive is the client who needs the endorsement and support of patrons in Beijing, which confers legitimacy and authority on the Hong Kong leader.[3] Under the chief executive, there are, in turn, a whole range of clients, including the members of the top policy-making body, the Executive Council, the appointed members of various advisory and consultative committees, and influential business and other pro-establishment elites. Friends and followers of the chief executive are rewarded for their support with various favors and preferential treatment.

After Tung Chee-hwa's resignation, Beijing endorsed the British-trained civil servant Donald Tsang (Tsang Yam-kuen) as the new chief executive to serve out the remainder of Tung's term. Tsang had served in a sequence of high-level posts dealing with finance and administration in both the colonial and SAR governments. He was reelected chief executive by the Election Committee on March 25, 2007, with 649 votes compared to 123 for his rival, Alan Leong of the Civic Party. This was the first time in the history of the HKSAR that the chief executive election had a candidate with political party affiliation. Leong's electoral participation was supported by moderate and mainstream democrats. The more radical democrats opposed the highly restricted "small circle election" and regarded Leong's participation as legitimizing an undemocratic electoral process.

Early in his term of office, Donald Tsang steered clear of controversial matters. But since his reelection in 2007, some of his initiatives have become more contentious. The most notable example was his expansion of the Principal Officials Accountability System (POAS), first established by the Tung administration to appoint loyal political supporters as the secretaries in change of important policy areas in the Hong Kong government. The POAS was designed in part to protect the chief executive from being directly criticized for policy mistakes. The appointees also formed a loose coalition that could strengthen the system's legitimacy among important sectors of Hong Kong society. Tung's POAS system handled appointment to all the key positions in the HKSAR government, such as the chief secretary for administration (the second most powerful office) and the secretaries of finance, justice, commerce, industry and manpower, economic development, education, and the environment, health and welfare.[4] These principal officials were hired on contractual terms, unlike civil servants who had permanent employment, and the length of their contract could not exceed the term in office of the chief executive who nominated them for appointment. In other words, they were political, rather than professional appointments.

In the summer of 2008, Donald Tsang expanded the POAS by adding seventeen undersecretaries and political assistants to the list of positions under its authority. But the fact that some of Tsang's appointees were foreign nationals, including those with Singaporean, British, and Canadian citizenship, and their exorbitant salaries aroused immediate public disapproval. Those undersecretaries who held foreign passports quickly renounced their non-Chinese citizenships. But the high salaries of the POAS appointees remained a source of public anger. Overall, the POAS became a patron-client mechanism for rewarding the Tsang's supporters rather than a system of appointing HKSAR principal officials on the basis of their merits and talents. Tsang's expanded POAS has proven to be as controversial as Tung's initial civil service reforms.

Interpreting the Basic Law

Three specific interpretations of the Basic Law by the Standing Committee of the National People's Congress (SCNPC) have been particularly controversial during the Tung and the Tsang administrations.

The first concerned the Basic Law's stipulation on the right of abode of mainland Chinese nationals in Hong Kong, which says that PRC citizens are allowed to live, work, and vote in Hong Kong under certain circumstances. In January 1999, the Court of Final Appeal, the highest judicial authority in Hong Kong, ruled that the right of abode also applied to children of Chinese nationals residing in the SAR. After the ruling, the HKSAR government estimated that 1.67 million mainlanders would flood into the territory and asked the SCNPC to review the matter.[5] In June 1999, the SCNPC overturned the decision of the Court of Final Appeals and allowed the HKSAR to invoke more restrictive measures on the right of abode.

Supporters of the SCNPC interpretation believed that it was necessary to stabilize Hong Kong by stemming the influx of a large number of mainland Chinese, a position, according the public opinion polls, favored by a majority of HKSAR residents. Opponents of the SCNPC ruling argued that it amounted to political interference with judicial independence of the Court of Final Appeal, and that the size of the projected influx of Chinese nationals was an exaggeration. They were most concerned about the implications for the preservation of the rule of law in Hong Kong.

The second interpretation of the Basic Law by the SCNPC that proved controversial in Hong Kong occurred in April 2004, nine months after 500,000 protesters had earlier taken to the streets to protest the Tung administration's effort to legislate Article 23, the anti-subversion law. In the aftermath of the success of those protests, Hong Kong democrats began to press for the direct election by universal suffrage of the chief executive in 2007 and of the entire legislature in 2008. The SCNPC settled the matter by ruling that such elections would violate the Basic Law. This hard line interpretation of the Basic Law coincided with the re-election in Taiwan of President Chen Shui-bian of the pro-independence Democratic Progressive Party (see chapter 16). Clearly, the SCNPC interpretation of the Hong Kong Basic Law reflected Beijing's determination to prevent the "Taiwanization" of HKSAR politics through the introduction of more democratic elections procedures for either the executive or the legislature.

The third controversial SCNPC interpretation of the Basic Law took place in April 2005, a month after Chief Executive Tung's resignation. Some members of the Hong Kong legal community pointed to Article 46 of the Basic Law, which states that the chief executive's term of office is five years, and therefore argued that Tung's successor should serve a full five-year term. Originally, the HKSAR government adopted this legal interpretation; nevertheless, after the HKSAR Secretary for Justice Elsie Leung visited Beijing, the Hong Kong government sided with Beijing's view that Tung's successor should serve only *the remainder* of his term before standing for reelection for a full five-year term, which is how the SCNPC ruled. The PRC was eager to establish the precedent that, in the event of any sudden resignation of the chief executive, they would have time to assess the new leader's performance before committing to a five-year term.

Opponents of each of these three interpretations of the Basic Law by the SCNPC believed they were based more on political considerations than on purely legal grounds. They saw them as a reflection of a worrisome trend away from the legal tradition inherited from the British that emphasized the rule of law over politics and toward the PRC's legal system in which politics can trump the rule of law. The clash between these two fundamentally different legal cultures remains a source of tension and controversy in Hong Kong politics.

Political Reform in Hong Kong

In November 2005, the Tsang government published a document on political reform in the HKSAR. The government's proposals included an expansion of the Election Committee that selects the chief executive from 800 to 1,600 members in 2007. It also proposed that LegCo be expanded to seventy members in 2008, with six elected by Hong Kong's local advisory boards, called District Councils, which are made up of both elected and appointed members. But the reform package did not gain the required two-thirds support of Legislative Councilors when they were presented to LegCo on December 21, 2005. It was rejected by a 34 to 24 vote with one abstention. Pro-democracy legislators opposed the reform proposals because they did not address their demand for the election of the chief executive by universal suffrage in 2012. The HKSAR government tried to lessen the democrats' opposition to its reform package by proposing that the appointed District Councilors would gradually be phased out and replaced by elected members. The democrats rejected this concession, however. This tussle over political reform further deepened the mutual distrust between the democrats and both the Tsang administration and Beijing.

In order to demonstrate to the public that the HKSAR government had not abandoned political reform, in mid-2007, the Tsang administration began a three-month public consultation process on the question of constitutional development in Hong Kong. In December 2007, Tsang submitted a report to Beijing saying that the Hong Kong public generally supported democratization of the electoral process with the eventual goal of universal suffrage in choosing the chief executive and the members of the Legislative Council. Many in Hong Kong wanted this to be implemented in 2012, but others wanted to move more slowly. Tsang concluded that these political reforms would have a greater chance of being accepted by the majority of Hong Kong people if they were set for 2017.

In response to the report, the SCNPC reached a decision on December 29, 2007, stating that the chief executive and the Legislative Council would not be returned by universal suffrage in 2012; that LegCo would retain the half-and-half ratio of members returned from geographical constituencies and functional constituencies in the 2012 elections; and that any amendment to the method of electing the chief executive must be reported to the SCNPC for a approval. This decision appears to pave the way for the possibility of directly electing the chief executive by 2017 and of the legislature by 2020. But the PRC itself will be going through a leadership transition in 2012 when Hu Jintao's term in office expires; it remains to be seen how the new power line-up in Beijing will handle the political situation in Hong Kong.

Identity is a very important factor in Hong Kong politics and is reflected in different views on political reform in the SAR. According to the survey findings of the Hong Kong Transition Project in June 2007, 37 percent of the respondents said they identified themselves primarily as Hong Kong persons, 29 percent saw themselves as Chinese, and 27 percent viewed themselves as Hong Kong Chinese.[6] Those citizens who tend to support the democrats are more likely to identify themselves as Hong Kong persons, whereas those who tend to vote for

Many people do not realize that there is another former colony besides Hong Kong that was returned to Chinese sovereignty and became a special administrative region (SAR) of the People's Republic of China in the late 1990s—Macao, a one-time colony of Portugal on the coast of China, about 37 miles southwest of Hong Kong. It is only 11 square miles in area, and has a population of a little over half a million; but it is one of the most densely populated places in the world. Macao has some similarities to the HKSAR, but also many fundamental historical, political, and economic differences.

The Portuguese first established a presence in Macao in the sixteenth century as a haven for shipwrecked sailors and then as base for trading with imperial China. Portugal gradually extended its activities in and control over Macao, and from the early seventeenth to the mid-nineteenth centuries, Portugal's relations with China were tense and fluctuating, with both sides claiming sovereignty over Macao. In the 1840s, Portugal was able to assert full colonial control over Macao as the Qing dynasty was in its period of rapid decline.

After Portugal became a democracy in 1974, it began to renounce its claims on its colonies. In 1976, China and Portugal agreed that Macao was a Chinese territory under Portuguese administration. The two countries reached agreement in April 1987 on the return of Macao to Chinese sovereignty, which formally took place on December 20, 1999. Beijing wanted to settle the question of Hong Kong's sovereignty before that of Macao.

Like Hong Kong, the Macao SAR has a Basic Law as a mini-constitution that grants it a great deal of autonomy, except in defense and foreign affairs. In all matters, the government of Macao, headed by a chief executive, is subordinate to that of the PRC. Despite one very high-profile corruption case in which a former senior government official was arrested in 2007 and sentenced to a long prison term, the Macao government has been relatively clean.

The SAR's first chief executive, Edmund Ho Hau-wah, a former banker, remained quite popular through his second term, which ended in late 2009. However, there was a mismatch between Ho's ability to lead Macao and the bureaucratic structure underneath him. Although there are signs of improvement, the Macao bureaucracy has been traditionally hierarchical, unresponsive, and slow to react to socioeconomic and political change, reflecting perhaps the persistence of the legacy of Portuguese rather than British colonialism. Edmund Ho was succeeded as Macao's chief executive by Fernando Chui Sai-on, who has a doctorate in public health from the University of Oklahoma.

But, in many ways, Macao's undemocratic but consultative and overwhelmingly pro-establishment political system is more akin to that of the PRC than to its Hong Kong counterpart. Like the HKSAR, the Macao Special Administrative Region (MSAR) has an executive-led administration that dominates the legislature, which also has a majority of pro-government and pro-Beijing members. Political parties only operate before an election and are disbanded afterward. Interest groups are mainly dominated by pro-Beijing trade unions and neighborhood associations. Although there have been some working class protests, civil society in Macao is relatively weak compared to Hong Kong, and its democracy movement is small and ineffective. There is also a lack of an independent mass media critical of the administration.

In March 2009, a tough national security law took effect in Macao after it was approved by an overwhelming majority of members of the Legislative Assembly. Civil society did not rise up against the bill, unlike the Hong Kong case with Article 23 of the Basic Law. In fact, many legal scholars in Macao supported the law. Critics argue that it outlaws ambiguous "preparatory acts" of treason, secession, and subversion—offenses

(continued)

MACAO: THE OTHER SAR (CONTINUED)

that can bring a minimum of three years and a maximum of 25-years imprisonment. Some Hong Kong democracy supporters fear that the enactment of the law is an attempt by the PRC to pave the way for "Macaonizing" the HKSAR in the future. To Beijing, however, its smooth enactment was one of the major achievements of the Edmund Ho administration in Macao.

The most unique thing about Macao is the importance of "**casino capitalism**" in its economy—and therefore in its politics, as well. Macao developed as one of the main gambling havens in East Asia during the Portuguese colonial era. But Macao's casino sector has undergone significant expansion and transformation since the 1990s because of the growth of tourism in South China and the influx of foreign investment in the gambling industry, including huge sums by Las Vegas companies. The Macao SAR is now home to the world's largest casinos, and its gambling revenue now exceeds those of Las Vegas and Atlantic City, New Jersey, combined.

During the 1990s, gang warfare between underground **triad organizations** over access to casino turf, particularly the VIP rooms where rich businesspeople gambled, became commonplace. The arrest in November 1999 and imprisonment of one of the most flamboyant triad bosses helped to decrease the gang violence by sending a strong message that China intended to crack down hard after Macao reverted to Chinese sovereignty.

In mid-2008 Beijing suddenly tightened the number of mainland visitors who were allowed to gamble in Macao, partly because of the need to control money laundering, cross-border crime, and illegal immigration. The central government was also concerned about the vicious competition among casino operators and the danger of an overgrown industry. The retrenchment policy initiated by Beijing and followed by the Ho administration has not really seriously affected gambling proceeds since Macao's casino sector relies much more on gamblers from Hong Kong and elsewhere than on those from the PRC.

the pro-Beijing party in elections are more likely to be Chinese identifiers. Similarly, those people who strongly oppose the SCNPC interpretations of the Basic Law tend to be Hong Kong identifiers, while those who support the SCNPC interpretation tend to have more Chinese identifiers. Moreover, those citizens who tend to support the double direct elections—universal suffrage of the chief executive and the direct election of the whole legislature—are more likely to be Hong Kong identifiers, whereas those who side with a more gradual and piecemeal approach to political reform tend to be Chinese identifiers.

Hong Kong: Semi-Colony or Semi-Democracy?

Under the prevailing situation in which the interpretation of the Basic Law is under the final jurisdiction of the SCNPC, and political reform ultimately depends on the will of the central government in Beijing, it could be said that the Hong Kong political system remains largely semi-colonial. The executive branch is more powerful than the legislature, and even in LegCo, pro-government and pro-Beijing elites can check the influence of the pro-democracy legislators. Advisory bodies and consultative committees are filled through political appointments with the people who favor the go-slow *status quo*, whereas the pro-democracy voices are politically excluded or marginalized.

Political parties remain relatively small and weak in the HKSAR. The largest party is the pro-Beijing Democratic Alliance for the Betterment and Progress of Hong Kong (DAB). The liberal, pro-democracy Democratic Party has suffered a decline in its popularity since the early 2000s, partly because of internal bickering and partly due to the rise of other pro-democracy parties, notably the Civic Party after the 2003 protests against the anti-subversion Article 23 of the Basic Law. The other pro-democracy parties have also been in decline, such as the radical party, The Frontier, and the Association for Democracy and People's Livelihood. The conservative pro-business Liberal Party is widely regarded as politically opportunistic, siding with the government strategically on some policy issues, but opposing it to polish its image to voters. Beijing views the DAB as its closest ally and the Liberal Party as available for political co-optation on some issues. In 2009, the Frontier merged with the Democratic Party and its key members joined the pro-democracy flagship party.

There are important non-party democratic elements in Hong Kong. Interest groups and the mass media, both of which are part of the SAR's strong civil society, are active and influential. In general, business interest groups tend to be far more powerful than the working-class groups because of the nature of the administration. Nevertheless, workers are well-organized and have their interests represented by two rival unions, the pro-Beijing FTU and the pro-democracy CTU. The FTU usually forms an alliance with the pro-Beijing DAB party in Legislative Council and other elections, whereas the CTU constantly supports the democratic camp in elections. Both trade unions compete fiercely for labor support whenever issues affecting working-class rights and interests surface. The CTU tends to mobilize disgruntled workers to protest against the government, but the FTU tries to moderate protests in order to avoid undermining the HKSAR authorities.

All in all, Hong Kong has maintained its long tradition of a lively, independent press. There are some concerns about media self-censorship in Hong Kong when it comes to reporting about political issues, especially by those outlets whose owners eye the lucrative China market and whose editors are the targets of political co-optation or pressure by PRC officials in the HKSAR. But many newspapers and other media sources often voice strong criticism of both the HKSAR and the PRC governments.

Public oversight of the government remains strong in some important regards, perhaps due to the British legacy of having a robust and respected Independent Commission Against Corruption (ICAC). Although the ICAC was plagued by internal management problems before the handover of Hong Kong, its performance remains relatively stable and commands the support of an overwhelming majority of the Hong Kong people. Other mechanisms that provide checks and balances against the abuse of power within the HKSAR political system include the Office of the Ombudsman and the Audit Commission. The ombudsman, who is appointed by the chief executive, serves as a public "watchdog" and handles complaints by individuals or organizations concerning maladministration by government departments and agencies; it also has some investigative powers of its own. The Audit Commission checks the budgets and expenditures of government departments. The HKSAR civil service remains relatively honest, capable, competent, and politically neutral. Although Tung's civil service reform negatively affected the morale of many public servants, Tsang, as a former senior bureaucrat himself, understood the need for stabilizing the civil service and maintaining the confidence of its members.

Overall, it may be said that Hong Kong has elements of both a semi-colonial and a semi-democratic political system. Beijing's strong hand in the executive-led system and the PRC's insistence on exercising its sovereignty over Hong Kong, particularly on matters concerning political reform, certainly limits the SAR's autonomy. On the other hand, there are significant degrees of civil liberties, media freedom, and the rule of law in the HKSAR.

Furthermore, there are also some elections that are highly competitive, and, perhaps most importantly, Hong Kong's civil society remains vibrant and assertive. It will be interesting and important to watch how semi-colonialism and semi-democracy interact in the future to shape Hong Kong's political development.

Notes

1. Suzanne Pepper, *Keeping Democracy at Bay: Hong Kong and the Challenge of Chinese Political Reform* (Lanham: Rowman & Littlefield, 2008), chapter 12.

2. Lo Shiu-hing, *Governing Hong Kong: Legitimacy, Communication and Political Decay* (New York: Nova Science, 2001).

3. Bruce Kwong, "Patron-Client Politics in Hong Kong: A Study of the 2002 and 2005 Chief Executive Elections," *Journal of Contemporary China* 16, no. 52 (2007).

4. Christine Loh and Richard Cullen, "Political Reform in Hong Kong: The Principal Officials Accountability System, The First Year (2002–2003)," *Journal of Contemporary China* 14, no. 42 (February 2005).

5. Sonny Lo, *The Dynamics of Beijing-Hong Kong Relations: A Model for Taiwan?* (Hong Kong: Hong Kong University Press, 2008), chapter 3.

6. Hong Kong Transition Project, "Hong Kong SAR: The First Ten Years after China's Rule," commissioned by the National Democratic Institute for International Affairs, June 2007, 29.

Suggested Readings

The Hong Kong Journal, http://www.hkjournal.org.

Lee, Leo Ou-fan. *City between Worlds: My Hong Kong*. Cambridge, MA: Belknap Press of Harvard University Press, 2008.

Lo, Shiu-hing. *Governing Hong Kong: Legitimacy, Communication and Political Decay*. New York: Nova Science, 2001.

Lo, Sonny Shiu-hing. *Political Change in Macao*. London: Routledge, 2008.

Lo, Sonny. *The Dynamics of Beijing-Hong Kong Relations: A Model for Taiwan*. Hong Kong: Hong Kong University Press, 2008.

Ma, Ngok. *Political Development in Hong Kong: State, Political Society, and Civil Society*. Hong Kong: Hong Kong University Press, 2009.

Manion, Melanie. *Corruption by Design Building Clean Government in Mainland China and Hong Kong*. Cambridge, MA: Harvard University Press, 2004.

Pepper, Suzanne. *Keeping Democracy at Bay: Hong Kong and the Challenge of Chinese Political Reform*. Lanham, MD: Rowman & Littlefield, 2008.

Tsang, Steve. *A Modern History of Hong Kong*. London: I. B. Tauris, 2007

Yee, Herbert. *Macao in Transition: From Colony to Autonomous Region*. London: Palgrave, 1999.

17

Taiwan

Shelley Rigger

In the summer of 2007, young people in Taiwan discovered an online game called "Click Click Click." The game is simple: visit a Web site (www.clickclickclick.com) and click a button. The site credits your click to your country; the winner is the country with the largest number of clicks when the game ends. In the first round of the game, "netizens" from eighty-four countries outclicked Taiwanese; in the next three rounds, Taiwan inched up to fifty-eighth place. Then, in round six, Taiwan caught fire. Taiwan's cyberspace lit up with Web sites and online videos exhorting young people to get on the site and "Click Click Click" for Taiwan. Taiwan leapt to third place, then second, then, in round seven, to first. Taiwanese logged 1.3 *billion* clicks in seven days.

Taiwan is an island of 23 million people; the winning total represented 55 clicks for every man, woman, and child in the country—in a game that few Taiwanese over thirty had ever heard of. How did Taiwan pull off this remarkable feat? And why?

The how is straightforward: once Taiwanese decided to get into the game to win, they launched an all-out assault. They used every available technology—word of mouth, viral video, email, text-messaging—to promote the game. They blanketed the Web with videos and graphics that urged "clickers" on. On the virtual world of the Internet, "Click Click Click" became a war fought by anime-style cartoon girls dressed (barely) in the national flags of the leading countries—Taiwan, Japan, and Hungary. As the competition heated up, amateur programmers built robot programs to run up vast numbers of clicks. When the game sponsor changed its software to stop the bots, Taiwan's programmers developed new ones.

Winning the game turned out to be a matter of human mobilization and technical skill—two things Taiwan is very good at. But why did so many people devote so many hours to an activity that most people would consider utterly pointless?

The "Click Click Click" craze is a testament to the power of fads, no doubt, and a tribute to the technical savvy of Taiwanese youth. But it also reveals a deep desire for international recognition that permeates Taiwan's society.

Taiwan is different from other countries; it is controversial even to *call* it a country. It has a government—democratically elected in free, fair, competitive elections—that makes and enforces laws, collects taxes, and sustains a modern military, but it does not have a seat in the United Nations or an embassy in a major world capital. Newspapers in mainland China refer to its government as the "Taiwan authorities," and put scare quotes around its leaders' titles: "president" Ma Ying-jeou and "premier" Wu Den-yih.

Although it is small geographically and demographically, Taiwan is one of the world's largest economies—it ranks in the top twenty in both gross domestic product (GDP) per capita and total trade and has the world's fourth-largest foreign exchange reserves—but Taiwan's national economic statistics are not reported by the World Bank. It was not until 2009 that it gained participant—not member—status in the World Health Organization, under the name "Chinese Taipei," and it is forbidden to join international agreements (it complies voluntarily with many conventions, even though it is denied the benefits of participation). The leading U.S. high tech companies depend on Taiwanese firms for engineering and manufacturing services, but a Taiwanese political leader can set foot in the United States only if he or she is on an approved stopover en route to another destination. Even the *CIA World Factbook* lists Taiwan in a special category, alongside the European Union.

Isolation makes Taiwanese work overtime to remind the world that "we are here." Their efforts range from the "Click Click Click" wars to the Taiwan government's quixotic campaign for UN participation—an effort that is now in its second fruitless decade.

Taiwan's exclusion from the world community is a product of history, but it is sustained and reinforced by the PRC government's unrelenting determination to deny the island international recognition. Its position is that Taiwan is part of China, and since the People's Republic of China (PRC) is the legal government of China, Taiwan's international representation should be channeled through Beijing. Although the PRC party-state has never governed Taiwan, its National People's Congress includes deputies claiming to represent the island, and Beijing requires international organizations to secure its permission before conducting any business regarding Taiwan. China calls this "exercising sovereignty"; Taiwanese call it "diplomatic strangulation."

Taiwan's unique international position makes it a fascinating place to study, while its complex relationships with the world's major powers make it an important geo-strategic player. It also is an economic powerhouse whose influence far exceeds its size. And it is an intriguing case for students of politics: a culturally-Chinese society that overcame colonization and authoritarianism to create a free-wheeling liberal democracy.

Taiwan to 1945

Taiwan is a volcanic island about 120 kilometers (75 miles) off the coast of southeastern China. At just under 36,000 square kilometers (13,892 square miles) in area, it is larger than Belgium, but smaller than Switzerland. From the perspective of comparative islands, Taiwan is about 15 percent the size of Britain. The island is mountainous, with peaks up to 4,000 meters (13,100 feet). Most of Taiwan's population lives on a broad plain on the west coast and in the northwestern basin where the capital, Taipei, is located. On the northeast coast, the mountains plunge straight into the sea; the southeastern plain is narrow and remote. With high mountains occupying most of the island, Taiwan's inhabited area is among the most densely-populated places in the world.

Four thousand years ago, Austronesian-speaking settlers from other Western Pacific islands began living in Taiwan. Their descendants, who belong to more than a dozen distinct groups, are collectively referred to as Taiwan's Aboriginal people. There are about 450,000 Aboriginal people living in Taiwan today.

Beginning in the sixteenth century, the Aboriginal people were joined by settlers from mainland China. Most came from Fujian, the Chinese province directly across the **Taiwan Strait**, the part of the Pacific Ocean that separates the island from the mainland. Eventually, the Aboriginal people living along the western plain were either assimilated or displaced,

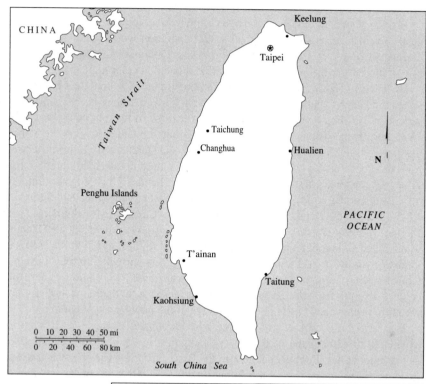

CHINA

Keelung

⊛ Taipei

Taiwan Strait

Taichung

Changhua

Hualien

N

Penghu Islands

PACIFIC
OCEAN

T'ainan

Taitung

Kaohsiung

0	10	20	30	40	50 mi
0	20	40	60	80 km	

South China Sea

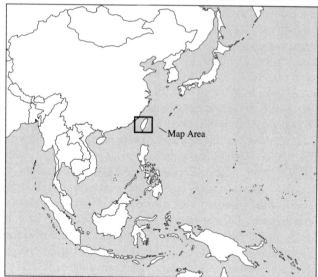

Taiwan

- Area: 13,892 sq. mi.
- Population: 22,975,000
- Ethnic groups: Taiwanese 84%,
  mainland Chinese 14%, indigenous 2%
- Total GDP at purchasing power
  parity: $738.8 billion
- GDP per capita at purchasing power
  parity: $31,900
- GDP by sector: agriculture: 1.5%;
  industry: 27.8% services: 70.7%
- Infant mortality rate: 5.35 deaths/1,000
  live births
- Life expectancy at birth: 77.96 years

• Data for 2008–09

Map Area

Map 5 Taiwan

and the region sprouted stable communities of Chinese migrants. In the mid-1500s, a passenger on a Portuguese ship passing by Taiwan called the island "Ilha Formosa," or beautiful island, giving it a name Europeans used for centuries.

In 1623, Dutch traders established a commercial colony in southwestern Taiwan. In the north, Spanish colonists launched a parallel operation with forts at Tamsui and Keelung. The local Chinese called the Spanish fort of San Domingo the "Red Hair Fort" in recognition of the Europeans' extraordinary hairiness and odd coloration.

In the early 1600s, the pirate Zheng Zhilong operated a large fleet in the Taiwan Strait. When the Dutch expelled him from his base in Taiwan, Zheng put his pirate armada in the service of the Ming empire. The Ming was overthrown and replaced by the Qing dynasty in 1644, but Zheng Zhilong's son, Zheng Chenggong, remained loyal to the Ming. Acting in the name of the Ming, Zheng Chenggong drove the Dutch out of Taiwan. He used his naval forces to keep Taiwan out of Qing hands for two more decades, but in 1683, forces led by Zheng Chenggong's grandson fell to defeat at the hands of the Qing admiral Shi Lang.

This historical episode bears uncanny parallels to events four hundred years later. In 1945, forces of the Republic of China (ROC) under Chiang Kai-shek took the island from a foreign colonizer (Japan). Within a few years, a new government (the PRC) came to power in mainland China, but Taiwan's leaders remained faithful to the ROC. Under the Chiang family "dynasty" until the late 1980s, ROC loyalists struggled to recapture the mainland while resisting Communist efforts to bring Taiwan under PRC control. Where the twentieth century diverges from the seventeenth is in the absence (to date) of a modern-day Shi Lang who brings the island back under the control of the mainland government.

Between these episodes of change and resistance, Chinese settlements on Taiwan expanded, first under the Qing, then under Japanese colonial rule. Japan seized Taiwan as war booty after it defeated China in the Sino-Japanese War of 1895. It used the island to demonstrate its prowess as a colonial power, building an extensive transportation infrastructure and agricultural processing industries. In the 1930s, at the height of its expansionist ambition, the colonial authorities launched a campaign to assimilate Taiwanese into the Japanese nation. Although the effort failed, Japan's influence on Taiwan was profound, and can be seen today in everything from cuisine to fashion, from literary tastes to law enforcement.

At the end of World War II in 1945, Taiwan was ceded to the Republic of China, which was still in power on the mainland. The ROC's ruling party was the Kuomintang, and its leader was Chiang Kai-shek. Chiang and the KMT had been engaged in a civil war with Mao Zedong and the Chinese Communist Party (CCP) more or less continuously since 1927, though the attention of both sides had been diverted to the war against Japan from 1937 to 1945. At first, Taiwanese were glad to see the era of Japanese colonialism end, but the ROC administration and military forces were exhausted by years of war and acutely aware of the islanders' long subjection to China's enemy. They treated the Taiwanese more as a conquered people than as liberated compatriots. Relations between the long-time residents (called **Taiwanese**) and the new arrivals (called **Mainlanders**) soon deteriorated.

In February 1947 tensions between the two groups erupted into violence when protests over police violence in Taipei mushroomed into riots that engulfed the island. When ROC forces returned a few weeks later to reestablish control, they rounded up thousands of suspected rioters, including much of Taiwan's political elite. Thousands were killed.[1]

The uprising—which is known today as the 2–28 Incident (it began on February 28)—set in place the themes that dominated Taiwan politics for the next four decades: a highly repressive single-party authoritarian regime under the Kuomintang, disproportionate political influence for the Mainlander minority, and a single-minded focus on re-instating the

Republic of China on the mainland. The needs and preferences of Taiwan's people were set aside; their energies and talents were to be harnessed to a grand mission: rescuing China from the "communist bandits" (*gongfei*), as the CCP was called.

Two years after the 2–28 Incident, ROC forces on the mainland lost to Mao's Red Army. With the People's Republic of China newly declared on the mainland, only Taiwan and a handful of outlying islands remained under ROC control. Nonetheless, the ROC government, with massive economic aid and strong security guarantees from the United States, set to work building Taiwan into an economic and military powerhouse that it imagined would one day be strong enough to battle back and reclaim mainland China.

Taiwan under Authoritarian Rule

In its heyday—roughly 1950 to 1980—KMT rule was a unique mixture of authoritarianism, rapid economic development, and popular mobilization. The ROC based its legitimacy on a democratic claim; its constitution established a five-branch, dual-executive electoral democracy with a full complement of civil liberties. To avoid implementing this system in Taiwan, the KMT invoked martial law and suspended the constitution. National elections, too, were postponed, because the ongoing "communist rebellion" made it impossible for Chinese living on the mainland to participate, and it would be unfair to have the whole Republic of China governed by people living in a single province (Taiwan). National representatives who were elected in mainland China in the 1940s and had followed Chiang and the KMT to Taiwan—including the National Assembly members who chose the ROC president—were to remain in office until elections could be held in their home provinces.

Challenging this restrictive political system was risky. The 2–28 Incident had shattered Taiwan's native-born leadership; when it was over, few Taiwanese dared to oppose the KMT openly. Because the slightest whiff of anti-government activism could result in a long prison term, the KMT's most vocal opponents were Taiwanese exiled to Japan and the United States. Nor were Mainlanders exempt from political repression. The KMT had been fighting communism in its ranks for decades, and the purges continued even after the party moved to Taiwan. Civil liberties, including freedom of speech, were minimal. Intense repression in the 1950s and 1960s earned those decades the nickname "White Terror" (as Chiang Kai-shek's purge of the CCP in the late 1920s was also called; see chapter 2), but politics remained closed well into the 1980s. It was not until 1984 that a leading scholar raised the possibility that Taiwan might be shifting from "hard to soft authoritarianism."[2]

Retaking mainland China was too great a task for Taiwan's Mainlanders (about 15 percent of the island's population) to accomplish alone. The mission would require active support and participation from the Taiwanese majority. To win over Taiwanese, the KMT used both economic and political means. In the early 1950s, it carried out a thorough, non-violent land reform program that paved the way for economic progress in the rural areas. It encouraged competitive local elections as a way of legitimating local government and identifying talented leaders. It encouraged export-oriented industrialization by promoting state-sponsored heavy industries and small and medium-sized family firms.

The combination of successful policies, a well-developed pre-war infrastructure, hard-working and nimble entrepreneurs, and ready access to the U.S. market drove double-digit economic growth and rapidly rising living standards and inspired the phrase "Taiwan's economic miracle."[3] In 2008, Taiwan had a GDP per capita (at purchasing power parity) of $31,900, very similar to that of France, Italy, and Japan. The Taiwan model of development is also noted for policies that promoted relatively high levels of socio-economic equality.

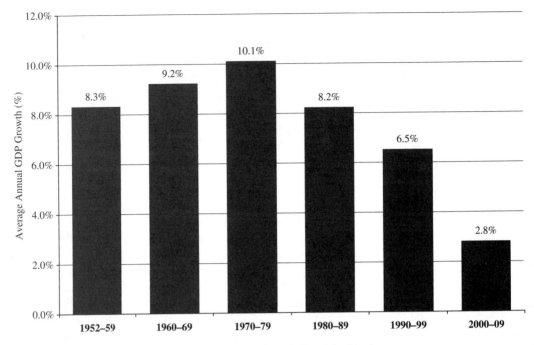

Figure 17.1 Taiwan's Economic Growth by Decade

As Taiwan's economy began to soar, the KMT's political might began to wane. By the mid-1970s, recovering the mainland was a distant dream, not least because many countries were recognizing Beijing as the legitimate government of China. In 1971, Taiwan lost its seat in the UN; a year later, U.S. President Richard Nixon visited China. In 1979, the Republic of China lost its most important diplomatic partner when the United States decided to recognize the People's Republic of China. The United States said it would not challenge Beijing's view that Taiwan is part of China (although it did not express agreement, either). Washington has continued to support Taiwan in unofficial ways—even selling weapons to the ROC military and maintaining a quasi-diplomatic presence in the form of the American Institute in Taiwan—but the loss of U.S. formal diplomatic recognition reinforced the growing sense that the KMT-led state was losing legitimacy.

As the idea of retaking the mainland faded, so too did the justification for suspending the ROC constitution. Seeing the change in the international climate—and feeling their growing economic clout—Taiwanese citizens began challenging the authoritarian system.

The Transition to Democracy

In 1975, Chiang Kai-shek died, and power passed to his son, Chiang Ching-kuo. The young Chiang had the foresight to recognize that history was turning against the ROC, and he launched a controlled unraveling of the authoritarian system aimed at rebuilding the KMT's battered legitimacy.[4] Chiang Ching-kuo expanded the number of Taiwanese in the party leadership and opened some seats in the national legislative bodies to direct election. Opposition activists probing the ruling party's tolerance for dissent found the boundaries expanding. While some ideas remained out of bounds (including communism and Taiwan independence), calls for democracy and justice for the Taiwanese majority met with an increasingly permissive reaction.

The reform process snowballed in the 1980s after an attempt to shut down the opposition in 1979 failed. Opposition politicians began running coordinated campaigns for local and national elected office—and winning. In 1984, Lee Teng-hui, a native-born Taiwanese politician educated in Japan and the United States, became Chiang Ching-kuo's vice president. When Chiang died four years later, Lee became the ROC's first Taiwan-born president.

In the early stages of democratization, the formation of opposition political parties was still banned under the terms of martial law. The KMT's opponents operated under the informal rubric of **dangwai**, or "outside the party." In 1986, *dangwai* politicians took the next step, and founded the **Democratic Progressive Party (DPP)**. Although the move technically violated martial law, the event went unpunished, and only ten months later, Chiang Ching-kuo terminated martial law. Within a few years, national legislative bodies were subjected to complete re-election, bringing into office a new generation of politicians elected by the people of Taiwan. In 1996, Lee Teng-hui added "first directly elected president" to his list of breakthroughs.

In 2000, the DPP candidate won the presidential election, ending the era of KMT rule. Single-party authoritarianism was gone, replaced by a fully functioning liberal democracy. Taiwanese today enjoy extensive civil liberties, and officials at all levels are accountable to the public through competitive, regular elections. Taiwan has been called "the First Chinese Democracy,"[5] both to make a comparison with the persistence of authoritarian rule on the mainland and to make the point that Confucian culture is not incompatible with democracy, as some scholars claim.

Taiwan's democratic transition reinvigorated its domestic politics, and it also attracted international support. Taiwan's transformation into a democracy reinforced America's commitment to protect the island from being absorbed against its will into a communist-led PRC.

Taiwan Politics Today

The ROC constitution adopted in 1947 is still the blueprint for Taiwan's political system. A directly elected president heads the national government and appoints a premier, who, in turn, names the Executive Yuan (cabinet).[*] The Executive Yuan is responsible for implementing the decisions of Taiwan's 113-member national lawmaking body, the Legislative Yuan. There is also a Judicial Yuan (to manage the courts), a Control Yuan (to supervise public officials), and an Examination Yuan (to run civil service examinations).

Taiwan's political institutions are a hybrid of presidential and parliamentary features, and recent amendments have added an additional layer of complexity. In theory, Taiwan's constitution divides power between the president and premier, with the president in charge of international affairs (including relations with the PRC) and the premier responsible for

---

[*] "Yuan," which literally means "board," as in "executive board," is adopted from the imperial Chinese system of government. The imperial government had a number of boards, such as the Board of Rites and the Board of Punishments, which advised the emperor. Sun Yat-sen adapted the terminology to the institutions of the constitutional republic established after the fall of the Qing dynasty in 1912.

domestic matters. In practice, however, Taiwan's presidents have played the dominant role, leaving premiers' authority limited.

Another perplexing feature of the system is the relationship between the premier and the legislature. In parliamentary systems, a prime minister (or premier) heads the government; he or she ordinarily is the head of the party that holds the parliamentary majority. If the prime minister loses parliament's support, the government is dissolved and new elections are held. In Taiwan, the premier is not subject to legislative confirmation; the president simply chooses the premier. If the Legislative Yuan does not approve of the president's choice, it may pass a vote of no confidence against the premier. In that case, the president may call for legislative elections. Thus, the legislature can "fire" the premier—who has relatively little power—but it cannot fire the president, who selects the premier. This provision limits the government's accountability to the legislature.

In 2000, Taiwanese voters elected their first non-KMT president, the DPP's Chen Shui-bian. Chen won a three-way race in which the KMT vote was divided between two prominent conservatives, Lien Chan and James Soong. Chen's 39 percent vote share provided only a weak mandate, and representatives of Lien's KMT and Soong's newly-formed People First Party (PFP) held a solid majority in the Legislative Yuan. During the eight years of Chen's presidency, this conservative majority stonewalled many of Chen's legislative proposals.

In early 2008, Taiwan held legislative and presidential elections. The KMT won both, ending the era of divided government. Still, the Chen years exposed a serious flaw in Taiwan's constitutional order. Divided government is possible in all presidential and dual-executive systems, but most have institutional devices to resolve conflicts between the executive and legislative branches. The United States has the presidential veto and the legislative override, for example, and the French system has a formalized structure for "cohabitation" in which the premier (representing the legislative majority) takes the lead during periods of divided government. Taiwan has nothing similar.

In the early 2000s, many Taiwanese hoped to use constitutional amendments—or even a new constitution—to resolve this and other institutional problems. But like many other issues, constitutional reform became entangled in the hot-button debate over Taiwan's international status. The PRC has had four constitutions in its sixty-year history, reflecting the fundamental political changes the country has experienced. But Beijing feared Taiwan was using a new constitution to establish a new country. Given President Chen's appetite for challenging Beijing—and Beijing's thin skin on the issue—many observers feared constitutional reform on Chen's watch could lead to a military confrontation. To prevent a crisis, the Legislative Yuan set a high threshold for constitutional amendment, effectively ending the constitutional reform debate.

The Independence Debate

Taiwan is the only country in the world that has all the attributes of a state—government, population, territory, military forces—except international recognition. As it is often said, Taiwan has *de facto* independence, but not *de jure* (legal) independence. It lacks recognition because Beijing insists it is a province of China, and "China" is the PRC. To have diplomatic relations with China—a rising global power—states must repudiate Taiwan. It is also important to acknowledge that Taiwan has not always been clear and consistent in its own message to the world about its status.

During the authoritarian era, the ROC wanted to be recognized as the government of all China. It refused to accept the existence of two Chinese states—the ROC and the PRC. It viewed the PRC as an illegitimate regime imposed by force on the Chinese people.

During the transition to democracy, many islanders began to question this characterization. While Mainlanders tended to accept the KMT's perspective, many Taiwanese thought defending the interests of the island and its people was more important than overthrowing communism and "saving" the mainland. Some people believed so strongly in putting Taiwan first that they advocated Taiwan independence, the permanent renunciation of unification. They wanted the international community to recognize that Taiwan was not—and never would be—part of China.

Taiwan independence is anathema to Beijing. Although the two sides have lived apart for more than sixty years, the PRC government does not like to admit they are separated; divorce is unthinkable. Chinese leaders insist that they will use any means necessary—including military force—to block Taiwan independence. In 2005, the PRC's National People's Congress passed legislation authorizing military action if independence is imminent. China has hundreds of short-range ballistics missiles aimed at the island backing up its threat.

Taiwanese are well aware of China's determination, and they take the danger seriously. For that reason, over the past decade, no more than 10 percent of Taiwanese have ever said they want to pursue independence right away. In that same period, however, the percentage that wanted immediate unification was even lower—below 5 percent. What Taiwanese *do* want is to maintain the status quo—to have the benefits of *de facto* independence (economic freedom and democratic self-government) without the risks of *de jure* independence.[6] There is no longer a big difference between Mainlanders and Taiwanese on this issue; nearly everyone now agrees that maintaining the status quo situation of the *de facto* independence that island has today is Taiwan's best option (see Table 17.1).

The fact that few Taiwanese are interested in pushing for *de jure* independence is good news for Beijing, but the declining enthusiasm for unification makes Chinese leaders nervous. What will they do if Taiwan makes a sudden lunge for independence?

In fact, it would even be difficult to recognize what steps would constitute "independence." Clearly, a declaration of independence by Taiwan would do the trick. Short of that, changing the name (from ROC to, say, Republic of Taiwan) or adopting a new national flag (they still use the original flag of the Republic of China founded in 1912) also would indicate a change. Other gestures—including constitutional reform—are more ambiguous. In 2008 Taiwanese voters considered a ballot measure instructing the government to seek UN membership under the name "Taiwan." The measure failed, but if it had passed, would it have constituted an act of independence? The answer is subjective, but Beijing believed it was necessary to oppose the measure—as it opposes all gestures toward independence—just in case.

Relations with the Mainland

Since its democratic transition, Taiwan's relationship with mainland China has changed radically. Under the authoritarian system, Taiwan treated the PRC as enemy territory, but democratization ushered in a more relaxed view. In 1987, Taipei lifted the ban on travel to the mainland that had been in place since the 1950s and thousands of Taiwanese made the trip. Many were Mainlanders hoping to reunite families divided by the civil war, but many others were Taiwanese who went as tourists.

The visitors included entrepreneurs who saw in China's fast-changing economy an investment opportunity. Rising wages and land prices on the island were starting to suffocate Taiwan's traditional manufacturers, but marrying China's low costs to Taiwan's know-

Table 17.1 Survey on "The Public's Views on Current Cross-Strait Relations," April 2009

"REGARDING RELATIONS BETWEEN TAIWAN AND MAINLAND CHINA, WHICH OF THE FOLLOWING POSITIONS DO YOU LEAN TOWARD?"

Unification as soon as possible	Maintaining status quo and unification later	Maintaining status quo and deciding on independence or unification later	Maintaining status quo indefinitely	Maintaining status quo and independence later	Independence as soon as possible	No response
1.2%	7.6%	35.0%	27.0%	15.1%	6.7%	7.4%
1.2%		84.7%			6.7%	7.4%

Source: Poll conducted by Election Study Center, National Chengchi University, Taipei, Taiwan; published in Taiwan Mainland Affairs Council News Release, April 23, 2009.

how and global connections offered a way forward. Taiwanese manufacturers soon became a leading force in the Chinese economy, and investment in the mainland became a critical factor in Taiwan's economic growth. As the second decade of the century began, the two were among each other's top trading partners, and Taiwan was almost certainly the first or second largest source of direct foreign investment in the PRC economy.[7]

The flood of Taiwanese visiting and investing in the mainland brought the two sides closer than they had been in four decades. President Lee declared the civil war over in 1991 and replaced the goal of recovering the mainland with peaceful unification. Representatives of the two sides began meeting in the guise of unofficial bodies to discuss issues ranging from the exchange of mail to criminal extraditions.

The conversations eased people-to-people relations and economic cooperation, but they also exposed profound differences in the two sides' goals. Beijing's idea of unification was to make Taiwan a province of the PRC, but when Taiwan's leaders spoke of unification, they had in mind a marriage of equals. Subordinating a democratic Taiwan to a communist PRC was unacceptable to a society that had only recently thrown off single-party authoritarianism. Eventually, the talks broke down.

Relations deteriorated further in the second half of the 1990s. Lee was growing anxious that Taiwan would be roped into a unification it did not want, so he looked to the international community to confirm the island's separate status. In 1999, he stunned Beijing by calling the cross-strait connection a "special state-to-state relationship." Fearing that Taiwan was on the verge of permanently discarding its Chinese identity, Beijing tightened its stranglehold on Taiwan's diplomacy. Economic ties between the two sides continued to develop, but political relations turned icy.

Campaigning for the presidency in 2000, the DPP candidate, Chen Shui-bian, called for increased economic engagement between Taiwan and China, but PRC leaders (as well as many Taiwanese voters) were convinced his real goal was Taiwan independence, a stance that had been part of his party's platform since 1991. As president, Chen found himself stonewalled by Beijing and by a Legislative Yuan dominated by his opponents. In response, he hardened his position, especially after his reelection in 2004. The PRC was especially agitated when Chen described the situation in the Taiwan Strait as "one country on each side." The result was eight years of stagnation in cross-strait political relations.

The combination of hot economics and cold politics drove competing trends in Taiwan's public opinion. During Chen's presidency, the Taiwanese became ever more convinced that the island's economic prosperity depended upon taking advantage of the economic opportunities on the mainland. At the same time, though, fewer and fewer Taiwanese felt themselves to be Chinese, and the sense that Taiwan should remain politically separate deepened.

By 2008, unification had become so unpopular that even the KMT presidential candidate, Ma Ying-jeou, refused to endorse it, promising instead to take unification off the table. The status quo—neither independence nor unification—had become the consensus preference of Taiwan's people. There was little the PRC could do to counter this trend, except to promote economic and social integration and hope that Taiwan would return to the fold someday. To improve its chances of succeeding, Beijing has worked with Taipei to expand cross-strait economic cooperation. In 2008, the two sides began allowing year-round direct flights, which slashed travel times (before, travelers had to switch planes along the way—usually in Hong Kong). They also reduced trade and investment restrictions and eased the rules for cross-strait tourism.

Overall, the early phase of Ma Ying-jeou's presidency saw rapid improvement in cross-strait relations. In addition to relaxing travel and economic restrictions, the two sides exchanged high-level visits, stepped up their quasi-official negotiations and opened direct talks between the Chinese Communist Party and the KMT. While most Taiwanese welcomed the reduced tension and enhanced convenience these developments ushered in, many also wondered whether Taiwan's concessions might outweigh its gains. According to his opponents, Ma's willingness to compromise with Beijing was naïve at best. At worst, they averred, his actions revealed a preference for unification that put him far from the popular mainstream. Claims that Ma might "sell out" Taiwan did not recede, in spite of the president's repeated denials.

One reason that Ma has been willing to make more concessions than his predecessors is the PRC's evolving position. In recent years, Beijing's rhetoric has shifted from insisting on achieving unification as soon as possible to opposing independence. While incorporating Taiwan into a unified China is still the PRC's long-term goal, the range of acceptable formats under which that goal might be achieved has widened. The KMT believes this new emphasis on patience and flexibility is real, which makes it safe to negotiate on issues short of unification itself. The DPP, in contrast, believes that PRC leaders cannot be trusted.

Ma's outreach to the PRC was no less welcome in Washington than in Beijing. During the Chen years, U.S. policy-makers found the ill will and lack of communication between the two sides dangerously destabilizing. Chen's behavior was hard to predict, and Chinese reactions were alarming. In that tense atmosphere, even a small misunderstanding or accident could have produced catastrophic results. By the end of the George W. Bush Administration (2001–2009), the United States was leaning hard on Chen to avoid actions and statements that might inflame the situation. The United States went to great lengths to welcome the new tone under the Ma administration.

Politics and Elections

During the authoritarian period, local governments were the focal point for political competition. Taiwan has twenty-five municipalities, including sixteen counties, five cities, two metropolises (Taipei and Kaohsiung), and two tiny islands near the mainland's Fujian coast. Some of these municipalities will be consolidated soon. Each municipality has an elected executive and council and various sub-municipalities (townships, towns, villages and wards) most of which elect their leaders, as well.

Before the DPP was founded, nearly all local politicians were KMT members, but the party organization in each municipality was divided into local factions. Although all were affiliated with the KMT, when it came to local elections, factions competed fiercely. Local factions might cooperate to help KMT candidates in national elections, but when opposition politicians began challenging the KMT in significant numbers, factions found ways to leverage those opposition candidacies for their own advantage. Local politics was an important training ground and venue for democratization, and as the scope of elections expanded, voters and politicians were well-prepared.

Taiwanese have participated in elections since the 1940s, so it is not surprising that they are skilled in the arts of campaigning and voting. During the period of one-party rule, campaigns revolved around "vote pulling." Candidates cultivated influential supporters—vote brokers—who mobilized their personal networks in support of those candidates. Successful candidates rewarded their vote brokers and supporters with targeted benefits—everything from public works projects to funeral wreaths. In small-town Taiwan, knowing a public official was a big deal, and politicians spent a huge amount of time and money serving their constituents.

To supplement this personalized politicking, Taiwanese politicians also used high-visibility techniques such as sound trucks, campaign flags, and rallies. As the island's population has grown and politics has become more sophisticated, parties and candidates have added mass media—TV advertising, media tours, endorsements—to their repertoire. Today, all these elements come into play in elections, and candidates spend their days racing from TV studios to stadium rallies to wedding feasts. In the 2008 Legislative Yuan election, one candidate in Taipei City followed garbage trucks through his district, shaking hands with voters as they came out to dispose of their trash (residents are required to put their trash directly in the truck at a scheduled time). (See Box, **Taiwan's "Hot and Noisy" Politics**.)

As in most countries, many of the issues voters care about are local. Economic development, law and order, and public services top the list in municipal elections. In national elections—legislative and presidential contests—Taiwanese voters pay attention to party, too.

After more than two decades of multiparty politics, the KMT remains the party of the establishment. It gets credit for many of Taiwan's successes over the years—especially the island's strong economic performance in the high-growth era—and while its opponents have tried to paint it as a pro-unification party, the party's platform puts it firmly in the mainstream. In his successful 2008 campaign, for example, President Ma Ying-jeou promoted "Three Nos": no independence, no unification, and no armed conflict with the PRC. He also promised to make it easier for Taiwanese to do business in the mainland.

Candidates associated with the KMT and its allies have won between 45 and 60 percent of the vote in every election since 2000. Only once—in the 2004 presidential race—has the DPP outpolled the KMT. The 2008 elections were the KMT's best performance in more than a decade; it won 53 percent of the legislative vote and 58 percent of the presidential vote.

The Democratic Progressive Party is known for promoting democratization, but it also has a reputation as a pro-independence party. The party's position is more subtle and moderate than this characterization implies, but perception is what matters in politics, and many Taiwanese voters perceive the DPP as recklessly pro-independence. Until 2004, one of the DPP's strongest cards was its reputation for incorruptibility—a sharp contrast to the KMT. Unfortunately, President Chen's second term was marred by scandals that tarnished his party's clean reputation. Since leaving office in May 2008, both Chen and his wife have been convicted of corruption involving money laundering, bribery, and embezzlement of government funds.

TAIWAN'S "HOT AND NOISY" POLITICS

In 2004, Taiwan's presidential election made headlines worldwide when the incumbent president and vice-president were shot while campaigning for reelection. The incident provoked a tsunami of conspiracy theories, mostly because the official account seemed so implausible. How could two politicians be shot in front of thousands of people without anyone—even the candidates themselves—noticing?

Chen Shui-bian, grazed by a bullet across his midsection, said he felt something when he was hit, but went on waving to the crowd for several minutes. When he finally looked down, he realized he was bleeding. Then he noticed Vice President Annette Lu bleeding from her knee. About that time, he noticed a bullet hole in the car window.

It's easy to understand why so many people scoffed at Chen's story, but if you've ever been to a Taiwanese campaign rally, you won't find it quite so hard to believe.

Although security procedures have tightened since, Chen and Lu were following standard Taiwanese campaign protocol on March 19, 2004: they were standing in an open Jeep, secured by a seat belt, driving through a tightly packed crowd with fire crackers raining down on them. The air was full of smoke, the noise was deafening, and there were explosions going off everywhere. No one could have heard a gunshot in the din.

Both candidates said they initially assumed their injuries were nothing unusual: just the typical dings from out-of-control bottle rockets. (Television cameramen trailing the candidates in another car reported smelling their own hair burning as smoldering fireworks wrappers fell from the sky.) It was only later, when the adrenaline wore off, that Chen and Lu recognized the nature of their wounds.

Crushing crowds and earsplitting noise are the *sine qua non* of Taiwanese political rallies. They are required, both literally and figuratively, to meet the Chinese definition of fun: *re'nao* (hot and noisy). A candidate who cannot provide them—along with a robust selection of food vendors and color-coordinated tracksuits for the staff—cannot expect to win an election.

Politics in Taiwan is a combination of door-to-door sales and traveling circus. The real mystery is how so many politicians make it to Election Day in one piece.

The DPP still is considered a young, outsider party; its biggest challenge is to convince voters that it is sensible and competent. Regrettably, Chen's presidency did little to advance that cause. Election analysts attributed the KMT's big wins in the 2008 elections to voter dissatisfaction with Chen's performance.

Beyond the two major parties, political parties have come and gone, but none has become a lasting force in Taiwan politics. The most important of the small parties are the People First Party (PFP), the Taiwan Solidarity Union (TSU), and the New Party, all of which grew out of splits in the KMT. As of 2008, both the PFP and the New Party had been reincorporated into the KMT, and the TSU was barely hanging on after losing all its legislative seats in 2008.

Conclusion

Taiwan's prosperous economy and successful democracy should make it a model for developing countries, but its troubled relationship with China has left it isolated, its achievements largely ignored. After worsening steadily for more than a decade, relations between Taiwan and China appear to have stabilized. The two sides depend on one another economically, and they have learned to communicate despite their differences. Nonetheless, those differences are profound. The PRC hopes to incorporate Taiwan into a Chinese nation-state with Beijing as its capital, while Taiwanese want to preserve their island's democracy. As long as China retains its nominally communist party-state political framework, a democratic Taiwan will need at least *de facto* independence. The still large gap in the level of economic development and standard of living between the PRC and Taiwan also presents a significant obstacle to unification. Resolving the standoff in the Taiwan Strait will require patience, flexibility, confidence and goodwill on both sides. In the meantime, Taiwan will continue to look for international affirmation and support wherever it can find it—whether in the UN General Assembly or on the "Click Click Click" Web site.

Notes

1. The most complete English-language account of these events is: Tse-han Lai, Ramon Myers and Wou Wei, *A Tragic Beginning: The Taiwan Uprising of February 28, 1947* (Palo Alto, CA: Stanford University Press, 1991).

2. Edwin A. Winckler, "Institutionalization and Participation on Taiwan: From Hard to Soft Authoritarianism?" *The China Quarterly* 99 (1984): 482–499.

3. Taiwan's economic development model is analyzed in detail in two books: Thomas Gold, *State and Society in the Taiwan Miracle* (Armonk, NY: M. E. Sharpe, 1986); and Robert Wade, *Governing the Market: Economic Theory and the Role of Government in East Asian Industrialization* (Princeton, NJ: Princeton University Press, 1990).

4. Accounts of Taiwan's democratization include: Linda Chao and Ramon H. Myers, *The First Chinese Democracy: Political Life in the Republic of China on Taiwan* (Baltimore, MD: Johns Hopkins University Press, 1998); Yun-han Chu, *Crafting Democracy in Taiwan* (Taipei: Institute for National Policy Research, 1992); Peter Moody, *Political Change on Taiwan: A Study of Ruling Party Adaptability* (New York: Praeger, 1992), Shelley Rigger, *Politics in Taiwan: Voting for Democracy* (London: Routledge, 1999); Denny Roy, *Taiwan: A Political History* (Ithaca, NY: Cornell University Press, 2003); Hung-mao Tien, *The Great Transition: Political and Social Change in the Republic of China* (Stanford, CA: Hoover Institution Press, 1989).

5. Chao and Myers, *The First Chinese Democracy.*

6. The Election Study Center at National Chengchi University maintains a database of surveys on these and other issues. The survey results are available in English on the ESC web site, under "Important Political Attitude Trend Distribution." See http://www.esc.nccu.edu.tw/eng/data/data03.htm.

7. It is impossible to state with certainty exactly where Taiwan ranks among international investors in China because a very large portion of inbound investment flows through offshore channels, including the Cayman Islands, British Virgin Islands, Hong Kong and Panama. Of this, a substantial—but unknowable—portion originates in Taiwan.

Suggested Readings

Andrade, Tonio. *How Taiwan Became Chinese: Dutch, Spanish and Han Colonization in the Seventeenth Century.* New York: Columbia University Press, 2008.

Bush, Richard. *Untying the Knot: Making Peace in the Taiwan Strait.* Washington, DC: Brookings Institution, 2005.

Copper, John F. *Taiwan: Nation-State or Province?* 5th ed. Boulder, CO: Westview Press, 2008.

Gold, Thomas B. *State and Society in the Taiwan Miracle.* Armonk, NY: M. E. Sharpe, 1986.

Goldstein, Steven M., and Julian Chang, eds. *Presidential Politics in Taiwan: The Administration of Chen Shui-bian.* Norwalk, CT: EastBridge, 2008.

Hsiao, Li-hung. *A Thousand Moons on a Thousand Rivers* (trans. Michelle Wu). New York: Columbia University Press, 2000.

Kastner, Scott L. *Political Conflict and Economic Interdependence across the Taiwan Strait and Beyond.* Stanford, CA: Stanford University Press, 2009.

Keliher, Macabe. *Out of China or Yu Yonghe's Tale of Formosa: A History of Seventeenth-Century Taiwan.* Taipei: SMC Publishing, 2003.

Rigger, Shelley. *Taiwan's Rising Rationalism: Generations, Politics, and "Taiwanese Nationalism."* Washington, DC: East West Center, 2006.

Roy, Denny. *Taiwan: A Political History.* Ithaca, NY: Cornell University Press, 2003.

Tucker, Nancy Bernkopf, ed. *Dangerous Strait: The U.S.-Taiwan-China Crisis.* New York: Columbia University Press, 2008.

Tucker, Nancy Bernkopf. *Strait Talk: United States-Taiwan Relations and the Crisis with China.* Cambridge, MA: Harvard University Press, 2009.

Wachman, Alan. *Why Taiwan? Geostrategic Rationales for China's Territorial Integrity.* Stanford, CA: Stanford University Press, 2007.

Timeline of Modern Chinese Political History

1760s–1790s	"High Qing"—the height of glory for China's last imperial dynasty.
1839–1842	The First Opium War; ends in an humiliating defeat for the Qing dynasty and the signing of the Treaty of Nanjing (1842), the first of the "unequal treaties" imposed on imperial China by Western powers.
1850–1863	The Taiping Rebellion nearly overthrows the Qing and leaves more than 20 million dead before it is suppressed.
1856–1860	The Second Opium War; China's defeat leads to more unequal treaties.
1860s	Empress Dowager Cixi, widow of Xianfeng emperor, becomes the "power behind the throne" of her infant son and the most powerful leader in China—a position she retains until her death in 1908.
1860s–1890s	The Self-Strengthening movement involves efforts to save the Qing by modernizing the economy and the military while preserving traditional Chinese values.
1894–1895	China defeated and humiliated in the Sino-Japanese War; loses influence in Korea and control of Taiwan to Japan.
1898	The Hundred Days Reform is proclaimed by the emperor, promising wide-ranging institutional changes, but the movement is crushed by the Empress Dowager Cixi, who places the emperor under palace arrest.
1899–1900	The Boxer Rebellion breaks out in northern China and is suppressed by Western military forces. The Boxer Indemnity further weakens the Qing dynasty financially.
1905	The imperial examination system is abolished as part of a last ditch futile reform effort to save the Qing dynasty. Sun Yat-sen establishes the *Tongmenghui*, or "Revolutionary Alliance" and calls for the overthrow of the Qing and the establishment of a republic.
1908	The Empress Dowager dies. but not before she moves to put another child emperor on throne, the three-year old, Puyi, who would be China's last emperor.
1911	Revolution breaks out in many parts of China; Sun Yat-sen becomes provisional president of a republican government before it comes to national power.
1912	The "Last Emperor" abdicates and the Republic of China is established.
1912–1916	General Yuan Shikai takes control of the Republic and tries to establish a new dynasty with himself as emperor.

1912	Sun Yat-sen founds the Kuomintang (KMT, Nationalist Party) to oppose Yuan's usurpation of power in the Republic of China.
1916–1927	The Warlord Era, which begins in the political vacuum left by Yuan Shikai's death. The Republic of China exists in name, but power is, in fact, held by numerous regional military leaders.
1919	The May Fourth Movement begins with protest against the terms of the Versailles Treaty and the weak leaders of the Republic of China, ushering in a period of political and cultural ferment.
1921	The Chinese Communist Party (CCP) is founded with advice and assistance from the Moscow-based Comintern (Communist International).
1924	The KMT and the CCP agree to a united front to oppose the warlords.
1925	Sun Yat-sen dies; Chiang Kai-shek takes over leadership of the KMT.
1926	The KMT-CCP united front begins the Northern Expedition from southern China in a military campaign to subdue the warlords and reunify China.
1927	Chiang Kai-shek turns against the CCP and unleashes the "White Terror," driving surviving communists underground or deep into the countryside. The CCP establishes the first of its major rural base areas in Jinggangshan.
1927–1937	The "Nanjing Decade": Chiang Kai-shek consolidates his position as the most powerful leader of the Republic of China and relocates the country's capital to the central Chinese city of Nanjing (Nanking).
1928–1934	The KMT carries out a series of "extermination campaigns" against CCP base areas. The CCP headquarters is relocated to a remote area in central China, which is called the Jiangxi Soviet.
1931	Japan begins its aggression against China, taking control of Manchuria in the northeast and establishing a puppet state, "Manchukuo," with China's "Last Emperor" as a figurehead ruler.
1934–1935	The Long March: the CCP is driven out of its Jiangxi Soviet base area by Chiang Kai-shek's forces and undertakes a 6,000-mile trek to the northwestern sanctuary in Yan'an; during the Long March, Mao Zedong moves to the top ranks of the CCP leadership.
1935–1945	The Yan'an period: a crucial decade in the development of the CCP, during which Mao Zedong becomes Chairman of the party and consolidates his political and ideological power; the CCP also greatly expands its popular support for its resistance against Japan and its program of reform.
1937	Japan invades China proper, setting off World War II in Asia; Chiang Kai-shek and the government of the Republic of China are driven to the far southwest and set up a wartime capital in Chongqing (Chungking). The Rape of Nanjing: Japanese forces carry out horrific atrocities against hundreds of thousands of Chinese civilians when they occupy the capital of China.
1945	World War II ends
1946	The Chinese civil war begins again after a temporary "truce" during the war against Japan and futile efforts by the United States to negotiate a KMT-CCP coalition government.
1949	The CCP wins the civil war and founds the People's Republic of China (PRC) with Chairman Mao as the leader and Beijing as its capital. Chiang Kai-shek and the government of the Republic of China retreat to the island of Taiwan.

1950	The United States and its allies block the PRC's effort to assume the "China" seat in the United Nations claiming it still rightfully belongs to the Republic of China.
	The People's Liberation Army invades Tibet; The Seventeen Point Agreement leaves the Dalai Lama in "charge" in exchange for Tibet's acknowledgment that it is part of China.
1950–1952	The period of the "New Democracy" in the PRC, which promises a mixed economy and a somewhat inclusive polity, although under firm control of the CCP. Land reform and other revolutionary programs begin.
1950–1953	The Korean War: China fights the United Nations forces under the United States to a stalemate.
1953–1957	China follows the Soviet model of development under a first five-year plan that involves a centralized economy, the nationalization of industry and commerce, and the collectivization of agriculture.
1956–1957	The Hundred Flowers movement: Mao invites criticism of the CCP's rule over China in order to shake up the bureaucracy and prevent discontent from boiling over.
1957	The Anti-Rightist campaign: in reaction to unexpectedly harsh criticism of the Hundred Flowers, the CCP strikes against critics.
1958–1960	The Great Leap Forward: Mao's campaign to accelerate economic development and bring true communism to China by relying on the labor power and revolutionary fervor of the masses; China is plunged into the worst famine in human history and a deep industrial depression.
1959	An uprising in Tibet against Chinese rule is crushed; the Dalai Lama flees to exile in India.
1961–1965	Mao retreats to the "second line" of leadership and turns economic policy over to Liu Shaoqi and Deng Xiaoping.
1962–1964	Mao grows increasingly unhappy with the policies that Liu and Deng have implemented to recover from the Leap and set China on a course of sustained economic growth.
	The Sino-Soviet split emerges: Mao concludes that the Soviet Union has betrayed communism and "restored" capitalism that benefits the party elite and exploits the workers.
1964	China detonates its first atomic bomb.
1966	Mao launches the Great Proletarian Cultural Revolution, an ideological campaign to get China off the "capitalist road" down which he believes Liu, Deng, and other top party leaders have led it.
1966–1968	The Red Guards emerge as Mao's mass ally in the Cultural Revolution and carry out a reign of terror against anyone and anything judged to be remnants of capitalism or imperial China. Liu Shaoqi and Deng Xiaoping are among those purged.
1968–1969	Mao concludes that the Red Guards and other rebels have gone too far and instructs the army, under his loyal subordinate, Lin Biao, to restore order. More than 20 million former Red Guards are sent for re-education in the countryside.
1969–1971	A period of military ascendency in Chinese politics; Lin Biao is named as Mao's successor.
1971	Sino-American détente begins after a long period of hostility since the founding of the PRC in 1949. National Security Advisor Henry Kissinger

makes a "secret" trip to Beijing (July 1971) to prepare the way for President Richard M. Nixon's historic visit in March 1972.

Lin Biao is killed in an airplane crash following an alleged coup to overthrow Mao, who had grown unhappy with Lin as his chosen successor.

The People's Republic of China assumes the "China" position in the United Nations General Assembly and Security Council, replacing the Republic of China (on Taiwan).

1972–1975	A momentous period of transition and tumult in Chinese politics: Radicals led by Mao's wife, Jiang Qing, fill part of the political vacuum left by Lin Biao's demise. Deng Xiaoping is restored to power to balance the leadership and help long-time premier, Zhou Enlai, manage the economy. China's relationship with the United States and the global community deepens.
1975–1976	The "showdown" between the radicals and more moderate CCP leaders intensifies.
1976	Zhou Enlai dies in January. A political "unknown," Hua Guofeng, is unexpectedly named to succeed Zhou as acting premier in a move by Mao, who is in deteriorating health, to balance power between radical and moderate leaders. The Tiananmen Incident: A mass outpouring of mourning for Zhou Enlai turns into a protest against Jiang Qing and other radicals and is suppressed. Deng Xiaoping is blamed for the Tiananmen Incident and again ousted from the party-state leadership. Hua Guofeng is made PRC premier and first vice chairman of the CCP, clearly emerging as Mao's successor. Mao Zedong dies in September. Jiang Qing and her closest radical associates (the Gang of Four) are arrested by Hua Guofeng with the support of senior party leaders. Hua Guofeng becomes chairman of the CCP.
1977	Deng Xiaoping is restored to his party and state positions by Hua Guofeng and gradually pushes Hua aside to become China's paramount leader, although he never assumes the top offices himself.
1978	A meeting of the CCP Central Committee in December marks the start of the era of economic reform and opening to the world.
1979	The Democracy Wall movement calls for greater political freedom but is suppressed. The United States and China establish formal diplomatic relations.
1980	Zhao Ziyang, a loyal protégé of Deng Xiaoping, replaces Hua Guofeng as premier of the PRC.
1981	Hu Yaobang, another Deng protégé, replaces Hua Guofeng as chairman of the CCP; the title of the head of the party is changed to general secretary in 1982. Deng Xiaoping replaces Hua as chairman of the Central Military Commission, thereby becoming the commander in chief of China's armed forces. CCP issues the "Resolution of Certain Questions in the History of Our Party since the Founding of the PRC," which blames Mao's political and ideological mistakes for the disasters of the Great Leap Forward and the Cultural Revolution, but concludes that his achievements far outweigh his shortcomings.

1987	Hu Yaobang is forced by Deng to resign as general secretary because he is said to be too sympathetic to student and intellectual calls for more democracy; Zhao Ziyang becomes general secretary and Li Peng becomes premier.
1989	Hu Yaobang dies in April.
	Students gather in Tiananmen Square to pay their respects to Hu Yaobang, regarded by many as a political reformer.
	The student gathering turns into huge demonstrations and protests against corruption and for democracy, eventually drawing people from nearly all walks of life and spreading to other cities during the spring.
	June 4th: The People's Liberation Army is ordered to clear the Square and does so with massive force, resulting in the deaths of a large number of protesters.
	Zhao Ziyang is forced to resign as CCP general secretary by Deng because of his sympathy and soft line toward the demonstrations; he is replaced by Jiang Zemin, party secretary in Shanghai, who also becomes chairman of the Central Military Commission.
	China enters a period of retreat from political and economic reform.
1989–1991	The collapse of communist regimes in Eastern Europe and the Soviet Union alarms China's leaders.
1992	During his Southern Inspection Tour of China's most prosperous region, Deng proclaims that economic reform must again become the country's highest priority.
1993	Jiang Zemin becomes president of the PRC.
1997	Deng Xiaoping dies; in the preceding few years, he had allowed Jiang Zemin to consolidate his own power.
	Hong Kong returns to Chinese sovereignty after nearly 150 years as a British colony.
2002–2004	Jiang Zemin retires. Hu Jintao becomes CCP general secretary (2002), PRC president (2003), and Central Military Commission chair (2004).
2007–2008	Hu Jintao "re-elected" to all of his leading positions, with his second and final terms scheduled to end in 2012–2013.
2008	Large scale unrest occurs in Tibet and is forcefully suppressed.
	Beijing hosts the Olympic Games.
2009	Large-scale unrest occurs in Xinjiang and is forcefully suppressed.
	China celebrates the 60th anniversary of the founding of the People's Republic.

Glossary

Note: This glossary does not include identifications of individuals. For lists of top leaders of the People's Republic of China, see Table 3.1 (1949–1976) and Table 4.1 (since 1976).

1911 Revolution   the process that began on October 10, 1911 ("Double 10"), with a series of mutinies and rebellions in several Chinese cities and culminated in the abdication of the **Qing** emperor and the founding of the **Republic of China** in February 1912.

2–28 Incident   events on Taiwan that began on February 28, 1947, when tensions between **Mainlanders** and **Taiwanese** erupted into widespread violence. Protests by Taiwanese over police violence in Taipei mushroomed into riots that engulfed the island. When **Kuomintang** forces arrived from the mainland to reestablish control, they rounded up thousands of suspected rioters, including much of Taiwan's political elite. Thousands were killed.

7,000 cadres conference   a massive gathering of officials from different institutions and administrative levels in the PRC in early 1962 to assess efforts at recovery from the **Great Leap Forward.** Mao offered a very restrained self-criticism, but also reasserted the correctness of the Great Leap policy line. The CCP leadership rallied around the Chairman, but Liu Shaoqi gave a speech critical of the Leap, which Mao later claimed caused him to begin to doubt Liu's political reliability.

administrative village   the unit of governance in rural China; technically, a "grassroots" unit below the formal government structure of the PRC. An administrative village is made up of one or more **natural villages**. There are more than 600,000 administrative villages in China.

All China Women's Federation (ACWF)   one of China's official **mass organizations**. The official mission of the ACWF is "to represent and to protect women's rights and interests, and to promote equality between men and women." It is a national organization with branches at every level of government. Like other mass organizations, the ACWF accepts the leadership of the CCP.

anarchism   from the Greek term meaning "without rulers"; a political philosophy that rejects all formal state authority as tyrannical and harmful to individuals. Anarchists believe society should be organized into small, voluntary, and cooperative self-governing units. Anarchism was popular in the first decades of the twentieth century among some

Chinese intellectuals who were looking for a solution to problems of late imperial and early republican China.

antagonistic contradiction   a contradiction between opposites that have no common ground and can only be resolved by force, compared with **non-antagonistic contradictions**, which can be resolved by discussion, debate, education, and other non-coercive means. For example, the contradiction between the **bourgeoisie** and the **proletariat** is antagonistic.

Anti-Rightist campaign   launched by Mao Zedong and the CCP in 1957 in response to the unexpectedly harsh criticism of the party's rule during the **Hundred Flowers movement.** It deeply touched intellectuals and other segments of the urban population in particular, and resulted in the extensive use of the "rightist" label, which would curse people so designated for the rest of the Maoist era. Many "rightists" were sent to the countryside for reform through labor, in many cases for more than two decades. Even more fundamentally, the campaign sent a chill of fear through society, especially among intellectuals.

Article 23   of the **Basic Law** of the **Hong Kong Special Administrative Region** (HKSAR) legislation that gives the HKSAR the power to enact laws on security issues such as treason and subversion against the government of the PRC, theft of state secrets, and the formation of political organizations with foreign ties. In 2002, the HKSAR government proposed enacting a tough new anti-subversion law under the terms of Article 23. The proposal created much controversy and protest by those who thought it would decrease democracy in Hong Kong. The government, in consultation with the PRC, withdrew the proposal after massive public demonstrations against it.

Asian financial crisis in 1997–1998   began in Thailand in July 1997 and spread to most of the other countries in East and Southeast Asia. Among the causes were bad government economic policies, overinvestment, and real estate speculation. The International Monetary Fund (IMF) helped bail out the worst hit countries. Hong Kong was seriously affected by the crisis, but China was not because of its controlled currency and other economic controls.

autonomous region (AR)   administrative units of the PRC with a high concentration of **ethnic minorities** and which are granted a limited degree of autonomy in economic, cultural, social, and other matters, but remain politically and militarily subordinate to the central government. China has five autonomous regions: Guangxi Zhuang AR, Inner Mongolia AR, Ningxia Hui AR, **Tibet** AR, and **Xinjiang Uyghur** AR.

baojia **system**   a system of community mutual surveillance first developed in China during the early **imperial period** and based on grouping together a number of households that are responsible for maintaining law and order by watching and informing on each other. Chiang Kai-shek tried to revive the *baojia* system in the **Republic of China** during the 1930s.

barefoot doctors   paramedics trained (usually by medical teams of the **People's Liberation Army**) to attend to the primary and preventive medical needs of people in China's rural areas during the Maoist era, especially in the early 1970s. Barefoot doctors were selected from among local residents, and the term "barefoot" refers to **peasants** in **South China** who worked without shoes in the rice paddies. They also promoted hygiene and family planning.

base area   a region in the Chinese countryside under the control of the **Chinese Communist Party** during the civil war against the **Kuomintang**. The CCP had numerous base areas in the period 1927–1945, the best known of which were the **Jiangxi Soviet** and **Yan'an.**

Basic Law   the so-called mini-constitution of the **Hong Kong** Special Administrative Region of the PRC. It is based on the "**One Country, Two Systems**" principle and provides a blueprint for maintaining Hong Kong's legislative, administrative, judicial, social, and economic autonomy under Chinese sovereignty. But the Basic Law empowers the **Standing Committee of the National People's Congress** of the PRC to interpret the provisions of the Basic Law, thus giving China the final say on all matters related to Hong Kong.

Beidaihe   an oceanside resort city near **Beijing** where the CCP leadership often held important mid-summer meetings.

Beijing   the capital of the **People's Republic of China**, and one of four **centrally administered cities**. Beijing literally means "Northern Capital." During the **Nanjing Decade** it was renamed Beiping, or "Northern Peace."

Beijing Consensus   a term sometimes used to describe the model of economic development being followed by the PRC that includes a commitment to innovation and experimentation; stable growth based on sustainable and equitable development; global integration with national self-determination; and strong government oversight of market reforms. It is often contrasted to the **Washington Consensus**.

Beijing Massacre   the military assault ordered by the leadership of the **Chinese Communist Party** on pro-democracy protesters in and around **Tiananmen Square** on June 4, 1989. Also called June 4, or simply 6–4.

Beijingology   an approach to the study of Chinese politics that emphasizes the analysis of the top leadership of the Chinese Communist Party, which is based in the national capital, **Beijing**. The term is an adaptation of "Kremlinology," which refers to efforts to understand politics in the Soviet Union (and, to a somewhat lesser extent, Russia today) by analyzing the words and actions of the top leaders who work in the compound of buildings in Moscow called the Kremlin.

"big bang"   an approach to economic development, especially in countries going through a post-communist transition from a **planned economy** to a **market economy**, that carries out widespread fundamental reforms simultaneously or in rapid succession. See **gradualism.**

big character posters (*dazibao*)   handwritten "documents" of oversized Chinese characters, often written on newspapers or large sheets of paper that make a strong public political statement. Although they have an earlier history in China, they were used most extensively during the **Cultural Revolution**, particularly by **Red Guards**, most often to denounce some person or group's ideological mistakes.

bingtuan   Chinese abbreviation for **Xinjiang** Production and Construction Corps, established in the early 1950s as places to live and work for demobilized soldiers and their families; designed to promote economic development and **Han** settlement in the far western region of China inhabited largely by **Uyghurs**. *Bingtuan* were initially mostly farms directly under the control of the **People's Liberation Army**. They are now largely civilian organizations and are involved in a wide range of economic enterprises.

blood heads   people in China who buy blood from poor farmers and resell it for a handsome profit to blood-products companies. They often use unsanitary equipment and methods, which has led to widespread HIV infections in donors that have been, in turn, transmitted to sexual partners and newborns. The problem has been most severe in Henan and adjacent **provinces** in central China where there are many "AIDS villages" in which a large percentage of the population is infected.

Blue Shirts   a clique of the **Kuomintang** that favored **fascism** as an ideology for the **Republic of China** in the 1930s. They were a paramilitary organization that drew inspiration from Benito Mussolini in Italy. The Blue Shirts were active in implementing Chiang Kai-shek's **New Life Movement**.

bourgeois liberalization   a term widely used by the CCP in the late 1980s to criticize intellectuals and others who were thought to be advocating political reforms that would challenge party leadership. The **Tiananmen Square** protests of 1989 were said to have been caused, in part, by the spread of bourgeois liberalization. See also **spiritual pollution**.

bourgeoisie   in Marxist theory, the ruling class in capitalist society. The bourgeoisie owns the means of production and employs and exploits the **proletariat** from whose labor they extract profits. It is not only the economically dominant class, but it also controls the state, which it uses as an instrument to protect its own power and property as well as to suppress the working class. Synonymous with the capitalist class. Mao applied the term more broadly to refer to those who used their authority for self-interest and to claim special privilege and higher status. There could be a bourgeoisie and bourgeois **ideology** even after private property had been abolished during the **socialist transformation** and the bourgeoisie as an economic class no longer existed. See also **class struggle, proletariat**.

Boxer Protocol   the peace treaty that the **Qing dynasty** was forced by foreign powers to sign in September 1901 after the suppression of the **Boxer Uprising**. Of all the Protocol's humiliating provisions, the most disastrous for China was a staggering indemnity to pay the cost of the war for the foreign powers, which proved a crushing burden to the imperial government's already crippled economy.

Boxer Uprising   also known as the Boxer Rebellion, or the Righteous Harmony Society Movement; took place in **North China** in 1899–1900. The name "Boxers" refers to the martial arts mastered by the rebels, which supposedly gave them protection against harm, even from bullets. The rebellion was aimed at Christian missionaries, Chinese Christian converts, and, initially, the **Qing dynasty**, but its causes lie more deeply in the deteriorating economic conditions in the rural areas, compounded by natural disasters. The Empress Dowager Cixi at first ordered the suppression of the rebellion, but then embraced it as an anti-imperialist movement. It was subdued by the intervention of Western forces after the Boxers attacked foreign diplomatic buildings in **Beijing**. See also **Boxer Protocol**.

BRIC   Brazil, Russia, India, and China, as an informal grouping of four large emerging economies.

Building Socialism with Chinese Characteristics   one of the two key components of **Deng Xiaoping Theory** (the other being the **Four Cardinal Principles**). The term conveys the idea that China must adapt both the theory and practice of **socialism** in its quest for modernization because of its relative economic "backwardness." This involves using whatever means are necessary, even capitalist ones, to promote development. There are, in turn, two components to building socialism with Chinese characteristics: reform of the economy by increasing the role of the market while reducing that of the state; and opening to the outside world by expanding China's involvement in the global economy. See also **cat theory**; **primary stage of socialism**.

Buyun experiment   elections that were held in 1998 in which all the voters in the villages that were part of Buyun **town** (in Sichuan **province**) went to the polls to directly elect the town leaders. This experiment with **direct elections** got much publicity at the time, but the central government soon ruled them unconstitutional and no such elections have been held since. However, the local leader who conducted the experiment, Zhang Jinming, has been promoted and continues as an advocate for more open election procedures at the local levels of government. See also **consultative election**.

cadre   any person in a position of authority. In China, not all cadres belong to the communist party and not all party members are cadres. The term encompasses officials from the very highest leaders to the lowest ranking and includes people in leadership positions in all types of institutions and settings, not just political.

cadre exchange system   a system of personnel management used in China in which leading **town** cadres, such as the town head and party secretary, are transferred to a different locality every 3–6 years. This system is meant to prevent cadres from developing local networks that might dilute their allegiance to higher-level authorities or provide opportunities for corruption.

campaign   see **mass mobilization campaign**.

capitalism   a type of economic system in which the means of production are, for the most part, privately owned and operated for profit. Economic activity is based on a free **market economy** in which the state plays a limited role in determining such things as production, distribution, investment, prices, supply and demand, and the allocation of labor. In **Marxism**, capitalism is the stage of human social and economic development that comes after feudalism and before **socialism**. It is a decisive period in history in which the **bourgeoisie** is the ruling class and the **proletariat** comes into being. Capitalism ends (and gives way to **socialism**) when the proletariat rises in revolution and overthrows the bourgeoisie.

capitalist roader   a label given to **cadres** in China who were accused of betraying socialism and advocating or following policies that would lead to a restoration of capitalism in the country.

casino capitalism   a system in which an economy and the government become heavily dependent on gambling in private casinos. **Macao** is an example of casino capitalism.

cat theory   based on Deng Xiaoping's famous saying that "it does not matter if it is a white cat or a black cat, as long as it catches mice"; in other words, it is results that matter when determining whether a policy is correct. The comment was made in a July 1962 speech on restoring agricultural production in the aftermath of the **Great Leap Forward** famine. Mao interpreted Deng's meaning as being that ideology did not matter in policy-making, and this statement was used against Deng in the **Cultural Revolution** as evidence that he was a **capitalist roader**.

Central Advisory Commission   established by Deng Xiaoping in 1982 as a CCP organization with little power, whose purpose was to ease elderly senior leaders into retirement by removing them from important positions, yet allowing them to retain some public visibility and prestige in an advisory capacity. It was abolished in 1992.

Central Commission for Discipline Inspection   the CCP organization charged with monitoring and punishing abuses of power, corruption, and other wrongdoings committed by party officials. Lower-level party organizations, including provincial, municipal, and county-level bodies, also have discipline inspection commissions that report directly to the commission one level above them.

Central Committee   the third-highest level of leadership in the **Chinese Communist Party**. It now consists of about 370 regular and alternate members who are high-ranking CCP **cadres** from around the country. It is elected every five years by the **National Congress of the CCP** and meets annually for about two weeks.

Central Cultural Revolution Group (CCRG)   became the *de facto* ruling body in China after the purge of Liu Shaoqi and other top leaders in 1966, although its power and that of all organizations was eclipsed by Mao's personal authority at the height of the **Cultural Revolution**. The CCRG was dominated by ideological radicals like Mao's wife, Jiang Qing, who was the effective leader of the group. It suspended operations in September 1969.

Central Military Commission (CMC)   the most important military organization in China. Technically, there are both a CCP CMC (formally, the Military Commission of the **Central Committee**) and a PRC Central Military Commission; in fact, the two bodies overlap completely in personnel and function. The current CMC has eleven members. CCP general secretary and PRC president Hu Jintao is the chairman, which, in essence, makes him the commander in chief of China's armed forces. All the other members are from the military. Sometimes referred to in English as the Military Affairs Commission.

Central Party School   formally called the Party School of the Central Committee of the Communist Party of China; located in **Beijing**; the highest-level institution for training CCP leaders. Party leaders from around the country take courses there for periods ranging from a couple of months to a couple of years on **Marxism-Leninism** and its Chinese adaptations, as well as in areas such as comparative political systems and theories, public administration, economics, law, and various policy-related subjects. Being the head of the school is an important position within the party leadership, particularly for rising stars, and has been held at various times since 1949 by such important figures as Liu Shaoqi, Hua Guofeng, Hu Jintao, and Xi Jinping, who is likely to become general secretary of the CCP in 2012. Mao Zedong headed the school in 1942–1947, when it was located in **Yan'an** and while he was consolidating his political and ideological authority within the party.

Central Special Case Examination Group   established in 1966 as the organ of an inner-party inquisition that directed the ferreting out, arrest, and torture of suspect **Central Committee** members and other officials. It was formally dissolved in December 1978.

Charter 08   a document signed by more than three hundred Chinese intellectuals and political activists, issued as a blueprint for democratic reforms in December 2008. Its leading signatories were detained and sometimes jailed.

chief executive   the head of the government of the **Hong Kong** Special Administrative Region of the PRC. The chief executive must be a Chinese citizen, at least forty years old, and have lived in Hong Kong for twenty years or more. He or she is elected for a five-year term by an Election Committee that currently consists of 800 members elected or appointed from various sectors of society, such as commerce, finance, labor, the professions, religion, and government. The composition of the Election Committee is closely controlled by **Beijing** and the candidate elected has to be approved by the government of the PRC. The **Macao** SAR of the PRC is also headed by a chief executive.

China Democracy Party   formed in 1998 as an open opposition party by former **Tiananmen Movement** activists. The party was initially allowed to register and open branches nationwide, but fearing that it was becoming too popular, the CCP banned the organization and arrested most of its leaders.

China Proper (or Inner China)   a somewhat imprecise geographic term that refers to the **provinces** of eastern and central China that became part of the Chinese empire early in its history and is largely populated by the majority ethnic **Han** Chinese.

Chinese civil war   the conflict between the **Kuomintang (KMT)**, led by Chiang Kai-shek, and the **Chinese Communist Party** (CCP), led after 1935 by Mao Zedong. There were two phases of the civil war: 1927–1937, beginning when Chiang Kai-shek unleashed the **White Terror** against the communists to the formation of a **united front** between the KMT and CCP to fight the Japanese after the **Xi'an Incident**; and 1946–1949, from the resumption of KMT-CCP hostilities following the surrender of Japan in World War II to the victory of the CCP and the founding of the **People's Republic of China**.

Chinese Communist Party (CCP)   founded in 1921; it has been the ruling party of the People's Republic of China since 1949. It currently has about 76 million members, making it by far the largest political party in the world, but still a small minority of the Chinese population, which is consistent with its self-proclaimed role as a **vanguard party**.

Chinese Communist Youth League (CCYL)   an organization of the CCP for people aged fourteen to twenty-eight. It is a training ground for future party members and leaders. In 2008, the CCYL had 75 million members. Some of China's current top leaders advanced their political careers by working as leaders of the CCYL. See also *tuanpai*.

Chongqing   a city in southwestern China to which Chiang Kai-shek and the **Kuomintang** retreated after the Japanese invasion in 1937. It became the wartime capital of the **Republic of China**. Today it is one of the four **centrally administered cities** of the PRC.

civil service examination system   the system for selecting imperial bureaucrats that was first established in the Han dynasty (206 BCE–220 CE) and lasted until 1905, when it was abolished as part of a futile effort to save China's last dynasty, the **Qing** (1644–1912). The exams mainly tested knowledge of Confucian texts and required years of intensive, highly specialized studying to prepare for multilevel examinations that few passed.

civil society   the social space occupied by private organizations and associations composed of civilians who join together to pursue a common purpose *other than the direct pursuit of political power* and which operate independently of government authority. Most simply, it consists of those associations that exist and operate in the space between the family and the state.

class struggle   the idea that exploited and exploiting classes are constantly engaged in conflict, for example poor peasants and landlords or the **proletariat** and the **bourgeoisie**. It is one of the central ideas of **Marxism**. Mao's elaborations on the Marxist theory of class struggle, especially that it continues even during the **socialist transformation** and after the elimination of private property, are defining features of **Mao Zedong Thought** as a variety of Marxism. It is also considered by the current leadership of the CCP as one of Mao's ideological errors and a cause of the **Cultural Revolution**.

"cleansing of class ranks" campaign   in 1968–1969, together with subsequent suppressions in 1970–1972, probably killed at least 1.5 million people. The targets were troublesome rebel elements or others who had earned the displeasure of local authorities during the **Cultural Revolution**, as well as ordinary criminals, imaginary counterrevolutionaries, and the usual suspects with bad class backgrounds.

collectives   a type of rural organization established in 1956–1957 in the second stage of the **socialist transformation** of the Chinese countryside that followed the formation of **cooperatives** in 1954–1955. Collectives were much larger—250 families—than the earlier cooperatives and more socialist in their organization; the collective not only owned the land, but members were paid only according to their labor with no account made of the amount of land or other resources that families had put in. Only a small portion of the collectively owned land was set aside for private cultivation. Also called Higher-Level Agricultural Producer Cooperatives (HLAPCs).

collective identity   a sense of belonging to a specific group based on some shared characteristic, for example, race, religion, economic class, culture, language, or gender.

collective ownership   a type of public ownership of property in a socialist economy that is between state (government) ownership and private ownership. In theory, the property is owned jointly by a group of people and is operated in their common interest rather than for the profit of any single individual. In China, rural land is collectively-owned by the entire village and is contracted out to individual families or used for other purposes such as building a collectively-owned factory.

collectivization   the transformation of private property, particularly land, into some type of public ownership. In China, the collectivization—or **socialist transformation**—of agriculture unfolded in three major stages that involved establishing **cooperatives** (1954–1955), **collectives** (1956–1957), and **communes** (1958).

communes   see **people's communes.**

Comintern (Communist International)   the organization established in Moscow in 1919 with the goal of supporting and spreading communist revolutions to other parts of the world. It worked with existing communist parties and sent agents to help establish such parties where they did not exist. Comintern agents were important in the founding and development of the **Chinese Communist Party,** though its influence diminished as Mao Zedong rose to power.

communism   in Marxist theory, the highest stage of human social development. It is the goal of and follows the **socialist transformation** of society. It is fundamentally egalitarian; power is in the hands of the producers, and the state withers away since there is no need for coercion in a truly classless society. Although reaching communism is the stated goal of all Marxist-Leninist political parties, including the Chinese Communist Party today, no country has ever claimed that it has achieved communism. The term is also often used as a synonym for **Marxism-Leninism**.

communist party-state   a type of political system in which a communist party, ideologically committed to some variant of **Marxism-Leninism,** has a monopoly of power and claims the right to exercise a "leading role" over the economy, culture, and other aspects of society, including politics.

communist period   Chinese history during which the **Chinese Communist Party** has been in power from the founding of the **People's Republic of China** in 1949 to the present.

"community" or *shequ*   a relatively new form of the lowest level of urban administration in China, first introduced in the 1990s to provide services for and as a means of control of workers laid off from **state-owned enterprises**. The *shequ* is intended to take over many of the functions that were formerly the responsibility of **work units**.

Confucianism   a philosophy based on the teachings of Confucius (551–479 BCE) and his disciples and interpreters that emphasizes proper and righteous social behavior, respect for and obedience to parents, deference to elders and superiors, the preservation of social harmony, and the value of education. Politically, it stresses that good government must be based on morality, including that of the ruler, not harsh laws. Confucianism deeply influenced the history and culture of China, as well those of the other countries in East Asia.

consultative election   a process of selecting **town** cadres—including the party secretary—in China that involves some direct inputs by all voters, but in which the final selection is left up to higher-level authorities and the deputies to the town **people's congress**. This process involves popular input into **cadre** selection, but does not cross the line of leaving the election totally up to a direct vote as was the case in the **Buyun experiment.**

contradiction   a crucial concept in **Mao Zedong Thought** (with roots in Marxist theory). It refers to the interacting opposites inherent in all things such that each part of the contradiction cannot exist without the other (the "unity of opposites"). It is also the interaction of those opposites that is the source of change and development, for example, in society, as well as in nature. For Mao (and Marx), the most fundamental contradiction in society is that between classes, such as between landlords and **peasants** and between the **bourgeoisie** and the **proletariat**, whose interaction takes the form of **class struggle.** See also **antagonistic contradiction.**

Cooperative Medical Scheme (CMS)   the system of health care in rural China in the 1960s and 1970s during the Maoist period that provided free or almost free basic-level preventive and curative services. About 90 percent of rural residents were covered. The CMS collapsed with the coming of **decollectivization** at the start of the **reform era**, leaving most rural residents uninsured.

cooperatives   the first form of socialist organization introduced in the Chinese countryside in 1954–1955. Cooperatives consisted of twenty-five to fifty families. Land, although still technically owned by the farmers, as well as tools and draft animals, were pooled. Members were paid partly on the basis of how much work they did and partly according to how much property they had contributed to the cooperative. Agricultural production was under the direction of cooperative officials. Formally called lower-level agricultural producers cooperatives (LLAPCs).

cooperativization   the process of establishing the rural cooperatives that was carried out in China in 1954–1955 in the first phase of the **collectivization** of the Chinese countryside and the agricultural economy.

"Criticize Lin Biao and Confucius" campaign   had little to do with either Lin Biao or Confucius; launched by Mao in 1974 because of his growing unhappiness with Zhou Enlai's policies and the political reliability of the **People's Liberation Army**. Lin Biao and Confucius were surrogates for criticism of alleged ultra-rightist mistakes by Zhou (who was attacked indirectly) and the PLA leadership. Although sometimes called a "second **Cultural Revolution**," it lasted less than a year and caused much less (though not insignificant) disruption.

county   the level of administration in the PRC below the **province** (and **autonomous region** and **centrally administered city**) and above the **town.**

Cultural Revolution   formally the "Great Proletarian Cultural Revolution," a political campaign and mass movement launched by Chairman Mao Zedong in 1966 to stop China from following both the bureaucratic Soviet model of socialist development and the Western "capitalist road" down which he had concluded some of his closest comrades were leading the country. There is a scholarly difference of opinion as to whether the Cultural Revolution occurred during the relatively short span of 1966–1969 or engulfed the whole decade of 1966–1976, including up to and just beyond Mao's death in September 1976. In either case, the Cultural Revolution was a terribly destructive period that combined elements of a witch hunt, a crusade, an inquisition, armed conflict, and cut-throat palace politics.

Dalai Lama   the spiritual leader of Tibetan Buddhism; from the seventeenth century to 1959 also the head of the government of **Tibet.** "Lama" is a general term referring to a teacher of Tibetan Buddhism. Dalai Lamas are believed to be the reincarnation of their predecessors. The current Dalai Lama (b. 1935) is the fourteenth in a line of succession that goes back to the late fourteenth century. In 1959, an invasion of Tibet by China's **People's Liberation Army** forced the Dalai Lama to flee to India (where his government in exile still remains). He won the Nobel Peace Prize in 1989.

dangwai   literally, "outside the party"; the general rubric applied to opponents of the **Kuomintang (KMT)** in **Taiwan** in the early 1980s, when the formation of formal opposition political parties was still banned under the terms of **martial law**. The fact that this was allowed by the KMT, then under the control of Chiang Kai-shek's son, Chiang Ching-kuo, was seen by some as an encouraging sign that democratization might be beginning. In 1986, *dangwai* politicians founded the **Democratic Progressive Party (DPP)**.

Daoist/Daoism   (Taoist/Taoism) an ancient Chinese school of thought and practice that combines elements of philosophy, religion, and folk beliefs. Dao (or Tao) literally means "the Way," and Daoism emphasizes harmony between humans and nature, the wholeness of the universe, spontaneity over thought, simplicity and truth, the rejection of worldly worries and desires, and achieving transcendence through the cultivation of moral character.

decollectivization   the process of dismantling the **people's communes** and establishing the **household responsibility system** in the Chinese countryside in the early 1980s that was a key part of the **market reforms** introduced by Deng Xiaoping when he came to power in the post-Mao era.

Democracy Wall   a name given to a 650-foot stretch of wall near **Tiananmen Square** in **Beijing**, where in late 1978–early 1979 there was an eruption of political posters by intellectuals criticizing Mao's mistakes and the neo-Maoist **"whateverist" faction**, as well as calling for democratization. Democracy Wall was shut down and several leaders of the movement were arrested after it had served Deng Xiaoping's purpose of isolating his leftist political opponents in the party leadership.

democratic centralism   the Leninist principle of how a communist party is to be organized and operate internally. The core idea is that the party should encourage open discussion and debate (democracy) while a matter is being decided, but once the leadership has made a decision, then all members are expected to accept and follow it (centralism). It stipulates that the individual party member is subordinate to the party organization and that lower-level party organizations are subordinate to higher-level organizations. Democratic centralism also provides for elections to leadership positions. In the practice of **communist party-states** such as China, the centralism part of the principle has far outweighed the democratic part. See also **inner-party democracy**.

Democratic Progressive Party (DPP)   one of the two major political parties in **Taiwan**, the other being the **Kuomintang (KMT)**. The DPP was established by **Taiwanese** opposition (*dangwai*) politicians in 1986 with independence for Taiwan as a major part of its platform. The DPP won the presidency with the election of Chen Shui-bian in 2000, who was re-elected in 2004, but lost the presidency (and control of the parliament) to the KMT in 2008. The party is still more cautious about ties with the PRC than is the KMT, but it no longer proposes outright independence for the island.

demographic transition   describes the "natural" shift in a country from high birth rates and high death rates to low birth rates and low death rates as a consequence of economic development and modernization.

Deng Xiaoping Theory   the official name given by the **Chinese Communist Party** to the **ideology** of Deng Xiaoping. Deng Xiaoping Theory was added to the constitution of the CCP in 1997 as a formal part of the party's guiding ideology. It can be said to consist of two main parts: **Building Socialism with Chinese Characteristics**, which involves the reform of the economy, including introducing elements of capitalism, and opening the country economically and in other ways to the outside world; and the **Four Cardinal Principles**, which lay out the political framework of Party leadership and the ideological conditions for reform and opening up. See also **cat theory**.

dependency ratio   the size of the working-age population (15–64) expressed as a proportion of the total population. The young (birth–14) and the elderly (over 65) are considered to be dependent on the working age (productive) population. Because of the **one-child policy**, China has a rapidly aging population, which will sharply increase its elderly dependency ratio. This is a challenge to the government in terms of providing elder care and social security.

developmental state   a government, usually an authoritarian one, that is strongly committed to and uses its power to promote national economic development.

dibao or **"minimum livelihood protection"**   implemented to provide subsidies to all individuals with incomes below locally determined poverty lines in urban China after the welfare elements (the **iron rice bowl**) of the **work unit** system were eliminated in the **reform era**.

dictatorship of the proletariat   the idea (first proposed by Marx) that after the **proletariat** (the industrial working class) has seized political power from the **bourgeoisie** (the capitalists), it—or the communist party on its behalf—will have to exercise strict control over the bourgeoisie and others who seek to overthrow the proletarian state. See also **people's democratic dictatorship**.

direct elections   an electoral system of choosing political officeholders in which the voters directly vote for the people or party that they want to see elected. Contrast with **indirect elections**.

directly administered city   one of four cities in China that are under the direct jurisdiction of the central government: **Beijing, Chongqing**, Shanghai, and Tianjin. They have the same administrative standing as **provinces**.

dynasties   the series of hereditary monarchies that ruled China from 221 BCE until 1912 CE. There were a dozen or so major Chinese dynasties, which lasted from under twenty years (the Qin) to two hundred (Tang, Ming, Qing), three hundred (Song), or four hundred (Han) years.

Eastern Turkistan Islamic Movement (ETIM)   a small militant **Uyghur** separatist group in the **Xinjiang Autonomous Region** supposedly affiliated with Al Qaeda that the United States Government declared to be a terrorist organization in August 2002 and which the Chinese government regards as a threat to its internal security.

ecological civilization   part of PRC president and CCP leader Hu Jintao's so-called **scientific outlook on development** and **harmonious socialist society**, which are the hallmarks of the platform of his administration and his contribution to the guiding **ideology** of the CCP. It emphasizes paying attention to the environmental consequences of economic growth and supports giving priority to **sustainable development**.

eight immortals   (or eight elders) eight very senior leaders of the CCP, including Deng Xiaoping and Chen Yun, who wielded great power in the 1980s and into the 1990s, even though they had mostly retired from their official positions.

eight model operas   the most famous of the very limited number of stage works approved for public performance during the **Cultural Revolution** by Jiang Qing. As with all authorized works of the time, they had revolutionary themes that praised the heroism of workers, peasants, and soldiers and highlighted the infallible leadership of the Chinese Communist Party. The titles of some of them are: *Red Detachment of Women*, *Taking Tiger Mountain by Strategy*, and *On the Docks*.

elitist coalition   a group of current Chinese leaders who prefer to continue giving priority to promoting development in the fastest growing and most modern parts of the country and are less concerned about problems such as inequality and environmental degradation. The elitist coalition represents the interests of entrepreneurs, the emerging middle class, and the coastal region. See also **populist coalition**; **princelings**.

ethnic minorities (or national minorities)   China's 55 non-**Han** ethnic groups that range in size from 16 million (the Zhuang) to under 3,000 (the Lhobo). See also **Tibetan**; **Uyghur**.

Executive Council (ExCo)   the advisory body that assists the **chief executive** of the **Hong Kong Special Administrative Region (HKSAR)** in policy-making. In that sense, it serves as the chief executive's cabinet. Members are appointed by the chief executive from among senior civil servants, members of the **Legislative Council**, and notable public figures, such as a university president. There are currently thirty members, including the chief executive.

export-led growth (ELG)   a strategy of economic development that stresses using exports produced by comparatively cheap labor to pay for technology imports that fuel modernization and shift the composition of GDP, first from agriculture to industry, and then to services. China's rapid economic growth has largely followed an ELG approach, but the global financial crisis that began in late 2008 forced the government to shift to a strategy that put more emphasis on domestic consumption.

extermination campaigns   efforts by Chiang Kai-shek to destroy the **Chinese Communist Party** by military force. There were five such efforts between 1930 and 1934. The

Fifth Extermination Campaign in 1934 drove the CCP out of their **Jiangxi Soviet** base and forced them to undertake their year-long **Long March**.

extraterritoriality   a concept in international law in which foreigners or international organizations are exempt or immune from the local laws of the country in which they are present. It may be applied to specific places, such as territorial concessions under the control of a foreign power. It may also mean the extension of the jurisdiction of a nation's laws to its citizens abroad, in which case if such a citizen committed a crime in a foreign country, she or he would be subject to the laws of his or her home country, not the country in which the crime was committed. Extraterritoriality was included in many of the **unequal treaties** imposed on the **Qing dynasty**.

faction   an informal group of individuals who are united by some common bond and whose purpose is to maximize their power, especially that of their own leader. Factions may be motivated by shared ideology, policy preferences, personal loyalties, or simply the desire for power.

Falun Gong   literally, "Dharma Wheel Practice"; a spiritual sect that combines elements of Buddhism and **Daosim** along with breathing exercises and meditation founded in 1992 by Li Hongzhi, a worker and musician turned spiritual leader. It gained tens of millions of followers from all walks of life both inside China and abroad. The Chinese government began cracking down on the group in 1999, which led to a silent protest by 10,000 Falun Gong followers outside **Zhongnanhai,** the CCP leadership compound in **Beijing**. The government then labeled the group as a dangerous religious cult and banned it. The ban remains in effect and the Falun Gong movement in China has been driven underground.

fascism   an ideology that exalts national glory and strong authoritarian government under a single party and a single leader. It is highly militaristic. Fascism is firmly anti-communist and believes in mutually beneficial economic cooperation between the state and the private sector.

floating population   the rural-to-urban migrant population, numbering 150 million, who have moved to China's cities in search of jobs since the 1980s. It is likely the largest population migration in history. Most migrants have insecure, low-paying jobs in the construction or service industries. In some of China's largest cities, they make up as much as a quarter or a third of the total population.

"Four Big" Rights   the right to speak out freely, air views fully, hold great debates, and write big-character posters; included in the 1975 constitution of the PRC—the so-called **Cultural Revolution** constitution because of its many radical features. These rights were removed when the constitution was thoroughly rewritten in 1982 after the Maoist era had ended.

Four Cardinal Principles   the ideological guidelines for economic reform spelled out by Deng Xiaoping in a speech in March 1979. In that speech he said, in pursuing modernization it was necessary for China to: (1) uphold the socialist road; (2) uphold the dictatorship of the proletariat; (3) uphold the leadership of the Communist Party; and (4) uphold Marxism-Leninism and Mao Zedong Thought. The CCP still emphasizes the Four Cardinal Principles as part of its guiding ideology.

Free China   that area of southwest China not under the control of the Japanese or the communists during World War II, but under the authority of the **Republic of China**. See **Chongqing.** The term was frequently used by the United States and its allies during the cold war to refer to **Taiwan** in contrast to the People's Republic, which was called "Red China."

Gang of Four   a label first applied by Chairman Mao Zedong in May 1975 to his wife, Jiang Qing, and her radical Shanghai colleagues, Zhang Chunqiao, Yao Wenyuan, and Wang Hongwen as part of a warning to them to stop their secretive factional maneuverings within the party leadership: "Practice Marxism-Leninism, and not revisionism; unite and don't split; be open and aboveboard, and don't intrigue and conspire. Don't function as a gang of four, don't do it any more, why do you keep doing it?" The label was then publically applied to them as part of a campaign of denunciation after their arrest in October 1976. The "Gang of Four" was put on trial in 1980 and sentenced to long prison terms for their political crimes.

general line   the overall policy direction set by the leadership of the CCP.

Gini Index   a statistical measure of the inequality of income distribution in a country. It ranges from 0 (perfect equality) to 1 (perfect inequality). China's Gini Index has been going up during most of the **reform era**.

"going out strategy"   China's push to purchase overseas firms, mines, and resources, locating its own companies overseas, and listing Chinese firms on global stock markets to acquire foreign capital. This strategy began in the 1990s, but has accelerated dramatically since the mid-2000s.

gradualism   an approach to economic development that implements reform in a cautious, step-by-step manner. China's economic reform are often characterized as being gradualist, in contrast to the **"big bang"** approach of rapid and multifaceted change undertaken by the former Soviet Union and many Eastern European countries after the fall of the region's **communist-party states**. But there have been "big bang" aspects to China's reform, such as the wave of privatization of state-owned and collective enterprises in the 1990s. See also **segmented deregulation**.

Great Leap Forward   (1958–1960) Mao's utopian push to accelerate China's economic development to catch up with the industrial powers and its ideological advancement into the era of true **communism**. The Leap was a **mass mobilization campaign** under party leadership that involved a radical reorganization of society, relied on labor power, and emphasized human will and revolutionary fervor to reach ever higher levels of production. It ended in one of the worst famines in human history and an industrial depression that wiped out nearly all the economic gains of the CCP's first years in power. See also **people's communes; Lushan Conference**.

Great Proletarian Cultural Revolution   see **Cultural Revolution**.

Great Wall   built as a fortification by various Chinese **dynasties,** beginning with the **Qin** (221–206 BCE), to keep "barbarians" from the north from invading China. Its stretches from the coast northeast of **Beijing** about 4,000 miles (6,400 km) to the west.

Greater China   usually refers to the PRC (particularly the southern **province** of Guangdong), **Hong Kong**, and **Taiwan**—and sometimes Singapore—particularly the close economic integration within the region.

guanxi   literally, "connections"; specifically, informal interpersonal relationships or networks. *Guanxi* can be based on a wide variety of connections between people, such as native place, school ties, or common acquaintances, and imply both trust and reciprocity.

guerrilla warfare   a method of warfare in which small, highly mobile units made up of fighters called guerrillas (the word guerrilla is derived from the Spanish meaning "little war") attack, harass, distract, or demoralize larger and stronger forces of the enemy. Guerrillas often rely on the support of civilians to provide them with food, medicine, shelter, and intelligence.

Han   the largest ethnic group in China, comprising about 92 percent of the Chinese people in the PRC. The name comes from the Han dynasty (206 BCE–220 CE), considered the greatest of China's early dynasties.

harmonious socialist society   the core of Hu Jintao's political platform as leader of the CCP and PRC, reflecting the proclaimed policy goals of his administration. It emphasizes righting some of the imbalances and problems of China's rapid economic growth since the 1980s, including income and development inequalities, especially between city and countryside, environmental degradation, and the collapse of the health care system.

High Qing   the period during the latter half of the eighteenth century when the **Qing dynasty** was at the height of its cultural, political, and economic glory.

higher-level agricultural producers cooperatives (HLAPCs)   see collectives.

Hong Kong   **a special administrative region**   of the PRC, formally known as the Hong Kong Special Administrative Region (HKSAR). It is a small area (420 square miles) located on the far southern coast of China with a population of around 7 million. But it is also a dynamic financial and commercial center and has a standard of living that is comparable to the United States and Japan. Hong Kong became a special administrative region of the **People's Republic of China** on July 1, 1997. For about 150 years prior to that, it was a colony of Great Britain. See **Basic Law: chief executive; Executive Council; Legislative Council; "One Country, Two Systems."**

Hong Kong Special Administrative Region (HKSAR)   see **Hong Kong.**

household responsibility system   the basic form of organization in China's rural economy since the early 1980s when the **people's communes** were abolished. In this system, individual households contract for "use rights" to the land, which is still owned by the village, and families make the decisions about crops, investment, savings, labor allocation, and marketing. There were brief experiments with this type of organization in the aftermath of the Great Leap Forward, but they were stopped by Mao, who regarded them as a "sprout of capitalism." See **decollectivization**.

hukou system   household registration system, first implemented in the mid-1950s as a way to control the movement of China's population and to prevent the massive rural-to-urban migration that plagued many developing countries. Each individual had either an "agricultural" or a "non-agricultural" registration (*hukou*), which dictated where he or she could, for example, live, work, go to school, receive health care, and get and use ration coupons. The system was very effective in achieving its purposes, but was criticized for the way it reinforced and compounded urban-rural inequalities to the great disadvantage of those with agricultural registrations. The *hukou* system began to break down in the 1980s with **decollectivization**, **market reform**s, and the need for labor mobility. The system is being reformed, but is not likely to be abolished.

Hundred Days Reform   a period in mid-1898 when the emperor issued edicts ordering far-reaching changes to save the **Qing dynasty** from further decline. Among the proposed reforms were modernizing the **civil service examination system**, the entire educational system, and the institutions of government. The reforms were brought to a halt when the Empress Dowager Cixi ordered the arrest of the reformers and put the emperor under palace arrest.

Hundred Flowers movement launched by Mao Zedong and the CCP in 1956 to "let a hundred flowers bloom, let a hundred schools of thought contend" as an invitation for freedom of discussion and debate about progress and problems in the first years of communist rule in China. The criticism was much more severe and extensive than the leadership expected, with the result that much of it was labeled as "poisonous weeds" (**antagonistic contradictions**) rather than "fragrant flowers" (**non-antagonistic contradictions**). The movement was shut down in 1957 and followed by the **Anti-Rightist campaign**, which suppressed and punished hundreds of thousands of people, mostly intellectuals.

ideology a systematic or comprehensive set of values and beliefs ("ideas") that provide a way of looking at and understanding the world or some aspect of it.

imperial period Chinese history from the establishment of the **Qin dynasty** in 221 BCE to the fall of the **Qing dynasty** in 1912 CE.

indirect election an electoral process in which persons elected to office are chosen, not by voters at large, but by members of a body that has previously been elected, sometimes directly and sometimes also indirectly. In China, for example, deputies to the **National People's Congress** are elected by the **people's congresses** at the provincial level, not by all the voters in the **province**. In the United States, senators were elected by state legislatures before 1913, and in many countries today, for example, South Africa, the president is indirectly elected by the national parliament rather than by all voters. See also **direct elections**.

inner-party democracy means allowing more open discussion and debate and more competitive elections *within* the Chinese Communist Party. It is aimed at enhancing the democratic aspect of **democratic centralism** without undermining the key principle of centralized leadership. According the China's current leaders, one of Mao Zedong's biggest mistakes was violating and destroying inner-party democracy in the CCP.

iron rice bowl the cradle-to-grave benefits and lifetime employment that were guaranteed to workers in **state-owned enterprises** and to a somewhat lesser extent to peasants in **people's communes** during the Maoist era. One major objective of the **market reforms** begun in the early 1980s was to "smash" the iron rice bowl, which was considered to have been a costly drag on enterprise and commune finances as well as a disincentive to labor productivity and efficiency.

Jiangxi Soviet also known as the Chinese Soviet Republic; the **base area** headquarters of the **Chinese Communist Party** from 1931–1934, located deep in the countryside of central China. The CCP was forced to abandon the Jiangxi Soviet under assault by Chiang Kai-shek's KMT army and to embark upon the **Long March** in October 1934.

job assignment system or *fenpei* system; a method of labor allocation used in China from the 1950s into the 1990s in which university students were assigned state sector jobs according to national needs upon graduation. This was in exchange for the free university tuition and housing they had received. Students had little choice over what jobs they were assigned or even where they were located.

joint ventures   companies that are partly owned by private foreign investors and partly owned by the Chinese government or a Chinese firm. When the PRC first opened to the world economy in the 1980s, all foreign investment had to be in the form of a joint venture, the share of foreign ownership was limited to less than 50 percent, and the Chinese partner was always a **state-owned enterprise** or other government entity. Now there are no such limits, although some sectors of the economy (especially the financial sector) remain restricted to foreign involvement.

Korean War   fought in 1950–1953 with the PRC and its ally, North Korea (the Democratic People's Republic of Korea), on the one side (with limited Soviet support) and, on the other side, the United States (acting under the authorization of the United Nations) and its ally, South Korea (the Republic of Korea). It began with North Korea's invasion of South Korea, which then led to the intervention of, first, the United States and then the PRC. It ended in a truce that left the political situation on the Korean peninsula essentially unchanged. For the PRC, the outcome was a victory, despite very heavy casualties (including one of Mao's sons), because it had fought the United States to a stalemate. The Korean War enhanced the legitimacy of the PRC internationally and the CCP nationally.

kowtow   literally, "knock head," also known as the "three kneelings and nine prostrations"; an act of submission performed by almost anyone who came into the presence of the Chinese emperor, or, more generally, by any commoner in the presence of an imperial official.

Kuomintang (KMT)   [*Guomindang* in *pinyin*] literally, "National People's Party"; founded by Sun Yat-sen in 1912 to oppose the usurpation of power in the **Republic of China** by the **warlord** Yuan Shikai. The KMT was taken over by Chiang Kai-shek after Sun's death in 1925. It then fought and, in 1949, lost a civil war with the **Chinese Communist Party**, after which it fled to **Taiwan**, where it headed an authoritarian government until democratization began in the 1980s. The KMT won the 2008 presidential and legislative election in Taiwan. Also referred to as the Nationalist Party.

land reform   the process of redistributing land from those who own a lot to those who have little or none. Land reform can be legal and peaceful, with landlords compensated for their property; or it can be extremely violent, with the land seized by force and without compensation. In China, most of the land reform carried out by the CCP in their **base areas** before 1949 and in the PRC in the early 1950s was of the latter type.

law of avoidance   a rule of the imperial Chinese government that someone who had passed the **civil service examination** and was appointed to an official position could not serve in his native **province** in order to lessen the chances of favoritism toward or pressures from his family. The PRC has implemented a version of this traditional practice in prohibiting officials in charge of investigating corruption from working in their own localities.

leading small groups   informal decision-making bodies set up by the CCP to deal with important issues that cut across bureaucratic and organizational boundaries. There are about ten such groups at the national level, including, for example, leading small groups on foreign affairs, on finance and economics, and on state security. Some leading small groups are more or less permanent and some are temporary. The main purpose of these interagency executive committees is to better coordinate implementation of policies among various top decision-making bodies such the **Politburo**, the **State Council**, the **Central Military Commission**, and the Ministry of Foreign Affairs.

Legalism an influential school of Chinese thought that, unlike **Confucianism**, emphasizes strict laws and harsh punishments as the only sound basis for government. Its "golden age" was during the **Qin dynasty,** when scholars were persecuted and books were burned.

Legislative Council (LegCo) the legislature of the **Hong Kong Special Administrative Region (HKSAR)**. It was first established while Hong Kong was a British colony. LegCo currently has sixty members with thirty chosen from geographical constituencies through **direct elections**, and thirty elected by functional constituencies such as industry, financial services, labor, education, sports, performing arts, culture, and publishing. It plays an important role in Hong Kong politics and governance, but it is limited in its power because of the executive-dominant nature of the political system, which gives great authority to the HKSAR **chief executive**.

Letters and Visits Offices government-run offices where Chinese citizens can lodge a complaint by making a petition to the authorities. Rather than going through the formal court system, petitioners seek official mediation through the Letters and Visits Offices to resolve problems such as local **cadre** abuse, labors disputes, and property rights.

Long March the epic and somewhat mythologized year-long, 6,000-mile trek of the Chinese Communist Party and supporters through some of China's most difficult terrain from their **Jiangxi Soviet** base area in central China to **Yan'an** in the northwestern **province** of Shaanxi. More than 100,000 people began the Long March but less than 10,000 made it to Yan'an. It was during the Long March that **Mao Zedong** moved into the very top ranks of party leadership.

lower-level agricultural producer cooperatives (LLAPCs) see cooperatives.

Lushan Conference an expanded meeting of the CCP **Central Committee** held in August 1959 to assess the progress and problems with the **Great Leap Forward**. Chairman Mao Zedong reacted furiously to criticism of the Leap by Defense Minister and high-ranking party leader Peng Dehuai. As a result, Peng and others were purged as part of an anti-rightist campaign within the party, and some of the radical aspects of the Leap were intensified until the reality of the famine forced a major policy shift in 1960.

Macao a special administrative region of the PRC. It is located on China's far southern coast about 37 miles southwest of **Hong Kong**. It is only 11 square miles in area, and has a population of a little over half a million. Macao became a special administrative region of the **People's Republic of China** on December 20, 1999. For about 150 years prior to that, it was a colony of Portugal, which first established its influence there in the sixteenth century. It is one of the world's great centers of casino gambling, which profoundly shapes its economics, politics, and relationship with the PRC. See also **casino capitalism**.

Mainlanders people on **Taiwan** who came to the island in the late 1940s as part of the **Kuomintang's** retreat from the CCP's impending victory in the **Chinese civil war** and their descendants. See also **Taiwanese**.

Manchus a non-**Han** ethnic group native to what is now the **Northeast** of China, formerly known as Manchuria. They conquered China in 1644 and established the **Qing dynasty**.

Mao Zedong Thought the official name given by the **Chinese Communist Party** to the **ideology** of Mao Zedong. Sometime referred to by foreigners as "Maoism."

market economy an economy in which market forces such as supply and demand and the profit motive (the "free market") rather than government policies and actions are the major determinant of economic outcomes. See also **capitalism**; **market reform**.

market reform   the process of making the transition from a **planned economy** to a **market economy** through policies that reduce the role of the government and increase the influence of market forces. It also involves a reduction in the amount of state- and **collective ownership** of property and other assets and increases private ownership.

martial law   a system of administration, usually invoked by a government in emergency circumstances, in which the constitution is suspended and military force is used to maintain order.

Marxism-Leninism   the ideological foundation of **communism** and **communist party-states**. It is based on the ideas of Karl Marx (1818–1883), particularly his emphasis on the role of classes and class struggle in history, and V. I. Lenin (1870–1924), notably his prescription for the organization of a revolutionary political party.

mass line   the Maoist theory of leadership (or **work style**) that emphasizes that officials must always remain in close touch with those they lead. It rejects both leaderless, spontaneous action by the masses and leadership that is aloof or divorced from the masses. It is one of the principles of **Mao Zedong Thought** that the current leadership of the CCP holds to be valid.

mass mobilization campaign   a style of policy implementation used by the **Chinese Communist Party** that combines leadership and direction from above and the mobilized involvement of people on the local level to achieve specific objectives.

mass organizations   in the PRC, associations that represent the interests of a specific constituency, but which are under the leadership of the CCP. The major mass organization include the **All China Women's Federation (ACWF), Chinese Communist Youth League (CYL)**, the All China Federation of Trade Unions, and the All-China Federation of Industry and Commerce.

materialism   the view that all things are based on matter, not ideas or ideals ("idealism"). **Marxism** offers a materialist view of history ("historical materialism") that sees change as based largely on stages of economic development and its impact on the class structure of society. References to Marxist materialism basically refer to the primacy the theory gives to economic aspects of human existence, sometimes called economic determinism.

May 16 Directive   (1966) formally, "Circular of the Central Committee of the Communist Party of China on the Great Proletarian Cultural Revolution," marked the formal announcement of the launching of the **Cultural Revolution**.

May 7th Cadre Schools   established in 1968 during the **Cultural Revolution** to train urban **cadres** to follow the **mass line** in carrying out their work. The bureaucrats were sent, for periods ranging from a couple of months to several years, to work and live among the masses, mostly in rural communes, while also engaging in political study and self-criticism. The name of the cadre schools came from a directive the Chairman Mao Zedong issued on May 7, 1966 to the **People's Liberation** that, in addition, to preparing to fight a war, it should become a "big school" by having soldiers engage in a wide-range of civilian activities, including agricultural production.

May Fourth Movement   roughly 1915–1924, a crucial period in China's political, social, and cultural development. The name of the movement is taken from the events of May 4, 1919, when students and others gathered in **Beijing** and other cities to protest the terms of the Versailles Peace Treaty giving Japan control of former German concessions in Shandong **province** following World War I. The major themes of the movement were national independence, dignity, and salvation. Many intellectuals were radicalized by the events of the time, one result of which was the founding of the **Chinese Communist Party** on July 1, 1921. See also **Twenty-One Demands.**

missing girls   the fact that in some countries there are many millions fewer females than there should be given natural sex balance ratios. See also **one-child policy**; **sex ratio imbalance**.

Nanjing Decade   the period from the establishment of the capital of the **Republic of China** at Nanjing by Chiang Kai-shek and the **Kuomintang** in 1927 to the takeover of the city by Japanese forces in 1937. It is considered by many to be a time of relative peace and development for China. Nanjing literally means "Southern Capital."

National Congress of the Chinese Communist Party   or National Party Congress, meets every five years for about one week. The most recent party congress (elected in 2007) had more than 2,200 delegates chosen in **indirect elections** by CCP organizations around the country. According to the constitution of the CCP, the national congress has the power to elect top leaders of the party, but most of its proceedings are symbolic and ceremonial, and the decisions it makes have already been approved by the CCP's higher-level organizations, including the **Central Committee**, the **Politburo**, and the **Standing Committee**.

National People's Congress (NPC)   the national parliament or legislature of the **People's Republic of China**. It consists of more than 3,000 deputies, elected every five years, and meets annually for about two weeks. According to the PRC constitution, the NPC has significant powers, such as electing the president and declaring war. While more active in recent years in shaping legislation and serving as a forum for discussion of important issues, it still operates within the framework of party leadership and is not a truly independent branch of government.

Nationalist Party   see **Kuomintang.**

natural villages   small rural communities in China that have emerged "naturally" over a very long period of time; in most cases, the PRC put several natural villages together to be governed as a single **administrative village**.

neo-authoritarianism   a school of political thought in China that borrows from traditional Chinese tenets of meritocracy, **legalism**, and hierarchy as the basis of a new form of party dictatorship. This school of thought is referred to as China's "New Right" and favors elite rule by **technocrats**, a strong military, and a **socialist market economy.**

neo-liberalism   an economic philosophy, and the policies that go along with it, that emphasizes free market **capitalism**, a limited role for the state in managing the economy, and unrestricted international trade.

New Culture Movement   a period of great intellectual ferment in China in the 1910s–1920s when intellectuals attacked Confucianism as the source of the nation's problems and lauded science, democracy, and other Western ideas. A wide range of philosophies from radical and liberal to conservative and reactionary were debated on college campuses. The movement included a language revolution that promoted a vernacular (*baihua*) writing style, in which the written language is the same as the spoken language, to replace literary Chinese (*wenyan*), a difficult grammatical form that was an obstacle to increasing the rate of general literacy. See May Fourth Movement.

New Democracy   the early period (1949–1952) of rule by the CCP after the founding of the People's Republic, when the party promised to go slow in the undertaking the **socialist transformation** of China and to maintain a mixed economy of both state and private ownership of property and include non-communists in the governing of the country.

New Life Movement   an effort by Chiang Kai-shek in the 1930s to resurrect Confucianism in the **Republic of China** in order to revive traditional values and cultivate civic virtue. It was part of an attempt to both bolster the legitimacy of his rule and to offer an alternative to communism.

new social strata   includes groups in Chinese society that have been created during the process of **market reform** and internationalization, most importantly private entrepreneurs, managers and technical staff who work for foreign enterprises, as well as professionals, intellectuals, and others who are self-employed or work outside the public sector of the economy. The **Three Represents** theory was an ideological rationalization for allowing members of these strata to join the CCP.

nomenklatura   a Russian term meaning "name list"; refers to several thousand high-ranking leadership (or **cadre**) positions in the party, government, and military, as well as large business firms, key universities, and other institutions that must be approved by the CCP **organization department** at the relevant level. This personnel management system was adopted from the Soviet communist party. Control of the cadre appointment process is one of the CCP's most important sources of power.

non-antagonistic contradiction   "contradiction among the people"; a difference that can be resolved through debate, discussion, and other non-coercive means because the opposing sides are still part of the "people" who support the revolution, **socialism**, and the CCP. See **contradiction; antagonistic contradiction.**

North China   the area between **Beijing** in the north and the **Yangtze River** in central China.

Northeast   the three **provinces** of northeastern China: Heilongjiang, Jilin, and Liaoning; formerly called Manchuria.

Northern Expedition   began in southern China in 1926 as a joint military campaign by the KMT-CCP **United Front** to advance against **warlord**-held cities with the goal of defeating the warlords and taking control of the government of the **Republic of China**. Drew to a close in 1927 when **Chiang Kai-shek** and the KMT established the capital of the Republic at Nanjing and technically brought an end to the **warlord era**. See also **White Terror**.

"One Country, Two Systems"   the principle, first enunciated by Deng Xiaoping in the early 1980s, and agreed to in essence in the **Sino-British Joint Declaration** of 1984, under which Hong Kong became a **special administrative region** (SAR) of the PRC. This meant that, although **Hong Kong** would become part of the PRC, **socialism** would not be implemented there and its capitalist system and way of life would not be changed for fifty years. The principle also applies to **Macao**, the other SAR of the PRC. It has been proposed by the PRC as the basis of an agreement for reunification with **Taiwan**, but Taiwan has not shown any interest in those terms.

one-child policy   the official population policy of the PRC since 1979. It stipulates that, with some exceptions, couples may have only one child. The policy has been implemented in various stages and by various means, ranging from coercion to monetary fines to education. China's population growth rate has decreased dramatically, but there is debate about whether it was the one-child policy or other factors that were the primary cause of fertility decline. The policy has also had important unintended consequences such as a **sex ratio imbalance** ("**missing girls**") and a rapidly aging population in terms of the percentage of people over the age of sixty-five, which will put a strain on China's woefully inadequate pension, welfare, and health care systems.

one-level-down management system   a system of personnel management used in China in which **cadres** at each level have the authority to appoint their own subordinates. For example, the head of a county government can appoint the head of the town government without seeking approval from higher authorities at the municipal or provincial levels.

open recommendation and selection   a process of selecting state and party officials that has been implemented in some towns and cities in China to increase competition, public input, and transparency in such appointments through the use of means such as written exam, candidate forums, telephone hotlines, and even televised debates. It does not involve **direct election** and the CCP **organization department** still has ultimate authority over the process.

"open sea" nominations   a process of selecting candidates for **village committee**.

operational code   the sum of beliefs of political leaders about the nature of politics and political conflict, the possibility of bringing about change, and the strategy and tactics required to achieve political objectives. The operational code of a leader influences decision-making and therefore has policy consequences. Perceptions of the "enemy" are an important part of an operational code.

Opium War   (1839–1842) between Britain and Qing China, caused by the clash between British insistence on being able to sell opium in China and Chinese efforts to halt the trade. It ended in a humiliating defeat for China and contributed significantly to the weakening and ultimate downfall of the **Qing dynasty**. A **Second Opium War** was fought with much the same outcome in 1856–1860. See also **Treaty of Nanjing; unequal treaties**.

Organic Law of Villagers Committees   first introduced in 1988 and revised in 1998; the legislation under which elections for local leaders take place in China's rural villages. An "organic law," in general, is a fundamental or basic law that specifies the foundation of governance, in this case, in China's villages.

Organization department   of the CCP is in charge of reviewing and approving all personnel appointments of leading cadres on the *nomenklatura* list. There are organization departments at most levels of the CCP from the top (the **Central Committee**) down to the county.

Outer China   a somewhat imprecise geographical term that refers to the vast but sparsely populated area to the west of **China Proper** and which was incorporated into the Chinese empire later in its history. The area has a large concentration of non-**Han ethnic minorities**.

path dependence   term used by political scientists and economists to indicate that decisions by policy-makers are often shaped or even limited by past decisions that were made under very different circumstances.

party congress   see **National Congress of the Chinese Communist Party.**

patron-client relations   (or clientelism) involves exchanges between a more powerful patron and a less powerful client. The patron may offer resources (such as land or a job) or protection to the client, while the client provides various services, including labor, personal loyalty, and political support to the patron.

peasants   generally, those who earn their living by working a relatively small amount of land and produce, just enough, if that, for the subsistence of their family. In the 1920s, Mao identified three groups of peasants in China: poor peasants who owned little or no land of their own and had to hire out their labor to work on land owned by others; middle peasants who can support themselves by working their own land; and rich peasants who (unlike landlords) still have to work on their land, but are also able to hire others to work for them. Mao Zedong Thought is, in part, characterized as a variant of **Marxism-Leninism** because of the important place it gives to peasants as a class in taking a leading role in the revolution to seize political power and in the **socialist transformation** of society.

People's Armed Police (PAP)   China's paramilitary force that is primarily responsible for internal security. It is estimated that there are about 1.5 million members of the PAP. It was the PAP that responded in force to the ethnic unrest in Tibet in 2008 and Xinjiang in 2009.

people's communes   the form of rural production and living that was established in 1958 during the **Great Leap Forward**. The communes virtually eliminated private property in the countryside and created larger (5,000–25,000 families) and more radical and egalitarian forms of living than the collectives that preceded them. They were designed to be comprehensive, self-reliant units that would pave the way to **communism** through agricultural, industrial, and ideological development. Although the people's communes were significantly scaled back in size, function, and authority after the failure of the Great Leap, they remained the highest unit of economic and social organization in the Chinese countryside until the beginning of the reform era in the early 1980s.

people's congresses   the legislative bodies of all levels of government in the PRC from the **National People's Congress** at the top and extending down to district people's congresses in the urban areas and town people's congresses in the rural areas. The people's congress is constitutionally empowered to supervise the work of the **people's government** at its level. Only town and district people's congresses are directly elected by all voters; other levels of people's congress are chosen by **indirect elections.**

People's Daily   the official newspaper of the Central Committee of the Chinese Communist Party.

people's democratic dictatorship   a Chinese Communist variation on the **dictatorship of the proletariat**. It is meant to convey that classes besides the proletariat, including the peasantry, revolutionary intellectuals, and other groups supportive of party leadership, are part of the "people" in whose name dictatorship is exercised over the enemies of socialism. It is also meant to imply that the "people" are able to enjoy democracy. Article 1 of the constitution of the **People's Republic of China** defines the country as "a socialist state under the people's democratic dictatorship led by the working class and based on the alliance of workers and peasants."

people's government   the executive branch of the government at all formal levels of the PRC political system, as in provincial people's government or town people's government. See also **people's congress**.

People's Liberation Army (PLA)   the combined armed forces of the People's Republic of China, including the army, navy, and air force.

People's Republic of China (PRC)   the formal name of China since the **Chinese Communist Party** came to power in October 1949.

permanent revolution   in **Mao Zedong Thought**, the idea that there will always be a need for revolution if human society is not going to stagnate, although the form of that revolution changes as society develops. Mao concluded that even after the overthrow of capitalism and during the **socialist transformation** of China, the permanent revolution would still take the form of class struggle between the **proletariat** and the **bourgeoisie**.

pinyin   the system of Romanization (or transliteration) used in the **People's Republic of China** to make the pronunciation of Chinese characters accessible to people unfamiliar with the language.

planned economy   or centrally planned economy, or command economy; an economic system that is controlled by the central government, which makes all important decisions concerning production, investment, prices, and distribution of goods and services. It relies on plans and commands, rather than the free market, to regulate the economy. Planned economies were key features of **communist party-states** such as the Soviet Union. The economic reforms introduced in China since the early 1980s have greatly reduced, but by no means eliminated, the role of planning.

plenum   or plenary session; a meeting of the CCP **Central Committee**, normally held annually between the elections of the Central Committee by the **National Party Congress**, which convenes every five years.

Politburo   or Political Bureau; the second-highest level of leadership in the **Chinese Communist Party**. It now consists of about two dozen members and generally meets monthly. See also **Standing Committee**.

populist coalition   a group of current Chinese leaders, mostly of humble origins, who want to shift China's policy priorities to address some of the serious problems, such as vast economic inequalities and environmental degradation, that resulted from the growth-at-any-cost strategy pursued for much of the last three decades. The populists often voice the concerns of vulnerable social groups such as farmers, migrant workers, and the urban poor and support great attention to the development of the inland regions of the country. See also **elitist coalition**; *tuanpai*.

pragmatist faction   or practice faction; a group of CCP leaders who early in the post-Mao era supported a return to a less ideological approach to policy-making under the slogan "practice is the sole criterion for testing truth." They were led by veteran cadre Chen Yun and were strong advocates of restoring power to Deng Xiaoping, who had been purged by Mao in April 1976. They were opposed by the neo-Maoist **"whateverist" faction**.

predatory state   a government that preys on its people and the economy for the benefit of those in power.

Presidium of the National People's Congress   the organization that presides over each session of the **National People's Congress** of the PRC. It sets the agenda and determines the process for legislation to be considered by committees and voted on. The Presidium also decides on the candidates for election to China's top leadership positions, including president, vice president, and the chief justice of the Supreme People's Court, although, in reality, these candidates are determined beforehand by the **Central Committee** of the CCP.

primary stage of socialism   or initial stage of **socialism**; declared by the CCP in the early 1980s to be where the PRC was in terms of its level of ideological and economic development. This provided justification for using aspects of capitalism and the market economy to promote China's economic development. It was said that one of Mao's biggest mistakes was to skip or compress this primary stage of socialism by eliminating all elements of capitalism (like the profit motive) and moving too fast from the mid-1950s in implementing China's **socialist transformation**.

princelings   an informal group, or faction, of current CCP leaders who are children of revolutionary heroes or high-ranking officials. They are mostly associated with the **elitist coalition** in Chinese politics.

proletariat   the industrial working class in a capitalist society, which Marx saw as the most exploited class in history and the most revolutionary. Mao used the term more broadly to refer to an **ideology** embracing revolutionary change that empowers the working masses. See also **bourgeoisie, class struggle**.

province   a level of administration in the PRC just below the central government. China has twenty-two provinces.

Qin dynasty   (221–206 BCE) regarded as the beginning of the Chinese empire and Chinese imperial history, even though Chinese cultural history dates back another 2,000 years. The Emperor Qin established the dynasty after defeating and unifying a number of small independent kingdoms.

Qing dynasty   imperial China's last dynasty, established by a non-**Han** ethnic minority, the **Manchus,** in 1644 and overthrown by the **1911 Revolution** that led to the founding of the **Republic of China** in 1912.

Rape of Nanjing   (Nanking), or Nanjing (Nanking) Massacre; occurred during a six-week period beginning in December 1937 when Japanese forces killed an estimated 200,000 to 300,000 Chinese and raped tens of thousands in their takeover of the city of Nanjing, the capital of the **Republic of China**.

rectification campaign   a **Chinese Communist Party** method of enforcing compliance of its members with the prevailing party **ideology**, policies, and leadership. The method was used both before the CCP came to power (most famously, in **Yan'an** in 1942) and afterward.

red and expert   the Maoist ideal for scientists, technical personnel, and other intellectuals: to combine both ideological commitment and knowledge of their field in the service of the country, the people, and the revolution.

Red Army   founded in August 1927 as the armed force of the **Chinese Communist Party**. It was the predecessor to the **People's Liberation Army.**

Red Guards   organizations of students committed to carrying out Mao's call for a **Cultural Revolution**. They first emerged in **Beijing** high schools and universities beginning in June 1966, but soon became a nationwide movement, though never under any kind of central direction. The Red Guards were responsible for the massive destruction of property and cultural artifacts as well as widespread brutal psychological and physical persecution of alleged class enemies. They engaged in increasingly violent factionalism and armed clashes until Mao decreed that order be restored in 1968 by the **People's Liberation Army**. The Red Guards were disbanded and more than 20 million of them were sent to the countryside to labor with and learn from the peasants.

reform era   the period in China since the late 1970s when Deng Xiaoping first introduced the dramatic economic changes that took the country in a very different direction from where Mao Zedong had led it. The reform era is said to have formally begun in December 1978 at the **plenum** of the CCP **Central Committee**. See also **Building Socialism with Chinese Characteristics**.

regional power hierarchy   the idea that there is an implicit ranking, rather than a balance, in the power relationship among countries in a region. The **tributary system** of imperial China in which other countries could trade with China as long as they recognized China's political and cultural supremacy was a regional power hierarchy. Some scholars believe that the recent rise of China marks the emergence of another regional power hierarchy in East Asia.

rent seeking   the introduction of government regulations that, in various ways, create conditions where officials can gain economic advantages ("rents") for themselves or their organization that would not occur in an open market situation.

Republic of China   the government of China following the overthrow of the **Qing dynasty** in the **1911 Revolution** until the founding of the **People's Republic of China** in 1949, following the conclusion of the **Chinese civil war**. Toward the end of the civil war, more than a million supporters of the ruling party of the Republic of China, the **Kuomintang**, and its leader, Chiang Kai-shek, fled to the island of **Taiwan**, where, with American support, they were able to establish a stronghold. The government of **Taiwan** still officially calls itself the Republic of China (ROC).

republican period   Chinese history from the establishment of the **Republic of China** in 1912 to the founding of the **People's Republic of China** in 1949.

residents' committee   a quasi-official unit of urban administration in China that functions below the **street office** and may encompass between 100 and 1,000 families. Residents' committees are made up of three to seven members, headed by a director, and carry out a variety of functions in the area under their jurisdiction, including organizing volunteer security patrols or cleanup squads, posting official announcements, hearing residents complaints and conveying them to higher levels, and even dispute mediation. The committee members are generally elected to fixed terms by residents. In some sense, they are the urban equivalent of **village committees**.

Resolution on Certain Questions in the History of Our Party since the Founding of the People's Republic of China   a major document published by the CCP in 1981 as the authoritative (and still largely upheld) assessment by the post-Mao leadership of the party's achievements and shortcomings since 1949. The Resolution acknowledged that Chairman Mao Zedong had made serious mistakes, but concluded that his achievements were greater than his failings. It also contained an assessment of **Mao Zedong Thought** that distinguished between those aspects that were wrong or taken to extremes and those that remain relevant today to the party's guiding **ideology**.

revisionism   a betrayal of **Marxism-Leninism** by revising its core principles. The CCP accused the Soviet Union of revisionism and the label was also applied to Mao's opponents in the **Cultural Revolution**.

Revolutionary Committees were created in 1968–1969 as the provisional organs of government to replace those destroyed by the **Cultural Revolution**. They consisted of representatives of the party, the army, and the "masses" and were established at the provincial, municipal, and other subnational levels of administration, as well as in schools, factories, **people's communes**, and other institutions. Initially, the military was usually the dominant force on these committees since it was their responsibility to restore and maintain order after the chaos of the Cultural Revolution. The Revolutionary Committees remained the primary administrative organs of the PRC until they were replaced by **people's governments** in the late 1970s.

rightful resistance a type of grassroots protest in which the protesters invoke national laws when they seek redress for abuses by local officials. Rightful resisters believe that the legal system and the national leadership are on their side. The PRC government usually permits this kind of protest, but some rightful resistance pushes the legal limits and sometimes goes beyond, in which case the it meets with state repression.

River Elegy a 1988 documentary that aired on China Central Television, scathing about China's cultural chauvinism and insularity (characterized as "yellow culture," reflecting the dull yellow color of the Loess Plateau in northwestern China where Chinese civilization began) and admiring of its cosmopolitan and overseas influences (called "blue culture" in reference to the seafaring and diasporic nature of this side of Chinese culture.) The program was initially supported by high-ranking CCP leaders, but after the **Beijing Massacre** in June 1989, it was banned and several of those associated with its making were either arrested or left the country.

scientific outlook on development the general rubric under which CCP leader Hu Jintao's contributions to Chinese communist **ideology** is put. It incorporates the idea of creating a **harmonious socialist society**.

Second Opium War fought in 1856–1860 between Qing China and Great Britain, which was joined by France. The cause had less to do with opium per se as with Western frustration with the lack of progress more generally by the **Qing dynasty** in implementing the terms of the **Treaty of Nanjing**, which ended the first **Opium War** in 1842. The war resulted in another humiliating defeat for the Qing and the imposition of another **unequal treaty**, the Treaty of Tianjin, which further opened China to foreign merchants and missionaries, legalized the opium trade, and ceded a second part of **Hong Kong** (Kowloon) to Britain.

Secretariat an important CCP organization that handles the Party's routine business and administrative matters. Secretariat members (there are currently six) meet daily and are responsible for coordinating the country's major events and important meetings as well as top leaders' foreign and domestic travels.

segmented deregulation an approach to economic reform that implements the new policies over time in different sectors of the economy or different parts of the country. The implementation of **Special Economic Zones (SEZs)** in China is an example of segmented deregulation. See also **gradualism**.

Self-Strengthening Movement a series of efforts undertaken roughly between 1861 and 1898 to save the **Qing dynasty** after it had been seriously weakened by external conflicts and internal rebellion. The movement was led mostly by powerful provincial **Han** Chinese leaders and aimed to strengthen China through economic and military modernization. Its approach was captured in the idea that Western techniques could be adopted for their "use" (*yong*) while Chinese learning could be preserved as the "essence" (*ti*) of the nation. It was generally opposed by the Empress Dowager Cixi and the conservatives in the Qing court.

Seventeen Point Agreement   formally, The Agreement Between the Central Government and the Local Government of **Tibet** on Measures for the Peaceful Liberation of Tibet; the surrender document signed in May 1951 by the **Dalai Lama**'s government and the PRC after the invasion of Tibet by China's **People's Liberation Army**. The agreement acknowledged that Tibet was part of China, but also stated that the Dalai Lama's position would not be changed and that Tibet's religion and customs would be respected.

Severe Acute Respiratory Syndrome (SARS)   a highly contagious, potentially fatal virus that first broke out in southern China in 2002–2003 and eventually led to 774 deaths worldwide. Chinese officials initially covered up or downplayed the severity of the epidemic, but were forced to confront it when it spread outside the country. The experience is considered a wake-up call to the PRC government that it must deal more proactively with potential and real epidemics, such as HIV/AIDS.

sex ratio imbalance   an unnatural ratio between males and females in a population, particularly as reflected at the time of birth. The natural gender balance is 105 boys for every 100 girls. China has recently had a sex ratio of 119 boys for every 100 girls, and in some places it has been as high as 130 boys per 100 girls. The cause of serious imbalance is the country's **one-child policy**. Many rural couples desperate to have a boy because of customary son-preference and economic necessity have resorted to female infanticide, abandonment of baby daughters, and more recently sex-selective abortion made possible by widely available and inexpensive ultrasound tests. See **missing girls**.

shequ   see **"community"**.

Sinification   the process of being *sinified*, that is being absorbed by, assimilated to, or deeply influenced by Chinese (Sino) culture, society, or thought. In the **imperial period**, both the Mongols and the Manchus were *sinified* after they had conquered China and established ruling **dynasties**. Likewise, Mao Zedong is said to have *sinified* **Marxism-Leninism** by adapting it to China's particular circumstances as a economically-poor peasant society.

Sino-British Joint Declaration   formally known as the Joint Declaration of the Government of the United Kingdom of Great Britain and Northern Ireland and the Government of the **People's Republic of China** on the Question of **Hong Kong;** signed in December 1984. It specified the terms under which the PRC would take over the sovereignty of Hong Kong on July 1, 1997. Hong Kong had become a British colony in stages during the nineteenth century. See **Opium War**; **Treaty of Nanjing**; **unequal treaties**.

Sino-Japanese War   (1895) sparked by competition between Qing China and imperial Japan over influence in Korea. Ended in a particularly humiliating defeat for China since Japan was viewed with disdain in the traditional Chinese worldview. One result of the war was that **Taiwan** became a colony of Japan and remained so until the end of World War II. The invasion and occupation of much of eastern China by Japan from 1937–1945 is also referred to as the Sino-Japanese War.

Sino-Soviet Split   the ideological conflict between the **Chinese Communist Party** and the Communist Party of the Soviet Union that began to appear in the late 1950s. The split involved a number of issues, including major differences over how to assess the international situation during the cold war and how to deal with the United States. Each side accused the other of betraying **Marxism-Leninism**. Hostilities reached the point of military clashes along the Sino-Soviet border in 1969. Relations between the two countries were normalized in the 1980s.

small and medium enterprises (SMEs)   enterprises of a certain scale in the PRC as determined by some combination of number of employees, capital, or the value of assets and sales volume. Since 1997, all SMEs in China have been privatized, leaving only large enterprises owned by the state. SMEs are one of the most dynamic sectors of the Chinese economy in terms of growth and innovation.

socialism   in Marxism, the stage of human history between capitalism and communism. See **socialist transformation**.

Socialist Education movement   (1962–1966) aimed at ideologically reinvigorating village **cadres** and combating corruption. It only reached about one-third of China's villages. Mao Zedong and Liu Shaoqi had some differences over how the movement should be conducted, which became a major source of Mao's growing unhappiness with Liu on the eve of the **Cultural Revolution**.

socialist market economy   the official designation given by the PRC to its current economic system. The implication is that the economy combines elements of both **socialism** and the free market (**capitalism**), but that the socialist or public aspect plays the leading role.

socialist transformation   the process of moving the country from **capitalism** to **socialism**, notably through the abolition of most private ownership, the nationalization of industry and commerce, and the collectivization of agriculture. Once socialism has been established, the ideological goal is to develop it further and prepare for the ultimate transition from socialism to **communism**.

soft power   the use of non-coercive means, such as diplomatic, cultural, and economic influence, by a state to advance its interests and influence other nations; contrast to hard power, which involves use of military means or threats and other forms of coercion.

South China   the area between the **Yangtze River** in central China and the country's southern borders.

Southern Inspection Tour   or Southern Journey, undertaken by Deng Xiaoping in 1992 to investigate firsthand the situation in China's most economically dynamic region in Guangdong **province**, bordering **Hong Kong**. Deng concluded that China needed to make economic reform and opening to the world its highest priority again after a period of retrenchment following the **Beijing Massacre** of 1989.

special administrative region (SAR)   administrative units of the PRC that have a significant degree of local autonomy in all matters other than foreign relations and defense. China has two special administrative regions: the **Hong Kong** SAR, a former British colony that returned to Chinese sovereignty in 1997; and the **Macao** SAR, a former Portuguese colony that reverted to China in 1999. SARs are much more self-governing than are the **autonomous regions** of the PRC, such as **Tibet** and **Xinjiang**. But ultimate authority resides in **Beijing**.

Special Economic Zones (SEZs)   or Export Processing Zones (EPZs); areas of the country that are allowed to implement incentives designed to attract foreign investment by firms that will produce goods for export. Such incentives may include tax holidays, low rents, guaranteed supply of materials and utilities, and inexpensive labor. The benefits to the host country include job creation and the transfer of technology and management skills. China's first SEZs were established in the early 1980s, followed by a rapid expansion of similar "open cities" and "development zones" in many parts of the country, but especially along the coast.

spiritual pollution   a term that was widely used in China in 1983–1984 during a campaign against ideas and influences, mostly from abroad, which, according to the CCP, contaminated the thinking and threatened the well-being of the Chinese people. It was a vague term that was applied to everything from democracy to pornography. See also **bourgeois liberalization**.

Standing Committee (CCP)   formally, the Standing Committee of the **Politburo** of the **Central Committee**, the most powerful leadership organization in the PRC. It currently has 9 members, headed by the general secretary, Hu Jintao.

Standing Committee of the National People's Congress (SCNPC)   is responsible for any issues that require congressional consideration when the full **National People's Congress** is not in session It generally convenes every two months, with each meeting lasting about one week.

State Asset Supervision and Administration Commission (SASAC)   the PRC government organization that oversees enterprises that remain under state control. SASAC covers five sectors of the economy—telecommunications, petroleum and refining, metallurgy (steel and other metals), electricity, and military industry.

State Council   the cabinet of the central government of the PRC. It is led by the premier, and consists of vice premiers; state councillors, who are senior government leaders with broad responsibilities; ministers or commissioners, who head functional departments such as the Ministry of Foreign Affairs and the National Population and Family Planning Commission; and a secretary-general who manages the day-to-day business of the Council.

state farms   huge agricultural enterprises run the by PRC central government. They are usually located in more remote parts of the country such as the **Northeast** and **Xinjiang**. They are run much like **state-owned enterprises**. The number of state farms has been reduced in the **reform era**, but, as of 2008, there were still 1,893 of them, employing more than 3.4 million people.

state-building   the process of establishing and strengthening the formal institutions and processes of government at the national and subnational levels.

state-owned enterprise (SOE)   a company that is owned and operated by some level of state administration. By the mid-1950s, all businesses in China had been nationalized and brought under the authority of state planning. SOEs received production quotas from the state, were supplied with all the inputs needed for production from the state, and had to sell its output to the state at fixed prices. Managers were appointed by the state. SOEs were not allowed to fail, and if they got into financial trouble, the state would bail them out. The economic reforms, particularly since the 1990s, have greatly reduced the number of SOEs in China and have streamlined those that still exist, as well as making them accountable for their bottom line. Tens of millions of workers have been laid off from closed or reformed SOEs. See also **iron rice bowl**; **work unit**.

street office or sub-district, the lowest official unit of formal urban administration in China. Chinese cities are divided into districts, which in turn are divided into sub-districts called street offices. The street office staff are government **cadres,** and there is usually a branch of the public security bureau at the street office-level. See also **residents' committee**; **"community"** (*shequ*).

struggle meeting a technique used by the **Chinese Communist Party** in which a person is subjected to intense criticism ("struggled") and sometimes physical punishment because of alleged political or ideological mistakes. The purpose is to elicit a confession ("self-criticism"), repentance, and compliance. Struggle meetings were used during **rectification campaigns**, **land reform**, the **Anti-Rightist campaign**, and most extensively during the **Cultural Revolution**.

Supreme People's Procuratorate the national-level organization responsible for both prosecution and investigation in legal matters. In some ways, its functions are similar to the U.S. Department of Justice, and its head, the procurator general, is roughly equivalent to the attorney general. There are procuratorial offices at the sub-national levels of government, including provincial and county levels.

sustainable development emphasizes the environmental consequences of economic growth and modernization and takes into account the imperative of maintaining resources and a livable world for current and future generations. See also **ecological civilization**.

Taiping Rebellion (1850–1864) a long and large-scale rebellion against the **Qing dynasty** led by a Christian convert, Hong Xiuquan, claiming to be the younger brother of Jesus Christ whose mission was to establish the Taiping ("Great Peace) Heavenly Kingdom on earth. Because of deteriorating economic and social conditions and its promise of radical changes, the rebellion gained a huge number of followers from among China's peasants. It conquered most of **South China** up to the **Yangtze River**, before it was undone by its own internal intrigues and discord and suppressed by armies let by powerful provincial **Han** Chinese leaders. The death toll from the rebellion is estimated to have been about 20 million. Although it did not succeed, the Taiping Rebellion greatly weakened the Qing dynasty.

Taiwan an island about 75 miles off the coast of southeastern China. At the conclusion of the **Chinese civil war** in 1949, the defeated forces of Chiang Kai-shek's **Kuomintang** fled to Taiwan. With American support, the KMT was able to continue governing Taiwan as the **Republic of China**. Taiwan is now an economically developed democracy that still calls itself the "Republic of China" and is *de facto* a separate and distinct political entity from the **People's Republic of China**. The PRC claims that Taiwan is rightfully a **province** of China.

Taiwan Strait or Formosa Strait, the 112-mile-wide stretch of water between the PRC and the island of **Taiwan**. It has been the site of several military and political crises, most seriously in the 1950s, and remains one of the strategically fragile parts of the world, despite much improved relations between the mainland and the island.

Taiwanese can refer generally to all the people who live on Taiwan, or more specifically, to those whose ancestors came to the island before 1945 or so. Taiwanese make up about 84 percent of the population of Taiwan, compared with the 14 percent who are **Mainlanders**, although these are much less important sources of **collective identity** than in the past.

technocrats   political leaders who were trained as engineers or scientists before beginning their careers in government and politics. In China, almost all top leaders are technocrats, though an increasing number have training in economics, political science, or law.

"Ten Thousand Character Letters"   a series of four underground pamphlets written by CCP intellectuals between 1994 and 1997 that were critical of the direction economic reform was taking in China. The authors complained of the decline in the state sector, rising foreign and private investment, and the declining hold of socialist **ideology** over society. This group of critics was referred to as China's "New Left."

Three-Anti campaign   a **mass mobilization campaign** against corruption, waste, and bureaucracy launched by the CCP shortly after the founding of the PRC in part to target **cadre** abuses of the **mass line**.

Three Gorges Dam   on China's **Yangtze River,** the largest dam and hydroelectric power station in the world. It was begun in 1994 and mostly completed by 2006 at an estimated cost of $39 billion. Its purpose is not only to provide a source of much needed clean energy to southwest China, but also to permit large ships to sail all the way from Shanghai on the coast to **Chongqing**, and to greatly improve flood control and irrigation. Critics of the dam point to the ecological and archaeological damage caused by the creation of gigantic artificial lakes, which also forced the relocation of 1.5 million area residents, mostly poor farmers. The construction of the dam was controversial both internationally and in China, but much of the internal dissent was suppressed.

Three Represents   former CCP leader Jiang Zemin's contribution to Chinese communist **ideology**. It means that the CCP should always represent China's advanced productive forces, advanced culture, and the interests of the overwhelming majority of the Chinese people. In essence, this was a reaffirmation of the absolute priority given by **Deng Xiaoping Theory** to economic development by any means, but also an ideological justification for allowing private entrepreneurs (capitalists) to be members of the CCP. Jiang's theoretical contributions were inscribed in the party (2002) and state (2003) constitutions and the CCP's guiding ideology was formally dubbed "**Marxism-Leninism**, **Mao Zedong Thought**, Deng Xiaoping Theory, and the important thought of the Three Represents."

Tiananmen Incident   events in April 1976 when hundreds of thousands of Chinese citizens spontaneously gathered in **Tiananmen Square** to demonstrate their affection for the popular premier (prime minister) Zhou Enlai, who had died in January. Not only were wreaths and poems lauding Zhou posted, but so, too, were scathing criticisms of Chairman Mao and his radical wife, Jiang Qing. After Jiang Qing ordered the removal of the wreaths that honored Zhou, people overturned a police vehicle and burned an official command post on the edge of the Square. The Square was finally emptied with a brief spasm of violence, but no one died and there were few arrests. The events were at first labeled as a "counterrevolutionary incident" and blame was placed on Deng Xiaoping, who was removed from his leadership positions by Mao. After Mao's death and Deng's consolidation of power, the official judgment of the "Tiananmen Incident" was reversed and it was called patriotic and revolutionary.

Tiananmen Movement   the largest mass protest in the history of the **People's Republic of China** took place in the spring of 1989. It began in **Beijing**, with university students gathering in **Tiananmen Square** in early April to commemorate the death of former party leader, Hu Yaobang, who they regarded as a reformer sympathetic to their desire for greater political freedom. The protesters set up camp in the square, and at one point attracted more than a million citizens from many walks of life expressing a wide range of grievances, including official corruption. The movement was crushed when the leadership of the CCP ordered the **People's Liberation Army** to clear the square on June 4th, resulting in a large loss of civilian life, known as the **Beijing Massacre**.

Tiananmen Square   the largest urban public space in the world (100 acres), located in the center of **Beijing**, adjacent to the front entrance of the Forbidden City, the one-time imperial palace. Tiananmen literally means "Gate of Heavenly Peace."

Tibet   a huge, sparsely populated area in China's far west, whose inhabitants are about 96 percent **Tibetan**. Its capital is Lhasa. Tibet was invaded by the **People's Liberation Army (PLA)** in 1951 and incorporated into the PRC. A major uprising against Chinese rule in 1959 was crushed by the PLA and the leader of Tibetan Buddhism, the **Dalai Lama**, fled to exile in India. In 1965 it was formally named the Tibet **Autonomous Region** (TAR). There has been extensive economic development in Tibet in recent years, and also extensive immigration by **Han** Chinese. The situation in Tibet remains politically volatile with frequent episodes of ethnic unrest.

Tibetan   one of China's fifty-five **ethnic minority** groups. There are altogether about 5.7 million Tibetans in China, 2.4 million of whom live in the **Tibet Autonomous Region**; the remainder—the majority—live mostly in areas called (in Tibetan) Kham and Amdo, which are now part of the **provinces** of Qinghai, southern Gansu, western Sichuan, and the northern tip of Yunnan.

Tibetan Plateau   a region in the far west of China that includes the **Tibet Autonomous Region** and parts of Qinghai, Gansu, Sichuan, and Yunnan. It makes up about 30 percent of all of China's area.

totalitarianism   a term used to describe a type of political system in which a single political party under a charismatic leader attempts to exercise total power over society and will use any means, including terror, to do so.

town and **township**   the lowest levels of formal government administration in rural China. Towns have a higher percentage of population with non-agricultural registrations (see *hukou* **system**) than do townships.

township and village enterprises (TVEs)   rural industries that are technically owned collectively by the township (**town**) or village and are not part of the state **planned economy**. TVEs expanded rapidly in the 1980s and were an important part of rising living standards in the countryside and of China's spectacular economic growth more generally. Beginning in the mid-1990s, most TVEs were privatized.

trading state   a country whose international commerce dramatically increases its national power. China is a contemporary example of a highly successful trading state.

Treaty of Nanjing   signed by the **Qing dynasty** and Great Britain in 1842 to end the first **Opium War**. It was the first of the **unequal treaties** forced upon imperial China by foreign powers from that time to the early twentieth century. Its main purpose was to open China to foreign trade. It also gave Britain the first part of what would become its colony of **Hong Kong**.

triad organizations   secret society criminal gangs that are active in Chinese communities in many parts of the world, especially in **Hong Kong** and **Macao**.

tributary system   the arrangement by which outsiders were allowed to conduct trade and other foreign relations with the Chinese empire, involving the giving of gifts (tribute) recognizing the superiority of and submission to the Chinese emperor.

tuanpai   literally, "League Faction"; an informal group of current CCP leaders who advanced their political careers through the ranks of the **Chinese Communist Youth League (CCYL)**. They are mostly associated with the **populist coalition** in Chinese politics.

Twenty-One Demands   a set of demands made by imperial Japan on the government of the **Republic of China** in January 1915, giving Japan territorial and other concessions in China. The weak response by the Chinese government led to widespread student protests, including those on May 4, 1919, which, in turn, gave rise to the **May 4th Movement**.

unequal treaties   the series of numerous agreements signed under military or diplomatic pressure in the nineteenth century by the **Qing dynasty** and foreign powers on terms that were very unfavorable to China and included economic, territorial, and other concessions that greatly weakened the imperial system.

unitary state   a type of political system in which all sub-national units of administration (**provinces**, states, etc.) are subordinate to the central government. The PRC is a unitary state. Compare with a federal system, like the United States, in which sub-national levels of government have considerable power.

united front   the communist party concept of joining together with other groups, even your adversaries, to fight against a common enemy and to achieve a common goal. There were two united fronts in China in the first half of the twentieth century: the First United Front joined the **Kuomintang** and the **Chinese Communist Party** in 1924–1927 to fight against the **warlords** and unify the **Republic of China.** The Second United Front (1937–1945) again brought the KMT and CCP together in order to fight the Japanese invasion of China. See also **Northern Expedition**; **Warlord Era**.

Uyghur   one of China's fifty-five **ethnic minorities**. Uyghurs are a Turkic ethnic-linguistic group who practice Islam. Most of China's 8.4 million Uyghurs live in the **Xinjiang** Uyghur **Autonomous Region**. There are also large populations of Uyghurs in other parts of Central Asia, notably Kazakhstan, Kyrgyzstan, and Uzbekistan.

vanguard party   the Leninist idea that a communist party should consist only of the most ideologically advanced and committed communists who are capable of leading the revolution to overthrow the old society and the **socialist transformation** of the country once political power has been seized. The CCP considers itself a vanguard party.

village   the basic social unit in rural China, made up of both **administrative villages** and **natural villages**. Villages are technically self-governed, although they fall under the jurisdiction of a nearby **town**. Village population is typically around 1,000 to 2,000. See **village committee**; **villager representative assembly (VRA)**.

village committee   the governing body in China's rural **administrative villages**. It consists of three to seven members, including the chair of the committee or village leader, vice chairs, an accountant, a female member who deals with family planning and women's affairs, and a person in charge of public security. In most of rural China, the village committee is directly elected by all eligible voters. Ultimately, the village committee is subordinate to the authority of the village communist party branch.

villager representative assembly (VRA)   monitors the work of the village committee, according to the **Organic Law of Villagers Committees**. Every five to fifteen households elect one representative to the VRA, which reviews annual village budgets, investment plans, and the implementation of national policies on the local level.

voluntarism   the concept that human willpower and determination can overcome any obstacles, or that the subjective can conquer the objective. **Mao Zedong Thought** is often said to put a great deal of emphasis on voluntarism, particularly the power of the masses when motivated by revolutionary spirit (and mobilized by the communist party) to achieve extraordinary economic or political results. Such voluntarism is contrasted with Marxist **materialism**, which emphasizes the objective limits, particularly economic, of human action at any given point in history.

warlord   is a person with power over a part of a country based on control of military forces who are loyal to the warlord rather than to the central government.

Warlord Era   the years 1916 to 1927 in China when political power was in the hands of regional or provincial military leaders (**warlords**) and the central government of the **Republic of China** was relatively weak.

Washington Consensus   policies promoted primarily by the United States, the World Bank, and the International Monetary Fund (IMF) that prescribe a **neo-liberal** approach to economic development, including reducing the role of the state in the economy and maximizing that of the free market, eliminating government subsidies, privatizing government industries and public utilities, and removing barriers to free trade and foreign investment. See also **Beijing Consensus**.

"whateverist" faction   a group of CCP leaders who in the early post-Mao era in 1977 pledged to "support whatever policy decisions were made by Chairman Mao" and to "unswervingly follow whatever instructions were given by Chairman Mao." The group, which have been called "neo-Maoists" because of their desire to continue some aspects of Maoist policies and **ideology** and preserve the Chairman's reputation included Hua Guofeng, Mao's successor as party chairman, Mao's personal bodyguard, Wang Dongxing, and the mayor of **Beijing**, Wu De. They were politically opposed by the **pragmatist faction**. The "whateverist" faction was gradually pushed aside after Deng Xiaoping returned to power in 1978.

White Terror   the suppression of the **Chinese Communist Party** by Chiang Kai-shek that began in April 1927 during the **Northern Expedition**. The terror nearly wiped out the CCP and forced most of the survivors to retreat to the remote countryside. Marks the beginning of the first stage of the **Chinese civil war** between the KMT and the CCP.

work teams   small groups of party **cadres** who are sent by the leadership to investigate, guide, and report on a situation. Work teams were sent to university campuses in **Beijing** at the outset of the **Cultural Revolution** in June 1966 to guide the **Red Guards**, but wound up clashing with the rebel youth. The teams were withdrawn in August 1966 and later accused of having tried, under the authority of Liu Shaoqi, to suppress the Red Guards.

work unit (*danwei*)   the place of employment for most urban Chinese citizens, particularly during the Maoist period when the work unit provided not simply jobs, but also housing, health care, education, daycare, pensions, restaurants, shopping, and vacation resorts, for their members. These benefits, along with permanent employment, made up the **iron rice bowl** that was a feature of urban (and to an extent rural) life in Maoist China. Work units were also important means of social and political control. Their importance has declined considerably during the **reform era**, but they still exert considerable influence on urban life for some citizens.

work style   in CCP terminology, the method of leadership that **cadres** use in carrying out their responsibilities and exercising their authority, particularly in relation to the masses. See also **mass line**.

World Trade Organization (WTO)   the international body based in Geneva, Switzerland, that regulates commerce among its 153 member states. Countries have to apply for accession to (join) the WTO. China acceded to the WTO in 2002 after agreeing to a large number of conditions to make its economy more open to trade. Formerly called the General Agreement on Tariffs and Trade (GATT).

Xi'an Incident   the kidnapping of Chiang Kai-shek in the northern city of Xi'an by Marshall Zhang Xueliang, a **warlord** ally of Chiang in December 1936. Zhang's purpose was to force Chiang to agree to a **united front** with the **Chinese Communist Party** to fight the Japanese, who were extending their aggression in China. Chiang did agree, but never really put his heart or forces into the fight against the Japanese, preferring instead to focus on what he thought was the more dangerous communist threat.

Xinhua   the New China News Agency (NCNA), the official news service of the **People's Republic of China**.

Xinjiang   an **autonomous region** of the **People's Republic of China**, with its capital in Ürümchi. It is a huge, sparsely populated area in China's far west (Central Asia). It is formally called the Xinjiang **Uyghur** Autonomous Region. About 69 percent of its population of 19 million consists of non-**Han ethnic minorities**, the largest of which are Uyghur Muslims, who make up 45 percent of the population. Oil and cotton have been the basis of recent economic development in the region. But it has also been the site of protest, sometime violent, by Uyghurs who oppose Chinese rule and ethnic conflict between Uyghur and Han residents. See also *bingtuan*.

Yan'an   the area in the northwestern **province** of Shaanxi where the **Chinese Communist Party** established their headquarters and most successful **base area** from 1935–1945. It was in Yan'an that Mao Zedong fully consolidated his ideological and political domination of the CCP.

Yangtze River   (Yangzi) the longest river in China (nearly 4,000 miles) and the third longest in the world. Its runs from its source in the far western **province** of Qinghai to the East China Sea near Shanghai.

Zhongnanhai   (literally, "Central and Southern Seas") the large walled complex of buildings in the heart of **Beijing** near **Tiananmen Square** where the **Chinese Communist Party** has its headquarters and where many of its top leaders both live and work.

Index